PUBLIC RELATIONS

Critical Debates
and Contemporary Practice

Edited by

Jacquie L'Etang and Magda Pieczka
Stirling Media Research Institute

Routledge
Taylor & Francis Group
New York   London

Editor:	Emily Wilkinson
Executive Assistant:	Bonita D'Amil
Cover Design:	Kathryn Houghtaling Lacey
Full-Service Compositor:	TechBooks

This book was typeset in 10/12 pt. Times Roman, Italic, Bold, and Bold Italic.
The heads were typeset in Americana, Americana Italic, and Americana Bold.

First published by Lawrence Erlbaum Associates, Inc., Publishers
10 Industrial Avenue
Mahwah, New Jersey 07430

Transferred to digital printing 2010 by Routledge

Routledge

270 Madison Avenue
New York, NY 10016

2 Park Square, Milton Park
Abingdon, Oxon OX14 4RN, UK

Library of Congress Cataloging-in-Publication Data
Public relations : critical debates and contemporary practice / edited by Jacqueline Yvonne
    L'Etang and Magda Pieczka.
      p. cm.
    Includes bibliographical references and index.
    ISBN 0-8058-4617-4 (casebound : alk. paper) – ISBN 0-8058-4618-2 (pbk. : alk. paper)
    1. Public relations. I. L'Etang, Jacquie. II. Pieczka, Magda.

  HM1221.P765   2006
  659.2—dc22

                                                    2005034330

10 9 8 7 6 5 4 3 2 1

PUBLIC RELATIONS

Critical Debates
and Contemporary Practice

Contents

Preface

This book began as a project to update and republish chapters from *Critical Perspectives in Public Relations* (ITBP, 1996) partly in response to many requests for the out-of-print edition. The project then became more ambitious, and we decided to invite a number of respected colleagues at various institutions and from a number of different cultures to share their work.

Looking back to the Preface of *Critical Perspectives*, it is clear that the field of public relations has developed and opened up and our intention here has been to build on that evolution. While we still believe strongly in raising questions and pursuing untrodden paths, our own work has taken a more empirical approach of late as reflected in our new contributions to this volume. Once again, we were keen to retain a critical edge but also wanted to include some empirical work, especially from the qualitative (largely critical) paradigm, since this has tended to be less well represented in public relations journals.

Acknowledgements are due to the following authors and publishers for permissions:
Sage Publications Ltd for their permission to reprint:
Pieczka, M., & L'Etang, J. (2001). 'Public relations and the question of professionalism' from R. Heath (Ed.), *Handbook of Public Relations*.
Sage Publications Ltd for their permission to use material from:
Pieczka, M. (2002). 'Public relations expertise deconstructed' that appeared in *Media, Culture and Society*. Vol 24, 1, pp. 301–323.
Palgrave Macmillan for their permission to reproduce material written for the book Anne Surma published with Palgrave Macmillan in 2005 *(Public and Professional Writing)*.

Every effort has been made to trace all copyright holders, but if any have been inadvertently overlooked the publishers will be pleased to make the necessary arrangement at the first opportunity.

We are, of course, primarily indebted to our contributors without whom this book would not have been possible. The project took longer to complete than envisaged and we are consequently grateful for their patience as well as their ideas! We should like to express our thanks to Alison Cooper, who copy-edited and formatted the manuscript and was an invaluable member of the team. We were encouraged by the enthusiasm and support of Emily Wilkinson, whose advice and guidance ensured the project reached conclusion.

Finally, this project would not have been written and edited without the support of our partners, Deek (Jacquie) and Ken (Magda).

—Jacquie L'Etang and Magda Pieczka
Stirling Media Research Institute

List of Contributors

Raymond Boyle, Professor and a member of Stirling Media Research Institute, University of Stirling, Scotland.

Vincent Campbell, Senior Lecturer in Media Studies in the School of Media and Cultural Production, DeMontfort University, Leicester, England.

Kristin Demetrious, Lecturer in the School of Communication and Creative Arts and member of the Corporate Citizens Research Unit at Deakin University, Australia.

Richard Haynes, Lecturer and Director of the MSc in Media Management by Online Learning and member of the Stirling Media Research Institute, University of Stirling, Scotland.

Julia Jahansoozi, Senior Lecturer at Lancashire Business School at the University of Central Lancashire and pursuing a PhD on a part-time basis at the University of Stirling, Scotland.

Richard Kilborn, Senior Lecturer at the University of Stirling and a member of the Stirling Media Research Institute, Scotland.

Larsåke Larsson, Associate Professor at Örebro University in Sweden.

Jacquie L'Etang, Lecturer and Director of the M.Sc. in Public Relations (full-time), University of Stirling, and a member of the Stirling Media Research Institute, Scotland.

Peter Meech, Senior Lecturer and Course Director of the BA programmes in Film & Media Studies and Journalism Studies at the University of Stirling, Scotland.

Judy Motion, Professor of Communication in the Department of Management Communication at the University of Waikato, Australia.

Magda Pieczka, Lecturer on the M.Sc. in Public Relations and member of the Stirling Media Research Institute, University of Stirling, Scotland.

Heike Puchan, Lecturer on the M.Sc. in Public Relations and member of the Stirling Media Research Institute, University of Stirling, Scotland.

Juliet Roper, Associate Professor in the Department of Management Communication at the University of Waikato, Australia.

Anne Surma, Lecturer in English, professional writing, and public relations writing at Murdoch University, Western Australia.

Donn James Tilson, Associate Professor of Public Relations at the University of Miami's School of Communication., USA.

C. Kay Weaver, Associate Professor in the Department of Management Communication at the University of Waikato, Australia.

PUBLIC RELATIONS

Critical Debates
and Contemporary Practice

Introduction

Students of public relations may have come across *Critical Perspectives in Public Relations*, a volume we edited, and contributed to, some years ago. This book represents a continuation of our interest in the subject and the work we and others have done in the field since 1996. Its title, *Public Relations: Critical Debates and Contemporary Practice*, signals the continued interest in a critical approach to the subject coupled with a conscious research engagement with contemporary practice. Here we preview some of the key themes and highlight some contributions as examples, although each section of the book has its own introduction which comments in some detail on each chapter.

The book presents the readers with a number of chapters which appeared in 1996 and more than twice as many new chapters. Many of the original chapters have been updated, but some were left in the original form (as explained in the introduction to the section 'Critical Perspectives Revisited'). This part of the book serves two purposes: it is a benchmark helping us to reflect on the developments in the field over, roughly, 10 years; it also ensures that important pieces, for example L'Etang's discussion of rhetoric or Meech's chapter on corporate identity which have become classics, well used by students and colleagues, remain accessible. In contrast, Pieczka's technical exposition of systems which forensically dissects the concept's origins, development, and use in public relations presents a major challenge to the dominant paradigm to which there has still not been an adequate response. The new chapters (the first four sections in the book) are a mixture of theoretical and empirical work. Some are conceptually focused, for example, the entire section 'Rhetoric, Ethics, Propaganda, and Publics'; others present results of empirical projects dealing with contemporary practice, for example, chapters in the sections 'New Directions' and 'Professionalism and Professionalisation'. Together they achieve, we hope, two main objectives: they extend the intellectual vocabulary and reach of PR theory by drawing on major writers and thinkers whose work has not been as well utilised

1

as it should be; and, they add to the body of knowledge on the history and sociology of the PR occupation.

Despite the diversity of interests and approaches, there are four main themes that run across the entire book: propaganda, history, PR industry, and PR practice. Propaganda and the associated concepts such as ethics, rhetoric, and discourse continue to haunt public relations. For some authors, they provide the sole focus of work (Weaver, Motion, & Roper; L'Etang); others run into them in the course of writing about the history of the field (Puchan) or while researching the occupation (Larsson). A welcome development in this area is the move away from debating how to distinguish public relations from propaganda. Instead, the authors reflect on why it is so difficult to achieve this aim and attempt to find ways of accommodating this, perhaps inescapable, ambiguity. The message is clear: there is no simple way of providing moral and intellectual comfort to practitioners. Consequently, the fundamental ethical questions have to be confronted daily in routine practice.

Historical research is represented here by four chapters which deal with a diverse range of material. Some focus on individual practitioners and their contribution to the development of the occupation, and in doing so reveal also something of an occupational culture. In Britain, the role of social networks, their cultivation, and meaning for the occupation are laid out for inspection. The influences of, and fascination with, intelligence activities for a generation of PR practitioners in the UK is another intriguing finding revealed here. Perhaps the most striking discovery for those not able to access German-language literature directly comes from the historical sketch of public relations in Germany. Puchan's discussion shows that although German practitioners and academics were well aware of, and sometimes influenced by, American developments, public relations in Germany has had a long and independent tradition both as practice and intellectual domain. This section is perhaps the most serious challenge to date to the primacy of American public relations widely accepted on the basis of comparatively rich historical research in the United States.

Another development which the book makes clear is the relatively relaxed attitude the authors take to the question of defining public relations. There is no major effort to offer a normative, totalising definition of what the practice is. Instead, a number of approaches are pursued helping authors to follow a range of interests in the field. For example, public relations is defined as communicative practice, an occupational group, or, indeed, an industry. If the first definition represents the 'discursive turn' in the field, the latter two lead to the sociology of public relations. Neither the term itself—the sociology of public relations—nor the kind of knowledge such labels usually cover have been apparent in public relations research so far.

Chapters gathered in the section on 'Profession and Professionalisation' develop a way of understanding practitioners' work which offers an alternative to understanding professionals through the typology of public relations roles which has supported much of the research on the occupation to date. The work offered by Pieczka attempts to analyse public relations practice by focusing on the key, and yet problematic, concept of expertise (knowledge) understood not as a rational, scientific system but a set of skills, conceptual frames, and the taken-for-granted knowledge developed and modified through commercial practice. Consequently, the economic basis of the practice, market, and competition—both symbolic and commercial—become highly relevant to our understanding of public relations.

'New Directions' offers four chapters which deal either with the ways in which PR has been extended into new specialised areas such as sport and documentary filmmaking or with newly articulated challenges to existing specialisms such as science, health communication, and public information. Most of the contributors to this section are not public relations scholars and they engage with the subject from their own specialist perspectives. The most striking effect of this work is to bring to us, students of public relations, a reflection on the role and effects of PR practice in popular culture, an area of social life with which we have not been overtly preoccupied.

Finally, a comment on our editorial policy: we have taken full advantage of the relative lack of restrictions on the length of contributions, which is particularly important for the empirically based chapters. We did not expect authors to have to squeeze substantial pieces of research into a short format, as is the usual practice with journal articles. As a result, readers can hear the voices of the informants and subjects of research projects much more directly and extensively. We hope this rich detail will be both stimulating and enjoyable. The readers will also find detailed introductions to all contributions at the beginning of each individual section.

Now, dear reader, it is over to you.

I

Rhetoric, Ethics, Propaganda, and Publics

INTRODUCTION

The book opens with the contribution of C. Kay Weaver, Judy Motion, and Juliet Roper which explores the semantic and philosophical relationships between public relations and propaganda. At the outset, the authors pose the challenging question: "Is there any substantive difference between propaganda and public relations once public relations is conceived of as a discourse technology of social governance?" The authors review historical intellectual developments in relation to public opinion linking these to symmetry, power, and the critiques of key social theorists Michel Foucault and Jurgen Habermas and theories of propaganda. As part of their overall critique, Weaver et al. cite Roper's argument that symmetrical communication is more likely to be used as a tool to maintain hegemony and suggest that in cases where symmetrical communication "does indeed involve the alteration of organisational practices in response to dissent . . . [it is] only so far as it is necessary to maintain what is essentially 'business as usual.' " Weaver et al. argue that public relations power is sourced in discourse, and they proceed to analyse public relations practitioners as "discourse technologists" (Motion & Leitch, 1996, p. 298) in developing an argument that "a key point in theorising public relations as discourse is understanding how discourse creates identity positions which then influence the types of social relationships that are possible within and outside that discourse." The authors thus explore the implications of discourse to extend our understanding of both propaganda and public relations.

Jacquie L'Etang also tackles the theme of propaganda to consider some of the methodological issues in defining the practice in relation to propaganda. Her starting point is take an essentialist approach and to identify the problems of analysis. She gives some attention to paradigm practices to suggest that too often discipline conventions and ideological baggage impede analysis and that greater transparency and reflexivity is sometimes required of researchers. Some emphasis is given to the relationship between education and propaganda, drawing on the controversial French theorist, Ellul (1962). The final part of the chapter presents empirical data from an oral history project thematising the views of practitioners from the 1940s and 1950s in relation to public relations and propaganda and drawing out an analysis of worldviews. Thus, the chapter gives some insight into the occupational mores, self-identity, and discourse of the post-war period in the formative era of professionalisation.

Anne Surma's contribution takes up the linguistic theme to explore public relations texts produced by a variety of organisations to communicate their social responsibilities. As part of her discussion, she presents qualitative empirical data on Nike's *Social Responsibility Report*. Surma draws upon a emergence of moral narratives and counternarratives. Her analysis concludes by suggesting that public relations practitioners are concerned "to establish and maintain ethical and mutually beneficial relationships ... might reflect less on their capacity to engage in the polished telling ... and re-telling of their preferred stories ... [and] focus more (and more) attention on exchanging and negotiating ... different, discontinuous and open-ended stories with those publics."

Julia Jahansoozi's chapter continues the relational theme foregrounding the role of interpersonal communication within the boundaries of defined publics. She reviews the innovative work of Ferguson, who as the first to introduce the idea public relations should focus on relationships argued that academics should "adopt the relationship as the unit of study." Jahansoozi provides a comprehensive review of a variety of theoretical developments from organisational, conflict resolution, public relations, marketing, and interpersonal communication sources. She argues that while "many relationship characteristics have been identified in the public relations literature, there [are] some gaps ... namely dialogue and transparency," suggesting transparency is a crucial part of the corporate social responsibility process. Finally, she presents a model to facilitate transparency.

Finally, Kristin Demetrious' work takes up the societal theme by exploring notions of advocacy and active citizenry "in wired and networked 'risk society'." She employs Ulrich Beck's theories of risk society (social domination by life-threatening byproducts of industrial society) and reflexive modernization to explore activism, corporate social responsibility, and public relations. She concludes that "'public relations' has specific connotations for activists as a self-serving capitalist activity deeply rooted in exploitative corporate history and tradition ... a void exists in the activist lexicon to describe their use of public communication."

1

From Propaganda to Discourse (and Back Again): Truth, Power, the Public Interest, and Public Relations

C. Kay Weaver, Judy Motion, and Juliet Roper
University of Waikato

Since Edward Bernays first introduced the term "public relations counsel" in his 1923 publication *Crystallizing Public Opinion*, public relations, although widely practised by corporations and governments alike, has monumentally failed to establish itself as of positive social utility and benefit. As L'Etang has stated, "It is something of a truism that public relations needs more public relations to increase public understanding of its role in society" (1997, p. 34). Indeed, public relations rarely enjoys good press and is continually maligned as little more than an industry of propaganda and spin that trades in lies and deceit (see, for example, Carey, 1997; Collison, n.d; Beder, 1997; Hager & Burton, 1999; D. Miller, 2003; Michie, 1998; Stauber & Rampton, 1995). This dismissive perspective is particularly likely to be espoused where there is an attempt to expose and/or oppose the messages constructed to garner public support for, for example, corporate or governmental policies and initiatives. Those objecting to the position advocated by the message are especially likely to encourage its casting aside as "propaganda" or "spin."

However, while public relations is popularly described as propaganda and spin, the "looseness" of these critical descriptions of public relations are not helpful to the development of a sophisticated understanding and evaluation of public relations as a particular form of communicative practice which purportedly advocates for not only organisational interests but also the public interest. Moreover, such dismissive labelling of public relations fails to accurately reflect how it might actually comprise part of the legitimate information management machinery of democratic societies, and how it attempts to gain public support for particular corporate, government, or for that matter even non-government organisations and activist practices. A related problem is the fact that the dismissal of public relations as "propaganda" and therefore "bad" reflects a particularly pejorative view of the term "propaganda" itself. As L'Etang (1997) has noted, it is a position that simplistically defines propaganda as lying which, by implication, places it in opposition to "truth." In reality, the practice of both propaganda and public relations is much more complex than is implied by the use of such black-and-white oppositional terms.

From a post-structuralist position, the notion that there is a "truth" which propaganda stands in opposition to is highly problematic. Post-structuralism regards all "truth" as socially constructed and contestable. As one of the key post-structuralist thinkers, Michel Foucault (1980), has argued: "Each society has its regime of truth, its "general politics" of truth: that is, the types of discourse that it accepts and makes function as true" (p. 131). In these terms it becomes very difficult, if not impossible, to argue that propaganda is necessarily a form of lying—or the promotion of "untruths." Instead, the issue has to be understood as a question of what is *accepted* as "truthful." How does this impact on our understanding of the role that public relations and, indeed, propaganda, plays in society and our ability to pass evaluative judgement on these communicative practices? Does this mean that we should simply regard the promotion of particular messages by public relations and propagandist practitioners as a legitimate part of the struggle in the effort to have society adopt a particular version of "the facts," or of one truth over another? And, what are the implications of adopting this position? These questions form the core concern of this chapter, wherein we draw on critical perspectives to theorise the similarities and differences between the communication practices of propaganda and public relations. By drawing on critical theory in this analysis, our aim is to explore how critical perspectives tend to position public relations and propaganda on a continuum, but also how they might provide pathways to theorise the role that public relations plays in the construction of knowledge and, therefore, notions of truth, power, and the public interest.

We begin the chapter with an exploration of how early 20th-century American public opinion theorists regarded propaganda and its allied occupation, public relations counsel, as vital to the effective working of democratic society. We then explore why "propaganda" has become a pejoratively loaded term and why, consequently, contemporary public relations theorists attempt to construct strict demarcations between propaganda and "ethical" public relations practice. After outlining how systems theorists argue that public relations can be practised ethically, we then examine these arguments in relation to Jürgen Habermas's theory of "communicative action," in which private interests and power relations are put aside in favour of open, informed discussion from which public interests will be determined. Although idealistic, the notion of communicative action is used as a benchmark for democratic processes, and ones which public relations practice are not necessarily in alignment with. Building on this critique of "ethical public relations," we then draw on the work of Michel Foucault and Norman Fairclough to outline how public relations can be understood as discourse practice that is utilised in efforts to legitimate or challenge social, cultural, political, and/or economic power. With this we are brought full circle back to the question of whether there is, in fact, any substantive difference between propaganda and public relations once public relations is conceived of as a discourse technology of social governance.

PROPAGANDA AND PUBLIC SOCIETY

The term propaganda has not always carried the negative connotations that it does today. Its origins lie with the 17th-century Roman Catholic Church, which established the "*de Propaganda Fide*" to "mobilize talented intellectuals of every sort into a vast social apparatus to persuade men and women all across the globe to believe in Christian doctrine or, if perchance they had fallen astray, to rekindle their faith" (Jackall, 1995, p. 1). Even in the secular society of the early 20th century, propaganda was still regarded as making an important contribution to the mobilization of public opinion. Indeed, early public opinion theorists, such as Harold Lasswell, Walter Lippman and the "father of public relations," Edward Bernays, regarded propaganda as vital to the workings of democracy through its advocating, for example, government and business policy developments to the "mass public."

For many American social theorists, this mass public was a cause for concern in the period of post-World War I when "Victorian ideals of an ordered society no longer held much sway, nor did the religious principles of delayed gratification and presumed hierarchies. It was unclear what would take their place. Anarchy?" (Tye, 1998, p. 94). Certainly the threats posed by a "burgeoning of militant working-class politics . . . fears of revolt from below" and "middle-class hostility toward big business" (Ewen, 1996, p. 60) were regarded by Progressive politicians as evidence of an increasing slide toward social disintegration and chaos. It was in this context that social psychologists, political scientists, politicians, and the corporate sector saw propaganda as providing a means of engineering public opinion, controlling the masses, and reinstating social order. As Ewen (1996) stated: "The dexterity with which a new class of experts could learn to manipulate symbols appeared to be the fortress that would protect the forces of order from the mounting tide of chaos" (p. 143).

However, in the early decades of the 20th century American propaganda practice did not focus on appealing to public rationale for support of political and/or corporate causes. Far from it. As a consequence of Freud's influence on psychological theories of the human mind—which posited unconscious instincts as determining individual behaviour—propagandists and early public relations practitioners focused efforts on appealing to public *emotion* rather than critical reasoning (Ewen, 1996). Indeed, the "public mind" was regarded as illogical and irrational and in need of governance from "responsible men" trained in decision making and leadership (Lippman, 1995 [1925]). As Ewen (1996) detailed, for Lippman, "The key to leadership in the modern age would depend on the ability to manipulate 'symbols which assemble emotions after they have been detached from their ideas.' The public mind is mastered, [Lippman] continued, through an 'intensification of feeling and degradation of significance'" (p. 335).

Those who regarded propaganda as a crucial tool in the maintenance of social order in the early 20th century were not advocates of participatory democracy. Lippman's (1995 [1925]) position on this is made abundantly clear in his statement that:

> When public opinion attempts to govern directly it is either a failure or a tyranny. It is not able to master the problem intellectually, nor to deal with it except by wholesale impact. The theory of democracy has not recognized this truth because it has identified the functioning of government with the will of the people. This is a fiction. (p. 51)

Lippman advocated a technocratic representative democracy where power resided in the hands of a small, intellectual elite (Ewen, 1996) and public consent to their rule was engineered. Harold Lasswell's position was very similar: "Regard for men in the mass rests upon no democratic dogmatisms about men being the best judges of their own interest. The modern propagandist, like the modern psychologist, recognizes that men are often poor judges of their own interests, flitting from one alternative to the next without solid reason" (1995 [1934], p. 24). From this perspective public interest is not debated, determined, and governed by the public itself but by an elite group. In these terms, the real value of propaganda lies *not* in its dissemination and promotion of *ideas*, but in its ability to orchestrate public opinion and social action that supported the ruling elite: "The propagandist is one who creates symbols that are not only popular but that bring about positive realignments of behaviour is no phrasemonger but a promoter of overt acts" (Lasswell 1995 [1934], p. 25). What is more, as McNair has previously pointed out, Lippman also advocated propaganda practices that "obscure personal intention, neutralise discrimination, and obfuscate individual purpose" (cited in McNair, 1996, p. 43).

While Lasswell, Lippman, and Bernays conceived propaganda—or as Bernays phrased it, "public relations counsel"—as essential to the management of information, the social engineering of consent, and as, therefore, a normative aspect of modern democratic society (Robins, Webster, & Pickering, 1987; see also Barsamian & Chomsky, 2001, chap. 6), their theories of the value of the propagandist psychological manipulation of people later fell into disrepute. This was largely as a consequence of the highly effective, and catastrophic, application and development of propaganda theory by Hitler and his Nazi propaganda chief Joseph Goebbels during the lead up to and during World War II. That there is a relationship between the American theories of propaganda and the Nazi propagandist practices is not denied. As Tye (1998; see also Bernays, 1965, p. 652) reported, Goebbels owned a copy of Bernays' *Crystallizing Public Opinion* and "while scholars still debate the extent to which the Nazis used Bernays's works, Goebbels did employ techniques nearly identical to those used by Bernays" (p. 111). In particular Goebbels, like Bernays, used "scientific" methods to psychologically manipulate the propaganda audience through means such as the constant repetition of a few relatively simplistic points.

Like the American political scientists and public opinion theorists, Hitler held a dim view of the general population's ability to make responsible rational decisions—describing them as a "great stupid flock" (Thomson, 1977, p. 117). Along with Goebbels, Hitler also—and again like the Americans—assigned enormous importance to the ability to manipulate the public mind through the use of symbols and emotional language. Both men also valued how propaganda could turn established "truths" on their heads through—as Goebbels is often quoted:

> a carefully built up erection of statements, which whether true or false can be made to undermine quite rigidly held ideas and to construct new ones that will take their place. It would not be impossible to prove with sufficient repetition and psychological understanding of the people concerned that a square is in fact a circle. What after all are a square and a circle? They are mere words and words can be moulded until they clothe ideas in disguise. (cited in Thomson, 1977, p. 111)

Goebbels' statement indicates a clear understanding of the significance that language plays in the effectiveness of propaganda and the establishment of (relativist) understandings of truth—an issue that we explore further below in relation to discourse and public relations. But it is also worth briefly examining how this theory of effective propaganda techniques—in terms of the perceived outcome of the repetition of the message—is dependent on a behaviourist stimulus–response transmission model of communication.

THEORISING THE PUBLIC: PROPAGANDA AUDIENCES

Within a transmission model of communication, communication is regarded as a one-way process in which an active "sender" communicates a message to a passive "receiver" whose behaviour is then affected by the message content. This model—closely linked to the popular use of propaganda techniques in the United States and Europe in the early decades of the 20th century and "the enduring notion of 'the public' as a vulnerable and persuadable lot 'at risk' from propaganda" (Brooker & Jermyn, 2003, p. 5)—has informed a large proportion of media effects research and theorizing. However, as Gauntlet (1995) explained, the model—often termed the "hypodermic model of communication effects"—is closely associated with:

> methods and assumptions which are inherited from the natural sciences, and are therefore of questionable applicability to the study of such complex systems as human psychology, behaviour and social life. Whilst natural scientists can generally hope to observe stable and verifiable effects of one object on another, similarly straightforward predictions about social action obviously cannot be made. (p. 9)

Nevertheless, in the 1920s this model held considerable sway in mass communication theory— as it would for several more decades. Indeed, Harold Lasswell argued that:

> The strategy of propaganda ... can readily be described in the language of stimulus response: the propagandist may be said to be concerned with the multiplication of these stimuli which are calculated to evoke the desired responses, and with the nullification of those stimuli which are likely to instigate the undesired responses. (cited in Robins et al., 1987, p. 3)

It is hardly surprising that there is a direct relationship between stimulus–response transmission theories of communication and the beliefs espoused by Lippman, Lasswell, and Bernays that propaganda makes an important contribution to democratic society given these theorists' perception of the public as a highly impressionable passive "herd" (Jackall, 1995, p. 358). Passive and irrational publics were regarded as in need of 'responsible' direction. What is more surprising is that despite the discrediting of transmission stimulus–response models and their replacement by transaction models in which there is "acknowledgement of the active receiver, the obstinate and recalcitrant audience" (Robins et al., 1987, p. 4)—a theoretical shift that began in the 1940s (Brooker & Jermyn, 2003), critiques of propaganda are still implicitly underpinned by the transmission model. Consequently, essentially behavioural models are used to cast propaganda as deliberate, manipulative, and, therefore, unethical persuasion. For example, Jowett and O'Donnell (1992) stated that the

> purpose of propaganda is to send out an ideology with a related objective ... [and] there is a careful and predetermined plan of prefabricated symbol manipulation to communicate to an audience in order to fulfill [the] objective. The objective that is sought requires the audience to reinforce or modify attitudes and/or behaviour. (pp. 2–3)

This explanation of propaganda clearly implies that the audience is a passive one, and that behaviour is open to modification by a message from what is constructed as a "powerful" *ideologically motivated* message sender. By defining propaganda in this way, Jowett and O'Donnell constructed all ideologically motivated messages as "bad", or at least ethically questionable, and in so doing imply that there are some forms of communication that are ("good" and) free from ideological underpinning. However, post-structural conceptions of culture contradict the argument that some communication can be "ideologically free," as *all* cultural activities, including communication, are 'always situated in specific social-historical contexts which are structured in certain ways" (Thompson, 1988, p. 361) and located within relations of power.

Jowett and O'Donnell (1992) also continually described propagandists as highly powerful and operating with conscious, deliberated self-interested intent. This notion is central to their definition of propaganda: "Propaganda is the deliberate and systematic attempt to shape perceptions, manipulate cognitions, and direct behaviour to achieve a response that furthers the desired intent of the propagandist" (p. 4). It is in these terms that propaganda is primarily associated with unethical communication and totalitarian regimes. However, some social commentators argue for the need to extend the association of propaganda to the strategic communication practices of democratic governments—such as, for example, those of President George W. Bush and Prime Minister Tony Blair in their campaigns to gain public support for the 2003 war on Iraq (Hiebert, 2003; D. Miller, 2003). Others have suggested that the communication practices used in environmental activist campaigns (Anderson, 1997; J. Palmer, 2000) and by non-government organisations and charities (Hutson & Liddiard, 2000) also make use of propagandist type approaches where the intention is to directly affect the emotions, attitudes, and behaviours of audiences.

However, the discrediting of behaviourist stimulus–response models of communication makes it much more difficult to explain the mechanisms by which recipients of propaganda messages can be persuaded to accept ideas or policies that do not, in reality, support their individual or collective interests. Under transactional theories of communication, audiences rationally chose to align with the message content and its senders' subject position as a result of some perceived benefit—be it personal, political, economic, social, or even pleasurable gain, for example, in doing so. This perspective becomes much less palatable, however, when used to explain the overwhelming effectiveness of the propaganda strategies deployed by the Nazis which mobilized public support for Hitler's dictatorship, the causes of nationalism, anti-Semitism, and mass genocide.

For many propaganda theorists, it is preferable to construct the public opinion that supported Nazi atrocities as the unwitting *victim* of an omnipotent monstrous power. Once pro-Nazi anti-Semitic opinion is theorised as anything less than the result of such extraordinary power, the astonishing intellectual legacy around propaganda left by Hitler and his Propaganda Minister Josef Goebbels has to be acknowledged. As Doob (1995) stressed: "Whether or when parts of [this legacy of propaganda] should be utilized in a democratic society are profound and disturbing problems of a political and ethical nature" (p. 192).

However, why the German public was seemingly willing to accept Hitler's message has to be considered in the wider context of the crippling effects of the post-World War I Treaty of Versailles on the German economy and employment, which in turn led to a groundswell in German nationalism. A more complex explanation of how Hitler's propaganda was effective would be that he engaged with an active, not passive public and that his messages resonated with commonly held public sentiments and national aspirations. Of course, Hitler's message was also soon underpinned by the suppression and censorship of anti-Nazi voices, threats, coercion, and violence (Marlin, 2002). Yet, it is Hitler's deliberate and so effective use of language and symbols which ensured public support for his horrific atrocities that has resulted in the term "propaganda" being associated with *unacceptable manipulation* of public opinion.

For the vast majority of propaganda and public relations theorists, certainly in the Western world, there is overt agreement that the type of propaganda practised by the Nazis has no place in a democracy. However, to simply say that propagandist practices are the prerogative of totalitarian regimes (see, for example, Jowett & O'Donnell, 1992) is indicative of a complete denial that propaganda could or, indeed, does play a part in democratic societies. This is a concern that Robins et al. (1987) raised when they asked: "Just how distinct is information management in the cause of democracy from dictatorial propaganda and information control? If there are those . . . for whom the principles seem clear cut, there are others who perceive a more muddy and ambiguous reality" (p. 15).

In an attempt to acknowledge that information management, or influence, does have a legitimate role to play in, for example, social and political relations, Jowett and O'Donnell (1992) described an arena for *ethical* influence—which they term "persuasion." Having defined propaganda as the *self-interested* attempt to manipulate the behaviour of others, they contrast this with ethical persuasion, which they conceive of as an "interactive or transactive" process:

> in which the recipient foresees the fulfillment of a personal or societal need or desire if the persuasive purpose is adopted. The persuader also has a need fulfilled if the persuadee accepts the persuasive purpose. Because both persuader and persuadee stand to have their needs fulfilled, persuasion is regarded as more mutually satisfying than propaganda. (p. 21)

Here Jowett and O'Donnell attempt to distinguish propaganda from legitimate practices of persuasion and influence. As we will discuss below, identifying what is ethical influence has come to play a major place in the development of public relations theory. However, we would argue that Jowett and O'Donnell's explanation of ethical persuasion could be seen at work in 1930s Germany, because supporters of Nazism viewed Hitler as potentially fulfilling societal needs by offering a way out of a crippling national economic depression. This suggests that propaganda in itself is not unethical. Rather, whether propaganda is ethical or not has to be assessed in relation to the context in which it is practised, the ends to which it is used, the quality of transparency in terms of the persuaders' openness about the 'ends' they are seeking to achieve, and, as far as one is able to judge, the consequences of those ends.

LEGITIMISING PUBLIC RELATIONS

As propaganda has become increasingly discredited as an unethical tool for the manipulation of public opinion, new models of supposedly ethical persuasion have been developed. These models have attempted to notionally distance public relations from propaganda (despite early public relations theorists regarding them as one and the same thing) and provide legitimacy for the public relations profession.

Four models of public relations practice evolved from Grunig and Hunt's (1984) use of functionalist systems theory in the development of a new conceptualisation of public relations. As Trujillo and Toth (1987) outlined, functionalists "are usually concerned with organizational effectiveness and efficiency as they relate to the 'bottom-line' financial health of the organization" (p. 202). Working from within the functionalist approach, systems theory specifically regards public relations as a means by which organisations can better manage uncertainties within their environments and so adapt and grow (Trujillo & Toth, 1987, p. 208). The four models of public relations that Grunig and Hunt (1984) developed are (a) press agentry/publicity, (b) public information, (c) two-way asymmetrical, and (d) two-way symmetrical public relations. It is the last of these, the two-way symmetrical model, that was deemed *ethical* and *best practice* public relations communication.

Although the term propaganda does not feature within Grunig and Hunt's outlining of the four models of public relations, there is certainly an acknowledgement that public relations is used in the attempt to manage information and public opinion to protect the self-interest of the client, organisations, or dominant coalition. For example, Grunig (2001) stated that:

> Practitioners of press agentry seek attention for their organisations in almost anyway possible, whereas public information practitioners are journalists-in-residence who disseminate accurate, but usually only favourable information about their organisations. With the two-way asymmetrical model, practitioners conduct scientific research to determine *how to persuade publics to behave in the ways their client organisations wish* (pp. 11–12, our emphasis).

Interestingly, research into public relations practice has found that "the dominant world view in public relations—the asymmetrical view [is] that public relations is a way of getting what an organizations wants without changing its behaviour or without compromising" (Grunig & White, 1992, p. 39). This suggests that not only are strategies associated with propaganda used in democratic nations, but also that public relations practitioners view their use as normative.

There is little question that modern public relations acts on the need to secure public acceptance of organisational policy, be it government, business, or not-for-profit. For some public relations and media theorists, the use of communication to persuade public opinion in this context is viewed as entirely acceptable practice. For example, McNair (1996) stated: "The public relations function is a necessary dimension of the modern political process, which has overall become more democratic, and not less, in the course of the twentieth century" (p. 53). This view is very much like that of Lasswell (1995 [1934]) in that it accepts public relations as necessary in spite of its propagandistic underpinnings. Indeed, as McNair stated, "As the producer and disseminator of symbols which can contribute to the building of unity and consent . . . the public relations worker is, of course, a propagandist" (p. 43).

Yet, as noted above, Grunig and Hunt (1984) promoted the notion of *symmetrical* communication as the model for *ethical* public relations, which, although never directly stated, could be construed as setting public relations apart from propaganda—especially in terms of its striving for a balancing of organisational and public interests (Grunig, 2001). Indeed, the process of symmetrical communication—which involves an organisation using public opinion research and engaging in public dialogue with stakeholders in the development of organisational objectives, clearly suggests a distinction from propaganda if we accept that propagandists are in the business of seeking to persuade, by one means or another, the public to buy into values or beliefs that benefit the interests of the propagandists over and above the interests of the public. As Grunig and White (1992) defined it, ethical public relations is, in contrast, "a symmetrical process of compromise and negotiation and not a war for power" (p. 39).

The idea of the two-way symmetrical communication model is that an organisation will engage with the public to assess what courses of action will work to benefit *both* the organisation and the public. Responding to public opinion may require that substantive changes are made to decisions about organisational direction and objectives. Grunig and White (1992) argued that, "In the long run the symmetrical view is more effective: organisations get more of what they want when they give up some of what they want" (p. 39). From this perspective, publics were perceived as active participants in dialogue leading to the formulation of organisational policy and goals. Consequentially, the public relations professional was positioned as aligned with a worldview that "presupposes that public relations serves the public interest, develops mutual understanding between organisations and their publics, contributes to informed debate about issues in society, and facilitates a dialogue between organisations and their publics" (Grunig & White, 1992, p. 53). In these terms public relations was cast as playing a very different role in society than that of propaganda. Its role is that of facilitator of dialogue working for the mutual benefit of both the client organisation and the public good.

As it was originally developed by Grunig and Hunt (1984), the symmetrical model of public relations practice can be seen as an attempt to advance public relations as an acceptable and ethical profession built upon democratic ideals. As Pieczka (1996) has argued, those who advocate for the legitimacy of public relations have been involved in a long campaign to distance the industry from any links to the practice of 'manipulative' propaganda and promote it as ethical, civilised, and even socially responsible. Indeed, acceptance of the role of public relations in the formation of public opinion and policy through open, democratic processes would provide legitimacy not only to the outcomes but also to public relations itself.

For critics of the "ethical" representation of public relations, predominantly insurmountable tensions exist between balancing the needs of public interest and self- or private interest within public relations practice, making the application of the dialogical symmetrical model an unlikely rarity and even something of a fantastical ideal (Leitch & Neilson, 1997; Weaver, 2001). Interestingly, these are the very same tensions identified by the German communication philosopher Jürgen Habermas in his attempt to theorise a public sphere—an ideal space in which citizens came together in a process he described as "communicative action" to discuss issues of public importance and political consequence.

A student of the Frankfurt School of social research, which promoted Marxist critique of Western capitalism, Habermas sought to provide a theory of civil society in which public opinion was not an outcome of partisan lobbying and strategic persuasive influence, but a result of rational public debate about what constituted "truth" and the collective good. The notion of "the public sphere"—an "open arena of debate" (Golding & Murdock, 1991, p. 22) accessible to the public in all of its diversity—was central to Habermas' theory of a just society. In this society, with full provision of information and with private interests put aside, public opinion was formed that in turn determined public policy.

Within Habermas' theory of the public sphere, a stable public consensus of opinion can only be derived from communicative action. In these terms the strategic intention of propagandists and even public relations practitioners can*not* be said to create true consensus, however effective they may be. As Mayhew (1997) stated:

> For Habermas, communication has its own imperatives, and if attempts to communicate violate its intrinsic character, they are deformed and ineffective in producing actual and stable consensus. Communicative action cannot employ force. Indeed, any mode of persuasion that falls short of a strict standard of reciprocity is coercive, even if its persuasive sway is not directly based on force. (p. 36)

It is through the process of communicative action, and the acceptance of a better argument based on claims to "comprehensibility, truth, rightness and sincerity" (Mayhew, 1997, p. 36), that policy is legitimated by citizens in terms of their accepting it as acting in the public interest (Habermas, 1976, 1996).

Habermas (1996) did, however, point to tensions between facticity and validity inherent in his (ideal) theory of the process of communicative action. The tension arises because the validity of truth claims will be under constant scrutiny in the light of counterclaims. He stated that, under ideal conditions, "the acceptance of validity claims, which generates and perpetuates social facts, rests on the context-dependent acceptability of reasons that are constantly exposed to the risk of being invalidated by better reasons and context-altering learning processes" (p. 36). Thus, the determination of what constitutes "the public interest" is contestable and context dependent, linked to the social norms of a given time and place.

As is evident, Habermas' theory of public interest as derived through communicative action is very similar to the theory of the formation of public interest within Grunig and Hunt's (1984) and Grunig and White's (1992) model of two-way symmetrical public relations. But to what extent do public relations practitioners genuinely engage in communicative action in the attempt to balance the requirements of legitimising the actions of the organisations that employ them with the public interest? One area of public relations in which this is a key strategic concern is in issues management, which is concerned with helping organisations to "make adaptations needed to achieve harmony and foster mutual interests with the communities in which they operate" (Heath, 1997, p. 3).

Heath directly related the concept and practice of issues management to public policy through the proactive management of key issues. If such issues were ignored then public policies might be developed in response. These would necessarily limit the ability of business to regulate itself. He stated that:

> The underpinning principle of issues management is not to avoid legislation or regulation but to balance the interests of all segments of the community so that each enjoys the proper amount of reward or benefit in proportion to the cost of allowing industry free rein to impose its own operating standards. (1997, p. 6)

From this perspective, Heath (1997) argued that where differences exist between perceptions of what companies are doing, and the community's expectations of what they *ought* to be doing, a "legitimacy gap" may be said to occur (see also Sethi, 1977). This gap results from, according to Heath (1997), differences of agreement over "fact, value and policy" (p. 4). For those public relations practitioners who advocate a two-way symmetrical model of communication, this poses the challenge of how to align the organisations's perspective with social norms and the public interest. Essentially this requires a dialogic process.

However, at this point it has to be said that the term "dialogue" itself is open to different interpretations of process and historicizing. For example, Habermas tracked the shift in dialogical processes from that of collaborative rational–critical dialogue where outcomes are jointly conceived to a negotiated compromise among interests from the period of the 18th through to the 20th centuries (Calhoun, 1992). Dialogue may thus be conceptualised on a continuum from collaboration—that is, working together to achieve a shared interest, to negotiated compromise where one or both parties make concessions. It is from the latter perspective that Heath (1997) suggested that dialogue is a process of "statement and counterstatement" (p. 365) where "[p]eople influence and are influenced. Judgement and conclusions are forged on the anvil of debate, negotiation and collaboration. Opinions change. Compromise is achieved" (p. 366). This is a process in which "reason takes the form of rhetorical rebuttal of rhetorical statement" (Mayhew, 1997, p. 48) and parties attempt to persuade one another of the validity of their perspective, protecting their own self-interest, and attempting to gain a position of power with, or over, others.

In these terms, however, two-way public relations practice does not accord with Habermas' theory of communicative action. Rather, public relations activity—especially in the context of the corporate and government sectors which are intrinsically connected to the concerns of economy and state, money, and power—falls under what Habermas defined as "strategic action." Strategic action is defined as that action which is "designed to achieve ends at the expense of other people" (Mayhew, 1997, p. 36). Yet, what also has to be considered is the lack of fit between the conception of the public interest within Habermassian theory of the public sphere and communication action, and the conception of the public interest in the two-way symmetrical model of public relations. As outlined above, in Habermas' model of the public sphere "people collectively determine through a process of rational argument the way in which they want to see society develop" (Curran, 1991, p. 83) and, therefore, what is in the public good or interest. In contrast, as Mayhew (1997) has argued, public relations professionals draw in a very narrow conception of the public interest and can do so because in their role as advocates:

> They are no more bound by detached, disinterested approaches to the facts than attorneys who argue on behalf of clients in courts of law. Providing selected truths in support of clients is entirely appropriate; it is up to the other side to present its own truths. (p. 203)

In these liberal democratic, adversarial, "market of ideas" terms, it is up to each party to bring to the debate points of argument which support their own position and which contest, challenge, or seek to modify the claims presented by the other party (Barney & Black, 1994). It is considered fair that you would not intentionally undermine your own cause by bringing to the discussion information that would work in the other party's favour and against your own interest. Rather, within the ideals of democratic liberal freedom of speech, each party is free to expose the weaknesses of the other in claiming their own moral authority, and it is up to them to do so.

This does raise the question of why the legal practice of advocating for the interest of clients is predominantly regarded as socially acceptable, whereas in the case of public relations such partisan advocacy is decried as unethical and propagandist. An important distinguishing feature of lawyers compared with public relations practitioners is, however, that the role of lawyers is to defend their clients' claim to innocence and their right to retain their life, liberty, and property until the state proves them guilty in the court of public opinion. This compares with public relations practitioners, who advocate for their clients, but not in a situation of protecting that client against accusation and punishment by the state and, moreover, not in a situation where clients' claims are thoroughly examined by an advocate appointed to work for the public interest. This is because, as Habermas and other media and communication scholars have argued, capitalist liberal democracy has failed to deliver a public sphere in which, through genuine public dialogue, rational consensus about what is in the public interest can be achieved. As Mayhew (1997) has stated, "Reason can only be realised in dialogue, and dialogue can only be institutionalised in society by providing strategically located public forums for expression and response, in which citizens speak freely about their socially located experience" (p. 48). Indeed, the professional communication industries of public relations, advertising, and marketing research have only further contributed to the erosion of the ideal possibility of the public sphere; and communication between citizens, governments, and corporations has become strategically invested with relationships of money, private interest, and, therefore, power. James Grunig (2001) acknowledged precisely this when he stated:

> Symmetrical public relations does not take place in an ideal situation where competing interests come together with good will to resolve their differences because they share a goal of social equilibrium and harmony. Rather, it takes place in situations where groups come together to protect and enhance their self-interest. (p. 18)

Consequently, public relations communication can be understood as the strategic attempt to control the agenda of public discussion and the terms in which discussion takes place. In these terms, public relations practitioners are complicit in the attempt to gain, and maintain, social, political, and/or economic power for the organisations that they represent. They do this by asserting the "common sense" truth value of what they stand for and communicate.

Considering public relations from this perspective, the concept of hegemony (Gramsci, 1971) provides a means of understanding how social power or dominance (without coercion or violence) can be achieved. Because dominant truths based in ideas can be challenged at any time and from multiple perspectives, hegemony is never static but must respond to such challenges through the making of concessions that will diffuse or absorb opposition (Hall, 1988). It is from this position that Roper (2005) argued that symmetrical communication, although conceived as a dialogic tool by which public relations can be practised *ethically*, is more likely to be utilised as a tool for the maintenance of hegemony. Certainly, dialogue can be undertaken in order to ascertain publics' concerns and responses to those concerns can be then negotiated. However, by making relatively small concessions in response to outside criticisms, organisations can undermine the arguments of their opponents and thereby strengthen their own positions. In this way power relations can be maintained rather than compromised. Thus, two-way symmetrical communication might involve the alteration of organisational practices in response to public dissent, but only insofar as it is necessary to maintain what is essentially "business as usual."

If, like Habermas, we are to argue that public relations practitioners play a key role in the maintenance of power without coercion and that their role is strategically invested, we need to examine the processes by which that strategy is effected. One key process is through construction and control of discourse.

PUBLIC RELATIONS AS DISCOURSE

While Habermas was concerned with theorising issues of influence in civil society, he did not develop a theory of discourse, and neither did he theorise the relationship between discourse, influence, and power. The reason for this, certainly according to Mayhew (1997), is that Habermas sought to maintain a space for reason and "true" rational consensus in society. This compares with Foucault, for whom the politics of truth, power, and knowledge were primary issues of concern. For Foucault, truth was not something that was "arrived" at through public discussion, but something that is "produced" through discourse.

From Foucault's perspective (1972), "Discourses are composed of signs; but what they do is more than use these signs to designate things"—they are "practices that systematically form the objects of which they speak" (p. 49). Thus, discourse structures how we know, understand, and speak about the world. Discourse is both a symbolic and constitutive system that structures knowledge and social practice. It is in these terms that Motion and Leitch (1996) argued that, "Public relations practitioners . . . play a central role in the maintenance and transformation of discourse" (p. 298). This perspective shifts the role of public relations from information management and control to the production, contestation, and transformation of ideas and meanings that circulate in society.

The task for public relations practitioners is to ensure that certain ideas and practices become established and understood and thereby attempt to gain the hegemonic advantage for their client in this discursive struggle. This is what Motion and Leitch (1996) alluded to when they stated that, "Public relations practitioners are involved in the maintenance and transformation of discourse primarily through the production and distribution of texts . . . strategically deploying texts that facilitate certain socio-cultural practices and not others" (p. 299). From this critical perspective public relations practitioners are theorised as working to (strategically) privilege particular discourses over others, in an attempt to construct what they hope will be accepted as in the public interest and legitimated as policy.

From this critical discourse perspective, public relations professionals are in the business of creating particular knowledge and identity positions which then influence the types of social relationships that are possible within and outside that discourse. Fairclough (1992) expressed these functions of discourse in the following terms: "The identity function relates to the ways in which social identities are set up in discourse, the relational function to how social relationships between discourse participants are enacted and negotiated" (p. 64). In this context public relations is understood as explicitly concerned with constructing knowledge, identities, and relationships that will work to facilitate particular sociocultural practices—those that work for the needs and interests of the client organisation (see, for example, Motion & Leitch, 1996; Motion & Weaver, (2005); Weaver, 2001; Weaver & Motion, 2002). However, for any one discourse to dominate over others requires that it be sanctioned as "the truth." This is not to argue the case for an essential "rational" truth of the kind that Habermas attempted to theoretically maintain. Rather, as Foucault (1980) has argued:

> There is a battle "for truth" or at least "around truth"—it being understood once again that by truth I do not mean "the ensemble of truths which are to be discovered and accepted", but rather "the ensemble of rules

according to which the true and the false are separated and specific effects of power attached to the true", it
being understood also that it's not a matter of a battle "on behalf" of the truth, but of a battle about the status
of truth and the economic and political role it plays. (p. 132)

Foucault is not interested in whether a discourse is true or real; he is concerned with the
mechanics whereby one discourse becomes produced as the dominant discourse (Mills, 1997,
p. 19). In order to maintain or transform social norms through discourse, a "regime of truth"
(Foucault, 1980, p. 131) must be established through relations of power.

The establishment of a regime of truth is "linked in a circular relation with systems of
power which produce and sustain it, and to effects of power which it induces and which
extend it" (Foucault, 1980, p. 131). Truth and power, therefore, are inextricably linked and
serve to reinforce one another. The struggle to establish a regime of truth is "about the status
of truth and the economic political role it plays" (Foucault, 1980, p. 132). What Foucault is
arguing here, and what is key to a discursive theory of public relations, is that truth is, in fact,
not itself the ultimate goal of a discourse struggle. Rather, establishing truth is a means of
legitimising, or normalizing, material practices. As Fairclough (1995) explained, "The power
to control discourse is seen as the power to sustain particular discursive practices with particular
ideological investments in dominance over other alternative (including oppositional) practices"
(p. 2). This makes clear the intrinsic connection between discourse and power.

Foucault conceptualised power as both organised and hierarchical within the context of
clusters of relationships. He also conceptualised power as relational in that both domination
and resistance are strategically coordinated (McHoul & Grace, 1993). That is, Foucault (1980)
saw individuals and organisations as deploying various discourse strategies to conform with,
circumvent, or contest existing power relations. In this context he argued that:

We must make allowances for the complex and unstable process whereby discourse can be both an instrument
and an effect of power, but also a hindrance, a stumbling block, a point of resistance and also a starting point
for an opposing strategy. Discourse transmits and produces power; it reinforces it, but also undermines it and
exposes it, renders it fragile and makes it possible to thwart it. (Foucault, 1978, vol. 1, p. 101)

Although the term "power" is traditionally associated with pejorative connotations of domination (just like propaganda), and is indeed even a much (mis)used concept in critical scholarship
where it has itself become associated with the essentialising and fetishising of "oppressed"
groups (Shugart, 2003), Foucault (1972) conceived of power as positive and productive. He
stated: "What makes power hold good, what makes it accepted, is simply the fact that it doesn't
only weigh on us as a force that says no, but that it transverses and produces things, it induces
pleasure, forms knowledge, produces discourse" (Foucault, 1972, p. 119). Discourse is the
vehicle through which knowledge and truth circulate and the strategic mode by which social, political, and/or economic power is maintained or transformed. Key to the acceptance
of these social meanings and interpretations of types of knowledge is the strategic linking of
the dominance with self- or public interest—which in turn explains their social acceptance. In
these terms public relations practitioners are involved in the strategic attempt to have particular
social meanings and interpretations of events, activities, or behaviours, for example, adopted
over others, meanings and interpretations which, in turn, affect "social interaction, . . . political
deliberation and decision making" (Fraser, 1989, p. 135).

This discursive hegemonic conceptualisation of public relations makes it difficult to argue
that there is any essential and substantive difference between public relations practices and
propaganda. The arguments about propaganda outlined above where the predominant concern
of critics was to decry propaganda as psychological manipulation can equally be applied to
public relations as discourse where hegemonic power is obtained by way of offering attractive

discursive positions for the public to identify with and subject themselves to. However, as we have argued, the psychological model—-especially since the discrediting of transmission theories of communication effects—can provide no explanation of why people accept propaganda messages.

Unlike the behaviourist models of propaganda and persuasion that fail to sufficiently explain public uptake of messages, the discourse model, "because of its lack of alliance to a clear political agenda, offer[s] a way of thinking about hegemony—people's compliance in their own oppression—without assuming that individuals are necessarily passive victims of systems of thought" (Mills, 1997, p. 30). That is, Foucault's view of power assumes an active participation in discourse by the public, whereby their part in the *relationship* is determined by whether or not a discourse resonates with their individual or collective subjectivities and perceptions of reality. From this perspective, the public itself takes an active role in the construction of reality and the discourses associated with that reality. However, we would argue that public relations (and, indeed, the closely associated industries of advertising and marketing) is involved in the attempt to govern our discursive understanding of organisational practice, for example, by "condition[ing] and delimiting[ing] the field of discourse within which our public and private conversations take place" (Goldman, 1992, p. 2).

Yet, we would also argue from a discourse theory perspective that the theory holds additional value in that it allows for the possibility that public relations discursive strategies might fail. While we would agree that powerful organisations (in hegemonic and economic terms) have extensively more resources from which to draw when trying to protect and enhance their own self-interest than do marginalised groups, their success is not *necessarily* predetermined given that the discourses promoted by an organisation are open to contestation and challenge. Again, unlike behavioural arguments, the post-structuralist Foucauldian discourse position argues that "Power is always a discursive relation *rather than something which a person or group wields or bears*" (McHoul & Grace, 1993, p. 21, our emphasis).

However, while discourse practice may be somewhat participatory, the ideologies of the social and economic contexts play a significant role in predetermining which discourses will achieve ascendancy. Therefore, the potential for collaboration across competing discursive positions is limited. Indeed, Deetz (1992) suggested that:

> An adequate theory of communication dealing with participation has to be able to assess whether or not people are able to represent their competing interests within the various institutions that compose society . . . It also has to do with deeper issues of whether or not people are able to openly form their own interests and whether they are able to contribute to the formation of meaning that enables them to represent the interests that they might have. (p. 109)

For Deetz (1992), as for Habermas, the emergence of the corporation "as the primary institution in modern society" (p. 109), and its whole machinery of promotion and publicity, has severely restrained the ability of the public to formulate alternative meanings and interests outside of those constructed and maintained by capitalism. This is due in part to the fact that the corporation has so successfully, in both discursive and material terms, constructed "the public interest" as intrinsically connected to "the corporate interest." Of course, the recent rise of the anti-globalisation movement does bear testament to the fact that the possibility for participation and the representation of competing or alternative interests does still exist.

CONCLUSION

As we have outlined, theories of propaganda very often position propagandists as possessing and wielding power, and succeeding in determining behavioural outcomes on the part of their audiences. While we reject the behaviourist underpinnings of this theory of propaganda effects, a view of propagandists and even public relations practitioners as being able to affect audience behaviour—against the interests of that audience—is not incompatible with a discourse perspective. In a situation of there being only a single discourse on an issue available that, for one reason or another, goes uncontested—perhaps because competing discourses have been discredited or the channels of communication closed down—audiences are more likely to accept and act upon the propaganda/public relations message. Certainly in dictatorial regimes this is how propaganda as discourse can be understood to work.

This is not to say that in democratic societies organisations do not similarly strive to have their "propaganda"—or singular discursive perspective—on an issue accepted by publics. The difference is that in the context of democracy other competing discourses (supposedly) also have avenues for expression and promotion. In these terms, discourse theory helps to move away from the notion of propaganda as deception and lying because it acknowledges the potential for competing discourses and competing truths in society: Multiple discourses circulate and compete with each other for hegemonic power and therefore there is a choice of meanings, identities, and realities available to audiences, not one all-powerful construction of reality. As is evident, discourse theory recognizes that power is present in all relationships, but that publics are able to choose to accept or reject a discourse according to whether it is perceived as being either in their own or the public interest. Yet we would also argue, in agreement with Deetz (1992) and Philo and Miller (2001), that Western corporate capitalism has succeeded in dominating the range of discourses, and indeed our material practices and notions of public interest, to such an extent that it is difficult for alternative discourses and practices to rise to any level of ascendancy without violence—as the 9/11 attacks on the World Trade Center demonstrate. Those attacks can be understood as an attempt to make America and Europe pay attention to accumulated Muslim resentments against a history of Western prejudice, exploitation, and anti-Muslim foreign policy in the Middle East. In effect, Al Qaeda's actions forced consideration, though not necessarily successfully, of how the West has crowded out alternative discursive meanings and visions of how societies can be managed socially, politically, economically, and religiously.

While the critical theory perspective drawn on here finds no substantive difference between propaganda and public relations, this is as a consequence of a rejection of the notions that propaganda *necessarily* operates counter to the public interest, and that public relations necessarily works *for* the public interest. As we have argued, the merits of propaganda and public relations practice can only be judged in terms of the contexts and ends to which they are used. This does not necessarily mean that because critical theorists might regard propaganda and public relations as part of a continuum, that we regard systems theorists constructions of symmetrical public relations as "a utopian attempt to make an inherently evil practice good" (Grunig, 2001, p. 16). Rather, we would argue that the critical discourse theory view of public relations, and indeed propaganda, provides a means of understanding the significance of the public relations contribution to the formation of hegemonic power, constructions of knowledge, truth, and the public interest. Understood in these terms, public relations becomes a tool of social power and change for utilization by not only those who hold hegemonic power, but also those who seek to challenge and transform that power and reconfigure dominant perceptions of the public interest.

2

Public Relations and Propaganda: Conceptual Issues, Methodological Problems, and Public Relations Discourse

Jacquie L'Etang
Stirling Media Research Institute

This chapter seeks to explain the problems that arise in trying to define public relations and propaganda as separate concepts. In other words: if they are the same, how are they different? This challenging task is made more so because for many public relations theorists and practitioners, the concepts arouse strong emotions. For contemporary public relations practitioners, the charge of propaganda is a threat to their self-image as aspiring professionals; for some journalists and media sociologists, the terms are interchangeable and public relations simply an outgrowth of capitalism, an instrument of domination, and a threat to the public sphere. Thus, we have a definitional issue that is already clouded to some degree by parties who have a clear self-interest in the debate: practitioners who seek legitimacy for their occupation; journalists, whose power to define news has been challenged and eroded by the emergence of organisational advocates; and media sociologists, some of whom may be inclined to lean towards conspiracy theories and demonisation. Finally, there is the response of public relations academics which has been largely to ignore the whole issue (many books on public relations do not even reference propaganda) or to position it solely as part of the occupation's history or as confined to political communication. This is largely a consequence of managerialist, functionalist, and technocratic thinking which has necessarily dominated a (predominantly American) scholarship largely subservient to the emergent semi-profession. In short, it appears that there is a contest over the meaning of "public relations" and "propaganda" between various actors, some of whom could be seen as ideologues. The purpose of this chapter is to try and understand that contest, the intentions and reasons for its existence, and to consider whether there are alternative routes to analysing the concepts.

Analysis of the relationship between public relations and propaganda seems to require consideration of historical events and their impact on ideas and definitions; communicative processes and techniques, especially those concentrating on persuasion and rhetorical techniques (see Weaver et al., this volume); conceptual frameworks that engage with epistemological questions of knowledge, truth, and interpretation (see Weaver et al., this volume); and morality (right or wrong, good or bad). A major challenge is whether it is possible to identify crucial characteristics or features that distinguish public relations or propaganda—the necessary conditions for each—whilst at the same time taking into account the historical and cultural background and the ongoing ideological struggle between proponents and opponents of public relations practice. Steering a course between criticism and apologism is unlikely to please anybody, but may be helpful in trying to piece together a more rounded understanding of the concepts. That, at least, is my aim.

The approach taken here is to begin with an historical review of the terms "propaganda" and "public relations" in an attempt to identify crucial points and contexts in which the terms became associated or disassociated. The broad political and historical transformations that facilitated the emergence of the concepts "public relations" and "propaganda" are sketched out, drawing examples from the literature that has explored their relationship. In particular the notion of public relations as education is given some reflection.

There is a more detailed exploration of the British scene in terms of the way in which the emergent occupation in the post-World War II era engaged with these concepts in terms of professional identity and the legitimacy or illegitimacy of the function. In this way some attention is given to public relations discourse (see Weaver et al. this volume) and the way in which the public relations occupation has sought to appropriate and legitimise a set of concepts or practices and thus gain an elite position in society through the attainment of professional status (see Pieczka and L'Etang, this volume, chapter 14). For decades practitioners have bemoaned the lack of 'public relations for public relations' but critics might suggest that the occupation is simply the respectable face of propaganda—"the public relations of propaganda." This chapter explores the conceptual and historical issues of this conundrum. The analysis is facilitated by the presentation of original and previously unpublished empirical data on public relations discourse in its formative post-Second World War period from an extensive sociohistorical project completed in 2001.

PROPAGANDA AND PUBLIC RELATIONS:
HISTORICAL CONTEXTS

Propaganda Paradigms in History

It is possible to identify various types of historical propaganda: religious, regime, colonial, territorial, royal, bureaucratic/administrative, political/ideological (governmental, NGO, terrorist), corporate, and activist. Within each of these domains opposing actors seek to persuade others towards their views on a vast range of topics such as resource allocation, safety of science and technology, health and anti-health. Propaganda has been communicated through a range of media: symbols, articles, books, literature, poetry, architecture, music, film, posters. Propaganda has been conducted in wartime and in peacetime in both totalitarian and democratic contexts. Perhaps a useful way to distinguish propaganda is to define it as monolithic communication on a grand scale that attempts to encompass all aspects of culture. Thus, propaganda is that which affects social construction to such a degree that its assumptions are welded to the taken-for-granted norms and values of the host culture and makes it difficult for deviant views to be expressed. Ultimately there is no "accommodation" process to be made by individuals, as the norms and values define their identity.

Methodological Issues

One of the difficulties that faces any historian of public relations is exactly where to begin. There appear to be two choices: one is to concentrate on the period when those terms were employed and when a discrete occupation appeared to emerge; the second is to identify the essential elements of practice and relate these to activities conducted in human society for aeons. Both approaches have pros and cons. Concentrating on the modern period seems historically more methodologically sound and recognisably linked to the contemporary scene. However, this approach does have disadvantages in that it encourages the view that public relations and propaganda are relatively new social practices. Yet it is clear that there are aspects of public relations practice such as argument and discourse which can be easily compared to Aristotle's ideas and Plato's critique of the speech consultants, the Sophists, can also be usefully applied to public relations consultants (see L'Etang, this volume, chapter 18). It seems that fear and criticism of persuasive communication and its ethics in society are universal problematics regardless of historical context or, indeed, terminology. This alerts us to the first methodological problem in discussing propaganda and public relations: historical explanation (events, concepts, debates) may tell us how and why concepts arose, were empowered by language to become part of discourse, ideology, culture, and the economy; but it cannot offer a typology of practice or guidelines for universal definitions or ethical judgements. History can only produce partial truths and contextual data about past events and is weak on prediction. This is one of the fundamental flaws with the traditional paradigm in public relations as laid out now almost infamously by Grunig and Hunt (1984) in that it attempts to encompass a typology of effectiveness, a typology of ethical practice, and historical explanation. The typologies are used as the basis for much deductive research which necessarily cannot incorporate the philosophical and historical reflection necessary for a fuller understanding of the practice and the (possibly conflicting) intentions and effects. My main interest at this point, however, is to elucidate and exemplify some of the key developments in the 20th-century evolution of the concepts of propaganda and public relations, from a largely, but not exclusively British perspective.

Thus far it has been established that there is a methodological tension between historical (time-line) and typological approaches. With regard to typological approaches there are some other technical considerations. First of all there is the question of the level of analysis which could be focused on the state, an ideology, an organisation, an individual, or a text. If we are making definitional judgements about such a pejorative term as propaganda, we need to be clear about the level and quantity of evidence that is required to support any claim. In other words, what are the necessary conditions? Second, a number of different disciplines can be brought to bear upon cases (and, at paradigm level I would suggest that it is useful to approach analysis in the field using case study approaches since those require triangulated multi-methods for a richer and deeper understanding): philosophy, psychology, sociology, politics, communications.

Philosophy can offer us understanding of universal concepts such as truth, deception, coercion, prejudice, fairness, right, wrong, good, bad. Such a focus might direct us towards identification of intent, the nature of established relationships, and areas of exploitation. This seems important given that the intention behind many of the efforts to define an activity as "propaganda" is primarily to condemn it on grounds of immorality. It remains the case that some who do so fail to explore the moral bases for their criticism and thus do not really advance our understanding of the concepts or develop sophisticated arguments. Psychology focuses usefully on cognitive processes and emotional influences that cause persuasion, social, and peer influences and could address questions about what it means to be propagandised, persuaded, or subject to public relations campaigns. This sort of approach has been applied to research into religious cults which explores questions of conversion and coercion in particular group settings. Sociology treats truth as a concept relative to a particular context but can explore general effects of society in relation to power-broking and, within media sociology, the way in which media are influenced by certain structural factors which may shape perceptions, media content, and potentially audiences. Thus, at a broad level it indicates patterns in society's information flow and structural impediments to communication, particularly the distorting effects of power. Media sociology has tended to take a critical and sometimes judgemental approach to public relations, particularly focused on political communication and the pejorative role of "spin doctors." The discourse of "spin doctor" is suggestive of webs of deceit, magic and manipulation, though to date there has been little analysis of the term, its origins, and denotative and connotative meanings. As one former prime ministerial adviser from the 1970s commented:

> The trouble is that now everything is being analysed as "what the spin doctor said." I marvel at the spin doctors . . . I don't know where the title came from . . . I have never been a spin doctor . . . in advising a minister—and this is legitimate spin doctoring—I would advise the minister as to the likely reaction to what he is going to say . . . so he can prepare himself for the supplementary question . . . I think it's making everybody too self-conscious . . . we're all psychoanalysts now . . . There is nothing new about it [spin-doctoring]. Nero I'm sure contemplated exactly how he was going to present himself . . . it has become a spurious science. (Interview, Henry James, 17/4/97)

Politics tends to take a more case-based approach and can offer insights into particular regimes and ideologies, analysing particular politicians and leaders and the promotion of ideology to control national and transnational cultures. Communications theory can work at a number of levels including direction, flow and force of communication, the nature of dialogue, distortions and barriers to communication, rhetorical strategies, and discourse analysis. While each of these approaches is highly informative and insightful, it is surely only by taking an interdisciplinary approach moving away from a media-centric approach towards a multi-factorial analysis that we can be in a position to make sensitive definitional judgements.

PROPAGANDA AND PUBLIC RELATIONS: INTELLECTUAL HISTORY AND PRAXIS

The origins of the term "propaganda" have been defined as doctrinal and ideological. Its religious origins (Jowett & O'Donnell, 1986, p. 15; Jackall, 1995, p. 1; M. Grant, 1994, p. 11) have been noted and have clearly tied the term to persuasion and influence on people's beliefs. But since social nomenclature changes to reflect cultural experience, the term has acquired negative connotations, but not in a very consistent way. According to Grant, while the *Oxford English Dictionary* in 1909 described propaganda as "any association, systematic scheme or concerted movement for the propagation of a particular doctrine or practice" (M. Grant, 1994, p. 11), she argued that it was not until after the First World War that criticism emerged of American, British, and German governments' manipulation of their citizens. The newly emerging science of social psychology legitimised fears of mass manipulation and were reinvented later by the emergent field of media studies. However, despite this early evidence that the term propaganda had been tainted with negativity, it is clear that publicists and public relations practitioners in non-governmental contexts remained comfortable with the term and, as will be shown later, as late as the 1950s, many public relations practitioners used the terms interchangeably. This suggests that despite constant attacks on its legitimacy as an occupation from the media (L'Etang, 2004, pp. 124–156), practitioners had sufficient social power and confidence not only to practice in a wide variety of contexts but also to start the process of professionalisation. Perhaps too much attention has been given to high-profile controversial crises involving politics and risk communication, and insufficient analysis made in more down-to-earth areas connected to the everyday reality of people's lives in relation to, for example, consumer products and services, leisure, entertainment, health, sport, and tourism. Improving our understanding of the communications in such areas and their intentions, persuasive efforts, media coverage, reception, and social impact might balance our understanding of the over-all role of persuasive communication in society and provide a counterpoint to some overtly negative and simplistic accounts.

There are two alternative approaches which would help redress the balance and provide a more richly coloured account of practice instead of the black-and-white images that persist. The use of case study methodology can provide a deep understanding of different perspectives in a debate contextualised by insights into organisational cultural practices, mores, values, and beliefs that influence actors and rhetors. However, it has to be borne in mind that "case study" conducted in the methodologically rigorous way required (Yin, 2003a, 2003b) using multi-methods, needs to be written up in a sufficiently reflexive and transparent way reveal-ing researchers' assumptions, explaining the relationship between researcher and researched, acknowledging the presence and influence of power, and so on (Yin, 2003a, 2003b). The case study approach could be taken within the ethnographic paradigm, a currently some-what underexplored approach in public relations. Hence, our understanding of public rela-tions practitioners as an occupational group is relatively limited since ethnography has not been employed as a research tool. While a few practitioners are high-profile individuals, rel-atively little is known of the culture and mores of the occupation. Only patient ethnography at the doctoral and post-doctoral levels could flesh out a broader picture of the occupation, and such projects seem unlikely in a research agenda driven either by functionalism (con-cerned with effectiveness and professional standing) or paranoia (concerned with demonising persuasion).

Understanding practitioners better and the opportunities and constraints on their work might be important in understanding key issues before condemning or condoning organisational communication. For example, since it has been suggested (Jowett & O'Donnell, 1986) that one of the major features of propaganda is that the source or sender of the message is not always identified, and since media may not always identify sources, it is important to know how an organisational position is arrived at (opportunities for dissent) and if efforts have been made to communicate "with," as opposed to, "to" stakeholders utilising forms other than mass media, and, if so, what views the stakeholders have of that communication. For this reason Habermas' Theory of Communicative Action (TCA) has become important to theoretical justifications for public relations practice if not (yet) to the practice itself. Critical theory is important, not only for the education of public relations students in order to help them identify problematic areas of practice, but also for practitioners in alerting them to the need for transparency. Burkhart (in van Ruler & Verčič, 2004) very usefully showed how transparency can be achieved in practice in terms of external audiences; a further step would be to reveal the process of internal policy formation and its rationale.

Determining intention in an organisational context is not easy, but is important is trying to understand the ethics of organisational communication. This issue has received attention in business ethics literature which has debated the epistemological merits of anthropomorphising organisations so that lawyers can assess the degree to which *mens rea* could be applied in the case of organisational misdemeanours (see L'Etang, chapter 21, this volume). Blaming a whole organisational culture for corporate wrongdoing is a crude approach, carrying within it the possibility of punishing those who are ignorant and therefore innocent of intention. Such considerations link quite naturally to the problems that challenge international law faced with unpleasant regimes of various persuasions that have perpetrated horrors on humankind.

The contemporary problem facing public relations is therefore that many basic definitions of propaganda could be equally used to describe public relations, and the crux for many has been identifying the difference between acceptable and non-acceptable persuasion. For example, Jowett and O'Donnell identified different aims such as the promotion of mutual understanding, the promotion of interactive dependency, and the promotion of one party's objectives against another's (1986, p. 22). Their framework of white, grey, and black propaganda has been widely cited in public relations texts and also overlaps with Grunig and Hunt's popular model. Jowett and O'Donnell defined propaganda as running

> the gamut from truth to deception ... it is ... value and ideology-laden. The means may vary from a mild slanting of information to outright deception, but the ends are always predetermined in favor of the propagandist. (1986, pp. 19–20)

The difficulty with this approach is highlighted by Motion et al. (chapter 1, this volume). If knowledge is socially constructed, then one person's definition of information or slanting may be different from another's. In other words one person's public relations may be another person's propaganda. Given the complexity of some debates—for example, in the field of science (see Campbell, chapter 11, this volume)—and the room for various interpretations, it is possible to see why discussion about the relationship between public relations and propaganda has shifted from complex methodological debate to becoming embedded in ideological difference. In other words, discussion has become less conceptual and more political, driven by a variety of agendas. So discussion about propaganda is not so much about method but has itself become propagandised. Describing an act as "propaganda" is a way of implying personal allegiances and oppositions, much less about understanding the form of communication and its ethics. The use of the term captures the orator, not solely the act that he or she intends to describe. Language speaks us.

An influential strand within debates on propaganda is traceable to its religious origins: its influence on core beliefs. For example, it has been suggested that the purpose of propaganda is to "build a movement or a following" whereas public relations is "to achieve consent" or "develop dialogue" (van der Meiden cited in Traverse-Healy, 1988a). Apart from the difficulty of distinguishing between "building a movement" and "achieving consent" (one seems to imply or infer the presence of the other), is it not the case that public relations is indeed concerned with "building a movement or a following" when carrying out the publicity function for a product, a service, and especially for campaigns of persuasive communication such as health campaigns. Yet as the literature on health promotion clearly shows, health promotion or health propaganda (as some have defined it) has moved away from individual behavioural change to facilitate worker effectiveness towards context-driven approaches which acknowledge social and economic environmental problems and seek to change those rather than focusing solely on individual change. Thus, health promotion "is a collective activity" (Webster & French in Adams et al., p. 12) which is socially constructed and requires engagement with values as well as evidence. Critical theorists in the field debate the extent to which this is achievable in the context of powerful medical and governmental agendas. This suggests a necessity for communicators to demonstrate their awareness of alternative perspectives and the reasons for them. Furthermore, it implies wider social responsibility for the content, form, and style of communications that take place. Revealing and communicating underpinning values explicitly together with agendas might therefore be an important part of distinguishing public relations and propaganda. And in current practice organisational communicators do go some way to doing this: it is an important part of organisational identity construction (see Meech, chapter 20, this volume).

The area of public relations that is more open to question is that of internal communication and organisational culture. Here there is clearly an area for possible communication distortion due to power, fear, and coercion. While media academics have necessarily given much attention to source–media relations and communication among elites, there has been little attention given to internal organisational propaganda. While Morgan (1997) argued that the inevitable multiple realities in organisations will be represented by aberrant or counter-cultures, the ethical position of public relations practitioners in relation to internal communications seems bound to be problematic. There is a tricky conundrum here between maintaining coherent identity and totalitarianism. On the one hand, as Meech points out (chapter 20, this volume), "Congruence is preferable for an organisation [in relation to corporate identity] since the exposure of a glaring discrepancy could indicate a lack of cohesiveness, or worse still, hypocrisy;" on the other hand, requirements to conform not merely to symbolic displays but to behaviour, values, and conventions does seem to contain problematic possibilities in terms of domination.

Well-known British practitioner Tim Traverse-Healy suggested that the legitimacy of the content and the societal importance of the concept to be inculcated was more important than the technique when he wrote in the International Public Relations Association "Gold Paper" that:

> It is quite clear that in early times emphasis was placed upon the unquestioned "rightness" of the doctrine to be propagated ... and the concomitant necessity to mankind or society of the belief being accepted by its members without question. And Belief without Question indicates Faith; and Faith is the Truth. Down the years this unswerving belief in the rightness of their particular brand of truth distinguishes the instigator of propaganda. (1988a, p. 5)

There are two difficulties here: first, beliefs may be either true or false regardless of the degree of faith placed in them; second, the argument seems to suggest that belief in a cause in itself defines propaganda. So if public relations practitioners happen to believe in the cause or organisation on whose behalf they are acting, then this, according to a publication emanating from the main international public relations body at one point in its history, would mean they are propagandists.

The focus on belief as an essential characteristic raises other issues. In a relativist context beliefs of all persuasions have legitimacy: it is a truism now that one person's terrorist is another's freedom fighter. In this context, maybe it is not so much *truthfulness* which counts but *rightness* in terms of moral position and behaviour. This would account for the very necessary ethical turn in terms of the analysis of organisational communication focusing on legitimacy, communication process, and intention but also requires attention to the morality of an organisation's overall purpose.

Some suggest that persuasion that is dependent on emotional appeals can bypass the rational faculties to provoke a knee-jerk and pre-conditioned response. This has especially been the case in discussing the communications of totalitarian states or states in conflict. There are some problems with this approach to communications. First, is it really possible to "bypass" rational faculties? What type of adult is one whose rationality can be bypassed? Surely we need our rational faculties to make sense of emotional experience and sensations and it is this aspect which distinguishes humankind from animals.

Second, it is an approach very much based on the hypodermic model of communication and mass media effects which assumes a passive audience and ignores the potential for alternative or aberrant readings of dominant presentations. Although historically this approach emerged from the analyses that followed Nazi and Communist propaganda, it still has some resonance today along with notions of "brainwashing" (especially utilised with POWs in Vietnam). Such dramatic cases necessarily attract condemnation but also seem to develop into caricatures that ultimately dehumanise. Perhaps this process usefully distances such behaviour from our own

lives. Either way, it seems more important to determine the extent of coercion or the freedom
to express alternative views.

EDUCATION AND PROPAGANDA

Public relations in the UK partly emerged out of concepts of democratic education for citizens,
and the educational aspects of public relations practice remain entrenched. Education is likely
to be seen as morally unproblematic, connoting positive values and thus beneficial to the public
relations of public relations in its quest for social legitimacy. However, the importance of the
educational concept for public relations' moral purity does require some interrogation, not
least because the role of education has been seen as an antidote to propaganda. However,
turning to the critical work of French social theorist Jacques Ellul, one discovers the reverse
thesis that suggests education is actually a necessary prerequisite for propaganda. Such a view
necessarily has implications for the ethics of PR practice and for its connection to propaganda.

The connection between public relations and propaganda is evident when we turn to the
educative aspects of each definition. The work of Ellul is significant and remains so. His radical
thesis was that propaganda was not only intrinsic to, but absolutely essential to democratic
society. Writing in 1962 (the original French edition was translated into English and published
in 1966), Ellul argued against the view that propaganda was intrinsically evil and concerned
with promoting untruths. Ellul's project was to go beyond an analysis of persuasion to identify
essential features of propaganda (of which persuasion was just one part). In particular he
reversed the common view that the role of education is to provide a defence against propaganda
and suggested education was actually a prerequisite of propaganda.

For Ellul, public relations was simply one element of propaganda. Methodologically we
can see that propaganda is tied closely to intention and source of one party and may include
a widespread vision that encompasses a culture whereas public relations tends to be more
narrowly focused and in contemporary Western society operates on behalf of a very great
range of interests (governmental, activist, corporate, terrorist). It is too simplistic to suggest
that public relations only supports those in power. Discussion of propaganda ought not to be
limited to the political domain and the activities of governments, politicians, "spin doctors,"
and journalists. Indeed, the issue of propaganda and indoctrination in the classroom was a
matter for considerable debate within the field of education in the 1970s. The role of education
in society has been a major focus for the sociologist Pierre Bourdieu, whose work has explored
the reproduction strategies used by dominant elites (Harkner, Makar, & Wilkes, 1990, p. 94).
The process of transformation of the dominant habitus to cultural capital demonstrates the
connection between education and propaganda. It is also useful in considering the role that
education plays in the process of professionalisation to which the public relations occupation
is now heavily committed. Public relations is an agent in the creation and dissemination of
concepts, but the occupation is also dependent on education to improve its status and as an
apparently benign justification or definition (with which Ellul would not agree) to gain social
respectability and legitimacy for practice. In public relations discourse the "educational" aspect
of the work is a taken-for-granted value that seems to have moral standing. It is the reproduction
of value-laden assumptions that Ellul warned us is the necessary function of propaganda.

Ellul's definition is drawn from the intellectual history of the concepts. Early practitioners
in the UK did indeed see propaganda as operating at a higher level (more "strategic" in today's
parlance) and something akin to the overall vision and mission of an enterprise. They separated
out the supporting disciplines of "publicity" (supply of information through specific media or
other techniques), "salesmanship" (promotion), "intelligence" (gathering information on current trends and policy, internal and external, and supplying this to public relations specialists),

and "public relations" (exchange of information to improve relationships); (L'Etang, 2004, pp. 24–26). Interestingly, some post-war practitioners, many of whom saw the concepts as inter-linked (unsurprising since a number had worked in propaganda functions during the Second World War), reversed the conceptual hierarchy and chose to see public relations as visionary and the over-arching concept, and propaganda, particularly "black" or deceptive propaganda, as simply one possible technique in the practitioner's armoury. In relation to this, Ellul argued that:

> Propaganda must be total... must utilise all of the technical means... all of these media... one leaves no part of the intellectual or emotional life alone... not one of these instruments must be left out: they must all be used in combination. The propagandist uses a keyboard and composes a symphony. (Ellul, p. 10)

The musical metaphor has also been used by public relations practitioners describing the practice, for example: "Professional public relations is like being the conductor of an orchestra... it requires a higher level of operation" (Warren Newman, Interview, 17/3/97).

Ellul argued that propaganda embraced psychological techniques, including those that were focused on educational objectives, psychological warfare, coercive reeducation and brainwashing, and also, "public and human relations [which] may shock some readers, but we shall show that these activities are propaganda because they seek to adapt the individual to a society, to a living standard, to an activity. They serve to make him conform which is the aim of all propaganda" (Ellul, 1966, p. xiii).

For Ellul education was pre-propaganda providing paradigms, frameworks, and "evidence" in the form of secondhand information to guide the individual's sense-making and provide a sense of community and belonging. Social education assists identity construction as well as providing personal connection with mediated events. Controversially, Ellul saw intellectuals as the most vulnerable group to propaganda because of their ready assimilation of large amounts of secondhand information (and his thesis here is even more relevant today with Internet dependence demonstrated both by academics and students), their arrogance in assuming themselves to have independent judgement, and their natural inclination to be opinionated.

Konrad Kelling, introducing Ellul's work, pointed out that:

> Modern propaganda has long disdained the ridiculous lies of past and outmoded forms of propaganda. It operates instead with many different kinds of truth—half truth, limited truth, truth out of context. Even Goebbels always insisted that Wehrmacht communiqués be as accurate as possible. (1966, p. v.)

Ellul classified the social role of propaganda with regard to its origins, purpose, and approach. He distinguished between "political propaganda" aimed at selling government policies at home and abroad from "sociological propaganda" which was designed to promote particular lifestyles, cultural values, and national identities produced by society (though these might be manipulated and articulated by government, for example, the American Dream, the British Council). He also delineated "agitation propaganda" which aimed to unify an audience against an enemy through demonisation (religious and racial dichotomies provide countless examples here) and "integration propaganda" designed to create a state of conformity to a new social order (post-devolution Scotland). A further feature of Ellul's framework was his distinction between "vertical" and "horizontal" propaganda. "Vertical propaganda" created fanatical support for a leader (this could apply to political or business contexts, for example, business leaders such as Richard Branson or Anita Roddick). In comparison to this, "horizontal propaganda" aimed to propagate group dynamics or egalitarian relationships (for example, the promotion of social practices such as children swearing allegiance to the U.S. flag in school). Finally, Ellul separated "rational propaganda" based on facts, figures, and logical argument and "irrational propaganda" based on emotions, patriotism, and mythical figures such as St George and the Dragon (the latter has cultural resonance in England, Catalunya, and Georgia). The weakness of the rational/irrational paradigm has already been discussed, but the broad sociological aspect of Ellul's framework is extremely useful in determining social or national trends that result from many individual actions, opinions, decisions and, maybe, accommodations to perceptions of dominant norms (Noelle-Neumann's thesis of the 'spiral of silence is of relevance here) (Noelle-Neumann, 1987).

It is worth noting that only very recently has Ellul made an appearance in the public relations literature. Zhang and Cameron (2004) applied Ellul's political and ideological framework to China to provide useful empirical data to support an analysis of the structural transformation of China's public sphere and the emergence of integration propaganda following those changes and new instabilities such as unemployment in the late 1990s (p. 313). While arguing that "nationalism is still the most powerful paradigm within which understandings of the past are popularly presented" (p. 315), Zhang and Cameron gave the example of China's Xia-Shang-Zhon Chronology Project to illustrate how archaeological and cultural events can be hijacked for the purposes of sociological and integration propaganda. Clearly the Beijing Olympics in 2008 heralds new opportunities in this direction.

Ellul's contribution can be seen as similar to ideas put forward by advertiser Charles Higham in the 1930s and the Scottish leader of the British Film Documentary Movement, John Grierson (whose archive at Stirling University is close to his birthplace). Higham was an enthusiast for film as a technique for government propaganda, community education, and the dissemination of ideas to educate the populace on a range of topics from hygiene and health to high and low culture and argued that publicity should be used "to formulate and inspire a collective aim or national idea" (Higham, 1920, pp. 80–82). These ideas seemed to anticipate those of two key figures in the formation of the public relations occupation in the UK (L'Etang, 2004 and chapter 8, this volume)—Sir Stephen Tallents, a high-level civil servant who wrote the blueprint for the British Council, *The Projection of England*, in 1932 and Grierson, who wrote and lectured extensively on the need to educate the masses to make democracy work.

Grierson's ideas about public relations developed throughout his life and encompassed definitions, theory, and practice. The main focus of his thinking could be described as social or democratic education, the role of propaganda, and social responsibility, and it is echoes of these that can be detected in public relations discourse.

> Democracy was in danger of collapse, because its citizens did not know how to make it work. The weakness, therefore, was essentially in the realm of public education and information. The vast possibilities of the new mass media . . . had not been spotted as the key to the problem. Film, because of its obvious mass popularity, and the vividness of the visual image . . . was an obvious choice as a medium in which to put the theory into practice. (John Grierson Archive G5:16:1, p. 1)

Grierson saw educatory films as a solution because it could "do something to bridge the gap between the citizen and the wide world" (John Grierson Archive G4:19:21, p. 3), because even "[i]f you can't teach the citizenry to know everything about everything all the time, you can give them comprehension of the dramatic patterns within a living society" (John Grierson Archive G4:19:21, p. 3). Grierson saw education as an instrument for social action (John Grierson PRO BT 64/86 6880, p. 2), declaring that:

> Its function is the immediate and practical one of being a deliberate social instrument—not dreaming in an ivory tower, but outside on the barricades of social construction, holding citizens to the common purpose their generation has set for them. Education is activist or it is nothing. (John Grierson Archive G4:19:1, p. 1).

Thus, education was seen as a key source for social change.

These themes were picked up by one eminent public relations practitioner in the mid-1950s, Alan Campbell-Johnson, who commented in what was described as "a philosophy of public relations" on

> the growing gulf between the active and passive elements in our community—the leaders and the led, the experts and the laymen, the players and the spectators. To cope with this cleavage, intensified as it is by the industrial and technical revolution around us is, I believe, the central function of public relations...the solidarity we seek can only be achieved by breaking up the mass into ever smaller and better informed groups, and re-asserting the final status and dignity of the individual's citizenship. (1956, p. 53)

Grierson saw propaganda as the means to educate the populace about complex social realities and defined propaganda as "the art of public persuasion" (John Grierson Archive G3A:5:1), a view shared by Fleetward Pritchard, an eminent public relations practitioner who ran one of the earliest agencies of the post-war era and was of the view that "[o]rganised persuasion is necessary to the proper integration of all civilised communities" (Pritchard, 1950, p. 20 in L'Etang, 2000, p. 84). Elsewhere Grierson defined public relations pragmatically, in terms of building particular relationships "good public relations, meaning good relations with the public, good relations with the responsible forces of society, good relations with the various forces of national leadership" (John Grierson Archive G:34:26). Definitions were much debated by the post-war generation of public relations practitioners, but typical examples included "the business of creating and maintaining...good relations with the public" (*Public Relations*, 1948, p. 1); "a two-way function... interpreting the understanding to the public... interpreting the public to the understanding.... aimed at enhancing the prestige of the trade concerned" (Murray Milne, 1950, p. 8); and "anything and everything that leads to better understanding between people" (*Public Relations*, 1955, p. 16).

Thus far, an attempt has been made to understand a variety of approaches to defining propaganda and public relations and the relationship between the concepts. A number of paradigms and methodological difficulties have been outlined. The importance of these debates relates to the ongoing public relations professionalisation project, which is inhibited by the connection with propaganda that is reinforced by those who define public relations solely as manipulation in the service of the powerful.

PROPAGANDA AND PUBLIC RELATIONS PRACTITIONERS' SELF-IDENTITY AND DISCOURSE IN THE FORMATIVE ERA OF PROFESSONALISATION

How have public relations practitioners understood the practice of propaganda in relation to their own occupation? This section draws on some historical data from the UK in which research in the Institute of Pubic Relations archives was complemented with in-depth qualitative interviews conducted with nearly 70 practitioners active in the field after the end of World War II during the crucial period of the occupation's establishment as a discrete field separate from publicity and advertising. Nineteen of those interviewed held the position of either President of the Institute of Public Relations (IPR, formed 1948) or of the international body International Public Relations Association (IPRA, formed 1955). Inductive analytical procedures were followed to code data from interviews and from the Institute of Public Relations' journals.

Following the style of Miles and Huberman (1992) tabulated quotes of representative discourse are presented under the following headings (which also form the structure of discussion):
(1) "Public Relations: Its Importance to the World (Ideological Justification), (*Public Relations*
1948–1955); (2) "Evangelism (Proselytism)" (*Public Relations* 1948–55); (3) "Debates over
Nomenclature and Difficulties in Defining Public Relations" (*Public Relations* 1948–55); and
(4) "Propaganda" (*Public Relations* 1948–55).

The purpose of presenting post-war data coded into key themes is multifold. First, it privileges key actors articulating values within the safe confines of their own professional journal.
Thus, it can be regarded as a reliable guide to these practitioners' social construction of public
relations and the dominant values of many who continued to influence the professional body
well into the 1990s (Tim Traverse Healy, Sam Black, and Joyce Blow are prime examples).
The quotations thus give insights into the problematics of public relations and propaganda as
experienced by those in practice as expressed in their own words. The tables, therefore, serve
another purpose of giving practitioners a voice in a way that rarely happens in public relations
research. As such it offers a small slice of public relations discourse and suggests some of
the difficulties and anxieties as the public relations occupation began to construct a formal
semi-professional identity.

The very first issue of the IPR journal was necessarily self-conscious and included attempts
to define the ideals and social role of the practice. The fundamental value that was highlighted
was that of truthfulness, as explained by the first editor, Bill Seymour:

> It is the responsibility of the serious practitioner . . . to convince those in authority that, whatever the objective,
> Truth is the best weapon. (Seymour, "Truth is the best weapon," *Public Relations* 1(1), 1948, p. 1)

TABLE 2.1
"Public Relations: Its Importance to the World" (Ideological Justification), *Public Relations*
1948–1955

"The beliefs we hold are as wide as our shades of public opinion; as varied as the work we do. But one belief we hold
in common—that the proper practice of public relations is of unassessable importance to the future of our world."
[Editorial, Warren Seymour, *Public Relations* 1(1), 1948, p.1]

"There is a need right through the country . . . for a more sensitive system of communication and, with the Cold
War which exists today between men and nations, Public Relations is the most important thing in the world." [First
Week-end School, *Public Relations* 1(4), 1949, p. 7]

"The need for public relations in the modern world is self-evident to the most myopic observer of the contemporary
world. I have referred to it as the dock leaf growing beside the bureaucratic nettle, but in our work we are in fact taking
sides in the perpetual war for the soul of Man . . . We shall not be content to act solely as a mediator in this struggle."
[The Presidential Address, Roger Wimbush, *Public Relations* 5(2), 1953]

"The function of the Institute must be to explain how important our job is; we must make people realise that. One
would think, in a world in which wars have been conducted solely by ideas, that public relations would be seen to be
one of the most vital jobs which today exist. But the truth has to be brought home. It is very necessary to make people
realise the honest importance of the work which we are setting out to do. People do not realise it, you know."
[Speeches at the Luncheon, Sir Stephen Tallents, *Public Relations* 1(2), 1948]

"It was vital to let the rest of the world—particularly the underdeveloped areas—know about the British way of
life . . . the problem was of world importance because knowledge of our democratic principles could be a most potent
defence against communism and a powerful weapon in the 'cold war.'"
["Public Relations in Industry," First Session of Conference, *Public Relations* 4(4), 1952, p. 2]

"Democracy vitally needs professional expert and technical advice if it is to hold the allegiance and maintain the
confidence of the people."
["Democracy Can Be Safeguarded by Public Relations," *Public Relations* Ian Harvey MP, 7(2), 1955]

TABLE 2.2
"Evangelism," (Proselytism) *Public Relations* 1948–1955

"If we do not believe in the worthwhileness of the organisations whose gospel we set out to deliver. Then not only shall we fail in our mission but we shall be unworthy of our craft."
[The Conference Speeches, Alan Hess, President, *Public Relations 3*(2), 1950, p. 6]

"If one might without levity define Almighty God as the Prime Organisation, then parsons have been public relations officers ever since Our Lord sent out the first apostles. One might even go further back and say that Moses was applying a special public relations technique when he displayed the Ten Commandments."
["You Make Me Feel at Home," Rev Dewi Morgan, Press Officer for the Propagation of the Gospel in Foreign Parts, *Public Relations 4*(4), 1952, p. 16]

"Faith, exemplified in our adherence to Christian principles and thought it . . . essential to the preservation of western life as we know it . . . the local Press of our country—and notably the London and Home Counties weekly Press with which I am most closely in touch—demonstrates unfailingly, week in and week out, the realisation of the high trust that is theirs. Despite newsprint shortages they manage to devote considerable space to the reflection of Christian thought and practice . . . building in this way a formidable rampart against the insidious workings of evil propaganda."
[Bulwark of Freedom, Gorge Dodson-Wells, PRO London Transport, *Public Relations 4*(1), 1951, p. 67]

"Although studying methods and ways and means is absolutely indispensable for mastering a profession, this line of study may only create experts and not apostles. Yet it is apostles which public relations needs. Apostles again need a philosophy."
["Aristocracy of Public Relations," M. J. Anema, *Public Relations 6*(3), 1954, p. 15]

"If we are to derive the fullest benefits from the Festival of Britain, we must project all that is best in our way of life, in our industries and services in our incomparably beautiful land."
[The Conference Speeches, Alan Hess, President, *Public Relations 3*(2), 1950, p. 5]

Public relations practitioners were thus positioned as ethical, righteous, and honest brokers who publicised information and improved understanding between various parties. In this lies the root connection to Grierson's democratic education (benign view of practice) and Ellul's propaganda (hostile view of practice). This has remained a fundamental problematic as indicated by the currency of the spin doctor debate alluded to earlier.

A dominant theme that emerged was of the ideological importance of public relations to the world. Public relations was seen as a conduit for the "right" ideas to prevail in society. A predominant ideal was that of "freedom." Public relations was presented both as a source of morally good ideas in itself and as a technique that could be favourably contrasted with "totalitarianism." The Cold War context and the fear of nuclear conflict in the newly post-nuclear world suggested to some an opportunity for the public relations occupation to move centre stage as a "group of crusaders" (Lipscombe, 1953, p. 1), whose role was to provide information and explanation and improve international communication. Public relations was to be the key agent to promote democracy over alternative systems.

Table 2.1 clearly presents public relations as a role that could save and promote democracy. Imbued in these quotes is a strong sense of nationalism (thus resonating Ellul's conception), British superiority, and the need for others to recognise the importance of public relations expertise, extraordinary in an era when Public Relations was not defined or analysed.

Linked to notions of ideological importance was that of public relations practitioners performing as evangelists both for causes and also for their own cause. Table 2.2 positions practitioners as believers and proselytisers in their cause. The selection chosen embody a certain self-righteousness as well as fear of the future, perhaps the consequence of Britain's loss of position in the world. There is at this stage a clear intent to inspire using religious and

TABLE 2.3

"Debates over Nomenclature and Difficulties in Defining Public Relations," *Public Relations*
1948–1955

"The public relations officer just like the good journalist for that matter, does carry a great responsibility for truth, and I think that he is very foolish if he disregards that responsibility. In fact, no public relations can be successful unless it is supported by the facts. I think that is absolutely fundamental. We should specify that the good public relations officer is one who is concerned with putting over facts which can be supported by truth."
[Eight Men in Search of an Answer." A recorded talk previously published by *The Manager*, R. A. Paget-Cooke, Director of Public Relations, Foote, Cone & Belding, *Public Relations* 6(1), 1953]

"Public relations is, fundamentally, an attitude of mind. You must have a passionate belief in your cause—and you must see the gulf in your cause—and you must see the gulf which separates the ideal from the actual, and, with cold professional objectivity, try to persuade the actual nearer to the ideal."
[John Pringle, PRO to the British Medical Association, Editorial, *Public Relations* 6(2), 1954, p. 33]

"The tag 'Public Relations' is a relatively new one to industry, and commerce, and precious few people have their minds made up about what it means." [Public Relations in Industry, Editorial, *Public Relations* 1(1), 1948, p. 4]
"A press agent . . . is surely one who is concerned solely with getting notices about an individual or an organisation into newspapers magazines and other periodicals. Whereas a Public Relations Executive is concerned with presenting an individual or an organisation to the public in every possible way, not only with the object of getting them talked about, but to explain policy, and help the public."
[The First Conference, Editorial, *Public Relations* 1(2), 1948, p. 1]

"The lack of a good common appellation makes it all the more necessary to keep the idea always firmly in our minds that Public Relations and Publicity are not two activities but two ways of pursuing the same activity."
[The Human Factor in Organisations, Editorial, *Public Relations* 1(4), 1949, p. 17]

"However we may ultimately define Public Relations—if we ever succeed in doing so at all!—there can be no question about the objective we wish to attain by practising it. That is to help people to understand the firm or organisation we represent and to feel a kind of warm, friendly glow towards it."
["Some Things They Said," Warren Seymour, *Public Relations* 2(3), 1950, p. 4]

"The best and shortest definition of Public Relations I have come across is this 'Good performance publicly appreciated . . . Public Relations is the two-way process of presenting an organisation in its true colours to the public; and representing to that organisation the public's opinion about it as a factor to be considered in the framing of its policy.'"
["Some Things They Said," *Public Relations* 2(3), 1950, p. 6]

"The problem in defining Public Relations arises from the different ways in which people may already regard it—as a philosophy, as a code of conduct, or as a set of methods."
["Some Things They Said," *Public Relations* 2(3), 1950, p. 6]

"First, the need for a definition of Public Relations. If Public Relations were a science we should, of course, have to find a definition, for indeed exact definition is, one might say, the corner-stone of any science. But in truth Public Relations is not a science; it is much more an art, or, more properly, a craft."
[The Conference Speeches, R. Stewart Foreman, Retiring President, *Public Relations* 3(2), 1950, p. 4]

"Unless some positive action . . . is taken, I see the dangerous likelihood that the term PR may become a fashionable attachment to a host of allied tasks, thus adding to the general confusion in the minds of management as to what precisely is the purpose of public relations."
["Thinking Aloud," *Public Relations* 5(1), 1952, p. 10]

"I think perhaps one of the weaknesses of the Institute is that Public Relations is so ill-defined."
["A Provincial Member is Disturbed," *Public Relations* 5(2), 1953, p. 17]

"To me, it means just what the words imply—the business of creating and maintaining, by all known and yet-to-be discovered methods, good relations with the public."
["Public Relations in Industry," Editorial, *Public Relations* 1(1), 1948, p. 4]

"He works outwards and inwards; the only one who looks at, and judges, the organisation and its performance from a detached point of view . . . He is responsible for the projection of his organisation to the outside world . . . from what he sees and hears and anticipates outside, he is equally responsible for projection inwards; he has a part to play in the shaping of policy, not just in its explanation and defence; perhaps a determining part."
["So a Public Relations Officer Was Appointed," Editorial, *Public Relations* 2(3), 1950, p. 1]

TABLE 2.3
(Continued)

"Public Relations has never been adequately defined, but it includes publicity and a great deal more besides . . . it has a two-way function—(1) interpreting the understanding to the public, (2) interpreting the public to the understanding. Some of the measures involved may be obvious and direct, others more subtle and indirect—all are aimed at achieving he one end—enhancing the prestige of the trade concerned."
["What They Said," *Public Relations* 2(4), 1950]

"Public Relations is usually spoken of by people in one of three senses—either as a philosophy, a code of conduct or a set of methods."
["Good Business," R. A. Paget-Cooke MBE, *Public Relations* 3(3), 1951, p. 9]

"Anticipated fireworks on the subject of the definition . . . As Public Relations Officer, our first duty is to be concise. Our object should be to enlighten our public, not to confuse and mislead by platitudes and meaningless dogma of which there is already too much in our public life. I view with misgiving all that has been said and written about the drafting of a suitable definition . . . Must we confess that we, the experts, find the writing of a few descriptive lines of plain English beyond out powers. If we are to be accepted in all seriousness as exponents of persuasion, we must act and think quicker than this. Our message must be Churchillian in scope and vigour. We are practical men attempting a practical job of work. There is no mystery. The Doctor treats disease. The Architect designs buildings. The Lawyer is an expert at law. And the Public Relations Officer persuades. I suggest we become realists and not visionaries."
["That Definition," Letter to the editor, *Public Relations* 3(3), 1951, p. 16]

"Public Relations are 'good deeds well told and publicly acknowledged.'" [Rene Elvin Crawford, *Public Relations* 6(3), 1954]

"Public Relations has suffered in the past from those who, on the one hand, have tried to make a cult of it, and from others who have maintained that there is nothing to it but publicity and unpaid advertising. Public relations embraces anything and everything that leads to better understanding between people."
["The Need for Mutual Understanding," Editorial, *Public Relations* 6(4), 1954, p. 1]

"Public Relations are human relations . . . there are very few communities or relationships into which public relations should not enter."
["Response," Rt. Hon. Viscount Swinton, Secretary of State for Commonwealth Relations, *Public Relations* 7(3), 1955, p. 16]

---

nationalistic references, pointing to a conformity and homogeneity that were under threat in the post-war world. Insecurity possibly underlies the appeal to traditional values, unsurprising as practitioners sought to earn a living in post-war society.

Table 2.3 is notable for its demonstration of how the post-war practitioners struggled to define their occupation and how diverse their approaches were in terms of pragmatism and idealism. While the public service ideal is still present, there are indications of approaches more focused on persuasion and promotion. Either way, the views expressed in this period were of a different order to those of the 1920s and 1930s, being less sophisticated (L'Etang, 2004, pp. 21–29). So it appears that public relations took something of a backward step or did not build on earlier work. The examples shown in Table 2.3 illustrate an inability to think about public relations work analytically even though practitioners could articulate ideals. The ideas expressed here seem to point to the conception of public relations as an art rather than a science.

The table offers a range of specific definitions and includes a greater focus on relationships and the role (but not the process) of interpretation. One quote comes close to notions developed in the 1920s and 1930s in linking internal and external issues and a number of quotes make a clear claim to a senior level status in the organisation. Themes of truthfulness, discursiveness, honesty, goodness, and understanding all emerge as key values at this point. Some of the definitions are so broad as to be meaningless, and one quote reveals frustration at the failure to define the practice or to spell out its *technic*. As one practitioner pointed out in some frustration: "We are practical men attempting a practical job of work . . . the Public Relations Officer persuades" (*Public Relations* 3(3), 1951, p. 16).

Finally, Table 2.4 compiles some key quotes linking public relations and propaganda. These show how practitioners of that era used the terms interchangeably as well as dichotomously. Perhaps the dominant theme that emerges in the Ellulian sense is that of integration propaganda and the promotion of certain values. The quotes selected illustrate the confusion and tension over terminology in establishing ethical communication. There is a sense of the struggle to establish an acceptable practice in the post-war world. Whether we have actually moved on in our understanding and analysis since this early period may perhaps be questioned, as this chapter has sought to suggest.

IMPLICATIONS

Pulling together the insights and values offered by these tables, it is possible to identify some key oppositions which go some way to explaining public relations' conflictual identity. These can be seen to be:

Faith/belief	vs the truth	
Art)	vs Science	
Apostles)		
Cult)		
A Christian God/religion	vs Propaganda	vs Religion *as* propaganda
Public relations	vs Propaganda	vs PR *as* propaganda
Public relations philosophy	vs Policy formation	
Personal belief in cause & intent to persuade	vs Truth and the facts: Presenting an/organisation in its true colours	
Promotion & enhancing prestige	vs Helping the public *and/or* Good relations with the public	

Extrapolating further from these, it seems that there are different motivational perspectives for public relations work which could be summed up as:

- Mystical/spiritual
- Relational/emotional
- Promotional/persuasive/policy drive/pragmatic

The exploration of broader, less rational aspects of public relations may help us understand the practice as a more finely textured part of human communication. Acknowledging a link to magic, witch doctors, and religion repositions public relations as a cultural practice.

This analysis therefore suggests a rather different and possibly more complex way of conceiving public relations and identifies some fundamental differences in thinking about public relations' role in society which perhaps have not been previously articulated and which open new avenues for debate. The approach taken here also refocuses the debate on public relations and propaganda—away from discussions of power, hegemony, and democracy towards a more anthropological approach.

TABLE 2.4
"Propaganda," *Public Relations* 1948–1955

"At another time we had an Institute of Public Relations just such as this—but with a much larger blessing and possibly a better title. It called itself the Congregatio De Propaganda Fide and it had, so help us, the actual illusion of a faith to be propagated."
["The Scope of the Film in Public Relations," John Grierson, *Public Relations* 3(1), 1950, p. 13]

"What is the attitude of the individual to organised persuasion? The very natural resistance to change and the personal objection to acting just as other people do. Propaganda inevitably acts slowly and will always act slowly when directed at men with minds of their own. The second thing about the individual's attitude to propaganda is the dislike of organised propaganda which seems to come from certain classes of the community. I refer particularly to university professors and schoolmasters whose job it is to teach and influence the young, to doctors who are responsible for guiding the public in matters of health, and to politicians who have their own ideas to propagate . . . people like these are, in a sense, all personal propagandists themselves and they may resent the way in which organised propaganda often interferes with their work. I cannot blame them for this. They are entitled to their own views but I do feel that their opposition to organised propaganda might be more specific and less generalised if they really understood the function it was performing for the community as a whole . . . I believe the public have a deep-rooted fear of all organised propaganda because they have seen how it has been misused, in war and peace, with fearful results."
["Persuasion," Fleetwood Pritchard, *Public Relations* 2(4), 1950, pp. 20–21]

"The whole public relations staff must be seen as active propagandists on behalf of their organisation, thereby setting an example to other employees to seize those moments in daily conversation which provide the opportunity for giving favourable information about their own organisation and the work."
["The Talks and Discussion," Leslie Hardern, PRO North Thames Gas Board, *Public Relations* 2(4), 1950, p. 13]

"In a propaganda-ridden age public relations must stand as a sign that public opinion—freely reasoned opinion, freely presented—will be properly considered by those responsible for policy, and will, if practicable, be translated into action to the mutual benefit of supplier and consumer. Conversely, it must stands as the guarantee that the information disseminated about policy, products and services . . . will stand the test of reasoned comparison, criticism and analysis. In the wider sphere of international affairs where the task is that of informing world opinion, the standard set must be equally high. In the integrity with which this aspect of public relations is performed is one of the main bulwarks of our Western way of life, culture and thought."
["Bulwark of Freedom," George Dodson-Wells, PRO London Transport, *Public Relations* 4(1), 1951, pp. 6–7]

CONCLUSION

This chapter has highlighted methodological problems in analysing the relationship between public relations and propaganda and drawn attention to historical problems for public relations' social legitimacy and the effects on practitioners' confidence. It has explored discursive struggles and attempts to make the practice socially acceptable and unproblematic. It pinpoints a crux in history when public relations was balanced between idealistic and technical conceptions as it struggled to find a place in the economy, the system of occupations (including professions and semi-professions), and the moral universe. It goes some small way to filling a gap in public relations literature by showing sufficient qualitative data that demonstrate the difficulties that practitioners of the day encountered in the contemplation of their working lives and the wider implications of their occupation.

In particular the chapter argues for a broader inter-disciplinary and multi-method approach to analysing public relations and propaganda and to tackle the relationship at all levels (state, government, organisation, group, individual, text, discourse) in order to improve our understanding of terminology and practice. It is suggested that much greater reflexivity is required by writers in the field and that other agendas sometimes dominate analysis in a way that is not particularly helpful. A more open and self-aware approach could further understanding. The work of Zhang and Cameron is highlighted as a rare example of public relations academics engaging fully with concepts of propaganda in their use of Ellul's framework to analyse Chinese social and political structures of communication and is seen as an encouraging example of inter-disciplinary engagement.

Ellul's ideas about the role of education in society have been given emphasis, not only because of their complex relationship to the ethics of organised communication but also to indicate to educators the potential for ideological agendas in their own teaching of public relations and the necessity to question taken-for-granted values and norms.

Finally, the chapter points to a need to understand the perspective of practitioners as they too struggle to come to terms with the nature and social role of their practice, its ethical implications, and connections with propaganda and the associated historical and ideological baggage. The need for such work is implied by the noticeable silence on the subject within the public relations literature and the extensive condemnation of the practice within media sociology. A combination of reflexive theoretical analysis combined with ethnographic research of particular cases could facilitate a fuller understanding of public relations and propaganda.

3

Challenging Unreliable Narrators: Writing and Public Relations*

Anne Surma
Murdoch University

Today, the practice of public relations is often popularly regarded as primarily, and in some cases exclusively, a function of (self-) promotion and publicity. This view can obviously work to the detriment of the profession in terms of its perception and credibility as a form of authentic relationship building.[1] It can also create difficulties, since corporate public relations has become increasingly concerned, as evidenced by various communication practices, to develop and enhance relationships with its publics and stakeholders through a range of social responsibility activities: corporate governance programmes, community relations activities, philanthropic investments, and so on.

The growth of the concept of corporate social responsibility can be traced back to the activist, civil rights, and feminist movements (C. E. Clark, 2000) and the growth of consumer awareness in the 1960s, and of environmentalism in more recent years (Meech, 1996a, p. 66). The developing understandings of the relationship between private and public spheres, the growing support for the struggle to overcome social, racial and economic inequities and forms of exploitation, and the increasing focus on various forms of sustainability have come out of those earlier movements, and have influenced much contemporary thought about the place and role of business in culture. As a participating member of society—one that owes its position to and draws considerable benefits from that membership—private business, as a consequence, is widely believed to have social responsibilities. As Birch and Glazebrook argue, "Corporate practices and policies can no longer ignore the social ethical, moral and, above all, cultural consequences of their partnership with society" (2000, p. 51). The authors also contend that

---

*This chapter is adapted from a chapter in the author's book *Public and Professional Writing* published by Palgrave in 2005 and is reproduced with the publisher's permission.

[1] For example, see Clare Duffield's (2000) sceptical view of multinational corporations' approaches to their contract workers' rights, wages, and conditions of work.

41

business is pivotal in the process of shaping, influencing, and "doing culture" (2000, p. 51), thus highlighting business's involvement with rather than distinction from society and social values. The term social responsibility, therefore, has now come to be generally understood to define "the attitudes and practices which distinguish those organizations which take heed of the wider consequences of their activities rather than being motivated by considerations of profit alone" (Meech, 1996a, p. 66).

This chapter focuses on public relations (print or online) texts, which an organisation or corporation circulates specifically to articulate directly or indirectly its understandings of its social responsibilities, and discusses the ways in which its writing of narratives is used as a specific rhetorical device to define itself to its stakeholders as a socially responsible moral agent. Public relations writing is proposed as a potentially valuable social activity involving the construction, circulation, and contestation of narratives. Such narrative texts specifically include social responsibility reports, documents that are becoming increasingly significant in a corporation's demonstration of its understanding and implementation of ethical, business-related practices. Many other public relations texts, such as employee newsletters, community relations brochures, client magazines, sections of annual reports, Internet sites, and so on, which devote space to describing issues related to social responsibility, are also implicated in this chapter's discussion.[2]

Through a critique of Nike's *Social Responsibility Report 2001*, the chapter goes on to suggest why the public relations rhetoric of organisations and corporations may regularly be perceived by various stakeholders as hollow rather than meaningful, self-serving rather than other-oriented.[3] It is argued that for corporations such as Nike who engage in public relations practices of articulating their moral identity through constitutive narratives, and who are concerned to have that identity acknowledged and responded to as genuine and socially engaged, the activity of imagining others (interested readers) requires (literally) giving agency to stakeholders whose voices would complicate those narratives and their meanings. Nike and similar business organisations require the dynamic involvement, in their texts, of those stakeholders with whom the business is significantly connected, and particularly with those who are either less powerful—those who may not fall into the categories of investors or satisfied consumers, and those who actively challenge or question the ethics of Nike's practices. The imperative of such involvement is highlighted by the recent lawsuit in which Nike's claims to be a good corporate citizen were disputed. In considering what might constitute meaningful and ethical approaches to public relations, the chapter concludes with some ideas for engaging in and enabling such approaches.

METHODOLOGICAL FRAMEWORK

As the points above imply and as the case study below will demonstrate, in this study, writing and the use of language are considered a crucial dimension of responsible and effective public relations theory and practice. As a result, a broadly critical discourse analytic approach frames and concentrates the examination of the Nike social responsibility document.

---

[2]Corporate social responsibility in this chapter is treated as a component of public relations. Compare Cynthia E. Clark (2000), who treats public relations and corporate social responsibility as separate disciplines and professional realms. Clark nevertheless argues that by acknowledging the similarities between them (specifically those relating to communication approaches and methods), researchers and practitioners can gain further insights into both corporate social responsibility and public relations.

[3]The choice of Nike as a case study was made on the basis of its public visibility and the availability of diverse and variously mediated (particularly Web-based) narratives about it, which would be accessible to readers. The choice is not intended to suggest Nike as necessarily any "better" or "worse" than other—large or small—corporations. See also Birch & Glazebrook, 2000, pp. 49–50.

Critical discourse analysis treats language, particularly public texts, as a form of social practice, and is concerned with the ways in which language organises and mediates (asymmetrical) relations of power between speakers or writers and readers, and the ways in which it naturalises particular ideologies (see Fairclough, 1995, 2001). Norman Fairclough has developed a 3-dimensional conception and method of discourse analysis, which serves to frame the scope of investigation. It consists of examining the interrelated instances of "(i) a language text, spoken or written, (ii) discourse practice (text production and text interpretation), (iii) sociocultural practice" (Fairclough, 1995, p. 97). Any such investigation, this chapter suggests, is enhanced by integrating ethical, imaginative, and rhetorical praxis. The relevance of ethics, imagination, and rhetoric to public forms of communication (its production, circulation, and interpretation), including public relations writing, is briefly outlined below. By extension, the usefulness of ethics, imagination, and rhetoric in contributing to the debate about effecting change in public relations theory and practice is described in the section that follows, in order to lay the ground for an inquiry into social responsibility texts as authentic moral narratives.

As a form of social practice, writing is an ethical activity: "Writing is an activity involving an ethical choice about what one is to be and what one is to do. At the point when you begin to write, you begin to define yourself ethically" (Porter, 1998, p. 150). However, this being and this doing are always defined and contextualised in relation to others; they are never isolated or independent activities. In other words, writing helps determine and modify social relations. Thus, a postmodern situated ethics is regarded as integral to the process of developing, and of analysing the functions and effects of, the rhetoric of social responsibility texts.

At the same time, writing is an imaginative activity, an attempt to make present (in the planning and formulating of texts) the actually or apparently immaterial: on the one hand, the various publics and the contexts of their interpretation of and responsiveness to written texts; and on the other, the rhetorical and moral issues at stake in specific communication and reception processes. Imagination is therefore linguistic in character (Kearney, 1998)[4] and, in this account, public relations writing is reconceived as constitutive of relations between self and other rather than as a process with exclusively instrumental ends. Such an orientation draws attention to the complex process of conceptualising an appropriate ethical and rhetorical relationship (text) between writers, subject, and readers. This clearly also involves the exercise of judgement, an activity which, as Hannah Arendt convincingly argues, has a dynamic connection with the activity of imagining (or, in her words, an "enlarged way of thinking"):

> The power of judgment rests on a potential agreement with others, and the thinking process which is active in judging something is not, like the thought process of pure reasoning, a dialogue between me and myself, but finds itself always and primarily, even if I am quite alone in making up my mind, in an anticipated communication with others with whom I know I must finally come to some agreement ... And this enlarged way of thinking, which as judgment knows how to transcend its individual limitations ... cannot function in strict isolation or solitude; it needs the presence of others "in whose place" it must think, whose perspectives it must take into consideration, and without whom it never has the opportunity to operate at all. (Arendt, 1968, pp. 220–221)

By implication, therefore, the use of rhetoric in public relations writing is necessarily sensitive to issues of social, economic, ethnic and sexual difference, to (inevitably) asymmetrical relations of power that either sustain or challenge those differences, and to the dangers of utterances that universalise, naturalise, or standardise knowledge and truth. It is concerned, therefore, with investigating the inscribed and interpretable effects (semiotic, practical,

---

[4]Kearney's (1998) exploration of what he calls a radical hermeneutics of imagination asserts the ethical and political imperative of imagining as principle and practice in the postmodern age.

cultural, subjective, and collective) of written language. This rhetorical approach, interwoven as it is with an ethical, imaginative stance, is alert to the relative power positions from which writers write and readers read. It motivates consideration of how far publics and stakeholders are enabled to become or have an interest in becoming active participants in the communicative process, and how far organisations are prepared or motivated to interpret their texts from the place of the other.

POSTMODERN—ETHICAL IMAGINATIVE AND RHETORICAL—APPROACHES TO PUBLIC RELATIONS PRAXIS

Tackling a topic evaluating the social and ethical functions and effects of corporate public relations narratives can be overwhelming, beset as any such attempt is by myriad and significant *other* narratives in this context: of late industrial capitalism; of governmental and corporate powers and their global ideological and practical reach, influence, and control (however indirect those are); and of widespread social and economic inequities. If it is agreed that capitalism dominates all other ideologies and that all political and philosophical beliefs and practices are subsumed by it, then there may be, understandably, a reluctance to put up any resistance against this grandest of stories.[5] In addition, it cannot be denied that conventional public relations practice (and even, until quite recently, most related theory) is largely driven to maintain or extend the stronghold of capitalist regimes (Holtzhausen, 2000, p. 97).

Moreover, is it possible *to enact* public relations through the written medium, in the face of the ubiquitous use of the interchangeable expletives, "it's just PR," "it's all rhetoric" and "they're just words?" People resort to such criticisms when they feel that the language of public relations texts—and the form and content they shape and represent—are remote from, or fail to adequately represent or approximate, the realities of their experience of a corporation and its practices. Nevertheless, a significant proportion of the relating with the public that organisations (and particularly large national and multinational ones) do today is necessarily activated and mediated through written print or online texts. Businesses and corporations spend vast amounts of money on producing public relations texts, so presumably they have a very strong interest in those texts offering meaning and value to their stakeholders. From this perspective, therefore, it is argued that language as rhetorical form and content should be used to represent, self-consciously extend and demonstrably complement the activities, relationships, attitudes, and beliefs it describes—the materiality of intersubjective experience.

It will become clear that the approach taken in this chapter highlights the fact that fundamental shifts in much conventional corporate public relations theory and practice—in the very idea of what relating to stakeholders involves and what its functions and objectives are—are absolutely vital as well. It would, of course, be absurd to suggest the potential for or possibility of a total overhaul of power within the capitalist systems in which public relations thrives. However, Foucault's description of power relations presents a scenario that makes the task of proposing and effecting such shifts a little less daunting:

> Power relations are not something that is bad in itself, that we have to break free of. I do not think that a society can exist without power relations, if by that one means the strategies by which individuals try to direct and control the conduct of others. The problem is not to try to dissolve them in the utopia of completely transparent

---

[5]As Lyotard remarks, "Our master is capital. Capital makes us tell, listen to and act out the great story of its reproduction, and the positions we occupy in the instances of its narrative are predetermined" (Lyotard, 1989, p. 140).

communication but to acquire the rules of law, the management techniques, and also the morality, the ethos, the practice of the self, that will allow us to play these games of power with as little domination as possible. (Foucault, 2000, p. 298)

To conceive of a notion of public relations writing praxis that proceeds "with as little domination as possible" and that functions to facilitate democratic processes of negotiation, dispute, and possibly reconciliation between an organisation and its stakeholders underscores the suggestions made through this discussion.[6]

Relatively recent moves by some public relations theorists in the United States, Great Britain, and Europe to reassess and reevaluate the theory and practice of public relations insist on a shift in both theoretical and practitioner perspective—from an organisation-centred approach to public relations to one that attempts to balance the needs of all players: the organisation, its diverse stakeholders, and the broader community (for example, see Holtzhausen, 2000; Daymon, 2000; Vercic, Van Ruler, Butschi, & Flodin, 2001). This shift is, of course, related to the belief that organisations are members of society and bear community responsibilities that go with that position. Also, with the development of public relations as an academic discipline, there has been a concomitant shift in the view of public relations as professional practice (the just-do-it approach) to public relations as "a conscious uncoupling of the intellectual agenda from the day-to-day thoughts, actions and preoccupations of practitioners" (Dozier & Lauzen, 2000, p. 4). Both these shifts have served to highlight the significance of public relations as having the potential to enact ethical, rhetorical, and imaginative praxis.

First, with the move to acknowledge the needs (the claims, the voices, the texts, the values, and the identities) of diverse publics as being as important as those of an organisation, public relations can begin to reflect on and work towards its (potential for) ethical and reciprocal engagements or exchanges with those publics. The ethical dimension of public relations defines the relationships between individuals, groups, and communities and corporations in terms of their relative power, and how this power, in practice, influences their mutual obligations, accountability, and responsibility as well as their respective degrees of interdependence with each other. Many organisations and corporations self-consciously declare their interest and investment in these relationships. For example, Jim Cantalupo, Chairman and CEO of McDonald's, writes in the introduction to the 2002 *McDonald's Social Responsibility Report*:

McDonald's has the honor of serving more customers around the world than anyone else. With this privilege comes a responsibility to be a good neighbor, employer, and steward of the environment, and the unique opportunity to be a leader and a catalyst for positive change. We recognize the challenges and the obstacles, but believe strongly in the importance of social responsibility. (McDonald's, 2002, p. 4)

And in the energy and petrochemical business, ExxonMobil's Chairman and CEO, Lee R. Raymond, announces in ExxonMobil's *2003 Corporate Citizenship Report Summary* that:

Our directors, management and employees understand that exemplary citizenship, including high standards of business conduct, effective corporate governance, sound financial controls, operational integrity and community engagement, is fundamental to sustained business success—and sustained business success is fundamental to good corporate citizenship. You cannot have one without the other. (ExxonMobil, 2004, p. 3)

---

[6]See Kevin Moloney (2000), who focuses on public relations in the UK context as socially pervasive practice. Moloney argues for a reconceptualisation of the profession so that, among other changes, the concentration of public relations activities in the hands of big business and powerful political and media institutions is more equitably distributed to include traditionally less powerful stakeholders and groups.

Similarly, the sports footwear, clothing, and accessories corporation adidas-Salomon's *Staying Focused: Social and Environmental Report 2003* declares that "while we have outsourced most of our production, we have not outsourced moral responsibility for the way in which our products are manufactured and distributed" (adidas-Salomon, 2004).

As has been established, ethics is an activity, and its writing one form of social practice. So there is a reasonable expectation on the part of readers and stakeholders that corporations writing about their ethical activity will bear out the claims made in their written texts as well as in other forms of practice. Thus, the fact that Shell, the global group of energy and petro-chemical companies, provides an e-mail facility on its Web site for people to post uncensored, publicly accessible feedback on Shell's activities[7] suggests that the corporation is interested in engaging with stakeholders, at least at the level of acknowledging and making available to others their views. How far those views might be debated and perhaps responded to or acted on by the corporation is another matter, however. This point indicates the crucial role of written communication as not only as a distinctive form of ethical practice but also as one necessarily coterminous with and contingent on other forms of social practice.

Second, the role of rhetoric in public relations—as *interactive* processes of communication and interpretation, involving the construction or inscription of knowledges, meanings, and values by one party and their various understandings or reinscriptions by other (supportive, antagonistic, indifferent, and so on) parties—also becomes crucial, and its dynamic links with ethical practice salient. In the domain of public relations, this relation between ethics and rhetoric is particularly important. Traditionally, discussions of rhetoric in relation to public relations have been limited to examining the legitimacy of rhetoric as persuasion. By contrast and more recently, some public relations theorists have countered this tendency and broadened the discussion considerably by engaging in debate that is sensitive to the ethical implications of rhetoric (see L'Etang, 1996, 1997; Heath, 2000). As Heath points out, "The rhetorical perspective assumes that ideas are not eternally dictated, mandated or taken for granted. They are subject to dispute" (Heath, 2000, p. 72). For example, rhetorical discourses in the community that foreground the significance of economic rationalism and profitability very often compete and conflict with those that emphasise the primacy of human rights or environmental sustainability.[8] The various interpretations of these discourses by different people in different contexts, and the subsequent impacts of those people's transformation of the discourses into particular actions or attitudes, will inevitably influence the relationship between one person and another, an organisation and its stakeholders, private business, and the community. Rhetoric as a sense- and truth-making technology clearly has dynamic ethical, material, and intersubjective effects.

It is important to notice in these accounts of rhetorical and ethical public relations communications that *consensus* and *mutual satisfaction* of all parties are not necessarily the desirable closures to be striven for. On the contrary, and as Lyotard points out in his discussion of the differend, such goals are misguided and may serve to disguise inequities and the difference in priority or interest that will still subsist at the end of any dispute: "A case of difference between two parties takes place when the 'regulation' of the conflict that opposes them is done in the idiom of one of the parties while the wrong suffered by the other is not signified in that idiom" (Lyotard, 1988, p. 9).[9] An ethical rhetoric in public relations texts is sensitive to that conflict

---

[7]See Shell's site at http://www2.shell.com/ home/ Framework, and click on the TellShell hyperlink.

[8]See Sharon Livesey (2001) for a discussion of the discourses of sustainability and their struggle with other (predominantly economic and rationalist) discourses in the evolving rhetoric of the Royal Dutch/Shell Group.

[9]And see Holtzhausen's (2000) use of Lyotard's notion of the differend. In her development of a postmodern approach to public relations, Holtzhausen rejects the idea that consensus and symmetry between practitioners and publics are either realisable or desirable goals.

and the power that might obscure its opportunities for exposure. Such sensitivity appears to be demonstrated by the skin and body care retailer, The Body Shop, for example, whose Web site carries both (management) statements about its approach to employee relations as well as comments (positive and negative) of Body Shop employees recorded in a survey (externally designed and administered) in 2000, on various aspects of their employment experience with and perceptions of the corporation (Kingston University, 2002). For example, one (corporate) employee comment from the survey, responding to a question about the company's effectiveness in facilitating communication and related issues, reads: "The Body Shop doesn't 'walk the talk', and is as bureaucratic, hierarchical, secretive as many other companies that don't attempt to make a public show of values" (Kingston University, 2002, p. 60).[10] Compare this with the Human Resources Director, Mark Barrett's, comment in a more recent, company-authored report: "The role of HR has been to help employees feel engaged in the business through improved and frequent communications, as well as direct consultation and the provision of wellbeing and other support programs" (The Body Shop, 2003, p. 4).

Interestingly, the juxtaposition of conflicting voices could here be seen to demonstrate the strategies implemented by The Body Shop in direct response to earlier articulations of employee dissatisfaction. It remains to be seen, however, in future reports and in its other business practices, whether the differences between The Body Shop management and staff (in perception and experience as represented through their various rhetorics) will be used to help transform employer–employee relations into a more productive and equitable association.

Subsequently and finally, the activity of imagining becomes important in exploring and evaluating public relations praxis—that process of putting oneself in the place of the other, thinking oneself outside the space of self-security and self-gratification—both in the activity of public relations as communicative and interactive process and as theoretical distancing. There is value to be derived from imagining in Holtzhausen's reflection on the future role of the public relations practitioner operating in a context of dissensus (rather than consensus): "This state of dissensus will inevitably place the public relations practitioner in a position of choosing sides and speaking out in the case of what he or she views as an injustice.... In [this] boundary-spanning function, a position of dissensus will force the public relations practitioner to recognise and respect differences on the side of both the organisation and its publics" (Holtzhausen, 2000, p. 108). The postmodern act of imagining entails an acknowledgement of diversity and dispute, and highlights the fact that situations can be promoted and created in which "new meaning" is produced "through difference and opposition" (Holtzhausen, 2000, p. 107). Public relations writing's capacity to genuinely imagine the place of the other in order for organisations and corporations to meet their various social obligations is still, as will be shown, severely limited. And if assumed as genuine one of Nike's (explicitly) stated (and other corporations' implied) goals as being "to see things through the eyes of the worker" (Nike, 2001, p. 27), then the ideas raised here may assist in extending that capacity.

PUBLIC RELATIONS, NARRATIVE, AND STORIES ABOUT MORALITY

Public relations writing organises and represents an organisation and its people, their situations, experiences, actions, and their effects over time through verbal patterns that give them order

---

[10]Of course, one comment cannot and should not be read as representative of widespread employee dissatisfaction. The quote rather serves to demonstrate The Body Shop's willingness to have other voices written into and read from its texts.

and coherence as a narrative. Such writing thus seeks to identify itself to its stakeholders.[11] The narratives may take the form of official public relations documents, such as reports, newsletters or Web site material, for example, produced by the organisation, as well as those constructed by marketing, advertising, the news media, activist groups, employees, subcontracted workers, consumers and, even by hearsay, through public and private conversation, rumour, speculation, and so on. The understandings and perceptions of an organisation circulating at any one time are largely developed through readers' and writers' interactions with such narratives: the stories encountered, responded to, and modified by diverse stakeholders. Inevitably there will be multiple narrative versions that help define the organisation's identity at a given moment, and these versions will vary depending on who is constructing, who is making sense of them. For example, for many Western consumers today, Nestlé, the world's largest food company, is commonly perceived through its marketing, advertising, and ubiquitous retail presence as a company producing a wide range of quality convenience foodstuffs: coffee, chocolate, yoghurt, infant formula, and so on. For consumers in developing countries and for an activist organisation such as Oxfam Community Aid Abroad, however, Nestlé is a disturbingly powerful corporation that has a monopoly on the milk production industry in countries such as Sri Lanka, and charges exorbitant and, for many potential customers, unaffordable prices for its product.[12] And yet for shareholders, Nestlé is a corporation whose healthy annual growth and profitable returns make it a very attractive company in which to invest.

Increasingly, and given the significant public expectation that they perform as responsible social actors (particularly following the recent and recurrent exposure of various and widespread malpractices), corporations tend to be regarded as unitary bodies, whose attributes and values resemble those of moral human agents. (Readers may consider, for instance, how often a corporation is referred to as "deceptive" or "greedy" or "caring" or "fair.") Moral agency can usefully be understood "as an effect of socio-historical interactions that reflect *processes* through which the boundaries of an actor are drawn and justified" (De Winter, 2001, p. 100). The corporation can therefore be regarded as a collective moral agent, "located within a specific set of historical relations with state and societal actors, and bearing the larger responsibility of contributing to social justice within the communities in which it produces" (De Winter, 2001, p. 101). While the representation of a corporation as a unitary actor can hide the complex network of relationships that together constitute the organisation, and while it might tend to obscure the agency and responsibility of individuals within it, it is this interactional process that results in the attribution of corporate moral agency (De Winter, 2001). Nevertheless, however powerful the organisation, and however influential it might be in constructing dominant, widely heard narratives about itself as a moral agent, the roles of readers and publics in interpreting those narratives into significant understandings of the organisation is crucial.[13]

This is not to ignore the fact that all interpreters and meaning makers are not likely to have the same degree of influence in representing their stories and their understandings of stories to others. In other words, the stories exchanged are not equally forcefully told, mediated, or understood: the capacity to disseminate preferred stories, the exposure of those stories to publics with different degrees of power, and the cultural credibility accorded to certain discourses harnessed to articulate stories, all help account for *how* or even *whether* stories

[11]See also Perkins and Blyler's discussion on the importance of professional communication "taking a narrative turn" (1999, particularly pp. 10–28).

[12]See Oxfam Community Aid Abroad's discussion of and involvement in the campaign on this issue (Oxfam Community Aid Abroad, 2002).

[13]See Mark Currie's discussion of the applications of narratology in studying contemporary culture (1998, pp. 96–113).

are communicated in the first place, and, if they are, whether they take hold in the social imagination.

The so-called McLibel case is an interesting, if quirky, example of the ways in which various stories and understandings of the fast-food corporation were transformed or modified by various stakeholders during the course of its protracted (two-and-a-half-year) libel case against two individuals, Helen Steel and Dave Morris, in England in the 1990s. Steel and Morris had been part of a group responsible for the publication and distribution of a leaflet called "What wrong with McDonald's—everything they don't want you to know." The leaflet claimed that McDonald's exploited children through its advertising campaigns and its staff through its work practices. It claimed the company's production processes were responsible for causing environmental damage and cruelty to animals. While the judge ruled against the fast-food company on some points, he did find that the defendants were guilty of libel on others. They were ordered to pay £60,000, but refused. McDonald's did not pursue the non-payment. The case also demonstrates the ways in which, in certain instances, the stories of relatively powerless underdogs can be used as an effective strategy to challenge conventional bases of control and influence.[14]

Postmodern accounts of narrative also alert us to the idea that the stories public relations constructs about an organisation are not definitive—in fact, they are only meaningful when endorsed, accepted, responded to, challenged, disrupted, contested, and so on by public readings of those narratives. All of this suggests the interpersonal process of telling and interpreting narratives—that it necessarily involves an engagement and an exchange between tellers and listeners, writers and readers And, moreover, public relations narratives—like all narratives— have gaps in them: public relations can never hope to tell the "whole" story, despite the fact that all kinds of narrative do, it seem, have that totalising impulse: "The formal project of narrative syntagmation [is] to encapsulate completely its descriptive object, i.e., to achieve a state of plenitude in relation to the narrating subject's appeal to the Other" (McQuillan, 2000, p. 20).

Stories about an organisation are likely to be appropriated by different publics within the context of cultural narratives that make those publics' own lives meaningful. Stories are only valuable in the moment(s) of their contact between writers and readers, and that contact generates variable degrees of tension, since narrative is reinterpretable and re-presentable by diverse readers as alternative narratives or counternarratives. "The condition of the counternarrative arises because the form of the narrative syntagm cannot express a totality of experience, although it attempts to disguise this necessary 'failing' in the imaginary figure of closure. Counternarratives are a necessary part of the communal narrative-matrix and are therefore necessary to the prolongation of inter-subjective experience" (McQuillan, 2000, p. 23). It is this concept of the counternarrative that further emphasises the pivotal—ethical—dimension of storytelling. These days, the most frequent and publicly visible or publicly accessible counters to corporate public relations narratives are those produced by activist organisations, such as Greenpeace and Amnesty International,[15] for example, who campaign on what they regard as the most critical gaps in corporations' narratives, in relation to environmental and human rights issues, respectively. Other activist groups, such as McSpotlight or the NikeWatch arm of Oxfam Community Aid Abroad, target or scrutinise the specific activities and draw attention to the absences or glosses in the narratives circulated by an individual corporation.[16] There is

---

[14]See McSpotlight's site, http://www.mcspotlight.org/case/trial/ story.html for an activist version of this case. No information from the corporation's perspective on the case could be found on McDonald's Web site.

[15]See Greenpeace's site at http://www.greanpeace.org/ and Amnesty International's at http://www.amnesty.org.

[16]See the *McSpotlight* site at http://www.mcspotlight.org/ and Oxfam Community Aid Abroad"s *NikeWatch* at http://www.caa.org.au/campaigns/nike/. Another activist site that must not escape mention here is the U.S. academic

also the Center for Media and Democracy's site, PR Watch, a non-profit, online organisation that reports on what it perceives as malpractices perpetrated by the public relations industry internationally.[17] And, of course, there are a host of other, more informal, counternarratives that will be generated—from private conversations in coffee shops (contemporary versions of the Habermasian variety) to public debates published in the news media, for example, that will each develop alternative understandings of what constitutes a meaningful story about a corporation.

The impulse of the counternarrative might otherwise be compared with the notion of dialogism, as Bakhtin uses the term. Bakhtin's reflections on language, and on novelistic discourse in particular, help to clarify the view sketched above of an essentially postmodern view of narrative and the meanings it generates in different contexts and by different writers and readers.

> The dialogic property of narrative, that is, its (internal or external) encounters with contradictory or competing meanings, ensures that the living utterance, having taken meaning and shape at a particular historical moment in a socially specific environment, cannot fail to brush up against thousands of living dialogic threads, woven by socioideological consciousness around the given object of an utterance; it cannot fail to become an active participant in social dialogue. After all, the utterance arises out of this dialogue as a continuation of it and as a rejoinder to it—it does not approach the object from the sidelines. (Bakhtin, 1981, p. 276)

Scrutiny of the public relations narratives circulated by organisations (through various media) about themselves—and particularly in relation to their self-description on issues of social responsibility—reveals that something seems to be missing. Why are so many publics' responses to stories of "good works" by a self-described ethically sound corporation often those of disbelief, cynicism, or distrust? Bakhtin's notion of dialogism, also a significant feature of his understanding of the relation between self and other, as manifested through narrative, again helps to clarify the problem:

> I am conscious of myself and become myself only while revealing myself for another, through another, and with the help of another... To be means to be for another, and through the other, for oneself. A person has no internal sovereign territory, he is wholly and always on the boundary; looking inside himself, he [sic] looks *into the eyes of another* or *with the eyes of another*. (Bakhtin, 1984, p. 287; italics in original)

The feminist philosopher, Margaret Urban Walker, throws further light on this idea of narrative as a responsibility to the other: "In all of its expressions, morality is fundamentally *interpersonal*; it arises out of and is reproduced or modified in what goes on between or among people. In this way morality is collaborative; we construct and sustain it together" (Walker, 1998, p. 10). In her "expressive-collaborative" view of morality, in which she argued that "a *story* is the basic form of representation for moral problems" (1998, p. 110), her comments have an important bearing on the social responsibility narratives of corporations.

Walker suggests that three types of narratives subsist and intertwine in our making of coherent moral stories of our lives: narratives of relationship, narratives of identity, and narratives of value. Briefly, in Walker's account, narratives of relationship are those of a "relationship's acquired content and developed expectations, its basis and type of trust, and its possibilities for continuation" (Walker, 1998, p. 111). Such narratives develop—are constructed from our experiences—out of our encounters with others, whether those are brief, episodic, or ongoing, for example. Our investments, responsibilities, obligations, and needs—practical and

---

David Boje's *Academics studying Nike*, at http://cbae.n msu.edu/~dboje/nike/nikemain1.html. Not only does the site offer access to a cornucopia of texts documenting a history of Nike's policies and practices, from an activist perspective, but it also carries links to several important related resources.

[17]See the PR Watch site at http://www prwatch.org/index.html.

ethical—both in individual relationships and between different relationships will necessarily vary and change over time. Through our relationship-centred narratives, our integrity is often put under pressure, since our decisions on how to move on with our stories are inevitably bound up with others' needs and situations. However, our narratives of moral identity, derived from the decisions and choices we make, the actions we take (or do not take) in our relationships with others, are concerned with defining how our specific moral attachments (our moral relationships) help define for ourselves and for others *who* we are: "where we stand and what we stand for" (Walker, 1998, p. 112). Spanning and supporting both these kinds of narrative is the narrative of moral values: the stories that articulate what holds meaning and significance for us, and what we come to deem important or less important through our history of relationships with others and through our (changing) understandings of who we are. "We learn progressively from our moral resolutions and their intelligibility and acceptability to ourselves and others who and how we are and what our moral concepts and standards mean" (Walker, 1998, p. 113).

This summary, although it cannot do justice to the richness of Walker's own account, nevertheless emphasises the centrality of the process of interaction between self and other for the development of moral narratives. The applicability of Walker's framework for such narratives constituted as written texts—representing rhetorically intersubjective experience— can be demonstrated by turning our attention to the case of a written document by Nike—its *Corporate Responsibility Report 2001*.

CORPORATE SOCIAL RESPONSIBILITY TEXTS AND THE CASE OF NIKE

Many corporations, having now assumed their roles as collective moral actors (by taking on the activities and the rhetoric of corporate social responsibility), have also, as has been described, assumed "an identity that cannot be delimited to their role as economic institutions maximizing the profits of stockholders" (De Winter 2001, p. 110). This complex identity, and the tensions and contradictions it articulates, is represented in the social responsibility texts of large corporations.

Typically in such texts, an organisation, through its self-representations as a moral actor engaged in significant relationships and attached to specific moral values, gives a narrative account of its history, current activities, and future plans in relation to social or community endeavours. These might include descriptions of work practices, environmental sustainability initiatives, community consultation programmes, and so on. There is one sense in which such accounts are necessarily self-sufficient and coherent: the documents stand as sense-making testaments to an organisation's efforts to "do the right thing" in its practices. However, while it is to be expected that the narrative discourses of marketing and advertising and even of publicity and promotion will be presented as self-assured, complete, and coherent (their functions and objectives most often support this approach, after all), corporate responsibility narratives describing the (first and foremost) ethical relationships between particular people in particular social, economic, and environmental contexts presented similarly have quite different rhetorical effects. In the latter case, the attempt to create the illusion of completeness, integrity, flawlessness, smoothness (with moral goodness implicit in those qualities) is problematic, and certainly one possible cause of public disbelief or cynicism. The "complete" story implies self-enclosure and immunity from interpersonal contact/contamination. It contradicts the notion of a moral narrative, because it entails leaving out of the story line those who would necessarily disrupt its flow or coherence. By extension, this approach produces distrust because the implication is that the story needs no readers to render it meaningful (to carry on, to develop, to disrupt, or to change the course of the story through their involvement in it), or to judge or evaluate it.

Precisely because such narratives as social responsibility documents *call out to the other for their legitimacy*, and because such texts represent (or stand in the place of) material or physical connection with other, they are bound—if they are authentic—to be tentative, incomplete and incoherent, in the sense of not "worked out," not finalised, not stitched up. Nike's report goes significantly further than many other corporations' reports in terms of its detailed (if selective) reflection on its activities and self-criticism of many of its past practices as well as the limitations of some of its present ones. Nevertheless, the report is imaginatively limited and its rhetoric therefore ethically questionable.

The *Corporate Responsibility Report 2001* is a slick publication (available in hard copy and online)[18] carefully designed, in true postmodern style, to simulate a well-used, crudely assembled, interdepartmental document. (The hard copy of the report, which is obtainable on request from Nike, is contained in a faux interdepartmental envelope.) "Admittedly it is incomplete, a bit of a mishmash" writes Phil Knight, Nike's CEO, in the "cover letter" attached to the inside cover of the hard copy document. As with its Web site, Nike in this document "consciously configures images as part of its public discourse" (Salinas, 2000, chapter 2, p. 5).[19] Thus, the report's visual impact is powerful and appealing: photos, maps, graphs, illustrations, and text are collated in a highly organised mock-up of chaos. As the introductory text (in a font recalling manual typewriter type and forming a palimpsest over a whole-page photo of boxes and shelves containing Nike office bric-a-brac) remarks: "Throughout this report you will see snapshots of Nike people working on corporate responsibility projects and programs, old files, e-mails, ticket stubs and the like. We thought it important for you to get the texture of this work as well as its substance" (Nike, 2001, p. 3). This suggests the self-conscious "play" of form with content, where the "substance" of corporate social responsibility is in part evoked by the "texture" of work in progress and of its innumerable, complex, and contradictory elements: people, places, statistics, technologies, products, ideas, values, issues.

The 55-page document covers five areas of corporate social responsibility: "Environment," "Labor Practices," "Nike People," "Community Affairs," and "Stakeholders." As well as presenting the mission or goals and giving an account of the company's (personnel, operational, administrative, and financial) activities in each of these areas, the document presents a narrative of its progressive ethical development and evolution. "The document you hold is our first step in systematically communicating the things we've done to evolve. ... We are, after all, just beginning to understand what a sustainable business means. ... For now, *it offers an honest self-assessment of our progress*" (Knight's cover letter, in Nike, 2001; my italics). This sets the tone for the reflections articulated in the document that follows: a tone that is both confessional and visionary, though largely self-oriented.

Also in his introductory letter, Knight quotes from the corporation's so-called Maxims: "Nike exists to pursue opportunity and enhance human potential" (Knight, 2001). Evident here is how the language of branding (see Klein, 2000, pp. 3–28)—evoking lifestyle, values, cultural beliefs, emotions—draws on the discourses of ethics and morality and of personal and social relationships. So there is an immediate connection between branding language and that

---

[18]The analysis in this chapter has been worked off a hard-copy version of the report, obtained from Nike. However, the report can also be downloaded from http://www.nike.com/nikebiz/nikebiz.jhtml?page=29.

[19]In his development of what he calls "a configural theory" for the design or writing and the critical reading of images, Carlos Salinas argues that images should be theorised as configurations, "as designed/written artifacts, rhetorically figured, representing particular ideologies and values, and projecting their make[r]'s ethos" (Salinas, 2000, abstract). He offers an astute reading of Nike's 1997–1998 Web site to concentrate his discussion, and makes a detailed critique of the company's representations of its labour practices.

of public relations, assuming public relations is understood as described above: as developing and negotiating ethical relationships between an organisation and its publics. Knight continues: "As a citizen of the world, Nike must Do the Right Thing—try to be transparent about what we are doing right, and about what we are doing wrong; embrace diversity; drive sustainability" (Knight's cover letter in Nike, 2001). It is interesting to witness here the shift from Nike's "Just Do It" culture to a "Do the Right Thing" culture, from the abstractly amoral to the explicitly moral speech act. Through the conflation of marketing or branding and corporate social responsibility discourses, Knight's letter attempts to sell the idea of his company's ethics—its moral goodness.

Repeatedly through the document, Nike confesses to and evaluates its responsibility for the negative impacts of past and present corporate social responsibility activities, and acknowledges that problems have not been eradicated. "How well do we do monitoring [of labour practices]? Not well enough" (Nike, 2001, p. 29). Here the rhetorical question-and-answer technique offers a clear instance of the company's impulse to self-assessment and even to self-recrimination: "By far our worst experience and biggest mistake [in relation to labour practices] was in Pakistan, where we blew it" (Nike, 2001, p. 30). However, these confessions do remain relatively comfortable and unthreatening, as the direct responses and judgements of others (for example, Nike's subcontracted workers, their families, communities, auditing and monitoring bodies) on these activities and their repercussions are excluded. Despite this, the Nike report certainly sets itself apart from reports such as McDonald's and ExxonMobil's, for example. Those companies use their reports very much as instruments of self-promotion and as expressions of corporate vision. The McDonald's report, as a case in point, makes no mention, with one exception (see McDonald's, 2002, p. 38), of any former or current practices that have been challenged by various stakeholders, although it does repeatedly stress that its corporate responsibility processes are part of its ongoing education and development. For example, the Chairman of the company's Corporate Responsibility committee, Walter E. Massey, describes the report as "a valuable roadmap that will enable McDonald's to measure its progress and enhance its standards of performance" (McDonald's, 2002, p. 5). And in relation to sustainability initiatives, the writer of the report comments that "we are embarking on a journey in which the answer are not obvious" (McDonald's, 2002, p. 18) and that "we are dedicated to learning" (McDonald's, 2002, p. 19). These kinds of visionary statements, by their self-conscious disconnection from those that are reflective, self-scrutinising or dialogic, tend to lack credibility.

In the Nike report's "Stakeholders" section is a clear illustration of the way in which a narrative of morality, such as Walker describes (see above), is significant in making coherent ideas about corporate relationships, identity, and value. The narrative opens with an admission that, in the past, Nike's relationships were largely financial- and stakeholder-focused. However, "we've learned the hard way that our view of the world was not as informed as it should have been. In the last few years we have had dialogue with the vast range of stakeholders in civil society" (Nike 2001, p. 54). Nonetheless, a comment suggesting Nike's discomfort with this claim of engagement in "dialogue" follows:

> If anything *the pendulum has swung too much the other way*, connecting with over 100 external non-profit stakeholder groups, including environmental organizations, human rights groups, students, colleges, trades unions, socially responsible investor groups, government, academia and consumers. Engagement ranges from information and dialogue to collaborative projects and multi-year programs. (Nike, 2001, p. 54; my italics)

A pie chart summarising the range of Nike's relationships is also depicted (Nike, 2001, p. 55). Values are enumerated systematically: belief in principle of engagement, seeking of

common ground, importance of relationship yielding "real value" (Nike, 2001, p. 54). Identity
through these pages emerges as the corporation's maturing moral identity—progressive, even
pioneering, in its efforts to forge links with a range of stakeholder groups and to establish a
global system of accepted social accounting principles. However, it seems that the narrative
lacks authenticity as a result of its singularity of voice and the absence of an acknowledgement
of the centrality of the interpersonal, or "moral life as a continuing negotiation *among* people"
(Walker, 1998, p. 60). We cannot claim to be authoritative judges of our own narratives or our
own identities; self-description is not enough, given that it exposes a lack or even an absence
of moral engagement with others. "Moral justification ... is from the first and at the last
interpersonal. It is with and from others we learn to do it, and learn that we must. It is to others
we must bring it back to do the work it is intended for: to allow and require people to account
to one another for the value and impact of what they do in matters of importance" (Walker,
1998, p. 114).

Only certain "people" are allowed into the pages of the Nike report as subjects: Nike management and staff. The texts of those with whom Nike's relationship has been and continues to
be notoriously fraught are absent, except in the abstract, that is. For example, the section entitled
"Labor Practices" is introduced by the Director of Corporate Responsibility Compliance, who
intersperses his discussion about the challenges of achieving approved working practices and
conditions with reference to the typical (female) "'Nike worker'": "You are 22 and single. You
are in the third year of your first job. You were raised on a farm. Your supervisor is a woman,
four years your senior. Your section leader is a foreigner. He doesn't speak your language
very well" (Nike, 2001, p. 26). By maintaining the Nike worker as a necessary or inevitable
stereotype (see Walker, 1998, pp. 165–170): "always one constant: a young woman, who is
22 and single. She is in the third year of her first job," the rhetoric minimises the potential for
readers to engage with the worker as a human agent; rather, she remains at a safe, immaterial
distance, despite the illusory effect, created by use of the second person, of her being directly
addressed by the writer. It is the writer who confidently asserts that, despite the fact that this
worker's occupation is "tedious, hard, and doesn't offer a wonderful future," she is "here of her
own free will" (Nike 2001, p. 26). Readers must resort to imagining the voice of a Nike worker
contesting this claim, challenging the denial of her moral agency and her language, arguing
against the smug view of those in positions of power that "the subordinated voluntarily serve"
(Walker, 1998, p. 166).

By stark contrast, the section "Nike people," which asserts personnel as the company's
most important asset, describes their diversity, opportunities for professional development and
the compensation and benefits awarded to them, begins with a first-person account by a Nike
employee. The rationale for this approach is explained at the outset: "We thought the best way
to introduce a section about Nike people would be to share a real story from a Nike person, and
hear from her about our unique corporate culture" (Nike, 2001, p. 40). Here, the writer clearly
understands the merits of "a real story" (as opposed to a hypothetical or stereotypical one) and
how, by offering a first-person account to represent personal experience, a subject is brought
up close for the readers. The distance of the faceless, impersonal other is thus overcome.
Predictably perhaps, the first-person account presented here (complete with a photo of the
individual Nike employee and her partner) paints a glowing picture of Nike as a progressive
and supportive employer. At the conclusion of her narrative, the employee remarks that "so
far my experience at Nike has been challenging, rewarding and unexpected. I am excited for
tomorrow" (Nike, 2001, p. 40). This summary remark, when set alongside that (third-person
account) describing the subcontracted worker's experience (of work that is "tedious, hard, and
doesn't offer a wonderful future"), produces a harsh dissonance.

In the "Labor practices" section Nike is frank about the dilemmas raised by its pull of responsibilities, particularly between workers and their local social and economic contexts on the one hand, and the company's business interests on the other (see Nike, 2001, p. 32). And the report in general demonstrates how extremely difficult it must be to make ethical decisions about labour practices, environmental sustainability, and so on, in the face of market logic and shareholder demands for profitability. Such awareness notwithstanding, the report's rhetoric still seems to favour a market and profit-driven over a humanitarian or ethical impulse. For example, also in the "Labor practices" section, an argument is mounted about why an increase in wages would disadvantage all stakeholders—even subcontracted workers who, on the face of it, might initially be perceived as being obvious beneficiaries of such a move. The argument is carefully presented through paragraphs constructing catch-22 market logic. The writer argues that increased wages would increase product costs, adversely affect the level of production and sales, and result in higher prices for consumers. The demand for products would consequently fall, and fewer units would mean lower earnings for shareholders and also "fewer jobs and lower earnings for Nike suppliers, employees and factory workers" (Nike, 2001, p. 39).

The above examination demonstrates that, like other comparable texts, Nike's document appears to draw largely on two types of discourse in its narratives. First is the discourse of marketing or branding, which, through the production and representation of "closed" stories, promotes its product as desirable for the consumer's integration into their aspired-for lifestyle, or for the investor's financial commitment to the corporation. Thus, through the use of marketing discourse, these two key groups of stakeholders are prioritised. Second is the discourse of ethics, which although apparently attempting to give an account of the company's moral relationships, identity and values, is subsumed by the discourses of marketing, advertising, and commerce; in fact, it seems that ethics and ethical behaviour cannot be thought of or articulated otherwise. "We run Corporate Responsibility like any other piece of the business. We have business plans, goals, action plans, timelines and measurables" (Nike, 2001, p. 1). In this account, ethics and ethical relationships are "managed" and apparently objectively measurable or quantifiable. It is evident that the public relations text is communicating on social responsibility issues that appeal particularly to *one* set of stakeholders (workers, community members, activists, concerned consumers) in a rhetorical discourse that most likely finds a far more ready understanding with *another* set of clearly *prioritised* stakeholders (shareholders, consumers, and so on). In other words, what do "business plans," "timelines," and "measurables" mean to Indonesian sports shoe factory workers who struggle to survive if they work under 60 hours a week in Nike contract facilities (in environments with substandard health and safety standards), and who are often forced to live apart from their children and families?[20] Quoting data, statistics, rules and regulations, codes and principles adhered to, as Nike's report does, is not enough to construct an ethical and imaginative narrative. How does such language connect to people's lives, emotional and practical experiences, beliefs and values?

There is a sense in which these two narrative discourses—of marketing and of ethics—have contradictory, or at least divergent, impulses. However, because marketing so often now, in its efforts to brand its products, draws on the rhetoric of human relationships, worldviews, and personal and social choices, in other words the language of morality, it becomes confused or conflated with ethical discourse. As a result, the rhetoric representing issues of corporate responsibility becomes absorbed into the branding process—"freed from the corporeal world of commodities, manufacturing and products" (Klein, 2000, p. 23). And people. In this scenario,

---

[20]For a detailed account of Nike and Adidas's subcontract worker conditions in Indonesia, see Connor, *We Are Not Machines* (2002).

the narratives of corporations' public relations texts can become almost completely obscured, and certainly alienated, from the very people and moral relationships they claim to be closely involved with and responsible to.

In a culture that demands that organisations present texts demonstrating their accountability and responsible and ethical practice, it can be conceded that they are easily tempted, even encouraged, to treat the process as a marketing exercise and to produce self-descriptive, self-supporting documents, whose priority or focus becomes to bolster promotional initiatives. Used merely as a marketing "ploy," however, social responsibility rhetoric proves to be a pitfall: "The adoption of social responsibility rhetoric is a double-edged sword. On the one hand, it allows corporations to insulate themselves from pressure by the [anti-sweatshop] movement since they can point to the rhetoric as evidence that they have aligned themselves with the movement's agenda. On the other hand, beyond indicating a possible internal reconstitution of corporations' self-identity, this language provides a significant point of leverage, a form of rhetorical entrapment, for the movement to hold corporations to their 'words', and is a basis for activists to make further demands for improved production practices" (De Winter, 2001, p. 111). Perhaps, rather than viewing its use of language as "rhetorical entrapment," Nike could exploit the opportunity that discourse offers to reevaluate and modify both its writing and its business practices.

Kasky v. Nike: COMMERCE OR PUBLIC DEBATE?

De Winter's words, quoted above, were prescient. Another—potentially highly significant—dimension to the corporate social responsibility discussion in particular, and public relations practice in general, has been added by the lawsuit brought by U.S. activist Marc Kasky against Nike, in which the former accused the company of false advertising. The ultimately unresolved case, which passed between various California courts and an oral review by the U.S. Supreme Court,[21] was finally concluded by an out-of-court settlement in September 2003, with Nike and Kasky agreeing that the company would donate $1.5 million to the Fair Labor Association[22] (see Nike, 2003; Liptak, 2003; BBC News, 2003; Milchen & Kaplan, 2003).

In 1998, Kasky sued Nike under California's Unfair Competition Law and False Advertising Law on behalf of the general public of the State of California (Goldstein, 2003, p. 65). Kasky alleged that Nike's circulation of press releases, (paid) advertorials, letters to the editors of newspapers and to university presidents and athletics directors concerning employee pay and working conditions, particularly in Southeast Asia, constituted false advertising.[23] Nike's defence was that the First Amendment of the U.S. Constitution protected the company from such claims.

Essentially, therefore, the case hinged on a debate about whether Nike's campaign of press releases, advertorials, letters, and so on constituted free speech, which is protected by the Constitution, or commercial speech,[24] which is subject to government regulation and prohibits

---

[21] For a detailed background to the case and its movement through different courts, see Goldstein 2003, particularly pp. 65–70.

[22] The Fair Labor Association (FLA) is a non-profit coalition of industry, non-government, and tertiary sector groups. The organisation exists to promote compliance with international labour standards and to improve working conditions around the world (www.fairlabor.org). The FLA has been criticised by various activist groups for its failure to effect full-scale improvements in labour conditions and wages for workers.

[23] See Goldstein 2003, pp. 65–66 for details of Kasky's allegations.

[24] The California Supreme Court defined "'commercial speech' to cover everything said by anyone 'engaged in commerce,' to an 'intended audience' of 'potential ... customers' or 'persons (such as reporters ...)' likely to

the issue of false and misleading statements. Nike contended that it was exercising its right to defend its business practices through engaging in public debate. The California Court of Appeal also held that Nike's statements "form[ed] part of public dialogue on a matter of public concern within the core area of expression protected by the First Amendment" (California Court of Appeal in Goldstein, 2003, p. 66). However, the California Supreme Court held that Nike, as a manufacturer, distributor, and retailer of sports shoes and apparel, is a commercial speaker. It also argued that Nike's statements were made to a commercial audience. Finally, the Court claimed that through a description of its labour policies, practices and factory working conditions, Nike "was making factual representations about its own business operations" (California Supreme Court in Goldstein, 2003, p. 68).

The fact that the case remained unresolved at its settlement means that businesses are likely to feel tentative or reticent about writing public statements on or commentary about their practices. In Nike's case, this is undoubtedly so. In its press release following the case's settlement, the company's Vice President and General Counsel, Jim Carter, indicated that Nike, together with other corporations, media organisations, and non-government organisations, "remain concerned about the impact of the California Supreme Court ruling on transparency— specifically companies who wish to report publicly on their progress in the areas of corporate responsibility." He disclosed that, as a result of that ruling, Nike would not issue its corporate responsibility report for 2002, "and will continue to limit its participation in public events and media engagement in California" (Nike, 2003).[25]

The *Kasky v. Nike* case raises some crucial questions that relate directly to the concerns of this chapter. Whether or not Nike's statements in its campaign were true or false was not addressed during any court hearing of the case, yet those statements were defended by the corporation as morally sincere. According to Thomas C. Goldstein, one of Nike's external counsel, Nike's statements "conveyed the view that Nike does act morally because its investments produce substantial economic and political benefits for workers and because it puts its best effort toward ensuring that employees at its contract facilities are paid fairly and treated well. None of the statements at issue appeared in advertisements of Nike's products or urged consumers to buy those products" (Goldstein, 2003, p. 65). Goldstein's statements reinforce the significance of Nike's intentions (their "best efforts") and make generalised assumptions about their effects ("its investments produce substantial economic and political benefits for workers"). But surely judgements about morality can only be made in terms of the *relationships* that obtain between the parties in question, and of the impacts of different parties' actions and their implications on those relationships? And ought not such judgements necessarily take into account the positions and the views of *all* those involved or implicated?

Jim Carter's comments on transparency quoted above are important, and Nike is to be commended for its attempts to be open and self-reflective about its business practices. All the same, moving towards transparency also means giving readers the opportunity to look at issues and experiences as those are written from different positions and different stakeholder voices,

---

influence actual or potential customers that conveys factual information about itself 'likely to influence consumers in their commercial decisions'" (in Goldstein 2003, pp. 70–71).

[25] In 2003, Nike released the first issue of *Nike responsibility*, an e-newsletter. In that issue's editorial, the Nike Corporate Responsibility Team comments that, with the settlement of the court case, "we are introducing new tools for dialogue with our stakeholders;" the newsletter and the company's corporate responsibility Web site (www.nike.responsibility.com) are two such tools. In the three issues of the newsletter produced as of June 2004, there is a significant focus on Nike's implementation of and involvement in several large-scale community-based initiatives around the world. While the level of the company's investment in such activities is undoubtedly impressive, the function of the newsletter appears to be exclusively self-promotional. Evidence of "stakeholder dialogue" is not so far in evidence.

not only from the viewpoint of the writers. As Foucault's remarks, cited near the beginning of this chapter, suggested, completely transparent communication is impossible to achieve. Nevertheless, others need to write and speak themselves rather than be written or spoken for by significantly more powerful voices and their preferred rhetorical discourses. If Nike is claiming to do the right thing, then the benefits of having others (apart from Nike-commissioned auditing agencies) endorse that through their own responsive commentary could be enormous. (And in the cases where respondents could not endorse the claims, they might offer Nike crucial direction on how to make its practices more equitable and ethical.) Of course, such a document would be unlikely to stand as a "successful" marketing tool, but as *Kasky v. Nike* has demonstrated, the confusion of marketing and moral discourses is always potentially fraught, particularly since the competing rhetorics draw attention to the demanding complexities of moral responsibility.

IMAGINATIVE TEXTS: A MEANINGFUL FUTURE FOR PUBLIC RELATIONS TEXTS

In its 2002 report, adidas-Salomon includes employee feedback (through direct quotation and summary) on the company's previous year's report. Several comments from employees relate to the issues concerning the company's responsibility for engaging more closely with the interests and contexts of less powerful stakeholder groups: "You have to divest yourself of some of your power by building a local process" and "You'd have greater legitimacy [if you included] more workers' voices" (adidas-Salomon, 2003, p. 23). In response to this feedback the company admits that "not all of [its] stakeholders have a voice" (adidas-Salomon, 2003, p. 22).[26] It makes this observation again in its 2003 report, with the comment that "the people who produce our products are an important part of our stakeholder community but we do not always hear their voices" (adidas-Salomon, 2004, p. 14).[27]

If contemporary public relations practices are genuinely attempting to establish and extend ethical and mutually beneficial relationships with their various publics—and given the exponential rise in corporate social responsibility initiatives over recent years, it might be assumed that they are—they might reflect less on their capacity to engage in the polished telling and (in many cases) monotonous and monologic retelling of their preferred stories. Instead, they might focus *more* (and more) attention on exchanging and negotiating of different, discontinuous and open-ended stories with those publics. In other words, there needs to be a different conception of and approach to the development, function, and useability of social responsibility texts.

It could, of course, be argued that given that counternarratives are circulating at the same time as a corporation's self-generated moral narrative, that there is no need to shift approach. As well as being able to read a corporation's account in its social responsibility documents, some stakeholders at least have relatively easy access to contradictory accounts prepared by various activist organisations, non-government organisations, and other interested parties. And yet in this scenario, the conflicting texts can remain out of touch: their dissonances may not be felt,

---

[26]The company goes on to report its 2002 launch of what it calls "stakeholder dialogues" — consultation meetings with key stakeholders in the regions of its outsourced labour activity (Asia, the Americas, and Europe; adidas-Salomon, 2002, p. 22).

[27]This latest document does contain an appraisal of adidas-Salomon's reporting processes by business-focused corporate social responsibility organisation, CSR Network Ltd (adidas-Salomon, 2004, p. 15), as well as summaries of stakeholder dialogues held with workers, non-government organisations, and other groups in the course of 2003 (see adidas-Salomon, 2004, pp. 13–17). However, a more diverse range of voices, quoted in context rather than summarised in abstraction, is yet to be recorded.

the tangle of their often competing and sometimes incompatible claims not confronted—and the dynamic complexities of moral relationships neither acknowledged nor communicated.

By incorporating dissonant, uncensored voices, the (rarely read) texts of those who would counter or challenge a corporation's claims in its moral stories, such open, shared documents (such as The Body Shop's employee stakeholder accounts or the employee comments included in adidas-Salomon's report, referred to above) will preclude that polished finished-ness, which is anathema to a text articulating moral relationships, and will extend the scope of potential contributors, readers, and respondent stakeholders. Those voices could include a corporation's employees, its subcontracted workers, workers' families, the community members inhabiting the environments in and around a corporation's production facilities, activist organisations, and other groups who present different accounts, broader perspectives, or alternative views. The *evolving, dialogic text* proposed could also be used as the location at which monitoring and auditing activities and reports by independent organisations are publicised and commented on by interested individuals or groups.

Perhaps only then will corporate social responsibility documents resemble more than a studiously manufactured "mishmash": the mess and clash of human relationships, the contradictions between capitalism and human welfare, the conflict between business and moral imperatives, obligations and responsibilities. All these will at least start the process of using texts not to distance themselves from their stakeholders but to bring them closer to them, even if only in closer conflict, so that new multi-authored stories may be imagined. Most importantly, such texts would lay the groundwork for discussion around why and how corporations and their stakeholders should go about developing and implementing better, more equitable, more humane business relationships.

4

Relationships, Transparency, and Evaluation: The Implications for Public Relations

Julia Jahansoozi
University of Central Lancashire

This chapter discusses the concept of organization–public relationships and the relational perspective. It reviews definitions of key terms such as organization, publics, and organization–public relationships within the public relations context. As a number of other fields use relationships as a fundamental concept, this chapter reviews literature from relationship marketing, organizational theory, conflict resolution, interpersonal communication, and public relations in order to identify relationship components (characteristics or elements) deemed necessary to build and maintain organization–public relationships. Dialogue and transparency are identified as relational elements that have been largely ignored in public relations literature on the relational perspective. Dialogue is considered essential for a relationship to exist and transparency is identified as a key relational condition that is connected to other relational characteristics such as trust, accountability, cooperation, and collaboration. Transparency also has "negative" coercive attributes as increased transparency may lead to lowering the level of decision making and increase self-censorship in an attempt to protect senior management from perceived negative societal consequences. A new phenomenon termed "stakeholder fatigue" is also briefly discussed, as is a summary of recent public relations research on evaluating organization–public relationships and possible evaluation methodologies.

THE RELATIONAL PERSPECTIVE

The relational perspective builds upon and transfers ideas based on interpersonal relationship initiation, development, maintenance, and dissolution from the individual level to organizations and publics. This may be problematic in that it is not as straightforward simply to treat an organization or a public as if it was an individual. Many models and theories of public relations involve the concept of communicating with groups, group dynamics and behaviour, and building relationships with specific groups or publics, a bias resulting from an emphasis on the media relations function. What has been sidelined is the central concept of the individual and interpersonal communication (persuasive communication) and interpersonal relationships which is emphasized once again in the relational perspective. Sriramesh's (cited in Taylor, 2001) personal influence model is based upon individual relationships between public relations practitioners and external publics. In reality these relationships are cultivated with "opinion leaders" or key representatives of targeted external publics. Public relations practitioners do not have relationships with publics; they build and nurture relationships with individuals within publics. Campaigns target individuals within defined publics in order to reinforce or change particular attitudes and the linked behavioural outcomes. Therefore, relationships are not with publics but with individuals identified as belonging to the particular public.

The relational perspective concentrates on the organization–public relationship and sees it as being central to the public relations function. Interest in public relations shifting over to a relational perspective is a quite recent phenomenon within the mainstream public relations literature. It has been identified as part of the natural evolution of the field as it moves away from technician practitioners toward strategic counselors (Heath, 2001a).

The first person to challenge academics and practitioners to take a fresh approach to public relations by focusing on relationships and also proposed that it was likely to be the most fruitful area for future theory building was Ferguson in 1984. She issued her challenge as a response to criticisms that public relations was not an area worthy of scholarship or theory building as it simply absorbed theories from related disciplines such as communications, management, and psychology. In order to identify areas of potential research for public relations scholars that were distinct from other disciplines, Ferguson attempted to categorize research published from 1975 until 1984 in the journal *Public Relations Review*. As a result of this categorizing, three broad categories emerged: introspective articles, the practice and application of public relations, and public relations theory development. Ferguson went on to identify three areas of scholarship that were unique to public relations and which she believed might be further developed into paradigms: social responsibility and ethics, social issues and issues management, and public relationships. She argued that the public relationships area had the most potential because of the primary focus on the relationship between organizations and publics. Whilst organizational theory specifically looked at the organization and sociology was concerned with social groupings (or publics), public relations could legitimately consider the actual relationship and adopt it as the unit of analysis. Ferguson proposed that the initial steps in developing the organization–public relationship theory would benefit from categorizing the types of public relationships that exist and also examining the relational elements such as satisfaction and control mutuality. For the underpinning theory Ferguson pointed to Scott (1983, cited in Ferguson, 1984, p. 17), who proposed that the relational and normative structures found in the interorganization field affected both the nature and type of relationship experienced. Organizational variables such as structure, values, goals, leadership, and management style need to be considered as they may have an effect on the type of relationship. For example, if the organization is hierarchical in structure and has an authoritarian management style, it would affect the relational elements found in the relationships it has with all its publics. Grunig (1983, cited in Ferguson, 1984, p. 18) suggested that environmental variables explained public relations behaviour far better than structural ones. Therefore, public relations variables were dependent upon the organization's environment, emphasizing the necessity of the boundary-spanning activity and careful analysis of external variables. The organization's relationship with its publics is linked to the nature of the external variables and their impact on the organization, but the organizational-level variables will dictate the tone of the actual relational elements or characteristics. Since 1984 there has gradually been increased interest in this "new" perspective, especially with regard to measuring and evaluating relationships, as public relations practitioners still need to be able to prove the value of their expertise to senior management and budgetholders.

The continued interest in evaluating organization–public relationships led Hon and Grunig (1999) to start to address the question: "Why is it important to measure *relationships* in public relations?" (p. 4). As the practice and academic pursuit of public relations matures and evolves, evaluating only the short-term outputs and even outcomes of specific public relations programmes is recognized as being shallow in that it provides no concrete information regarding the actual state of long-term relationships (Hon & Grunig, 1999). If public relations is to be taken seriously as a management function, then the focus must shift to ongoing monitoring through continual measurement and evaluation. Only this can provide an accurate assessment of the organization's long-term relationships with its publics.

While measuring and evaluating outputs is the most basic level in assessing the success or failure of a particular public relations programme or campaign as opposed to measuring the success of a strategy (as outputs are the visible results of a particular public relations programme such as news releases and feature articles), measuring and evaluating outcomes (such as attitude and behaviour change) provides a far more sophisticated look at whether the persuasive communication message was successful. Most public relations evaluation centres on measuring the tactics used and whether they were successful—for example, whether the news release was picked up in the target media. Very seldom is the strategy evaluated, which would entail examining the actual outcomes. Measuring and evaluating outcomes involves looking at "whether target audience groups actually *received* the messages directed at them ... paid *attention* to them ... *understood the messages* ... and *retained* those messages in any shape or form" (Hon & Grunig, 1999, p. 4). Measuring outcomes also requires looking at the actual organization–public relationships to see how they have been affected. Most public relations strategies revolve around building or maintaining a particular relationship or sets of relationships, yet these relationships are not evaluated before the programme is launched or after it is completed.

This ties into the research around persuasive communication and hinges upon the origins of public relations in mass media, which emphasises "an interest in message design and dissemination to achieve awareness (publicity and promotion at their best), to inform, and to persuade—even manipulate" (Heath, 2001b, p. 2). The role of public relations practitioners as persuasion gurus should be relinquished or at least take a back seat to the relational perspective, which enables practitioners to identify mutual values, interests, and benefits between the organization and its publics so that "win–win" situations result.

Heath (2001b) suggested that academics' interests ought to lie in the conflict reduction paradigm, which fits well with the relational perspective. By reducing conflict with publics, practitioners move towards a "revenue generation paradigm" (p. 2) as costly crises are averted. To do this requires investing in building and maintaining positive relationships with key publics. This logically leads to the need for an appropriate methodology for measuring and evaluating the organization–public relationship.

Huang (2001a) found that the effect of public relations on conflict resolution was mediated by the organization–public relationship. Not only does public relations increase the organizational effectiveness by building and maintaining positive relationships between the organization and its strategic publics (Grunig, Grunig, & Ehling, 1992), but it also can be used to reduce the organization's costs due to issues management and crisis aversion (Grunig, Grunig, & Verčič, 1998; Heath, 2001b). Using the relational and cost reduction paradigms of public relations, it can be proposed that public relations is responsible for building and maintaining positive relationships between organizations and publics and thereby manage and reduce conflict. Positive relationships are those that benefit the organization and do not hinder its objectives. Whilst there may be times when there is disagreement regarding these objectives and consequences or implications that may result from them, members are able to work through them in a constructive manner that strengthens the offering, producing the ultimate "win–win" situation. It would then seem logical that a negative organization–public relationship could be described as having a high degree of conflict in it or alternatively that a positive relationship would possess a minimal amount of conflict.

Whilst Ferguson (1984) first introduced the concept that public relations should focus on relationships and indeed adopt the relationship as the unit of study, J. Grunig and Hunt (1984) defined public relations as the "management of communication between organization and its publics" (p. 6), which only implicitly refers to organization–public relationships. Interest in the relational paradigm diminished until the late 1990s as Grunig and Hunt's focus on the management of communication became the dominant perspective that forged ahead whilst Ferguson's became less influential. Positioning public relations as a strategic communication management function catered to the occupation's desire to be taken seriously by senior managers and be recognized as part of the management team as opposed to skilled technicians. Hutton (1999, p. 212) blamed Grunig and Hunt's four models of public relations for strangling theoretical developments, particularly those in the relational perspective, by proclaiming communication as being the core of public relations. Instead, communication should be viewed as a necessary tool for developing and maintaining organization–public relationships and to promote mutual understanding. The continued focus on communication overshadowed Ferguson's correct conclusion that the organization–public relationship was core to the public relations function. By the late 1990s the relational paradigm was resurrected by Hon and Grunig (1999) and Bruning and Ledingham (1999) as interest in evaluating organization–public relationships increased after Grunig and Hunt's (1984) four models were found to be unsatisfactory and limiting.

KEY RELATIONAL DEFINITIONS

Before examining key relational elements and possible evaluation and measurement techniques, it is important to explore what key terms such as "organization," "publics," "relationship," and "organization–public relationship" are understood to mean within the public relations context. Relational characteristics are discussed in literature covered from related disciplines such as relationship marketing, organizational theory, conflict resolution, and interpersonal communication. Much of the work done in related disciplines is relevant for public relations and furthers the understanding of relational characteristics as well as building and maintaining "positive" relationships.

Organizations

Organizations can be defined as being "goal-directed, boundary-maintaining, and socially constructed systems of human activity" (Aldrich, 1979, cited in Aldrich, 1999, p. 2). By "goal-directed" behaviours, Aldrich is creating a distinction between other social collectivities such as family groupings. Individuals who are members of a particular organization behave in ways that lead to fulfillment of the organization's goals, even if on a personal level they may not fully agree with them. Recognizing and maintaining the boundaries of an organization is important as it separates out and makes the distinction between members and non-members. This separation helps to identify the boundaries of the organization within its environment. Aldrich's definition is simple and, given the criteria Grunig and Hunt (1984) provide for identifying active publics, it could be argued that active publics are in fact organizations.

Publics

Whilst Grunig's theory for identifying publics may be useful for the developing theories of public relationships, it is at times problematic in that it is crisis-focused and active publics are purely reactive. Grunig and Hunt's (1984, p. 144) definition of the term publics is preoccupied with "active publics" who are directly interested in the organization's activities.

Publics consist of individuals who detect the same problems and plan similar behaviours to deal with those problems. Thus, we can define a public as a loosely structured system whose members detect the same problem or issue, interact either face-to-face or through mediated channels, or behave as though they were one body (Grunig & Hunt, 1984, p. 144).

Vasquez (1993) reinforced the idea that publics exist only if there is a problem and defined a public as being made up of "individuals that develop a group consciousness around a problematic situation and act to solve the problematic situation" (p. 209).

Hallahan (2000, p. 499) noted that this focus on active publics was troublesome in that it did not acknowledge or even consider the importance of inactive publics in influencing the organization's decision-making process. The preoccupation with active publics is understandable when the public relations function is purely reactive in nature and is responding to crises, but with the desire to move in a more strategic and proactive direction it becomes crucial to evaluate relationships with non-active publics as well. Grunig and Hunt's definition builds on historical definitions (Dewey, 1927; Blumer, 1966) that connect the term "public" with "issue." The actual term public has more recently become blurred and is interchangeably used with the term "audience." Public relations practitioners also use demographics such as age, gender, education level, and socioeconomic status in order to identify recipients of a message in much the same way marketing tries to segment the population. Hallahan (2000) and Vasquez and Taylor (2001) argued that as the term "public" is used so liberally and has been expanded to cover such concepts as audience, market segment, community, constituents, and stakeholders, the accuracy of meaning is lost in the ambiguity.

Hallahan argued there are limitations with Grunig and Hunt's (1984) symmetrical model of public relations and situational theory as it assumes that publics are actively engaged and are motivated to participate in some way and that prediction is only possible for identifying when a public might shift from an inactive to active state and interact with the organization. Hallahan's assumptions differ in that he proposed that not all public relations activities are directly connected to issues or crises and that some activities exist purely to build positive relationships where the organizational interests are best served by meeting the public's needs. Many organizational relationships exist at a low level with publics that do not require extensive knowledge of the organization, and in these circumstances information is then offered on a "need-to-know" basis. Hallahan differentiated between publics by the activity–passivity levels and provided an updated definition of the term "public" to reflect this: "a group of people who relate to an organization, who demonstrate varying degrees of activity–passivity, and who might (or might not) interact with others concerning their relationship with the organization" (2000, p. 502). Hallahan tied his definition and understanding of how publics behave with the elaboration likelihood model (ELM) developed by social psychologists Petty and Cacioppo (1986, cited in O'Keefe, 2002, pp. 137–161), which explains how the level of personal involvement is linked directly to the way people process information and with attitude and behavioural change. Individuals with high levels of involvement with the particular issue will process the message/information via the central route which entails engaging with the argument at a cognitive level. In order to target these individuals, the persuasive message needs to be directly relevant and also contain a two-sided argument. Individuals with low levels of involvement will process the message/information by the peripheral route which makes use of cognitive shortcuts and stereotypes which are used to filter the message. Changes in attitude and behaviour using the central route tend to be more effective in the long term. The ELM works on an individual level to reinforce or change behaviour and in the public relations context, the central route is used mostly as it cognitively engages people who have a high level of involvement and who are considered to be "active" publics. The peripheral route is often used by advertisers as it works to familiarize a particular message with an audience that is characterized by having "low involvement." Celebrity endorsement is a tactic which uses the peripheral route as it makes use of cognitive shortcuts and stereotyping as assumptions are made with no supporting evidence in tow.

Organization–Public Relationships

Like most concepts in public relations, there is no single definition for relationship that is unilaterally accepted. Interpersonal communication literature describes that relationships exist between two or more people when there is a link between them that mutually serves a purpose over a period of time (Coombs, 2001). For a relationship to exist, both parties need to be aware of each other and also aware of their interaction and understand it as a two-way process. One-way relationships exist in that they tend to occur when one party identifies that it would like to have a relationship with another party and therefore engages in relationship "grooming" strategies to "woo" the other party and gain their interest and attention in order to start building a relationship. Ledingham and Bruning 2000 defined relationship with regard to public relations as being the "state which exists between an organization and its key publics in which the actions of either entity impact the economic, social, political, and/or cultural well-being of the other entity" (p. 160). Broom et al. went further and proposed a definition of the specific organization–public relationship as:

> Organization–public relationships are represented by the patterns of interaction, transaction, exchange, and linkage between an organization and its publics. These relationships have properties that are distinct from the identities, attributes, and perceptions of the individuals and social collectivities in the relationships. Though dynamic in nature, organization–public relationships can be described at a single point in time and tracked over time. (2000, p. 18)

In order to describe the organization–public relationship, the relational elements or characteristics deemed essential for a relationship to exist need to be considered. Relational characteristics are discussed in literature from "neighbouring" disciplines such as marketing, organizational theory, conflict resolution, and interpersonal communication as well as more recently within public relations. Key relational characteristics are identified as being common within the interdisciplinary literature, with some having more of an emphasis than others. The relational characteristics are those elements that are crucial for a "positive" relationship to exist and flourish. Without the presence of the relational characteristics, the relationship will falter and, if not attended to, ultimately dissolve.

MARKETING LITERATURE

Marketing literature and scholarship is moving aggressively into what has traditionally been viewed as public relations territory and in doing so is methodically reinventing itself as public relations, according to Hutton (2001, p. 205). Public relations academics have failed to collaborate with related disciplines, such as marketing, which has led to public relations being blinkered and isolated from parallel developments in neighbouring disciplines (Heath, 2001c, p. 184) and has laid the way open for marketing to expand its borders and include public relations academia and practice within its intellectual domain. This gradual hostile "takeover" was initiated by the advertising industry in the 1980s and 1990s as conglomerates decided to include public relations within their extensive offerings and the term "integrated marketing communications" (IMC) was born (Duncan, Caywood, & Newsom, 1993; Lauzen, 1991; Rose & Miller, 1994; cited in Hutton, 2001, p. 205). IMC changed the relationship between public relations and marketing from that of rivals jockeying for organizational recognition and budget towards marketing re-creating itself as public relations.

While Ferguson in 1984 championed the relational perspective for public relations as an area of research that could be owned by the discipline, the previous year a marketing academic, Berry (cited in Buttle, 1996, p. vii), had already coined the phrase "relationship marketing." As public relations evolves into the relationship management and organization positioning strategic functions (Cropp & Pincus, 2001, p. 198), marketing is also steering a parallel course and could be accused of hijacking public relations' territory (Hutton, 2001, p. 205). As marketing reinvents itself and updates its definitions, it has been argued that the field has recognized the value of public relations and is attempting to own it and rebrand it, leading to some debate regarding jurisdiction. This jurisdiction battle is more serious than the weight it receives within public relations as it has implications for the future of the discipline and practice. The abduction of public relations by marketing is occurring at both the tactical and strategic levels. Marketers who only understand public relations to mean media relations and publicity have already incorporated it into the "marketing mix" by adding it as the fifth "p" to the product, placement, packaging and price mantra, and have reduced the public relations function to being purely technical. If public relations is unable to identify and claim its territory as a management function, then the evolution of the discipline will regress and public relations will end up being subsumed into marketing communications.

However, the other perspective is that marketers cannot be "taking over" public relations as they are unaware of what public relations fundamentally is about and do not bother to use public relations academic sources to understand the discipline properly. Marketing's lack of acknowledgement that it is shifting into public relations territory therefore is mainly a consequence of public relations' failure to educate marketing and other business disciplines as to what public relations is and does. Public relations is equated with publicity and is then only used to boost a marketing campaign by securing "free advertising" in the editorial pages. Marketing, like public relations, is simply operating in a rather blinkered way and is unable to step outside of its own paradigms. Academics disciplines need to break through the "fire walls" and subject politics and become more interdisciplinary and collaborative where there are common or parallel paths.

Like public relations, marketing is a relatively new distinct discipline, established in the 20th century. Whereas public relations is considered to have its academic roots in psychology, sociology and communication science, marketing grew out of selling and advertising and to gain credibility as a business discipline established a connection with economics by focusing on market behaviour (Sheth & Parvatiyar, 2000, p. 119). Perhaps this partially explains why marketing's position as a management function is secure while public relations battles to prove its value to management. Relationship marketing is viewed as a paradigm shift from transactional marketing with a new focus on developing and maintaining mutually beneficial relationships (Grönroos, 1994). This move from on–off transactions to developing relationships is very similar to the shift to the relational paradigm in public relations. For marketing, however, this shift mirrors the previous practice of direct marketing, which allows the formation of relationships that go beyond isolated transactions.

Historically, the transactive paradigm came into being as a result of mass production, wholesaling, and the utilization of middlemen who were removed from the organization (Sheth & Parvatiyar, 2000, p. 124). The drive towards developing relationship marketing has been largely fuelled by the proliferation of high-quality competing products and services that are available to customers. Building relationships with customers provides a competitive edge, as long-term relationships with customers are hard to crack or steal. Relationship marketing is touted as the future of marketing, and the focus upon relationship building is not only a differentiator between competitors but is also an attempt to increase customer retention. Value is increasingly found in having relationships as it is believed to increase brand loyalty and it is much more cost-effective for organizations to retain customers than recruit new ones. The nature of marketing has changed as it has gone from "mass marketing" to highly targeted and personalized marketing. Information about individual customers is used to tailor both marketing strategies and the direct tactics employed. The relational perspective in marketing shifts the entire focus from customer acquisition to customer retention. Sales representatives become customer relationship managers as retention becomes the main concern (Buttle, 1996, pp. 1–13). The use of computers and customer relationship management (CRM) software has made it much easier to track and segment customers in order to increase sales opportunities over the customer's lifetime.

As the relational perspective increases in popularity, more marketing theorists (such as Cannon & Sheth, 1994; Christopher, Payne, & Ballantyne, 1991; Grönroos, 1994; O'Neal, 1989, cited in Sheth & Parvatiyar, 2000, p. 138; as well as Berry, 1983; Jackson, 1985; Morgan & Hunt, 1994; Håkansson, 1982; cited in Buttle, 1996) are exploring relationships and key relational elements such as trust, customer satisfaction, and the impact upon retention, and profitability. Duncan (1993) defined integrated marketing communications as "the process of strategically developing and controlling or influencing all messages used to build and nourish relationships with customers and other stakeholders" (cited in Hutton, 2001, p. 211). As marketing shifts toward the relational perspective, Buttle (1996, p. vii) defined relationship marketing (RM) as "the development of mutually beneficial long-term relationships between suppliers and customers." The evolution of marketing from a transaction-orientation model towards a relational paradigm that revolves around the building and maintenance of mutually beneficial relationships is currently embedding itself into the newly revised definition of marketing. Morgan and Hunt (1994, p. 22, cited in Buttle, 1996, p. 3) removed the focus on suppliers and customers from the definition and redefined it as "all marketing activities directed toward establishing, developing and maintaining successful relational exchanges."

However, marketing is not moving away from its customer-centric orientation, even if it appears to be given Morgan and Hunt's (1994, p. 22, cited in Buttle, 1996, p. 3) identification of 10 publics for RM to focus on that includes suppliers, competitors, non-profit organizations, government, employees, and customers. Morgan and Hunt are simply expanding the role of marketing and suggest that in order to improve customer relationships other organizational relationships need attention as well as these relationships and cannot be viewed in isolation. RM focuses on three main relationships: the company/intermediary relationship, the company/consumer relationship, and the company/employee relationship (Buttle, 1996).

A definite change from the previous transaction-orientation model, which is supported by Naudé and Holland (1996), who highlighted the impact of technological advances on marketing and explained the shift to the new relational paradigm. Relationships in the business-to-business (B2B) arena are now based on information exchange as opposed to human interaction purely between buyers and sellers. Marketing managers are now expected to set up social, organizational, and IT networks as well as develop and maintain these relationships. This "new" focus is all part of the shift toward the network/relational paradigm (Morgan and Hunt, 1994) which emphasizes the importance of relational elements such as trust, commitment, and satisfaction.

In the marketing relational paradigm, organizations are required to become trusted collaborators in order to be effective in the global competitive environment. Morgan and Hunt (1994) theorized that commitment and trust are necessary in order to have a successful relationship where collaboration can occur. Commitment and trust are key elements for any relationship as they are needed for maintenance of the relationship, encouraging a long-term view as opposed to a short-term one, and also allow for certain risks to be taken because of the belief that other parties in the relationship will not take advantage of the situation. Having a long-term view and nurturing the relationship by providing and showing commitment allows for the development of deeper levels of relationships. Commitment is defined as "an exchange partner believing that an ongoing relationship with another is so important as to warrant maximum efforts at maintaining it; that is, the committed party believes the relationship is worth working on to ensure that it endures indefinitely" (Morgan & Hunt, 1994, p. 23). The trust element is conceptualized as existing when there is reliability, confidence and integrity. Morgan and Hunt conducted a preliminary investigation using in-depth interviews which informed the quantitative questionnaire used to test whether trust and commitment were simply two independent variables or whether they were central for having a positive relationship. Trust was found to have a stronger effect on achieving collaboration and cooperation compared with commitment (Morgan & Hunt, 1994). Both trust and commitment were found to be mediating variables.

Trust is considered to influence commitment (Achrol, 1991; Morgan & Hunt, 1994). In relationships where there is a high degree of trust present, parties are more likely to make a firm commitment to the relationship and invest appropriate resources to maintaining and developing it further. This is reflected in the notion of reciprocity found in social exchange theory, where people agree or negotiate upon the boundaries, rules, and regulations for each individual relationship. Parties in the relationship must exchange resources within an agreed or appropriate amount of time that is either equivalent or equal in value to balance the exchange. A clear link must be made between the resources exchanged; otherwise one party may be unaware that an exchange has taken place and therefore not reciprocate (Heath & Bryant, 1992).

Atuahene-Gima and Li (2002) questioned the evidence for the strong normative bias that exists in relationship marketing literature toward the importance of trust in relationships and proposed that very little empirical evidence exists to support the high value placed on it. This position draws on Dirk's (1999, cited in Atuahene-Gima & Li, 2002) review of management literature, which finds little evidence of a direct, positive relationship between trust and performance. But is performance the same as outcome? A task might be performed perfectly and yet the desired outcome might not be achieved. Quality control ensures that the process is performed to the highest possible standard. Whilst trust increases collaboration and commitment leading to improved performance, coercion also may increase performance, so it is important to identify what variable is actually at work. Atuahene-Gima and Li (2002) cited the research of Dalstrom and Nygaard (1995) as providing a differing view on the trust–performance relationship in that the cultural context becomes critical. The notion of abusing trust is touched upon by Noteboom (1996, cited in Atuahene-Gima & Li, 2002). Trust is only likely to be abused when there is little chance of detection, and therefore transparency may solve this issue (Jahansoozi, 2002).

The Darwinian perspective of marketing emphasizes the survival of the fittest and supports exchange relationships that provide a direct benefit for the organization. Any relational strategies such as cooperation and collaboration that strengthen an organization's position and help it survive in a highly competitive market environment are utilized. Darwin considered this perspective for the survival of species in his seminal work *The Origin of Species*, originally published in 1859 (Burrows [editor], 1982). Darwin's survival perspective is built upon by Dawkins with his "selfish gene" argument. It is the inherent selfishness that evaluates what gain lies in any exchange, including cooperation and collaboration that encourages and ultimately leads to relationship formation (Dawkins, 1989). In short-term relationships there is no trust as the parties involved consider the transaction as unique, not to be repeated in the future, and therefore selfish interests are met first and foremost. Here cooperation and collaboration are not linked to altruism as the relationship is over as soon as it is no longer cost-effective. The role of altruism is limited in this perspective as it revolves around self-interest or, at the very least, mutual gain. The selfish gene argument posits that relationships exist solely to further one's aims and as soon as the benefit from the relationship declines the relationship is dissolved. So cooperation and collaboration only exist whilst the benefit to do so is clearly demonstrated. In this perspective, corporate social responsibility only occurs in order to "sweeten" local communities and allow corporate interests to operate unhindered. As soon as more profit can be made elsewhere, corporate interests disengage from the communities they both supported and were supported by. A recent example is the shift of utility and banking call/contact centres from the UK to India, despite record profits. Other companies such as Shell are attempting to foster sustainable development projects in the communities they operate in (or impact) so that the projects are able to continue to exist long after the oil giant has left the area. Again, this is not entirely altruistic. Shell needs local cooperation in order to keep production costs to a minimum but has discovered that philanthropy is short-term and when in the future money goes to another worthy project bad feeling results from the previous receivers, as expectations were set.

Although this survival model based on the selfish gene argument has a winner and a loser, there is a "win–win" model which links this line of thought with literature on negotiation and conflict resolution (Fischer & Ury, 1991) and economic theories which predict and analyze strategic behaviour such as game theory (von Neumann, 1937, cited in Parkin & King, 1995, p. 351). Economists have studied the competitive behaviour of organizations operating within the same market since the 1830s (Parkin & King, 1995, p. 348) and developed models that were based upon the beliefs regarding the expected behaviour of the other parties involved. Game theory provides a method for analyzing strategic behaviour and includes the prisoners' dilemma game and Nash equilibrium. These models consider "strategic behaviour," or behaving in a way that acknowledges the anticipated behaviour of others and the interdependence of the actors involved. Nash equilibrium posits that employing a strategy that is the best solution to the strategies adopted by the other parties in the relationship ultimately results in no party going after what could be considered to be their selfish interests. In other words, both parties recognize that they will not be able to get everything they want so instead they compromise in order to get the best possible outcome. Nash equilibrium occurs when the organization takes the best possible action given the action of the public, and the public takes the best possible action given the action of the organization, and therefore both parties end up with a satisfactory outcome (Parkin & King, 1995, p. 353). For the relationship to survive, both parties must not pursue their "selfish interests" but instead must compromise so that they both can achieve satisfactory outcomes. Cooperation exists in long-term relationships where trust is experienced and parties in the relationship know what to expect from each other. For relationship marketing to be successful, the chosen strategy must overcome the inherent selfishness and drive to exploit opportunities and short-term profits, and instead compromise and cooperate, thereby building long-term relationships.

Central to marketing theory is the concept of "mutual satisfaction," which differs from the concept of "mutual understanding" found in public relations. Mutual satisfaction occurs when both parties in the transaction believe they have received fair treatment. It can be questioned whether the satisfactions are really mutual or equal as is implied as they are not the necessarily the same. One set of satisfaction falls to individuals such as customers and the other set belongs to the corporate organization. Both will have different needs that require satisfying, which does not mean they are mutual or equal in weighting. Mutual understanding does not imply that both parties have satisfaction, but that they understand each other's position regarding the particular situation or issue. In order for mutual satisfaction to occur, there needs to be an understanding of the other party's desires and aims in order to reach a position where satisfaction occurs. Buttle (1996) proposed that relationship management is more about concern, trust, commitment, and satisfaction than straightforward transactive interactions. Murphy (1996) also included mutual trust and loyalty, interaction and dialogue, commitment, and satisfaction with the other parties in the relationship as elements of a relationship. The concept of mutual understanding is not found in relationship marketing but is central to many definitions of public relations as it is concerned with understanding the organization's publics and facilitating their understanding of the organization by managing relationships with them.

Grönroos (2000) discussed the nature of the dialogue process of "relationship marketing." Starting from the obvious premise that all forms of contact with an organization include a communicative element, Grönroos took this point further to emphasize the dialogue process being one that creates two-way, or even multi-way, communication processes. Whilst not all communication activities between an organization and its publics are two-way, investment and effort should be made in creating opportunities for dialogue and thereby strengthening the organization–public relationship. Surprisingly, marketing literature seems to be overlooked by most public relations scholars, and yet with the focus on relationship management it is developing a parallel course. Many of the relational elements identified as being critical for relationship marketing are equally important for organization–public relationships, which supports the premise that literature on relationships can be transferred across domains as long as there is sensitivity regarding the context and intent behind building and maintaining the relationship. Public relations academics and practitioners have perhaps ignored recent developments in marketing and are guilty of reducing it to the transactive paradigm much in the same way marketing reduces public relations to media relations and publicity.

ORGANIZATIONAL LITERATURE

Literature on organizational theory that has had the biggest impact upon public relations theory is largely connected to systems theory. Systems theory had its origins in biology and is based in part upon the idea that organizations can be compared with organisms as they are both self-contained entities that strive for equilibrium with their environment. Initially it was assumed that organizations operated as "closed systems" able to control the environment they functioned in, and were therefore able to meet their organizational goals and missions without input from the external environment (Grunig, Grunig, & Ehling, 1992, pp. 71–74). D. Katz and Kahn (1978) moved to the "open system" perspective, which acknowledged that organizations interacted with an external environment containing other organizations and publics. The "open system" perspective understands that the external operating environment exerts a level of influence and control over the organization's goal-meeting activities.

The concept of "system" has a history stretching back over 300 years. It was translated into the domain of organizational theory in the 1950s and emerged as general systems theory. Pieczka's (1996) analysis of the historical origins of the systems approach distilled the literature and the various models into three categories: equilibrium, homeostatic, and the process or adaptive system (Buckley, 1967, cited in Pieczka, 1996, p. 126). Pieczka found that these models corresponded directly with Gharajedaghi and Ackoff's (1994, cited in Pieczka, 1996, p. 126) models: mechanistic, organismic, and "social system." The equilibrium or mechanistic model, with roots in mechanical physics, uses the laws of motion (Kepler and Newton) to explain social interactions and is interested in the efficiency of the system. The homeostatic or organismic model grew out of the age-old comparison of society to a living organism. Society, like any organism, is interested in growth and survival. The process or adaptive system model views society as a system of interdependent and cooperating parts and social networks and is interested in development.

Much of public relations literature discusses the systems theory approach for looking at the organization and the publics within its environment (Pieczka, 1996, p. 144). Public relations practitioners enter the picture in the "boundary-spanning" role (Grunig, Grunig, & Ehling, 1992) as they help and enable the organization "to manage its relationships with groups in the environment" (p. 67). The role for public relations practitioners is effectively to limit this external influence and control that the environment is able to exert and place the various relationships into a state of harmony, which allows the organization to pursue its goals with the minimum interference or obstruction. This harmonious state also saves the organization in question money in the long term, as it reduces the amount of litigation, lawsuits, and changes to operating procedures both locally and globally (Heath, 2001b). Once in this state of harmony, the organization is able to pursue its goals effectively and maintain its license to operate. However, maintaining the harmonious state requires ongoing relationship management in order for small adjustments to be made proactively when issues are first picked up on the radar instead of adopting a defensive tactical position as the result of a crisis or imbalance in the organization–public relationship.

Whilst it is obvious that most organizations would prefer to be completely autonomous to get on with the primary organizational goals and to fulfill the mission statement (Mintzburg, 1983), the reality of the situation insists that organizations are interdependent upon other organizations and groups operating in the external environment. It is these relationships with other organizations and groups operating in the external environment that must be effectively managed to create harmony and balance:

> Building relationships—managing interdependence—is the substance of public relations. Good relationships, in turn, make organizations more effective because they allow organizations more freedom—more autonomy— to achieve their missions than they would with bad relationships. By giving up autonomy by building relationships, ironically, organizations maximize that autonomy. (Grunig, Grunig, and Ehling, 1992, p. 69)

Here Grunig, Grunig, and Ehling (1992) are proposing that the underlying motivation for building relationships is for the organization to retain its autonomy. The real motivation is therefore power. There is an understanding that in order to have power over how the organization operates, the organization must foster positive relationships to build trust and allow for operational autonomy. This idea promotes "exchange" relationships that provide benefits to the organization and links back to the selfish gene argument and marketing's survival paradigm, which does not tolerate altruism as an explanation for organizations building mutually beneficial relationships.

Theories of organization relationships drawn from organization theory validate the notion that there is a distinct link between strong and positive relationships (those relationships that aid organization goals and which are perceived to be working well) between an organization and its publics and the ability of the organization in question to be effective (Grunig, Grunig, & Ehling, 1992). Organizational theory has developed a body of knowledge on organizational relationships. Aldrich (1975, 1979, cited in Grunig, Grunig, & Ehling, 1992, p. 83) identified four relational dimensions: formalization of the relationship, intensity of the relationship, level of reciprocity, and standardization of the relationship. Aldrich's relational dimensions have similarities to Ferguson's (1984) relationship attributes which could be used to evaluate a relationship: the dynamic/static nature; open/closed; satisfaction; power ratio; and understanding, agreement, and consensus. Grunig, Grunig, and Ehling (1992) added trust and reciprocity to the list, while Pfeiffer (1978), Oliver (1990), Grunig, Grunig, and Ehling (1992), and Jensen (1997) added legitimacy. Jensen proposed that organizational legitimacy was strongly linked to the organization's strategic concept regarding what it is and that it is not the same concept as legal legitimacy. If the organization's publics accept its strategic concept within the specific parameters of its operations, then the organization has legitimacy within the public sphere.

Organizational literature, especially the systems theory approach, provides a view for looking at the organization and the publics within its environment and provides an easy way for practitioners to survey and conduct environmental scanning and boundary-spanning activities. When issues are identified before they develop into full-blown crises, there is an opportunity for the organization to resolve the potential crisis using conflict resolution strategies and techniques, which are very similar to those advocated in relationship management. Many of the relational elements discussed in organizational theory resonate with the relational perspective in public relations. The systems perspective allows for the identification of key publics in the organization's environment. Once these key publics are identified, relational grooming activities can occur, leading to the development of strategic relationships.

CONFLICT RESOLUTION LITERATURE

Conflict resolution literature is useful for public relations in that it provides insight into managing levels of conflict within relationships. In order for organizations to be successful in their local and global markets, they must concentrate on developing and maintaining relationships with key publics both at home and abroad. Any conflicts among or between publics and the organization need to be resolved quickly (Plowman, Briggs, & Huang, 2001). Understanding how conflict resolution and negotiation strategies are employed has become of greater importance for public relations scholars and practitioners, especially with regard to the relational perspective. Stroh (1999, cited in L. A. Grunig, 2000, p. 77) proposed that changes occurring in an organization's environment were the main catalyst or instigator of conflict in the organization–public relationship if left unmanaged. In order to be proactive and counteract change, public relations practitioners need to be able to effectively evaluate their organization–public relationships and move towards scenario planning (Stroh, 1999, cited in L. A. Grunig, 2000, p. 77; White, 2001). Issues/crises usually occur after management has made a decision and not considered the impact upon affected publics. When change in the environment surrounding the organization–public relationship occurs, a level of conflict resolution needs to be engaged.

Literature on conflict resolution and negotiation also highlights key relational elements such as openness, trust, and mutual understanding as being essential for a good working relationship (Fisher & Brown, 1988). Both parties involved in the relationship must be open to listening to each other. The concept of trust in conflict resolution is connected with risk assessment and accountability and not with issues of morality. For example, the organizations involved can be trusted to carry out what has been mutually agreed upon and that there is little chance of a "nasty" surprise or the playing field suddenly changing. Fisher and Brown (1988) emphasized that mutual understanding was crucial for the working relationship to prosper and that there was a direct link between mutual understanding and a healthy and productive relationship. Newcomb (1953, cited in van Ruler, 1997, p. 254) coined the idea of co-orientation as a communication model in which symmetrical communication was critical for developing understanding between parties (Pieczka, 1996, p. 151). Understanding the thinking and reasoning of the other party in the relationship will decrease the chance that a crisis will occur due to a simple misunderstanding and lack of empathy. Public relations practitioners need to be able to understand where their organization's publics are coming from in order to develop and maintain mutually beneficial relationships. If one party of the relationship feels that the other is uninterested and unwilling to invest time and effort into understanding the issue or concern, then it is likely that the relationship will not be positive or long-lasting (Fisher & Ury, 1991).

Another important relational element identified in conflict resolution literature was communication. When relationships collapse or are dissolved, the cause is often attributed to either a lack of communication or a complete breakdown of communication, suggesting that without communication there is no relationship. Fisher and Ury (1991) described negotiation as a "process of communicating back and forth for the purpose of reaching a joint decision" (p. 33), which can be seen to be very similar to Grunig and Hunt's (1984) two-way symmetrical model which "is based on research and that uses communication to manage conflict and improve understanding with strategic publics" (J. E. Grunig, 1992, p. 18). Fisher and Ury (1991) suggested that there are three main problems with communication that lead to a breakdown of the process: first, the parties involved may not be communicating with each other as each side has mentally written off the other party and is purely going through the motions of communicating in order to maintain the facade; second, both parties may not be actually hearing what is being said; and third, misunderstanding and misinterpreting what is being communicated. This third point is particularly apt for cross-cultural communication and supports Huang's (2001b) efforts to include a relationship dimension reflecting the Asian culture. Numerous examples exist in the area of international relations and diplomacy where relationships were destroyed by ignorance surrounding the connotations and/or meanings of certain words and gestures in different cultures.

Psychologists and therapists have a clear understanding of another aspect of communication—listening. Active listening skills, popular in the area of crisis counseling, aid in the understanding and perception of the other party's concerns and position. By repeating back what is being said, the other party is reassured that you are listening and have heard them and it also increases their level of satisfaction with the communication process (Fisher & Ury, 1991; VWSAC, 1994). Many misunderstandings happen simply because the act of listening did not occur. Face-to-face communication is still the best form of communication, especially in a conflict situation, as non-verbal communication cues can be assessed and can make a significant difference to the meaning. Mutual understanding is important for a relationship to continue to exist. If one party feels that the other fails to understand their position, the relationship is in jeopardy. Both parties must endeavor to understand each other's position and active listening techniques provide an easy way to establish clearly that concerns have been heard.

Power dynamics between relational parties also has implications for the relationship. More often than not, power is unbalanced within the relationship, which can lead to a breakdown. For example, the organization may have far more in the way of resources compared with the particular strategic public. While no relationship will succeed if all the power is on one side, parties in the relationship need to achieve agreement without feeling coerced into it. Whilst both parties in the relationship are aware of the power ratio, there needs to be agreement on the power balance within the relationship (Canary & Stafford, 1992). If it is perceived that all the power is located on one side of the relationship, compliance may take place but the other party may feel coerced or bullied into agreement. Coercion and bullying are both remarkably effective in organizations for gaining compliance, particularly in terms of work output; however, as soon as the threat is removed the compliance ends—making it an effective tactic in the short term only with any hope of future collaboration forfeited.

Conrad (1985, cited in J. E. Grunig, 1992, p. 315) described the concept of collaboration as a strategy employed in conflict resolution as follows: "All parties believing that they should actively and assertively seek a mutually acceptable solution and be willing to spend large amounts of time and energy to reach such an outcome." Collaboration can occur only in a climate of trust. The parties involved need to be able to trust each other enough to work together towards mutual objectives. In an organization–public relationship, both sides must understand that for a positive outcome they will need to collaborate on some level. Obviously, the level of collaboration will affect the outcome as well as the relationship itself. Mutual understanding helps to identify the level of collaboration possible between the parties. In conflict resolution literature the key relational elements of trust, openness, communication, mutual understanding, power, and collaboration have all been identified as having an important bearing upon relationships between people. Many of these concepts translate directly into public relations as it must be remembered that organization–public relationships are essentially relationships between people who simply represent other entities.

INTERPERSONAL COMMUNICATION LITERATURE

Historically, public relations depended heavily upon mass communication for its theories, which is understandable as the majority of public relations practitioners initially came from a journalism background. As the relational perspective became more influential, public relations academics turned to interpersonal communication theory, which investigates different factors that are involved in improving relationships (J. E. Grunig, 1990; Heath & Bryant, 1992). L. A. Grunig (2000) and Huang (2001b) suggested that the resurgence of interest in the public relations relational perspective in recent years was built upon the foundations of interpersonal communication and the work of Stafford and Canary (1991), who directly influenced Huang's research on the key relational elements of trust, control mutuality, commitment, and satisfaction. Whilst the relational elements of trust, control mutuality, commitment, and satisfaction are discussed in marketing, organizational theory and conflict resolution literature, the concept of mutual influence is not. Mutual influence is the cornerstone of interpersonal communication, which entails that the parties involved in communicating have the ability to influence each other's attitudes and behaviour (Coombs, 2001). Both parties need to have the ability to influence each other; if not, the relationship becomes unbalanced and can lead to breakdown as coercion results when only one party has the ability to influence the other.

Initially in the field of interpersonal communication, work on relationships was dominated by social psychologists as opposed to communication scientists (Duck, 1984). Duck proposed that one of the main problems with research in the area of social and personal relationships was the fact that the concepts of relationship were very diverse and that social psychologists and communications scientists mostly viewed relationships as being in a static state with "automatic" consequences resulting from the qualities of the parties involved in the particular relationship. Duck pointed out that the important influence of "time" was neglected in research conducted up until the mid-1970s. Duck viewed relationships as processes that possess certain qualities or elements.

Ledingham (2000) utilized an interpersonal relationship model by adapting it to the organization–public relationship and outlined the 10 phases relationships pass through in an unmanaged lifecycle—in the "coming together" and "coming apart" process. At its peak, the organization–public relationship basks in the "fidelity phase," where the public is loyal to the organization and the organization in return is committed to the public's interests; the elements of "mutual trust, openness and commitment are perceived as operating" (Ledingham, 2000, p. 45). Reaching and sustaining the "fidelity phase" with organization–public relationships is the ultimate goal for public relations practitioners operating within the relational perspective.

Interpersonal communication literature emphasizes particular relational elements. The relational element of trust was deemed critical if the environment contained risk and there was the possibility that self-interest could direct the relational goals and ultimately lead to mistrust by the other partner and a breakdown in the relationship (Miller & Rogers, 1976, 1987, cited in Heath & Bryant, 1992, p. 176; Canary & Cupach, 1988). Trust is built up or "banked" over a period of time, which is linked with credibility and is necessary for resolving conflicts or communication problems (Plowman, Briggs, & Huang, 2001).

Stafford and Canary (1991) defined the interpersonal relationship element of control mutuality as "the degree to which partners agree about which of them should decide relational goals and behavioural routines" (p. 224). Control mutuality includes the notion of power as each party in the relationship agrees and understands that one has the rightful ability to influence the other or agree upon the power balance (Morton, Alexander, & Altman, 1976, cited in Heath & Bryant, 1992, p. 163; Plowman, Briggs, & Huang, 2001). Domineering behaviour and coercive tactics are often used in relationships where control mutuality is lacking. Habermas' theory of communicative action recognizes that relationships require symmetrical communication (dialogue) to take place as it encourages the parties involved to develop a deeper understanding of the "other's" position, leading to increased empathy. The concept of control mutuality is linked with Habermas' theory as relational parties are seldom equal and one party will almost certainly have access to greater resources and power. Habermas proposed that as rational beings we seek to reach a position of agreement through symmetrical communication. When the relationship is unbalanced as a result of access to resources, power communication becomes asymmetrical and irrational and leads to the relationship breaking down. Openly recognizing where the power lies in the relationship facilitates achieving the desired relational outcome (L'Etang, 1996b, p. 121).

Along with control mutuality, commitment, liking and relational satisfaction are other elements identified (Stafford & Canary, 1991). Most of the research on commitment is based on social exchange theory and is found to be positively associated with satisfaction and long-term investment in the relationship (Rusbult, 1983, cited in Stafford & Canary, 1991, p. 224). The perceived level of commitment was found to be directly related to the strength and stability of the relationship by Lund (1985). The degree of liking is dependent upon the perception of the efforts that one party has undergone to maintain the relationship by the other involved party. Relational satisfaction deals with the rewards or benefits for remaining in the relationship outweighing the costs. As long as relational satisfaction is maintained, it is likely the relationship will continue to exist (Stafford & Canary, 1991).

Morton, Alexander, and Altman (1976, cited in Heath & Bryant, 1992, p. 163) also included communication as a defining element of relationships, specifically the type of communication that occurs. Taylor and Altman (1987, cited in Heath & Bryant, 1992, p. 167) provided a simple formula: "Relationship outcomes = rewards − costs." The reward/cost ratio could be used to measure each specific relationship to gage whether it is a positive or negative relationship. Only when the rewards are more than the costs involved in sustaining the relationship can the relationship be said to be satisfying.

PUBLIC RELATIONS LITERATURE

Public relations literature on the relational perspective has drawn from interpersonal communication, organizational theory, marketing, and conflict resolution literature. The organizational perspective has been the main focus in much of the literature in the public relations body of knowledge and is based on the work of Grunig and Hunt (1984). Using systems theory as the foundation, Grunig and Hunt (1984) developed four models of public relations, which simultaneously described the evolutionary process of the occupation. Grunig and Hunt (1984) proposed that the two-way symmetrical model was best practice for public relations, being the most ethical and effective of the four models. Leitch and Neilson's (2001, pp. 127–138) critique of the two-way symmetrical model is derived from the understanding that within the systems framework publics exist only when the organization has identified them. Viewing publics from the organization's position is problematic as they are then considered to be equal participants in the dialogue or relationship. When power is omitted from the relationship, it is then possible to assume that an organization and its publics are able to meet on equal footing and are able to develop mutually beneficial outcomes for recognized problems. However, in reality this is not the case as usually the organization has access to far greater resources. The concept of power is ignored in the organizational perspective as the organization tends to deal with publics in much the same way it would deal with other organizations, which is why there is confusion with defining publics without there being an issue, linking back to Hallahan's (2000) work on identifying inactive publics. As the relational perspective has become more popular, publics are finally being viewed from a different standpoint—that of the publics themselves (Leitch & Neilson, 2001). This in part is due to globalization and communication technology, which have allowed global movements to operate at the local, national, and international level, promoting collaboration between publics. This has caused a shift in power relations between the organization and its publics as publics have increased access to resources and information, and are in a much better position to form coalitions with other publics that share a similar worldview.

The organizational perspective acknowledges the publics only once they have been identified as such. While different types of publics such as latent and active are strategically identified, they are treated as if they are on an equal footing with the organization. This perspective does not consider the balance of power between the organization and its publics or between publics (Leitch & Neilson, 2001). Leitch and Neilson (2001) explained that this is the key reason why evidence to support the two-way symmetrical model was, and remains, scarce in practice. While the communication process between an organization and its publics may very well be symmetrical, the relationship between them will not be.

"Organization–public relations refers to relations between organizations and publics that are defined as internal to neither the organization nor other system organizations" (Leitch & Neilson, 2001, p. 131). Using the relationship management perspective that looks at the relationship as the unit of analysis, there is the potential to identify an appropriate framework or methodology to effectively evaluate the relationship between an organization and its publics. Since Ferguson in 1984 proposed that public relations should shift its focus to the organization–public relationship, other public relations scholars have taken the banner and have started to examine relationship antecedents, concepts, and consequences in more depth using quantitative methodologies (Hon & Grunig, 1999; J. E. Grunig & Huang, 2000; Ledingham & Bruning, 2000; Broom, Casey, & Ritchey, 2000; Huang, 2001a, b). One of the reasons that scholars have enthusiastically adopted the relational perspective is that it provides public relations practitioners with the ability to "utilize quantitative evaluation methods to track relationship changes over time" (Bruning & Ledingham, 1999, p. 158). This is a welcome departure from previous quantitative evaluation methods such as counting press clippings, which has long been discredited mainly because of its failure to link media coverage to its possible effects, such as changes in the levels of awareness, public's attitudes, and behaviours. However, as the methods employed are still quantitative they do not provide a rich description or understanding of the organization–public relationship, as would be the case if qualitative methods were used instead. The relational perspective with its quest to understand and describe organization–public relationships implies the need for qualitative methodologies.

The relational perspective has the potential to shift public relations practitioners away from using persuasive communication as a tool to manipulate public opinion toward building and maintaining mutually beneficial organization–public relationships. By effectively managing relationships with strategic publics, public relations practitioners are able to influence positively their attitudes and behaviours in the long term. It is the public relations practitioner's role to identify strategic publics and manage the organization's relationships with them in order to ideally achieve a stable equilibrium within the system or operating environment. To do this effectively each relationship must be viewed separately, and the elements of the relationship need to be evaluated in order to have an understanding of the present state of the relationship.

By effectively managing the organization–public relationship, the attitudes and behaviuor of members of strategic publics can be influenced. Findings from Ledingham's (2001) study of government–community relationships reinforce the thought that relationship management and the relational paradigm offer a useful way to understand and explain the behaviour of a strategic public. Social exchange theory was shown to be particularly useful in explaining the behaviour of the strategic public within the context of the relationship. Kovacs (2001) examined the strategies and impact of six activist groups on the British broadcasting policies and programming and found that their success over time was attributed to relationship building. She suggested that good relationship building and maintenance induced collaboration, producing a "win–win" situation for resolving conflict, which in the long term was more effective in producing behavioural change than confrontational approaches often used by environmental activist groups. Bruning's (2002) investigation into the relationship–attitudes–behavioural outcome link examined the student–university relationship attitudes affect on retention rates. Bruning (2002) suggested that relationship attitudes are directly linked with behavioural outcomes and can be quantitatively measured.

Drawing from the literature reviewed from the disciplines of marketing, organizational theory, conflict resolution, and interpersonal communication, public relations scholars interested in the relational perspective have started to identify the antecedents, characteristics, or elements that when present together produce the constituents of a positive relationship. Grunig, Grunig, and Ehling (1992) identified reciprocity, trust, credibility, mutual legitimacy, openness, mutual satisfaction, and mutual understanding as being the most important. Hon and Grunig (1999) went further to identify a total of six attributes: control mutuality, trust, satisfaction, commitment, exchange relationship, and communal relationship. Huang (2001b) used trust, control

mutuality, commitment, and satisfaction as key relational features derived from Western literature and in dealing with cross-cultural relationships added the "face and favor" attribute as the
fifth dimension, which reflected Chinese social psychology. Huang's (2001b) "face and favor"
relationship dimension was based upon Hwang's (1987, cited in Huang, 2001b, p. 68) social
psychology model of "face and favor" in the Chinese society. This model explained the use
of personal social connections and networks in locating resources or obtaining favours from
others in positions of authority or power (Huang, 2001b). Huang's addition of a cross-cultural
attribute is important as it highlights the necessity for considering cross-cultural attributes
when identifying the elements of the relationship to be evaluated, as many relational elements
such as transparency are culturally specific.

Broom, Casey, and Ritchey (2000) suggested that relationships are both formed and maintained by an ongoing process based upon mutual adaptation and contingent responses, which
enable the relationship to reach homeostasis. It was also proposed that the relationships between
an organization and key publics could be studied as distinct and separate from the perceptions
of the state of the relationship held by the parties involved.

DIALOGUE AND TRANSPARENCY AS
RELATIONAL CHARACTERISTICS

Whilst many relationship characteristics have been identified in the public relations literature,
there appear to be some gaps in the lists of relationship characteristics, namely dialogue and
transparency. Communication is touched upon in some of the literature surveyed on conflict
resolution and interpersonal communication, but it is barely touched upon as a relationship
characteristic with regard to public relations. Yet surely for a relationship to exist, there must
be a level of communication occurring. Dialogue is a form of communication most applicable to building and maintaining relationships (Kent & Taylor, 2002), and without it there is
little chance of the relationship surviving, much like a relationship without trust. Kent and
Taylor (2002) clarified the concept of dialogue in public relations and described it as "one
of the most ethical forms of communication and as one of the central means of separating
truth from falsehood" (p. 22). The shift in public relations toward a relational perspective
emphasises the use of communication as a tool for resolving conflicts and building and maintaining relationships with strategic publics. Kent and Taylor (2002) found that whilst dialogue
is mentioned as a concept in public relations literature, what is actually meant by it remains
unclear.

The study of dialogue, like public relations, traces back to philosophy, rhetoric, and psychology (Kent & Taylor, 2002). Dialogue is considered to be the most ethical form of communication in that the "truth" of an issue has an opportunity to be heard. Kent and Taylor (2002)
suggested that today our concept of dialogue is based heavily on the work of the theologian
Martin Buber. Buber viewed dialogue as being essential for a relationship to exist and that
it required both openness and respect. Buber believed that dialogue required elements that
have also been identified as relational characteristics: reciprocity, mutuality, commitment, and
openness. Dialogue is not the means to an end but rather the end goal itself, with the relationship facilitating the process (Buber, 1982, cited in Kent & Taylor, 2002, p. 324). Dialogic
communication requires the parties involved to be willing to negotiate in order to reach a position that is mutually acceptable. By communicating back and forth in a symmetrical manner,
both parties are able to construct a deeper understanding of the other's position and discover
"common ground" by not immediately rejecting the other's position and increasing empathy
for each other.

Whilst dialogue can change the type of organization–public relationship by shifting the focus onto the relationship and developing mutual understanding, it is unable to make the organization behave ethically towards its public or react to an issue (Kent & Taylor, 2002). Transparency is required for the realization of this outcome as it exposes organizational behaviour and encourages ethical decision making, which more likely to occur in organizations that operate in a transparent environment. It is because of the many benefits transparency brings to organization–public relationships that it has resulted in being hailed as the saviour against all corporate and government evils as its power lies in it being perceived as "an antidote to mismanagement and corruption" (von Furstenberg, 2001, p. 106). Governments, corporate conglomerates, and NGOs have all called for greater transparency in the operational side of things and reinforced the view that it is considered to be the universal cure for unethical practice and the only way to restore a damaged reputation.

Transparency Related Outcomes

Transparency is very important for organization–public relationships and can be viewed as a relational condition or variable that is a prerequisite for other relational elements such as trust and commitment. It provides the atmospheric conditions that allow trust, accountability, cooperation, collaboration, and commitment to flourish.

Trust, accountability, cooperation, collaboration, and commitment are all components of "positive" organization–public relationships. Transparency instills a level of trust that is crucial, especially for organizations that have experienced crises and need to rebuild their reputations. Transparency is necessary in order for publics to trust that ethical communication and decision making is taking place within the organization. As Grunig (cited in Center & Jackson, 2003, p. 14) proposed, decisions or policies often create problems and active publics, which lead to the emergence of issues and, without action, can turn into full-blown crises. However, if the organization–public relationship is "positive," there will be transparency, communication, trust, cooperation, satisfaction, and commitment as well as other relational characteristics present. Increased dialogue with active publics feeds into the organization's decision-making process, enabling it to deliver in what many cases is considered to be the "least-worst" possible option. Survival will often depend upon the organization's ability to predict the consequences of such decisions or policies amongst its key publics.

Transparency is considered a necessity for public relations practitioners interested in opening up the decision-making process and ensuring accountability and in preempting issues and averting expensive crises. Decision making requires communication, information, and knowledge, which provide more choices. If the process is transparent, then publics are able to view the interaction and internal behaviour and can decide whether the organization actually does what it claims to be doing. This process feeds into corporate social responsibility (CSR), as transparency forces the organization to consider ethics and values in relation to its own operations as well within its entire supply chain.

Transparency can be defined as a relational characteristic as well as with regard to environmental conditions and organizational processes. Florini (1998, p. 50) defined transparency as being the opposite of secrecy in that the internal processes are purposefully exposed to the external world. As public relations practitioners collaborate and facilitate work in teams, internal transparency increases.

A more in-depth definition is provided in the IMF Code (1999, pp. 1–2, cited in von Furstenberg, 2001, p. 112) that defines transparency as being far more than simply releasing information into the public domain. It is also described as being an environmental condition that exists and within which the organization operates. Thus, transparency has an impact on both the internal and external processes:

> an environment in which the objective of policy, its legal, institutional, and economic framework, policy decisions and their rationale, data (related to the proper exercise of agencies' functions), and the terms of agencies' accountability, are provided to the public on an understandable, accessible and timely basis.

Von Furstenberg (2001, pp. 107–108) traced the origins of the concept of transparency to positivist philosophy and classical liberalism as a rationalist promise to limit and reduce abuses of power. In this capacity, transparency acts to reveal abuses of power and show accountability. Transparency provides the economic and civil benefits resulting from predictability, trust, and credibility. These benefits raise transparency onto a moral and ethical platform, which is why from the Western perspective it should be applied internationally and across the board, with little regard to its incompatibility with other cultures.

Transparency contributes to the organization's reputation management through numerous benefits enjoyed by transparent organizations: increased trust, credibility, cooperation with key publics, reduced information and transaction costs, and lowered risk premiums. Von Furstenberg (2001, p. 108) acknowledged the good that transparency instills and credits it with reducing the levels of corruption and bad practice that flourish in opacity. When one organization commits to having a transparent approach, often its competitors will feel coerced into complying or else risk being perceived as "hiding something." Technological advancements have been crucial in extending transparency as interested publics can quickly and easily compare competitors. The Internet was partially responsible for the drive toward transparency in organizational behaviour. Information accessibility has forced organizations to rethink the potential outcomes of decisions and choices.

Transparency is a choice, encouraged by changing attitudes about what constitutes appropriate behaviour. Transparency and opacity are not either/or conditions; instead they represent the opposite ends of a continuum (Florini, 1998, p. 50) with perhaps a translucent category at the mid-point. Here the transparent organization is defined as one where both the internal and external processes are transparent. The translucent organization is one where either the internal or external processes are transparent, but not both, and the opaque organization is where both the internal and external processes are hidden or secret. It is likely that most organizations would be considered to be translucent given the above criteria.

Christensen (2002) analyzed the notion of transparency as both an organizational condition as well as a business strategy and questioned whether transparency is a condition or adoptable strategy. He proposed that corporate communication is a result of transparency as a condition and that "contemporary organizations not only describe their communication environment in terms of transparency but also prescribe transparency in communications as the proper managerial response" (p. 2). This idea links back and connects with Grunig's (2001) symmetrical and ethical communication model by using transparency as an environmental condition in order to promote ethical decision making as the correct managerial response.

Christensen was critical of van Riel's (2000, p. 158, cited in Christensen, 2002, p. 163) assumption that transparency is a "basic requirement" for organizations operating today and questioned where this condition for operation originates and whether it is a preexisting condition or simply a survival strategy adopted during a crisis of trust. Christensen (2002, p. 163) argued that whilst transparency is often presented or introduced as an environmental condition that shapes an organization's communications, it is at the same time an "assumption necessary for organizations to pursue and justify their corporate ambitions." As a condition that shapes organizational behaviour, transparency can be viewed as part of a persuasive response-shaping process, which is most effective when situations are radically new or when there is a new development within the organization's environment, which agrees with it being utilized as a survival strategy (Miller, 2002, p. 7). The organization is "socialized" to be transparent—otherwise the consequences are negative, relationships with key publics are destroyed, and its licence to operate is withdrawn.

Christensen (2002) differentiated between internal and external transparency. He argued that whilst the condition of transparency does not equate with self-transparency, where organizations are internally transparent, corporate communications with its overall ambition of coordinating and managing all organizational communication under one corporate identity has the underlying presupposition that the organization is self-transparent, which is seldom the reality (p. 166). With multiple realities the idea of one single perspective is impractical and unsustainable. Christensen argued that ambiguity can be far more productive as it allows the coexistence of multiple perspectives within an organizational entity. The more defined the identity becomes, the more difficult it is to manage. Also, as transparency increases there is also more exposure to pluralism and multiple voices as opposed to the corporate communications ambition of "one voice."

Organizational transparency is based upon the assumption that external publics have access to the information and are also capable of processing it. It also assumes that access to more information allows publics to develop a more sophisticated understanding of the organization and the complex issues it faces. Frombrun and Rindova (2000, cited in Christensen, 2002, p. 265) proposed that as information availability increased there was also an increase in trust and credibility and a decrease in the alienation of strategic publics; however, too much information is overwhelming. Also, there is the incorrect assumption that communication equals information.

Reducing communication to purely information is problematic. Some organizations and, more importantly, individuals and/or groups only understand communication with stakeholders as the way to send information, adopting a conduit metaphor where messages are merely transferred from the sender to the receiver based upon the Shannon–Weaver model of communication (Fawkes, 2001, p. 13). However, Christensen (2002, p. 165) suggested that reception theory is more relevant as it highlights the important point that receivers interpret messages in a creative and self-referential manner and are able to construct meaning that cannot be controlled or even completely determined by the sender. It is the publics' ability to process information and construct the resulting meaning (Iser, 1974, cited in Christensen, 2002, p. 165).

Literature on transparency tends to deal with economic concerns such as the necessity of financial transparency or with corporate social responsibility initiatives because of the cost-reduction paradigm as crises are expensive to weather and expose the organization to unnecessary risk. Because of the link between transparency, trust, and accountability, there is naturally a strong interest in it as a solution for instantly restoring confidence to the organization–public relationship. In cases where natural disasters have caused a crisis, if the organization is responsive and transparent about its actions they are usually supported and embraced by the community. Transparency enables organizations that have been faced with a "man-made" crisis to have the world witness that they are making up for their sins and are setting "right" what was perceived to be "wrong." It is required for repairing damaged reputations where trust is minimal or even completely lost. This restorative power or quality of transparency permits organizations to rebuild trust by exposing accountability. Whether it is increased confidence in the organization's environmental and labour policies/practice or increased investor confidence, transparency builds trust. Organizations are pressured into becoming more open by revealing the internal decision-making processes and operations to interested publics such as activist groups and nongovernmental organizations (Florini, 1998, p. 50). The recent lack of investor confidence attributed to the exposure of illegal accounting practices, for example at Enron, has led investors to "put their money where transparency allows some predictability about the likelihood of returns. Thanks to globalization, they have a lot of options, creating a powerful economic incentive for ever higher degrees of disclosure" (Florini, 1998, p. 56). Organizations can no longer afford to be opaque, as transparency has related outcomes that claim to provide more benefit than cost.

Transparency increases the level of trust in an organization. As publics are demanding ethical behaviour from organizations, transparency becomes a necessity in order for the organization to gain the trust that it is doing what society expects of it. Trust is built when publics are able to discern that what the organization says is actually true. For many organizations, transparency translates into open accounting practices and CSR. Corporations such as Enron and WorldCom provide recent examples of organizations that effectively lost their license to operate mainly due to the lack of transparency involved in their accounting practices and triggered the demand for transparent operations globally. Transparency has become critical for trust to be maintained in relationships between publics and corporations. Revelations regarding Enron, whilst shocking, were also portrayed as an exception. However, with Xerox, WorldCom, and, more recently, Shell, the threat is very real and is not just confined to one particular area. Trust in the corporate world is decreasing and cynicism is increasing. Without transparency there is little trust, which is important for both cooperation and collaboration to occur. Trust is also the foundation of a positive relationship.

Along with increasing trust, transparency also increases the level of accountability in an organization. Many different publics have a vested interest in encouraging organizations to embrace transparency. Financial investors both demand transparency from publicly listed companies and are required to be transparent themselves after recent allegations and court cases regarding conflict of interest as financial analysts promoted IPOs (initial public offerings) whilst their colleagues at the same financial institutions were responsible for those floatations. Coombes and Watson (2001) found in a McKinsey survey on corporate reform in the developing world that greater transparency or disclosure ranked most important amongst reforms within a company's control. As the recognition of the importance of transparency increases, there are obvious implications for public relations practitioners working in the areas of investor relations or financial public relations, where publics are already demanding transparency. Pressure from financial analysts and shareholders for increased financial reporting regulations indicates that there is a strong suspicion that appropriate information is not being disclosed (Ho & Wong, 2001). Global business and investors require the uninterrupted free flow of information, making transparency a necessity. Ethical funds continue to gain interest with fund managers and investors, as shareholders are more informed and concerned about corporate social responsibility issues along the entire supply chain.

As transparency increases the level of trust, this in turn has an effect on the level of collaboration and cooperation in organizations (Parks & Hilbert, 1995, cited in de Cremer & Dewitte, 2002). Transparency is very important for collaborative work, which requires the involved parties to trust that what is being done is being done to the agreed standard. Because transparency makes it clear where accountability lies, people are more inclined to do a good job. If individuals and organizations are required to be accountable for their decisions and actions, then it is likely that they will conform and cooperate if cooperation is perceived to be positive. Once it is clear where accountability lies, cooperation is more likely to occur, as a level of trust exists. Because transparency increases trust, it is key for determining levels of cooperation. Organizations and publics regularly are required to cooperate in mixed-motive situations. De Cremer and Dewitte (2002, p. 542) stated that expectations concerning reciprocity may ultimately influence the level of cooperation. A high level of transparency and trust will lead to a high level of cooperation. Opaque organizations do not promote high levels of trust; in fact the reverse tends to be the result, which may lead to a negative downward spiral of low trust leading to low levels of cooperation just when it is crucial for the organization to survive a crisis situation. Without trust collaboration is minimal, as people do not want to work with untrustworthy colleagues or institutions. Transparency rebuilds trust where it is lacking and provides an environment where collaboration can exist, as it exposes what is going on and therefore increases the level of trust.

The Dark Side of Transparency

Transparency is often viewed as a "quick fix" solution that makes accountability abundantly clear by providing a scapegoat and thus exonerating an organization from its crimes or misdeeds. The drive for corporate and organizational transparency has been fuelled, and largely made possible, by the advances in communication technology and specifically the Internet (Florini, 1998, p. 52). Transparency enforces the maintenance of standards via the underlying coercive threat of exposing bad practice: regulation by revelation. In this way it is similar to "self-censorship" where individuals and organizations censor themselves, thus ensuring that society or the government does not do the censoring for them. However, this only works when there is enough interest in what is revealed to spark or "kick-start" a reaction of some sort—for example, boycotts or a drop in share value—and it focuses only on the observable behaviour and not the actual intent that lies behind it.

In addition to not being transparent at the source, there are other negative consequences regarding transparency. Whilst the IMF promotes transparency, it also acknowledges that there is a cost in that it can lower the decision-making quality: "[T]he rationale for limiting some types of disclosure arises because it could adversely affect the decision-making process and the effectiveness of policies" (IMF, 1999, p. 8, also cited in von Furstenburg, 2003, p. 112). Unsavory or difficult decisions may be put off or not even made for fear of the media and the ensuing public outcry when in reality those decisions might be better for the survival of the organization in the long term.

Transparency becomes easier to establish if it is done in a climate of reciprocity, or otherwise organizations may feel vulnerable regarding competitors (von Furstenberg, 2001, p. 113). Individuals are also likely to censor what they say or may perceive what others say in a negative light by adding value judgments contributing to possible organizational depression, which affects individual and group performance. Political correctness could negatively influence transparent behaviour and lead to the inhibition of creative and innovative outcomes, or worse, to social conformity. Therefore, transparency operating in a climate of political correctness could be highly oppressive and possibly lead to, or result from, behaviourist approaches to leadership rather than constructivist ones.

Florini (1998, p. 60) emphasized that because transparency only exposes behaviour and does not shed light upon the actual intent behind the behaviour, hidden agendas remain undisclosed. This relates to criticisms regarding sender–receiver models where the connotative meaning of the message is undisclosed and therefore inhibits appropriate interpretation and the construction of meaning.

Von Furstenberg (2001, p. 107) argued that transparency is a relational variable that is culture bound and derived from 300 years of European and American social philosophy and is therefore not applicable given the impact of globalization on organizations. Like Florini (1998), von Furstenberg (2001) was concerned that transparency only reveals the behaviour and not the intent behind it. Organizations such as the EU, IMF, and donor countries can impose transparency upon "weaker" or more vulnerable cultures as a form of "cultural imperialism" by pretending it is for their own good, whereas in reality there is another opaque vested interest at work. Organizations are forced into transparency, except perhaps for NGOs and organizations with good reputations as it is assumed they are ethical and that they are doing good work. Von Furstenberg's main argument against the popular uptake of transparency is that the actual term "transparency" has been overused and as a result has become watered down and meaningless.

Von Furstenberg warned that transparency comes at the cost of privacy and control (2001, p. 108) and that it is important to keep in mind the vested interests behind it. Because of the inherent dangers involved, it is crucial to determine who gives transparency, who benefits from it, "and up to what point the benefits to one side exceed the costs to the other" (p. 108). There may also be a point where too much transparency, as mentioned earlier, actually hinders the purpose by watering down the decision-making quality. This may be heavily influenced by developments and access to technology where information overload, without the possibility of discriminating between what is relevant and what is noise, confuses and hinders the construction of meaning or—even worse—prevents it, resulting in social apathy. A possible role for public relations practitioners could be to help filter information, which enables others to construct meaning, energizing the social engagement.

For practitioners interested in increasing or decreasing transparency within the organization's internal and external processes, the public relations catalyst model, depicted in Figure 4.1

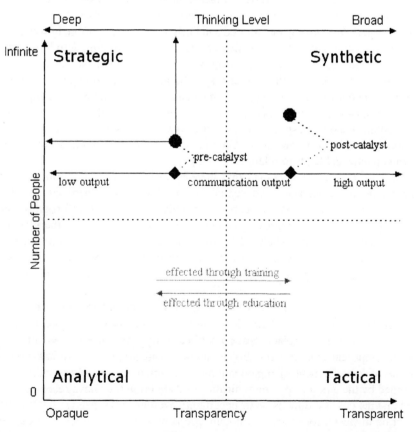

FIGURE 4.1.   Public relations catalyst model (Jahansoozi & Koper, 2004). The blue circles denote the organization.

(Jahansoozi & Koper, 2004), provides a pragmatic and descriptive approach. By simply increasing the number of people involved in an activity and increasing the communication output, transparency increases. If the organization considers itself to be too transparent, it can decrease collaboration and the number of people involved.

This model is concerned with thinking levels and the differences between analytical and tactical thinkers. Communication in this example is used as a catalyst to instigate the change toward strategic and synthetic levels of operation. For example, if an organization such as an engineering company found itself to be highly analytical in its approach toward problem solving and relationship building, it would be operating in the lower left-hand quadrant of the diagramme. In order for the problem-solving activities to become strategic, more people need to be involved, which increases the level of internal transparency and moves the organization into the top left-hand quadrant. The organization is translucent at this point as only the internal processes are transparent whilst the external processes remain opaque. To remedy this communication output needs to be increased, moving the organization away from the analytical/strategic side toward the tactical/synthetic side, where both the internal and external processes are transparent.

STAKEHOLDER FATIGUE SYNDROME

As practitioners become more interested in managing the organization's relationships with its publics and invest resources into engagement activities, there is also the risk of overengagement. Initially the targeted public may be flattered and intrigued by the attention; however, when they start to feel inundated with communication and relationship-building activities, "stakeholder fatigue" may set in. Stakeholder fatigue occurs when organizations solicit too much contact with key publics. The organization's keenness to build and maintain "positive" relationships with these key publics results in the actual mismanagement of the relationship. The magnitude of communication activities becomes overwhelming and leads to disengagement. Many publics are interested only in specific areas of the organization's operation and prefer to obtain information on a "need-to-know" basis. Communication that deals with peripheral operations is most unwelcome and leads to relationship fatigue.

Christensen (2002, p. 165) argued that there is an implicit assumption in the literature that external publics both want and demand organizational transparency, which is established via communication. Communication is readily equated with information, and hence the reasoning that external publics want more information. However, there is a backlash occurring as publics are overwhelmed by the amount of communication and information sent their way (e.g., Shell's Athabasca Oil Sands Project—"stakeholder fatigue syndrome" was a result of strategic publics being overwhelmed by the organization's well-meaning attention).

Some of the assumptions that lead and shape organizational strategies for coping with transparency as an environmental condition are linked with society's expectations regarding democracy and a free marketplace. But do publics really want unrestricted communication? There is no empirical evidence for this assumption and terms such as stakeholder fatigue indicate the mismanagement of organization–public relationships where publics have been overwhelmed by the amount of communication and attention they have received. Christensen proposed that the cultural dimension of uncertainty avoidance (Hofstede, 2001, pp. 145–199) should not be mistaken for interest in organizations by external publics, and that except for a select few special interest groups who construct their own meaning, most external publics simply want assurances that the organizations they interact with are behaving in a socially acceptable and responsible manner.

RECENT PUBLIC RELATIONS RESEARCH ON EVALUATING RELATIONSHIPS

In the last 5 years interest in evaluating the organization–public relationship has increased. A number of quantitative studies have been conducted that use various scales that measure many of the relational elements or characteristics previously outlined. However, the studies reviewed all evaluated the organization–public relationship solely from the perspective of the particular public involved. None of the studies so far have included both the organization's perspective as well as the public's perspective and very little qualitative research on the organization–public relationship has been conducted, resulting in a major gap in this area. As public relations falls within the domain of social research, particular research questions require specific approaches. Quantitative methods are singularly useful for identifying factors or variables that may influence an outcome or in enabling a level of prediction (Cresswell, 2003, pp. 21–22). However, qualitative methods are best for understanding a new concept or phenomenon, such as the actual organization–public relationship, as this research approach is exploratory in nature and seeks to understand and describe the actual relationship. To understand an organization–public relationship, it is crucial that the relationship is the phenomenon that is explored from both the perspective of the organization and the particular public.

Research conducted by Ledingham, Bruning, and Wilson (1999) found that the longer the organization–public relationship existed the more expectations the public had regarding the organization and its responsibilities, which is congruent with interpersonal relationships and intuitively is what one would expect. Bruning and Ledingham (1999) developed an organization–public relationship scale and used it to determine the status of a relationship. The relational elements of trust, openness, involvement, investment, commitment, reciprocity, mutual legitimacy, and mutual understanding were included as part of the survey instrument, which they found could measure the influence that perceptions of the organization–public relationship had on consumer attitudes. The results supported the idea that organization–public relationships were multidimensional in that there were professional, personal, and community relationship dimensions. Each dimension had different expectations from the public, which translated into different strategies that could be employed by the organization to maintain or improve the relationship. For example, the professional relationship required the organization to invest financially in the relationship, personal relationships required trust between the organization and the public and that the organization was willing to invest time and be emotionally engaged with the public, while the community relationship needed the organization to be open with the community, invest in CSR programmes, sponsor events, and in general engage with the community and its development.

Further quantitative research conducted by Bruning and Ledingham (2000b) using the same scale and data set examined the ways in which relationship attitudes affected satisfaction evaluations. The research indicated that satisfaction with the organization was influenced by the key public members' perceptions of the relationship, which would be expected, as satisfaction is a relational element and if the relationship was perceived to be unsatisfactory then it would be rather odd if the public was still satisfied with the organization. However, as the research was meant to explore the attitude towards the relationship in order to assess whether it affected satisfaction levels, a qualitative approach would have yielded a more in-depth view, and if there were areas in which levels of satisfaction towards the organization were low the reasons why this was the case could be explored, described, and understood.

Again using the Bruning–Ledingham Relationship Scale, Ledingham (2001) carried out a further study, which looked at the perceptions of public members. Despite a low response rate (17%) for making generalizations, Ledingham concluded that the scale was an effective tool for assessing relationship quality and predicting the behaviour of a strategic public. Bruning (2002) provided additional evidence that a positive organization–public relationship influences the public's behaviour, which provides further support for the utilization of the relational perspective by practitioners interested in changing or reinforcing behaviour. Bruning, Langenhop, and Green (2004) again found that the public's perception of the organization–public relationship influenced their behaviour towards the organization.

Huang (2001b) developed a cross-cultural multiple-item scale, the Organization–Public Relationship Assessment (OPRA), similar to the Bruning–Ledingham Relationship Scale for measuring the organization–public relationship but which included a cultural variable. Initially Huang used a pilot survey to test the OPRA scale and then conducted qualitative in-depth interviews in order to assess the validity of the scale, which she then refined to include a Chinese cultural variable called "renqing" ["favour"] and "mianzi" ["face"] and again used as a survey to measure a public's perception of a particular relationship with an organization. The OPRA was found to be a reliable and valid scale for measuring the organization–public relationship in Taiwan. Whilst Huang's study employed a qualitative method, the research design was primarily quantitative in its approach.

The key weaknesses in the quantitative research conducted so far is the fact that it is still very much a one-sided analysis using predetermined instruments that provide statistical data. This type of data does not provide a description of what the relationship is like and what it means for those involved in it. For a comprehensive relationship analysis, a qualitative co-orientational approach that assesses all the actors in the relationship and their perceptions of it would provide a more holistic view (Broom & Dozier, 1990).

ANALYZING THE ORGANIZATION–PUBLIC RELATIONSHIP USING MULTIPLE PERSPECTIVES

Broom and Dozier (1990) were amongst the first in public relations academia to discuss ways in which it is possible to analyze the relationship between a particular public and an organization and built upon and promoted McLeod and Chaffee's (1973) coorientational model. As a starting point, it becomes necessary to first know what it is that the public knows about the organization as well as what the organization knows about the public—and in particular about the issue that may have created the public—for example, an environmental issue. This feeds into audits that research the position of the organization and its public. Individual members of the public are surveyed to find out their position, and the distance between the organization and the public's position can then be calculated. This type of audit is referred to as a "gap analysis." Broom and Dozier (1990) criticised this approach, as it is only useful if the public relations objective is that of changing the public's position. It finds out how far removed the public's views are on an issue from those held by the organization, in order to close the "gap," usually by changing the views of the public. The coorientational approach, however, provides a more holistic view as it measures both parties' perceptions of the relationship.

Once the perceptions of the organization and the particular public are analyzed, it is possible to calculate the coorientational variables, which McLeod and Chaffee (1973, pp. 483–488, cited in Broom & Dozier, 1990, p. 37) referred to as agreement, accuracy, and perceived agreement.

Agreement is understood to refer to the degree that the organization and public agree or at least have similar views regarding the particular issue. Accuracy is understood to refer to the degree that one side is able to correctly estimate the views of the "opposing" side. Finally, perceived agreement refers to the degree that one side's views match what they perceive to be the other side's views. These three variables also provide room to consider inaccurate perceptions, true consensus, dissensus, false consensus (when an organization "pretends" to hold the same views as the public and even provides evidence in the form of actions and policies when in reality this is just done to "fool" the public), and false conflict (when both sides agree but one side inaccurately perceives the other side's views as being different).

Until Verčič and Tkalac's (2004) research on the communication behaviour between the Slovenian and Croatian "general" publics, very few studies employed the coorientation approach, which is surprising as it exposes the different perceptions of the coorientational indicators (as defined by McLeod & Chaffee, 1973, cited in Broom & Dozier, 1990, pp. 82–83). This again highlights the fact that although public relations is positioned as being interdisciplinary, models such as the coorientation model which hail from the interpersonal communication domain have largely been ignored.

In analyzing the organization–public relationship, it is also important to remember that the organization's environment contains multiple publics. As Springston and Keyton (2001) pointed out, most public relations models focus on one-way and two-way communication scenarios. However, these models are inadequate to explore the complexities found in relationships with the organization and conflicting publics. The organization's relationship with one public will have implications for its relationship with other publics, and depending upon the relationship between the publics related to the organization, managing these relationships in harmony (or a state of equilibrium) might not be possible. It also needs to be recognized that many publics have relationships with each other that may be completely independent of the particular organization. Also, it is possible that an organization's relationship with another organization could create conflict and hostilities from a public that previously it had no relationship with. For example, the Royal Bank of Scotland was targeted by animal rights groups because of its relationship with Huntingdon Life Sciences, an organization that uses animal testing practices. Just as organizations do not operate in isolation, neither do publics and stakeholders. The implications are that stakeholder groups and publics are connected whether or not they realise it. The organization's relationship with one stakeholder will have an affect on another and the same goes for identifiable publics. Relationships do not occur in isolation or sterile bubbles.

Springston and Keyton's (2001) public relations field dynamics (PRFD) provides another method for understanding the complexities of the multi-public environment. Based on group dynamics theory, PRFD measures the organization and its publics at a particular point in time, or across the entire development of an issue. PRFD is able to assess types of coorientation as it describes the publics' perceptions of the current situation, the best possible scenario, and the worst-case scenario, which makes it valuable for scenario planning exercises. PRFD provides another useful instrument for assessing the perceptions of multiple publics towards each other as well as towards the organization.

Research using the coorientational approach has analyzed the relationship between the organization and public whilst referring to a particular issue. Minimal research has been done using the coorientational approach to assess the actual quality of the relationship, focusing on the relational elements of trust, satisfaction commitment, control mutuality, dialogue, and transparency. Using PRFD it is possible to triangulate the coorientational approach by assessing the relationships between the publics as well as the organization to see if it agrees with the assessment of the organization–public relationship.

IMPLICATIONS

Public relations has struggled with an identity crisis and has failed to adopt an accepted definition of what it is nor agreed to what it does. While public relations is interdisciplinary, it remains blinkered to developments in related fields and neighbouring disciplines such as marketing with its emerging relationship marketing paradigm. Ferguson's (1984) challenge to academics and practitioners to take a fresh approach to public relations and focus on the organization's relationships with its publics instigated interest in identifying relational elements and quantitative instruments to measure them. If public relations practitioners want to gain recognition from senior management, they will have to prove they can offer strategic advice relating to the continued survival of the organization. Instead of being used as a promotional aid for marketing, public relations should be responsible for identifying key publics and stakeholders and managing relationships with them in order to reduce conflict situations. By doing this practitioners will move towards a "revenue generation" model by increasing goodwill and understanding between the organization and the publics who grant its licence to operate.

Whilst relational elements such as trust, commitment, mutual satisfaction, and control mutuality have been identified (Hon & Grunig, 1999), relational elements such as dialogue and transparency have been neglected in recent research on organization–public relationships—and yet both are central for the grooming, developing, and maintenance of important relationships. The shift in public relations toward a relational perspective emphasizes the need to use dialogue to resolve conflicts whilst building and maintaining relationships with strategic publics. Transparency provides conditions that allow trust, accountability, cooperation, collaboration, and commitment to grow but can also act as a coercive force. Publics and stakeholders are demanding transparency as a result of bad corporate practices that have had an impact on the social and economic environment. Transparency verifies that an organization is behaving ethically both locally and internationally and actually doing what it says it is doing. Social and environmental change has forced organizations to reevaluate their business practices as various crises have led to a lack of trust in organizations and increased cynicism regarding organizational behaviour. Organization–public relationships are now considered to be very important for the organization's ability to successfully meet its mission objectives and they are ignored at the organization's peril.

Evaluating the organization–public relationship has recently been the focus for a number of studies. Quantitative methodologies have almost solely been utilized for examining and exploring organization–public relationships and yet the relational perspective implies a need for qualitative work. Academics and practitioners should want to understand how organizations and strategic publics perceive the relationship they have with each other in order to be able to diagnose the health and survival of the relationship. It is important to understand what the relationship actually means, how it is perceived, and how meaning is constructed and what that meaning is for those involved. It is all well and good to be able to quantitatively measure a relational element such as trust and assign it a number on a scale but what does this really mean, why is this the situation, what was the reason for this to happen, and so on. The relational approach to such an in-depth interest in the phenomenon appears better served by qualitative research. By utilizing a coorientational approach, differences in agreement, accuracy, and the perceived agreement of the other relational party exposes inaccurate perceptions each side has of the other side's views. This analysis allows practitioners to zone in on where perceptual differences exist and are therefore in a position to resolve issues by addressing the cause before it develops into a crisis.

The relational perspective of public relations is key for future theoretical advancements and also for defining the field and setting up its jurisdictional boundaries. If public relations continues to fragment and divide into specialist areas such as public affairs, corporate social responsibility, investor relations, and so on, then it is likely that it will not survive as a distinct discipline. The relational perspective fundamentally unites the specialist areas together, as regardless of the area of practice or context the focus remains on the organization–public relationship.

The relational perspective allows public relations to draw upon other disciplines also interested in the dynamics of interpersonal relationships, such as marketing and interpersonal communication, without being subsumed by them because of the unique organization–public relationship focus that only public relations offers. Practitioners need to be aware of developments in neighbouring fields and also to recognize and adopt skills that are of great benefit for developing and maintaining relationships such as negotiation, conflict resolution, and counselling skills. The relational perspective allows academics and practitioners the room to explore the organization, its publics, and the relationships they all have and share with each other in order to gain a holistic view and understanding of the actual environment the organization operates in. This overall view enables practitioners to understand the relationships between different groups and the organization and to prioritise them according to the level of importance and impact upon the environment. It also allows for the development of proactive strategies for grooming, developing, and maintaining organization–public relationships, which are critical for the organization's survival.

The relational perspective increases organizational effectiveness by building and maintaining critical relationships with the organization's strategic publics. By facilitating and maintaining "positive" relationships with key publics, public relations practitioners are able to proactively position the organization, reduce the risk of conflict, and avert costly crises. The relational perspective also contributes directly reputation management. By managing the organization's relationships with important groups, there is far less likelihood that a "man-made" crisis will develop and harm the organization's reputation. Current research has ignored qualitative approaches, creating a major gap, and therefore future research should initially focus on qualitative approaches before further replication of the multiple dimension organization–public relationship scales is done in other sectors and cultural contexts. As public relations continues to evolve, it is clear that there is far more to it than simply managing the communication between an organization and its publics and that the relational perspective is really the only way forward for the discipline.

5

Active Voices

Kristin Demetrious
Deakin University

Advocacy and active citizenship are essential elements of democracy in the 21st century. This chapter explores the changing definitions of citizenship in wired and networked "risk society" and how these new definitions affect the perception and practice of contemporary public relations. It explains why activists have ignored the constructive activities of the public relations industry and why the public relations industry has ignored the constructive activities of activists. In particular, it examines Ulrich Beck's theories of risk society and reflexive modernisation—an innovative theoretical perspective on these relationships and activities that provides a lens to view activism and other institutions in society such as public relations. Beck's theories make an important contribution to a redefinition of public relations and its relationship to grassroots activism and changing notions of citizenship in the 21st century. They forecast the growth of grassroots activists and their capacity to generate change in society, the types of issues they seek to promote, and the reason why they are gaining power in this area. Beck provided a framework to understand how and why new forms and expressions of organizational communication are emerging.

MY PLANET

Log on; scroll down; create a Web site, bulletin board, homepage, blog, or chat room; access vast mines of information; amplify your message—be a citizen of the bright planet. Loud, insistent and precocious, civil society and its manifestations—once random and disparate—are increasingly organized and relevant to state and business sectors in the 21st century. Paradoxically, the proliferation of new social groups is both facilitated and necessitated by the Internet, the global system of computer networks. Virtual communities have propagated into

93

virtual cities as the interactive functions of the Internet redefine traditional communication. Rheingold's *The Virtual Community* (1995) looked at the potential of the new technology to create a digital democracy where new forms of community can flourish:

> The remarkable degree of citizen tool building in the Net, particularly tools that enable wider and wider segments of the population to make use of the new resources, is a de facto argument for keeping a widely accessible Net open for citizen experimentation. (p. 108)

Five years later, the potential of the Net's citizen-building capacity was explored by Naomi Klein (2000), who detailed several case studies that demonstrate the sophisticated use of the Internet as a tool for mobilizing support and gathering and disseminating information. For example, she argued that Nike changed its policy on labour reforms in response to pressure exerted via the World Wide Web (2000, p. 393). Similarly, Shell responded to the shift in activist power by a counter-Internet strategy involving monitoring all online discussion of Shell's affairs (2000, p. 394).

Civil societies' experimentation with cyberadvocacy in tandem with other social impacts has led to concepts of "citizenship" being rethought. One example is where traditional definitions based on membership criteria like the inclusion of a nation-state are being challenged to expand and accommodate the rights and responsibilities that constitute full membership of a *global* society. In the past, the term "second-class citizens" has been associated with structural and attitudinal divides in the areas of race, gender, and sexuality that result in members' partial rights in society. But the rapid economic, technological, and political changes taking place have created a new chasm between the Internet "haves and have nots." Tagged the digital divide today, it is relevant to ask, Does a group's limited access to modern technology and knowledge disenfranchise them from their rights as citizens? Manuel Castells (1997) discussed the impact of new technologies on social movements. Castells looked at the impact of new technologies, particularly the Internet, in relation to the achievement of social movements' objectives. Like Rheingold, Castells argued that the Internet, characterised by unprecedented decentralisation of stakeholders, is an ideal tool for grassroots activists to develop virtual communities and powerful Web sites to communicate with their publics. However, Castells' discussion of the democratising potential of the Internet is grounded within the consequences of creating technoeconomic dependencies for all citizens. He asked does the Internet simply entrench the dominant cultures in new forms so that people and groups with limited technocultural capacity are further socially excluded in new forms.

Castells' analysis (2001, pp. 248–256) is based on U.S. data collected in 2000 and tells us that overall, 41% of households had Internet access. Castells examined several factors that influence access and equity to the Internet. Some of his findings include:

- *income*—70.1% of people had access to the Internet who earned over $75,000 while only 18.9% had access who earned less than $15,000.
- *education*—74.5% of tertiary-educated people had Net access, while 30.6% of high school-educated people and 21.7% of those who did not graduate had Internet access.
- *age*—26.9% of people over 50 had Internet access compared to 56% of 18–24-year-olds.
- *unemployment*—56.7% of employed people had access compared to 29% of the unemployed.
- *ethnicity*—50% of White Americans, 49.4% of Asian Americans, 29.3% of African Americans, and 23.7% of Hispanics had access.

Accessibility is one of the key assumptions about the Net. But Castells' findings tell us to be a fully participating and active cybercitizen you must have the capacity to do so. This can depend on a range of variables including health, income, and ethnicity. Clearly, this is critical information for public communicators in both planning and conducting campaigns. Using Castells' analysis, it is easy to understand how this accessibility can be limited:

> The fact that the rise of the Internet took place in conditions of social inequality in access everywhere may have lasting consequences on the structure and content of the medium, in ways that we still cannot fully comprehend. This is because users shape the Internet to an even greater extent than any other technology because of the speed of transmission of their feedback and the flexibility of the technology. (Castells, 2001, p. 255)

As a result, Castells argued that this distorted access to new technoeconomic systems will simultaneously:

- increase wealth and poverty
- increase productivity and social exclusion.

Exposure to these factors will depend on where in the world you live and what group you belong to within that region.

Castells (2001, pp. 265–266) also argued that the decentralised organisational structure of the Internet is shaping the digital divide. In his view, social unevenness will occur to a greater extent because the Internet's global network characteristics that create flexibility and mobility reinforce its own economic dominance. This will mean other forms of economy will be less competitive and marginalised as the Internet becomes the lifeblood of economic production. Education, information, science, and technology become critical investments in society for creating value. The global distribution of access to the Internet will determine, entrench, and extend global divisions.

Castells' intense and bleak analysis of "network society" helps place the Internet within wider social and technoeconomic development contexts of the 21st century. His views extend understanding beyond the privilege of circumstance and confront the massive inequity and entrenchment of new practices that may set social and political agendas for future generations. There is ample evidence civil society is increasing, and taken on face value it may appear that the Internet has created an e-topia for grassroots democracy. But the new democracy is within a new, complex, and untested context that may pose more problems than it solves. Public communicators are challenged to consider the new ways cyber inequity may impact on stakeholders and be addressed to promote and foster contemporary citizenship in meaningful and sustainable ways.

RISKY BUSINESS

If the world is changing, what relationship is there for public relations? Extending the concept of citizenship beyond inclusion and exploring the role of the Internet in the development of civil society is an important step in an examination of the role of public relations and its relationship to democracy in the 21st century. But Ulrich Beck's work *Risk Society Towards a New Modernity* (1992) also has particular relevance to developments in public communication. The two underlying themes in Beck's work are the notion of risk society and a new era in modernity, "reflexive modernization." In the world Beck describes, old hierarchies of social order based on centralised techno/scientific knowledge and economic power have changed to a new order of decentralised knowledge, of social and political power. In this new political culture (1992, p. 185), those outside traditional political systems or civil society are powerful determinants in decision making and change. Collision of risk society with what Manuel Castells termed network society (1997) forms a powerful, new reflexive civil society. The sophisticated use of public communication will be central to the maintenance of this position.

Beck defined a "risk society" as one dominated by life-threatening byproducts of industrialized society (1992, p. 19). According to Beck, the sophisticated medical and techno/economic advances society tags as "progress" are causes of serious risk. Beck's new definition of risk is as something unseen, concealed in long periods of incubation; for example, radioactivity. Risk is also insidious and may be linked to products and practices traditionally considered "safe." For example, once regarded as a useful fire retardant, asbestos is now known to cause serious health problems. Industrial activity motivated by notions of progress and in fact the very act of risk minimisation itself, is the cause of risk. Risk, in Beck's definition, will emerge to threaten humanity on global scales. It will outlast generations and continue to threaten the unborn in different times and places. New societal divisions or "social risk positions" (1992, p. 23) will emerge based on the extent of exposure to risk (for example, the difference between the first world/third world impacts of risk so tragically demonstrated in Bhopal, India).

According to Beck the "dictatorship of scarcity" (1992, p. 20), that is, the premise that need or lack of any commodity required for our survival dictates production, has given way to the technoeconomic development which produces "hazards and threats" to an extent previously unknown. Beck characterised risk in this sense as impacting widely on humanity. Rather than having its genesis in underproduction and the practice of "making nature useful" that is characteristic of scarcity society risk, it will have its very basis in overproduction and modernisation.[1] Today, insurance and legal professions use standards and rules to regulate and maintain justice and financial insulation for individuals and institutions affected by risk. In "risk society" these standards are not adequate to protect groups and individuals. How is it possible to estimate a potential risk emerging in another place or time, or as an unintended byproduct of an attempt to alleviate some harm? In this environment the institutions that measure risk and compensate for injustice are unable to cope. For example, inadvertent biological and economic byproducts of the nuclear accident at Chernobyl present many new and unidentified international legal issues. New ways of calculating risk will have to be developed as the "unknown and unintended consequences come to be a dominant force in history and society" (1992, p. 22).

For Beck, the powerful institutions of industrial society such as governments and corporations produce these global risks and hazards (1992, p. 21). However, the impact of the risk they create will not be absorbed solely by disempowered publics, as was the case in the scarcity society. Afflictions will no longer be tied to place of origin. For example, unintended byproducts of the genetically modified foods will spill out into ecosystems, unable to be contained. Risk will cross traditional class boundaries that protect power elites from consequences of their action. It will claim them as the victims of their own mistakes. This situation is significantly different from "risk" in the "scarcity society." There, hazards and risk were obvious and "assaulted the nose and ears." They were often caused by lack of hygiene or "under supply" (1992, p. 21) and localised in effect. They could be defined and minimised by personal choice. Indeed, as Beck pointed out, risks and hazards were often associated with bravery and adventure.

---

[1]Beck prefered the term "modernisation" to describe the period of modernity. Modernity can be defined as a post-Enlightenment Western view of progress achieved through the advancement of scientific rationality.

Beck's "The Reinvention of Politics Towards a Theory of Reflexive Modernization" (1994) describes two distinct periods of modernity. The delineation of these periods helps to clarify the points of transition from scarcity society into risk society:

1. The first and foreground position of modernisation exists largely in the third world or places where the social production of wealth and the social production of risk take place under the "dictatorship of scarcity." Working safely from this point, modernity takes place with a claim of providing new wealth and therefore emancipation from poverty. Beck referred to this as the "residual risk society."
2. The second period describes modernity in the West where the "dictatorship of scarcity" has lost its immediate relevance. (In many ways people have become preoccupied with the overproduction of wealth. Beck cited the example of obesity now preoccupying consciousness more conspicuously than hunger.) In this second period, the unwanted side effects and unintentional byproducts of modernity now complicate the primary human objective of "making nature useful." (1994, p. 5)

It is worth stopping for a moment to clarify the meaning of the term "reflexive." According to Beck, the concept of reflexivity does not imply "reflection" but rather "self-confrontation" (1994, pp. 5–6). Scott Lash and Brian Wynne (Beck, 1992, p. 2) offered a more succinct definition of reflexivity as a widespread public critique of science whose occurrence is evidence of society's evolution.

Therefore, "laypeople" in post-scarcity society, it may be supposed, are likely to question or scrutinise claims made under the banner of science.

To understand the rise of subpolitical culture and the rise of new social movements, Beck (1994, p. 13) introduced the notion of "individualization." He pointed out that this does not mean "unconnectedness" or "isolation and loneliness" as the word may suggest, but rather industrial society "disembedding" understood social patterns like marriage, gender roles, and class-based relationships and "re-embedding" new ones. However, the emphasis is on the individual to create and signify his or her meanings and ways of living; "individuals must produce, stage and cobble together their biographies themselves" (1994, p. 13). An example might be redefinition of traditional gender-based parenting roles in family life based on changes to workplaces and expectations. According to Beck, the industrialisation process has changed traditional roles and collective and understood ways of living. These changes are forcing us to think up unique and individual ways to live, parent, and have relationships.

For Beck, there is a strong relationship between individualisation and the rise of new social groups:

> The individualized individuals, the tinkerers with themselves and their world, are no longer the "role players" of simple classical industrial society, as assumed by functionalism. (1994, p. 16)

Beck supported his view by citing that it was citizen-initiative groups who tabled ecological issues on the public agenda in the 1980s: "They were the ones who put the issue of an endangered world on the agenda, against the resistance of the established parties" (Beck, 1994, p. 18).

For groups to achieve change in Beck's "reflexive modernization" model, boundaries across subsystems will merge. These boundaries will be based on mutual social needs as well as economic. They will be in areas such as family, transport, consumption, pedagogy, wages, and employment (1994, p. 136). For Beck, these new system patterns may contain a number of contradictory elements (for example, indigenous Australians in partnership to restore native vegetation with the mining company who occupies their traditional land).

These alliances will transcend (traditional) borders and may create a perception of "possible ambivalence" (1992, p. 29).

Beck described five stages developing these intersystemic mediating institutions:

1. Demonopolisation of expertise and the democratisation of "knowledge."
2. Social standards of relevance that dictate participating groups structures.
3. Awareness of open decision-making structures and agency to create change.
4. Central role of public dialogue and uncontrolled media in setting debates.
5. Self-legislation and self-obligation in the creation of new norms for discussion and communication. (1994, p. 30)

While Beck's ideas provide exciting new frameworks to view developments in public communication activity in the 21st century, Deborah Lupton (1999) outlined several key arguments to challenge Beck's ideas. Lupton saw inconsistency in views of risk as, on the one hand, strengthening inequity and on the other "democratising, creating a global citizenship." She also cited lack of acknowledgement that reflective critiques of science and social movements were found in earlier modernity and are not unique to late modernity. Furthermore, she criticised Beck for portraying simplistic representations of modernity and failing to acknowledge that industrial society was more complex than credited. She asked, If the agency of the self-reflexive individual is both borne out of social and economical privilege, are people increasing there as Lash puts it, "reflexivity winners and reflexivity losers?"

But what are the impacts of these changes on civil society? Citizens' initiative groups or grassroots activists will play an increasingly important role in the emerging risk society and the management of communication will be integral to that role (Beck, 1992, p. 185). Beck's ideas have helped form the view that in scarcity society activism is a marginal activity practised by isolated groups. These groups exist on the fringes of the "legitimate" institutions. These are largely governmental or corporate institutions that society invests with the authority to create and implement change. They proclaim legitimacy either through their right to exercise power by public mandate or by the provision of products and services of "benefit" to society. According to Beck, in the post-"scarcity society" risk will be open to social definition: it will be tied to the construction of knowledge and the key areas of communication, science, and law will determine what society sees and understands to be risk. "(T)he mass media and the scientific and legal professions in charge of defining risks become key social and political positions" (1992, p. 23). From this I infer that activists will have a far more rigorous role in challenging and interrogating legal and scientific "knowledge" and in dealing with critical power positions now occupied by the media.

Grassroots activism in the new risk society, characterised by their very lack of legitimacy, will play an increasingly important role in developing and exercising independent knowledge. Beck defined new risk as imperceptible and occurring in other times and places. My view is that new activists will need to develop greater sophistication and "expertise" to understand, predict, and disseminate information through an increasingly decentralized mass media. Reflexive activism will develop a new significance in the definition and social explanation of risk, precisely because it is so difficult to for the public to detect. Complex risk will result in activists interrogating issued knowledge by risk-producing organisations and developing the means to disseminate information to the public. This is what Beck termed, reflexive modernisation.

At the nucleus of this is the existence of an articulate, educated, and persistent public who oversee the techno/scientific-economic growth with an increasingly cynical and practised eye. The evidence of fallibility of legitimate institutions is mounting. A litany of tragically bungled scenarios linked to technoeconomic development assaults us in the mass media daily. Decisions undertaken in either good or bad faith are justified at the time on sound scientific knowledge. Therefore, the construction of knowledge and its interpretation and dissemination for the public is now a legitimate function of activism. Public communication is central to this task. Without sophisticated understanding of the mass media, and knowledge of what messages to construct and the means by which to send them, activism will be little more than an occasional burr in the side of big business and governments.

Social movements—ad hoc, reactive, poorly resourced in both time and money, and with no ostensible links to dominant coalitions—have been dismissed as falling too far out of the paradigm to fit with most public relations theories. However, with the impetus of a new social hierarchy heralded by Beck, activism is the dynamic new edge of the newly defined area of public communication. It is precisely because activists are perceived to be independent of any economic self-interest that they have gained legitimacy to dissect and describe and advocate social, economic, and cultural impacts in the public sphere. "Lay opinion," once a dismissive term for those outside professional domains who proffered erroneous views on issues and affairs not in their sphere, has reinvented itself as "reflexive modernization." This now denotes critical, thinking, and skeptical citizens who have a right, if not an obligation, to comment on the technoeconomic and scientist movements. For Beck the critical transition of a passive to active public took place in the 1960s:

> Until the sixties, science could count on an uncontroversial public that believed in science, but today its efforts and progress are followed with mistrust. People suspect the unsaid, add in the side effects and expect the worst. (1992, p. 169)

In Beck's new risk society and the era of reflexive modernisation, public communication and its use by grassroots activists is precisely the area that should now receive attention. The far-reaching global effects of many new risks mean that international boundaries are no longer barriers to global communities that link contested issues. Resources for grassroots activists, in isolation so meagre, can now be pooled as global communities weave networks through new tools of electronic technology. The means to develop alternative "expertise" and counter arguments pitched by the techno/scientific and economic stakeholders is also facilitated by the digital and decentralised media, given impetus by "social risk positions." Activists now research and analyse other related issues and/or campaigns. Activists now study the communication processes. Activists now develop expertise and share information with other activists. "Sub-politics . . . means shaping society *from below*" (Beck, 1994, p. 23).

Using Beck's theory to extrapolate future developments, this chapter asserts that grassroots activists will play an increasingly critical role in public debate of issues tied to the unseen and hidden side effects of the scientific/techno industry. These will include three key areas: environmental hazards such as acid rain, salinity, and the destruction of flora and fauna habitat; ecological threats such as global warming; and biological threats such as disease and the unwanted heath impacts of new developments and technologies. Grassroots activists will contribute to the construction of knowledge with unprecedented sophistication. With redefined "legitimacy," grassroots activists will challenge traditional notions of knowledge and the powerhouses that have protected them. They will understand the role of the media in setting public agendas and debates both from a long-term and short-term strategic perspective. They will become adept in the traditional areas of public relations such as relationship management and use of specialised communication tactics. Grassroots activists will significantly contribute to the generation of change and lead to the greater decentralisation of power in 21st-century society.

THEORETICAL PERSPECTIVES OF THE PUBLIC RELATIONS INDUSTRY

Applying the ideas of Beck to notions of public communication, it may be supposed that "PR" is a product of scarcity society where the primary focus was "making nature useful" to provide wealth to escape from poverty. Despite the fact that the word "public" implies affecting all people, for many "public relations" is traditionally associated with the activities of large corporations and governments. Mainstream public relations literature (Wilcox, Ault, Agee, & Cameron, 2000; Hendrix, 2001; Cutlip, Center, & Broom, 2000) provides only limited attention to activists' use of public communication. To understand why, it is necessary to examine the embedded ideas that shape views of "public relations" found in statements like this:

> Public relations practice is the art and social science of analysing trends, predicting their consequences, coun-seling organization leaders, and implementing planned programs of action which serve both the organization's and the public interest.[2]

In this definition the "organization" and the "public" are two separate domains of self-interest. However, this does not necessarily imply conflict; indeed, it is explained that social analysis and the management of programs of action can serve *both* organisation and public interest. This view is consistent with the notion of pluralism. Pluralism largely developed in the United States and is both a political philosophy and ideology that asserts power is distributed and exercised between several participants or groups (Abercrombie, Hill, & Turner, 1984, p. 314). For pluralists, conflict of self-interest between groups is not of primary importance. Smith (1993, p. 25) pointed out that while pluralists do not regard all groups as equal, they do consider that power is generally dispersed and available in different forms that allows influence to be exerted in democratic societies. Smith (1993, pp. 16–17) also noted how pluralists emphasise the importance of "countervailing powers" to explain the constraints on certain groups from having too much power and influence:

> Pluralists argue the existence of one group is usually matched by an alternative countergroup (Galbraith, 1953; Smith, 1976). So, for example, in the case of the abortion issue the development of the pro-abortion lobby led to the creation of the anti abortion lobby (Marsh & Chambers, 1981). Even if countervailing groups do not emerge, powerful groups are also externally checked by the existence of potential groups.

This is consistent with Drucker's (1989, p. 73) view, who argued that to be effective, pluralist institutions must only focus on their specific interests. For Drucker, an U.S. example is how the politically focused racial desegregation debates were positioned in American schools. He argued that the broader ideological and social agenda in effect weakened the central school "function"—to teach children.

This valuable insight into how pluralists view the world shows us why they are not partic-ularly concerned about the asymmetry of power between groups, and why they do not seek to represent all. This may explain why PR has traditionally been focused around the activities of large state and business organisations. For a pluralist, an activist group counterweights a

---

[2]Definition source: World Assembly of Public Relations in Mexico City, 1978.

corporation's relative power. Beyond this, the state acts as society's safety net so that "the very system of government provides for the representation of a plurality of interests" (Smith, 1993, p. 17). Therefore, it could be assumed from a pluralist view that the activist groups may have other relationships that also wield power.

Smith outlined several key criticisms of pluralism, including the simplistic and naïve assumptions about all groups' ability to access power and resources and "the tendency to treat business as just another interest group" (1993, p. 27). Smith argued that the failure to recognise that business has advantages and access to unusual and privileged resources and information is an oversimplification that reflects "insufficient attention to the structural and ideological context and the interests and activists of bureaucracy and the government" (1993, p. 25).

Charlotte Ryan (1991) shed further light on pluralism, activism, and public communication[3] (p. 12). Ryan maintained that under the pluralist model there is recognition that power is shared unequally, but that this power asymmetry is not a problem pluralists recognise in the overall agency to create change. Indeed, if it is assumed that much of the public relations *not described* is embedded in activism, for example, anticorporate or environmental campaigns, then it is also often as business managing the process of activism as a negative element in achievement of corporate objectives.

The following Official Statement of Public Relations from the Public Relations Society of America appears in key public relations texts, including Wilcox, Ault, Agee, and Cameron (2000), Hendrix (2001), and Cutlip, Center, and Broom (2000). It states that we live in a "pluralistic" society and cites a various institutions as evidence of this. It demonstrates the extent to which this view is entrenched in public relations discourse and literature.

> Public relations helps our complex, *pluralistic* society to reach decisions and function more effectively by contributing to mutual understanding among groups and institutions. It serves to bring private and public policies into harmony.

> Public relations serves a wide variety of institutions in society such as businesses, trade unions, government agencies, voluntary associations, foundations, hospitals, schools, colleges, and religious institutions. To achieve their goals, these institutions must develop effective relationships with many different audiences or publics such as employees, members, customers, local communities, shareholders and other institutions and with society at large. (Hendrix, 2001, p. 4)

Hendrix called this a "comprehensive description" of the field of public relations. Indeed, he devoted the remainder of the book to the practice and process of public relations in large organisations. There is no further examination of society, agency, or power and its distribution. From this it may be concluded that public relations operates and is described from a largely pluralist perspective in dominant discourse.

Further evidence of public relations and its association with pluralism can be found in Grunig and Hunt (1984). In this work they develop a conceptual framework consisting of four models of public relations: publicity/press agentry, public information, two-way asymmetric, and two-way symmetric (1984, pp. 27–43). Grunig's two-way symmetric model of public relations can be criticised as simplistic as it assumes that power is shared equally in society and that "symmetry" between organisations and publics is achievable. Furthermore, Grunig and Hunt do not discuss the issue of group power and privilege and the ethics of changing public opinion and behaviour. This is precisely because under the pluralist model the problems associated with the distribution of power are not seen as a central issue. Public relations educators and practitioners use Grunig's models to describe the role and function

---

[3]Ryan did not refer to "public relations" as such but to generic communication.

of public relations, for example, Wilcox, Ault, Agee, and Cameron (2000). Grunig and Hunt (1984) contains a number of references to activism. This work has historically made an important contribution to public relations study and provided a theoretical anchor for subsequent public relations texts, including Cutlip, Center, and Broom (2000) and Wilcox, Ault, Agee, and Cameron (2000). In this work, Grunig and Hunt developed a succinct definition of public relations that has potential to include activism: "the management of communication between an organization and its publics" (1984, p. 6). Taken at face value, this definition could equally apply to grassroots activism as any other sector of society. However, Grunig and Hunt largely excluded activism in their application of this definition and only discussed it in the context of *challenges* to organisations (1984, p. 320). This is also the case in Grunig (1992). In this work Larissa Grunig gave more detailed reference to activism, but once again it is from the point of view of corporate management of activism. Larissa Grunig attempted "to help practioners deal in more than an ad hoc way with the opposition their organizations face from activist groups" (1992, p. 503). This fact contributes to the relative silence about grassroots and other forms of activism in dominant public relations discourse. Later Grunig works (2000) demonstrate that even if "activism" can be accommodated within current public relations theoretical frameworks, grassroots activism faces particular complexity in the administration of power. "Except, perhaps, for small community groups, most activist groups are powerful organizations in their own right" (2000, p. 43).

The role of activism in the broader sociopolitical culture of the United States was examined by Robert Heath (1997). He represented activists as legitimate contestants struggling for limited power resources and key to the notion of democracy. Heath provided a useful framework to dissect the stages of activism as strain, mobilisation, confrontation, negotiation, and resolution (1997, pp. 164–179). However, Heath's objective was to provide a secure proactive corporate credibility strategy and can therefore be situated within Beck's notion of scarcity society or residual risk society.

Dozier and Lauren (2000) expanded the intellectual boundaries set by Grunig and Hunt by describing public relations as a "professional activity" and an intellectual domain (p. 4). They argued that public relations is dominated by narrow industry views and needs more intellectual leadership as it matures (2000, p. 20). Likewise, an alternative view of the theoretical underpinning of public relation was taken by Holtzhausen and Voto (2002). They considered the "dominance of modernist perspectives in public relations" and advocated more postmodernist stances for public relations practioners. They defined modernism as seeking to apply universal explanations that privilege management discourse and goals as "natural" and legitimate and forecasted a new era that predicts a principally "activist" role essentially distanced from the self-interest of the organisation for public relations practioners (2002, p. 58). The perspectives of both Dozier and Lauren (2000) and Holtzhausen and Voto (2002) come close to dealing with PR within the contemporary context of Beck's risk society and reflexive modernisation.

So it would seem that much of 21st century PR is a leftover from the days when Beck believed the state, civil, and business sectors nurtured and tolerated a culture that sought to "make nature useful" to escape "the dictatorship of scarcity." But Habermas (1989a) added another edge to this analysis when he highlighted the impact of this for citizens' ability to have a voice in contemporary democracies. He argued that today when important questions are raised for society, the public sphere—the fragile conceptual space where public debate and dissent occurs—is now hijacked by distorted influence of commercial special interest grown fat in the culture of scarcity society and which has only their own limited and specific concerns at heart. Habermas' views also help explain why the traditional definition of public relations is not inclusive of activists' use of public communication. Organisations' specialised self-interest is at odds with and undermines the broader public's common self-interest. So while theoretical definitions of PR could apply equally to activist or corporations as "organisations," they do not. Instead, the majority of traditional literature and discussion devoted to public relations deals with the subject as a professional offshoot of corporate business and avoids any rigorous discussion of civil society and public communication.

THEORETICAL PERSPECTIVES OF ACTIVISM

So far I have talked about changing notions of citizenship and also how public relations has traditionally regarded activism. Now I want to talk about how activism has traditionally viewed areas like public relations. But to understand this, it is necessary to examine some of the principle themes which have shaped activism. Civil society and their relationship with contemporary society can also be viewed from a Marxist perspective:

> In the Marxist scheme, the ruling class of capitalist society is that class which owns and controls the means of production and which is able, by virtue of its economic power thus conferred upon it, to use the state as its instrument for the domination of society. (Miliband, 1969, p. 23)

Marx's ideas shed light on a range of activist attitudes and stances. In particular his theory of workers' systematic exploitation by industrialist owners of production clarifies their adversarial positioning (see McLellan, 1984). Workers for example, represented by trade unions struggle to achieve better working conditions like shorter hours and more money in opposition to capitalists seeking to maximize their business profitability. The legacy of these beliefs and attitudes is a continuing antagonistic relationship between workers and owners of capital still palpable today. Activists who mount campaigns often view corporations as capitalist structures with simplistic exploitative relationships to communities. Hostility erupts and each party reacts in adversarial roles with predictable communication tactics and strategies.

Naomi Klein (2000, p. 444) described the mayhem and violence that erupted in 1999 when activist movements formed a coalition against globalisation policies of multinational corporations. Tagged the "global carnival against capital" (2000, p. 444), the protests focused on European stock exchanges and the headquarters of corporate multinationals. They also included protest by Bangladesh garment makers against labour conditions. In Montevideo a protest against child labour used in the arms trade was held. This example shows that economic and social practices and views Marx described in the 19th century are still active in society today.

Bergmann (1993, p. 9) exposed the inadequacy of Marxism to explain recent relationships between political action and social change. "Marxism . . . has problems with social movements other than those inextricably linked with working-class interests, or with movements which express forms of social and political conflict that do not sit neatly within the class parameters which confine orthodox Marxism."

Marx's ideas clarify the reason why activists tend to overlook the achievements of the public relations industry. They explain this is because of public relations' strong association with the corporate world and the "domination" of workers. So when activists discuss "public relations," it is often only as a *victim* of the public relations industry. "Management" of communication is therefore given limited attention and description in activism literature.

Traditional critics of PR often reflect a Marxist perspective. Joyce Nelson (1989) provided a contemporary alternative view of activism and public relations. Her work challenges the belief that we live in an open society and exposes the dark side of public relations in series of case studies. She argued that the mass media are responsible for public misinformation and the maintenance of corporate power elites, particularly in regard to social movements (1989, p. 131). Nelson looked at the mobilisation of environmental activism in America and corporate public relations responses to this perceived threat. She talked about the subterfuge of corporate "greening" as a tactic to disguise objectives and deflect criticism. Building on this theme, John Stauber and Sheldon Rampton's *Toxic Sludge Is Good for You!* (1995) presented a view of public relations as unethical and manipulative in relation to activism. They argued that public relations practioners bow routinely to the self-interest of their employers. This leads to unscrupulous behaviour and deliberate harm to the reputation of the opposition (1995, pp. 3–4). This book provides valuable examples of corporate anti-activism strategies such as "astroturfing" (1995, p. 79) and "greenwashing" (1995, p. 125). Astroturfing is "fee for service" artificial grassroots public support offered by public relations companies. It manifests itself as "genuine" public support of corporate programs channelled through mass media. Greenwashing is the use of public relations to deceive the public into believing that corporations are actively environmentally responsible. But while activism is a major focus of the work, Stauber and Rampton do not discuss "public relations" as a legitimate function of social movements. Nor do they have a firm theoretical grounding for their ideas. Like Nelson, their work is inclusive of activism only as a victim of the public relations industry. Stauber and Rampton's work has shock value and an arresting set of examples. However, it does not delve deeply into the issues of power and its distribution.

Ewen's work (1996) is a far more comprehensive and overarching analysis of the public relations industry than Nelson (1989) or Stauber and Rampton (1995). Ewen's book examines public relations' implications for democracy in 19th- and 20th-century America, notions of power, and agency and activism. Ewen explored the concept of public relations as a mechanism for control in industrial society. He argued that the intersection between democracy and the rise of the media resulted in public relations as the new controlling force in society (1996, p. 51). Ewen's work starkly clarifies why activism has received either negative or no attention in conventional public relations literature. Klein (2000) tracked the rise of "anti-corporatism" activism in Western culture. Her work seeks to look behind the glossy face of global corporate monopolies. She revealed exploitative labour policies and practices and the cultural side effects of rampant consumerism. Klein's work adds to Castells' in the examination of further contemporary case studies and examples of corporate responses to Internet activities used by activists. Klein (2000, p. 80) also provided evidence that Habermas' notion of the public sphere has particular relevance to today's brand name-dominated culture. Her discussion of "culture jamming" (2000, pp. 279–309) documents challenges to brand name saturation of public space by grassroots activists. "Culture jamming" is additional text introduced to corrupt or distort brand name messages. It aims to politicise the decoder and challenge passive acceptance of advertisers' messages. Klein also raised the issue of asymmetry in power relationships in public communication.

These examples explain why when activists discuss "public relations," it is often only as a *victim* of the public relations industry. The Marxist perspective explains that this is because of public relations' strong association with the corporate world and the "domination" of workers. Public relations is limited by its definition of an "organisation" as resource rich and proactive, and its notion of strategic management. The field of public relations is also profoundly rooted in the corporate history of the United States. This means public relations discourse is often described from a pluralist perspective and seen as the antithesis to activism. Consequently, many activists fail to identify their public communication activities as "public relations" simply because of its association with big business, manipulation, and undemocratic practice.

WHERE TO FROM HERE: RISK SOCIETY
AND CHANGING NOTIONS OF PR

The notion of "corporate social responsibility" (CSR) opens up new territory for PR and reflects a blurring of the boundaries between business, the state, and civil society that validates Beck's predictions about the emerging risk society and reflexive modernisation. With its notions of the common good and mutual obligation, CSR promotes a distinct change from pluralistic and Marxist views that traditionally silo the activities of each sector.

Using Beck's ideas, it could be argued that CSR is the manifestation of modernity in the West where the "dictatorship of scarcity" and the primary objective of "making nature useful" has lost its foothold. Furthermore, the complications such as the unwanted side effects and unintentional byproducts of modernity Beck described as characteristic in this second period (1994, p. 5) appear to be the very areas that have provided the impetus for CSR. Castells' findings on the relationship of the Internet with society locate individuals' and groups' agency to create change in their capacity to participate in the network society and explain the rise of powerful groups in the West that was the momentum for CSR.

L'Etang (1996a) explored the historical roots of corporate social responsibility's moral dimension brought to bear by articulate social movements and explained how this has led to the softening of the perceived boundaries that separate the powerful institutions from other parts of society:

> The sense of obligation was nourished by social activists in the 1960s and 1970s, many of whom criticized the role of large corporations and power elites in society and argued that political and economic justice could only be achieved through a distribution of goods and power. These sorts of arguments tend to promote an idea that increased power should bring with it increased responsibility and an obligation not to exploit or take advantage of individuals and small communities. (p. 85)

Beck's idea of risk society has some unique attributes. First, a "risk" is defined as something hazardous, global in scale, insidious, and perhaps slowly incubating to threaten in different times and places. Second, "society" is defined as new publics unbound from tradition, articulate and empowered to define and challenge knowledge and reflexively mobilise to act on issues of risk. The following examples of "PR" discussed within the context of contemporary CSR literature reflect how risk society and reflexive modernisation is manifesting itself and in the process changing traditional definitions of public relations:

Implicit in Thomas and Eyres' journal article (1998, p. 11) is the view that *traditional public relations* struggles to deal well with the new corporate citizenship culture because it continues to act as servant of a dominant master culture that is predicated on profits and expansion. They argue that mainstream corporate PR is ineffective within the context of "media-savvy" "pressure groups" like Greenpeace who in 1995 demonstrated new activism's ability to set powerful public agendas by forcing Royal Dutch Shell to change its plans to sink the Brent Spar, a redundant oil storage plant, in the North Sea.

> In response to these pressures companies can choose to continue to externalise the vast majority of social and environmental costs. They can hope that using "stealth" marketing and public relations will enable them to head off any threats. However it is clear that these techniques are not sufficient. Take PR. At the heart of most companies public relations functions are ultimately aimed at providing a justification for corporate policy rather than providing mechanisms for dialogue. They also seek to polish up the good aspects of the company and put a gloss on the bad aspects. They do not seek to ensure that the company understands the needs of its stakeholders and consistently meets their needs. (1998, p. 12)

Andriof et al. (2002) analysed why current practice and thought within public relations is no longer adequate to house new perspectives on corporate citizenship and corporate responsibility. In particular, they discussed the notion of the boundary spanner—a common theme within much PR literature, describing someone with one foot in and out of the organisation. They discussed the evolution of notions of reactive and proactive approaches to relationship management to a higher level of interactive engagement: "A second feature of this shift of definition is the recognition of power relationships and interdependences: that is, a movement towards a more systemic understanding of the relationships that exist among organizations and their stakeholders in societies, particularly important in any kind of relationship or engagement process" (p. 23).

But the fact that good news is tarred as spin and seen as an inevitable byproduct of the public relations industry is discussed by Bliss (in Andriof and Waddock, 2002, p. 252), who raised the need for a sophisticated understanding of the notion of stakeholder in order to be able to communicate in the new ways. For Bliss the rise in citizen organisations like Greenpeace and Amnesty International, combined with changes to information technology, has profound implications for business, particularly in the area of communication. Like Andriof and Waddock, Bliss discusses the adversarial paradigms that have historically existed between business and activist groups that result in boycotts, pickets, demonstrations, and anti-corporate Web sites, and counselled a new, more collaborative approach that embraces the notion of stakeholders resulting in joint task forces, policy dialogues, and stakeholder engagement.

These ideas link to Beck's who predicted that activism will become centrally important in the interpretation and communication of risk. He foreshadowed the growing power of the mass media and public communication to construct and define knowledge in the new social order:

> As the risk society develops, so does the antagonism between those afflicted by risks and those who *profit* from them. The social and economic importance of *knowledge* grows similarly, and with it the power of the media to structure knowledge (science and research) and disseminate it (mass media). The risk society is in this sense also the *science, media and information* society. (Beck, 1992, p. 46)

In the West, risk society now intersects dynamically with network society, fuelled by the decentralisation of media power through the Internet and the creation of powerful and articulate online communities. This has particular consequences for contemporary activism and PR. From this discussion, three dominant themes have emerged: grassroots activism and its changed relationship with public relations; new corporate cultures in risk society; and the sometimes times contradictory role of the media and new communication technologies in shaping contemporary democracy.

Organisations that operate with a standard PR approach in the changed social and political landscape face the prospect of PR as ineffective or, worse, counterproductive. But there is a new additional hazard within the network/risk society and that is the possibility that new forms of PR will adopt the CSR and corporate citizenship discourse while acting within the narrow capitalist frameworks; and in this latest guise undemocratically influence control in society. Too slick, brash and glossy, PR can be seen as a victim of its own success. As quality of life and citizenship become central to 21st-century society, public relations must respond to the challenge and evolve to create new meanings.

PUBLIC COMMUNICATION

This chapter has attempted to explain historical and theoretical contexts that affect ways activism and PR operate and are perceived. It has exposed the important theoretical contradictions in pluralism and in Marxist social theory that have led to the marginalisation of grassroots activists' use of public communication in both public relations literature and activist literature and the stagnation of traditional "PR." In particular, it has established that "public relations" has specific connotations for activists as a self-serving capitalist activity deeply rooted in exploitative corporate history and tradition. "PR" for activists is therefore a loaded term. A void exists in activist lexicon to describe their use of public communication. Because of this it may be concluded that activist discourse and literature does not deal comprehensively with the issue of public communication, nor does public relations literature deal adequately with activism. For some, PR is now increasingly simplistic and counterproductive within contexts of CSR for business. This chapter argues that if advocacy and active citizenship are essential elements of democracy in network and risk society, then it is increasingly relevant to critically examine traditional PR and develop a wider conception of public communication as an ethical activity fundamentally embedded in all social, economic, and political environments.

II

Histories

INTRODUCTION

The histories presented in this section give singular insight into three different cultures. Heike Puchan makes an invaluable contribution to the literature by drawing together a range of important German sources in her review of German intellectual thought on public relations, or "Offentlichkeitsarbeit." Her review encompasses both a conceptual discussion of propaganda and a consideration of the legacy of the Nazi era. In her discussion of German history, she evaluates its impact on conceptions of public relations, highlighting semantic debates and the "propaganda-phobia" that dogged the early years of public relations. She notes that public relations activities were present in Germany from the Middle Ages and documents in more detail activities from the mid-19th century such as the establishment of corporate public relations in a number of important companies. As in the UK, the Great War led to a major expansion in governmental public relations, especially in press relations, although the Weimar Republic's guarantees for freedom of the press and freedom of speech were short-lived and did not survive in Nazi Germany. A discussion of the expansion of public relations practice in post-war Germany includes relevant empirical details in terms of numbers and professional structures. Finally, Puchan reviews the development of public relations theory in Germany and elucidates theoretical conceptions that explored the social role of public relations (from social theory), practice-based conceptions, and those which drew from organisational or marketing theory. The important influence of structural functionalism on German authors is highlighted. Influential writers, and in particular Oeckl, Ronneberger, and Ruhl, are discussed in relation to U.S. intellectual developments in a critical review suggesting that German authors have been particularly influenced by Niklas Luhmann and Jurgen Habermas. This explains why German academics have been so focused on "the function and role of public relations in a pluralistic society."

Lårsake Larsson presents an historical sociology of public relations evolution in Sweden. He records key developments in the evolution and presents empirical data resulting from a project in which public relations consultants and journalists were interviewed about their relationship and the impact on, and consequences for, democracy of the public relations industry's activities. As part of his analysis Larsson reviews concepts of public opinion in relation to publics, arguing that the dominant paradigm in public relations has underplayed the importance of the general public: "in Europe, and not least in Nordic countries, the dismissal of the general public (citizenry) seems alien and incorrect, for this concept constitutes such a basic dimension of our society where all citizens are assumed to be communicated with on democratic matters." The empirical data cover a range of important issues in relation to democratic practice: public relations' social and democratic roles, how public relations practitioners construct and influence opinion, opinion polls, the advantages of the resource-rich, transparency, and ethics. Larsson identifies a number of important problems for democracy that arise from the existence of public relations practice, "the sector's lack of transparency . . . the regimented culture of influence created by this sector that floats freely between different interests in society, with the result that ideological values and political identities are increasingly eroded."

Jacquie L'Etang takes as her focus the evolution of public relations in Britain, highlighting contributions and ideas of key individuals in that history. The research on which the chapter is based employed oral history (within the sociological historical paradigm) as the main method, and the purpose of the chapter is to give space to a variety of (sometimes competing) voices. Thus, the chapter is empirically based and descriptive, not theoretical. The chapter begins with a brief overview of key historical developments in public relations from the early 20th century, leading in to a discussion of public relations' role in "promotional culture" (Wernick, 1991). The chapter then explores a number of themes and career trajectories of key individuals under the headings "Act I: spooks and spies: dramatic personae;" "Act II: myths, mentors, and public relations culture;" Act III "Culture Club(land);" "Act IV: articulating principles and explaining practice: education, educators, and authors;" and "Act V: women in public relations."

Donn Tilson defines a unique type of public relations which he terms "devotional-promotional," defined as a "campaign that is religious in nature . . . [which] may seek to instil great love or loyalty, or zeal for a particular individual, living or deceased or for a specific religion or faith" (Tilson & Chao, 2002). His ambitious qualitative project explores the campaign of the Catholic Church and the Spanish government to establish and maintain allegiance to St James domestically and internationally. Tilson employs Koehn's covenantal model of public relations as part of the basis for his analysis which explores the role of relics, saints, and pilgrimages. Controversially, Tilson disputes the common interpretations in the public relations literature with regard to the Catholic Church's Sacred Congregation for the Propagation of the Faith and the term "propaganda," which he analyses in the historical context of the time. Tilson links an impressive range of historical detail with concepts of identity, cultural identity, cultural change, and the nation-state and its "mythico-cultural apparatus" (Schlesinger, 1991) as he recounts the story of a thousand-year campaign. Finally, Tilson links his discussion to present-day campaigns and reflects on the potential for covenantal public relations to achieve legitimacy for public relations practice. Thus, Tilson's chapter opens up public relations and religion as a major new area for empirical and conceptual research.

6

An Intellectual History
of German Public Relations

Heike Puchan
Stirling Media Research Institute

The assumption that public relations was an American invention brought to Germany and the German-speaking area after the second world war seemed to be a dominant one in the second half of the 20th century, accepted and perpetuated by scholars and practitioners alike. Albert Oeckl, for example, one of the foremost writers of public relations in post-war Germany, wrote that public relations as it is understood today, was initiated due to many "practical suggestions of the occupying powers and particularly the Americans after the monetary reform in 1948 and then during the initiation of the first German parliament and the government in 1949" (Oeckl, 1994, p. 14).[1] In the last decade, however, more German scholars have come forward and demonstrated that public relations has a rich history in Germany, both from an intellectual and practical point of view. Kunczik, for example, in his detailed history of German public relations up to the 1920s, demonstrated that public relations efforts both in politics and business can be traced back to the Middle Ages, but were particularly prevalent during the era of industrialisation (Kunczik, 1997). The lack of English writing on German public relations, however, remains a problem and hence many interesting developments in both public relations practice and theory remain inaccessible to non-German speakers. This chapter provides a brief overview of the history of public relations and conceptual developments in Germany with a view to highlighting characteristics that both define and transcend the German-speaking area. The aim of this chapter is not to deliver a comprehensive account of the history of German public relations theory and practice, but to introduce and analyse some of the milestones that have shaped its development. This chapter will also demonstrate a distinct rupture and disconnection in the development of public relations activity in the 19th and early 20th centuries and the development of the modern, post-war public relations profession, due to the devastating impact of the propaganda machine of Nazi Germany.

---

[1] All translations from German to English were carried out by the author.

111

TERMINOLOGY—"ÖFFENTLICHKEITSARBEIT" OR PUBLIC RELATIONS

An interesting starting point for the discussion of German public relations history is the term itself. The English term "public relations" was first introduced by Carl Hundhausen in 1937 in a special report in a German advertising magazine (*Deutsche Werbung*), where he portrayed public relations as an art. Hundhausen explained that public relations aims to "create a favourable public opinion through the spoken and written word, through action and visual symbols for the organisation, its products and services" (Hundhausen, 1937, p. 1). However, during the Nazi regime, the term "public relations" was deemed highly undesirable and remained largely unknown. Carl Hundhausen reintroduced the term in an essay in 1947 (Oeckl, 1964, p. 95). However, there were many voices against the use of the English terminology. One of the most often cited reasons against was the fear of lack of clarity of what public relations would actually entail. Some claimed "public relations" was simply advertising in disguise (Gross, 1951, p. 7) or was carrying undertones of the widely feared propaganda. Journalists particularly were highly critical of the connotations of the word "public relations." Journalists and practitioners alike were searching for a German equivalent that would better capture its essence to the extent that there was even a competition in the German news weekly *Die Zeit* to find an appropriate and valid translation (*Die Zeit*, 22/02/1951). However, the competition was less than successful and no first prize was given. The reluctance to accept the English term and its connotations led to the introduction of a new, German term—"Öffentlichkeitsarbeit," which translates as "working with the public." Today, both the English and German terms are used interchangeably.

PUBLIC RELATIONS AND PROPAGANDA

The differentiation of public relations and propaganda has been a focus of attention for public relations scholars and writers around the world for decades. This feature is particularly apparent within the German context of public relations activity following World War II. The Nazi regime made considerable use of their ministry of propaganda and following the establishment of peace, it was evident that everyone involved in public relations activity was anxious to differentiate and to distance the term public relations from the negative and unsavoury image associated with the Nazi propaganda machine. The term propaganda reeked of a time when the only role of the media was to mould the public for the purposes of a Nazi worldview and where education and information campaigns were designed to benefit only the ruling elite.

Noelle-Neumann summarised it very appropriately when she diagnosed a "propaganda-phobia" in Germany (Noelle-Neumann, 1971, p. 176). Oeckl, for example, described propaganda as the "unconditional infiltration of purposive views with the goal of alignment without any consideration for one-sidedness or distortion of the truth" (Oeckl, 1964, p. 61). He understood propaganda as an instrument of totalitarian regimes. Similarly, Jahn noted that propaganda aims to "ease the thought processes of the human mind with the final aim of completely switching off individual thoughts" (Jahn, 1953, p. 55). According to the author, the "poisoning of the souls" that took place during Hitler's rule could only be healed through the creation of real trust (Ibid.). Ahlers described propaganda as a "thing full of aggression and maliciousness" (Ahlers, 1979, p. 189).

Even much later, public relations practitioners and scholars alike tended to insist on a clear distinction between public relations and propaganda. Barthenheier insisted that "Propaganda is the communication behaviour of totalitarian states" (1988, p. 36), and Buß could not accommodate a modern understanding of public relations with the term propaganda: "Propaganda polarises, radicalises and emotionalises and this cannot be the objective of public relations" (Buß, 1992, p. 20).

Despite propaganda-phobia, there are some, such as Maletzke, who in his discussion of "propaganda in a western democratic context" saw it as a legitimate element of political communication (Maletzke, 1972, p. 157). Interestingly, the German Federal Armed Forces use propaganda and public relations interchangeably (Kunczik, 1993, p. 16) and the Federal Constitutional Court, in paragraph § 32 BwahlG, understands propaganda as an important aspect of modern democracy when it refers to political election campaign elements such as posters, leaflets, and stalls (Schürmann, 1992, p. 72).

The list of attempts by German authors to define public relations and to differentiate it from propaganda could fill a chapter on its own, but as Kunczik stipulated, it is ultimately a play with semantics (1993, p. 15). In addition, however, it also portrays the signs of the early stages in the development of an emerging profession or discipline which is trying to demarcate its borders and to justify its existence. In 1983 Binder diagnosed that public relations/Öffentlichkeitsarbeit was suffering from an identity crisis which has led to an obsession with defining the practice and distinguishing it from related fields to the detriment of further development. Some of the symptoms of this neurosis are clearly still evident today.

A BRIEF HISTORY OF PUBLIC RELATIONS

The development of public relations in Germany is undoubtedly linked to its political history and the development of press and press freedom. In his comprehensive history of pre-war German public relations, Kunczik traced German activities in the field back to the Middle Ages (Kunczik, 1997). However, in this context it seems appropriate to start at a time when more concerted communication efforts of both public and private organisations appeared, that is, during the middle of the 19th century, just before the establishment of the German Reich in 1871. One of the main developments to foster increased media and also public relations activity was the new media law introduced in the German Reich (Reichspressegesetz) which paved the way for a less restricted, less censored, and more open provision of news content. Early public relations activity can easily be divided into three categories: governmental and political public relations, corporate public relations, and municipal public relations. Governmental public relations in the 19th century consisted mainly of press relations activity. The Prussian government in particular recognised the importance of liaising with writers and publishers in order to communicate with and influence its citizens. During the politically challenging times of the 1848 March revolution, they established the first institution for the observation of the press. Another similar institution was founded by the Ministry of the Interior, called the Literary Cabinet (Literarisches Kabinett). Its main role was twofold: first, to analyse any press coverage and second, to influence journalists' reporting in order to obtain positive press coverage, if necessary even through bribery (Groth, 1948; Kunczik, 1994).

The new government of the German Reich additionally established a press office in the Foreign Ministry. One of the main forces behind this was Imperial Chancellor Bismarck, who aligned and combined foreign political action, diplomacy, and media campaigns (Schöneberger, 1981). One of the innovations of the press office was press conferences with carefully selected journalists; however, as Schöneberger pointed out, manipulation and corruption were rife (1981, p. 21). Another important step in the development of governmental public relations was the establishment of a press office of the navy under the leadership of Admiral Alfred von Tirpitz. He saw the importance of gaining public acceptance for the plan of an increased German naval fleet and made use of a variety of instruments such as lectures, speeches, and press relations in order to swing public opinion. Later on, he also established the position of information officer for all of the larger ships of the German navy. He supported the idea of increased exchange with journalists and the importance of provision of information (Kunczik, 1994, p. 116). In addition to media relations, he also instigated concerted efforts to liaise with the public at large and organised public guided tours on the ships, concerts, and other interaction with local communities.

Governmental public relations opened another chapter in its history with the establishment of a war press office in October 1914. It was not until the establishment of the Weimar Republic, however, that freedom of the press and freedom of speech were provided with a legal foundation and framework. Paragraph 118 of the new constitution promised a change both to media and public relations activity (Kordes & Pollmann, 1989, p. 14). This newfound freedom from censorship and manipulation lasted for only a short time. In 1933, censorship again took hold, when, after the burning of the Reichstag in Berlin, Hitler brought in emergency laws. This signalled the start of a new era of the propaganda machine under the Reich Ministry of Public Information and Propaganda in Nazi Germany where newspapers were either censored, banned, or streamlined into governmental instruments of manipulation (Kordes & Pollmann, 1989, p. 14).

In terms of corporate public relations, the famous steel company Krupp must be highlighted as one of the initiators and leaders in the field (e.g., Kunczik, 1994; Wolbring, 2000). Krupp has been described as a company that was aiming to create and maintain a positive image amongst its customers, workers, and the community. Alfred Krupp, who himself led the company's public relations activities for a long time, was clear about the importance of the role of public relations at an early stage. To him, the creation of a strong image was of utmost importance and he made use of blatant symbolism to achieve his aim. In 1851, Krupp took part in the world exhibition in London and displayed an immense cube of steel which weighed 2,000 kilograms, the biggest steel cube that had ever been manufactured (Kunczik, 1994, p. 192). In addition to further symbols of the company's manufacturing prowess, Krupp also employed techniques such as open days/ guided tours and press relations. He went on to establish the first corporate press relations department and saw the necessity of employing a dedicated press relations officer.

A wide range of other companies showed early attempts at public relations activity including the biscuit manufacturer Bahlsen, Maggi, electronic giants AEG and Siemens, Henkel, or tradesman Roselius of the coffee company HAG. Astrid Zipfel, in her comprehensive book on public relations in the electronics industry, noted that at Siemens, as early as the 1860s, the establishment of a positive, long-lasting image was valued over short-term financial gains. Newspapers were seen as an invaluable resource in creating such an image (Zipfel, 1997, pp. 33–44). In 1899, Siemens employed a dedicated press relations officer and 3 years later established a more comprehensive department for press relations (Centralstelle für das Pressewesen). Zipfel also clearly demonstrated that Siemens had embarked on international public relations activity very early on as the company expanded in the international market (Zipfel, 1997). Corporate public relations activity received a great boost during the 1920s, which saw enormous economic developments, and many corporations followed the example of leaders such as Siemens or AEG and established press offices and communication departments.

A third area of early public relations activity in Germany can be located in the municipal sector. During the late 19th century, several towns had expanded economically, politically, and culturally in importance. Consequently these towns (e.g., Freiburg, Magdeburg, Munich, Kiel, Aachen, and Erfurt) all established press offices with the initial aim of providing information to citizens and visitors and to liaise with the press as well as to carry out research (Istel, 1974, p. 11). Municipal public relations activity gained increased importance during the Weimar Republic as publicity was seen as crucial instrument in establishing a democratic system within the municipal or local government sector (Kunczik, 1994, p. 181; Liebert, 1995).

The gradual development of a public relations industry came to an abrupt halt with the arrival of national socialism in 1933. The Reich's Ministry of Public Information and Propaganda put a stop to the freedom the media had experienced during the rise of the Weimar Republic and used both press and broadcast for the distribution of Nazi propaganda. On a corporate level, many communication departments remained, but their work was tainted by the propagandistic climate of the Hitler regime.

After the end of World War II, Carl Hundhausen und Albert Oeckl were amongst the first to reintroduce public relations into Germany. Both had worked in public relations during Nazi rule and were eager to both practice and analyse this new form of public communication. Hundhausen and Oeckl were typical of early public relations experts who combined a practice and theory-orientated career. In the 1950s, public relations work in Germany was dominated by press/media relations and early practitioners understood PR as promotional work to create trust. Pioneer practitioner Georg-Volkmar Graf Zedtwitz-Arnim, for example, coined the phrase "Do good things and talk about it" (Zedtwitz-Arnim, 1961).

CURRENT PROFESSIONAL AND OCCUPATIONAL STRUCTURES IN GERMANY

The accurate size of the current public relations industry in Germany is very difficult to estimate. Several recent studies provide insights into these numbers and figures, but a comprehensive study of the industry is currently still lacking. The number of public relations professionals is estimated to be sitting at above 20,000 (Bentele, 1998), but many speculate that the real figures are much higher than that. However, only around 20% of those are affiliated with professional organisations. Around 2,300 are members of the professional body Deutsche Public Relations—Gesellschaft (DPRG; Reineke & Eisele, 1994). Interestingly enough, many of those are also members of the Deutsche Journalisten Verband (djv), the professional body of German journalists.

The DPRG was founded in December 1958 in Cologne, with Carl Hundhausen, then public relations director of the company Krupp, as its president. The aim, according to Hundhausen, was to keep the profession free from "chancers" and "imposters" (Hundhausen, 1959, p. 8). The other major aim was to define public relations as a distinct professional activity and delineate the area from advertising and journalism. One of the main problems was the strict rules for membership laid down in the constitution of the DPRG in 1958. In order to become a member, the constitution demanded that any PR person needed to fulfil the criteria of having accumulated at least 5 years' practical experience in addition to being in a management role. This quickly led to criticism of elitism and exclusivity of the DPRG. Today, entry criteria are much different and there are options such as junior memberships for students which have made the DPRG accessible to all. Despite this, membership numbers today are still relatively low overall. In addition, there is also the association of public relations agencies (Gesellschaft der PR Agenturen—GPRA), which currently has a membership of 26 agencies and 1,200 full-time staff (http://www.gpra.de/gpra/basisinfo/zahlen_f.htm).

Since the 1980s, public relations is taught in a wide range of universities and polytechnics as part of various degree programmes (e.g., journalism, communication studies, advertising, or business studies), although the number of dedicated public relations degrees is still relatively small. Programmes are available at the University of Leizpig and the Free University of Berlin and also at polytechnics. Röttger, in her assessment of the education status of public relations professionals, found that although most practitioners had very high educational qualifications, only around 14% had reached a high level of specific public relations education (2000, p. 317).

THE DEVELOPMENT OF PUBLIC RELATIONS THEORY AND CONCEPTUALISATION IN GERMANY

Although public relations activity, as discussed above, can historically be traced back centuries, the actual theorisation seems to have begun much later and a systematic analysis did not start until the 1970s. Below, I introduce a number of German-speaking authors and their analyses of public relations who have been selected either on the basis of having clearly shaped the debate or for being exponents of a particular school of thought within the discipline. A number of German writers and scholars stand out as having instigated particular developments in the theoretical analysis of public relations, such as Albert Oeckl and Carl Hundhausen in the post-war period and Franz Ronneberger in the early 1970s. Both Oeckl and Hundhausen came from a more applied perspective whereas Ronneberger, based at the University of Erlangen/Nürnberg, can be identified as one of the first academic scholars to develop a draft of a comprehensive public relations theory (Ronneberger, 1977).

Oeckl, in his 1964 *Handbook of Public Relations*, stipulated that public relations will have a positive influence on a modern society where citizens feel disconnected and disenfranchised. Oeckl saw public relations as a major aid to improving education and information amongst the population. He also saw public relations as a necessity for developing and nurturing political and social consensus in modern society (Oeckl, 1976). He developed a formula that highlights his main ideas: Public Relations = Information + Adaptation + Integration (Oeckl, 1976, p. 15).

Often described as a "cultural pessimist" (e.g., Kunczik, 1993), Oeckl saw the role of the public relations practitioner as more comprehensive, more complex, and at least as important as that of the journalist (Oeckl, 1988). He felt that the public relations practitioner's job required a much broader education, including the study of psychology, media, and social sciences. What is very interesting to see is that Oeckl also considered PR people to be in a better position and also more able to spend time and effort researching specific issues and to gain greater access to sources. This would effectively put them ahead of journalists in terms of research capabilities. What he failed to point out, however, was the potential lack of distance and objectivity that might impact on PR practitioners' work. Oeckl hoped that over time a more friendly and collegiate relationship could develop between journalists and public relations practitioners to the benefit of a society that could be engaging in greater dialogue which could lead to enhanced harmonic relationships between various interest groups.

Although branded with the "cultural pessimism" stamp, Oeckl seems to have assigned great hopes to the power of public relations. In his book *PR Praxis* (1976), he developed 15 principles for public relations practice which have been described as "an ideology for the profession" (Kunczik, 1993, p. 113), but did not constitute a comprehensive theory as such. However, there have been many elements of Oeckl's approach that have been described as highly relevant for further theoretical development of the discipline. His work emphasised that public relations activity comprises a wider spectrum of tasks than journalism and highlighted public relations' management orientation. Some authors have pointed out that Oeckl's theory contains a number of elements of the PR approach developed much later by the Americans Grunig and Hunt. For example, his 15th rule for public relations was:

> The decisive rule for public relations is: public relations is two-way communication, it is information flow in both directions, it is dialogue. Hence, it has...to achieve its threefold task: information, adaptation and integration. (Oeckl, 1976, p. 305)

Criticism of Oeckl's "ideology" has been raised with regards to a number of points. First, it has been doubted whether public relations can actually contribute to a broad "public interest" as it will always be used for particular organisational and individual interests. Additionally, the assumption that public relations' research and writing will contribute more to an informed society than journalism remains doubtful and unproven. However, Oeckl became one of the most influential public relations writers and remained the most often cited author up to the early 1990s (Arlt, 1998, p. 68).

Another influential author from the same era is Carl Hundhausen. Hundhausen has been described as one of the most influential people in the continued development of public relations in post-war Germany as a long-standing public relations director of the company Krupp and also as the first president of the professional public relations body DPRG. Hundhausen, who was strongly influenced by the American Bernays, developed a set of principles for the profession in his 1969 book. Although the title features "theory and systematic analysis," the book can be better understood as a collection of ideas and thoughts about the profession. As Kunczik put it, Hundhausen "merely pointed out the complexity of a pluralistic society in which there are continuing tensions and conflicts between the interests of smaller groups and the interest of society as a whole" (Kunczik, 1993, p. 117). The central task of public relations, according to Hundhausen, is the "engineering of consent" (gleaned from Bernays) amongst involved parties, groups, or organisations and the most important aim of public relations is the achievement of "harmony" through adaptation.

Hundhausen based his 1969 principles on the ideas he had developed for the creation of "public trust" which he had formulated back in 1951. Hundhausen saw public relations as a holistic task and role for the whole organisation. Only in cooperation with other departments or sections of an organisation could public relations be successful (Hundhausen, 1951). Like Oeckl and well before Grunig and Hunt in 1984, he lent public relations a clear management dimension.

Both Hundhausen's and Oeckl's writings demonstrate a relatively early, practice- orientated approach to public relations theory. A common characteristic of their understanding is that public relations activity is perceived as a vehicle for creating trust and consensus in order to secure the acceptance of the relevant organisation or person.

The first systematic development of public relations theory in Germany did not appear until the 1970s. Broadly speaking, the development has focused on several perspectives: organisational theories, marketing-orientated theories, and society-related theories.

Ronneberger's work *Legitimation durch Information* (1977) shaped the public relations debate for a long time to come and became the basis for one of the major strands of public relations theory—a society-orientated theoretical approach to public relations. His early theoretical work clearly links public relations with a democratic and pluralistic society and hence follows the demands of the education and research section of the professional body DPRG for a theory of public relations that would justify its contribution to society at large. According to Ronneberger, in a modern pluralistic society, public relations assumes a crucial role in the negotiation process of competing interests of various players. What set Ronneberger's approach apart is that public relations was clearly seen as a societal function and not as a function of individual organisations or institutions.

There are clear connections with Niklas Luhmann's (see, e.g., Habermas & Luhmann, 1971) functional–structural systems theory in which the development of society is interconnected with the development of communication methods and processes (Kunczik, 1993, p. 126). Luhmann had pointed out that in an increasingly complex system there was a likelihood of different states of information amongst various parts of the system unless organisations could develop a communication system that would counterbalance this information deficit, including planned communication efforts (Habermas & Luhmann, 1971, p. 44). Ronneberger saw public relations as a counterbalance to such an information differential. What sets Ronnberger's theory apart from earlier writers is that—although he clearly saw public relations as a way of integrating various interests—its main aim is to create a consensus on the basis of the lowest common denominator. A total agreement, adaptation, and integration of interest is clearly understood to be unrealistic. On the contrary, public relations' role, according to Ronneberger, is to highlight and clarify differences in a public discourse (Ronneberger, 1977, p. 7). Critics of Ronneberger's approach have focused mainly on two areas. His theory has been criticised for failing to assess the question of differences in access to communication in that not every actor and every organisation will have equal chances to participate in the communication process (Kunczik, 1993, p. 128). Others have criticised the failure to distinguish between mass and interpersonal communication or to acknowledge that poor public relations might actually be more likely to muddy the waters than to contribute to a truthful and balanced public discourse (e.g., Scheidges, 1991).

Based on this earlier theory, Ronneberger and Rühl developed a macro-social, society-related theory which became one of the most well-known and most comprehensive within the society-related theorisation of public relations (Ronneberger & Rühl, 1992). Ronneberger and Rühl's theory drew upon a wide range of disciplines such as sociology, social psychology, economics, communication studies, political science, and linguistics and aimed to integrate them with a systems approach. Ronneberger and Rühl described public relations as an "emerging reality" (1992, p. 19) and pointed out that public relations in its contemporary form is a completely new form of communication that had to be invented from scratch (Ibid.). Public relations can only be understood in the context of the historical development of a social reality that is becoming increasingly complex (Ronneberger & Rühl, 1992, p. 43). The authors held a number of "megatrends" responsible for the emergence of the public relations phenomenon: a shift in education processes from rote learning to reflexive learning, increased computerisation and mediatisation, increased permeability of borders both Europe-wide and worldwide; increased international competition, increased industrialisation of leisure organisations, and a qualitative expansion of mass communication (Ronnberger & Rühl, 1992, p. 20). Public relations, according to the authors, can only be understood in the context of a modern, affluent society where life is dominated by freedom, peace, and security (Ibid., p. 19). Ronnberger and Rühl clearly adopted a very optimistic—some would even say utopian—worldview of Western late 20th-century society. Public relations, according to the authors, centres around communicative acts which are offered for the orientation of people in an increasingly complex world (Ibid., p. 46). They also observed that effective participation in public discourse in such a society is only possible in a mediated public sphere (Ibid., pp. 51–52).

Adopting Niklas Luhmann's systems theory, Ronneberger and Rühl described public relations as an autopoietic system which is self-creating, self-organising, self-sustaining, and self-referential (Ibid., p. 89). The authors identified three structural dimensions in which public relations can be observed and which also allow for specific inter-relationships with other social subsystems (Ronneberger & Rühl, 1992, p. 249). The macro-level focuses on the relationship between public relations and society at large. The meso-level focuses on those autopoietic relationships between the PR system and other functional systems of modern society via markets. Lastly, within the micro-level, intra- and inter-organisational relationships are found which focus on the variety of public relations tasks according to the demands of a functionally differentiated, technologically advanced society. In order to achieve those tasks, public relations has partially adapted a number of journalistic techniques and also developed its own specific techniques.

Ronneberger and Rühl's theory has clearly been a milestone in the development of German public relations theory. The authors were the first to attempt a comprehensive analysis of public relations within the context of its societal function. However, their theory has not been without criticism. First, there are those such as Kunczik (1993, p. 243) who have argued against the authors' unconditional use of Luhmann's systems theory. Luhmann's understanding of autopoietic systems as a "supertheory" (Luhmann, 1984, p. 19) has been criticised as aiming to provide universal explanations, but being empirically impossible to prove. Others, such as Röttger, bemoaned the fact that Ronneberger and Rühl's theory remains very general and unspecific as far as the micro-level of public relations is concerned (Röttger, 2000, p. 32). Röttger pointed out that Ronneberger and Rühl on the whole fail to discuss the role, shape, and function of public relations in the organisational context. What public relations activities of organisations might look like and on what basis organisations choose to carry out particular public relations is largely down to the fantasy of the reader, according to Röttger (Ibid.).

A further systems theory in the functional–structural tradition was developed by Werner Faulstich (1992) in which he made use of a previous approach by Ragnwolf Knorr (1984). Faulstich defined public relations as interaction between system and environment. This differentiates his approach from Ronneberger and Rühl's, who allocated public relations a system's character. According to Faulstich and Knorr, public relations assists individual social systems in its aim to maintain and steer its interactions with the environment in order to safeguard its existence (Knorr, 1984, p. 12). In Faulstich's theoretical approach, the "environment" is to be understood as a complementary term to "system," consisting of a number of overlapping systems with different meaning and importance for public relations. Public relations has to face the challenge of dealing with the variety of differing environmental systems and hence has a number of roles to fulfil. As Faulstich put it, public relations is "interaction in society" (1992, p. 50). The difference between public relations and similar disciplines such as marketing is derived from the target publics towards whom the interaction is directed as well as the type and shape of the interaction. Faulstich saw public relations as a necessary development arising through the emergence of the information society in the 20th century (Faulstich, 1992, p. 42). Information society has led to the production of such a high level of complexity that the necessity for a regulatory instrument was created. Public relations roles, tasks, and techniques hence emerged as mechanisms to manage the increased complexity of society as the overarching system (Ibid., p. 60). The question, according to Faulstich, is not whether an organisation is carrying out interactions, but whether those interactions are consciously designed and implemented. "A company, an organisation, a club can't not carry out public relations" (Faulstich, 1992, p. 50). Faulstich's theory has attracted criticism on a number of accounts. First, there is the tendency to overly focus on public relations as interaction which ignores or denigrates communicative processes such as mass communication. Second, Faulstich has been accused of confusing public relationships with public relations. Szyszka pointed out that although obviously no organisation exists in a vacuum, that does not necessarily mean that it will inevitably and consciously use public relations techniques to manage those relationships (1998, p. 70). Others have criticised on the basis that according to more recent understanding of functional–structural systems theory, system and environment cannot "interact" as Faulstich proposed (e.g., Röttger, 2000; Schweda & Opherden, 1995).

Ulrich Saxer, also in the tradition of the functional–structural systems concept, put forward his theory of "public relations as innovation" (1991, 1992). The starting point for his theory is that public relations has to be understood in the context of a theory of evolving societies. He called for an understanding of public relations and related areas such as advertising and journalism to be identified and analysed as "differing social systems in their varying social phases" (Saxer, 1991, p. 275). He added innovation theory to systems theory to help categorize and more fully explain societal developments. Saxer understood public relations campaigns to be strategic systems which can be used to generate social change or, if necessary, hinder social change according to the aims of the organisation. Hence, he distinguished between innovative and stabilising public relations systems (Saxer, 1992, p. 51). Saxer stipulated that systems theory is particularly useful for the explanation of public relations as it is allows us to establish connections between micro- and macro-level theoretical approaches as long as the action within the system and the system–environment interaction are treated equally. He also concluded that systems theory offers a synthesis between the more organisational-orientated American public relations research and the more societal-orientated German approaches.

Anna M. Theis (1992) described public relations from the perspective of organisational sociology as an instrument for environmental control. Organisations try to instrumentalise the power of the mass media in order to prevent/avoid confrontations. According to Theis, this is "contingency management." The aim is to stabilise relationships between organisations and environmental sections concerned with mass communication. Crucial for Theis' understanding of public relations are trust and truthfulness. Organisations are dutybound to release information about themselves in order to avoid discrepancies between portrayed image and reality (Theis, 1992, pp. 31–32). The maintenance of the image requires the organisation, according to Theis, not only to communicate particular aspects of the organisation to the environment through public relations efforts, but also to "manage" the image by working behind the scenes and keeping information out of the public sphere (Ibid., p. 33). Theis' work clearly defines public relations' main aim as control of the environment rather than crisis management or social responsibility. Kunczik assessed that this was not a new idea, but had already been suggested at the annual sociology conference in 1930 (Kunczik, 1993, p. 194). However, Theis' understanding of public relations has to be seen as important in the sense that it shifts its role and importance once again from a societal to an organisational context.

In the early 1990s, a move towards a different approach to public relations was made by Roland Burkart and Sabine Probst, who introduced the concept of consensus-orientated public relations (verständigungsorientierte Öffentlichkeitsarbeit VÖA). The concept arose as a result of the evaluation of public relations work for the implementation of landfill projects in Austria (Burkart & Probst, 1991; Burkart, 1993b). At the heart of the concept lies the aim to reduce conflict of interest between actors through consensus, the actors being organisations and various target publics. The authors based their ideas on Jürgen Habermas' "theory of communicative action" and applied elements of his work to public relations. However, Burkart later (1996) elaborated that consensus-orientated public relations is also modelled on the "symmetrical communication" favoured by Grunig and Hunt (1984). Burkart and Probst's approach can be understood as a situational approach to public relations which allows for the resolution of particular crisis situations that might arise between an organisation and its target publics.

Consensus-orientated public relations is based on the assumption that social change has necessitated a different outlook for organisations' interaction with its target publics. The authors stipulated that in an era when citizens around the world are increasingly aware of threats and dangers posed through, for example, environmental problems, organisations will have to be prepared for active resistance of publics. Consensus-orientated public relations could be effectively used in such crisis situations, according to Burkart, to negotiate and overcome conflict (Burkart, 1993a). The aim of this approach to public relations is to create a mutual understanding of the involved parties with regard to the conflict situation in hand on the basis of trust and also mutual understanding of legitimacy of interests. Core terms of the approach are understanding and consensus. These can only be achieved, according to Burkart and Probst, if all participants are concerned with communicating in a comprehensible, truthful, and accurate manner (Burkart & Probst, 1991, p. 59).

The consensus-orientated public relations concept consists of four phases: information, discussion, discourse, and—the ultimate goal—the mutual definition of the situation in which both sides agree on the arguments that have been put forward, accept the trustworthiness of the involved parties, and accept their interests as legitimate (see Burkart & Probst, 1991, p. 72). This builds the foundation for negotiated decisions and solutions. Public relations' role in this process is to facilitate the process rather than to influence the result or outcome. Burkart later qualified the definition of success for the consensus-orientated model, however, by adding that it might not always be possible to achieve complete understanding; sometimes involved parties will only reach an understanding by "agreeing to disagree."

Critics of the consensus-orientated public relations model have raised a number of issues, the most pertinent being the idealistic nature of the concept. To create mutual understanding and consensus might not be achievable in all or even many circumstances as the issues at hand (e.g., global environmental issues) might be far too fundamental and non-negotiable (e.g., Dorer, 1997; Kunczik, 1994).

Further criticism is directed at the practicality of solutions that might follow such a mutual understanding and consensus. Even if parties agree on the actual definition of the situation, they might not agree on particular programmes of action. In addition, many felt that the organisational context was insufficiently taken into account within the consensus-orientated public relations concept. Burkart and Probst assumed a management function for public relations for organisations partaking in consensus-orientated public relations, but at the same time stated that public relations will only have a mediating role in the process. They failed to acknowledge the potential of public relations to influence the decision-making process in an organisation where PR is a management function. Hence, public relations might falsely be portrayed as a value- and interest- free mediator (Kunczik, 1994).

Despite criticism, Burkart and Probst's model added a different dimension to public relations theory. Their model has to be understood less as an ideal for general public relations practice than as a specific situation-orientated model for resolving crisis through negotiation. It provides insights into how organisations and publics might be able to enter into a fruitful process of communicative interaction.

CONCLUDING REMARKS

Public relations practice and theory in Germany has a rich history which dates back well into the 19th century, if not beyond. Early corporate, governmental, and municipal activities to communicate with customers and citizens have been plentiful and can clearly be analysed and interpreted as public relations activities. These can well be regarded as German public relations' roots and foundations and deserve further consideration and integration into the theory-building process.

As shown above, German public relations research, like British research, is still a relatively new field. Particularly in comparison with related areas such as journalism, it attracted relatively little attention until the later years of the 20th century. In the early stages of public relations theorisation, German roots have often been neglected and public relations was introduced as an

American or British invention. This might well have been because of the fear of the connection that might be made to the propaganda machine of the Nazi Germany, but also because of the role that corporations such as Krupp played in both World Wars.

Initially, as demonstrated in what could be called a "pre-theoretic analysis of public relations," by for example Oeckl and Hundhausen, the literature was dominated by the provision of prescriptions for practitioners. Oeckl adopted similar assumptions as his American counterpart Bernays with regards to the existence of a mass society. Public relations was seen as an opportunity to improve information and to achieve dialogue between organisations and the public. Oeckl was also one of the first to introduce the management character of public relations.

Academic analysis and theory development have since been dominated by society- and democracy-orientated approaches such as Ronneberger (1977), Ronneberger and Rühl (1992), Faulstich (1992), and Knorr (1984). However, during the last decade theories have been put forward which aim to add an organisational dimension to the analysis of public relations (e.g., Röttger, 2000; Theis, 1992; Saxer, 1992).

Many of the German authors of public relations theory can be characterised as utilising or being embedded in the framework of functional–structural systems theory (e.g., Ronneberger's legitimation through information; Ronneberger and Rühl's theory of public relations as a system, Saxer's PR as innovation, or Theis' theory of environmental), which distinguishes them from the structural–functional school of American scholars such as Grunig and Hunt (1984). Of primary concern in the analysis of these German authors is the actual function of public relations for society or the organisation. Of particularly important influence on public relations researchers and their attempts to produce comprehensive analyses of the public relations function has been Niklas Luhmann's understanding of society, social systems, and organisations and Jürgen Habermas' theory of communicative action.

Despite a growing field of theoretical analysis of public relations in Germany, particularly since the early 1990s, many scholars (e.g., Röttger, 2000) bemoan the lack of concepts that focus on public relations as an organisational function. German public relations theory development can still be regarded as being predominantly concerned with the function and role of public relations in a pluralistic society.

7

Public Relations and Democracy: A Swedish Perspective

Larsåke Larsson
Örebro University

What role does public relations play in society and democracy? Does it support and serve as a condition for a working liberal democracy, or is its democratic function problematic and perhaps even threatening? How does the PR opinion process work? And what role does journalism play in the opinion process?

Public relations has grown into a significant and powerful industry during the 20th century, particularly during the latter half of the century, not only in the United States but also internationally as well. While PR operations do still constitute part of the in-house activity of organizations such as private corporations and public institutions, they are increasingly set up as independent consulting firms. As such, they can be said to have become a new and important actor in the democratic process.[1]

This chapter discusses the role of public relations in society and democracy, first through a review of the literature on this subject and secondly through a presentation of a Swedish research project on the PR industry that includes this question. In this project, PR consultants and the journalists (the group with whom they work most closely) were interviewed about their relationship and the impact on and consequences for democracy of the PR industry activities.

THE SWEDISH PR INDUSTRY

Public relations in Sweden came into existence in the 1940s, much later than in the United States and Britain but also than in Germany, where PR actually started earlier (Ewen, 1996;

---

[1] Organizations refers to all kinds of organized groups/entities in society, for example, political parties, government agencies, local authorities, corporations/companies, industry groups, unions, interest groups, non-profit organizations.

L'Etang, 1998, 2004; Davis, 2002; Oeckl, 1964; Bentele & Wehmeier, 2003). A distinctive feature of the Swedish PR history compared to many other countries is that public relations started within state authorities and is in line with the development and growth of the governmental sector at different levels. Swedish pioneers worked mainly in the large state-owned corporations such as Swedish Rail, Swedish Post and the National Board of Health, besides in a government information office during the war period. These men—for they were all men— were mostly press officers, but their work also often included information and 'propaganda' direct to the general public.

PR competence began to spread across a wider spectrum of activity after World War II, and a formal professional association was established in 1950.[2] At that time, the job title was still press officer. The first consulting firms in Sweden—a couple of one-man bureaus—came into being in the 1950s. A few new firms were established over the next decade, but their number remained low well into the 1970s.

Not until the 1980s did a 'real' consulting trade with companies offering a broader service base begin to take shape. Interestingly, many of these PR companies were started by people who had worked in the political sphere, primarily for conservative organizations as well as think tanks and business groups. During the 1980s some of the large international PR firms also established offices or bought into companies in Sweden (e.g., Burson & Marsteller, Hill & Knowlton). Over the course of the following decade, alongside a long period of economic growth, the market for PR services nearly exploded and several companies were established, often relatively small at first but growing very rapidly. Mergers, acquisitions, and breakups were very common at this time (and still are). The industry was visibly volatile. In this climate, the larger Swedish PR companies grew quite steadily.

Looking at the figures, the number of individuals working as Swedish PR consultants more than tripled during the 1990s, rising from about 200 in 1990 to about 1,100 in 2000. The increase occurred mainly during the latter half of the decade. Earnings increased fourfold during the same period, from about $30 million to $130 million. As of 2005, it is estimated that there are about 150 PR firms in the country. Just over 300 firms formally identify themselves as working with PR in their annual reports, but for many of those PR constitutes only a smaller portion of activity (i.e., advertising firms). Most of the PR firms are small, employing only one or two people, while about 60 firms have 3–4 employees or more. Of the consultants practising today, about a quarter work at the three largest PR companies—Kreab, JKL, and GCI Rinfo—which also account for a third of the industry's total income.

Over the past few decades, then, and with increasing rapidity, Swedish corporations, government institutions and non-governmental organizations have shifted from in-house PR activity to the commissioned services of PR firms. The landscape of public relations in Sweden today is beginning to resemble the picture in the United States, where consultants constitute a significant share of the entire PR and information sector.

THEORETICAL POINTS OF DEPARTURE

The PR and information industry has in many countries grown considerably during the last decades (Franklin, 1994; Bennett & Manheim, 2001). England has seen a tenfold increase in the number of PR consultants during the 1980s and 1990s (Davis, 2002). And in the Scandinavian countries the development is the same, as Allern (1997) observed for Norway and which we have just seen above for Sweden.

---

[2]The Swedish Public Relations Association, which is still the name in English, changed its name in 1991 to *Sveriges Informationsförening* (Swedish Information Association).

Public relations as a societal phenomenon and international business has brought itself to an important position with respect to its political and cultural impact and power, especially as it works within the same arena as political and societal actors.

Public Opinion and Opinion Constructing

Contemporary men not only live in an information society but also in an opinion society, the Swedish researchers Holmberg and Weibull (1998) claimed. In this society, opinions and images are the functional equivalent of the land in an agricultural society and steel in an industrial society. Public opinion, however, is a central element in our society.

What exactly is a (public) opinion? At the surface we all seem to know, and in short there is an agreement that "the term refers to the opinions of a number of people" (Childs, 1965, p. 348f). But beyond this basic definition, the meanings differ. Herbst (1993) identified four types of opinions—the majority, aggregation, consensus, and reification models. The first means elections and the second opinion polls; the third can be referred back to the thoughts of Habermas and the last to Lippman (1922/1997) and his ideas that public opinion is a projection of what (elite) observers perceive to be an opinion. The aggregation model is today an almost hegemonic one (besides formal elections), but there are scholars who have opposed this view, most firmly Blumer (1948) and Bourdieu (1979), claiming that polls do not measure opinions.

Another question is whether a public opinion is something people by themselves form around social matters or if opinions are instrumentally constructed by special interests—like trade and industry, organizations, and political parties—and diffused to the public in order to grow into a wide opinion. Several scholars have, in studying the information and opinion process, explored processes of construction and developed theories, such as agenda building (Cobb & Elder, 1972; Weaver & Elliot, 1985), information subsidy (Gandy, 1982), and primary definers and framing (Hall et al., 1978/1993; Gitlin, 1980; Entman, 1993).

The public opinion process has two meanings or phases: the process itself and the consequences of the process. It is a dualism between "the actors forming and expressing public opinion and the actors to whom it is addressed, or between the expression and realization of public opinion" (Splichal, 2001, p. 27). In the second sense, Herbst found in a study of various actors' perception of the public opinion process that for political staffers, public opinion was what the media displayed and those issues driven by interest groups. For journalists, it was above all the same as their own imaged views and the content of interpersonal conversation with people they happened to meet (Herbst, 1998).

Opinions are increasingly created and constructed by experts such as information staff, PR consultants, and spin doctors. Norris (2000, p. 173) noted that "the techniques of spin-doctors, opinion polls, and professional media management are increasingly applied to routine everyday politics." These actors have almost been equal to the politicians in a permanent campaigning around opinions, she argued. Another opinion builder—or frame builder—is think tanks. These have been "important means through which business can disseminate its perspective on public policy," (Smith, 2000, p. 167f). In sum, Herbst (1998, p. 2) claimed that "the processes of 'constructing' public opinion have vital implications for democratic theory and practice."

The Relationship Between Public Relations and Journalism

Public opinion is above all processed via mass media—for the public from those who want to raise an opinion and for the politicians and other decision makers about what opinions there are in society. It demands contacts and relations between the actors in the opinion process and the media. As public opinion mostly is processed this way, the media also *becomes* opinion.

And, as Jamieson (2003) and Waldman (2003) noted, the more important the role of public opinion in society, the greater the potential for the impact of journalism.

A large number of studies have been carried out through the years on the contacts between political and institutional decision makers and journalists. Research shows almost unanimously a close and tight relationship, depicted by Gans' often cited dance metaphor of it taking two to dance. The two parts depend on each other for exchanging information and media space (Cohen, 1963; Tunstall, 1970; Sigal, 1973; Gans, 1979; Fishman, 1980; Blumler & Gurevitch, 1981, Ericson et al., 1989; Cook, 1989). German studies (e.g., Kepplinger & Fritsch, 1981) and a Swedish study give the same picture of a more or less symbiotic relationship (Larsson, 1998). On the other hand, corporate sources have weaker affinity with news producers, except for the business news, according to Davis (2002, p. 175), viewed from a British horizon.

Studies of the relationship between public relations and journalism describe a relationship of intense contacts as well (McNair, 2000; Davis, 2002; Larsson, 2005). The rationale here is also information/news against publicity. But, as McNair noticed, neither can be seen as needing the other too much. Managing the delicate balance between dependence on and distance from the media is an important element in the legitimation of both categories of communication professionals. Moreover, the (political) journalists need PR actors and spin doctors for it positions them as victims rather than villains (McNair, 2000, p. 136f).

PR actors have been extremely successful in producing "real news," Davis concluded, not only by writing press releases and inventing events, but also in creating experts, institutions, and statistics for journalists. This goes hand in hand with the overall decline in the level of news-gathering resources for the media. Public relations has thus "worked to erode the autonomy of journalists at the micro level" (Davis, 2002, p. 172). The information subsidy theory seems to be more accurate than ever.

Several academic sources claim that public relations and spin doctors today are a serious problem for journalism. This phenomenon has led journalism to become an alienated and cynical force in society (Blumler & Gurevitch, 1995), "turning people off citizenship rather than equipping them to fulfill their democratic potential" (McNair, 2000, p. 8). Street is in line with this, claiming that "the spin doctor has become a cultural icon, a symbol of the new cynicism about modern journalism . . . leading gullible journalists to half-truths and bare-faced lies." From this follows that "journalists are the lapdogs of partial interests, not the watchdogs of the public interest" (Street, 2001, p. 145f). The consequence is, with complementary words of Davis (2002, p. 173), that "The liberal description of the fourth estate media, based on an image of an independent autonomous journalist seeking out news, has been severely undermined." But for McNair these problems are balanced with the media's ability to disclose the manufactured news; the media increasingly undermines these excesses from public relations and "stays alert to its abuse" (McNair, 2000, p. 175).

PUBLIC RELATIONS AND DEMOCRACY

What role does public relations play in society and democracy? This question about the PR phenomenon and the PR industry has met diametrically opposed academic notions. On the one hand, we can note a liberal market-oriented tradition, while on the other hand we observe a more critical school that has emerged in recent years.

A number of democratic values and criteria are frequently mentioned in the literature (see, e.g., Beetham, 1994). The last Swedish commission on democracy included among its criteria for democracy meaningful popular participation, political equality, and transparency. These criteria—particularly equality, and transparency together with Dahl's (1998) further requirements of increased awareness, control of the political agenda by the people, and above all enlightened understanding—provide much of the evaluative framework of this study.

Public Relations as a Support for Democracy

The first line of thought is the classical one, that this industry constitutes an important support for a liberal democracy, serving different interests by helping them articulate their views and thus be seen and heard in the political debate. This view goes back to the childhood of PR and appears in most textbooks. This view has influenced thinking on public relations ever since this type of operation began in the late 1800s (see, for example, Cheney & Vibbert, 1987). Tedlow, who wrote an early history of PR, viewed public relations as "an indication of the health of American democracy" (1979, p. 209).

Moving to PR research of today, with Grunig as the most prominent spokesperson, the view of public relations is essentially the same, that is, it is a support for democracy in the sense that this function assists different interests in communicating and articulating their views. J. Grunig (1989) applied the concept of interest-group liberalism, in which the political system is an open playing field with free competition between different groups possessing similar opportunities to participate.

For most modern PR writers, there is no general public or general public opinion. "There is no general public," said Grunig and Hunt (1984, p. 138), and Cutlip et al. (2000, p. 383) argued that "there is no such thing." And Davis (2002) observed that PR actors in operation are not interested in a general public. For the founders of PR, however, there seems to have existed a general public (see Bernays, 1923). Over the course of its journey since the 1920s, the American concept of PR appears to have lost the general public, most likely affected by the marketing tenets of segmenting customers into as many delimited target groups as possible. Several researchers, however, have criticized this notion in more recent years (i.e., Leeper, 2001; Leitch & Neilson, 2001; see also Rakow, 1989). Leitch and Neilson (2001, p. 130f) argued that PR researchers have turned their backs on democracy by excluding the general public.

In Europe, and not least in the Nordic countries, the dismissal of the general public (citizenry) seems alien and incorrect, for this concept constitutes such a basic dimension of our society where all citizens are assumed to be communicated with on democratic matters. The German term for public relations—*öffentlichkeitsarbeit*—literally means "public work" and can be explained as "working in public, with the public and for the public" (Nessman, 2000, p. 200). Public relations in the European environment is thus "concerned with issues and values that are considered publicly relevant, which means relating to the public sphere" (Verčič et al., 2001, p. 376). In other words, public means publics in the U.S. context, but is connected with the public sphere in (at least several) European countries.

Public Relations as a Problem for Democracy

The other line holds that the PR industry is a threat or at least a problem to democratic society since it is a sector that builds and creates opinions, seeking to influence and steer political decisions, but lacking in democratic accountability and transparency. Public relations practitioners constitute an expertise that acts outside the realm of traditional organizations and steers opinion without being involved in the issues themselves. The fact that they steer opinion without a democratic "mandate" and without themselves being engaged in the issue will henceforth be referred to as the legitimacy issue.

The critical voices follow two lines of direction. One addresses the influence PR exerts on the realm of ideas, that is, the opinion-building effects of corporations and institutions, while the other is concerned with PR's lack of responsibility for society and democracy. Critics do not constitute an integrated research group or school, but rather consist of voices from other disciplines such as history, cultural studies, and political science. This disciplinary mixture is particularly noticeable in terms of scholarship on opinion effects, while research and debates surrounding the more ethical issues also tend to be conducted by PR researchers.

PR's Influence on Ideas and Opinions

A central aspect of public relations has from the beginning been to build or construct public opinion, even though it is performed in a segmented way. J. Grunig noted that "In essence, then, public opinion is both a cause and effect of public relations activities" (1997, p. 4).

The discussion broadens even further in its consideration of consumer society. Stuart Ewen pointed to what he considered to be the central consequence of industrial society—namely the development of a consumer society over the past century. In his view, consumerism has become a decisive force in modern socialization, where industry has consciously nurtured a philosophy about a commodity life for all people with the help of consumption and its requisite advertising (Ewen, 1976).

Ewen anticipated the observations and conclusions of several later researchers on the advertising and promotional culture of our time, such as Schudson (1986), a media sociologist, and culturally oriented researchers such as Wernick (1991), Fowles (1996), and Mooij (1998). Wernick observed the way in which consultants now not only act within a commercial economic sphere but also in a political and public sphere, as agents of political organizations in a larger sense. The "promotionalization" of the former sphere has spread into the non-commercial sphere (Wernick, 1991). In the same spirit, Deetz (1992) claimed that production interests have colonized society and public decision making, and Turow (1997) noted that advertisers now influence social debate and people's way of thinking as a whole.

Mayhew concluded that the public discourse has been fundamentally altered by the practices of public relations, advertising, and market research. The democratic foundations of debate and influence in society no longer take place in the form of a conversation between people, but have become instrumental activities steered by professional experts, creating what he called "the New Public." Public relations professionals take no responsibility for balanced, objective presentations, but see their role as advocates of selected truths before the court of public opinion. The principles that guided the early advocates and fathers of public relations—including honest representation to the public, two-way communication, and commitment to the public interest—have not been realized, Mayhew (1997, p. 202f) wrote.

Within the field of political communication, the question of professionalization of the field has long been intensively discussed. For example, Sabato observed over 20 years ago that political actors more and more have handed campaign planning over to consultants. He saw several dangers to democracy in this involvement in the political process, such as the dependency on more or less debatable opinion surveys, negative campaigning, pseudo-news and other types of false information, and what he called tunnel-vision campaigns with narrow (conflict-oriented) issue ranges. In general, he believed, campaign consultants have contributed "to the darker side of politics" (Sabato, 1981, p. 322).

Mancini and Swanson (1996) claimed that the use of experts and consultants is one main characteristic of the development of political campaigns in recent years, besides among other things increased distance from voters and the increasingly political function taken on by the media. The use of consultants implies that election campaigns have become even more oriented toward marketing and advertising and dependent on opinion surveys and the manipulation of opinion figures. Experts contribute to the development of "spectatorship," where election campaigns have become characterized more by spectacle than by political action (Mancini & Swanson, 1996; Swanson & Mancini, 1996).

The critique of the PR's culture of increased promotion and advertising does not go uncontested, however. Certain anthropological research points out that material assets have always given social meaning to people. And Meijer claimed that a "consumer culture may produce citizenship" and that "new cultural values need new products to come alive." She argued that advertising acts as a legitimate source of discussion among citizens and therefore fulfills Habermas' criteria for a public sphere (Meijer, 1998, p. 239).

PR'S SOCIAL AND DEMOCRATIC ROLE

The other critical view addresses the demand for corporations to take responsibility for society and democracy. Within organizational research, Deetz argued that corporations must include the general public among their stakeholders, since "corporations are political sites, because they make critical decisions for the public" (1995, p. 173). Turow (1997) observed that advertisers, through segmentation and efforts to maximize market shares, exploit social problems and contradictions and distance people from each other rather than improve society.

In PR circles, a social and democratic debate was started with Kruckeberg and Starck's *Public Relations and Community* in 1988. However, it was not until the mid-1990s that the "uprising" gathered momentum, when a sudden tidal wave of books and articles were published on the topic of corporate social responsibility and democratic participation (see Leeper & Leeper, 2001, note 6ff). L'Etang, while pleading for the need for corporations to seek to encourage good citizenship and help the functioning of democratic institutions, stated that "the role of public relations itself is . . . intrinsically undemocratic" (1996a, p. 105).

Social responsibility means, among other things, that companies plan *with* the community and help the community develop social resources and institutions. And it means encouraging employees to become active in their environment and in the democratic process as well (Culbertson & Chen, 1997; Leeper, 2001).

In Ewen's second review of the PR industry, conducted 20 years after his first book, he focused more deeply on democracy-related issues, not to say dangers or hazards. He found that the industry's will and capacity to shape the public and society had become increasingly pervasive, sophisticated, and expert-oriented. He asked: "Can democracy exist when public agendas are routinely predetermined by 'unseen engineers'?" And, with John Dewey behind him, he gave his answer: "For this situation to change, the public sphere—currently dominated by corporate interests and consciously managed by public relations professionals—must revert to the people" (Ewen, 1996, pp. 409, 411).

For some, the theory of social responsibility is so central that they suggest it serves as a foundational theory for public relations (Leeper & Leeper, 2001). In recent years, this model has been incorporated into the concept of communitarianism (Leeper, 2001), a sociological school of thought dating from the mid-1800s and serving as a counterpoint to liberalism (see Etzioni, 1998) that has become a theoretical trend within PR research.

SWEDISH PR CONSULTANTS AND DEMOCRACY

A research project on the Swedish PR industry has recently been studying the history and development of the business, its work and methods, and, most importantly, its role in society and democracy (Larsson, 2005). The study was mainly conducted through interviews and case studies, but it also examines media coverage of the PR industry and documents (at PR firms and the PR Association).

Method and Design

In the PR project, personal (deep) interviews were conducted with 64 actors over a period of 4 years (2001–2004). Twenty were PR consultants, 8 information managers and officers, 5 former information managers and now independent advisers, and 17 journalists. In addition, 14 PR pioneers or veterans who built the PR industry in Sweden have also been interviewed, many of whom are well-known names in the country. The journalists reflect a broad spectrum—newspaper, radio, and television reporters and editors specializing in public affairs and/or business reporting.

The inclusion of journalists in the design of the study is a result of the theoretical question concerning the relationship between various actor groups in society. Journalists are a particularly important actor group in this nexus given the role that they play vis-à-vis PR professionals.

This chapter focuses on only one part of the research project: the role of PR in society and democracy. It does not seek to answer the question of whether PR constitutes a help or hindrance to democracy in any absolute sense. Rather, it reports the views of PR practitioners and journalists regarding this question. The group information managers and officers were principally interviewed for other parts of the project and hence are referred to in a very small degree in this chapter. The following report of the results aims at using the interview material (the statements and quotations of the respondents) in a substantial way.

One conceptual issue must be clarified. In this project, terms like "opinion-constructing," "opinion building," and "opinion work" refer to activities aimed at influencing citizens or sub-sections thereof (most often carried out through the mass media but also including advertising and event-making, etc.). The term "lobbying," on the other hand, refers to activities aimed at influencing decision makers such as politicians and government officials. By operating within the corridors of power, lobbying seeks to achieve more direct policy outcomes, while opinion-building activities seek to mobilize and steer public opinion in a way that will in turn create a favorable climate for policy decisions. Both methods aim to bring about certain decisions or other types of measures that favor the represented group, but they operate in different arenas and use different methods.

RESULTS OF THE STUDY

The Swedish PR industry in general and the consultant corps in particular is, as already mentioned, a young industry in Sweden, especially compared to the United States. Almost all of the pioneering consultants are still alive. Interestingly, very few of the consultants have been exclusively in this job—many have worked as information officers before becoming consultants or wandered back and forth between professional roles. Some were previously journalists, but they have not been able to switch back to journalism. Among the younger subjects, there are several who have gone directly into consulting after graduating from university, in essence becoming advisors without having acquired practical experience (Larsson, 2005).

THE DEMOCRATIC ROLE OF PR CONSULTANTS

How do PR practitioners and journalists view the role of public relations in society and democracy? This is an overall question of the study. The interviewees were presented with and asked to comment on the two contrasting conceptions of the societal role of PR as discussed above, that is, the positive liberal view and the critical view.

It is easy to imagine in advance that consultants will uniformly defend their operation as supportive of democracy, and not unexpectedly, many of them do believe that PR "serves a purpose for democracy" and "is a completely legitimate democratic activity." For some it is "completely alien" to see things any other way, in one case meaning that those who see PR as a democratic threat "suffer from a regrettable form of madness," since all actors must have the right to influence opinion in society. It is a "completely natural consequence of living in a market economy." Typical viewpoints are:

> We are a guarantee for liberal democracy and an additional source of different voices, a spotlight beaming light on issues and emphasizing different things and expanding the information base of decision making. (Consultant 1, 5/11/01)

> We are a result of democracy in society . . . I believe that much of what we communicate to patients (re medication) or the general public is information they should have for their own well-being. (Junior consultant 1, 11/11/01)

But there are nonetheless quite a few consultants who expressed a degree of doubt alongside their general optimism—a point to be noted is that those who did so were women in the field:

> We do not damage democratic processes. On the other hand, I don't think it's appropriate to say it is completely benign, either . . . The debate is too simplistic when people claim that PR is a precondition for democracy. It is a problem for democracy in terms of opinion-constructing. (Female PR firm executive, 6/12/01)

> Consultants can be a guarantee for democracy, because one gets an open debate. However, this requires both ethics and high competence and experience. The risk is that we end up with something opposite, unfortunately . . . There are too many flashy things, too much money in all this. If things move too much in this direction, then I think consulting operations can become a threat, without a doubt. (Female senior advisor, 28/3/01)

A number of interview subjects further discussed the conditions under which PR could strengthen or weaken democracy. One of them suggested that it is "important to reflect and see what you're doing as one makes a powerful impact on opinion about an issue," and one of the pioneers reflected:

> If there is some kind of information vacuum, or if viewpoints missing from the public debate are brought to the fore through the efforts of consultants, then they contribute to the general discourse. However, if they see their task only in terms of effectively expressing selected manufactured messages, then yes—they are the gravediggers of democracy, as I see it. (Elder consultant 'doyen', former PR company executive, 21/3/01)

Some of the subjects placed some "blame" on clients, criticizing what they see as poor social responsibility displayed by some companies. One of them claimed that it was important for the occupation that PR practitioners be perceived as good members of society so as not to damage the occupation's image, "but those in the business world must also [do so]." According to these voices, it is not so much the consultants who are the democratic problem, but the companies involved. One consulting veteran said, with apparent irony:

> I often meet with the boards of directors of various companies . . . and there I encounter viewpoints concerning their role in society which, quite frankly, I find difficult to understand how they can exist. The only topic where they consistently display true ability is in their concern for their shareholders. (Senior adviser, former information manager, 28/3/01)

When the conversation shifted in emphasis from the more general discourse on democracy to the issue of consultants as a power factor in society, the statements became more polarized. Some denied that they are a power factor. The statement "I can't see the PR industry as a power in itself" is typical in this regard. Some conceded that "knowledge is power and we possess knowledge, so therefore I think we have a certain power." A few interview subjects, however, were more explicit about the scope and nature of PR power:

> PR companies are clearly a political power factor. I think this is something that must be discussed and not swept under the carpet. What methods do we use? Are they hidden, open? What is the purpose? Do we have a mandate to go in and do certain things? (Consultant 2, 25/9/01)

What do the journalists and editors say about the democratic role of consultants? One can imagine that they would tend to be more critical, and some certainly did exhibit these tendencies, in words like "It is a threat to democracy that you can buy your way to opinion power." Particularly journalists writing for the more left-leaning press took the discussion in this direction:

> There is still a difference between opinion activities conducted by a membership-based group that says that "we want to work for this" and activities conducted by PR companies, which are based on money. . . . That's a big difference, and in that way, PR firms can naturally be a threat to democracy—in any case the democracy we have come to know in Sweden. (Political editor, 12/12/01)

> Basically I think the phenomenon itself (PR consultants) is terrible, but what can you do? It's a part of society as it now stands, and it is a powerful part . . . This isn't how society should be organized—we thought society should be organized according to a party system. The parties should discuss, journalism should question, citizens should form their own view of the whole thing and then one should arrive at a decision. When things are happening beyond the purview of the public, it is a threat to democracy. (Journalist, evening paper, 12/12/01)

But most of the journalists interviewed embrace the liberal notion and more or less accept the PR industry as a legitimate actor that fills a democratic function. The preeminent argument is that "PR can be a help to those who otherwise wouldn't be seen or heard," as a well-known political TV reporter said, together with other colleagues:

> It is not a problem for democracy that companies and organizations want media exposure and influence over decision makers. That itself is a precondition of democracy. The fact that they sometimes move via PR offices . . . doesn't strike me as problematic, either. (Editor, evening paper, 12/12/01)

> I don't see them as a threat to democracy. They are a threat to democracy if we (the media) as recipients of their information are not capable of reporting it fairly and independently. If that is the case, those who pay the most money to the best PR consultant will be the ones who get their information across in the long run. (Business TV reporter 28/5/02)

The positive view expressed by journalists tends to be more focused on the practical aspects of consulting work as opposed to the larger issue of their role in democracy. As two journalists put it, "they do a lot of the footwork" and "they are a type of lubricant, they know all the technicalities." Others echoed this sentiment. But at least one added: "On the other hand, it is of course not good that they are pseudo-journalists."

The oldest of the interviewed journalists, a retired but still active business editor, offered a reflective sequence of thoughts on the matter. At first he said that it seems far-fetched to discuss the PR industry as a problem. However, he added: "Imagine if it turns out that my cohorts and I have been manipulated over the years without realizing it!" Although he then came to the view that this is not likely, he spent quite a while reasoning around this topic.

Along with activities surrounding opinion creation, the PR industry also engages in lobbying efforts. In this study, the definition of lobbying was limited to direct personal influence on decision makers, while opinion work pertains to influence aimed at the general public or portions thereof. While only a few consultants in the sample said that they refrain from opinion activities, more reported that they and their firm do not practice lobbying. This does not mean, however, that they are critical of or opposed to the phenomenon of lobbying—not even the older ones, who otherwise voiced more scepticism about PR activities:

> Lobbying activities are part of the democratic system, part of the discourse, the social dialogue. I think we should strive to make it part of the public discourse. (Senior freelance 1, 28/3/01)

> I think that lobbying is absolutely legitimate—all this talk about it being a threat to democracy and that only rich corporations can afford them is a load of crap. (Senior freelance 2, 8/5/01)

One argument in favor of lobbying is the notion that decision makers *want* the contact and information provided by lobbyists: "Many of those who are lobbied appreciate receiving the information." Some of the subjects, however, expressed reservations such as government decision makers getting very tired if there are too many "well-trained guys running around slipping in some formulations." Others expressed clear conditions for an acceptance of this phenomenon. One of these conditions is adherence to the industry's ethical rules. Another is transparency: "When I am in contact with politicians I am very clear about what I stand for, what I'm doing and on whose behalf I am working." Despite these slight reservations, however, two arguments dominated the lobbying discussion. The first is that lobbying by consultants is simply an outsourcing of the organization's government relations activity. The second argument is that lobbying activity provides a foundation for more pluralistic decision making and thus enhances democracy.

Among the journalists, opinions about lobbying were quite diverse. For some, PR and lobbying are one and the same, while others see the two as separate, with lobbying as an 'influence industry' in its own right. In both cases lobbying is seen as a natural consequence of a democratic society. The key is transparency:

> Lobbyists who do not make clear why they are there and what their goals are, are very dangerous. They are extremely treacherous. They elude the democratic process. (Political TV reporter 28/5/02)

Thus far, the discussion has focused on the two groups' views on the PR industry as a whole and on its democratic role. Within this general framework, however, a number of more specific issues can be identified. These include: (a) opinion-building activities, (b) opinion polls, (c) resource distribution, (d) transparency, and (e) ethics. Views relating to these five issue areas are presented below.

CONSTRUCTING AND INFLUENCING OPINION

The first issue deals with the opinion activities of PR consultants and the fact that their efforts to steer opinion are for hire and thus operate outside the traditional nexus of interest representation. All of the PR consultants interviewed—with a couple of notable exceptions—stated that opinion-constructing operations are an assumed and legitimate task for PR companies. Typical remarks included "it's a part of our task," "opinion building is generally included in our communication tasks," and "opinion-constructing activities are very important, very key, they are fundamental" for the trade.

The question of legitimacy—that is, the problem that they act without an underlying democratic mandate and without being "genuinely" engaged in the issues they promote—is something most of them did not seem to understand, or else they considered it irrelevant and uninteresting.

Generally, the rationale consisted of the notions, on the one hand, that the freedom to create opinions is part of a democratic society, linked to freedom of expression, and, furthermore, that acting as advisors and providing services to various interests is a central task of consultants. Many interviewees argued that it does not matter if it is the consultant or the client who is responsible for opinion activities:

> Ultimately it doesn't matter if an organization has its own employees working on opinion-building or if it goes through a consultant. The purpose is the same and the client is ultimately the same. The dilemma arises when a consulting firm acts in its own name, speaking through its own people without acknowledging on whose behalf they are acting. (Senior independent consultant, former PR company executive, 14/11/01)

> Many organizations would never be heard at all if they didn't get help expressing themselves and finding the right channels to get their message through. (Veteran consultant and former information officer, 4/4/01)

One exception to the view of opinion constructing and lobbying as legitimate PR activities was that of an older consultant and former information director of a state-owned corporation, who expressed doubt about these activities as appropriate tasks for public relations. Another exception was the head of bureau that mainly deals with market-oriented PR and brand-name issues who has a journalist background. Claiming that his firm does not engage in such activities, he expressed a clearly negative view of opinion-constructing operations, which he regards as efforts "to try to influence legislation in undemocratic ways."

Among the journalists interviewed, there was no noticeable aversion toward the opinion-constructing activities of the PR industry, in words such as "it is a legitimate occupation" and "it is completely OK to hire someone who is an expert in communication." Most of those addressing this issue believe that creating opinions is part of a democratic society and they accept that companies and organizations enlist the help of consultants in this work. "Democracy presupposes opinion-building," said one TV journalist, who added that this applies to the private sector as well as the public sector. Another journalist stated that such activities have always been fuelled by political organizations but that corporations "are more noticeable now than they were a few years ago." Most, however, mentioned some form of nuance or variation, particularly on the question of available resources:

> I don't think I have a problem with the fact that they sometimes use PR firms because these possess a certain knowledge or communication channel that they don't have. Rather, the issue is who commissions the task and to what degree is it steered by money. (Political editor, 12/12/01)

Open opinion-building—where it is clear whose message it is—is easier to handle. It is more difficult with hidden activity because it is harder to know the source. I generally don't like opinion activities, though, since there will always be groups in society unable to buy power. (News desk head, 12/12/01)

Some of the journalists discussed issues of principle. One editorial writer saw as the main problem that consultants are not engaged in the issues and that they steer opinion for one issue and organization one week while "the next week (they) work for another organization." Still, many cited the responsibility of journalism as well, saying it is up to the journalist to identify and monitor movements in opinion: "It is the media's problem." They stressed the importance of "increasing awareness at the news desks about this" so that one does not "become part of the process."

OPINION POLLS

A particular problem in opinion work is the extent of opinion polling. Today, such polls belong to the standard arsenal of opinion work: "Polls are conducted all the time." But they have, according to veterans, existed as an instrument since the beginning of the PR industry. "It was something we emphasized most strongly," said one of the founders of the PR profession in Sweden, meaning that he and his colleagues pleaded heavily for this type of input at that time (1960s). A prevalent view is that opinion polling has become more common over the last 10 to 15 years. Among the older consultants, however, there were views such as "I rely less and less on hiring different survey institutes" because their quality is lower and surveys are "a fairly expensive method and have lost some of their effect." For most interviewees, however, opinion polls are an obvious method:

A clear tool we have is surveys, especially in terms of opinion building. We conduct lots of surveys ... and it's been really easy to get the large media to pay attention to them. I view this merely as high marks for the fact that we have had good ideas from the beginning. (Junior consultant 2, 12/11/01)

Several consultants, particularly those with more experience, actually expressed themselves in doubtful or questioning terms when it came to opinion polls. A question was asked whether this PR method is defensible in light of the fact that most of them are produced to generate desired results. They agreed that they are often "rigged" in a planned way, and one consultant reasoned that one can make surveys to "get exactly the results you want," a view reinforced by several colleagues. Another discussed the subject in more practical terms, like "surveys are not intended to find something out but to become a top story."

This is one of the classic ways to get a particular issue onto the agenda—you contract an opinion poll and then report those portions of the results that support a certain thesis on a certain issue. (Senior freelance consultant, former PR company executive, 14/11/01)

I think there are some who behave overtly unethically ... It is a clear fact that many opinion polls are contracted in order to support a particular position, then they are sent out as a news item. (Veteran consultant, former information officer, 4/4/01)

The notion that it is up to journalists to scrutinize and critically monitor opinion polls was dominant among the PR group. The role of the PR consultant is to get material into the news media, and this role exists alongside the journalists' and editors' role of selecting newsworthy material. For this reason, they argued, it is important that the polls generate newsworthy results. At the same time, some consultants felt that journalism often has difficulties in tackling this type of material. Referring to the fact that opinion data are often constructed in a biased way, one of the senior consultants commented that "it amazes me that the qualified national press journalists . . . don't understand this but rather fall like skittles every time one of these polls comes along."

Many journalists expressed awareness of the opinion strategies of the consulting world in general and of surveys in particular. Most of them interviewed in this study were critical of polling, claiming that they are aware of the underlying motives:

> There is an increasing tendency in PR to use opinion polls to create news value . . . They are always carried out with the aim of generating a positive result. (Editor, morning national paper 11/12/01)

> It's problematic, actually. You have to keep your eyes open in terms of the study itself and whose interests it serves, particularly if it is conducted properly. I think lots of stuff slip through, both here and elsewhere in the media. (Editor, computer magazine 18/6/02)

> They don't ask questions directly, but pose them in a context they have constructed at the request of an interest group or party. In that sense people are lured into responding . . . yes or no to a constructed question whose aim is to generate a particular answer. These opinion surveys can be extremely dangerous and one should be careful to keep them at arm's length. (Political TV reporter 28/5/02)

Some journalists were uncertain about whether they could treat polls critically in their work, while others were confident in their ability to do so. The problem is that the material is so well suited for the journalistic narrative: "It's a huge problem. I would say it is the greatest problem because they almost always fit so well into the news dramaturgy" (Political editor, evening paper).

The figures and simple tables associated with opinion polls are ideally suited to media logic and media dramaturgy. Several of the journalists interviewed discussed the issue in these terms. One commented that "there is a temptation in the simplified quantitative" and that "as soon as there are some numbers there is the guise of objectivity that is attractive and easy to write about." Another, an editorial writer at an evening paper, concluded: "It does seem to be the case that the need for media dramaturgy is sometimes greater than the weight of source scrutiny."

ADVANTAGE OF THE RESOURCE-RICH

Another problematic issue for PR consultants is the risk that only those interests with ample resources can avail themselves of such services, a dynamic that widens the visibility and influence gap between rich and poor organizations. Quite a few of the consultants raised this issue on their own, stating that this does in fact seem to be the case: "We are paid by those who can afford to pay—it's a bit crass but it's true." Some believe that this is either acceptable or unavoidable, while others see a problem in this relationship: "I see the democratic dilemma in that companies who can afford it can commission a PR firm while others can't." It is primarily among the veterans that one finds the frankest statements in this regard:

> It seems easy to say that everyone has the same chance and that it is open, but it is clear that this is a resource issue and I don't see this as unproblematic. (Female freelance adviser 29/3/01)

> It is the rich who can afford the services of expensive consultants, while it is very difficult for the small and weak in society to make themselves heard with the help of consultants. . . . The gap is increasing, and injustices are reinforced in the sense that the resource-rich can increase their lead by purchasing highly skilled consulting services. (Senior freelance consultant 26/4/01)

At this point, the consultants interviewed discussed and compared the "opinion power" of the resource-rich versus the resource-poor. Many argued that supposedly "weak" interest groups, particularly activist groups, are equally if not more visible in the media debate than resource-rich companies—completely in line with one of Grunig's theses. "An organization for or against something that is a bit heart-breaking can get an amazing amount of coverage," one said. Some claimed further that "corporations have less means at their disposal to express themselves than do activists" and that certain weak interest groups have an easier time in gaining ground in the media than richer actors:

> The forest industry in Sweden get less publicity for their opinions than a field biologist who chains himself to a helicopter. Or some other green activists who climb up a chimney or a person from an international organization who sits on a rubber raft and circles around a boat. (Veteran consultant and former information officer, 4/4/01)

> There is also power in not having any money.... It isn't money that matters but rather the legitimacy that can be established around their interest. Organizations for the disabled have had enormous success while it is perhaps more difficult for Volvo ..., despite the fact that they have unlimited resources. Capital should be measured not only in dollars and years but also in terms of emotional weight. (Consultant 1, 15/11/01)

Few journalists brought up the resource issue, although an underlying sense of resource inequalities was present in several interviews. One of them said:

> I think it's important to keep in mind that PR is money-driven. That is the big difference between PR and other types of opinion constructing activities. (Business TV reporter, 28/5/02)

TRANSPARENCY

One assumption of a democratic society is that debate and other processes take place openly and with transparency. Participants should clearly identify both themselves and their intentions, and there should be no hidden agendas. With PR, it is often someone other than the client that presents him or herself in the debate—the consultant or, more typically, someone else acts as the messenger. Many PR consultants do not see this as problematic, except in terms of lobbying, where the dominant view appears to be that the client should speak directly. But the picture is not so simple. A number of interview subjects discussed how they have acted on behalf of their client. Some expressed very firm views:

> The problem with opinion construction occurs when there is a hidden agenda, when you don't know the source of the message. That definitely happens. (Senior consultant, former PR company executive 14/11/01)

> If opinion building takes place openly, that's good. However, if you use decoys and stay hidden in the back-ground and the aim of the opinion constructing isn't brought forth ... then that's bad. (Consultant 3, 13/12/01)

One of the problems deals with the using of other spokesmen with "higher credibility than the client to speak out themselves." Spokespersons can be well-known individuals such as celebrities, cultural personalities, or researchers. They can also be organizations with high credibility and high "conscience status," such as environmental, foreign aid, disability, and other socially oriented organizations. In addition to seeking allies and getting them to testify on behalf of proposed activities, another approach is to get the desired spokespersons to somehow act on their own initiative to mobilize opinion. Here the strategy is to "inspire to initiative, to create movement from below, grass roots initiative." A primary tactic is to get the allies to sign debate articles, preferably in the large national newspapers. PR firms write the articles either alone or in collaboration with the signatories. "The debate article is often, just like the press release, written by the PR firm," said one consultant. Another respondent claimed that almost all articles in the DN Debate pages (the most prestigious debate arena in the largest national morning paper, *Dagens Nyheter*) are written by PR consultants.

The journalist group expressed some scepticism about PR transparency: "There is a lot of hidden PR activity that you don't see." Several are clearly critical of the alliance strategies of PR consultants, particularly if the collaboration is hidden or unstated. Not all journalists are critical, however. One debate editor sees no problem with signatories who have not written the articles themselves, as they, in his view, in some way mostly sympathize with the issue.

ETHICS

In recent years, PR ethics has become one of the most hotly debated issues in Sweden as well as abroad. A number of debaters have questioned the ethics of the industry, particularly when PRECIS, the professional association of Swedish PR companies, revised its ethical rules in 2002. According to critics, these changes weakened the ethical standard, for example, by declaring less transparency at the member firms and less responsibility for society.

Interestingly, most consultants firmly regard a strong ethical standard as a required condition of their work. Many raised this issue without prompting. Ethics "are a strong reflection of both individual morals and the morals of the company," said a still-active pioneer. The issue of ethics is seen in different ways. While some discussed it in terms of ethical codes adopted by the industry on a national and international level, others discussed it in terms of personal moral values. One pattern that emerged, however, is the tendency for the issue to be discussed in greater depth by the older and more experienced consultants:

> It's fundamental because it's part of the operation, ethics and morality—one must have it, not only on paper and rhetorically but in practice as well. (Senior consultant, former information manager, 28/3/01)

> As long as you can maintain ethics, it's OK. It is quite right to ensure that all voices come into the arena and that all opinions come to the table, but when the process takes place in a veiled sense, then I object, and I know of and can name various examples of consultants. (Veteran information manager, 29/3/01)

The interviews revealed a certain lack of depth and clarity surrounding the definition of ethics and ethical rules. In many cases the statements were vague, such as the comment that "it's a strong gut feeling." When asked whether they discuss ethical issues at the office, responses like "yes, absolutely, something pops up quite often" were typical.

For some, ethics is mainly a question of which tasks one can and cannot accept. Not unexpectedly, working on behalf of a clearly non-democratic interest is considered unethical. Many also mentioned tobacco companies as unacceptable clients, and some mentioned oil companies. Many consultants said that their firms allow individual employees to refuse tasks that run counter to their personal morality, such as promoting nuclear energy or certain types of consumer products.

Very little mention was made of procedural issues, that is, the appropriateness of certain strategies and methods. Some discussed ethics in terms of how information should be formulated and presented, like "For me, ethics means that information is accurate, true, factual and not biased."

> Opinion-constructing must—of course!—fulfill ethical requirements of truth and relevance. Otherwise it is propaganda. The more skilful one is, the more important it is to live up to ethical demands. (Senior consultant 2, 15/15/01)

Several critical views were expressed on the subject of ethics, one of which is a general criticism over the lack of debate on ethics within the PR industry and at individual companies. Criticism was also directed at the inadequacy and inefficacy of formal ethical norms and regulations, including the international codes and the codes of the Swedish professional organizations:

> There is too little ethical debate in this guild ... The old rules that have been in the books since the 1950s are no longer relevant to how things work today. I think you have to keep this kind of debate alive if you are going to remain credible. (Veteran information manager 30/3/01)

> There are no good ethical rules. They are too fuzzy ... they are so abstract that you can interpret them however you like. It's not possible to say that this is right or wrong based on the rules, so I don't think they are much good. It should be clear what we are and what we stand for. (Female consultant, PR firm executive, 6/12/01)

Most PR firms abstain from party political tasks. Several reasons were given for this policy, including the argument that employees should not be forced to work against their own political views. Underlying this position is the perhaps more essential desire to avoid being overtly associated with a particular party. It is worth recalling that several of the more well-known firms in Sweden were established by people working in organizations closely tied to political parties, particularly conservative ones. So while they do not hesitate to conduct work that supports a political or ideological agenda, they avoid tasks which are purely party political.

SUMMARY OF RESULTS

This research project represents the first attempt to study the Swedish information and PR consulting sector. The findings are, except for documents and records, based on interviews with PR consultants, journalists, and information managers.

To begin with, it is clear that the Swedish PR industry rose through close associations with the political sphere. Several consultants, among them those who now own the largest companies, had previously worked in political organizations, especially conservative ones. Some had also worked in journalism. Thus, many PR professionals work to exert influence on those spheres where they have been brought up.

Turning to the relationship between consultants and journalists, contact between the two groups seems to vary. While some consultants claimed to be in frequent contact with journalists, others said that they have more modest contacts (but then often others in their PR firm have more contact). In general, the relationship appears to be cooperative rather than competitive and virtually pretty close, a pattern that reinforces other research conducted on the relationship between institutional and journalistic actors (see, for example, Sigal, 1973; Gans, 1979; Ericson et al., 1989; also Larsson, 1998, 2002). However, the relationship can hardly be described as symbiotic, as between politicians and the media. Contact between the groups is seldom driven by direct interpersonal connections—ongoing one-on-one relationships between journalists and PR consultants are rare. Here it is mainly a matter of telephone and e-mail contact, mostly from the consultant side, with different media and news desks depending on the subject and matter of influence.

In terms of the respondents' general views on the role of PR in democracy, the study confirms the expectation that PR consultants are for the most part uncritical of their profession. Most of those interviewed see themselves clearly as a support to the democratic process of interest articulation. With only a few exceptions, they see no democratic problems with their activities. In response to the assertion that consultants are "undemocratic," in the sense that while working to influence society and politics they operate without a democratic mandate (based on membership or electoral support) and without a genuine engagement in the issues, the most prevalent argument is that their commissioned services are simply an outsourcing of work that would have been conducted by the client company or institution anyway.

It is interesting to note what appears to be a generational difference in the consultant corps whereby the older respondents appear more likely to express some misgivings about PR's contribution to democracy than do their younger colleagues. The same observation can be made of the female respondents compared to men. The consultants expressing concern over the democratic impact of PR are particularly critical of opinion-constructing activities. Some voiced concern over the issues of transparency, ethics and what might be called the problem of the unlevel playing field—that is, the more money an organization has, the easier it is to hire PR experts to gain access to the media and decision makers. Many respondents stated that PR activity must be ethical, though even when being prompted to elaborate on what ethical practice actually is, statements about ethics remained vague and general.

The journalists interviewed in this study displayed a basic acceptance of PR operations in Sweden. Quite a few even believe that PR consultants help ease the journalistic workload, although others, particularly those from the more leftist press, expressed concern over the democratic implications of PR's opinion and lobby activities. Several journalists are very sceptical of PR efforts to steer opinion and are particularly negative toward PR-based opinion polls.

These findings can be compared to the studies of Herbst (1998) on the views of different groups—including journalists—about public opinion in the democratic process. In her study, journalists expressed a basic faith in consultants (lobbyists in her terminology), both in terms of their function as information providers and as representatives of different opinions. Lobbyists are seen as more useful than press secretaries since they tend to have information on upcoming issues and debates, for example. Like their Swedish colleagues, the journalists in Herbst's study were skeptical of polls as news material, although they, like their counterparts, displayed ambivalence in this regard since they would use this material if it provides a good story.

The fact that many journalists in the present study are uncritical of the media influence of PR consultants is interesting. Journalists have long accepted that public and private organizations actively seek media coverage in their opinion-forming activities and that not all, or perhaps most, news is purely journalist-driven. It would also appear that they accept the influence of hired consultants who seek to create opinions for strictly strategic purposes, who do not necessarily share the views they attempt to spread in the media, and who often use hidden methods and fabricated messengers.

Apparently journalism as a whole—the democratic diffuser and monitor of information—does not see the activities of consultants as problematic. Perhaps they do not want to know about it, since recognition of this would create economic, ethical, and professional problems. The journalist corps, with some exceptions, appears to lack self-reflection and criticism in terms of their relationship to the PR industry.

DISCUSSION AND CONCLUSION

Communication and PR consultants have grown strong during the 1990s, in Sweden and Scandinavia as well as in Europe. Assisting corporations, government authorities, interest organizations, and political parties in their efforts to influence public opinion and political decision making, the consulting sector has become a new and important actor alongside the traditional players in the political game.

For Sweden's part, important changes have taken place in the political setting. Whereas previously Sweden's political interest representation landscape could be described as a combination of parliamentarism and corporatism, a greater degree of fragmentation has occurred which has rendered the system somewhat more pluralistic at the expense of umbrella corporatist structures. In other words, the previous situation of nearly universal institutional representation is increasingly characterized by the participation of non-institutional actors. In this setting, there is an increased competition for influence over public opinion and legislative decisions, and hence the growth of opinion-building and lobbying activities. This development has led to a situation described by some as "opinion society" (Holmberg & Weibull, 1998), where the image of a phenomenon is increasingly more important than its substance, just as a brand label is increasingly more important than the product.

Here is where PR consultants come in, helping clients build a favorable public opinion. This development can be seen as a professionalization of the production of ideology and opinion formation in society. Organizations hand over their opinion activities to external experts instead of using their own actors. Consultants can operate from a more hidden part of the stage, and their activity carries with it certain democratic disadvantages, such as the lack of a mandate from citizens or membership groups and the fact that their engagement in issues is contracted rather than "genuine." They certainly act on behalf of a client, but they also appear as their own driving force in the public discourse.

PR consultants have established themselves as a significant actor in the democratic process through their special "competence" in mobilizing public opinion and lobbying decision makers. They have altered the cast of characters as well as the stage upon which the public discourse takes place. The question is whether this new societal phenomenon implies that the public discourse is being transformed. This is, in any case, what Mayhew (1997) meant by his term the New Public.

Opinion activities can be seen both as a goal and a means. They are a means in the sense that they mobilize opinion with the aim of swaying politicians and other actors to make decisions favoring the client. But opinion activity can also be a goal in itself in the sense that a favorable image enhances the status and power of the client in society generally.

The handing over of interest articulation and opinion constructing to external actors implies not only that organizations part with one of their basic ideological functions, but also that a new profession arises with its own experts. Opinion building has thus been professionalized with its own corps standing outside the organizations that are bearers of different ideologies, societal ideas, and issues. These consultants create an opinion-building competence independent of the client and subject. To be seen is to have power, as Thompson (1995) proclaimed. There is reason to assert that this sector has grown so strong that one can speak of a *fourth actor* in Swedish society, aside from the collective citizenry, the media, and parties and organizations.

Several democracy problems can be identified in terms of the growth of the consulting industry. One applies to the sector's lack of transparency, meaning that they can act without being seen and beyond scrutiny—and without needing to take responsibility in public. Another problem is the regimented culture of influence created by this sector that floats freely between different interests in society, with the result that ideological values and political identities are increasingly eroded. A basic democratic question is whether the production of ideology can and ought to be professionalized.

From the study presented, it seems fair to suggest that PR consulting activities could carry the risk of weakening basic democratic values such as equality between groups and the demand for openness and transparency. What can be stated with some certainty is that the PR consulting industry has become a power factor in Swedish society and that it exerts influence on democratic processes in Sweden.

8

Public Relations as Theatre: Key Players in the Evolution of British Public Relations

Jacquie L'Etang
Stirling Media Research Institute

This chapter aims to sketch out briefly the key influences on the development of British public relations and to identify some of the dramatis personae who shaped those developments. Elsewhere I have recounted in detail the key political, economic, and social developments which led to the evolution of the new and distinctive occupation of public relations (L'Etang, 2004). Here the historical context is purely backdrop and this chapter foregrounds the key actors and actresses who defined and defended the new occupation from its opponents (largely consisting of the media) and who instigated the professionalisation process through the establishment and development of the professional body in the UK, the Institute of Public Relations (IPR). Thus, the focus is on key historical figures within the IPR. The theatrical metaphor is appropriate since public relations practitioners, like lawyers, may appear on the public stage, defend their clients, prosecute opponents, and need to respond to public opinion. The marketing side of public relations can be seen as front-of-house. The public side of the work is complemented by much behind-the-scenes work, which does not solely consist of rehearsal for public performance but also of research and understanding of discourse, scripts, emotions, and the perspectives of other parties. Production and direction processes are intrinsic to analysis and creativity. Public relations practitioners, like actors, are concerned with method, technique, and practice. There are moments of "showtime" during "beauty parades" (pitching) and internal presentations. There is also specialist work behind-the-scenes which presents some challenges to democratic practice: the area of lobbying, which focuses on communication between elites.

This chapter is largely based on nearly 70 oral history interviews gathered during the 1990s and focuses on the crucial 1940s, 1950s, and 1960s. As far as possible the actors speak for themselves, although critical commentary is also provided to contextualise the data. Very little of this empirical material has been previously published and it is presented here as a way of balancing a number of imbalances in currently published literature on the history of public relations, which tends to focus on the United States. Valuable histories of U.S. public relations

143

have been written by Cutlip (1994) and there have also been some excellent monographical books and articles (Hiebert, 1966; Tedlow, 1979; Pearson, 1992; Marchand, 1998). There has also been an attempt to colligate historical detail by thematising and characterising some structure onto historical events, for example, Cutlip (1994). Grunig and Hunt (1984) went further by linking historical periods with certain types of public relations practice, implying an ethical progression in practice over a period of time. The difficulty with such approaches is that in attempting to delineate a story and characterise phases of development, the historian's schema are likely to shape interpretation. As Pearson perspicaciously noted:

> The need to find answers is an important part of the historian's motivation. Burke (1957) suggested that all writers, including those who write history, write to work through personal problems. And Wise (1980) argued that the text of historical scholarship needs to be understood as a personal response on the part of its author to contemporary situational exigencies, just as primary recorded texts of historical characters need to be understood as situationally conditioned ... No single, obviously correct public relations history exists; rather, there are a plurality of public relations histories. (Pearson, 1992, p. 112)

Critical work on public relations history has been conducted by the social theorist Stuart Ewen (1996), and Larry Tye's biography of the very well-known U.S. publicist Ed Bernays presented an initial and fascinating glimpse into the archive of this dominant (and domineering) figure (Tye, 1998). In my own research (L'Etang, 2004) a broad-ranging narrative is constructed linking the evolution of the public relations occupation in the early 20th century to key political, economic, social, and technological developments informed by methodological approaches drawn from sociological history and focusing on a key concern of public relations practitioners: that of professionalisation. This chapter is rather different and aims to flesh out for the record some of the main characters who influenced the development of the profession and the social world they inhabited. Thus, the emphasis is on partial and reflexive interpretations of British public relations practitioners of an earlier age, their self-identity, their heroes, their aspirations, and their self-identity.

BEHIND THE SCENES—RESEARCH METHOD

Being privileged to meet and listen to so many from the formative generation was a fascinating insight into other worlds and an earlier age. All the interviews were tape-recorded, transcribed, and sent to interviewees for them to read and comment upon. Since many were in their late 70s and 80s, this process enabled them to add further details, correct mistakes, and to indicate any material which they did not wish attributed. Many were extremely generous with their time and also took pains to send me supplementary material, to lend me books, and, in a number of cases, a fruitful and extensive correspondence developed.

There is, of course, one important caveat. As one interviewee pointed out with some acerbity, "You are too late, they are all dead!" And, of course, it was true that I was indeed unable to interview many participants in the creation of the public relations scene: public relations began in Britain in the 1920s and my interviews were largely conducted in the mid-1990s. The majority of those I interviewed had entered public relations after the Second World War and, of these, it is those with good luck and the strongest genes that have necessarily shaped the tale. Likewise, those who deposit material in archives are more likely to become the focus of research. And, I could not fail to be aware that those I interviewed were past masters and mistresses of impression management and the opportunity that my project offered for their place in history to be recorded. The interview material I collected was partial but colourful, and conveyed the atmosphere and concerns of the times most vividly. I was also made aware of rivalries and factions in a way that did not always emerge so clearly in the institutional sources I used to triangulate my historical project. Here I have chosen to present insights from key characters on major themes that affected the occupation and to draw out some underlying issues, for example, in relation to gender and class. In selecting the "key characters," I have focused on the names of those given most emphasis by all those I interviewed. Methodologically this could be considered "snowballing the snowballs" (!) since all interviewees were asked to recommend other potential sources for interview. The initial list came from a mailing to the Institute of Public Relations targeting those with membership dates in the 1950s and a necessarily filtered list given to me by Sam Black, then Honorary Professor of the University of Stirling. Those sampled included 19 former Presidents of the Institute of Public Relations, six holders of the Stephen Tallents Medal, 12 Honorary Fellows, and three Presidents of the International Public Relations Association (IPRA).

This chapter consists of memories, opinions, judgements and autobiographical quotes, interwoven with some contextualised material. To an extent this chapter focuses on the social and cultural aspects of public relations history in Britain. Data have been interpreted from a critical perspective framed by the historical sociological paradigm. Interpretation was informed by postgraduate education in the fields of history, social justice and public relations, and experience of teaching public relations at the postgraduate level since 1989 on Britain's first postgraduate degree in the subject. There were two important close relationships with well-known British practitioners appointed as Honorary professors at the University of Stirling for several terms of office, Sam Black and Tim Traverse-Healy (the latter also held a Visiting Chair at the University of Stirling during 1994), which facilitated a deep understanding of two leading lights of the Institute of Public Relations' post-war generation and their perspectives on public relations, education, and theory. Tensions between education and practice were also experienced during the early 1990s and I was very active in the now defunct Public Relations Educators' Forum in an era when the Institute of Public Relations often appeared to try and control the curriculum. Thus, in writing this chapter I experienced conflicting emotions. As far as possible I have tried here to be fair and accurate, while at the same time presenting an overall flavour of the period drama: The Early Years of British Public Relations.

THE BACKDROP

The key structural elements which drove the development of public relations in Britain in the 20th century were democratisation, widening franchise, colonialism and (later) decolonisation, international tensions resulting from ideologically driven power blocks, historical grievances, and war (both total and Cold). In addition there was technological change which facilitated the process of cultural exchange and globalisation begun by the earliest explorers, merchants, and colonisers.

While wartime produced inevitable distortions of communication through the devious use of communication to mislead the enemy, reassure the national public, lead public opinion in several countries simultaneously, maintain support of existing allies and cultivate new allies, peacetime also presented international challenges which meant that diplomatic practice increasingly had an important role in international media management.

The concept of propaganda as a negative and morally wrong practice became more common throughout the 20th century (see discussion in L'Etang, chapter 2, this volume). Yet the complexity of modern life required governments and organisations to communicate with stakeholders and a democratic context created the expectation that they would at least be informed, if not consulted about ongoing issues. The horrendous effects of two devastating world wars within 21 years of each other raised many questions and contributed to political change. For example, a second "Khaki election" of 1918 (the first was after the Boer War) had a much widened franchise (all men over 21, all women over 30), which trebled the size of the electorate, and in 1928 there was a further expansion to include women over 21, which meant that voting was finally a right for adult citizens. Political division on class lines, the growth of the trades union movement, and the increasing confidence and growth of the embryonic Labour Party were important factors in considerable social and economic change such as improved housing, education, and social welfare. Diversity of interests had implications for promotional roles and media relations. For example, the Trades Union Congress (TUC) and the Labour Party subsidised *The Herald* for a number of years and the impetus for the highly influential Beveridge Report was the consequence of political lobbying by the TUC at the Ministry of Health in 1941 (K. Williams, 1998, pp. 65, 137). The 1945 general election was a landslide victory for Labour and brought in a government that implemented improvements in social welfare and education, changes likely to lead to a much more critical and active citizenry. On an intellectual level, the development of the Frankfurt School can be seen as particularly important in facilitating change and alternative lifestyles that became fashionable in the 1960s. Widening choices and increasing diversity in popular culture were important in challenges to orthodoxy and social conventions.

The process of industrialisation and modernisation had considerable implications for mass communications and the increase of political democracy was "matched by the concomitant growth of state power" (Ward, 1989, p. 2). Nationalisation and denationalisation resulted in considerable struggles in communicative space for legitimacy and control. Post-war industrial processes translated wartime technological developments into peacetime products. Rapid commercialisation of these was achieved through the creation of new markets and the growth of consumerism: both required communication as a fundamental plank in the process of Britain's economic recovery. Part of the social change and consumer expectations which accompanied the arrival of new products and services was a greater awareness of the process of identity construction via product purchase. Management and marketing language have permeated private space and individuals now commodify themselves as they compete for jobs, promotion, social cachet, or celebrity such as that achieved through reality TV. Young children learn skateboarding tricks because they hope for sponsorship, and even supposedly left-wing academics use promotional techniques and media publicity to enhance their position in order to compete for promotion on what are ideologically Thatcherite assumptions. By 1991 Andrew Wernick had published his seminal text *Promotional Culture*, which explored the cultural impacts of advertising:

> To facilitate an analysis of the relation of advertising to ideology, and of both to the maintenance of the capitalist order, which can take account of the particular way that advertising articulates with social values and, through that, with the wider processes of social reproduction. (Wernick, 1991, p. 24)

Wernick's thesis was subtly different in approach to earlier critical work by social theorist Stuart Ewen, who argued that political and commercial requirements for familial consumption transformed advertising from an agent of consumer demand to an agent in the "management of consciousness" (Wernick, 1991, p. 25). However, for Wernick, advertising's ideological influence was a side effect rather than an intent:

> [Advertising's] raison d'etre is not as a socialising or propagandising agency at all. Those who shape and transmit its symbolic material have no intrinsic interest in what, ideologically, that material might mean.

> Advertising is an entirely instrumental process. You promote to sell. You sell to get money, in turn to get more money or else to exchange it for something else. In this, the mobilisation of affect through the invocation of values is strictly a tool. (Wernick, 1991, p. 26)

So to some degree Wernick let advertising off the hook of social responsibility or charges of manipulation emerging from Marxist-influenced critics. Because Wernick reduced advertising to a mere technique or process, it became possible to identify public relations as ideologically influential and strategic discipline or partner (because according to Wernick advertising is simply one tool alongside others such as exhibitions, Web pages, e-mail, media relations, etc). Wernick did not use the term public relations, but "promotion," which he defined as follows:

> Promotion crosses the line between advertising, packaging, and design, and is applicable as well, to activities beyond the immediately commercial. It can even (as in "promoting health") be used in a way which takes us beyond the competitive exchange altogether. For current purposes, though, I have confined it to cases where something, though not necessarily for money is being promoted for sale—while recognising that the metaphorical diffusion of the word, wherein it has come to mean any kind of propagation (including that of ideas, causes, and programmes), reflects a real historical tendency for all such discourse to acquire an advertising character. (Wernick, 1991, p. 182)

Wernick explored the notion that promotion has gradually (and he was keen to avoid periodization) become a cultural dominant structuring process which infiltrates society's values and processes. Yet, as he pointed out:

> Promotion—unlike any cultural movement—is not only not a class phenomenon, it is not an expressive one either . . . [it] is a mode of communication, a species of rhetoric. It is not defined by what it says but by what it does. (Wernick, 1991, p. 184)

Yet questions as to the impact of public relations—"what it does" (from the practitioner's point of view, the effectiveness of programmes)—remain a relatively under-researched and unresolved area.

These very broad questions about the emergence and rationale for an occupation called "public relations" suggest that the study of practitioners and the practice should be central to contemporary sociological concerns, yet at present there is a major gap in terms of ethnographic social scientific research in the field. This means there is less in the way of inductive research focused on practitioners and the work they do; hence the significance of Pieczka's contributions to this volume (see chapters 15, 16). This historical chapter and chapter 2 on PR and propaganda aim to give some partial insight into the world, values, culture, and ideology of practitioners from the 1950s and 1960s in the context of those times.

THE PROLOGUE

The earliest evidence of public relations work, as opposed to advertising and publicity, emerged in Britain in the 1920s and 1930s in local and central government. Putting to one side for the moment the importance of communications in wartime, British government found itself increasingly required to communicate with citizens following democratisation, widening franchise, and increased social and economic legislation. The influence of civil servants on the formation of the public relations occupation and core concepts such as exchange of information, managing public opinion, and internal and external intelligence gathering were well developed and articulated in the journal *Public Administration*, which from 1923 had published "a succession of able articles, concerning Public Relations, a subject hot from the oven, or perhaps still in the mixing bowl" (Simey in L'Etang, 2004, p. 24).

The collaboration between senior civil servant Sir Stephen Tallents (Secretary of the Empire Marketing Board in the mid-1920s) and the leader of the British Documentary Film Unit, John Grierson, was also highly significant in elaborating principles and practice of public relations. Tallents wrote the blueprint for The British Council (founded 1934) in his pamphlet *The Projection of England* in 1932, which emphasised the importance of cultural projection and publicity for a nation's identity, self-image, economics, and politics and argued that promotion was essential to achieve diplomatic advantage. His ideas were ultimately picked up in higher political echelons and were influential in making the notion of peacetime propaganda acceptable to many who thought it was inappropriate for democracies. He was President of the Institute of Public Relations in 1948 and 1952 (though according to one source, "Stephen Tallents was President twice because we couldn't agree on who to ask"). Grierson, a Scot, benefited from Tallents' patronage but his influence was much wider than the films for which he is largely remembered. He was an energetic person who wrote extensively on the subjects of public relations and propaganda and gave an inspirational address to the Institute of Public Relations in 1950 that had considerable impact on the–then President Alan Hess. The Grierson Archive (based at the University of Stirling) contains many papers that demonstrate Grierson's contribution to the intellectual development of public relations. Grierson's energy and enthusiasm for his subject are apparent and the impact of his ideas to some degree guaranteed due to his access via Sir Stephen Tallents (mentor and to some degree official sponsor of his work) to elite circles in British government and key contacts in British business (L'Etang, 2000).

Grierson corresponded with a range of interested parties—for example, Christopher Mann, Publicity and Press Agent during 1930 (G2:22:9)—and lectured and published his ideas on a range of topics including propaganda and public relations (G4A:3:2), propaganda and education (G4:19:5), public information (G4:20:13), communications in diplomacy and international relations (G4:20:22), communication and democratic practice (G4:19:11), and art as communication (G4:21:4). He travelled extensively and lectured internationally, advising other governments on documentary film as public information; for example, in 1939 the New Zealand Public Relations Council gained support from the Minister of Lands in charge of tourist and health resorts to seek Grierson's services (G3:15:17). Grierson's legacy was his ability to see the significance of the public relations role in democratic society and to argue for its extension to the highest levels bearing major responsibiity for democratic education. His long-lasting contribution to professional public relations was to add to practitioners' idealism about their social role and their sense of grandeur and appropriate place in society. Others who took up this particular theme and were inclined to ponder on the "philosophy" of public relations within the Institute included Alan Hess, Roger Wimbush (President 1951–1952), R. A. Paget-Cooke (President 1959–1960), and Tim Traverse-Healy (President 1967–1968).

In the private sector there were some individuals working in the areas of transport (notably London Transport, Southern Railways, Port of London) and utilities (Gas, Light & Coke), but there were few consultancies pre-war (L'Etang, 2004, pp. 51–57). Exceptions that were founder organisations of the IPR were Hereward Phillips Ltd, LPE (London Press Exchange) and F. C. Pritchard Wood and Partners Ltd (*Public Relations*, 1(1), 1948, pp. 16–17). LPE and Pritchard Wood began as advertising agencies and LPE contained some influential and important figures in public relations history. Most important from the point of view of the intellectual development of the field was Mark Abrams, an economic researcher from the London School of Economics who, in the 1930s, developed much of the necessary statistical knowledge (professional expertise) that can be applied to public relations work. Others may have been more colourful characters, but Abrams was quietly influential behind the scenes and in 1939 became Head of Propaganda Research for the BBC, in 1941 took a similar post at the Foreign Office, and ended the war in the Psychological Warfare Branch at Supreme Allied Headquarters (L'Etang, 2004, pp. 31, 103). A range of advertising agencies moved into public relations in the 1950s (see L'Etang, 2004, pp. 103–105), thus influencing its culture and shifting the focus of practice towards marketing-orientated concerns. Post-war, the contraction of journalism led to an influx of ex-journalists whose skills enabled them to mimic news source styles and offer clients publicity opportunities that seemed tantamount to free advertising (L'Etang, 2004, p. 124). The marriage of marketing and media relations appears to have shaped strongly the character and development of public relations over the next 30 years or so away from its origins as strategic intelligence gathering, democratic education, and citizen feedback.

ACT I: SPOOKS AND SPIES: DRAMATIS PERSONAE

One of the most important features of public relations history which has not been forgotten but is quite difficult to track is that of the cadre of practitioners who worked in the capacity of intelligence officers or spies as well as public relations practitioners. The reason that this is so inevitably intriguing is that it clearly contradicts the commonly assumed dualism between propaganda and public relations. For such men, the overlap between public relations and propaganda work (see chapter 2, this volume) was part of their biography. While there are examples from the Great War such as Sydney Walton, whose career included political public relations and consultancy (for details, see L'Etang, 2004, pp. 52–53), the focus here is on those figures who influenced notions of public relations in a key period of expansion and the early professionalisation process. As well-known pre-war practitioner Hereward Phillips explained:

> The [Second World] war saw the real creation and establishment of public relations in Britain. For months before the outbreak a picked team had been planning the organisation of a comprehensive Ministry of Information, covering all means of communication. There was also a Department of Political Warfare responsible for underground propaganda. Elephantine, bureaucratic—it was easy to criticise the Ministry of Information, but from it emerged a thorough technique, the best of which has been carried on in the present Central Office of Information. It was during the war that every Government Department appointed public relations officers, often with substantial staffs. Few of the people appointed had special qualifications for the work, but as the years passed they began to make themselves useful in many different ways—preparing literature, visual material, producing films. (*Public Relations*, April 1961, p. 12)

The best-known of those involved in intelligence operations was Colonel Maurice Buckmaster, who was Head of Special Operations Executive (SOE) "F" (France) Section responsible for dropping British spies into France in the Second World War to work with the French Resistance Forces. Subsequently, he worked in public relations for Ford (UK) and the French champagne industry. He became a Fellow of the IPR in 1954 and was President from 1955–1956. In a letter to me, his son—also a public relations practitioner—suggested that:

> The networking or "réseau" pattern that my father "operated" was not so dissimilar to those he operated with Vera Atkins as "F" section. (Private correspondence 31/1/97)

This is the only concrete example I have been able to trace of a "concept" being translated from intelligence to public relations. The main connection is simply that which is contained in the curriculum vitae of a number of practitioners and the power this part of history has played in public relations mythology, at least for one generation. To my knowledge, none of those practitioners committed their ideas about public relations and propaganda to paper, and the only practitioner from the war and pre-war period to do so was John Grierson (as discussed earlier), up to and including his period as Director of Mass Communications at UNESCO.

While much of Buckmaster's appeal can be attributed to his impressive war record, some could be attributed to his socially elite status and access to influential people; for example:

> Networking is not a new invention ... He was a member of "Pop" (slang name for the invitation-only exclusive club The Eton Society) when he was at Eton and I guess knew all sorts of people around this scene. He very much had that view of the gentleman and what the gentleman did and what the gentleman didn't do ... He was an important figure in the business and the sort of man who added lustre to the PR business and part of the PR industry's own public relations ... He and Alan Campbell Johnson were the two people who had status already. (Interview No. 35)

Buckmaster's mythological status was enhanced by a review of Buckmaster's book *Specially Employed* (1953) about the underground since in France which concluded 'members of the Institute can be very proud of the part played by their colleague, Maurice Buckmaster (*Public Relations* 5,(2), 1953, p. 21).

According to his son, Buckmaster collaborated with a number of practitioners, including the well-known Bryan Samain (Chief Publicity Officer for The Cementation Group of Companies), and socialised with, among others, the distinguished war veteran Bill Simpson, pre-war practitioner Freddy Gillman, Alan Eden-Green, Roger Wimbush, and Tim Traverse-Healy (Private notes attached to correspondence 3/2/97).

Buckmaster's influence continued into the 1960s, as PR author Pat Bowman recalled:

> He was a great PR man, a great guide and mentor to many of us in my generation ... he was the man who introduced me to my first literary agent along with Nigel Ellis for the books we wrote together. (Interview 28/9/96)

A well-known practitioner and President of the IPR from 1957–1958, Bill Simpson also had an impressive war record and public persona beyond public relations (he appeared on *This Is Your Life* in April 1961). Shot down in France "a war pilot hero, had his hands and face burnt in the war, a gallant officer" (Alan Campbell Johnson, Interview, March 1994). Though severely wounded, he managed to make contact with the Resistance and in his autobiography recalled "movingly of the many friends he made in the Resistance, operating under the hands of the Vichy government" (*Public Relations*, January 1956, p. 2). Simpson was recruited to work for British European Airways by a former Intelligence Officer in 1948 and joined the IPR due to the influence of Maurice Buckmaster and Alan Campbell Johnson, thus illustrating networking in practice. His background included journalism (*Sunday Express*) and advertising (E. Walter George), and he understood the expansion of public relations post-war as being the result of:

> people looking around for something to do and this was a natural [development] ... it coincided with the beginnings of the new BBC which was able to say a little more than they had been while the war was on ... there was a general sort of sprouting of information ... censorship had stopped. (Interview 14/2/97)

And he defined the public relations role both in tactical and in strategic terms, again showing that public relations in Britain was understood by some organisations as a sophisticated concept relatively early in the practice's history: "a matter of relations with the media, films, but also political; I mean I worked only for the Chairman and was in all the top consultations" (Interview 14/2/97).

Simpson also shared something of the motivation and idealism that lay behind early practitioners' views of public relations' role in society: "I think everything that went on in our minds was conditioned by the appalling war, the appalling effects of it and wanting to make a slightly better world. I know it sounds a bit pompous" (Interview 14/2/97).

Simpson interestingly characterised practitioners as "mostly upper middle class professional people who hadn't got a particular profession" and proposed the unusual insight that public relations grew in response to expansion of the middle class "which had become very powerful and still is very powerful" (Interview 14/2/97).

Freddie Gillman OBE was a local newspaper journalist from 1915–1939 and during the war worked in a variety of posts in Fighter Command and the Air Ministry, where he finished the war as Deputy Director of Public Relations. He made an effort to record some of the key points in public relations history building on the published work of senior civil servants Sir Tom Fife Clark (COI and President 1958–1959) and F. D. Bickerton (Ministry of Pensions).

There are a few other examples of men with backgrounds in Intelligence (I did not come across any examples of women), mostly tracked through obituaries and some of the interview data, although some interviewees did not wish to be named when discussing such matters. A typical unattributable comment was the insight from one interviewee that "when I visited Voice & Vision, the public affairs man was the former head of military intelligence or communication... at the Ministry of Defence" (Transcript 37). One acknowledged example of the intelligence intake was Denys Brooke-Hart (IPR President 1962–1963), who "served throughout the war in special operations in the Intelligence Service" before working in the oil industry and forming his own consultancy, Brooke-Hart. Later he was Chairman of Brooke-Hart/Ruder Finn Int. (in New York) and Vice-President of Ruder-Finn in the United States (*Public Relations*, October 1962). During the war he was: "One of the first members of 'the Phantoms', that highly mobile intelligence and communications force, the envy of many in the many theatres of operation. He got an immediate award of Military Cross at Arnhem—for an outstanding feat of leadership, skill and communications" (*Public Relations*, 13(4), 1961, p. 43).

Jack Beddington, who had worked for Shell pre-war as head of Advertising and Film (1927–1946), became Head of the Film Division in the Ministry of Information and post-war worked for the consultancy Colman, Prentis, Varley and later still chairman of Voice and Vision. Another example was Allan Ashbourne, who closed his publicity business in Nottingham in 1940 to join the Ministry of Home Security with responsibilities encompassing civil defence at home and abroad, including a period as Civil Defence Commissioner for Palestine (*Public Relations*, April 1962). Gerald Samson was a Far Eastern correspondent and war correspondent for Reuters before working for Air Ministry Intelligence (*Public Relations*, 22(2), 1969, p. 25) prior to his career in consultancy. Others included Arthur Wallis—"I was channelled into propaganda warfare [in MoI]... I was a journalist in the provinces before the war" (Interview in IPR archive, unreferenced)—and E. D. O'Brien, a Fellow of the IPR who had a background in Conservative Central Office and later set up his own consultancy, but during the war "was vigorously engaged in trying to keep the press in the neutral countries in sympathy with the United Kingdom" (*Communicator* 1979).

Arthur Cain, a very keen PR educator, was remembered by many as a great character, born in 1903, whose early career was as a railway engineer. After joining the police, he became a Detective Inspector in special branch "dealing with Ramsay MacDonald and Gandhi among others" (*Public Relations*, 15(3), 1998, p. 14) and his duties also included, very ironically, shadowing John Grierson.

A curious and probably forgotten member of the IPR was Ellic Howe, whose wartime pseudonym was Armin Hull, under which name he was responsible for printing black propaganda for Sefton Delmar. "Black" material did not acknowledge the source was British but purported to be of German origin and conveyed via underground sources. For example, faked issues of the German astrological periodical *Zenit* were produced along with prophetic verse in the style of Nostradamus (One of Hitler's advisers in the early part of the war was the Swiss astrologist, Karl Ernst Krafft) (Howe, 1967, p. 12).

Others involved in the shadowy world included Eric Stenton, whose career included periods in the Intelligence Corps and BBC External Services (*Communicator*, March 1979, p. 8), and Alan Hadden, who post-war became a Manager, Employee Information Division, Industrial Relations Department, Shell who said: "As Colonel Buckmaster has told you, I am an erstwhile journalist, a one-time propagandist" (*Public Relations*, 11(2), 1959, p. 14). Lionel Altman "was over four years in Intelligence during the war ... a lot of the time in the war people were involved in political public relations and many of them did go into PR" (Interview in IPR archive, unreferenced).

These examples indicate conceptual and applied overlaps between the fields of intelligence and public relations since these named individuals were able to progress coherently from one domain to another. The evidence suggests certain common concepts, information and interpretation (analytical skills), use of networks, communication skills, and also a degree of censorship or subterfuge. At the outset, then, there was a tension between some of the origins of public relations and espoused ideals of transparency and honesty. It is little wonder that public relations has struggled to separate itself from propaganda. The wartime activities of some public relations practitioners are a crucial part of public relations mythology in the occupational culture and link it to more noble ideals of heroism and self-sacrifice. The agent, hidden from the public view yet working in the public's benefit, ties in to Griersonian notions of an elite group of communicators responsible for public education and the practice of good democracy.

ACT II: MYTHS, MENTORS, AND PUBLIC RELATIONS CULTURE

Alan Campbell-Johnson (CIE, OBE, Legion of Merit USA), a much revered pre-war practitioner and President from 1956–1957, articulated a common view in identifying Sir Stephen Tallents as a key champion for public relations:

> Tallents' prestige was important for the founding of the Institute and [Richard "Dick"] Forman got him to take the front line role. Forman was the second President and it was essentially Forman who activated the IPR and got all the local government men to come in and support PR. (Interview March 1994)

Bill Simpson (IPR President 1957–1958) concurred: "Tallents was a key man, pure as pure and a very nice fellow, a knighthood and highly respectable and he set a very good tone" (Interview 14/2/97). Similarly, Nigel Ellis (IPR President 1971–1972) described Tallents as, "a lovely man, gallant, judgement delightful, imposing" (Interview 30/8/96).

Campbell-Johnson was educated at public school (in UK context that means private school as opposed to state school)—Westminster and Oxford. Between 1937 and 1940 he was political secretary to Sir Archibald Sinclair, Liberal leader, and wrote biographies of Anthony Eden and Lord Halifax. His war service in the RAF included 4 years on the Headquarters Staff of Lord Mountbatten at Combined Operations and South-east Asia Command. From 1947–1948 he was Lord Mountbatten's Press Attaché in India. His diary of that period was the first authoritative account to be published of the transfer of power in India. Pre-war, Campbell-Johnson had worked for a press syndicating agency and later joined Richard Forman at the London Press Exchange. In the latter stages of the war, Campbell-Johnson became Mountbatten's Public Relations Officer when he was Viceroy of India during the crucial transfer of power to India and post-war set up his own business with the support of the advertising company Macy's with "an extremely able woman named Athena Cross... until 1951 when [she] left my business to re-join her husband who had been in government PR" (Interview March 1994). Campbell-Johnson's main clients were Esso and Procter and Gamble and his subsequent close friendship with John Hill ensured a stream of work via Hill & Knowlton as that consultancy appears to have adopted the notion of "think global, act local" as early as the 1950s. Even in his 80s, Campbell-Johnson was carrying out work for Coca-Cola.

Author and educator Pat Bowman remembered Campbell-Johnson and Buckmaster as inspirational. As he explained:

> They were the kind of men who'd got the weight, the gravitas, as well as the technical competence to impress managements whether they were on the staff or whether they were consultants. (Interview 28/9/96)

This quote hints at the difficulties encountered by practitioners attempting to establish their craft as an organisational necessity at the highest level.

Campbell-Johnson cited Sir Fife Clark (President 1958–1959) as a key influence in the IPR:

> He effected the transfer of the Ministry of Information into a peacetime instrument (Central Office of Information (CoI)). He was very much a background man, he never had an interest in promoting himself. He had been PR under both Churchill and Attlee and he was knighted [for his work]. (Interview March 1994)

Likewise, Eric Gould, who joined the IPR in 1954, claimed:

> The people who were held in fairly high regard at that time were Stephen Tallents and Sir Fife-Clark... they were the leading lights... another one quite high on the list was Maurice Buckmaster... those three stand out in my mind... others were Alan Campbell-Johnson, Bill Simpson, Paget-Cooke, Alan Eden-Green, Freddie Gillman, Denys Brook-Hart... and Colin Mann. (Interview 20/3/97)

Fleetward Pritchard was chief of one of the leading advertising and publicity agencies pre-war and was a key figure who wrote and gave inspirational speeches on the topic of persuasion in the post-war era. His pedigree was described admiringly by Traverse-Healy: "He became adviser to the Ministry of War Transport. He had a double MC in the First World War, had two degrees at Cambridge, one in economics and one in mathematics" (Interview 25/6/91).

Edward Rawdon Smith, the first Public Relations Officer of London Transport and PR adviser to the English Electric Group, was recognised posthumously for his sophisticated abilities in the field when it was written:

> If public relations is the engineering of consent then Rawdon Smith was one of the great "engineers" of consent. As time passes it will be seen that he was a pioneer and perhaps the founder of public relations, in its real and best sense in this country. (Obituary, *Public Relations*, January 1958)

Tim Traverse-Healy was a very helpful source for a number of other key personnel whose careers had straddled wartime and peacetime public relations, and the following interview extract highlights the elite connections of key pre-war practitioners suggesting that public relations in the UK was initiated from centres of social power:

I never met ... Sir Basil Clarke [who] ran the first public relations consultancy [in the 1920s] ... Dick Forman ran the London Press Exchange, Alan Campbell-Johnson set up his own outfit after the war, Hereward Phillips who set up had been public relations adviser to the Indian Government, Freddie Lyons started in about 1926, the leading parliamentary lobbyist was Commander Chris Powell of Watney and Powell who had been political correspondent I think for the old *News Chronicle* ... Howard Marshall who had been with the Ministry of Food became public relations chief of Richard Thomas and Baldwins, a great steel company in Wales ... [there was] Sydney Wynne who'd been in the Ministry of Supply and was Ernie Bevan's son in law ... Mike Williams-Thompson who'd also been in Supply who began his own company called Sydney Barton ... Rawdon-Smith who'd been adviser to London Transport before the war and then done work with Antony Eden, the Prime Minister and he set up his own company just after the war called Rawdon Smith and Associates with John Inglis-Hall and Dick Paget-Cooke ... Lex Hornsby who'd been running the Ministry of Labour PR ... Then there were certain personalities whose influence was fairly dominant because they were powerful people and they spoke with authority about business and [these included] Sydney Rogerson of ICI, the famous Jock Bremner of British Rail, Clem Leslie of the Treasury and there was Leslie Hardern of the North Thames Gas Board who was also President of the Wine and Food Society. (Interview 25/6/91)

Traverse-Healy's own career began at Aims of Industry, an organisation which supported free enterprise and opposed nationalisation. Traverse-Healy's role was to organise meetings and speakers (L'Etang, 2004, pp. 85–88). A Founder Member of the Institute, he was fascinated by the world of propaganda and spies and particularly admired Buckmaster. Later in life, Traverse-Healy wrote a pamphlet for the International Public Relations Association exploring the relationship between the concepts (Traverse-Healy, 1988a).

Another well-remembered practitioner was Colin Mann, "who always had a carnation and [was] very much the debonair political young sprig" (Interview Herbert Lloyd 19/8/95) and "had a cigarette holder and the half-filled glass and monocle" (Interview 18/3/97). Mann worked for the Press and Receptions Department of the British Council from 1938–1942 (thus reinforcing the connections between cultural diplomacy and public relations established by Tallents) before doing war service as a rating non-commissioned sailor in the Navy from 1942–1946. In his later career he was Public Relations Officer to the Conservative Party, then after a spell in consultancy (Head of Lintas Information Services and Chief Executive of E. D. O'Brien) was personal assistant to the Prime Minister Sir Antony Eden, after which he became Head of Advertising and Publicity at J. Lyons & Co, then Head of PR at Heinz (*Public Relations*, April 1962, p. 25). Maurice Buckmaster's daughter remembered that her father "thought that Colin Mann was a good chap and [so he] helped and promoted him" (Interview 28/8/96). Mann was one of the earliest practitioners who argued that the IPR should try and get a Royal Charter, according to Joyce Blow (Interview 31/10/96).

R. A. Paget-Cooke (IPR President 1959–1960), whose career encompassed Edmundsons's Electricity Corporation, the Federation of Master Printers, the consultancy Foote, Cone and Belding, Bowater Paper Corporation and Voice and Vision (known irreverently as "Vice and Vision" and a subsidiary of Colman, Prentice and Varley), was one of the cohort who "went straight from the army after demobilisation in 1946" (*Public Relations*, 12(1), 1961, pp. 26–27).

Perhaps one of the weaknesses of oral history is the tendency for interviewees to recall the past through rose-coloured spectacles and glamorise the origins. One example of this is the romantic view put forward by Joyce Blow:

When I got involved [in PR] it was a heroic period of public relations [due] to the fact that a large number of the senior people in public relations were people who had distinguished themselves during the Second World War, the Maurice Buckmasters, the Alan Campbell Johnsons, the Freddie Gillmans, the Bill Simpsons, oh legion, you know. And they were people who were used to being in senior positions and mixing with famous people and some of them like Buckmaster were old Etonians. Public relations immediately post-war was sort of full-grown. In the 1950s we had our annual dinner one year at the Mansion House and one year at the Guildhall—hundreds of people, white tie and decorations. A very different world but one in which I think the leading people were a part and therefore public relations was on the right side of the fence and not the wrong side of the fence. (Interview 31/1/96)

Although Blow acknowledged that "this sounds as if I'm extolling the British class system which I'm not," she clearly conveys a sense of public relations' potential for power and influence at that time. She herself regretted the loss of influence which she linked to the growth of marketing and pubic relations' subordination to that function. Another of her generation of post-war practitioners, Tim Traverse-Healy, concurred with her view:

I think we were much better placed. I think we were doing much more to position public relations within the movers and groovers and opinion leaders in London—it's where the power is—who were decision takers. We had a much better entrée than we have now. (Interview 13/9/95)

In addition, he detected an interesting shift in the client–consultant relationship over the years:

We were all moderately tough people and we were not sycophantic, if anything we were a rather arrogant crew and nowadays all this scurrying around for business and clients and [the notion that] the customer's right. I don't give the client what he asks for, I give him what he needs! It's at the heart of that relationship and I think we lost a bit there. The public relations business isn't what it was . . . we've a tendency [now] to be very subservient. There was much more belief that [the] craft was a strategical advisory thing and less emphasis on it as a communications [activity] and I think the balance has changed. (Interview 13/9/95)

This view was shared by Ivy Lee Jr who wrote to me that:

Today I believe public relations is often involving advertising and promotions. My father's concept of public relations basically involved policy . . . the last public discussion that my father had on July 4th, 1934 was before The American Club in London' (private correspondence 29/9/1998)

However, a different view was offered by Dennis Buckle:

In the very early days, we were really just "fixers," people who went and talked to the press and talked to other people whom we wanted to listen to the stories we had to tell them, making contacts and acquaintances with people in the media. There wasn't a great deal of skill about it. The skill didn't come into it until those of us in the early days had a bit of experience and began to learn through trial and error and until people started organising training courses in the late '50s, early '60s. (Interview 26/9/97)

There was also a sense of shifting sands in terms of public relations' reputation and practice. Interviewing a range of practitioners whose experience stretched from the early 1940s to the present day, it seemed as though each generation saw itself as the Golden Age of PR and those preceding or succeeding it as lesser mortals. So, the post-war generation regarded the local government PROs as very important in the formation of the IPR, but had no sense of those from the 1920s and 1930s or their intellectual contribution to the concept and practice of PR. And as recently as 2004, the IPR journal *Profile* published an article which asked, "How can we identify the next generation of internal communication specialists?," in which the author recounted:

At the recent PR Week Awards I bumped into some old internal communication friends. And, as we tend to do when we meet, we started to moan about the shortage of good people coming up in the profession. (Fitzpatrick, 2004, p. 19)

A number of those interviewed who had entered practice in the 1950s decried practice in the 1960s or 1970s and saw the post-war period through a rosy glow. Yet one of the most influential pre-war public relations practitioners, Hereward Phillips, was most critical of this 1950s generation, arguing:

> The post-war years began with a background of the achievements of the Ministry of Information and the hundreds of public relations people in Government Departments and the Services. But in 1945–46 neither industry, local government, nor any other organisation yet had any understanding of public relations; nor did they appear interested. The progress of public relations received a serious setback about this time. Hundreds of people coming out of the Services, without knowledge of newspapers or other media, and only a smattering of an idea of what it was all about, decided they were God's gift to public relations, or that public relations was an easy way of earning money. Many of these people were engaged to handle public relations and, failing to achieve anything, the whole practice came under a cloud. (*Public Relations*, April 1961, p. 12)

However, it is useful to contextualise this quote by noting that a number of pre-war practitioners apparently did not feel they had been sufficiently consulted or involved in the setting up of the IPR, which some saw as overly dominated by local government officials. As Traverse-Healy remembered:

> Some of those who were older like Colin Hurry and Colin Wintle and Michael Romaine and to some extent Rawdon Smith tended to stay out of it because they thought they were already moderately well-known and successful and didn't really want to associate themselves with the new boys. (Interview 25/6/91)

Consequently, a number of key pre-war consultants chose not to join the IPR or did not do so until a number of years after its establishment, and even Sir Stephen Tallents was at least temporarily a rather reluctant President on the grounds that he was no longer involved in mainstream public relations (L'Etang, 2004, p. 64). Former IPR President, Bill Simpson, confirmed this impression:

> I know it sounds a bit pompous but we didn't like the idea of people who were purely promoting a product. This has changed now, even politics is a product! [We were] opening society up and helping to promote business but doing it in a way that wasn't the hammer blows of highly expensive advertising campaign but something a little more subtle and trying to do it honestly rather than in a sinister way. (Interview 14/2/97)

Interestingly, two key figures prominent in the IPR for much of their careers, Sam Black and Tim Traverse-Healy, both revered particular American practitioners: Traverse-Healy admired Earl Newsome and Sam Black, Ed Bernays and both made efforts to keep in touch with their idols. Sam Black corresponded regularly with Ed Bernays and exchanged visits (Sam Black Collection, Media Archive, University of Stirling), and Traverse-Healy "made 17 crossings on the old Queen Mary" (Interview 13/9/95). On the one hand this suggests some sharing of concepts and techniques; on the other, it could be seen as personal promotion and the achievement of personal cachet both in the UK and the United States. The need for self-publicity was essential for those in consultancy, as illustrated by one senior practitioner's memories that:

> There were some people much publicised because their photographs always appeared in *Advertisers Weekly* or *World's Press News* ... Tim Traverse Healy was one of those people and Colin Mann (from the consultancy Carl Byoir) and Herbert Lloyd (a visionary and dynamo who worked very very hard). In those days if you went to the States to do business you were normally photographed on the steps of the British Overseas Airways plane going into first class accommodation with the caption that "Colin Mann is going on a fact-finding mission in the US" but in fact it was probably a jolly or a holiday! Because they worked in agencies they had staff who could send their pictures off. (Interview March 1997)

This suggests the cultural and even class divide between consultancy and in-house practice.

This was not the only instance of factionalism. When the IPR was formed in 1948, there was a (failed) attempt to distinguish public relations practitioners from publicity officers and to exclude the latter. Others also had the experience of having their applications for membership rejected. Henry James, later Press Secretary to Prime Minister Thatcher, applied to join the IPR in 1954 when he was a press officer in the Ministry for National Insurance but was refused entry because "they didn't regard government communications as public relations" but then: "In 1976 when I was Director General of the Central Office of Information (CoI) I was invited to join them [and] I found myself President within two years which was a bit of a shock!" (Interview 17/4/97).

Likewise, Herbert Lloyd (IPR President 1968–1969) had a similar experience when he approached the IPR in 1957 as an ex-lawyer who had been appointed as public relations officer for the Law Society and "was told in no uncertain terms that I would need to attend night school first" (Interview 19/8/95).

ACT III: CULTURE CLUB(LAND)

Clubs appear to have been, and remain, an important feature of the public relations culture. There are two types of clubs: the first is the traditional British gentleman's club, usually based in London, to which entry is restricted either by a particular form of education (Oxford and Cambridge), military background (the In and Out), class, and usually gender (Travellers, Athenaeum)—although most usually established a sitting room for ladies accompanying gentlemen (though they were restricted to that area of that building and certainly could not use the library or other facilities). Practitioners aspiring to this social status join, but more importantly publicise, their membership of such establishments as it is an important part of their identity construction both personally and professionally. The second type of club has been that set up within the public relations occupation and is typified by some sort of restricted entry.

The culture of "clubbability" appears to have been an important feature in British public relations, which raises sociological questions about the class origins and connections of practitioners, an aspect of public relations which is so far unresearched. A useful theoretical focus here might be Bourdieu's notion of distinction and its processes. Interview data on class appeared mixed and further research is clearly needed. One question to consider is whether public relations practitioners are so concerned for social status and legitimacy that they make more of conformity to social graces and conventions than is actually the case. Clearly, during the period when public relations practitioners spent much of their time in pubs and clubs with journalists, there would have been pressure on practitioners, regardless of parental background, to gain the necessary social skills. As Sam Black remarked:

> If you're good and you know the right people it helps up to a certain extent, but it is useful and you can cultivate friendships and one thing one does is join societies ... we have to take advantage of our natural qualities or social contacts or family contacts—there's nothing wrong with that but that isn't going to get you very far if that's all you've got ... I'm very far from the... country squire background but never found it a disadvantage when working on conferences with the British National Export Council with lots of high-up people ... I was very shy when I was younger but I think I was able to conquer it by forcing myself to speak in public and so on. (Interview 25/6/91)

"Clubbability" was also relevant to networking, including networking at elite levels already noted as important to public relations practice. As Alan Campbell-Johnson pointed out: "As a result of my work in India I knew Francis Williams very well (the equivalent of the man who does the 10 Downing Street job) a very powerful man" (Interview March 1994).

Campbell-Johnson had a lifelong interest and passion for liberal politics. He had a connection to Charles Masterman CMG (responsible for information work during the Great War) and worked unpaid for Archie Sinclair MP for a period. He therefore had a good understanding of the political elite and always maintained an MP as adviser to his consultancy on Parliamentary procedures and processes including William Duthie, Lady Tweedsmuir, Lord Straubenzee, and Nick Scott (Interviews March 1994 and 22/8/95).

Campbell-Johnson also saw that connections could be used to leverage a more public profile for the occupation and so during his presidency organised a fabulous dinner which his previous employer, Mountbatten, attended. As he remembered:

> We had it at the Savoy and it was very big stuff. There were one or two critics who said we were overdoing it but I said that if we really want to get national we'd better do something on this scale. I did that deliberately, to blow us out and give us a bit more national status which is what it did—it was a big occasion. (Interview 22/8/95)

Networking was initially facilitated by the preponderance of practitioners based in London, as Traverse-Healy pointed out:

> After all you were all working within two square miles of each other in London and we tended to know each other . . . [we met in] pubs mostly. Some of us were smarter than others and were members of clubs and some were pub people and then the Institute developed. (Interview 25/6/91)

So clubs were partly a space for networking but also for individual and collective identity construction. The establishment and growth of the Institute did not, apparently, adequately fulfil such needs and clubs remained a feature of public relations culture. For example, in the 1960s there was The PR Club founded by Maurice Buckmaster, Francis Butters, John Fowler, John Kaiser, Frank O'Shanohun, Michael Rice, Hugh Samson, Francis Schuster, and Arthur Wallis. Membership of The PR Club was limited to 15 members and those

> men and women engaged in PR practice in an independent agency or unit connected with an advertising agency; who are employed in the most senior positions (e.g. Head of PR Department, Chairman, Managing Director, PR Director) within the profession; and who are acceptable to the majority of existing members. (Archival material supplied by Nigel Ellis)

Warren Newman, President of the IPR in 1987, illustrated the enduring nature of this aspect of public relations occupational culture when he commented in 1997:

> There are a number of private clubs within public relations which tend to operate by invitation only. These are dinner clubs and suchlike [and] they have two functions: one is to recognise that people have reached a level of seniority in which they are invited in and welcomed into such exclusive groups, the other function is a headhunter network because in public relations, perhaps more than many [occupations] the role of the headhunter is important and you've got to have places where they can gather their intelligence . . . There are a small number of headhunters who are well-known within the industry [who] have established direct contact and who could certainly ask "Who's part of your dinner club?" There mere existence of these small exclusive groups provides the necessary foundation for the headhunters to build their intelligence network. (Interview 17/3/97)

Peter Earl (IPR President 1977) suggested that the clubland culture continued well into the 1980s:

> In the mid-eighties a number of us who were doing roughly comparable jobs formed ourselves into an informal dining club and met four times a year [it was] called the Charing Cross Club [of which] I was a Founder. There are quite a lot of dining clubs within public relations [based on] self-interest, at one time all the nationalised industries got together... I used to meet with my competitors in the telecommunications field because I felt it was very useful to know one's competitors. There was something called the Apostles for people who worked around Fleet Street. [Dining clubs] are more common at the senior level. (Interview 12/4/97)

Tony Spalding saw the club era as very much part of public relations' evolution in the UK:

> It was run like a gentleman's club the way PR was done in those days... I'm involved in the Charing Cross Club for all the top in-house practitioners, we have BBC, British Airways, we have BoC, we have Guinness, we have Sainsbury's, Vauxhall, BICC, Coca Cola. There are about fifteen or sixteen of us who meet once every two or three months to have dinner. There are two women. The fur flies, the conversation ranges from changes of newspaper attitudes to covering the business or the current controversy. (Interview 13/3/97)

One rather bizarre example of the "club culture" is perhaps the Leo Club for those within the Institute born under that astrological sign of the zodiac, which holds an annual and rather expensive lunch (at least for those on academic salaries!) during the period in question (Personal correspondence with Doug Smith and Iain Smyth 1996 and 1997).

Earl also expanded on the role of socialising as a public relations technique to influence elites and suggested that this approach had been responsible for the expansion of public relations at a senior level in organisations in Britain:

> I think I was probably one of the first to be appointed at Board level... in order to get the Managing Director better known I organised a series of private dinner parties at the Dorchester for eighteen people at which we would get a principal guest, like a former Prime Minister or someone of that calibre and mix the guests up as chairmen of companies, leaders of trades unions, clerics, artists—people who were absolutely at the top of their tree. We had 48 of those dinners so we had several hundred very very top notch people, many of whom saw what the Standard Telephones and Cables (STC) were doing and decided they were going to make [public relations] appointments at senior level in their own companies, including Rank, Courtaulds, ICI. (Interview 12/4/97)

This evidence suggests that a major structural feature of public relations culture is that of clubs for a variety of purposes: contacts, networking, informal learning and education, socialising. All the more pity, then, that at present there has been no research into this aspect of the public relations occupation. For example, qualitative, ethnographic research would shed light on the role of clubs in fostering and maintaining occupational culture and promoting certain types of practice.

ACT IV: ARTICULATING PRINCIPLES AND EXPLAINING PRACTICE: EDUCATION, EDUCATORS, AND AUTHORS

Who were the thinkers and writers in British public relations? The demands of business practice meant that many never committed their ideas to paper, but a number of practitioners did so with enthusiasm. Their efforts were crucial to the attempts to professionalise which I have explored at length elsewhere (L'Etang, 2004, pp. 186–220) and were linked to efforts to define an occupation, establish boundaries, and limit entry. Training courses and qualifications were one part of this professional project, but a number of individuals put considerable individual effort into writing articles and books, a considerable workload carried in addition to their paid employment. Some of these authors and their works are highlighted here, again in an attempt to correct the notion that public relations practice and concepts are solely an American invention, an impression which can be hard to counter in the face of the dominant American academic industry.

As already noted, there had already been academic and practical literature published on the role and scope of public relations in the 1920s and 1930s by a variety of authors in the journal *Public Administration* (L'Etang, 2004, pp. 23–26). This work encompassed strategic concerns of intelligence gathering and linking external and internal communications while monitoring public policy and public affairs and the issues of the day. A similarly thoughtful piece was written by a barrister, P. A. Wilson, who contributed a chapter on "Public Relations Departments" to a book written by a number of lecturers from the London School of Economics entitled *Some Modern Business Problems* (Longman, 1937). Wilson took an economic approach to public relations, arguing that public relations was required in imperfect markets and that political lobbying and media relations were necessary techniques for business organisations to thrive and benefit from public goodwill. In contemporary terms, Wilson's argument suggested the means for an organisation to achieve "licence to operate." Wilson's analysis captured the necessary requirements for anticipation, responsiveness, and dynamism in the field at both a conceptual (economic) and a practical level.

There is a notable rupture in the limited literature between pre-war and post-war publications. The sources above, together with Grierson's extensive archive, show engagement with what we would now see as strategic concepts and theory. The post-war literature is of a very different order, focusing on function and technique and generally atheoretical. That some of these early ideas have been lost has probably contributed to the notion that it was the Americans who largely developed public relations theory.

It was not until 1949 that a specialist pamphlet, *Public Relations and Publicity*, was published by the Institute of Public Administration. Written by the distinguished practitioner J. H. Brebner OBE (whose pre-war career included the Post Office and contributing to the establishment of the Ministry of Information in 1937), it argued for an understanding of attitude formation, the press, the ability to interpret "the human factor" in organisations, and the skill of interpersonal communications to overcome boundaries between different groupings of people important to an organisation's success. The pamphlet argued for the need for organisations to formalise their approach to relations with their overlapping publics in ever-changing circumstances.

An autobiographical work was written by the former Chief Information Officer from the Ministry of Supply in 1946–1949, Richard Williams-Thompson. In his book *Was I Really Necessary?* (1951), he reflected upon the changing role of the civil servant and his opposition to the concept of centralised information services, which he believed were dangerous for democratic practice. Thus, he represented a lone critical voice and apparently was an isolated representative of the inter-war era when many thought peacetime propaganda inappropriate to democracies.

The Institute itself was the next to produce a publication tailored to fit its own training courses (L'Etang, 2004, pp. 186–201). *A Guide to the Practice of Public Relations* was published in 1958. The book was introduced by Stephen Tallents, and the opening chapter by Lex Hornsby defined public relations as "the deliberate, planned and sustained effort to establish and maintain mutual understanding between an organisation and its public" (Hornsby, 1958, p. 8). A focus on relationships was implicit rather than explicit and greater emphasis was given to process and method than principle. Essentially the book was a pooling of experience of those who had knowledge of various media (press, broadcast, film, photography, print, exhibitions, advertising, house journals, business presentations), media relations specialists, and those who worked in different contexts (central and local government, trade associations). There was no attempt at theory although there was a useful chapter by the Director of the Market Research Society, Graeme Cranch, which took a more analytical approach and included some basic methodology. Other authors (in order of chapter publication) were R. A. Paget-Cooke, H. J. Bradley, John Pringle, Barbara Fell, Vera Watkins, A.W. Pragnell, K. Lockart Smith, John C. Shepherd, Iain MacPhail, Trevor Jones, Leslie Room, Ian Harvey, John Wales, Bernard Smith, Paul Reilly, Stephen Heald, A. A. McLoughlin, and Sam Black, to record their names for posterity.

Once the Institute's own qualifications were established, there was clearly a market for books and a number of practitioners contributed their ideas to print. Two prolific authors were Sam Black and Frank Jefkins, both of whom were heavily committed to the educational project as part of public relations professionalisation. From the evidence available, it would seem that Jefkins became more heavily involved in teaching activities, especially overseas (although Sam Black also ran his own courses in London for overseas practitioners well into the 1990s). Norman Hart was another important author (who wrote and edited many introductory books in the 1980s such as *Strategic Public Relations* and *Effective Corporate Relations: Applying PR in Business and Industry*) and he, like Sam Black, became associated with a university via an honorary professorial appointment in the 1990s (Hart at Leeds in 1998; Black at Stirling a decade previously).

Important texts by IPR members included *The Handbook of Public Relations* by Nigel Ellis and Pat Bowman (an edited and practical technique-driven text focused on media relations first published in 1963 but with several editions). For the record, authors contributing to Bowman and Ellis' text were: Tim Traverse-Healy, Ivan Piercy, R.E. Polendine, H. W. Shirley Long, Claude Simmonds, Barrie Pepper, T. Hampson, R. F. Owen, K. J. Ley, Peter Hunt, Charles Elliott, John St John Cooper, Stewart McConville, T. W. Burnett, Douglas Bentley, Alec Davis, Geoffrey Bensusan, Derek Dutton, K. Lockart Smith, Ted Jones, Ann Roush, Norah Owen, A. S. H. Bodden, Andrew Reid, Peter Stattersfield, Maurice Buckmaster, Douglas A. Cole, Marie Jennings, Kenneth Bartlett, Colin Norton-Smith, Bryan Samain, and Margery Weiner.

Author Pat Bowman commented in an interview that:

> There were very few books on the subject. One of the reasons Nigel Ellis and I settled down to write some books was because we saw there was a need. A lot of emphasis was on practice and on broad experience of industry, commerce, government, local government. [There was] far less communications theory than now. Academics hadn't got as far as that. (Interview 29/8/96)

Curiousl*y, Public Relations in Business Management* by James Derriman (1964) took a different and more sophisticated approach structured around different publics, yet this book does not seem to have appeared in multiple editions as did some others.

Of the early post-war generation, other authors included the irrepressible Herbert Lloyd (President 1968–1969), who collaborated with his son to write several editions of *Teach Yourself Public Relations* (Hodder & Stoughton, 1963) which ran to several editions well into the 1980s. The 1989 edition incorporated some very basic notions of communications theory, included a model of practice and management feedback adapted from Reginald Watts PhD (President 1989), and focused heavily on the media. It included a number of useful checklists for practice but did not include material on research or evaluation.

The gently witty Basil Saunders was lead author of the tongue-in-cheek *Bluff Your Way in PR* (Ravette Books, 1991). Ideal airport reading, this pocket book does contain some interesting stereotypes of PR culture and should not be dismissed out of hand for the insights it offers therein.

Sam Black wrote numerous publications translated into many languages. His first book, *Practical Public Relations*, was published in 1962 and became the standard text for IPR Diploma candidates. He also published *Public Relations in the 1960s, Public Relations in the 1970s, Public Relations in the 1980s, The Role of Public Relations in Management, Exhibitions and Conferences from A to Z, Exhibiting Overseas—A Marketing Shop Window*, and *The Businessman's Guide to the Planned Economy Countries*. Black's approach (drawing on the 1989 version of *Practical Public Relations*) was similar to that of the IPR book in focusing on techniques and domains of practice. While there was nothing on evaluation as such, it did include a brief summary of questionnaire methodology.

Black played an important role in the development, establishment, and professionalisation of the embryonic public relations industry in Britain through his books (published all over the world in many languages), his role on the IPR education committee for many years, and his enthusiasm for the development of university courses. He had an unusual background. Born in 1915 to Russian parents, Lionel Tcherny and Sophia Divinskaia, the family moved from Baku, Russia to England around 1912, took British citizenship, and changed their name to Black (the English word for Tcherny). He qualified as an optician and spent 5 years in the Royal Army Medical Corps. In 1955 he went to work for the British Electrical and Allied Manufacturers' Association, during which time he collaborated with other companies and trade associations on an exhibit for the World Expo at Brussels. He subsequently established his own consultancy, the Sam Black Organisation Ltd.

Books published by post-war practitioners are notable for their functional focus on technical aspects of the job. Most describe key media and various communications techniques (exhibitions, press conferences, photography), often focused on form and layout rather than intention and communication process. The books are set out as templates of practice focusing on checklists and administrative detail. It was evidently too early for communication and media theory to have much input. So the books conform to a very strong genre that still exists today. However, an analysis of that genre and deconstruction of its discourse is still awaited.

ACT V: WOMEN IN PUBLIC RELATIONS

It is strange today, in an era when 90% of a class of public relations students will typically be female, to realise that half a century ago women were relatively scarce in the field. The gradual influx of women into public relations seems to have coincided with the recovery of the British economy, the translation of wartime technological developments into new domestic goods, the growth of consumerism, and the belief that only women could market to women. As Gina Franklin, President of the Association of Women in Public Relations (AWPR), explained:

> Thinking women have a unique property to offer to big business. We as women know the kind of attitudes women are likely to take up regarding new developments, new processes and are therefore in a position to advise. Women are extremely conscientious, and if they "fall in love" with a product, or believe in it, they can produce miracles of resourcefulness. (*Public Relations*, October 1963, p. 8)

Trying to recapture something of the her-story of public relations in Britain is a challenge. Drawing on a range of interviews, it seems that key names in the 1940s and 1950s included Rose McDenell, Molly Clucas, Anne Little, Anne Leam, Pat Hardy (English Electric), Elizabeth Elliot (Bowater Scott), Pam Grey (Formica), Janine Roxborough-Bunce (Elizabeth Arden), and Gina Franklin (originally in high fashion but later the formidable Director of Link Information Services, owned by Unilever). Within the IPR, female membership was low in the early years.

Of the 142 Founder Members of the Institute listed on 16 August 1948, only nine were women: Nancy Warner Debenham, Esta Eldod, OBE, Sylvia Clarissa Forman, Marjorie Eileen Green, Joan Mary Kitching, Elisbeth Ruth Littlejohn, Yvonne Marie-Aimee Moyse, Margaret Stevens, and Vera Hope Watkins. Unfortunately, the IPR journal, *Public Relations* did not list the organisations for which these women worked. One of these, Esta Eldod, had expressed some concern for the lack of opportunities open to women within the IPR before she emigrated "to take up an interesting married life in Brazil" (*Public Relations*, 3(3), 1951, p. 11).
Eldod wrote that:

> It has always been my regret that the profession of public relations, as represented by the members of the Institute, has shown a distinction between men and women officers, by refraining from voting a woman PRO on to the Council. This year I agreed to be a "guinea pig" as a test case, and I am sad that I have to leave this country with the feeling that my own profession is non-progressive ('Some correspondence', *Public Relations*, 3(3), 1951, p. 11)

The President, Alan Hess, replied:

> Positively there are no mixed feelings about my reaction to your disappointment that the members of the Institute of Public relations have given you the impression that they have shown a distinction between men and women officers. I believe you are over-sensitive on this point as I am quite sure everybody recognises the valuable contribution to British public relations which has been made by the leading women PROs including yourself, and that there was no distinction intended at all. Plainly, when only a certain number of vacancies exist and there are vastly more applicants than seats, a number of disappointments must ensue and I feel quite sure there is nothing whatever of a sinister nature in the coincidence that women candidates failed to secure the necessary support. ('Some correspondence' *Public Relations*, 3(3), 1951, p. 11)

Thus at this stage of its history, social norms which tended to exclude women from fast career progression, and, in this case, to exclude them from representing their own occupation, prevailed.

It was not until 1975 that there was a female President of the IPR, Margaret Nally, and the second was Norah Owen a few years later for an 18-month term from 1981–1982.

Margaret Nally (IPR President 1975–1976) was in the Wrens in the war as a radio mechanic, and after some experience in freelance journalism moved via secretarial work into a public relations role in an advertising agency in the mid-1950s and the IPR around the same time. On women in public relations in that era, she commented:

> There were not many women and most were dealing with beauty or fashion. I was dealing with things that were definitely not what would be regarded as women's interests. I was a good attender at IPR events and I stood for Council and got on. When I worked at Aubrey and Turner I used to do some modelling for them to save some money, sometimes we used myself on photographs on the PR side. A lot of them regarded me as a fairly good-looking woman whom it would be useful to have at the dinner table . . . there were a number of times when one or two of them, I think, regarded me as a bit of decoration to help with being hostess at the annual dinner. It was rather a disadvantage that I was quite good-looking. It can be a battle sometimes to get yourself taken seriously—you were not treated as a PR person but as a woman. (Interview 20/8/95)

Her account on the one hand distances her status from that of lowly woman to honorary man in terms of the content of her work, yet at the same time she could not fail to be aware of her femininity and the effect it had on men of that era. One sensed she both enjoyed and resented the position this gave her.

Nora Owen (IPR President 1981–1982) worked in fashion journalism at *Harper's Bazaar* and the *Sketch* when, "I was offered this job to head up the fashions account at W.S. Crawford" (Interview 16/8/95), and then worked for a fashion consultancy, Newslines, which was subsequently taken over by Charles Barker. One of Owen's inspirations was the extraordinary American practitioner, Eleanor Lambert, "one of the 'greats' of fashion PR in the States" and still alleged (à la Bernays) to be working at the age of 95 (Interview 16/8/95).

One former journalist made the switch to public relations because: "My lifestyle wasn't very conducive to marriage and I had been doing some publicity work on the side...in the fifties there were jobs galore and there was no problem getting into PR via a PR section of an ad agency" (Interview 18/3/97).

Thus, it seems women were ghettoised in the early years even though some men practising in the era claimed it was "a sexless trade" (Interview 29/8/96) and "it doesn't matter what sex you are" (Interview 30/8/96).

A key figure in the IPR for many years, Joyce Blow, started her career in 1950 doing vocational training with the John Lewis Department before becoming a secretary in the publicity department of the Federation of British Industry (FBI, predecessor of CBI) working for F. L. Stephens, "a moving spirit in setting up the IPR" (Interview 31/10/96). But she moved on after 9 months because despite having a degree in classics and history from the University of Edinburgh, she got the message that "You will never get an executive job in the FBI because you are a woman" (Interview 31/10/96). She got a job as Assistant Press Officer at the Council of Industrial Design (precursor of the Design Council), joined the IPR as an Associate Member, and quickly became involved in committees—including the one which put together the IPR's edited text on public relations that was published in 1958. Among her achievements was that of the first woman to be elected to the Council of the IPR. Ultimately she became frustrated with the limited opportunities for women and entered the Board of Trade at the level of Principal; she remained in the civil service for the rest of her career as an administrator. As she pointed out:

> The thought that my life should be restricted by some sort of external power which says that although I spent three years studying 60BC to 90AD all I'm fit for as a woman is to run a cosmetic account was something that really I thought was too much. (Interview 31/10/96)

Barriers to progress came from social context, as Joyce Blow pointed out: "What used to be said when I tried at one stage to get into consultancy was 'Oh, well super, we'd love you to come and work for us but I'm not sure how happy our clients would be' " (Interview 31/10/96).

It is worth counterpointing this account with the inclusion of evidence of sexist attitudes within the public relations occupation, as evidenced by one retiree:

> I think some of them [women] come in as secretaries and find they can do rather more. I had a splendid and formidable middle-aged lady as my secretary and when I left she took over from me as public relations manager. I think a lot of women have come in this way, but for others it is a fairly attractive way of life as they see it. It is regarded as fashionably acceptable...amongst their friends I would think—does that sound belittling and demeaning because there are lots and lots of all-female consultancies who are marvellous on fashion and arranging cocktail parties and all the rest of it but I don't think would be able to get down to the real nitty gritty major public relations problems that are occurring within business and companies today. I remember reading in the *Daily Express* that some debutante had got fed up doing the season and Daddy was going to set her up in business as a public relations consultancy. (Interview March 1997)

According to this account socialising by women is personal entertainment, yet socialising by men in clubs and pubs was regarded as a serious and legitimate business function in the context of public relations work.

The fact that Blow (the first woman to be elected to the Council of the IPR in 1956), who clearly had exceptional capabilities, was eventually driven to leave the field speaks volumes.

That she retained her influence in the IPR committee (especially on the influential Education Committee) decades after she had left the field (well into the 1990s) also speaks volumes.

FEMALE CLUBBABILITY?

In 1962 the Association Women in Public Relations was formed, "on a restrictive membership of thirty" clearly mimicking the exclusive clubland approach that still held sway in much public relations practice. Founder members were Anne Little (Joint Managing Director, Brunskill Little), Thelma Stevenseon (Director, Brunskill Little), Norah Owen (self-employed consultant), Rose MacDonnell (PR executive at Colman, Prentice & Varley, Advertising and PR agency), Patricia Hardy (PRO, English Electric), Gina Franklin (MD Link Information Services, subsidiary of Lintas advertising agency), and Joyce Blow (Press Officer, Council of Industrial Design). The first President was Gina Franklin.

According to Mary Gilbert, writing in the *IPR* journal in October 1963, the AWPR was designed to offer women:

> unusual opportunities for widening experience through interchange, safeguarding high standards, furthering knowledge in the field and consolidating professional contribution. Its formation is one more proof—if proof be needed—that women take their profession seriously and regard it with definite continuity and not just something decorative to do for the time being. (*Public Relatoins* 18/1/1963, p. 7)

However, membership was restricted to 30 and Phyllis Oberman recalled: "AWPR has always been a separate organisation [from the IPR] and is meant to be of interest to senior women practitioners. You join the AWPR by invitation [and you need] referees. I was proposed by Pam Grey" (Interview 18/3/97).

Thus, it seems that AWPR should not be regarded as a supportive women's group aligned to feminist principles but simply another example of a public relations networking culture that formed cliques and elites like an amoeba reproducing. Even in the 21st century membership is capped at 150.

Nora Owen was one of the Founder Members of AWPR:

> I was asked to join and I did become President and I did get slightly irritated about the attitude towards women because it didn't seem to me to matter whether you were male or female in PR really . . . it was felt that it was a sensible thing to have an association other than the IPR which was terribly male dominated so that we could get together and have chats . . . it is still in existence but to my mind it never really worked out properly. I was President for a while but I was never really happy about it because I never know what a "feminist" is. I don't think men and women should be separated in their work. (Interview 16/8/95)

In fact, Owen later resigned because she thought that AWPR "had become a little bit 'wimminish' . . . Men and women in PR are now more or less interchangeable and I frankly cannot now see the necessity for a 'women only' group any longer" (internal historical correspondence 13 January, no year specified).

Leading woman Margaret Nally "didn't get involved [with AWPR] as "I joined the Press and PR Branch of the NUJ and tended to be mixing with a group of men than with the rest of the women" (Interview 20/8/95), possibly implying a belief that men and men's work was superior to women and women's work.

The barriers to entry of AWPR prevents us from seeing it as some kind of early feminism: instead women practitioners chose to simply copy the exclusive networking structure which enveloped them in their working lives within PR culture. No sense of community seems to emerge from descriptions of the AWPR in the 1950s and 1960s, no culture of mentoring or supportiveness, or of giving those behind them "a leg up." Even as late as 1986, correspondence was received by the then-membership secretary commenting on an application for membership:

> I am strongly of the opinion that [the applicant] is much more involved with promotional activities than with public relations matters and from what I read on her application form, consider her a "light weight." I was under the impression that the Association wished to raise the calibre of membership and the only way to do this is to select people who possess the qualities and experience which will meet that objective. (AWPR archive cited in Foley, 2004)

In an era when formal qualifications were not available, "calibre" was understood by those who were part of public relations culture, even though the term "calibre" was not defined. The notion of being of the "right calibre" does seem to have been part of the discourse of public relations that has remained to the present day, especially in discussions about new or recent applicants to the field. How those distinctions are made and implemented is an aspect of public relations occupational culture that remains uncovered.

EPILOGUE

The chapter has presented some insight into the cultural scene of public relations in the post-war era. It has clarified a number of characteristics of PR social history and culture: its romanticism and attachment to the era of military intelligence and the downplaying of its more sophisticated intellectual history that actually lay in the bureaucratic intelligence of the 1920s and 1930s; the loss of its intellectual position and content due to rank commercialism and the influx of ex-journalists in the 1960s; its class consciousness, parochialism, and conventionalism; its cliquey structures and occasional (and sadly unquotable) bitchiness. The expansion of public relations in the UK post-Second World War can be explained in terms of the major structural changes in postwar society. Post-war public relations practice became an unsophisticated affair and few practitioners reflected on how their work fitted in to democratic society. Nevertheless, even in these brief snippets we can see the development of an occupational culture with some sense of history, a fraternity of networks, an absence of sorority, a recognisable domain of work—a stage.

9

Devotional-Promotional Communication and Santiago: A Thousand-Year Public Relations Campaign for Saint James and Spain

Donn James Tilson
University of Miami

Individuals and corporate entities communicate for various reasons—to record, inform, educate, entertain, and persuade (Bivins, 1995)—largely depending on the context of the communicative moment. Persuasive communication, which intends to influence the attitudes and/or behaviour of publics, also may be considered promotional in nature in that it attempts to advance an idea, an individual, a product or service, or an organization, usually in a positive manner. Commercial, governmental, and nongovernmental organizations often use such promotional communication to create, advance, and sustain corporate identities as the central component of a strategic public relations plan. These campaigns may be directed by the promotional sector—advertising, public relations, or marketing—within a society (Tilson, 1999).

A particular form of promotional communication, *devotional-promotional communication*, may be used also to inspire allegiance to an individual, political entity, or religion (Tilson, 2000). For example, a devotional-promotional campaign "that is religious in nature, may seek to instill great love or loyalty, enthusiasm, or zeal for a particular religious individual, living or deceased, or for a specific religion or faith" (Tilson, 2000, p. 1; cited in Tilson & Chao, 2002, p. 89).

This study examines the devotional-promotional campaign of the Catholic Church and the government in Spain, particularly the Ministry of Culture, Social Communication and Tourism in Galicia, to establish and sustain the identity of and allegiance to Saint James (Santiago) domestically and internationally. The study critiques past and present campaigning and examines the effects of the campaign. The study is one of the first of its kind to examine religious devotional-promotional public relations campaigns (see also Tilson & Chao, 2002) and represents a significant contribution to the profession's body of knowledge.

METHODOLOGY

A combination of various qualitative methods was used in this study to obtain data on the Church–State devotional-promotional campaign in Spain and its effects on key publics. A textual analysis of corporate media, including electronic material, provided insight into the various strategies, tactics, and messages employed as well as the key publics targeted by such media. Written surveys and face-to-face interviews of key corporate figures also were conducted to further probe the development of public relations strategies and effects. Field observations of selected religious sites provided further data on the design and use of such sites.

A THEORETICAL APPROACH

A review of the research and professional literature fails to find any mention of significant public relations theory or research concerning religious communication. Generally speaking, as an area of public relations research—and communication research overall—religion is unexplored territory.

A discussion of appropriate definitions and paradigms of public relations may be useful at this point. The essential nature of the profession has been variously defined as one of persuasion, advocacy, public information, image/reputation management (Hutton, 1999), education, community service, and issues management, among other interpretations (Botan, 1992). More recently, another view has emerged—*relationship management*—that considers "public relations as an exercise in identifying mutual interests, values and beliefs between a client-organization and its publics" (Hutton, 1999, p. 208). Such an approach envisions a relationship built upon "mutual trust, compromise, cooperation" given that "public support and consent are vital to the organization in achieving its long-term objectives" (ibid, p. 208). Trust has been defined as "the extent to which both management and publics express willingness to make themselves vulnerable to the behavior of the other—confidence that the other party will take its interests into account in making decisions" (Grunig & Grunig, 1998, p. 4). Recent research has reported "trust is an important foundation for relationships" in international settings (Hung, 2000, p. 6), and "that key public member perceptions of trust, openness, involvement, investment, and commitment influence evaluations of satisfaction with the organization" (Bruning, 2000, p. 6; Bruning & Ledingham, 1998; Bruning & Ledingham, 2000a).

If we can view "the process at the center of public relations—using communication to adapt relationships between organizations and their publics" as a valid interpretation of the profession, then, as some have argued, "the public relations function is ancient, dating from early Egyptian and Mesopotamian civilizations, and far predating the business perspective . . . used in different ways by . . . governments, religions and corporations" (Botan, 1992, p. 153; Grunig & Hunt, 1984). Indeed, as Botan (1992) argued, "Adopting a definition of the practice not tied to any one set of assumptions, particularly the assumption that public relations is a management function, . . . expands the set of historical examples that can be used to inform current public relations research and practice" (p. 153). Some have contended that, given the persuasive nature of the communication used to establish and maintain relationships, "public relations is . . . deeply rooted in the rhetoric of antiquity" (Brown, 2003, p. 230) and can be traced back to philosophical and theoretical origins in ancient Greece (Jowett & O'Donnell, 1992). Still others suggest that "monuments and other art forms of the ancient world . . . reflect early efforts at persuasion" and "pyramids, statues, temples, tombs, [and] paintings" are examples of "early techniques and tools" of public relations-like practice (Newsom, Turk, & Kruckeberg, 2000, p. 32). As Wilcox, Ault, and Agee (1992) noted, while "none of these [early] endeavors was called public relations . . . their purpose and effect were the same as those of similar activities today" (p. 36).

A trust-based *covenantal model* of public relations has been suggested as a theoretical ground for the profession (Koehn, 1994; cited in Baker, 2000), a model that has particular relevance to religious devotional-promotional communication. Koehn (1994) argued that "professional practices qualify as morally legitimate because, and to the extent that, they are structures to merit the trust of clients" (p. 8; cited in Baker, 2000, p. 5). Professionals establish their authority "because they are experts . . . or service providers" who make "a public promise to serve . . . a particular (client) good" and who "dedicate their lives to promoting" that interest (Koehn, 1994, pp. 15, 59, 69; cited in Baker, 2000, pp. 6, 9, 10) in a proactive manner. Moreover, "persons become clients because they seek some good they lack and are unable to provide for themselves . . . (and) become the minister's congregant, the doctor's patient and the lawyer's advisee" (Koehn, 1994, p. 58; cited in Baker, 2000, pp. 8–9). According to Koehn (1994), the profession, or public promise, however, must be "to furthering an end which is genuinely good" and "desirable in its own right"—"health, salvation, or justice"—if a practitioner is to have the requisite moral authority inasmuch as "the pledge would not ground authority if the promised good were actually an evil" (pp. 69, 88, 153; cited in Baker, 2000, pp. 10, 12, 13).

Baker (2000) argued that "in order for public relations practice to move to professional status, and . . . into a covenantal model," the profession "must devote itself to a particular human good or need (as . . . the clergy to client spiritual well-being)" that is grounded in a "public pledge to serve this need" and "practices . . . that foster strong and effective relationships" (pp. 18, 23). Baker noted that, while "it might be more appropriate in the PR setting to speak of 'fostering' relationships rather than of 'promoting' them . . . the terms . . . can be used somewhat inter-changeably with regard to defining public relations . . . (and) are . . . harmonious with the covenantal model" (2000, p. 15).

The devotional-promotion campaign for St. James throughout history has been premised upon just such a covenantal relationship between the faithful and their God through the intercession of their clergy, a relationship inherent in the Judeo–Christian tradition of faith. Following the flood described in Jewish scripture, or the Old Testament, God established a covenant with Noah, blessing him, his sons, and his descendants, vowing "that never again shall all bodily creatures be destroyed by . . . a flood" (Genesis 9:11). The covenant later was extended to "Abram (and) your descendants" (Genesis 15:18), renewed through Isaiah following the collapse of the northern kingdom of Israel to Assyria in the 8th century B.C.—"my love shall never leave you nor my covenant of peace be shaken" (Isaiah 54:10)—and again through Ezekiel during the Babylonian captivity of Israel, with the promise "to restore you the land . . . so that they will live according to my statutes . . . thus they shall be my people and I will be their God" (Ezekiel 11:17, 20–21). Early Christians considered themselves to be "the children of the prophets, and of the covenant which God made with our fathers" (Acts 3:25), and Jesus to be "the mediator of the new covenant," a "high priest" who, through his death—"the blood of the everlasting covenant"—restored mankind's relationship with God (Hebrews 7:26, 12:24, 13:20).

In this sense, the Catholic Church's public relations campaigning for St. James in Spain can be considered covenantal relationship-building in that, through these efforts, the Church calls its various publics (Catholics, non-Catholics, nonbelievers, etc.) into a positive relationship with St. James, the Church, and, ultimately, with God. Such religious devotional–promotional public relations campaigns can be viewed as proceeding within a covenantal relationship established on the foundation of clergy–congregant trust, offering the promise of fulfilling "client" needs considered mutually and inherently good. Proceeding on faith, public relations within such a context can be both relationship-building and persuasive or promotional in nature; the two functions need not be mutually exclusive and may, in fact, serve to enhance each other.

RELICS AND PILGRIMAGE

An understanding of devotion to relics and saints, as in the case of St. James and other venerated figures, is, in fact, virtually impossible unless such behavior is viewed within the frame of a covenantal relationship. According to Catholic doctrine, saints are those faithful whom the Church has officially recognized as having "practiced heroic virtue and lived in fidelity to God's grace;" moreover, "the patriarchs, prophets, and certain other Old Testament figures have been and always will be honored as saints" (United States Catholic Conference [USCC], 1994, p. 21). In a devotional-promotional sense, "the Church . . . sustains the hope of believers by proposing the saints to them as models and intercessors" (USCC, 1994, p. 219), whom the faithful turn to for help in times of personal difficulty. Relics are defined as "the corpse of a saint or any part thereof . . . (which) in their cases may be exposed on an altar during sacred ceremonies, presented to the people for veneration, carried in procession . . . but only those may be publicly honoured for which a proper authentication is held" (Attwater, 1961, pp. 423–424). However, as O'Donnell (1999) noted, "Homage or respect is not really paid to an inanimate object, but to the holy person, and indeed the veneration of a holy person, is itself honour paid to God" (p. 1).

But, as Melczer (1993) noted, "Relics, as wine, do not travel well" (p. 2). In reality, "pilgrimage and relic are the two sides of the same coin. The one is conditioned by the other: the essential mobility of the pilgrimage is a function of the essential immovability of the relic; and the fixedness of the latter is predicated upon the mobility of the former" (p. 2). Indeed, "the word *pilgrim* comes from the Latin *peregrinus* or *traveler*," with the true journey being not merely an outwardly physical one but also an interior one (Beckwith, 1999, p. 20). A "mystic bent of mind" that inclined medieval pilgrims toward visiting saintly remains to touch them—physical contact being "a condition sine qua non"—also inspires the faithful today (Melczer, 1993, pp. 1, 3). Modern-day pilgrimages are daily phenomena worldwide that draw faithful across the religious spectrum to sites considered sacred. As Reverend Peter F. Vasko, president of the Holy Land Foundation and pilgrimage director, noted, "Jews go to Jerusalem; Hindus visit the Ganges; Muslims make their way to Mecca, Buddhists to Sarnath and members of the Tenri-Kyo of Shintoism to Tenri Shi in Japan" (Vasko, 1999, p. 1).

DEVOTION AND PERSUASIVE COMMUNICATION

Covenantally inspired devotion requires individuals and structures to institutionalize and operationalize God's call to holiness. The corporate promoters, the entities that are formed, and, indeed, the communicative process employed are, in the case of Christianity, a consequence of the origins and nature of the faith. The Catholic Church considers herself to be "apostolic . . . in that she remains through the successors of St. Peter and the other apostles, in communion of faith and life with her origin; and in that she is 'sent out' into the whole world" (USCC, 1994, p. 229). In the beginning of his ministry, Jesus "appointed twelve, whom also he named apostles, to "go into the whole world and proclaim the good news to all creation" (Mark 16:15). In being sent to "make disciples of all the nations" (Matthew 28:19–20), the apostles later "consigned, by will and testament . . . to their immediate collaborators the duty of completing and consolidating the work they had begun...that on their death other proven men should take over their ministry" (USCC, 1994, p. 228). Hence, the Church teaches that "the bishops have by divine institution taken the place of the apostles as pastors of the Church" (USCC, 1994, p. 229). The "good news" eventually was written and compiled as the various books of the New Testament—"eternal 'press releases'" (Coup de Frejac, 1999, p. 2)—for the purpose of evangelization—"these have been recorded to help you believe" (John 20:31).

As the Church expanded over the centuries, a formal entity was established in 1622—the Sacred Congregation for the Propagation of the Faith—by Pope Gregory XV to communicate the faith. Today, that function has further expanded to include the Pontifical Council for Social Communication, which oversees a global network of corporate intranet, print, and broadcast media, such as Vatican Radio and Fides, the Vatican's missionary news agency. As the Most Reverend Robert F. Morneau (2000) noted, "Would not St. Paul, if alive today, be on television and sending out epistles via the Internet?" (p. 14).

Unfortunately, the purpose of the Congregation, and even its name, has been misreported in various public relations texts. Wilcox et al. (2000) mistakenly referred to the organization as "the College of Propaganda," arguing that "the church was among the first to use the word *propaganda*" (p. 27). Verčič, Grunig, and Grunig (1996) similarly misreported that "the word propaganda came into the vocabulary when the Roman Church named its standing committee of cardinals in charge of missionary activities...little more than a symbolic expression of inquisitionist behavior" (p. 43). It should be noted, however, that the Congregation was not a tool of "inquisition;" according to Attwater (1961), "inquisitionist behavior" long predates the Congregation, with ecclesiastical tribunals of inquiry having originally been established as early as 1229 in southern France (pp. 255–256). Moreover, the purpose of the Congregation was "to be the organ for coordinating missionary enterprise" in non-Christian lands and in countries that had become Protestant (J. Kelly, 1986, p. 279), training priests for such work, and supervising their activities. In this sense, *propagate* meant to transmit and to foster Catholic teaching, an objective no different than other present-day religious organizations, like the Billy Graham Evangelistic Association, which declares that "our task is...to tell the whole world of Christ...through television, radio, motion pictures and literature" (Graham, 2000a, p. 1). It was not until the 20th century—largely during or after World War I—that the term *propaganda* assumed its modern-day negative, unethical connotations (Doob, 1966) "as the deliberate and systematic attempt to shape perceptions, manipulate cognitions, and direct behavior to achieve a response that furthers the desired intent of the propagandist" (Jowett & O'Donnell, 1986, p. 2; cited in Wilcox et al., 2000, p. 227).

While some may argue that all religious communication should be considered "propaganda," it should be noted that "propaganda...is not about communication between organizations and their publics; it is about discommunication. Its first aim is to dissolve communication between people in order to disable their ability to form publics" (Verčič et al., 1996, p. 42), hardly a description of communicative activity that fosters relationships between religious institutions and their publics and builds communities of faith. While, historically, "PR-related activities have been used to promote religion throughout the ages" (Newsom et al., 2000, p. 33), such efforts need not be viewed as being inherently unethical. While some will argue that "propaganda, in the broadest sense of the word, also includes...public relations" (Wilcox et al., 2000, p. 227) inasmuch as "the effort *to persuade* underlies all public relations activity" (Newsom et al., 2000, p. 32), propaganda and persuasive communication are not synonymous. As Wilcox et al. (2000) noted, propaganda is used "to deceive and mislead the public" while "persuasive messages require truth, honesty, and candor" (pp. 229–230). Indeed, even though "an evangelist...is one who proclaims the Gospel to those who have not accepted it, with the goal of persuading them to accept Christ" (Graham, 2000b, p. 2), the Church has always maintained that such efforts are to be done in a spirit of truth. For example, Jesus exhorted his apostles to "Say 'Yes' when you mean 'Yes' and 'No' when you mean 'No' (Matthew 5:37), and Paul charged his followers to "profess the truth in love... let everyone speak the truth to his neighbor (Ephesians 4:25). Furthermore, as Verčič et al. (1996) noted, inasmuch as propaganda intends to create "constraints... on [lateral] communication" (p. 44) and "lateral communication is considered to be at the core of what public relations professionals do" (p. 46), any organization or nation-state that "permits only propaganda as a form of organizational communication could not practice the generic principles" (pp. 41–42) inherent to excellent public relations, which, at its center, values symmetry of communication (J. E. Grunig, 1992). Practitioners who use communication "to manipulate publics for the benefit of the organization" (Grunig, 1989, p. 18; cited in Tilson, 1999, p. 69) soon find themselves steered "toward actions that are unethical... [and] socially irresponsible" (Grunig & White, 1992, p. 40; cited in Tilson, 1999, p. 69). Rather, Wilcox et al. (2000) argued, as professionals, "public relations practitioners must conduct their activities in an ethical manner" (p. 229). Certainly, while "public relations construed as rhetoric" argues from an exclusively client-centered perspective that "the truth" is relative and "that there is no one overall standard with regard to those interests on behalf of which public relations operates... and no one overall standard for public relations practice itself" (L'Etang, 1996b, pp. 115–116), such a worldview represents public relations only in its most "primitive" model—"press agentry, publicity-seeking"—which, as asymmetrical communication, can be considered as synonymous with propaganda (Verčič et al., 1996, p. 41).

In keeping with a symmetrical approach to public relations, the process of persuasive communication can be viewed as a proactive symbiotic relationship between source and intended publics. Indeed, Miller has proposed "a model of persuasion which entails active participation by the persuadee, who in effect self-persuades... given the opportunity to become involved in the creation of the persuasive message" (as cited in L'Etang, 1996b, p. 118). As such, as L'Etang (1996b) noted, "persuasive acts might be judged in terms of the relationship between the parties concerned and their views of each other (a co-orientation approach)" (p. 119). Such a conceptualization best describes religious devotional-promotional public relations campaigns—like that of St. James—that proceed within a covenantal relationship established on the foundation of clergy–congregant trust and with the willing participation of all parties.

ST. JAMES: LIFE, DEATH, AND REDISCOVERY

According to Walsh (1991), St. James and his brother, St. John Evangelist, were fishermen with their father, Zebedee, and the third and fourth apostles called to be "fishers of men" (see Matthew 4:19) by Jesus after two other brothers, Peter and Andrew, were recruited on the shore of Lake Genesareth in Galilee (Thurston & Attwater, 1996). Peter, James, and John were considered "the inner ring of the disciples" (McBirnie, 1977, p. 87) as they were the only apostles present with Jesus on four intimate occasions—the raising from the dead of Jairus' daughter and the cure of Peter's mother-in-law by Jesus, Jesus' transfiguration on Mount Tabor, and Jesus' agony in the Garden of Gethsemani (Ruffin, 1997). James' mother, Salome, also followed Jesus, "providing for him, and was one of the women who stayed with Jesus as he was crucified, when the apostles, including her son James, had fled" (Catholic Online, 1999, para. 10). About 14 years later, in 44 A.D., James was the first apostle to be martyred; Eusebius notes (also Acts 12:2) that King Herod Agrippa I "made a determined attack on certain members of the Church, killing James the brother of John with the headman's sword" (Eusebius, 1981, p. 81).

The disposition of St. James' body after his death has been a matter of dispute and tradition as is the New Testament's silence on the "lost years" of his life between Pentecost and his death. McBirnie (1977) noted that "the absence of the name or the record of activities of so prominent an Apostle... in the book of *Acts*... could have some significance" and speculated that he might have visited and preached to the Jewish colonies in Spain and "upon his return to Jerusalem... James could have been accused by Herod... of spreading sedition" among the Jews in Spain (pp. 104–105). Thurston and Attwater (1996) noted that "according to the tradition of Spain, he made an evangelizing visit to that country... the earliest reference to this is... in the later part of the seventh century... in an oriental... source" (p. 183).

Religious or holy cards on sale in the Santiago de Compostela Cathedral gift shop also note that "a very old tradition claims that St. James preached at the Iberian Peninsula and that he wanted his disciples to move his corpse to Compostela when Herod Agrippa I ordered to behead him" (*St. James the Apostle*, 1996). As Thurston and Attwater (1996) elaborated, "According to the tradition of Spain, dating from about 830, the body was translated first to Iria Flavia, now El Padron, in Galicia, and then to Compostela... Spanish scholars champion the traditional view most strenuously" (p. 183). *The Golden Legend*, a compilation of French stories translated into English by William Caxton in 1483, in describing the *translatio*, explains that two of St. James' disciples laid his relics in a sarcophagus (the site was a Roman cemetery) and over it built an altar and a small chapel (Starkie, 1957).

The tomb was soon forgotten and covered over by forest until its rediscovery in 813 by a hermit, Pelayo, who "lived in a church dedicated to St. Felix ... situated at Libredon" (Otero, 1998, p. 4). Interrupted from his prayers "on successive nights [by] a series of inexplicable lights and sounds that seem to emanate from a nearby wood," Pelayo and his brother hermits alerted Theodomir, the bishop of Iria Flavia (ibid, p. 4), and led him, his entourage, and workmen to the site. Here, they cleared away the undergrowth to find a building in ruins with an altar and a lower-level crypt with three burials (Otero, 1998) and a piece of parchment in the sarcophagus identifying the remains as St. James and his two disciples (Starkie, 1957). The altar was used as the main altar in three successive basilicas built over the burial site until its transfer in 1105 to the adjoining Monastery of St. Pelayo, a community of Benedictine monks entrusted with the care of St. James' relics since their discovery (Otero, 1974). The relics of St. James and his two disciples remain today in a silver urn in a crypt directly beneath the present-day cathedral's main altar.

With the discovery of St. James' relics, the stage was set for the next phase in the development of Spain's "organizational culture." As a "founding event," it was an essential first step in "the mythic process of social self-identification" that ultimately forms the "personality of a group, whether a tribe, a nation, or a corporation" (Kendall, 1996, p. 202). More important, however, it was the *interpretation* of this event by Church–State promoters that was to play a critical role in the formation of Spain's mythological history as indeed the "collective 'schema'" of an organization's culture includes "what an organization *makes* of the facts" of its origins, a process that "gives an organization a vital self-consciousness" (ibid, pp. 200, 202). As Brown (2003) noted, "The historical Jesus was of course necessary for the development of Christianity. But even he wasn't sufficient. History required Paul... [to create Christianity's] theology, churches and governance" (pp. 232, 234). Building a distinctive mythology for Spain would require Church–State promoters to interpret the finding of the tomb with stories and rituals that, over time, would shape the character of the nation.

ST. JAMES, THE *RECONQUISTA*, AND NATION-BUILDING

Bishop Theodomir announced the discovery to Alfonso II, king of Asturias and Galicia, who "readily understood the political significance of the discovery and eagerly seized upon it... for the sake of the consolidation of his fragile kingdom" (Melczer, 1993, p. 13). Van Herwaarden (1980) explained that, at the time of the discovery of St. James' tomb, "Frankish influence in north-west Spain was... considerable" and "the news of the discovery... became for Alfonso II the starting-point for a new emphasis on the independence of his kingdom" (p. 17). This "aspiration to independence" was "a reaction against foreign influence, especially that of the Franks" (ibid, p. 17). Given that "no part of Spain was more heartily and thoroughly Spanish than this north-western country," the battle cry of "patriots and loyalists" soon became one "to denote exclusiveness, 'Spain for the Spaniards!'" (Stone, 1927, pp. 186–187). Belief in St. James, according to Simmons (1991), "served as a rallying point for the standard bearers of a newly emergent Hispanic nationality" (p. 23). Today, Spain is "often referred to as 'the land of Saint James the Great'" with his tomb at Compostela being "an important source of national identity" (Rosiko, 2000, p. 32).

The discovery also gave impetus to the *reconquista*, or liberation of Spain, from Muslim occupation. Nearly a hundred years earlier, in 711, the Islamic general Tariq crossed the Straits of Gibraltar from Morocco, and, within 3 years, Muslim forces had subdued the entire peninsula except the northern fringes on the Atlantic and Mediterranean coasts. The Muslim occupation represented a "major threat to the survival of a Christian way of life and civilization," and people "placed their hope for survival on the protection of Christian rulers and their armies" (Kinast, 1999, p. A23). The rulers and chroniclers of the remnant Christian northern kingdoms considered that they had a "mission to restore the Christian state that had existed before 711" (Vincent & Stradling, 1994, p. 47). The discovery of St. James' tomb was "a stronghold with which to fight against the Muslim invasion... Santiago was the main hope to cling on to" (Ministerio de Economía y Hacienda, 1995, p. 5). As Frey (1998) noted, "belief in the apostle's presence in Compostela bolstered the Christian drive south and the repopulation of the peninsula, which ultimately led to the expulsion of non-Christians from Spain in 1492" (p. 11). The *reconquista* actually had begun earlier in 718 with a victory by Pelayo, a Visigothic noble and the first of the Christian kings, in Covadonga in the northern Cantabrian mountains, when the Kingdom of Asturias was emerging (Starkie, 1957). By 1040, nearly one third of the Iberian peninsula was reconquered (Vincent & Stradling, 1994).

To aid in their liberation of Spain, Christian forces needed to counter the spiritual power of Islam, which fueled its military successes. The Muslim leader Abderrahman I founded in Cordoba a mosque with a shrine that "contained some of the bones of the Prophet Mahomet... these relics became the envy... of all Spain. Pilgrims came from all over Europe to pray at the Holy of Holies... and Moslems... drew their moral strength from the relics" (Starkie, 1957, pp. 21–22). It should be recalled that "Muhammad... had urged his followers to fight for Islam" and had begun his ministry "leading his followers in raids against Meccan caravans" (Stewart, 1967, pp. 18, 40). The successful raids "strengthened Muhammad's claim that he was the apostle of God" even as he assured his warriors that "if killed in battle they were sure of going to heaven... in fact, *jihad*, or 'holy war,' narrowly missed being the sixth pillar of Islam" (ibid, p. 40). After his death in 632, Muslim troops, "bearing the Koran and the sword" and shouting "Allahu Akbar!" ("Allah is most great!"), began their invasions of the Byzantine and Persian empires (ibid, pp. 35, 54).

Certainly, the notion of a militant faith was neither original nor unique to Muslims. Old Testament or Jewish scripture is replete with stories of God fighting alongside the Israelites.

Stone (1927) recalled that "the angel of the Lord went before the camp of Israel at the time of the Exodus" (p. 174), and Boadt (2002) noted that "Israel used battle language" in scripture, particularly in Psalms where "psalmists ask God to ... punish the wicked with terrible violence" (p. A18). During World War I, British troops rallied to victory in Mons around visions of St. George even as French soldiers were inspired by St. Joan of Arc and St. Michael the Archangel, "who appeared to them ... and led them on to victory" (Stone, 1927, p. 175). Even today, Palestinian suicide bombers invoke Allah's blessing, and "the contemporary militant Ulster-Protestant slogan, 'For God and Ulster', reveals national and religious aspirations have all too often been interwoven" ("Who Was JONAH?," 2002, p. 37). Pope John Paul II has declared that "it is a profanation of religion to declare oneself a terrorist in the name of God, to do violence to others in his name. Terrorist violence is a contradiction of faith in God" ("Reconciliation, The Only Road to Peace," 2002, p. 13). Spain soon "learned from the Moors" the "curious custom" ["intermingling of religious and military motives"], and launched its own counteroffensive (Simmons, 1991, pp. 13, 15). Sadly, Spain's struggle with Islam "produced a hardening of the faith and an intolerance toward others, leading to the widespread notion that Spaniards were the new chosen people of God ... pride and arrogance characterized the ruling classes ... as well as the conquistadors who opened a new kind of crusade against ... the Americas" (ibid, p. 15).

Not surprisingly, the Spanish forces found their "champion" in St. James. King Alfonso II informed Pope Leo III and Charlemagne of the discovery of St. James' tomb (McBirnie, 1977) and ordered the construction of a church on the site, a monastery and cloister for its guardians, and a fortified wall around the area (Starkie, 1957). More important, he declared the apostle the patron saint of Spain, a devotional designation that is still invoked today. Priests give pilgrims who visit the cathedral, as the author did in June 1999, a prayer card that reads, in part, "Oh glorious Spanish Nation strengthened with such a Patron ... because of his intercession the Almighty has done such great favors for you" [author's translation] (*Vigor del Camino*, 1999).

Actually, according to Mullins (1974), "the idea of St. James as the champion of Christianity in the fight against the Infidel" had been "first planted in the popular mind" by St. Beatus of Liébana, author of the *Commentaries on the Apocalypse* in 776 (p. 12). Beatus, a learned monk and scholar, "was an impassioned advocate of the Santiago legend," and it was he "who in the years immediately before the discovery prepared the atmosphere of excitement which overtook the Christian world when the news broke that the body really was in Spain" (ibid, p. 10). With the Moorish invasions of northern Spain, St. James "took his place on the battlefield as though he had ridden straight out of the pages of Beatus's *Commentaries*" (ibid, p. 12). Moreover, the notion of St. James as patron of Spain also predates its official proclamation by King Alfonso II and the discovery of St. James' tomb. Van Herwaarden (1980) explained that an Asturian–Galician hymn, *O Dei verbum patris ore proditum*, written as a homage to Asturian King Mauregatus, who successfully defended his kingdom against a Berber invasion, contains a reference to St. James as patron of Spain—"our protector and patron helper" (Melczer, 1993, p. 12). Written about 788, following the King's death, the hymn associates Mauregatus, "defender of Christendom in north-west Spain," with St. James in this struggle (van Herwaarden, p. 17).

Military battles and pilgrimages to St. James' relics soon followed, with Santiago de Compostela becoming "the most popular place of pilgrimage whose importance was only preempted by Jerusalem and Rome" (Cruz, 1984, p. 109). Christian soldiers rode into battle with the cry "Santiago y cierra Espana!" ("St. James and Close Spain!"), believing that St. James "was fighting alongside them" (B. Smith, 1984, p. 69). According to Stone (1927), "like St. Martin of Tours and St. George of England and other saintly military commanders, he generally appeared on horseback: fierce as the west wind, swift as the lightning's flash" (p. 174). Chroniclers recorded that in 845, at the battle of Clavijo, near Najera in Leon—" the first, largely mythical turning point in the military fortunes of the Christians" (Melczer, 1993, p. 66)—St. James appeared to King Ramiro I before the skirmish, promising him victory, and then rode with his forces to defeat Caliph Abderrahman II "on a white charger, having in one hand a snow-white banner [with] a blood red cross, and in the other a flashing sword" (Starkie, 1957, p. 23). The victory is commemorated in Spain annually as a feastday on May 23, with special Church liturgical services (Barbe, 1998). Over the ages, countless visual impressions in Spain have celebrated his patronage as warrior, from stone reliefs on royal chapels (Granada) and royal hospitals (Burgos), statues atop churches (Sevilla), portable figures carried in processions (Asturias), to prayer cards. To further underscore the Church–State devotion to St. James, a sculpted portrayal of the Clavijo apparition and an equestrian statue of St. James grace the 18th-century Rajoy Palace, once the Archbishop's residence, seat of Compostela's town council and the regional government of Galicia, located directly across from the cathedral (Otero, 1998).

The notion of the "sword-wielding apostle who personified both the manly and religious ideal incorporated in the concept of *Hispanidad*, or Spanish selfhood" (Simmons, 1991, p. 15) was one used to advantage years later by Francisco Franco. After the Civil War, "Santiago Matamoros became a politically potent symbol to advance the nationalist policy . . . of Franco" who "consciously allied himself with Santiago . . . as the savior and unifier of Spain" (Frey, 1998, p. 238). He restored both St. James as the patron of Spain and the annual tradition of a "national offering" of money to the saint (instituted by King Philip IV in 1646) and sponsored research on the pilgrimage (Frey, 1998). Franco visited Compostela in 1954 with members of his Falange Party, squadrons of city police, government ministers and foreign guests, and, during the liturgy, made the national offering "in an eloquent speech describing Spain's crusading spirit on behalf of the Church in the great days of her Empire and in the recent Civil War" (Starkie, 1957, p. 318). The tradition of the national offering continues today, and military units from throughout Spain regularly march on pilgrimage to Compostela to pledge their allegiance to St. James and the nation. A portrait of Franco and his army "represented as modern warrior-pilgrims of the Church militant under the protection of the apostle himself who flies overhead on his white charger" hangs in the Historical Military Archives in Madrid (Mullins, 1974, p. 15).

In another sense, the incarnation of St. James, while serving a political purpose, also reflects the covenantal relationship of Spanish faithful with their God, a relationship that is part of the nation-state's cultural identity. As B. Smith (1984) noted:

> The adoption of Santiago as the patron saint of Christian Spain, and the Spanish concept of him as both a spiritual and a corporeal figure, seem to provide early evidence of a cultural trait peculiar to Spaniards; unwilling to worship their God and saints from afar, they brought them down to earth. Not only did Santiago ride with them, but their art reflected this need for realism even in their spiritual world. (p. 69)

This Spanish mixture of faith, militancy, and nationalism by the 11th century was being copied throughout Europe. As Simmons (1991) noted, "The crusading zeal that burst forth in Spain and the rest of Europe . . . coincided with a revival of popular faith, papal reform, an expansion of the cult of saints, an enlarged devotion to pilgrimages, and a proliferation of ecclesiastical construction . . . it was during this same period that many parts of the Santiago legend . . . first gained currency" (pp. 13–14). For example, in the mid-11th century, Walsingham, England became "one of the four great pilgrimage sites of the Middle Ages" (Zeno, 2000, p. 17), built as a replica of Mary of Nazareth's home. During the next 250 years as England unified and matured into a world power, "all eight English kings journeyed to Walsingham,

bringing valuable jewels ... petitioning Our Lady for success in military campaigns and re-
turning in thanksgiving for prayers answered" (ibid, p.17). Seemingly, the old Roman Empire
was being reconstituted into new nations, with faith as a key building material in the process.
Also, in a communicative sense, it would seem that the devotional-promotional activities of the
religious and political advocates of St. James had found a receptive and trusting public in those
who needed both spiritual and physical assurance that a benevolent divine patron watched
over them and their nation. Embodying this covenantal relationship between the faithful and
their patron, clergy and political leaders alike represented themselves at once as both intercessors and "experts ... or service providers" dedicated to "furthering an end which is genuinely
good ... health, salvation, or justice" (Koehn, 1994, pp. 15, 153; cited in Baker, 2000, pp. 6,
12, 13). In this way, they fostered vital relationships with their faithful subjects and furthered
devotion both to St. James and *reconquista* Spain.

In the course of conducting the *reconquista* and the devotional-promotional campaign for
St. James over the centuries, Church and State promoters have fashioned a distinct cultural
identity and a nation-state. As Drijvers (1992) noted, "'Culture' is more than language alone
and includes the way a group of people live and live together, share experiences, materialize
these in expressive symbols, and shape time and space around them" (p. 195). And, more
important, particularly as it concerns Spain, Gormly (1999) observed that "most who study
culture ... see religion and culture as inextricably interwoven ... Religion is a potent cultural
force that affects behavior and imparts moral views and values into the public realm" (p. 24).

Nation-building is the process by which "diverse societies, regions, and groups within a
country are linked into a national-state system" (Morrison, 1989, p. 18). Nancy Morris (1995)
defined "nation" "as a self-defined community of people who share a sense of solidarity
based on a belief in a common heritage and who claim political rights that may include
self-determination" (p. 12). The "self-definition" "is usually based on some combination of
objective characteristics of history, language, culture, and territory" (ibid, p. 12). Moreover,
the process of "defining collective identity involves establishing the distinction between group
members and outsiders, 'us' and 'them';" indeed, a "shared perception of uniqueness and a
shared pride in that uniqueness see to rest at the core of collective identity" (ibid, pp. 8, 156).
It is a phenomenon that spans history from *reconquista* Spain to European decolonization in
the 1960s to modern-day identity struggles in Puerto Rico and Quebec (N. Morris, 1995).

Some have suggested that the nation-state is "a communicatively constructed entity" in
that communication channels "transfer information from one group or network to others and
buil[d] the relationships necessary for attaining national goals" (Taylor, 2000, p. 187; Deutsch,
1963, 1966). As Taylor (2000) noted, "relationships create social integration" and a "collective
consciousness that ... lead[s] to national integration" (p. 187; Deutsch, 1963, 1966). Moreover,
as Taylor (2000) noted, effective nation-building requires that "relationships ... be negotiated
between individuals ... and governments" and such "negotiation involves compromise, trust,
and respect" (p. 207), much like the foundation necessary for a covenantal relationship that
underlies effective religious devotional-promotional communication.

In a sense, the nation-building process is similar to the approach taken to establish
corporate identity defined in the broadest terms as "everything from products or services ... environments ... and information ... to behaviour ... the aggregate of an organization's activities and artefacts, everything it does and says, both deliberately and unintentionally,
built up over a period of time" (Meech, 1996a, p. 72). As Meech (1996a) noted, "In order to
survive and prosper, an organization needs to know what its *raison d'être* is and to ensure as
far as possible that all groups with which it is strategically involved do too" (p. 67). Given
a strategy "to generate both an awareness of and a positive attitude towards" itself, an organization strives through its corporate identity—"considered a potential asset in a competitive

environment"—to distinguish itself from others "and to provide its own members with a collective sense" (ibid, p. 67). It could be said that an organization, much like a nation-state, is
"a communicatively constructed entity" endeavor—to foster "relationships [that] create social
integration" (Taylor, 2000, p. 187).

Inasmuch as communication between government and its citizens is at the center of nation-
building, a public relations approach to the process should focus on such relationships (Taylor,
2000). Various studies have examined the role that public relations and communication in
general play in the nation-building process (Van Leuven & Pratt, 1996; Van Leuven, 1996;
Taylor & Botan, 1997; Taylor & Kent, 1999), including government campaigns to attract
investment and to build civic support on social issues. Still other government campaigns,
such as one in post-World War II Malaysia and another in the new republic of Singapore,
have focused on creating "shared values, a common will, and a single national identity" (Van
Leuven, 1996, p. 209). In much the same way that *reconquista* communicative campaigns
sought to rally Spain, these two campaigns for "political stability and national unity" were
intended to combat and drive out "enemy forces;" the first campaign endeavored "to wage
psychological warfare against the communist guerrillas by convincing Malaysians that the
British, and not the Chinese communist guerrillas . . . eventually won World War II over Japan"
while the second attempted to "preclude the build-up of Communism in Singapore" given the
level of "communist infiltration activities" predating the formation of the republic (Van Leuven
& Pratt, 1996, pp. 95, 97; Van Leuven, 1996, p. 209). As in Spain, Van Leuven and Pratt (1996)
noted:

> People accepted these campaigns because they symbolized the establishment of a national culture, with national
> interests being placed above separate sectional, ethnic, or linguistic interests. Because they believed in the end,
> people apparently did not object to the fact that the means to the end was one-way persuasive communication.
> (p. 98)

While conflict may appear to be ideological in nature, as with Singapore and Malaysia, or
religious as with *reconquista* Spain, Coup de Frejac (1999) suggested that "a misunderstanding
between two politics" and not cultural differences is at the origin of conflicts between cultures,
nations, and ideologies inasmuch as all these "have their 'politics' which are synonymous with
the struggle for power" (p. 7). Indeed, modern-day struggles "for formal differentiation from
existing states" by groups of ethnically, linguistically, or religiously distinct people are essentially "movements for political independence" (N. Morris, 1995, p. 9). Moreover, when such
movements inevitably "activate forces of political and military coercion," these pressures on
identity not only "can generate a vital counter-pressure" but also "may strengthen that identity
rather than diminish it" (ibid, pp. 7, 9, 168). In such conflicts, Coup de Frejac (1999) noted
that "the cultural dimension is frequently evoked and exploited" as "politics . . . us[es] . . . one
of the most powerful weapons ... culture as part of the arsenal" (p. 7). Inasmuch as feelings of
national identity generally are expressed through the use of various "'mythico-cultural apparatus': symbols such as language, flags, and anthems" (Schlesinger, 1991, as cited in N. Morris,
1995, p. 14)—"which have gained their meaning and their power through social interaction"—
political leaders can exploit such symbols to strengthen and to rally identity in a "defensive
response to the fear of cultural displacement" (N. Morris, 1995, pp. 161, 166). Indeed, Morris
(1995) observed that, in response to "political coercion" by the United States to "Americanize"
Puerto Rico's culture, island "political elites . . . have consistently sought to defend" Puerto Ri-
can identity (p. 168) using its distinctive Spanish language, flag, and other symbols. In a sense,
the *reconquista* in Spain can be viewed as a struggle for political power rather than a religious
war, with both sides attempting to use their full array of cultural weapons to advantage. In

this respect, St. James and Muhammad become more than just cultural symbols—they are transformed into veritable weapons of war.

Employing culture as a weapon, as in the case of Singapore, Malaysia, *reconquista* Spain, and other developing nation-states with low literacy levels, often requires using alternative channels of communication—oral community presentations (Van Leuven, 1996; Van Leuven & Pratt, 1996) and folk forms of entertainment such as dance dramas and songs (Reddi, 1978)—to reach rural and urban populations; in some cases, as in Malaysia, "local religious ... leaders ... were recruited to bolster campaign credibility" (Van Leuven, 1996, p. 211). In much the same manner, popular devotion to St. James (and to Spain) was cultivated by roving troubadours, poets, and clergy through song, "miracle stories," and sermons. Moreover, even as such interpersonal, folk forms of communication build a national organizational personality, they also serve to create further rituals, interpretations of past events and leaders, and stories that become part of the nation-state's mythological history and cultural self-consciousness. Artistic forms of expression, or "visual constructions," in particular, as Abraham (1999) noted, also can serve "as tools for achieving particular cultural agendas" (p. 7), specifically, "for advancing some moral, religious, political, or psychological purpose" (Schamber, 1991, p. 19). As a people materialize their culture, storytellers, whether they are artists, poets, public relations professionals, or journalists, craft the visual and verbal elements of their materials into "touchstones for the collective memory" of their target culture, reinforcing the self-consciousness of a nation-state (Silcock, 1994, p. 4). Indeed, over the course of 1,100 years, by proactively promoting popular devotion to St. James, both Church and State have generated as well as inspired a virtual torrent of communicative material—written, oral, and visual.

For example, in compiling a bibliography of works about Santiago dating from the inception of pilgrimages in the 9th century, Dunn and Davidson (1994) have identified more than 5,000 references, from pilgrims' travel journals to Church documents to mass media articles in 12 different languages. They also noted a resurgence in scholarly and popular media activity on the subject within the last decade. Such materials serve to further recycle, embellish, and imbed "the cult of Santiago" with its cultural trappings into the national psyche and that of devotees globally. Ultimately, all such communication serves not only to further popularize the saint and Santiago de Compostela but also, in a devotional-promotional sense, to advance the process of covenantal relationship-building between the faithful and St. James, the Church, and, ultimately, with God as well as to call new generations into relationship. And, as with the announcement of the finding of St. James' tomb, Church–State promoters have played an important role in publicly campaigning for their favorite saint and city.

CHURCH–STATE PROMOTERS
AND DEVOTIONAL CAMPAIGNING

Both Church and State have encouraged pilgrimages to Compostela in a variety of ways over the years and have done so effectively. Indeed, the number of official pilgrims (those receiving certificates of completion from Church officials) has increased from a low of 100 in 1974 to more than 10,000 in 1992 (Dunn & Davidson, 1994). Some 99,000 pilgrims visited Compostela in 1993 (Dunn & Davidson, 1996), and, in 1999, there were 155,000 pilgrims (Pousa, 2001).

As an encouragement to visit Compostela, according to Starkie (1957), "a pilgrimage could be [a] means of atonement [for sins], and so absolution was frequently granted to Papal Bull, upon condition that the penitent should visit certain holy places" (p. 62). Special moratoriums were granted to debtors if they were away on pilgrimage, and "university professors in Spain "might be lawfully excused from . . . giving . . . lectures . . . if . . . on pilgrimage to . . . St. James" (ibid, p. 68). However, "devotion to St. James constituted the primary motivation for undertaking the pilgrimage" (Melczer, 1993, p. 39). According to Dalrymple (1992), "Mass pilgrimage . . . in the eleventh century . . . was inspired first and foremost by devotion: People really did believe in saint's relics, that they had a spiritual power and could act as divine go-betweens in the quest for personal salvation" (p. 116). Even today, more than half the pilgrims who visit the cathedral's office to receive their *compostela*—a replica of an 11th-century document verifying the completion of their pilgrimage—"say they walk for 'religious reasons' when questioned by church officials" (Winchester, 1994, p. 69).

To further encourage pilgrims to Compostela, Pope Callistus II initiated in 1119 the "Jubilee or Holy Year Privilege," granting a plenary or full indulgence to travelers who visit the cathedral (and pass through its "holy door" with the proper intentions) in a year in which the feastday of St. James—July 25—falls on a Sunday (Otero, 1998). In 1179, Pope Alexander III declared that the observance be celebrated in perpetuity (Concello de Santiago Departamento de Turismo, 1994). In recent years, the Holy Year, or "Jacobeo" (Latin for James), has been celebrated in 1971, 1993, 1999, and 2004. The next Holy Year will be celebrated in 2010.

It was during the late 11th to early 12th centuries that Compostela enjoyed a veritable "golden age" under the skillful leadership of two bishops, Diego Pelaez and Diego Gelmirez. Pelaez, with support from King Alphonse VI, began with a "conscious and aggressive program of dignifying the apostolate of St. James" and "exaltation of the city . . . as a 'second Rome'" (Melczer, 1993, p. 21). In 1078, "the building of the vast Romanesque Cathedral was begun," and, in 1095, Pope Urban II transferred the bishopric see from Iria Flavia to Compostela (ibid, p. 22). Bishop Gelmirez assumed control in 1100, and "bolstered Santiago as a kind of second epicenter of Western Christendom and realistically evaluated the pilgrimage to St. James . . . as perhaps the most important tool of power at his disposal" (ibid, pp. 22–23). During this time, the road to Compostela became "an extremely efficient means of scientific, artistic and literary communication" (Ministerio de Comercio y Turismo, 1995, p. 2).

It was during his administration that perhaps the most famous promotional manuscript for St. James, the *Liber Sancti Jacobi* or *Codex Calixtinus* (named in honor of Pope Calixtus II), was produced in 1130. The manuscript actually is a compilation of previously existent material into five books that include St. James' biography, sermons, hymns, and the first travel guidebook of St. James' Road, presumably written by Aymery de Picaud, a French cleric and Pope Calixtus' chancellor (Starkie, 1957; Dunn & Davidson, 1996). Its importance, according to Dunn and Davidson (1996), cannot be underestimated as it "codified the pilgrimage to Compostela . . . practically everything since that creation is imitation, commentary or exegesis of the original work" (p. xxvi). The *Liber* "was written . . . in order to boost the pilgrimage to the tomb of St. James" inasmuch as it "was intended by . . . Cluny to be an account of the great pilgrimage written at the height of its fame;" the monks of Cluny, "who looked after the roads and hospices in France and Spain," "were especially interested in pilgrimage" and "compiled books of instructions for travellers" (Starkie, 1957, pp. 40, 64). According to Otazo (1972), "Cluny was Compostela's manager and business associate . . . and acted much like a XX century travel agency . . . promot[ing] the pilgrimage to Santiago in all of her dependencies throughout Europe" (p. 42). Picaud detailed four of the principal routes—all French—which "became the most renowned roads perhaps largely because of how they were described" (Dunn & Davidson, 1996, p. xxv). In describing the pilgrimage routes to Compostela, Picaud "introduced the golden age of the cult," and through circulation of the book, "wider significance was given to . . . the Apostle" (Starkie, 1957, pp. 1–2). Book IV of the *Liber* was considered "beneficial to the shrine, to the clergy, and to the city" for, in its text, "Charlemagne ordains that all powers ecclesiastical and civil in the Peninsula should be subject to the see of Compostela" and that "all should pay an annual tithe to Santiago" since "it is of equal status with Rome" (C. Smith, 1996, p. 31).

The *Liber* "was copied... for diffusion in France... for the clergy and chroniclers [and noblemen];" its book of sermons "was clearly for use by the clergy in their preaching on the Saint's special feasts" while another book of the saint's miracles "provided attractive materials for the same sermons (C. Smith, 1996, p. 27). Since "the great majority of simple folk... had probably never before left their native provinces... much reassurance would have been necessary... the pilgrim's parish priest could presumably give this with some confidence" (ibid, p. 23).

The communicative process used to promote pilgrimages to Compostela is similar to that conceptualized by Roper in his "Concentric Circle Theory" (1954). Propagated by disciples or promoters, ideas and influence move outward from a center of "Great Thinkers" (Einstein, Adam Smith) to "Great Disciples" (Oppenheimer, Lincoln), "Great Disseminators" (national figures in politics, media, and industry), "Lesser Disseminators" (local editors, clergy), "Politically Active" (civic leaders), and, finally, to the "Politically Inert" (popular majority). An organization influences the members of any one particular circle—who, in turn, influence others in their circle and those in the next adjoining circle—by directing "a message... [to the immediate target group] in a medium they understand and respect" (Roper, 1954, p. 31). While Roper contended that such messages can be communicated via "class media," he also observed that the "interaction of neighbor upon neighbor" often serves to disseminate ideas throughout society "without any apparent influence of the mass media" (ibid, p. 25). The best approach, concluded Roper, is to use influentials "respected by the particular target group" in a mix of interpersonal and mass-mediated communication (ibid, p. 32).

Indeed, as various "influentials" (Church and government officials) have disseminated key messages about St. James in Spain to publics in adjoining "circles," they have used commentaries about and visits to St. James' tomb by yet other "influentials" as "celebrity endorsements" or "testimonials" in their corporate publicity—a promotional tactic most commonly used, of course, in commercial advertising. Throughout the centuries, Compostela has attracted numerous "celebrity" pilgrims, particularly royalty who, with their visits, served as promotional endorsements for St. James even as they sought his "endorsement" of their administration. According to Dunn and Davidson (1996), a record of early medieval pilgrims to Compostela is a veritable "who's who list" of Spanish and other European royalty: Alfonso VI, Fernando II, Alfonso IX, Violante (wife of Alfonso X) of Spain; Luis VI, Louis VII of France; Frederick I, Leopold VI of Austria; Sancho II of Portugal; and Empress Matilda (daughter of Henry I of England). In addition, cardinals, dukes, and others, including St. Francis and Erasmus (who wrote of his travels), joined the thousands of pilgrims who journeyed annually to the city (Starkie, 1957). Modern-day celebrity pilgrims have included Pope John Paul II, who visited Compostela in 1982—the first Pope to do so—and again in 1989. Ten years later, in 1999, to encourage pilgrims to visit Compostela during the Holy "Jacobeo" Year, he issued a Vatican document on the benefits of pilgrimage to shrines in 1999. Prayer cards distributed to cathedral visitors included his message—in actuality, a promotional endorsement—about Compostela:

The Road to Santiago created a vigorous spiritual and cultural current of fertile interchange among the peoples of Europe. But, what pilgrims truly sought with their humble and penitent attitude was that testimony of faith that seems to resound in the Compostelean stones with which the Basilica of the Saint was built [author's translation] (*Vigor del Camino*, 1999).

King Juan Carlos I attended St. James' feastday ceremonies at the cathedral on July 25, 1999, and made a special visit to embrace the statue of the saint behind the main altar as is the custom of pilgrims—a photo opportunity that generated considerable news coverage worldwide ("Juan Carlos y Santiago Apostol," 1999). Earlier, in June, members of the rock band the Rolling Stones also "paid honor" to St. James by visiting the cathedral and "kissing the saint" prior to their concert in the city, which similarly attracted media attention (Sotelino, 1999, p. 16).

Such visits are none other than advertisements, which are circulated to opinion leaders, the media, and the general public via institutional newsletters, bulletins, news releases, and prayer cards—not to mention medieval art, poetry, sermons, miracle stories, and music about St. James (as contained in the previously mentioned *Liber Sancti Jacobi*)—in an attempt to attract pilgrims. And, as the media produce stories of such events, the coverage, because of its perceived objectivity, further becomes a form of *third-party endorsement*, "bestowing legitimacy and newsworthiness" on the "product" (Wilcox et al., 2000, p. 225).

The Church, and the Papacy in particular, has continued to promote St. James and pilgrimage in various ways ever since. During the late 1870s, scientific excavations were conducted to find the "lost" tomb of St. James, and its rediscovery prompted a resurgent promotional campaign by the Church; the Archbishop of Compostela, Juan de Sanclemente, had hidden the relics in another tomb in the cathedral in 1588 when Sir Francis Drake and his Armada threatened to sack the city (he burned St. Augustine, Florida, to the ground in 1586). Pope Leo XIII sent a special commission to verify the relics and declared with the Archbishop of Compostela their authenticity in an Apostolic Letter, *Deus Omnipotens*, on November 2, 1884 (Starkie, 1957). According to Dunn and Davidson (1996):

> Other Cathedral personnel . . . worked . . . through the first decade of the twentieth century publishing records and old documents, writing on various aspects of the history of the . . . Cathedral and the Saint enshrined there. In all these publications and activities we discern a concerted effort to promote the pilgrimage to Compostela. (p. xxix)

In 1940, on the eve of the Feast of St. James, Pius XII proclaimed his "virtual" pilgrimage "to take up his staff to go as pilgrim . . . in spirit" to Santiago" (Starkie, 1957, p. 59). Pius XII, in a worldwide radio broadcast in 1948, told a postwar audience that pilgrimage to Compostela "had the noble function . . . of relieving the unfortunate and comforting all . . . and will continue to be a blessing for the world" (ibid, p. 59). According to McDowell (1991), Pope Pius was "the first Pope to become widely known through radio and television . . . and used the media to promulgate his concern with liturgy" (p. 193).

In more recent years, both Church and State have endeavored to promote devotion to St. James. To celebrate the Holy "Jacobeo" Year in 1971, for example, Spain's Information and Tourism Ministry sponsored the publication of a major compilation of historical and cultural information on St. James. The work, *Santiago en Toda Espana, en Europa y en America*, documents the artistic, religious, and cultural expressions of devotion to St. James in Spain and throughout Europe and the Americas. Various chapters were written by scholars, clergy, and government officials, including the Ministry's Secretary General; according to the Ministry, the book was published for "religious and patriotic reasons . . . exalting the spirit of St. James and the patronage of the Apostle in Spain" (Information and Tourism Ministry, 1972, p. 5).

For the 1993 Holy "Jacobeo" Year, according to Dunn and Davidson (1996), "both the Spanish government and the Catholic Church made great press about the anniversary, holding grand celebrations, aiding in providing lodging and . . . helping to mark the routes leading to

Compostela ... Popular singer Julio Iglesias was the celebrity representative, in an effort to reach out to a wide audience" (p. xiv). Additionally, Compostela's Archicofradia and the Xunta, or government of Galicia:

> embarked on a course of editing and publishing materials dealing with the pilgrimage to Compostela, from reports on the statistics gleaned in surveys in Compostela to republications of seminal works, such as the Spanish translation of the *Liber Sancti Jacobi* ... the expositions and exhibitions ... were done with great ... fanfare ... Almost every major town along the Road to Compostela ... now has an association and an accompanying bulletin. (ibid, p. xxxvii)

One of the joint projects in particular was the publication by the Xunta and the Compostela Archbishopry of a book, *Santiago e America*, detailing the importance of St. James in the Americas; the publication accompanied an exhibit in the Compostela Monastery of St. Martin Pinario (Dunn & Davidson, 1996).

As part of the preparations to celebrate the 1999 Holy "Jacobeo" Year, the Galician government (Xunta) provided funding to remodel the Monastery of St. Pelayo's Museum of Sacred Art, adjacent to the cathedral, according to Sister Encarnacion Senande (personal interview, 17/6/1999). The Xunta, together with Spain's Ministry of Foreign Affairs and Iberia, Spain's national airline, also organized a "promotional exhibit" on Jacobean influence along the various pilgrimage routes; works of art and a scale model of the cathedral toured 13 cities in Europe, the United States, and South America (Xunta de Galicia, 1999, para. 2).

Additionally, Tur-Galicia, a public–private organization, promoted Holy Year celebrations through various corporate workshops and conventions; familiarization trips for travel agents and the media in Spain and Latin America; participation in "ferias," or religious feastday events in Spain; and public exhibitions and programs at its tourism office, Casa de Galicia, in Madrid (Xunta de Galicia, 1997). According to the Galician government, tourism is revitalizing the regional economy, with the area now ranking seventh as a tourist destination in Spain. Holy Year 1993 attracted 7 million visitors to Galicia and generated more than 38 million hotel overnight stays (Xunta de Galicia, 1997). With the designation of St. James' Road by the Council of Europe as the "First European Cultural Itinerary" in 1987, and, in 1985, by UNESCO as a World Heritage site—"one of the pillars of the development of Europe's history and cultural identity" [author's translation]—both the Xunta and Tur-Galicia invested additional monies in infrastructure and promotional campaigns to attract tourists to Santiago de Compostela in 1999" (Xunta de Galicia, 1997, p. 387). According to Jose Agra Adan, an officer in the Ministry of Culture, Social Communication and Tourism, Xacobeo 99 (Jacobeo) broke all records for attendance, attracting more than 11 million visitors to the region and generating 500,000 million pesetas ($280 million U.S.) in revenue (personal online interview, 19/10/2000; Pousa, 2001).

Development of devotional-tourism as a natural resource by Galicia's Xunta has proceeded in earnest as the region has gained in autonomous status. Following the death of General Francisco Franco in 1975 and the establishment of a constitutional monarchy in 1978, specific broad powers were granted to various "autonomous" regions of Spain, which, in the case of Galicia, elected its own parliament, supported by a president and executive cabinet. The Ministry of Culture, Social Communication and Tourism is one of the departments that constitute the executive branch of regional government. According to the Xunta, tourism development that capitalizes on the region's distinctive culture and tradition, particularly in rural areas, is one of the central objectives in its strategic plan (Xunta de Galicia, 1997).

CONCLUSION

The 1,100-year devotional-promotional campaign by both Church and State for St. James is remarkable not only for its duration and crafting, but also for its effect upon pilgrims and nonpilgrims alike. It would seem that the covenantal relationship that Church–State promoters have so carefully fostered over the years has indeed blossomed into maturity. The fruit of the Road or *Camino* of St. James—in effect, an ancient Internet—can be seen throughout history in the political, economic, cultural, social, and religious development of Europe and of Spain in particular. Certainly, one cannot truly understand the culture and society of Spain without having first intellectually "embraced the Saint." Over the centuries, in the course of nation-building and religious devotional-promotional campaigning by Church–State promoters, the identities of St. James, Santiago de Compostela, Galicia, and Spain have become intertwined as one. Whatever the particular moment in history—the *reconquista*, the "golden age" of Compostela, or post-Civil War Franco Spain—St. James has ridden—or has *been* ridden, as it were—to the rescue of the nation. Personified as the living spirit of Spain, it is little wonder that St. James is the patron saint *par excellence* of the nation and its ambassador of goodwill (and tourism) to the world. Moreover, through modern technology, St. James' *Camino* since has been extended via video productions and Web sites that create a "virtual *Camino*" for would-be pilgrims to travel the Road as armchair spectators and to "virtually" embrace the saint. Seemingly, the Twelve Apostles' mission to proclaim the "good news" to the "ends of the earth" now can be accomplished electronically.

Future research would do well to examine fully the direction and nature of Church–State campaigning for St. James, comparing campaign plans perhaps for the most recent Holy Year—2004—with those for the next Holy Year—2010—in an attempt to detail the role of Church–State promoters and adjoining circles of influentials, including celebrity pilgrims, and to identify any significant shifts in messages, channels of communication employed, or key publics targeted given the development of Galicia as an autonomous region and the advent of new technologies including the Internet. Furthermore, inasmuch as it has been posited that the process of persuasive communication, and devotional-promotional communication specifically, can be viewed as a proactive symbiotic relationship between source and intended publics, an analysis of the interaction between these parties and their co-orientation would be helpful in gaining a greater appreciation of not only the formation of persuasive messages but also of the covenantal relationship upon which religious devotional-promotional public relations campaigns are built. With 14 Holy Years occurring in the 21st century (the next two in 2010 and 2021), there will be ample opportunities to explore Xacobeo campaigning, campaigners, and publics.

In the final analysis, as evidenced by the historic campaigning for St. James, public relations efforts cannot be successful unless built upon a covenantal relationship between practitioner and "client." In that respect, the promotional efforts for St. James reflect and enhance the trust that is the foundation of the relationship between the Church and its faithful. A review of the nature of that bond should not only serve as something to marvel at but also something to strive for in all public relationships, if indeed public relations would truly be a profession to be respected by society.

III

New Directions

INTRODUCTION

This section is dominated by the contributions of established media sociologists, all of whom have taught and supervised many students on the M.Sc. in Public Relations at the University of Stirling. The editors' intention here was to encourage inter-disciplinary work and debate and, in particular, to benefit from insights from one of public relations' sister disciplines. This was seen as a positive collaborative move in that the work showcased here explores a variety of aspects of public relations practice and shows clearly that media sociology's role in public relations need not be restricted to critique of public relations' social role, often focused in the political domain.

The first chapter, written by Richard Kilborn, begins by the author explaining the historical overlaps between public relations and documentary filmmaking that took place in the UK in the 1930s and 1940s and showing the entanglement between documentary film and propaganda. Kilborn then proceeds to consider the present-day reputational implications for public relations practitioners who facilitate documentary production by opening up their organisations to filmmakers. A number of examples are given to illustrate the analysis. The chapter deftly illustrates the fact that changes in the media and the production of programmes that entail interest groups has meant that public relations has become reinvolved with documentary in a more obviously contemporary and professional role.

Vincent Campbell makes a crucial intervention in public relations thinking by highlighting the challenges facing communicators in the area of science. Campbell convincingly argues that "scientific communication" is not confined to scientific subjects but affects "almost every feature of modern society [and] probabilities of particular risks (or opportunities) are often implicitly or explicitly discussed in all sorts of media output." As Campbell points out, media representation of risk and scientific issues shape public, political, and corporate agendas, which thus has major implications for public relations practitioners representing a variety of players in such debates. Campbell carefully outlines a number of approaches that have been taken in considering problems in the communication of science, and explores the reasons for media misrepresentation of science as well as issues surrounding the public misunderstanding of science and the implications for communication campaigns. Finally, the chapter raises the fascinating spectre of the influences of the sociocultural context upon what might be defined as "serious" science, arguing, possibly counterintuitively, that "a focus by communication professions purely on data and evidence in scientific campaigns is likely to run into problems."

Raymond Boyle and Richard Haynes straddle public relations, sports studies, and media sociology in a chapter which begins by mapping the rise of promotional activities in football with a special focus on public relations and its relationship with other parts of the entertainment industries. This analysis is achieved through an exploration of the relationship between football journalism and public relations and the presentation of case studies that illustrate the role of public relations in football scandals. Finally, the chapter indicates the potential of the field for elucidating the relationship between promotional activities, public relations, and the football industry and highlights future lines of research.

The final chapter in this section picks up on themes identified by Campbell, Boyle, and Haynes in an attempt to open up the areas of sport, health, and tourism and the intersections between them (health tourism, sports tourism) for public relations research and analysis. The author argues that sport, health, and tourism play central parts in culture, international communications, media, business, economics, and politics and, at an individual level, are an important component of individual identity construction. The chapter therefore emphasises sociocultural activities that shape and describe interest groups (publics) and debates (rhetoric) at the level of everyday life and discourse. These topics are complex and attractive because they touch so many aspects of life, but also because it is clear that they are important to so many citizens. Focusing public relations analysis at this level of society may reveal different aspects of the range and depth of public relations' role in culture than a concentration on corporate or political public relations. As part of this grass-roots approach, the chapter highlights the importance of lifestyle media. The chapter also indicates that sports and tourism literature have, to date, given very little attention to public relations and suggests that both sports and tourism practitioners could benefit from a deeper understanding of the field.

10

A Marriage Made in Heaven or in Hell? Relations Between Documentary Filmmakers and PR Practitioners

Richard Kilborn
Stirling Media Research Institute

This chapter reflects on the relationship between the work of documentarists and the operations of the public relations industry. Though not intended primarily as an historical survey, the chapter attempts to throw some light on the changing nature of this relationship from the early days—when documentary filmmaking was largely dependent on various forms of industrial, commercial, and government sponsorship—to the situation today, when documentary film and programme makers rely much more on television for the funding of their projects and the airing of their work. These changes have, naturally enough, had consequences for the ways in which public relations practitioners have sought to exploit documentary in their ongoing attempts to promote the interests of those they represent.

In seeking to illuminate various aspects of the relationship between those who undertake public relations work and the documentarists with whom they seek to collaborate or whose ear they try to bend, the chapter also draws attention to instances where the relationship breaks down. It chronicles instances where PR persons are called on to intervene after film or programme makers have produced allegedly biased or distorted accounts of a client's activities and where a public relations exercise has to be launched in order to repair or limit the damage. Though such instances are comparatively rare, the fact that they do occasionally occur has given rise to a certain amount of suspicion between documentarists and the institutions or organizations that agree to be filmed. It is for this reason that, from the outset of any filming project, both sides have to have a clear understanding of the terms and conditions under which the filming occurs. Film and programme makers need, for their part, to have the assurance that, in producing their documentary accounts, they have not been inveigled into merely serving the promotional needs of publicity-hungry companies or institutions. The latter, on the other hand, need to be reassured that once they agree to be the subjects of a documentary investigation, their interests and activities will not be misrepresented.

INTRODUCTORY REMARKS

The last few decades have seen an exponential rise in public relations activity, as companies and organizations have sought to "manage" their relationships with variously defined publics with which they are seeking to communicate. In the attempt to secure promotional advantage, no efforts are spared to ensure that companies, institutions, and individuals gain the much desired oxygen of publicity (Michie, 1998, pp. 1–17). The public relations industry can, in this respect, be regarded as an integral part of the "promotional culture" which has become such a significant feature of contemporary Western societies (Strinati, 2000, pp. 235–236). One consequence of these developments is that PR practitioners have to be adept at maintaining good working relations with the media professionals whose work can exert a powerful shaping influence on public understanding and opinion.[1] A further consequence is that the vehicle we have come to know as the "public relations machine" is now in perpetual motion. As the authors of a recent article on the rise of the PR industry in Britain observed:

> There is almost no issue of consequence for business, government or pressure groups which has not been attended to by promotional professionals... It is clear that PR and public affairs have seeped into the very fabric of policy and decision-making in Britain and in the European political arena. (Miller & Dinan, 2000, pp. 27–28)

Whilst the fundamental goals of public relations (those of promoting a better understanding or otherwise defending the interests of the organizations they represent) may not have changed radically over the years, the transformations which have taken place within the media and broadcasting environment—especially those resulting from the increasing deregulation and commercialization of broadcast services—have arguably facilitated the work of PR practitioners. Indeed, concern is often expressed that the provision of allegedly "informational" material is now overly determined by persuasive, promotion-seeking agents. Spin doctoring, lobbying, and various types of news management and PR activity have become so much a part of our contemporary consumer-oriented culture that disquiet is voiced in some quarters about the threats this might pose to the democratic process (Miller, 1998b, p. 65; Schlesinger et al., 2001, pp. 14–15). Anxieties are furthermore expressed that audiences and readers may not always be sufficiently aware of the role played by diverse promotional agencies in the production of various types of media material. Of special concern to some commentators has been the type of public relations activity where information beneficial to particular interest groups is fed to news organizations that do not always choose to provide adequate acknowledgment of its origins. As Eldridge et al. have observed:

> We should notice, in particular, the role that public relations agencies play in the preparation of video news releases. These are pre-packaged news stories prepared on behalf of business or other interest groups which are then sent to newsrooms or transmitted by satellite to TV stations throughout the world... These "story segments" can be shown on news programmes without attribution, and to that extent can be described as a hidden form of manipulation. (Eldridge et al., 1997, p. 101)

For no small number of observers, it is the fact that these practices are hidden from view that creates the biggest threat. In most forms of advertising, or so it is claimed, consumers are left in no doubt about the intentions of the information-providers. With news reporting and

---

[1]This also includes the practice of journalists and documentary filmmakers giving media training to business executive and captains of industry to ensure that they give a good account of themselves when appearing in TV interviews or documentary accounts of their activities (Miller, 1998b, p. 75).

other types of "factual" media output, however, audiences allegedly have a different set of expectations about the status of the material. Consequently, the unacknowledged involvement of invisible persuaders is potentially more invidious (Michie, 1998, p. 6). Evoking a scenario where groups of powerful but largely anonymous players succeed in effecting leverage over those who are claiming to report objectively on important issues of the day acquires therefore something of the quality of a nightmare vision.

Whilst properly drawing attention to the manipulative activities of these hidden persuaders, one should also bear in mind that the last few decades have also brought greater levels of awareness on the part of media consumers about how information is disseminated and promotional advantages sought. In making this point, however, one has to be cautious not to overstate the power that consumers have. Even allowing for apparently growing public scepticism about, say, the broadcast media's claims for the impartiality of its news and current affairs broadcasting, this heightened media savviness does not necessarily mean that the public is any more privy to the diverse, and not always transparent, operations of the public relations industry.

If it is the case those responsible for generating news and current affairs output for television networks are constantly being solicited by publicity-seeking organizations, is it not reasonable to suppose that those producing more extended forms of factually based programming such as documentary will be similarly targeted? Documentary film and programme makers may persuade themselves that they are able to maintain a vigorously independent stance in their coverage and analysis of events, but, as the following pages will reveal, they may be just as vulnerable to attempts on the part of their subjects to gain promotional advantage from media exposure.

THE DOCUMENTARY MISSION TO RAISE AWARENESS

Documentary film has a long and chequered history. Like most other media forms it has, over the decades, gone through significant transformations. Not only has it actively sought new ways of representing the real (Nichols, 1991), but it has also had to adapt to a series of institutional demands concerning the functions it has been required to fulfil.

The origins of documentary can be traced back to the latter years of the 19th century when it first became possible to document and chronicle events occurring in the sociohistorical world using the newly emerging technologies of cinematography. Much of the early documentary work attempted to capitalize on the novelty value of the medium, as audiences were enthralled to see filmic representations of everyday reality. Some of the early travelogues and ethnographic accounts also presented fascinating insights into distant lands and exotic cultures (Jacobs, 1979, pp. 2–11; Barnouw, 1974, pp. 3–30). Many of the early documentarists sought to promote their work on the strength that it offered audiences an essentially different sort of media experience to the one provided by the increasingly popular fiction film. It was not long, however, before it began to be recognized that documentary could be exploited for both educative and promotional (public relations) purposes.

Various factors and circumstances led to the recognition that documentary had great potential as a consciousness-raising instrument. Developments in film-recording technology, and especially the coming of sound in the late 1920s, produced a heightened sense of realism for documentary audiences and meant that filmmakers could experiment with new ways of representing the real. It was, however, developments in the sociopolitical and economic domain which prompted governments and other bodies to utilize mass media to "educate" the public as to what courses of action were being contemplated on their behalf and to seek their consent for the measures being undertaken (Barnouw, 1974, p. 81).

It is against this background—the state's need to secure a much greater degree of public involvement in the democratic enterprise—that the great flowering of socially educative documentary work produced in Britain during the later 1920s and through the 1930s has to be understood. What is sometimes underestimated in some historical surveys of the period is the extent to which this work of civic education (using film as a consciousness-raising medium) was dependent in no small measure on ideas emanating from the United States. The key idea—that of winning consent for the actions of democratic government by all available means—had already been persuasively articulated by Walter Lippman in his highly influential *Public Opinion* (1922). Lippman's principal thesis was that democratic ideas and ideals would have to be actively promoted in such a way as to enable citizens to feel a greater measure of involvement in the operations of the complex modern state (McNair, 1996, p. 35; Ellis, 2000, p. 21). John Grierson, founding father of the British Documentary Movement and an influential figure in the international development of documentary, openly admitted that it was Lippman's work which provided the vital impetus to his own thinking on the uses to which documentary might be put (Hardy [ed.], 1966, pp. 150–151, Ellis, 2000, pp. 21–24). In developing his ideas on how documentary could be used in the task of "imaginative civic education" (Corner, 1996, p. 22; L'Etang, 2000, pp. 83–90), Grierson was also influenced by other more business-oriented philosophies to which he was exposed during a 3-year stay in the States. An important impetus to the growth of documentary, as it developed under Grierson's nurturing influence, was thus the exposure of one of its leading exponents to American ideas on techniques of persuasion and the use of the mass media to accomplish both educative and propagandist goals.

On his return from the United States, Grierson began to give more active consideration to the instrumental use of film in this broad task of civic education. He linked up with like-minded individuals who were also intent on harnessing the power of the mass media (especially film) for consciousness-raising ends (L'Etang, 2000; 2004, pp. 32–38). Grierson himself showed considerable public relations prowess in forging alliances with key government officials and civil servants and persuading them of the role that documentary film could play in illuminating and explaining the work being undertaken by democratic institutions (Grierson in Hardy [ed.], 1966, p. 146).

It was largely as a result of Grierson's influence and vigorous campaigning that the movement which came to be known as the "British Documentary Movement" (BDM) was set in train. The movement was born out of the recognition (or claim) that cinema could exert a powerful influence as a medium of social propaganda. Films produced by the BDM in the late 1920s and 1930s such as *Drifters* (1929), *Night Mail* (1936), and *Song of Ceylon* (1935) have now entered the established canon of documentary work and are seen to have had a shaping influence on the developing language of documentary. It is important to recognize, however, that all these films owe their being to various types of *sponsorship*. They must be seen as products of a symbiotic relationship between sponsoring agencies such as the Department of Overseas Trade or the Empire Marketing Board and a group of highly motivated filmmakers anxious to explore both the aesthetic and consciousness-raising potential of a medium that was beginning to exercise a powerful hold over the public imagination (Swann, 1989, pp. 12–13). The hope was that, in exchange for contributions to the funding of documentary projects or for assistance provided to the filmmaker in gaining entry into institutions or organizations from which access otherwise might be barred, film or programme makers could be relied upon to produce an account that would provide reasonably positive media exposure for the subject under documentary scrutiny.

This is not to say that there were not initial qualms about using film for public relations and publicity ends. Slowly but surely, however, individual civil servants (possibly mindful of Lenin's dictum that "of all the arts, for us the cinema is the most important") began to recognize that film could play a significant role in their public relations operations. The Empire Marketing Board—set up to boost British and Empire Trade and Industry in the face of American competition—was one of the first departments to use film documentary to these ends. Besides drawing attention to specific products and services, films made at the behest of the EMB also fulfilled the more broadly defined PR task of soliciting consent and of creating a favourable climate of opinion for the ideas and practices for which the Government needed to have widespread public support.

The success of the Empire Marketing Board in using film for promotional and publicity purposes—together with the more general recognition of the persuasive power of film—had the effect of encouraging other institutions and agencies to include film (and more specifically documentary) in their publicity and public relations operations. Thus, it was that during the 1930s public relations practices became ever more closely allied with the activities of documentary filmmaking. Individual government departments (such as the Post Office) also began to set up their own film production units in order to ensure a greater measure of control over potentially unreliable filmmakers. By the same token, government civil servants within these departments actively campaigned for the use of film in the important task of external and internal public relations.

HE WHO PAYS THE PIPER...

As already signalled in the introduction to this chapter, the relationship between documentarists and those who broadly represent PR interests has always been a slightly uneasy one. Though the BDM filmmakers of the 1930s were wont, for understandable reasons, to claim they had developed good working relations with government and commercial sponsors, the relationship between the filmmakers and their various sponsors was always prone to strains and stresses. The primary explanation for this is that, whilst both "camps" recognized that they shared certain common goals (e.g., reaching out and finding the ear of a number of defined publics), there was still a considerable divergence in their respective aspirations as to make for a problematical relationship at times. Apart from those occasions when filmmakers are employed on propaganda missions or on corporate profile-raising tasks, documentarists have always wanted to emphasize that the accounts that they render are their own "creative treatment of actuality" (Grierson, 1966, p. 13). Thus, whilst a sponsor may be able to define the broad parameters within which commissioned documentarist can work, filmmakers will always wish to underline that their accounts do not simply represent the views of a sponsoring agent.

Even though there can often be friction in the relationship between sponsors and documentary filmmakers, it is relatively seldom that these tensions are played out in the public domain. It is precisely *because* these conflicts rarely become matters of public knowledge that we need to discover more about the reasons for the breakdown in sponsor/documentarist relationships. One of the tasks of documentary scholars, therefore, has been to throw more light on the precise leverage which sponsors have been able to exert over filmmakers and on the degree of freedom accorded to filmmakers in the course of their documentary explorations. Work published to date provides some reinforcement for the view that, especially in the early days of documentary, sponsors and public relations agencies were able to exercise greater leverage than the filmmakers themselves were willing to acknowledge (Swann, 1989, pp. 176–179; Winston, 1995, pp. 35–36). Documentarists for their part have likewise always been reluctant to concede that they may have relinquished critical or authorial freedom as a result of the sponsoring agreements into which they entered. What emerges from the analyses of scholars such as Winston and Swann, however, is that there was always a "quid pro quo" in the relations between documentarist and sponsor. Thus, even during the period when documentarists appeared to have gained unprecedented support from government departments anxious to capitalize on the persuasive power of film, there were always strings attached to the monies given. At the same time, filmmakers also had to display considerable public relations skills in maintaining an adequate level of support in the light of the growing scepticism of sponsors about the actual benefits of this form of sponsorship.

In 1930s Britain, it was not long before those government agencies responsible for initiating and funding sponsored documentary projects became quite sceptical as to whether these documentaries were actually raising public awareness and whether the hired documentarists could be relied upon to carry out the remits with which they had been entrusted. Take, for example, the series of documentary films made during the 1930s by the government-sponsored GPO Film Unit. The declared aim of the unit was to publicize the work of the Post Office and to inform the public of the impressive achievements of Government in the wider communications field. For a time the relations between filmmakers and sponsor had been especially close, with key members of the unit having been transferred to the Post Office payroll. Though the work of this unit was generally highly regarded (it produced among other things the well-known documentary *Night Mail* [1936]), it was not long before cracks and fissures began to appear in the relations between sponsors and filmmakers. As one commentator has observed:

> The Post Office was the leading exponent of the use of modern public relations by official bodies. Film was an important public relations tool that had been largely developed by the documentary movement. When the opportunity came to place film policy under the direct control of the civil service, [however], it was eagerly grasped by the Post Office. *In the final analysis, the Post Office preferred to control its own publicity rather than delegating it to a group of filmmakers with definite ideas of their own concerning the use of film publicity* [my emphasis]. (Swann, 1989, p. 78)

Another point worth underlining in this respect is that, even amongst members of the BDM filmmaking community, there was considerable divergence of opinion as to how beholden documentarists should be to their sponsoring agents. Grierson for his part was always eager to talk up the educational benefits accruing from documentary, whilst playing down the role of the sponsoring agent. Several of his contemporaries, however, took the arguably more circumspect view that their work was quite heavily constrained by sponsor requirements. Writing in 1935, the documentarist Paul Rotha, for instance, observed:

> It is a significant fact that it is primarily the industrialist and the Government official and *not* the educationalist who are today making possible the development of the cultural film by providing the all-important means of production. Ostensibly serving the needs of propaganda or, if you prefer it, furthering the aim of public relations, documentary is at the same time fulfilling a definite instructional purpose. It is being enabled to do so by the financial resources of industry and commerce, an aspect of education and propaganda that is worth considerable contemplation. (Rotha, 1952, pp. 27–28)

Rotha's words make clear that industrial, commercial, and government sponsors were certainly counting on specific promotional benefits from their investment. This highlights the importance of focussing on the funding mechanisms that operated during this period of documentary history. The filmmakers who belonged to the BDM, for instance, were well aware of what was expected of them in exchange for being given quite generous funding. For the most part they were able to reconcile their own values and beliefs with those of the government departments who were anxious to "build up mutual sympathy and understanding between the people and the work of the public services" (Rotha, 1952, p. 59). It was only when projects were mooted where documentarists were asked to incorporate transparently political messages into their films—such as those that unambiguously promoted pro-Empire beliefs—that relations between filmmaker and sponsor became strained. An additional reason for this was that most BDM filmmakers were politically on the left and thus had an understandable desire that their films should promote pro-labour and reformist ideas.

By the later 1930s documentary was being increasingly pressed into service as a propaganda vehicle (Barnouw, 1974, p. 139). What was formerly the GPO Film Unit became the Crown Film Unit and the work of documentarists became subject to a more explicit set of government-determined objectives. The war created new challenges but also new opportunities for documentarists, and during this time public relations officers and documentarists worked very closely together as concerted efforts were made to maintain public morale. Whilst the war provided a healthy boost for documentary and public relations activity, it is significant in the light of our present discussion that even during this period doubts were raised as to whether some filmmakers were sufficiently "on message" to carry out the propaganda tasks with which they were entrusted. Humphrey Jennings, notable for films such as *London Can Take it* (1940), *Listen to Britain* (1942) and *Fires Were Started* (1943), was, for instance, occasionally subject to criticism that his films were too poetic and that they did not hammer home their propagandist message with the required urgency (Winston, 1995, pp. 106–107).

A BRAVE NEW WORLD?

The course of documentary in Britain during the period 1925–1945 had been determined—sometimes in ways that the filmmakers were not always willing to concede—by the desire of government departments and public utilities companies to use film as a vehicle for propagating particular ideas. In the immediate post-war period, however, the support that had been once provided by government PR departments and agencies began to fall away. This was accompanied by the recognition on the part of both PR professionals and documentarists that alternative ways would have to be sought to communicate more effectively with the public. For instance, it was acknowledged that there had been considerable elitism in the way that Grierson and some of his followers had sought to "instruct" ordinary members of the public in ways that society could be improved. Many of the BDM documentaries—though claiming to speak to and for the common man—had adopted a preacherly, patronizing tone which could well have blunted their edge as socially educative vehicles (Swann, 1989, p. 178).

It was not just the decline of official public relations and government sponsorship that impacted on documentary in the immediate post-war era. Commercial and industrial organizations became, if anything, more sceptical of the public relations and promotional benefits to be derived from sponsored documentary. In the pre-war era, a man like Grierson had been able to deploy his formidable array of public relations and organizational skills to facilitate the collaboration between industrial or government sponsors and documentary filmmakers. Now, in a more austere economic climate, harder-nosed attitudes started to prevail. To an increasing extent, doubts began to be cast on the effectiveness of film as a promotional vehicle and much closer attention was paid than hitherto (especially in the United States) to devising better ways of *distributing* the films, so as to maximize their impact.[2] This led in many cases to far more money being spent on distribution and subsidized exhibition than on the cost of the

---

[2]There had also been opposition in various government quarters to the use of film as part of government public relations campaigns. Among other things, the cost-effectiveness of film was often questioned. Referring to the early work of the EMB, for instance, Swann noted that even then there had been "many clashes between those who favoured

original production (Barnouw, 1974, pp. 219–220; Rotha, 1952, pp. 227–228; Swann, 1989, pp. 107–108).

Slowly, however, as nations sought to recover from the traumas of war and to rebuild their shattered economies, documentary film began to be used once again for a series of promotional and public relations purposes. In contrast to the 1930s, however, when documentary makers had relied primarily on enlightened state sponsorship to fund their projects, now in the post-war period it was the publicity divisions of large industrial concerns and corporations which turned to documentary to assist in the task of building brand awareness and of generally creating a favourable company image.[3] Some of the larger oil companies had already become involved in various forms of sponsored documentary before the war (Swann, 1989, p. 41), but these same organizations now began to use film more extensively and systematically. Companies such as Shell, for instance, sponsored a whole series of documentary films celebrating the technological achievements of the new age, especially the development of oil-dependent transport systems and communications networks. Such films, whilst not specifically advertising Shell products, were clearly designed to lead audiences to obvious conclusions about the contributions being made by Shell to the national economy and to the public good (Barnouw, 1974, pp. 213–216). The same thinking had also been behind projects initiated by sponsors of earlier BDM films such as the Gas Council (the publicity arm of the British Commercial Gas Association). *Housing Problems* (1935) is a case in point. The first part of the film provides a graphic description of the parlous living conditions in which many citizens were living at the time (Winston, 1995, pp. 43–45), but the promotional payoff (for the Gas Council) comes in the latter part of the film when a brave new world is conjured up with better-designed and more efficiently (gas)heated homes. Such documentary projects where the sponsoring agent is inferentially associated with the solution to a particular societal problem were the favoured option in the early phase of sponsored film. They avoided the potential crassness of direct advertising. Besides allowing filmmakers a certain creative leeway, it also enabled them to claim that their work had a wider social and educative value than that of merely serving the public relations or publicity needs of the sponsors (Rotha, 1952, p. 204).

One of the best early post-war examples of film being used to serve promotional ends is Robert Flaherty's *Louisiana Story* (1948). This sponsored documentary provides a good illustration of the "inferential" benefits that a commercial company, in this case Standard Oil, sought to obtain (Jacobs, 1979, pp. 186–188). *Louisiana Story* is an account of oil exploration in the bayous of Louisiana, though the narrative focus of the film is less upon the rapaciousness of the modern petrochemical industry and more upon how large stretches of the natural landscape have remained unspoiled and intact, despite the entry of the oil seekers. The promotional message which audiences could derive from this film was that the oil industry did not pose a serious threat to the environment and that the drilling operations being undertaken could even be seen to enhance the beauty of place. *Louisiana Story* can, in this respect, be regarded as a particularly astute piece of public relations work, since it did not specifically require the filmmaker to sing the praises of the oilmen. Those in Standard Oil who had commissioned the film knew that the romantically inclined Flaherty had a track record of making non-polemical films about man's relationship with Nature and wild places. They could confidently predict therefore that, in asking him to make a film about oil exploration in

government publicity and thought films a particularly valuable form of publicity, and those who thought publicity and films were expensive luxuries" (1989, p. 31).

[3] In the majority of cases, the participation of an industrial sponsor was clearly identified, though in some cases the sponsoring agent preferred to remain anonymous, thereby raising interesting questions about the legitimacy of a practice which attempts to present essentially promotional material in the guise of formats which claim to be "factually based."

Louisiana, he would follow the same line as he had done in earlier work—*Nanook of the North* (1922) and *Moana* (1926)—where he had enthused about the beauty of wild places and of the human struggle against adversity. There was thus no need, as it were, to contractually oblige Flaherty to produce an identifiably pro-industry account. He could be relied upon to convey a sponsor-friendly message: that modernizing influences do not sound the death knell for traditional ways of life and that it is possible to reconcile the incursions of technology with a love of and respect for the natural world.

TELEVISION: THE NEW FORCE IN THE LAND

Without a shadow of a doubt, however, the most significant development affecting the relationship of public relations and documentary in the post-war era has been the inexorable rise of television. Just as in earlier times government public relations officers and others had sought to use film to serve a range of promotional needs, so over the last 5 or 6 decades we have witnessed a systematic attempt to exploit the medium of television as a public relations or promotional tool. It is important to bear in mind here that television operates from a different institutional basis to film. It has moreover had to devise different ways of communicating with its audience. PR practitioners have consequently had to factor these differences into their calculations when attempting to use television for promotional ends (Bowman, 1988, pp. 245–248). An intimate knowledge of the workings of television has therefore become an essential prerequisite of successful public relations activity. It is certainly no coincidence that it is nowadays frequently the case that those with considerable firsthand experience of working in television take on important secondary roles as PR consultants, assisting companies in their planning of public relations campaigns.

Broadcasting has, of course, developed in markedly different ways according to the different socioeconomic systems which had gained ascendancy in various geopolitical areas. For several decades broadcasting practices in Western Europe were determined primarily by the public service model, according to which broadcasters were committed to producing programmes which, in equal measure, informed, educated, and entertained their audience.[4] As far as broadcasting in the UK is concerned, early TV documentaries put out by the BBC gained the not undeserved reputation of providing viewers with valuable insight into events at home and abroad about which citizens living in a democracy needed to be kept informed. Having said this, however, there is less evidence of political influence (coercion?) being brought to bear on TV documentarists than was the case with documentary filmmakers during the 1930s. One of the reasons for this is that public service models of broadcasting have, generally speaking, been subject to strict forms of regulatory control, with firm limits being set on the type and amount of promotional and advertising activity that can be undertaken. As is well known, however, these restraints have been significantly loosened in the last 2 decades. In an age of increasing commercialization and with the media industries becoming ever more global, we are now witnessing the introduction of many more forms of sponsorship, both open and hidden, into TV programme making.

The strict guidelines under which the majority of broadcasters in Western Europe have been required to operate is in stark contrast to the situation obtaining in the United States where a far more commercially oriented broadcasting model has developed. In such a system there have

---

[4]This commitment to produce, among other things, programming that was socially educative suggests a certain affinity with the work of the British Documentary Movement, which was likewise dedicated, in part, to the task of cultural and social enlightenment (E. Bell, 1986, pp. 65–80).

been relatively few opportunities to develop styles of documentary that one could claim to be "socially educative." It is largely for this reason that, in the context of U.S. network television, the documentary genre has become relatively emasculated. Broadcasters have, by and large, sought not to cause undue offence to the various sponsoring and advertising agencies on which they have come to depend for their financial well-being. Serious documentaries could simply not be relied upon to deliver audiences in the required numbers. As one broadcasting historian has commented:

> Broadcasters [in the United States], licensed to serve "the public interest," considered documentaries obligatory, but were not happy about them. They represented a large investment, which was often lost. For financial security, most documentaries were designed to be suitable backdrops for advertising, but topics chosen to this end—i.e., not likely to stir up public relations crises—tended to lose audiences. (Barnouw, 1974, p. 227)

Work which did have a genuinely critical edge tended, therefore, not to get commissioned or aired by the major U.S. networks, as broadcasters deliberately sought to avoid the stir which a controversial documentary with an investigative agenda might provoke. It is as a consequence of this that American film and programme makers with a serious social or political agenda have turned increasingly to non-broadcast outlets for airing their work, a development which has, in turn, resulted in a relatively flourishing independent documentary film sector (Corner, 2000).[5]

PUBLIC RELATIONS ATTEMPTS AT DAMAGE LIMITATION

Organizations and companies—whether in the public or the private sector—have always been aware, of course, that their activities and affairs can be subject to press and media scrutiny. This is one of the reasons for employing PR personnel in the attempt to preempt or defend them against unwelcome media intrusion. In such a climate of apprehension, one of the roles of a public relations person is to anticipate, second-guess, or forestall the attempts of journalists/documentarists to uncover information that could reflect negatively on that company or organization. Documentarists, for their part, have become equally adept at breaking through the protective shields which companies erect. They may resort to various types of subterfuge (including secret filming) in order to gather evidence for their investigative reports. Such "sting" operations can be highly damaging to a company's or individual's reputation. In a recent (October 2002) BBC *Panorama* investigation, for instance, which looked into the relationship between the Jockey Club and the betting industry in the UK, a secretly filmed interview with a Jockey Club official, during which he made derogatory comments about some of his colleagues, led to that person's resignation soon afterwards. This was in spite of the fact that the Jockey Club had been otherwise extremely cooperative with the filmmakers in the putting together of the programme.

Major battles have been fought as documentarists have attempted to discover information that they suspect is being withheld for no good reason. Sometimes the battles are fought over the issue of access, whilst at other times the battleground shifts as PR practitioners attempt to prevent the publication or screening of potentially damaging revelations. Some of the most

---

[5]Some of the U.S. networks provided a fillip to documentary filmmaking by contracting series of documentaries from such filmmaking teams as Drew Associates. Problems arose, however, when the revelations of the documentarist conflicted with the interests of the sponsoring agent. Witness the celebrated case of *Happy Mother's Day* (1963), a documentary that never made it to American TV screens (Rosenthal, 1988, p. 300).

furious rows took place in the United States during the later 1960s and 1970s over the production and screening of documentary work that projected a very different picture of military activity in Vietnam and Cambodia than the one emanating from government sources. Documentaries which proved to be especially controversial were those which not only attempted to "correct" government proposed versions of events, but also sought to expose the diverse manipulative ways by which government had attempted to pull the wool over the eyes of the populace. The best example of this is provided by the CBS documentary *The Selling of the Pentagon* (1971), a film that created a major furore when it was first screened. The film sets out to describe the activities of the public relations arm of the Department of Defense, in particular the latter's orchestrated attempt to promote a positive image of war whilst disguising the vast fortunes being made by armaments and weapons manufacturers (Jacobs, 1979, pp. 518–520).

The growing number of documentarists who have succeeded in exposing the crimes and misdemeanours of companies or governments has led to various cat-and-mouse games being played out between public relations departments and programme makers. It is for this reason that nowadays companies attach much greater importance to the need for being aware of how exactly the media operate, not only to seize promotional advantages as and when they arise, but also to be in a position to enlist the media's help in confidence-restoring exercises in the wake of negative publicity. Given the likelihood that certain institutions will, at some point, come under heightened media scrutiny, a favoured strategy of public relations practitioners has been to act preemptively in order to guard against potentially damaging revelations finding their way into the public domain. If a documentary filmmaking team announces, for instance, that it is working on a project which focuses on some aspect of a company's activities, both sides will enter into a series of negotiations concerning the "rules of engagement" under which the programme makers will operate. Questions of access will be discussed as well as issues such as who will be allowed to speak on the company's behalf. Such initial negotiations are always important from a public relations point of view. The granting of total access might be seen as too bold or risky a strategy, whilst attempts to place curbs or limits on the documentary investigators might arouse suspicions that the company had something to hide.

What some PR officers sometimes fail to recognize in their dealing with documentarists, however, is that the reticence they display in their negotiations with a team of film or programme makers can itself sometimes become part of the film maker's narrative project. The documentary career of filmmaker Nick Broomfield, for instance, has been built on his much publicized on-screen attempts to penetrate the protective screen of minders and PR people (Bruzzi, 2000, pp. 171–180). Likewise, Michael Moore's hugely successful documentary *Roger and Me* (1989) focuses on the energetic efforts of the questing filmmaker to outwit a retinue of PR men and women in his mission to gain an audience with the head of General Motors, Roger Smith. Some of the most humorous scenes of this film are those that focus on the despairing attempts of PR staff at General Motors to stave off Moore's unwelcome advances.

LETTING THE CAMERAS IN: THE GAINS AND LOSSES

In spite of the negative publicity which can arise when, say, dubious business practices are exposed, the risks associated with *not* complying with a programme making team's requests for access or information are nowadays usually judged to be greater than allowing the cameras in. From the company's point of view, it is preferable to be able to negotiate the terms of access or to agree where filming can take place rather than fall victim to a "sting operation" where programme makers may resort to other means (e.g., secret filming) to produce an account which may prove to be potentially quite damaging and may even require the launching of a major PR damage limitation exercise. As some of the examples to which I shall presently refer illustrate, such a strategy is never entirely risk-free, but public relations personnel are usually confident that they will be able to "manage" the relationship with documentarists in such a way as to minimize the likelihood of any major embarrassments.

There is also recognition on the part of companies that nowadays subject themselves to documentary scrutiny that, in exchange for the incoming programme maker being granted a reasonable degree of access, they would be expected to cede editorial control to the programme maker. This means in practice that, whilst company staff may at a later stage in the production process be invited to check for factual errors or inaccuracies, they will in no way be allowed to suggest significant changes to programme content.[6] From the company's point of view, it is therefore imperative that from the outset the aforementioned "rules of engagement" for filming and interviewing are clearly established, in order to forestall any later complaints that reasonable access had been denied or a distorted picture projected.

To illustrate some of these points, let me comment briefly on some specific instances where companies and organizations have had salutary experiences as a result of their involvement in documentary projects. The first of these relates to the case of *The House* (BBC 2, 1996), a six-part documentary series that went behind the scenes at the Royal Opera House, Covent Garden. At the time of filming, the Opera House was about to undergo a major refurbishment exercise with the aid of a $78 million grant from the National Lottery fund. From the Opera House's point of view, one of the principal motivations for allowing the cameras unprecedented access was to help rebuild the image of a once highly respected British institution which had recently been exposed to much negative publicity on account of its alleged elitism and of the high level of subsidy required to support its activities. In the words of Jeremy Isaacs, at the time the general director of the Royal Opera House:

> I thought it would be good for a TV audience to see how we use the public money ... It is inevitably a selective insight. But I want people to remember that, at the end of the year we balanced the books—quite an achievement. (Gillard, 1996, p. 20)

Though *The House* secured some prime-time exposure for the activities of the Opera House and gave viewers insight into the logistical challenges of running such an organization, the series also exposed a number of organizational shortcomings and tended to confirm the view already circulating in the print media that this was a crisis-ridden institution. After the series had been screened, those at the Opera House who had agreed to allow the cameras in were far from convinced that this had been a wise decision. Jeremy Isaacs, who before joining the Opera House had been chief executive of Channel 4, took some responsibility for this. In his own self-castigating words:

> I learned what I should have known: there is no such thing as a fly-on-the-wall documentary. The camera is not a passive observer. It's a provoker, a modifier of opinion and behaviour. All of us were in some way, acting to camera. (cited in Gillard, 1996, p. 20)

---

[6]In the attempt to maintain the trust of their subjects, many contemporary documentary programme makers will arrange for the pre-transmission viewing of the final edited work. This gives those who have participated the opportunity to correct any factual inaccuracies. It is important to recognize, however, that this in no ways signifies a ceding of editorial control.

Isaacs and his team also conceded that they had underestimated the extent to which contemporary documentarists are not so much interested in objectively chronicling events as of producing lively audience-grabbing programmes that meet the "factual entertainment" criteria imposed by TV executives. What those managing the affairs of Covent Garden (including those who were directing its public relations) had failed to recognize was that the programme makers would be magnetically drawn to the crises that were regularly besetting the Opera House at the time. To this extent any promotional public relations gain would be likely to be cancelled out by the more unflattering revelations that the programme makers might come up with.

Companies that seek to achieve promotional gain by inviting the cameras in will also do well to elicit information from the documentary team about the slot in which the resultant programme will be accommodated. Recorded material can be shaped and edited to serve a variety of ends, and organizations that agree to have their activities scrutinized have a right to be given a clear indication of the precise use to which the material will be put. Conversely, the programme makers have a right to expect that they will not always be steered in particular "safe" directions by members of the organization's public relations department. Both parties stand to gain from this exercise, but not necessarily in ways which each might imagine. As Michael Waldman, documentary director responsible for *The House*, has perceptively observed:

> It is too simplistic to argue that TV's aim is merely to expose and make a splash, its purpose entirely at odds with the interests of any organization, or individual. Documentary styles range from hard-hitting investigative exposé to PR puff. And the public's response is not necessarily predictable: *an honest defence to an investigative attack can prove beneficial to the subject; blatant hagiography almost always strikes a false note.* I always make it clear in negotiating access that it has to be a "warts and all" portrait, and it likely to be all the more credible for that [my emphasis]. (Waldman, 1997, p. 16)

Waldman's observations alert us to an important aspect of the relationship between documentarists and the public relations personnel representing a particular company's interests. In order to avoid later recriminations, there has to be a reasonable degree of trust on both sides concerning the other's motives. This may on occasion necessitate a formal agreement that governs some part of the filming process or which places limits on access to people and places. Such agreements are intended to safeguard the interests of all involved parties, but organizations can also gain a further measure of reassurance from the knowledge that programme makers working for broadcasters in the UK have to conform to the quite rigorous codes of practice laid down by regulators. These prescribe, among other things, the ways in which programme material is gathered and the treatment of individuals or organizations that appear in these programmes. The informed consent of all featured participants has to be gained (see Hibberd et al., 2000), but the key to the success of any documentary enterprise in which an organization is profiled is the formation of a trusting relationship between programme makers and their subjects. In Waldman's words:

> In making a series like *The House*, my colleagues and I were not unaware of the strength of certain eyebrow-raising scenes. Equally, we were determined to show the humour, passion and vitality of the place (quite apart from its artistic excellence). I make programmes, which endeavour to understand, not accuse. A relationship of trust should be beneficial to both sides, though understanding does not preclude criticism. I hope that, if and when I view films with their subjects, they might be delighted or disappointed, amused or embarrassed, but will not be able to say that I abused their trust. (Waldman, 1997, p. 16)

As Jeremy Isaacs' earlier cited remarks testify, there will always—depending on whether you are producer or subject under investigation—be differences of opinion concerning the accuracy of the picture that emerges from a documentary account. Such is the desire of

CONCLUDING REMARKS

For those institutional or company representatives entrusted with public relations or promotional tasks, the proliferation of what are sometimes called the "softer" forms of documentary may not be an unwelcome development. It makes it less likely that damaging revelations will enter the public arena, and it may even make it that much easier to gain some promotional or public relations benefits. For other commentators, however, this blunting of documentary's cutting edge and its absorption into a now largely entertainment-led television culture has brought with it a new set of problems. It has potentially devalued the currency of documentary, making it less likely that it can any longer be employed as a socially educative or consciousness-raising tool. The growing awareness on the part of the audience that factual programming on TV is projecting an increasingly sanitized view of the contemporary world might also be regarded as having negative consequences for any democratizing role which the media might be expected to fulfil.

At the same time, there are some who believe that the changing landscape of television also has certain negative implications for the practice of public relations. Those involved in PR activities are, among other things, concerned to maintain a level of public confidence in the activities of an organization or institution. Measured in these terms, the increasing volume of factual programming designed to promote the "feel-good" factor may, paradoxical as it may seem, not always bring the anticipated promotional gains. There is some evidence to suggest, for instance, that in a celebrity-obsessed culture where merely appearing on television is rated as a creditable achievement, there may be a growing reluctance on the part of some institutional representatives to appear in programmes that are primarily designed as lightweight entertainment vehicles. Audiences are also beginning to take a generally more sceptical view about these softer lifestyle and reality formats. As a consequence, they may be less disposed to give due recognition to the type of programme which is actually more deserving of their serious attention. The views expressed by the director of a documentary series on the nursing profession are sufficiently revealing in this respect to be quoted at some length. Talking about her experiences in putting the series together, the director Jenny Abbott observed:

> We felt it important for the series to reflect the [less attractive] realities of nursing. Nursing is a highly skilled and complicated job, but it involves hard, unglamorous work ... but even this is a toned-down "television" version of what really happens. In fact when the students saw the finished series their main comment was that it should have been grittier ... I suppose the current fashion for docu-soap is in some ways responsible for the fact that viewers will complain when confronted with a documentary that reveals a less palatable reality. Too many documentaries now are sanitized acceptable representations of society that will make popular teatime viewing ... Despite the popularity of docu-soaps there is a danger that they will put off a certain section of society from wanting to take part in documentaries—people who don't want to be stars, who aren't exhibitionist, who are worried that they won't be portrayed seriously and that complexity will be sacrificed for entertainment. These are often the people we should be making documentaries about. (Abbott, 1998, p. 15)

These comments of an experienced documentarist should be taken seriously. They alert us to the problems that arise when a powerful medium such as television becomes increasingly bound up with the values of promotional and consumer culture. It also may in part explain why some documentarists—disturbed by the requirement of mainstream television that factual/documentary work should become increasingly accessible and entertainment-oriented— are seeking alternative outlets such as the Internet for distributing and airing their work.

With television's seemingly irrevocable transformation into a ratings-driven vehicle for entertainment delivery, it would be foolhardy to deny that many in the PR industry will not be displeased that things have taken this turn. The fact that an increasing number of programme makers seem to be prepared to work collaboratively with companies towards a common aim is very much grist to the PR mill. The fact remains, of course, than public relations is about something more than the garnering of free publicity. Audiences also have to be credited with having the intelligence and insight to see through—and occasionally be frustrated by—these bland, unchallenging forms of programming (see remarks of Jenny Abbott cited above). A more productive type of public relations work is one in which there is a greater understanding (on the part of the incoming documentary team and of the "host" institution) about what each stands to gain. Those representing the company will need to be reassured that the incomers will not be operating with preconceived notions, whilst the documentarists will need to be given the type of access that allows a fuller picture of the company's operations to emerge. That there occasionally can be tensions in this relationship is evidenced by the controversies that have occurred when companies feel they have been misrepresented or when documentarists feel that they have been duped by publicity-seeking individuals or organizations.

Whilst public relations officials may sometimes be concerned about the degree of control they appear to be ceding to a third party in their dealings with documentarists, the potential public relations gain of more committed involvement cannot be underestimated. Documentary—at least the more traditional, thought-provoking forms of documentary which have developed in public service models of broadcasting—remains one of the TV genres best equipped to enable viewers to engage seriously with a range of issues in the contemporary world. Documentaries are arguably one of the few television genres that help viewers to reach a better understanding of how institutions operate and what is required of the individuals who work there. It is only when one begins to consider the function of documentary in these terms that the full public relations potential of the genre can be appreciated. As the veteran British documentary filmmaker Roger Graef commented soon after completing a documentary series about the prison service:

> Documentaries are concerned with the impact of decisions on people's lives—in contrast to the litany of facts and figures that litter our screens in a form we can seldom digest or remember. Documentaries about public institutions translate these abstractions into everyday experience . . . Why do normally closed institutions let filmmakers in when the results are not predictable and not always flattering? The case I put to such bodies as the prison service is that the public impression gained only through headlines—usually bad news—is too crude to be accurate. The media shorthand used to describe troubled institutions leave out the human dimension which allows the public to identify with their predicament and whatever efforts they make to resolve it. (Graef, 1993, p. 30)

To some PR practitioners, this may be a persuasive argument for cultivating good working relationships with documentarists. In spite of this, documentary and public relations remain, at heart, uneasy bedfellows. Their underlying aims and objectives are sufficiently at variance with each other as to introduce friction and uncertainty into the relationship. Given the commercial imperatives that dominate the new media order, however, it is unlikely that we will see a letup in attempts by PR practitioners to use all the means at their disposal to seek the considerable gains that media exposure can bestow. The particular attraction for participating companies is that, in contrast to earlier forms of sponsored film, exposure in the form of a televised documentary is obtained at little or no cost to the participant. There are, of course, attendant risks in getting involved in an exercise which is essentially broadcaster-led and where the odds always seem to be stacked in the programme-makers' favour. Sometimes, as instanced by those investigatory probes which expose company misdemeanours or institutional shortcomings, documentarists and public relations practitioners are thrust into a much more hostile relationship with each other, as the one group seeks to defend the company they represent against the other's attack. The fact remains, however, that the growing sophistication of promotional strategies and the noticeable convergence of the PR and journalism industries (Miller, 1998b, pp. 75–76) means that, in most cases, those handling the public relations affairs of companies and institutions no longer view the arrival of a documentary film crew on their premises with fear and trepidation, but as yet another marketing opportunity.

11

Science, Public Relations, and the Media: Problems of Knowledge and Interpretation

Vincent Campbell
De Montfort University

I wrote in the colloquial tongue because I must have everyone able to read it...I am induced to do this by seeing how young men are sent through the universities at random to be made physicians, philosophers and so on; thus many of them are committed by professions for which they are unsuited, while other men who would be fitted for these are taken up by family cares and other occupations remote from literature. The latter are, as Buzzante would say, furnished with "horse sense," but because they are unable to read things that are "Greek to them" they become convinced that in those "big books there are great new things of logic and philosophy and still more that is way over their heads." Now I want them to see that just as nature has given to them, as well as philosophers, eyes with which to see her works, so she has also given them brains capable of penetrating and understanding them.

—Galileo in Drake, 1957, p. 84

Galileo is one of the most important figures in human history, and his 17th-century concerns expressed here about the desire to communicate his findings with a wider audience, one less versed in the technical vocabulary and conceptual understanding of scientific processes, remain central in the communication of science today. When Galileo published his work, the book was the only mass medium (newspapers followed only a few years later), subject to strict controls from authoritarian monarchical and papal regimes that dominated Europe at that time. Despite the secularisation of many parts of modern society, the popular communication of science retains the problems Galileo speaks of, and these have arguably been compounded by developments in mass media rather than alleviated. If Galileo were alive today, whilst he might marvel at the means through which to disseminate scientific knowledge, he might also be dismayed by the lack of public awareness of at least some kinds of scientific knowledge.[1]

---

[1] In a 1998 poll conducted by the National Science Foundation, for example, 52% of people did not know that the Earth goes around the sun once a year (NSF, 1998).

But problems in scientific communication go further than people's lack of basic scientific knowledge. Almost every feature of modern society has a scientific dimension, such as in the routine themes of much news media reporting of risk. Probabilities of particular risks (or opportunities) are often implicitly or explicitly discussed in all sorts of media output, from tragic cases of child abduction and murder to the chances of winning a national lottery. Media representation of risk and other kinds of scientific issues potentially shape public, political, and corporate agendas in problematic ways.

Problems in the communication of science have been widely discussed, and it is possible to categorise the range of interpretations that have emerged into a few distinct positions. The first position blames problems in scientific communication on the media, arguing that the media routinely, and often deliberately, misrepresent science (e.g., Glasser, 1999; Murray, Schwartz, & Lichter, 2001). A second position argues that scientific communication is problematic because of the complex nature of scientific knowledge and the scientific process, a complexity that media professionals and the public lack understanding of (e.g., Gilovich, 1991). A third argument identifies science as an essentially political arena, where vested interests compete for definitional control over a topic or event, thus shaping its representation in the media and reception by the public (e.g., Miller, 1998b, 1999). A final factor to be considered in this chapter is the effect of the sociocultural context in which scientific information occurs, a context that includes popular beliefs and their representation in popular culture (e.g., Turney, 1998).

"THE CULTURE OF FEAR": BLAMING THE MEDIA

Media misrepresentation of scientific issues is a central aspect of concerns about scientific communication, and has been for many decades stretching back at least to the 1960s (Dornan, 1990, pp. 48–49). Such critiques rest on normative assertions about what the media should be doing with regard to scientific information, particularly information of potential public importance, such as the reporting of risk. Here is a typical assertion of this kind:

> [T]he media's role is important enough that they have a responsibility to try to improve risk coverage, particularly related to risk assessment and numbers. Reporters must realize that even if they cannot place important risk assessment information into stories because of space or time limitations, they must understand this information to ask the right questions of sources and be sure they cover all of the important points. (Friedman, 1994, pp. 203–212)

The misrepresentation of risk essentially can take two forms, either overrepresentation or underrepresentation. Much of the news media appear to significantly overrepresent certain kinds of risks, far in excess of their relative likelihood. Such misrepresentation is not inconsequential, clearly tapping into public fears and political agendas. An obvious example is the representation of child abduction and/or murder. Most developed nations have had particular cases of this type that have generated intense media coverage, public debate, and often political intervention. In Belgium, for example, revelations in the case of child abductor Marc Dutroux in the mid-1990s generated mass public demonstrations concerned with police incompetence and possible corruption. In Britain in 2000, the abduction and murder of Sarah Payne by a registered sex offender generated public protests in several towns and cities over the release of convicted paedophiles back into the community. Similar protests occurred in Italy the same year, and both the British and Italian protests were fostered by highly emotive and partisan newspaper campaigns. In the United States, a number of cases, and public responses to them, have seen a flurry of new state laws named after abduction and murder victims, such as Jenna's Law in New York, Amber's Law in Texas, and Stephanie's Law in Kansas (Glasser, 1999, p. 63). In the summer of 2002 the abduction and murder of two young girls allegedly by their school caretaker prompted the UK government to conduct a country-wide re-vetting procedure of all schools' staff, a measure which left many children unable to start the new school year on time.

Undoubtedly, the abduction and murder of a child is one of the most traumatic crimes for anyone to be confronted with, and each individual case is a terrible tragedy for all involved. Yet the reams of coverage that individual cases generate, whilst reflecting the undoubted tragedy of such crimes, arguably contribute to a significant misrepresentation of the chances of this occurring, and at the same time deflect attention away from a more persistent and worrying aspect of child murder. Glasser cited several examples of the tendency for media hyperbole, often driven by parents of victims who become de facto "expert" commentators. Media celebrities play along with these celebrity victims, like this example from talk-show host Geraldo Rivera in 1997:

> This isn't a commentary, this is reality: they will come for your kid over the internet; they will come in a truck; they will come in a pickup in the dark of night; they will come in the Hollywood Mall in Florida. There are sickos out there. You have to keep your children this close to you [he gestures with his fingers]—this close to you. (Glasser, 1999, p. 64)

The trouble with such hyperbolic rhetoric is that it not only exaggerates one particular risk, but also misrepresents some of the real causes of child murder. Of the 64 million or so children in the United States, the proportions murdered are tiny, and the proportions killed by strangers even smaller (Glasser, 1999, p. 61). US Department of Justice, Bureau of Justice Statistics provides detailed statistical information about such crimes on the Internet, and the data clearly

TABLE 11.1
U.S. Homicide Victims Under 16, Who Knew the Offender (for years between 1976–1999 by victim age)

Age	Known		Stranger/Unsolved	
	Number	Percent	Number	Percent
0	5,178	85.6%	871	14.4%
1	3,004	87.2%	442	12.8%
2	2,419	85.5%	409	14.5%
3	1,452	81.9%	320	18.1%
4	987	79.2%	259	20.8%
5	741	77.6%	214	22.4%
6	542	72.2%	209	27.8%
7	509	71.2%	206	28.8%
8	472	70.5%	197	29.5%
9	435	66.3%	221	33.7%
10	435	66.2%	222	33.8%
11	430	63.2%	250	36.8%
12	606	62.9%	358	37.1%
13	832	58.1%	599	41.9%
14	1,456	56.3%	1,129	43.7%
15	2,314	51.8%	2,153	48.2%
16	3,563	48.9%	3,717	51.1%

Sourse: US Bureau of Justice Statistics (http://www.ojp.usdoj.gov/bjs/homicide/homtrnd.htm)

show just how much the media focus on child abduction and murder is misplaced. Table 11.1 shows the distribution of murders of children under 16 between 1976 and 1999. A simple, if rather chilling, pattern is evident that the younger the child, the more likely the killer is to know the victim. As children get older the propensity for murder by strangers increases, but the context of murders of teenagers also begins to change, as the data suggest that around a quarter of murders between 14 and 17 are gang-related.

Moreover, looking simply at the raw numbers, despite the unquestionable tragedy for the victims and their families, cases of child murder have been thankfully rare across this 23-year period, particularly in the age range of many of the high-profile media cases (circa 6 to 12 years old). Looking more specifically at infanticide, defined by the Bureau of Justice as children 5 and under, the proportion of children killed by strangers is extremely small, as shown by Table 11.2.

In only 1 year in this 23-year period were parents responsible for less than 50% of murders. The Bureau summarised the data as follows:

> Of all children under age 5 murdered from 1976–99: 31% were killed by fathers, 30% were killed by mothers, 23% were killed by male acquaintances, 6% were killed by other relatives, [and] 3% were killed by strangers. (Fox & Zawitz, 2002)

To put some raw numbers to this, in 1998, for example, of 571 (solved) murders of children under age 5, only eight were committed by strangers, compared to 363 committed by parents.

TABLE 11.2
Percentage of Homicides of U.S. Children Under Age 5 (by relationship with offender)

Year	Parent	Other family	Friend/ acquaintance	Stranger	Unknown	Total
1976	57.3%	7.8%	19.5%	3.3%	12.1%	100.0%
1977	59.1%	6.1%	20.2%	4.1%	10.4%	100.0%
1978	56.8%	6.4%	22.0%	4.0%	10.8%	100.0%
1979	47.3%	9.0%	22.8%	3.8%	17.0%	100.0%
1980	54.0%	7.5%	20.7%	2.8%	15.0%	100.0%
1981	57.0%	7.7%	24.0%	1.6%	9.7%	100.0%
1982	57.9%	4.3%	22.2%	2.4%	13.1%	100.0%
1983	58.7%	5.3%	22.9%	2.3%	10.8%	100.0%
1984	52.4%	7.8%	26.0%	2.7%	11.1%	100.0%
1985	61.8%	4.7%	23.6%	1.7%	8.1%	100.0%
1986	56.1%	5.6%	24.0%	0.9%	13.4%	100.0%
1987	57.9%	6.3%	23.2%	2.2%	10.3%	100.0%
1988	52.8%	5.8%	27.4%	1.1%	13.0%	100.0%
1989	57.1%	6.6%	22.4%	2.0%	12.0%	100.0%
1990	52.2%	5.7%	24.1%	1.5%	16.4%	100.0%
1991	54.4%	6.2%	24.1%	2.6%	12.6%	100.0%
1992	53.3%	4.5%	24.6%	4.1%	13.5%	100.0%
1993	49.9%	4.3%	28.3%	3.0%	14.6%	100.0%
1994	51.9%	5.5%	25.2%	3.0%	14.4%	100.0%
1995	52.3%	7.1%	23.7%	6.0%	10.9%	100.0%
1996	50.2%	6.0%	29.8%	2.4%	11.6%	100.0%
1997	56.9%	6.2%	23.5%	2.3%	11.1%	100.0%
1998	55.7%	4.2%	26.5%	1.3%	12.4%	100.0%
1999	56.6%	7.8%	22.9%	2.0%	10.8%	100.0%

Source: U.S. Bureau of Justice Statistics (http://www.ojp.usdoj.gov/bjs/homicide/homtrnd.htm)

The U.S. media, therefore, should be focusing far more heavily on parental murder of children, as it occurs far more frequently than stranger murder. Ironically perhaps, one of the highest-profile child murder cases of recent years in the United States, the JonBenét Ramsey case, has generated coverage from the widespread assumption that JonBenét's parents were responsible. Yet the evidence in that case is highly contested, and hence there remains no prosecution even though the murder was committed in 1996. It also remains an atypical example of a high-profile child murder case where parents are represented as the prime suspects.

It is difficult to be certain about the reasons behind this trend of the media focusing on the much rarer occasions of stranger murder of children, but one contributory factor may be the relative difficulty of how to police parental murder of children compared to the threat of strangers. Most of the new legislation and calls for legislation in countries like the UK and the United States concerns communities' rights to know about the presence of convicted sex offenders amongst them, but such measures do nothing about those who have yet to be caught, and nothing about parents abusing their own children. This would be a strong example of what Glassner called "metaphoric illnesses"—social constructions that exist "to help us come to terms with features of our society that we are unprepared to confront directly" (1999, p. 153).[2]

The cycle of media saturation coverage, public anxiety (even hysteria), and knee-jerk political decision making has been seen time and time again in many countries, as all sorts of issues become moral panics. On occasion news media have gone further than merely overrepresenting particular risks, and have engaged in the act of turning hypothetical risks into stories. One notorious case of this occurred in the United States in 1980 when a Pulitzer Prize-winning story by Janet Cooke about a young child with heroin addiction turned out to have been faked (Reinerman & Duskin, 1992). In that case the presumption of the possibility of child heroin addicts prompted a faked story, even though subsequent investigations of the City of Washington, where the imaginary child was supposed to live, found no child addicts at all. Critics of the media point to cases of fabrication, exaggeration, and distortion of scientific information, and degrees of risk as strong evidence for the news media being key to problems in the wider dissemination of scientific knowledge and understanding.

REASONS BEHIND MEDIA MISREPRESENTATION OF SCIENCE

One potentially straightforward explanation for media misrepresentation, assuming this is indeed what occurs, stems from the requirements of news media. As Hansen argued, "Science is, in news terms, a slow process of small incremental developments; and rarely, if ever, does science happen in the form of a continuous series of significant or major developments synchronized to the 24-hour time-cycle of press reporting" (1994, p. 115). Anderson concurred, citing the example of environmental issues like global warming, and stating that "a fundamental difficulty has been that while environmental issues tend to be drawn-out processes which are not clearly visible, the media feed upon short, sharp, highly visible events" (Anderson, 1991, p. 465).

Yet not all authors agree. Cracknell argued to the contrary when he stated, again speaking of environmental issues, that:

> Environmental issues are often mediagenic, the stories they provide frequently have good pictures and can be conveniently symbolized, for example, seabirds stranded in oil slicks, the menacing shape of a nuclear power plant. (1993, p. 6)

---

[2]Amongst his examples, Glasser rather contentiously, but persuasively, includes Gulf War syndrome (1999).

What these comments highlight is the tension between those aspects of science that are difficult to communicate through the news media, such as the incremental development of evidence in support of hypotheses, and those events that concretise scientific issues and concerns. So, global warming is difficult to elucidate in a news article of a few hundreds words or 2 minutes of broadcast air time, but a natural disaster or major incident of pollution like an oil spill does fit the parameters of news media limitations. Similarly, the complexities of illegal drug use or child murder are difficult to articulate compared to stories focused around individual cases (real or otherwise).[3]

Science arguably does not fit straightforwardly into news production processes and also has the added feature of being a highly specialised area of professional practice and knowledge quite different from that of journalism. Studies comparing the attitudes of scientists and journalists towards scientific news are revealing in this regard. Studies in Germany (H. P. Peters, 1995) and the UK (Gunter, Kinderlerer, & Beyleveld, 1999) have compared attitudes of scientists and journalists towards the reporting of science in the news. Many scientists feel some antipathy to journalists, regarding journalists as people who, deliberately or otherwise, trivialise, sensationalise, and distort scientific information. Peters' survey suggested that scientists have a paternalistic attitude towards journalists, expecting them to generally support the goals of scientists in their presentation of science news, to try and influence public opinion, and, as is the convention in the publication of scientific papers, to give the scientists the chance to review articles before publication (H. P. Peters, 1995, p. 42). Journalists' views of scientists, on the other hand, include the opinions that they suffer from being "long-winded, afflicted by jargon, difficult, and being hung up on detail and accuracy" (Gunter et al., 1999, p. 376). Peters indicated that these differences may "indicate a struggle for control over the communication process" (1995, p. 42) between scientists and journalists. Gunter et al., asserted that:

> These differences partly can be explained by the influences of the respective professional cultures. Journalists consider scientists to be passive sources who are used by them to perform the media function of informing and entertaining the public and criticising elites. Scientists, in insisting that the mass media should operate similarly to scholarly journals, will inevitably get into disputes with journalists. Scientists and journalists do not work in the same way and according to the same rules or objectives. (1999, p. 377)

Both the production and presentation of science news are shaped in part by journalistic values as to what constitutes interesting, entertaining, and informative news (Murray, Schwartz, & Lichter, 2001, p. 52). That scientists do not easily gel with journalists in terms of professional attitudes and values may therefore additionally contribute to apparent distortions of scientific information in the news media.

PUBLIC MISUNDERSTANDING OF SCIENCE

Differences in the professional practices and competences between scientists and journalists lead to another potential contributing factor to the problem of scientific communication. The scientific process is a very particular method of gathering knowledge, one which few outside science have much familiarity with. It is argued by some that what is taken as ignorant or

---

[3]The same could be said of many areas including, for example, the complexities of American–Cuban political relations symbolised in the case of Elian Gonzalez a few years ago. Tomlinson has made an interesting case for seeing this kind of individual case-based reporting as a form of "'regulating' the tacit moral order of a community" (1997, p. 68).

deliberate misrepresentation of science is nothing of the sort. Instead, it merely reflects the widespread misunderstanding of science in the public at large.

A frequently occurring example of public, and media, misunderstanding occurs in the area of judging probabilities (particularly important in questions of risk). Take, for instance, this comment from Steven Morris, a journalist with the broadsheet British newspaper *The Guardian*:

> Typical, isn't it? Scientists have pinpointed the day when Earth is in danger of being hit by an asteroid the size of an office block. And it has to be at the weekend. Put the date in your diary—Saturday, September 21 2030. Forget about the lie-in, that boozy lunch with friends down the pub—if pubs still exist—and that shopping trip. (6/11/00 p. 5)

Morris' flippancy is supported later in the article when he says the chances of the asteroid, 2000 SG344, hitting the Earth are 1 in 500 (ibid.). Since the late 1990s, observation of asteroids orbiting near Earth has produced many alerts about possible collisions with Earth. Most, like the recent NT7 2002, are found on subsequent analysis to be very unlikely to hit, at least in the near future, and this too may contribute to the comic indifference expressed by Morris. Yet, as many astronomers have lamented, this indifference is massively misplaced. One in 500 seems like long odds, yet they are tiny compared to the 1 in 14 million chance of winning the jackpot in the British National Lottery,[4] yet every week millions of people in Britain buy tickets (without checking the skies for falling meteorites).

SOME FUNDAMENTALS OF PUBLIC MISUNDERSTANDING OF SCIENCE

Of course, the Earth being hit by an asteroid or winning the National Lottery are not events people might necessarily relate, but this kind of misperception of probability is widespread. There are other instances of general misunderstanding and misinterpretation of causal relationships and probabilities. A good example is a widespread tendency to underestimate the likelihood of coincidences (Gilovich, 1991; Martin, 1998). Most readers will have experienced instances of coincidence such as thinking of an old friend just before bumping into them or them telephoning you. Gilovich gave an interesting example of Nobel Laureate Luis Alvarez, who was once reading a newspaper article that set him off thinking about an old acquaintance. On turning the page, to his great surprise he saw an obituary of that very person (1991, p. 176). Being scientifically minded, Alvarez did not assign some kind of paranormal explanation of this coincidence; instead he produced a estimated calculation of the likelihood of thinking of someone just before finding out they have died—suggesting a figure for the U.S. population of approximately some 3,000 instances of this per year, or almost 10 *every day* (ibid.).

Alongside the underestimation of the likelihood of coincidences, humans also display a tendency to overestimate the presence of patterns in events. A good example of this is known as the "clustering illusion" (Gilovich, 1991, pp. 11–19). In many sports the idea of streaks and slumps is a significant feature, with the statistics for individual sportspeople dominated by measures of success or failure. In basketball, scoring streaks are often characterised as the player having the "hot hand" (essentially the perception that players who have scored with their previous shot are more likely to score with their next shot, sometimes leading to a hot streak of scoring). Gilovich's statistical analysis of one team's scoring throughout a season

---

[4]The chances of winning the smallest prize available on the National Lottery are 1 in 54.

showed this not to genuinely occur, but the perception amongst sports fans and professionals was too strong for this evidence to be accepted by them (ibid., p. 17).

One reason why this is the case, and indeed a possible reason behind differential treatment of the chances of asteroid strikes and lottery wins, is that humans have the tendency to remember confirmations of beliefs whilst non-confirmations are ignored (Gilovich, 1991, pp. 64–65). To give a simple example, we tend to remember those times when the phone rings when we are in the bath or working and thus generate a (false) theory about the phone "always" ringing when otherwise engaged, whilst ignoring the many more times when the phone rings and there is no issue in answering it. Exactly the same is true for things like dreaming/thinking of people who you then hear from/bump into, or relating predictions from astrologers/tarot readers to events in one's life.

This has very little to do with issues of media misrepresentation or a lack of science education in schools, and much more to do with the inherent evolutionary biases of human minds. Humans are not particularly good at performing serial calculations, the kinds that today we have computers do for us and would include highly accurate measurements of probability. On the other hand, humans are extremely good at parallel calculations, which are very useful for pattern recognition systems (Johnson, 2001, pp. 126–127). Humans are highly pattern sensitive, such as being able to recognise human faces and social hierarchies. This ability has been very useful in human evolution, a good adaptation to early human environments, but it is not that good for genuinely understanding causal relationships and probabilities.

One problem in this approach revolves around how scientists are allegedly immune to these apparently human tendencies (Miller, 1998a, p. 218). There appears to be a kind of implicit categorisation of scientists as having sufficient "correct" knowledge, whilst the wider public are somehow deficient (ibid.). Yet, some argue, not unreasonably, that the recognition of limitations in normal human perceptual processes have only been revealed through the accumulated knowledge provided by scientific observation, experiment, and education. For example, the clustering illusion is only evident today because statistical methods of analysis have revealed perceptions of some patterns like the hot hand in basketball to be *demonstrably* wrong. Thus, an education in science does not so much make scientists immune from these kinds of errors but, as in the case of Luis Alvarez mentioned above, arguably more able to effectively investigate and comprehend phenomena (Gilovich, 1991, p. 189). Critics of this approach are surely confusing the recognition of limitations in normal human perceptions with some kind of normative judgement in which scientists are claiming superiority over "ordinary" people, and valuing a particular (scientific) form of knowledge over others. Such normative judgements when made are illegitimate, but identifying features in human perception that skew our everyday interpretations of phenomena is entirely legitimate.

CONSEQUENCES FOR PRODUCTION AND RECEPTION

One of the consequences for scientific communication in terms of both how issues and events get represented by the news media, but also how they may be interpreted by the public, lies in what Sandman has dubbed a focus on "outrage" rather than the "hazard" (1994). As already mentioned, the conventions of news media create a tendency for event-related reporting of scientific issues, so concerns about pollution or global warming, say, are routinely articulated in relation to particular instances of pollution (e.g., the Exxon Valdez disaster) or extreme weather (e.g., the widespread flooding in Europe in the summer of 2002). Sandman's work as both risk communication practitioner and analyst has led him to conclude that reporting, particularly of environmental risks, is heavily focused on concerns about a particular event and not on genuine questions of risk. He stated:

> What happened, how it happened, who's to blame and what the authorities are doing about it all command more journalistic attention than, say, data on toxicity. (1994)

But this is not only a feature of how journalists treat issues and events. Based on particular studies conducted by Sandman, he argued that the provision of more technical information, that might be "expected to reassure people," does not seem to have any impact on audiences' concerns (ibid.). He argued that "in their focus on outrage rather than hazard, journalists are at one with their audience" (ibid.). Sandman does not offer a reason why this might be the case, but in relation to the characteristics indicated above, a key factor would seem to be the overemphasis on confirmatory cases. Whether it is cases of child abduction and murder by strangers, or at the more positive end of human affairs cases of people winning lottery jackpots, the focus of public (and media) emphasis is on those confirmatory cases of fears or desires. The likelihood of such events occurring becomes almost an irrelevance for media and public agendas once such an event has occurred, and so does technical detail about the circumstances of that particular event's occurrence. Instead, according to Sandman, by focusing on particular incidents both media coverage and audience responses arguably consist of four elements: "(1) alarm over reassurance, (2) extremes over the middle, (3) opinions over data, and (4) outrage over hazard" (ibid.).

For those charged with the professional responsibility to try and disseminate scientific information, such as public relations and information officers, this would seem to offer significant hurdles in achieving effective communication with target audiences. A further complication lies in the modes of communication themselves and how the public interprets communication messages. The persuasive communication industries—advertising, marketing, and PR—remain dominated by highly simplistic and mechanistic approaches to the construction of persuasive communication campaigns. Assumptions about what information to convey and how to convey it, in the scientific sphere anyway, rest upon assumptions of addressing deficits or gaps in audiences' knowledge about a topic, that rely upon logical reasoning and rational comprehension within audiences' reception of messages. In other words, to ape Sandman's typology, there is a focus in persuasive communication in science on (presumed) reassurance through concentrating on the most likely outcomes, based on presentation of accurate data.

Part of the problem with this approach, however, lies in the gap between scientific processes of knowledge construction and everyday processes of knowledge construction. An equally large part lies in the gap between the construction of scientific communication messages and audience interpretations of those messages, whether that communication comes through the news media, and therefore journalists' frames, or through governmental or organisational information, framed by public relations and other persuasive communication specialists. In the latter case, some very high-profile governmental communication campaigns have failed dramatically despite apparent care having been taken over the construction of communication content in terms of its reassurances and factual accuracy, due to unanticipated audience responses. A notorious example would be efforts by the British government in the 1980s and 1990s to inform the British public about HIV and AIDS. Research by Kitzinger into audience responses to media coverage and government information campaigns regarding HIV and AIDS offers important evidence for this (1990, 1993). Her research found that audiences consciously or otherwise often tend to reproduce an issue in terms of the interpretive frameworks offered by the news media, but a significant proportion of an audience will interpret information in an oppositional manner. Kitzinger stated:

> Audiences selectively highlight, oppose or reconstruct statements and they are able to deconstruct dominant themes and to construct alternative accounts drawing on personal experience, political belief or a general critique of media or government sources. (1993, p. 300)

This ties in with one critique of presumptions of public inadequacy concerning scientific knowledge, which argues that the role of personal experience as a form of knowledge can play a powerful role in the interpretation of scientific communication, allowing for the sometimes legitimate rejection of official or expert interpretations (see Johnson, 1993).[5] In Kitzinger's work this was evident in some oppositional responses to British government advertising about HIV. One print advert used in the late 1980s consisted of a blank background with the words "Two Eyes," "Nose," and "Mouth" arranged on the page to very superficially resemble a face. The main caption stated: "How to recognise someone with HIV" (this is reproduced in Kitzinger, 1990, p. 331). The intent was to suggest to audiences that those with HIV did not conform to any prior stereotypical image (often confused with that of images of those in the final stages of full-blown AIDS), but for some participants in Kitzinger's study a diametrically opposite interpretation emerged, with one stating that the meaning of the advert was an instruction, telling you to "look at their eyes, look at their nose, and look at their mouth and if they look queer you dunnae bother going near them" (in Kitzinger, 1990, p. 332). This "wrong" interpretation of the advert was interpreted by Kitzinger as being fostered by a combination of preexisting news media stereotypes, personal experiences, and reproduction and dissemination of distorted images amongst the public (ibid.).

So, the production of scientific communication cannot be conducted according to simple assumptions about target audiences' knowledge deficits. Even a high level of simplification in campaigns like the one above does not automatically prevent contestation and oppositional reading by audiences, so technical complexity is not necessarily a fundamental reason why public misunderstanding of science communication can occur. In other words the public cannot be blamed simply for a deficit of particular kinds of knowledge, as members of the public actively utilise a range of experiences, beliefs, and information sources in their interpretations of science communication messages (Miller, 1998a, p. 218).

DEFINITIONAL STRUGGLES: THE POLITICS OF SCIENTIFIC COMMUNICATION

So far, these approaches have essentially focused on individual parts of the communication cycle. Critics of the media focus almost exclusively on media organisations, what they are doing wrong, and what they should be doing instead. Such authors do not always consider issues of reception by audiences or issues of self-presentation by the scientific community. Similarly, approaches which highlight common unscientific features of public attitudes and understanding also arguably underplay the role of scientists and communicators in influencing public understanding and attitudes through shaping the dominant interpretive frameworks offered by the news media, and shaping other elements of public discourse. There is a third way of looking at the problems of scientific communication which recognises that media coverage of science is no different to any other media topic, such as politics or crime. In such areas, research suggests that media representation depends on the results of competition and

---

[5]This has been seen very recently in Britain with persistent public concern over the measles, mumps, and rubella (MMR) vaccination and possible links between it and the onset of autism, despite reassurances from government and scientists.

negotiation between a range of vested interests trying to get their interpretation accepted as the definitive interpretation of an issue or event.

What such research highlights is the fallacy presented by some critics of the news media (e.g., Murray, Schwartz, & Lichter, 2001) who argue that the facts of any particular issue or event are incontrovertible and could and should have been represented as such by the media. This is a fallacy in two regards. First, such assertions betray an oversimplistic conception of science as a discipline of certainty and unambiguity, a lapse which scientists themselves often make (Miller, 1998a, p. 212). Such a view presumes that in any issue or event there are incontrovertible facts allowing for a *particular* explanation/interpretation to be correct. Yet if science is being conducted properly, then scientific knowledge is always contingent or provisional (ibid.). In other words scientific knowledge is based upon the current state of available evidence for theories, but evidence yet to be gathered may cause a paradigm shift in our understanding of any particular issue (e.g., the theory of continental drift was widely disparaged by the scientific community until journeys to the deep ocean floor discovered the mid-Atlantic ridge, offering strong evidence supporting that theory). Thus, scientists often present their research, quite appropriately, in highly qualified ways. In news media terms qualification ("might") is akin to ambiguity, and less preferable than certainty ("will"). Out of qualifications and contingent evidence stems not only possible ambiguity but also possible disagreement amongst the scientific community, and this too can become part of media representations of an issue, even when those disagreements are about questions of detail and not about fundamental principles. A good example here would be creationists' opposition to the teaching of evolutionary theory in some American states. Creationists have won over some local politicians through highlighting disagreements between leading evolutionary theorists, such as those between Stephen Jay Gould and Richard Dawkins, even though such disputes are about fine details in how evolution works and not about the viability of evolution itself as a theory of life on Earth.

Second, because any event or issue has consequences in the way that it is represented, those involved will, to varying degrees, attempt to influence the representation of that event or issue in a way that suits them. In the above example, evolutionary theorists' legitimacy is challenged by creationist ideas so they have a vested interest in contesting creationist rhetoric, which many of them (including Dawkins, and the late Gould) have done. This makes the communication of science not a straightforward reporting of facts, but a site of contestation between a wide range of (often conflicting) goals and objectives including those of scientists, journalists, governments, corporations, pressure groups, and so on. Thus, as Schlesinger, and Tumber pointed out, "Those seeking access to the media *must* engage in the active pursuit of definitional advantage" (1999, p. 264, emphasis added).

Science routinely becomes part of domestic political agendas, as for example in the public health scare around BSE ("mad cow disease") in the UK in the 1990s. As such the professional conflicts between scientists and journalists, which make communicating science through the media difficult enough, are often exacerbated by this competition for definitional advantage. In the last 30 years or so, a persistent site of definitional struggle has emerged over health and environmental risks. In such contested areas, the communication of particular issues rests not so much on the science but on the relative effectiveness of the communication strategies used by the competing groups. Miller's analysis of the definitional struggles in Britain around the public health risk of BSE, for example, argues that to some extent "risks are represented according to the outcome of promotional strategies and their negotiations with the media" (1999, p. 1252). In other words, news media representations are influenced more by how those sources are able to interact with journalists in ways conducive to the news media than by any simple relationship to "reality" or the "truth," or even to the dominant scientific interpretation of the day.

Miller has modelled this negotiation of promotional strategies into a dynamic "circuit of communication" (1998a, p. 210). He suggested that the communication of science is the result of a complex interaction between four sets of actors: social and political institutions, the media, the public, and decision makers (ibid.). It is important to note here that scientists themselves are not merely neutral bystanders subject to the whims of politicians, interest groups, and journalists in the definitional conflict over their discoveries or inventions. As Lievrouw pointed out:

> Scientists (especially those engaged in expensive, labour- and resource-intensive projects) are often involved in constructing representations of their ideas that will "read" well with audiences beyond their colleagues and that can be assimilated into the popular culture at large. (1990, p. 8)

The implicit point here is that scientists are often in competition for funding for research and institutional maintenance, and this is often as much a factor in proactive communication as any desire to see ideas adopted or advocated practices accepted.

Quite apart from the already mentioned conflict of interests between scientists and journalists, the range of potential vested interests in the dissemination, or non-dissemination, of particular information creates a highly competitive environment in which scientific communication is produced. Social institutions, whether they be governments, universities, businesses, pressure groups or other bodies, can be differentiated not only in terms of their particular positions on an issue, but also in their resource capacity to promote their interpretation of the issue at hand. For those institutions that are "resource-rich," there is an automatic advantage in their favour (Miller, 1998a, p. 212). Governments, for example, and large corporations are able to draw on significant financial resources to construct communication campaigns and PR strategies to try and counter oppositional points of view and ensure they can set the agenda (or at least set the media agenda).[6]

For those lacking the financial resources or political authority enjoyed by corporations and governments, challenging dominant interpretations around scientific issues is more difficult but by no means impossible. For decades the tobacco industry, for example, was able to manage media and policy agendas against the growing evidence of health risks from smoking, and it is only recently that anti-smoking campaigners have began to shift the political agenda towards the liability of tobacco companies for suppressing the potential risks of smoking. One of the interesting things about those groups challenging dominant social institutions in areas of science is that in order to compete effectively in terms of shaping media representations of science (and other forms of public discourse about science), such groups have to engage in promotional strategies and campaigns that potentially take them away from the scientific basis of much of their opposition to "official" interpretations. A good example here would be in the evolution of campaigning strategies in the environment movement. Groups like Greenpeace and Friends of the Earth have grown from very small beginnings in the 1960s and 1970s into global organisations with large popular followings,[7] and many successful changes in national and international environmental policies. Yet the strategies developed by some of these groups often problematise the scientific aspects of their causes, as they are forced to use more dramatic strategies to engage the interest of the news media and the public.

A good example here would be the case of the Brent Spar incident in 1995. This was an oil storage platform in the North Sea which its owner, oil giant Shell, and the British government (whose waters the platform was in) agreed should be disposed of at sea. The environmental

---

[6]Details of how some governmental and business organisations have tried to do this in recent years have been outlined by Stauber and Rampton in their acerbically titled *Toxic Sludge Is Good for You* (1995).

[7]For example, having once been a small, marginal environmental group, by the early 1990s Greenpeace was a global pressure group, with some 400,000 members in the UK alone (Baggott, 1995, p. 169).

pressure group Greenpeace objected in principle to dumping in the deep sea, and mounted a campaign to publicise this action and try to prevent it, employing a wide range of communication strategies. Alongside a sophisticated news management strategy, involving holding press conferences, having media-savvy spokespeople appear on news programmes, and issuing press releases, they also engaged in a traditional tactic of resource-poor or "outsider" organisations—direct action (W. Grant, 1995, p. 20). Filming themselves, and with invited news media on board one of their ships, Greenpeace activists landed on the oil platform, in the wake of water cannon from Shell/UK government ships. Through this strategy, Greenpeace was able to turn the incident into a major news story and incident of significant policy controversy. Bennie commented:

> Nor were the tactics of Greenpeace new—its creation of dramatic pseudo-events was a tried and tested formula. However, its skilful public relations campaign appeared to have special resonance and seemed to project the issue onto the public agenda in a uniquely dramatic fashion. (1998, p. 397)

It would later emerge that the scientific claims behind the Greenpeace campaign were highly suspect—for example, their estimates of the amount of oil left in the platform were based on measurements taken with a jam jar on a piece of string—and turned out to be very inaccurate. But the images generated by the activists on the rig being blasted by water cannon had, by the time this problem came out, forced Shell and the government to back down in light of growing public disapproval of their policy. This event stands as a very clear example of how, on occasion, non-institutional sources can wrestle the agenda from the control of institutional authorities, but it also shows how that contest for definitional control of events and issues as represented in the media can override the scientific component of an issue or event, even when that is a key—or even *the* key—component. In this way even groups with access to scientific knowledge about an issue, and genuine pro-social intent, can end up being diverted by the competition for definitional advantage into a focus on—to use Sandman's terms—alarm, extremes, opinions, and outrage, rather than on reassurances, balance, data, and the hazard.

FRED FLINTSTONE'S LEGACY: THE SOCIOCULTURAL CONTEXT

A final and far more diffuse factor that may problematise the communication of science stems from the sociocultural context. Scientific approaches to understanding are not the only the ones extant in modern society. A wide range of other approaches exists, many fundamentally at odds with science, and some actively engaged in assaults on science (like creationism, mentioned earlier). Popular beliefs, particularly religious beliefs, provide a highly problematic context for the dissemination of scientific information, as Galileo found to his cost in the early 17th century. Yet researchers in contemporary science communication often disregard this, as Johnson pointed out:

> The hazards field's unduly narrow emphasis on probability may explain why researchers have scorned the idea that cultural taboos shape risk perception at least as much as uncertainty. What one should not think about may be more vital than how well one knows what one does think about. One cannot assume that effective hazard response depends only upon knowing probabilities, nor that other kinds of knowledge offset a deficit in statistical skills. Yet, the one-dimensional view ignores the likelihood of multiple knowledges and ignorances. (1993)

The tensions between scientific developments and traditional moral and ethical values, let alone the traditional understanding of the way the world is, are also articulated in popular culture—most notably in the genre of science fiction. Popular fictional representations may then in turn impact on the representation and articulation of scientific issues, although this dimension has often been ignored by previous research (Dornan, 1990, p. 51). A striking example of this has been explored by Jon Turney in looking at the way Mary Shelley's novel *Frankenstein* has repeatedly been used since its writing in 1818 to frame debates about scientific developments, particularly in the areas of biotechnology and medicine (1998). A recent and overt example of this was the British news media's dubbing of GM produce "Frankenstein Foods."

More recently Cohen and Stewart have written a serious investigation into possibilities of the existence and nature of extraterrestrial life (2002). Interestingly, they couched their discussion in relation to a wide range of science fiction aliens, highlighting the plausibility of some and the inadequacies of others. When discussing H.G. Wells' *War of the Worlds*, apart from dismissing the novel's dénouement of earthly bacteria killing the Martian invaders as scientifically implausible, they acknowledged that the novel "has given us an icon for creatures from other planets that continues, subconsciously, to influence our thoughts about alien life" (Cohen & Stewart, 2002, p. 2). Through the late-19th-century novel, the infamous Orson Welles' radio version of the 1930s, to contemporary variations on the theme in movies like *Independence Day*, the iconography of invading aliens from Mars and beyond has played a very significant role in contemporary Western culture. At least since the end of World War II, the existence of aliens has seeped from popular fiction into cultural beliefs with the rise of ufology and the emergence of groups of alleged alien "abductees." Such beliefs have persisted and grown in recent decades, despite their contravention of current scientific understanding. For example, the belief that alien civilisations are visiting Earth is problematised by the vast distances between stars and the massive energy costs to traverse such distances (Thorne, 1994, p. 82; Ferris, 1999, p. 88). Even the idea that there could be intelligent extraterrestrial life out there is a contentious point, since there is no credible evidence so far (UFO sightings and alien abductees not being regarded as credible by the scientific establishment).

The point here is that popular culture, whether it be in the form of popular fiction, beliefs, or a combination of the two, regularly impacts on media representations and public interpretations of science. This occurs through the already identified importance of personal experience and knowledge used by audiences (and journalists) in their responses to scientific information. Bodies assessing levels of public understanding of science have made throwaway remarks regarding the impacts of popular culture on scientific knowledge, such as the National Science Foundation's comment in a 1998 survey of public attitudes:

> Perhaps reflecting the legacy of Fred Flintstone, only half of the Americans rejected the statement that "the earliest humans lived at the same time as the dinosaurs." (pp. 7–8)

Our conceptions of the nature of dinosaurs, and the small detail of the 60 million years or so separating humans from dinosaurs, may indeed be influenced by fictional representations like *The Flintstones, One Million Years BC, Jurassic Park*, and *Walking With Dinosaurs* (allegedly dubbed by the BBC's Natural History Unit as "Making it up as you go along With Dinosaurs"; Cohen & Stewart, 2002, p. 40). The problem is that cultural experiences and representations are caught up somehow in the already quite complicated circuit of communication in which scientific messages get constructed, disseminated, and received and interpreted.

Moreover, it could been argued that representations of popular beliefs and pseudo-science (like ufology and parapsychology) fit more easily the desired parameters of not only fictional forms like Hollywood films and TV series like *The X-Files*, but also the narrative conventions of factual news media forms like documentary (Silverstone, 1986; Y. Campbell, 2000). As such the communication of "proper" science is complicated further, as the primary routes of factual media dissemination are being equally, or perhaps even to a greater extent, used to represent pseudo-science and popular beliefs (see Dawkins, 1998 for a critique of this).

A good recent example of how popular culture and "proper" science interact in this complex and problematic way occurred in 2004, with the release of the Hollywood film *The Day After Tomorrow*—a natural disaster movie that sees most of the United States destroyed by freak weather caused by climate change, although that change is displayed as occurring in a few hours, rather than the more scientific time scales of decades or longer. Opinions amongst the scientific community were divided in terms of the film's relative merits, with concerns over its scientific accuracy tempered by the high profile a big box office Hollywood film could bring to the topic of climate change. For instance, Tony Juniper, director of Friends of the Earth, said of the film:

> Science alone has failed to convince politicians and international companies with the power and influence to make a difference. The film will reach entirely new audiences that may not have heard about global warming. We hope it will help to create a much-needed sense of urgency to fight climate change in the real world, especially in the US. (*Guardian*, 19/5/04, p. 14)

On the other hand, Stephen Weller, Director of Communications for the International Policy Network, said:

> During the past few years, a plethora of green groups have blossomed in Britain and across the globe, emitting copious amounts of hot air, burning up millions of dollars to alert the public that we are all about to toast, freeze or drown from global warming, and that we have brought this horror upon ourselves. Now Hollywood has turned this poster child into a multimillion dollar enterprise. It is simply manna from heaven for campaigners. Some environmental organisations have billed the film as "a teachable moment," hoping for mass conversions to their belief that climate change mitigation is the world's most urgent priority. (ibid.)

Whether for good or ill, the impact on the climate of public opinion created by pieces of popular culture, like Hollywood films, have to be integrated into the dissemination of science and into models attempting to understanding the processes of scientific communication.

CONCLUSION

Problems in the communication of science can arise for a range of reasons. Most of these revolve around perceptions of deficits in terms of knowledge in and interpretations of science. Some critics blame the news media for misunderstanding science and representing scientific issues according to journalistic rather than scientific values and goals. Others point to problems in the public understanding of science, rooted in the common perceptual processes that shape how we perceive and interpret the world around us. Such ideas are problematised by the realisation that scientific communication is not a simple arena of facts and fallacies, but instead a site of definitional struggle, with a variety of vested interests, including scientists themselves, vying for definitional advantage in the representation of scientific issues and events. As such, scientific communication in the media may be shaped more by the interaction of competing interests than by the "facts" of the issue at hand. Finally, and often missed in evaluations of science communication, audiences draw on a wide range of experiences and information sources in interpreting science communication messages, including the welter of ideas and images flowing from popular culture and popular beliefs. Sometimes the communication of science is seen merely as a linear exercise in ensuring the "facts" are disseminated accurately, and in achieving this successful reception of the message will occur. In fact, what occurs in scientific communication is a complex interaction of frameworks of knowledge construction and interpretation, of which science is just one. Scientific knowledge and interpretation, therefore, has to compete with a range of other frameworks and cannot be expected to automatically achieve definitional dominance. A focus by persuasive communication professionals purely on data and evidence in scientific campaigns is likely to run into the kinds of problems encountered by the British government in the late 1980s around HIV/AIDS campaigns, unless the wide range of heuristics that come into play in the course of scientific communication are acknowledged and accommodated.

12

The Football Industry and Public Relations

Raymond Boyle and Richard Haynes
Stirling Media Research Institute

A football club would not have seen the wisdom of having a PR 15 years ago. Football is just starting to come out of the dark ages.
—Max Clifford, PR agent, cited in O'Connor, 2002.

The last decade has seen an explosion in the growth of the football industry both in the UK and across Europe (Fynn & Guest, 1999; Horrie, 2002). Driven by money from television—for example, the 2001 3-year BSkyB-English Premier League deal is worth £1.6 billion—the game remains key "media product" across a range of platforms despite the Europe-wide fall in the value of football rights in 2002 (Boyle & Haynes, 2004). What also makes this football–business–media nexus such a compelling area for research is the high news value of football, both in the UK and across the globe.

Two related features are of particular interest in this chapter. One is mapping the rise of promotional activities in and around the sport. This relates to the broadcasters, the clubs, the players (concerned with image rights), and football's new stakeholders such as City investors and shareholders. The other area relates to the growth of specific public relations activity around the sport. To what extent has PR in football actually simply meant promotional activities? Or are aspects of PR activity associated with other sectors of the entertainment industries becoming prevalent within the football industry?

The chapter is divided into three sections. The first examines the changes that have occurred in the football industry over the last decade or so. It outlines how the role of PR has become more important as the business of football has increasingly interfaced with financial and political arenas. The commercialisation of the sport and the rise of elite clubs as global brands have also helped extend the role that PR has within the football industry.

The next section specifically looks at the changing relationship between football journalism and PR activity. It focuses on the growing tensions between these areas as clubs attempt to

222 BOYLE AND HAYNES

exert more control over the management of news related to their activities. Section 3 contains two case studies that examine the role PR plays within the arena of football scandal and high-media-profile controversy. It documents the issues—such as that of reputation management associated with the release in August 2002 of a highly controversial autobiography by the Manchester United captain, Roy Keane. This section also charts the role of PR in the trial of the two Leeds United players, Jonathan Woodgate and Lee Bowyer, which dominated both the front and back pages of national newspapers during 2001, with the ramifications for the reputation of the club still being felt over a year later.

While this chapter maps the emerging relationship between promotional activities, PR and the football industry, it also attempts to highlight what we view as the key areas requiring research and investigation over the next decade as the sport continues to grow.

SECTION 1: THE FOOTBALL ECONOMY AND THE GROWTH OF PR

The decade since 1992 has seen football in Europe and England in particular, transformed into a multimillion-pound business (Horrie, 2002). Key to this has been the vast sums poured into the game from television, and BSkyB specifically. In the space of a few short years, a club such as Manchester United has seen its earnings from television revenue grow from £500,000 (pre-1992) a year to over £20 million (2002). When this is allied to the growth in commercial sponsorship and the aggressive branding and marketing of the FA English Premier League both domestically and internationally, then a booming industry has been created, one in which the players are the stars and £30,000 pound a week salaries at the elite end of the game became commonplace. In this process BSkyB has also become one of the most profitable television companies in the world and helped alter the ecology of British broadcasting (Horsman, 1997).

Crucial in this process has been television, which both helped transform football into "media product" and also aggressively hyped and promoted the game and its stars. Of course many media outlets had a vested interest in promoting the sport, with the News International empire (the home of BSkyB) stretching across a newspaper market which has always been an important site for the promotion of the game.

The 1990s saw clubs rush to float on the stock market as the value of football television rights continued to spiral. Football and its stars such as Eric Cantona moved out of the back page ghetto they so often occupied in newspapers and onto the pages of glossy magazines and billboards. High-profile international football media events such as the 1996 European Championships staged in England and the 1998 French FIFA World Cup all added to the extensive media profile and exposure that football enjoyed.

As money flowed into the higher echelons of the sport, there was an accompanying growth in the companies involved in the promotion of football and media events. These companies became involved in one or several of the following activities: *sponsorship, event management, public relations, licensing, rights management, marketing research*, and *brand management* (Rines, 2000). Many of these activities are often found under one umbrella organisation or in partnership between corporate groups.

While some of these organisations emerged from traditional sports sponsorship and management companies, others are specifically interested in sports content and media rights acquisition and management, and the development of sports-driven television and online services. For example, a key growth area has been in the use of public relations to enhance the growing number of high-profile football sponsorship agreements, which often involves in-house PR personnel working with agencies specialising in sports sponsorship.

Sponsors associate with sport because of the audiences they attract and the positive image sport carries more broadly in the public's mind. Managing brands at times of crisis has become a more sensitive issue for football sponsors, as we discuss later in the case of Leeds United.

These changes in the football economy have resulted in a range of stakeholders becoming involved with the sport. Football clubs can now find themselves having to communicate with a growing range of publics: their supporters, shareholders, employees, sponsors and commercial partners, the City, the media—local, national, and in some cases international—and the local community, to name just some of the areas with which a club may be involved.

Yet despite the growing complexity of running a football club as part of a PLC (public limited company) or a commercial business, public relations has, until relatively recently, been absent from many clubs. As Patrick Harverson, former *Financial Times* journalist and then Director of Communication at one of the largest football clubs in the world, Manchester United, suggested:

> I think it is fair to say that football at all levels—clubs, leagues, national associations—has been slow to embrace public relations. For too long the sport took its customers—the fans—for granted. However, that has changed, and many clubs and other organisations are know becoming increasingly sophisticated at dealing with the public, the media and the other "stakeholders" in the game. ("Harverson writes PR role." 2002)

Other major clubs, such as the 2002 English double-winning side Arsenal, have only developed a press and PR office as recently as 1999. It now employs seven people and works closely with the club's marketing and broadband sections of their commercial operations. In many ways the development of in-house PR culture within football is in its embryonic stage. It also appears to have been driven primarily by the changing economic environment within which many clubs now operate.

Yet the idea of football club Public Relations Officers (PROs) is not new. As far back as the late 1940s and early 1950s, Santiago Bernabeu, the man who helped create the modern-day Real Madrid, appointed a PR chief, Raimundo Saporta—one of whose key talents was that of a formidable networker—to help the club cultivate friends in high places, including General Franco and the Spanish royal family (Ball, 2001, pp. 142–143). However, for most clubs up until the 1990s, a PRO simply meant an ex-player who would be around on match days to talk with some of the supporters and the corporate sponsors. While corporate hospitality remains an aspect of football PR, with former players regularly used by clubs on match days to mingle with corporate guests, it is but one small part of a larger, more complex practice.

Until relatively recently, football took its core support for granted. Being a football supporter was all about loyalty—you did not change your team if it performed poorly; you were a fan for life. This loyalty was often abused by those who ran football (Conn, 1998). Ironically, while many supporters have been uncomfortable with what they view as the rampant commercialisation of the sport over the last decade or so, the growth of football PLCs has resulted in those fans who are shareholders having at least to be treated seriously by most of the clubs (see Hamil et al., 1999, 2000).

FOOTBALL: THE FINANCIAL AND POLITICAL ARENAS

In recent years the business dimension of football has become more pronounced. Examples of this incorporation of football into the financial sector are widespread: clubs listing on the Stock

Exchange, hostile takeovers, a globalised market for players, football clubs as brands, and so on. In addition, the central role that the sport plays as key "media product" for organisations such as BSkyB has resulted in vast sums being put into the game to secure live television rights. The 2001–2004 English Premier League deal cost BSkyB £1.1 billion. With such amounts of money involved, various forms of lobbying surround the run up to every new deal. As the value of sports rights has fallen across Europe, the run up to the 2004 deal in England saw extensive lobbying and the strategic placing of stories about the proposed value of the deal, as the League attempted to talk up the value of its product.

However, while football at the highest level is now clearly a business, it is not *just* a business. Football's importance, and the extent of the media coverage it receives, cannot be reduced simply to economics, but rather reflects its wider social, political, and historical importance. As noted above, perhaps the key distinction between football and more conventional businesses is the inadequacy of the concept of the customer to describe football supporters.

Patrick Harverson, then Director of Communication at Manchester United and responsible for the club's public relations, is well aware of this issue:

> A big challenge has been to tackle the perception of Manchester United as two different, often conflicting, entities: the football side and the business/plc side. Our message is there is only one United, with the business and football arms of the club working together to achieve the same aim: success on and off the pitch. Our point is that we cannot have a successful, well-run business without a successful, well-run team, and vice versa. ("Harverson writes PR role." 2002)

As the elite football clubs such as Manchester United and Real Madrid increasingly view themselves as global brands, the promotion of the club as a commercial entity can often run contrary to the emotional and cultural aspects of the clubs which they seek to establish in order to retain and develop their fan base. It is not only football clubs that perceive themselves in this context. Leagues such as the FA Premier League also seeks to develop their brand in particular within the international television marketplace. This is a market which, in 2002, was worth £600 million a season in television revenue alone as the league sells the rights to 152 countries (Campbell, 2002b, p. 20).

This increase in the number of clubs that are part of a PLC structure means financial reporting has become important for generating confidence in the football economy. Research has also indicated that this aspect of the football industry has resulted in some clubs requiring a particular financial public relations capacity (Boyle, Dinan, & Morrow, 2002). Clubs like Manchester United outsource their financial PR, using the London-based Holborn Public Relations agency, while in Scotland both Shandwick and Media House have been involved in the financial aspects of the football industry there.

Of course, clubs having close links with the City predate the recent boom in the football industry—Tottenham Hotspur floated on the stock market as far back as the early 1980s—but the level of institutional investment in the clubs was scant compared to the involvement that currently exists. In addition, the role of media companies as investors and shareholders in football clubs, something which has been a recent phenomenon in the British game, has also complicated the picture and increased the need to manage financial news (Boyle, 2000).

As the game among the elite clubs has evolved into an increasingly global business, driven by television and commercial sponsors, it tends to mitigate against the voice of traditional supporters being heard. Exceptions do exist. The successful PR battle to influence public and political opinion waged by the Independent Manchester United Supporters Association in 1998/1999 ultimately helped block BSkyB's attempt to buy Manchester United and in so doing fundamentally changed the shape of football ownership in the UK. Central in this success was the ability of these supporters—who were well connected in both the political and media spheres—to organise a PR campaign that influenced the climate of social and political opinion with regard to the merits of the BSkyB bid (Walsh & Brown, 1999; Horrie, 2002, pp. 232–253).

In the past, newspaper owners have exerted influence through their newspapers in promoting (or indeed rubbishing) attempts by rivals to control football clubs. In the early 1990s, Robert Maxwell's *Daily Mirror* supported his proposed takeover of Tottenham Hotspur, while Rupert Murdoch's *Sun* newspaper backed his business associates Alan Sugar and Terry Venables' bid to control the club (Horrie, 2002, p. 101). A public relations battle to secure the hearts and minds of supporters was fought out on the back pages of Britain two largest-selling newspapers.

Transfer speculation is increasingly sensitive information, both for supporter confidence and increasingly for financial backers and markets. Leaking interest in a player to the press is a mechanism of forming general interest and associating a move in the mind of a player. Football agent Eric Hall admitted to a FA enquiry into corruption in the game in the 1990s that he often placed stories in the papers to "hype transfer deals or create expectations of higher fees" (Horrie, 2002, p. 149). How clubs manage this process is very interesting, not least because there are new regulations on the movement of players and the protocols associated with this process.

Morrow (1999) has argued that with more clubs becoming PLCs that this has meant that a public relations strategy has been forced on some of them by the need to manage potentially sensitive financial information. This is particularly important when, as Michie suggested, much of the reporting in the business pages of newspapers is attributable to PR sources (Michie, 1998, p. 25). Thus, changes in the wider financial structure of the football industry have forced clubs to address the issue of financial and City PR, something which goes with the territory of being a PLC. It should, however, be noted that this aspect of PR activity remains the domain of a number of elite clubs, and the vast majority of clubs view financial PR activity as of no relevance to them.

The recent collapse in the value of football television rights across Europe has included a number of spectacular casualties (Campbell, 2002a). In Italy, Fiorentina, one of the major clubs in Seria A, has gone bust despite being the 14th richest club in the world in season 1999/2000 (Moore, 2002). A revamped new club began the 2002 season in Italy's part-time league. The collapse in television revenues means that few clubs are going to seek to float on the stock market in the near future. Those that have find their shares have plummeted in value over the last couple of years, while a number of media companies, such as the American cable company NTL, seek to liquidate their stakes in a number of clubs (Banks, 2002). All this helps reinforce the trend that more traditional aspects of PR activity involving club sponsors and match day promotions are likely to remain more important for most clubs than City and corporate PR.

Football Governance and PR

The governance of football itself has become an increasingly important issue in sports, news. Due to the commercial imperatives of professional sport, the way sport handles its business aspects has increasingly come under media focus (Bower, 2003). Allegations of corruption (involving organisations such as FIFA) or mismanagement (such as the Football League's handling of the ITV Digital fiasco when the company collapsed owing millions of pounds to football clubs) have made governing bodies acutely aware of the need to manage their relationship with the media. The broader image of football and sport is at stake, and administrators are under public scrutiny as much as leaders of the corporate world.

It has become clear that there is an increasing importance placed on the role that public relations can play as governing institutions in football seek to modernise their structures. Zwirek (2002) has clearly documented how the English FA has placed public relations at the centre of its strategy to revolutionise the game from national to grassroots level in that country. Much of this has been driven by their then Chief Executive (CE), Adam Crozier, who was appointed in 2000. Crozier, at 36 the youngest CE ever at the FA, was headhunted from his post as Chief Executive at the advertising agency Saatchi & Saatchi.

Under Crozier, the FA implemented a more proactive communication strategy and restructured their communication organisation. Their Communications Office was headed by the former BBC journalist Paul Newman and focused on working with the professional media. They had a Public Affairs section, which included their Customer Relations Unit, dealing with the wide range of public and community-based work carried out by the FA. Finally, they had an International Relations Unit, which focused on the international politics of the game and the vital lobbying and liaison activities required with international bodies such as UEFA and FIFA. This also includes networking with organisations such as the powerful G14 group of elite European clubs that has become an important body in shaping change in the European game. Under the auspices of an Executive Director David Davies, another former BBC journalist who we have elsewhere (Boyle & Haynes, 2000, p. 148) referred to as a sporting spin doctor, the FA's range of PR activity employed a staff of 22 in their Internal/External Affairs Division.

What is significant about the FA "revolution" is that it has become one of the few major sporting governing organisations in the UK which clearly views the role of public relations as a central aspect of its wider strategic goals. The analogy with the role that public relations plays in the highly mediated world of politics was not lost on the then Chief Executive. As Crozier himself has noted:

> You realise in football very quickly, because of all the different sections of the game and the world outside, which is so interested in it, that you are in a very political arena, and in all sorts of ways. [ ] As in politics, I suppose I had to understand how politicians work. (cited in Lawton, 2002)

Indeed, this need to understand the machinations of the political arena is increasingly important for an organisation such as the FA, charged with overseeing the game at all levels in England. While football has always interested politicians to some extent, the profile of the game means that few can choose to ignore it.

However, the departure of Crozier from the FA in 2002 and the subsequent 20$cut in staff (including the departure of Paul Newman in April, 2003) have severely set back the "modernising" culture initiated by Crozier. These cuts of £13 million a year have become necessary as the FA seeks to fund projects such as the new Wembley stadium. However, Crozier's departure was more symptomatic of the wider power struggle between the traditional governors of the sport in England, the FA, and the new powerbrokers of the Premier League who would rather run the sport to serve their own particular interests (Bower, 2003).

In their study of FIFA, Sugden and Tomlinson (1998) have shown how lobbying, PR activity, and politics are all intertwined at the highest levels of the world game. As part of the wider creative and cultural industries, football events are increasingly viewed as important generators of employment and income streams for cities and countries around the world. The UK government backed England's failed bid to stage the 2006 FIFA World Cup in that country. When UEFA announced that Portugal would stage the 2004 European soccer championships, economists correctly predicted an extensive public and private investment in the country's telecommunications, tourist, and communications infrastructure. With five new stadia planned to be built for the tournament (at a cost of (£207 million) shares rose steeply in the construction industry. Thus, a political PR capacity is vital for any footballing organisation such as the FA which must interface with government at various levels.

More recently, the Football Associations of Scotland and the Irish Republic put together a bid to host the 2008 European football championships. This involved an extensive PR campaign initially to secure high-profile political and commercial backing and support within the countries themselves, and finally to convince UEFA that such a bid could be a major sporting and commercial success for the game. The Edinburgh-based sports marketing and consultancy group RiverGani Communications (www.riversgani.co.uk) and Craigie Taylor International (CTI), the Surrey-based PR and sponsorship organisation (www.craigietaylor.co.uk), were both involved in the promotion of the 2008 bid. The latter was involved in a range of activity across a number of commercial arenas mostly focused on sponsorship management (including raising awareness of Vodafone's sponsorship relationship with Manchester United).

The fact that CTI generates most of their business outside sporting activity is a good example of how many PR and promotional agencies have diversified into sport, and football in particular, as the commercialisation of the game has increased over the last decade or so. There clearly now exists a PR market for those with specialist expertise in the footballing or sports arena. Established PR agencies such as Hill & Knowlton Public Relations operate a sports marketing and sponsorship division which seeks to build brand awareness for a range of sporting organisations and sponsors including the involvement of Adidas as a major sponsor in the 2002 FIFA World Cup. Other agencies such as Ketchum (www.ketchum.com)—voted *PRWeek's* 2002 agency of the year—have launched a dedicated sports PR unit, the Ketchum Sports Network, to generate more business for the company in this particular sector of the market. Central to their portfolio is their ability to use public relations to generate greater awareness or value from any sports sponsorship relationship a client may have.

SECTION 2: PR, JOURNALISM, AND THE COMMODIFICATION OF FOOTBALL

Alex Ferguson has long understood that football is unlike many other specialist areas of journalism, where reporters will find alternatives if one source is denied to them. In effect each club is a local monopoly. (Crick, 2002, p. 524)

JOURNALISTIC ACCESS AND CLUB PR

There has long been a symbiotic relationship between the print media and football (Boyle & Hayes, 2000, pp. 21–26). The sport remains a vital component in helping to sell newspapers. While this has historically centred on the tabloid end of the market, the last decade has seen the broadsheet market for sports coverage, and football in particular, expand, aided and abetted by the vast sums of television money which have flowed into the game in England (Boyle, Dinan, & Morrow, 2002, pp. 166–169).

However, tensions are clearly developing between sections of the media and football clubs as the latter attempt to exert more control over what they view as their intellectual property (IP). This has involved a number of elite clubs developing their own media capacity (Boyle & Haynes, 2002). This process begins to call into question some well-established relationships which have traditionally seen the print media in particular expect access to players, managers, and information from the club.

Certain clubs such as Arsenal, Manchester United, Chelsea, Liverpool, and Celtic have been actively developing their own media capacity, often forming partnerships with particular media companies such as Granada Media (Boyle & Haynes, 2002). As the marketplace for football rights continues to evolve, these clubs wish to retain more individual rights to exclusive material which they will seek to communicate to their supporters through the club's online and offline media channels. In the longer term, they view this as a potentially lucrative income stream. Part of any content package must of course include news and information.

As Patrick Harverson, then Director of Communications at Manchester United, has argued, a balance needs to be struck between general media access and the club's retaining and exploiting content for their exclusive use:

> That is an increasingly contentious issue, what's happening is that football clubs and individuals, the sports stars, are waking up to the value of the rights that they own [ ] for decades we've essentially allowed the broadcasters to exploit that and now of course in recent years the broadcasters been paying a lot of money for that, it's a perfectly sensible two-way business there and without sounding too passé it does all come back to striking the right balance. What we don't want to do is build an internal media structure that cuts the external media out of the equation because that would be stupid. Partly because our internal media to be honest doesn't reach that many people, how many programmes do we sell, the website or MUTV cannot compete with BBC or the *Daily Telegraph* or *The Sun* so you'd be foolish because there is no doubt the broadcasters and the newspapers are a great shop window. (Interview with authors, 25/4/2002)

Other football clubs such as Chelsea appear to be less well disposed to continuing to allow unfettered access to newspaper journalists.

Chris Tate, Managing Director of Chelsea Digital Media at the English Premier League club Chelsea, is strident in outlining how he views the relationship with the media has changed over the last decade:

> Why should we give access to certain newspapers really who are trading on our name, our football players, our brand to sell their newspapers? If you were an official partner, if you have invested in the club like BSkyB, then fine, yes, come along, you're very welcome and that extension runs into associated newspapers. If you happen to be the *Daily Mirror,* an example of a newspaper that's not allowed in here then sorry you can't come along to training or get interviews after that but out of common courtesy the club will always provide press tickets for people who wish to do match reports and we always provide players, relevant players, to do a press conference afterwards along with the manager. (Interview with authors, 8/4/2002)

Of course, this position is not viewed favourably by newspaper journalists in particular. Journalist Ewing Grahame then of the Glasgow-based *Herald* newspaper has attacked the tightening of news management by Celtic in recent years. He argued that the club's strategy is one that seeks to control the media:

> With an overmanned, inefficient bureaucracy, dozens of jobs were created on Celtic films, the Celtic website, the Celtic newsroom, and the PR department. One applicant for the role of chief press officer was told that the intention was to get rid of newspapers, or at least the need for them. (Grahame, 2002)

There is a certain irony in this journalistic attack as in the past the club became notorious for the deluge of leaks and rumours that used to pour out of Celtic onto the back pages of Scottish newspapers. This was a state of affairs which newspapers were more than happy to exploit. What Grahame seems to fail to realise is that Celtic is simply doing what most other major football clubs are also implementing. At Manchester United, for example, their Director of Communication, former journalist, outlined a club position that would more than likely be echoed at a club such as Celtic:

There's no doubt the media is not happy with it (less access) and I don't blame them for being unhappy but we have a right to do what we're doing. There is an issue here of delivering the news to our fans unhampered and untainted by the spin of the media because a real problem for me in my job and for us as a club is the way the perception of us is shaped by the way we are portrayed by the media. This is often negatively, so the tabloids will take something a player says and turn it around into something he didn't say quite happily because it's a much better story and it's sensational [ ] So that gives us good reason to use our own media to deliver (exclusive content) as well as the commercial reasons which is to obviously drive subscriptions and sell things, but it's about striking the balance and I think it will take some time before everyone works it out. (Interview with authors, 25/4/2002)

It is not simply the print media that are likely to become concerned with this development. Neil Fraser, Head of Sport at BBC Scotland, is also aware of the difficulties faced by that organisation as it attempts to compete journalistically in an increasingly complex football rights market.

I mean I think there's a general concern that we don't get the access to clubs that we once did and I think for them it's likely to continue in that sense. I think if you're a rights holder you've got a stronger negotiating position and you say well we're the rights holder, we've got access but where the trouble begins is if you're not a major rights holder it becomes very hard, you're negotiating position becomes very weak, you might then just get into press conferences. Television in particular, generates a lot of features, background stuff and player profiles and so on and if you don't have access to them to get in and get pictures then you're struggling basically. (Interview with authors, 12/3/02)

There seems little doubt that over the next few years the battle lines will continue to be redrawn as clubs seek to extract commercial value from all their assets, while media institutions (in particular those not holding specific coverage rights) will argue for the importance of continuing to journalistically report on all aspects of the football industry.

Transfer Speculation

Rowe (1997) highlighted that "soft news" predominates on the back pages of newspapers. In football reporting, transfer speculation takes up much of this "sports gossip." This most banal form of sports reporting has an important role in football subculture and opinion formation among supporters. It connects fans to the hopes and aspirations of football clubs, and the way in which the industry disseminates this information, which can be very sensitive both economically and culturally, is interesting to analyse.

There are certain distinctions to be made regarding the forms of media and how they report on transfers—arguably the press have become important "talking shops" for speculating which players are moving where, closely followed by radio. TV tends to have less speculation on transfer moves due to restraints on time of TV sports news—one exception being the recent transfer of Rio Ferdinand from Leeds United to Manchester United in July 2002. Furthermore, a distinction can be made between national and local media. Local media will tend to have more intimate connections with individual clubs and will have their ear to the ground once transfer speculation begins.

Related to this, of course, is the long tradition in football of players and managers leaking stories to their favourite journalists or newspapers. Sir Alex Ferguson at Manchester United was happy to have *The Manchester Evening News* run with the headline: "Fergie: I'll quit in pay wrangle," when he wanted a new pay deal with the club finalised in 1996 before leaving for a holiday. More recently, the former Hibernian manager Frank Sauzee employed a PR consultant to raise his concerns on the sports back pages about the club's delay in agreeing to a severance deal following his sacking. In these cases the added publicity helped agreements to be reached quickly as both clubs wanted to minimise any poor publicity.

Why is this transfer speculation an issue for PR? The main public for transfer speculation are the fans. Clubs have to be careful how they leak information to the media; they are aware that fans like to hear that the club is attempting to sign a player but are cautious not to incite too much excitement in case a particular deal does not materialise. A case in point was the attempts by Leeds United to sign a new manager in 2002. An earlier public move in 1998 to coax Martin O'Neill to Elland Road from Leicester City had failed when O'Neill rejected their approach, leaving the Yorkshire club to fall back on an alternative choice, David O'Leary. This not only led the club to backtrack on earlier statements that O'Leary would not be offered the job, but also undermined the status of O'Leary once he was given the job.

Leeds was more cautious when they attempted to lure O'Neill once more from Celtic in 2002, letting media speculation take its own course—signaling their interest without actually making a formal approach. O'Neill privately rejected the approach once more—allegedly through his close friends—but because no formal approach had been made Leeds did not end up with egg on their face. This version of events is disputed by Bower (2003, p. 298), who claimed that O'Neill did meet Risdale and did accept the job, only to later change his mind. (When this story broke, O'Neill threatened to sue the author.)

As the money involved in football has escalated, clubs have developed more formal relations with the media. The beat journalist still exists and may have an inside track on developments in a club, but because of the increasing media focus on football, clubs realise that they have to communicate to various publics through a range of formal PR activities. In addition, there are now more media outlets to service which are covering football, including a new online media community. Press releases and press conferences are now commonplace. New signings will be paraded in front of the media with structured events, including media briefings, Q&A sessions, photo calls, and press packs.

SECTION 3: FOOTBALL ON TRIAL: CASE STUDIES IN FOOTBALL PR

"Football's very bitchy. It's not like Hollywood." (Vinnie Jones, cited in Anthony, October 2001)

CASE STUDY 1: FOOTBALL ON TRIAL: SCANDAL, CELEBRITY, AND PR

As in other areas of the entertainment industry, the reporting of celebrity is central to the football–media nexus. Recent studies on sports stars and celebrity reveal that the contemporary media focus on sporting achievement and personality tell us much about popular culture and wider social relations (Van de Burgh, 2000; Whannel, 2002a). As Whannel (2002b, p. 49) identified:

> Stardom is a form of social production in which the professional ideologies and production practices of the media aim to win and hold our attention by linking sporting achievement and personality in ways which have resonances in popular common sense.

In this respect the construction of sports celebrity has become formalised and normalised in the production and consumption of media sport. As in other areas of the entertainment industry, the exposing of the private lives of sportspeople to public gaze has become increasingly commonplace over the last decade or so. This process driven by the proliferation of media outlets and the increased media exposure given to sport means that footballers are not immune to this exposure, and are increasingly in the public eye often beyond the world of football.

Crucially, football stars provide fans with a key point of identification as the bearers of entertainment and sporting narratives (Whannel, 1992). Stars, with their cachet as celebrities, have been integral to the new promotional culture that pervades the contemporary football industry. The heavy investment of television and sponsors in the industry has created an era of football millionaires with all the material trappings. The contemporary footballer can be nominally defined by superstardom and material excess in stark contrast to the "organic" football heroes of previous generations.

The intensity of media focus brings with it an increasing need to manage celebrity and defend the blurred boundaries of the public and the private. The use of agents and publicists has become standard practice for Premier League footballers as they attempt to juggle their commitments and responsibilities to football club, sponsors, agents, fans, family, and friends. Footballers are commodified as performers, role models, corporate assets, and even, in the case of David Beckham, famous husbands.

In this context football stars go to extreme lengths to protect their reputations and privacy. For example, the Manchester City player Gary Flitcroft took out an injunction to prevent press revelations of sexual impropriety at a lap dancing club and David and Victoria Beckham's attempts to control their image as a celebrity couple by both contractual and legal means have been well documented (Whannel, 2002b). However, limiting public disclosure of the private lives of celebrity footballers has largely been negligible and is the meat and drink of much tabloid gossip.

Moreover, when footballers have scrapes with the law—drunk driving, recreational drug use, criminal violence—the stories surrounding these scandals have increasingly come under the media spotlight and subject to public interest. As Rowe (1997) has outlined, the celebrity sports scandal presents the media and the public with an opportunity to scrutinise sporting heroes. The sports scandal highlights the tension between the elevated status of stars and their fall from grace as mere mortals. As Rowe argued:

> The media scandal is [..] a way to "truth," a means by which the public façade is penetrated and privileged access gained to the domain of the private. (Rowe, 1997, pp. 205–206)

While sports scandals may contribute to the surfeit of media scandals under the common themes of sexual misconduct, financial impropriety and corruption, most football stories tend to reflect on improper conduct more localised to the context of the sport.

The notoriety of footballers for drinking binges and gambling addictions are the mainstay of football scandals and fuel the stereotypical image of the professional player represented in popular drama series such as the ITV drama production *Footballers' Wives*.

Similarly, violence on and off the pitch has come under increasing focus within the coverage of football. Television in particular ritualistically scrutinises the level of violence in the game and the ability of referees to control and penalise players. This media spotlight on violent conduct and reckless tackles (especially the cynical use of the "professional foul") has definitely led to the introduction of new stringent laws by the world-governing body FIFA and the instigation of universal reward for "fair play."

Football clubs are without doubt sensitive to the revelatory stories of individual players, particularly where some crime or misdemeanor has taken place. The management of how these events are reported has increasingly preoccupied clubs and their public relations activity.

Driven in part by the competition for stories between media outlets and the commercial value now attached to the image rights of some of the elite players such as David Beckham, there is an inherent tension around footballing celebrity. They want (and need) public media exposure, but at the same time they need to control any adverse publicity. This skillful management of publicity is becoming an increasingly important aspect of any PR activity associated with elite football players.

We now turn our attention to two recent instances in order to illustrate how football scandals have emerged as a central component of everyday sports news values and how football clubs have attempted to manage the flow of information in their efforts at damage limitation.

The first focuses on revelatory admissions by Manchester United and Republic of Ireland footballer Roy Keane in his ghosted autobiography (2002) that was serialised in August 2002 in the *News of the World* and *The Times* prior to its subsequent publication. The second reviews the public relations crisis faced by Leeds United after the trial of Jonathan Woodgate and Lee Bowyer over the course of the 2000/2001 and 2001/2002 Premier League seasons. In both instances, we analyse the increasing importance of public relations activities as a defensive mechanism to gossip and scandal in football journalism.

CASE STUDY 2: FOOTBALL ON TRIAL: KEANOGATE

Footballers are no strangers to courting media attention to garner and reinforce their celebrity status when it suits them. However, since the 1960s the intense media spotlight on football stars means that they must expect as much bad publicity as good. As entertainers and role models, the media has assumed a public right to know about all aspects of their behaviour both on and off the field of play. One way in which footballers have attempted to control the flow of information about them and their personal life is through the publication of memoir and ghosted autobiography. The expansion in football publishing during the 1990s, instigated by the fanzine movement (Haynes, 1996) and Nick Hornby's *Fever Pitch*, has been substantially fleshed out by a boom in revelatory autobiographies by some of the Premier League's leading players.

Autobiographies that caused a stir on publication include those by Arsenal captain Tony Adams (1999), who struggled against alcoholism, and Jaap Stam (2001), who revealed an illegal approach by Manchester United in his transfer to the club. The latter was serialised in the *Daily Mirror* before publication and written without the consent of the Manchester United management, who flatly denied Stam's version of events. This did not prevent the shock sale of the Dutch international almost immediately after the book was published, reflecting the club's dismay and embarrassment at the revelations, although the £15 million move to the Italian club Lazio was officially put down to financial pressures (Crick, 2002, pp. 541–543).

As the Stam case highlights, the reportage of sports scandal aims to throw negative publicity in the face of an individual or a club invariably through a process of naming and shaming. The selection of stories as scandals is frequently premised on a set of conflicting sports values of competition (the drive to win) and fairness (connected to the altruistic ideology of sport as inherently good). Again as Rowe concluded:

> The media are key conduits in the communication of the meaning of the sports scandal, patrolling and marking the ethical frontiers of sport and switching between official and popular discourses and private and public domains in a relentless quest for the "truth" of the day. (Rowe, 1997, p. 219)

The truth, of course, can often hurt, both for those being publicly exposed and those who publish the revelations in the first instance. The serialisation of the Manchester United player Roy Keane's (2002) autobiography in the *News of the World* and *The Times* prior to publication by Penguin offers an interesting case study of reputation management spinning out of control.

Keane had built a reputation within the game and its supporters as a dedicated, almost obsessive competitor and was widely viewed as the "linchpin" in Sir Alex Ferguson's successful reign as Manchester United manager. Keane's combative style of play had repeatedly led him into trouble with referees and disciplinary action from the FA, but he always enjoyed the full support of his manager and the club. Keane parachuted himself into the media spotlight prior to the 2002 World Cup in South Korea and Japan, where he was to captain the Republic of Ireland. In a much publicised vitriolic spat between Keane and the Irish manager Mick McCarthy, Keane was released from the squad and sent home before the finals began amid speculation that he would retire from international football.

The events sparked a series of articles on Keane focusing on his mental attitude, which did little to endear the player to his otherwise adoring public. In this context, the serialisation of Keane's autobiography on the eve of its publication, and more significantly a new Premiership season, was a classic case of commercial opportunism by the publisher. In serialising the rights to the press, Penguin had managed to recoup £150,000 of the £1.4 million in royalties that had been paid up front to Keane and sports journalist Eamon Dunphy, who had ghostwritten the book. Serialisation also served to publicise the book in the most sensational and dramatic circumstances.

The *News of the World* had focused on the "juicy bits" from the book, which included revelations of his conflict with McCarthy and claims that certain Manchester United players had compromised their competitive spirit because of their fame and fortune. However, the most sensational headlines came from his confession that he had intentionally sought to injure the Manchester City player Alf-inge Haaland in a reckless challenge during a Manchester derby in 2001. Keane's honesty regarding his challenge on the City player soon spiraled out of control as information of his malicious attack became headline news across the UK media. The admission of premeditated violence was roundly denounced by most sports commentators and prompted debate as to Keane's character.

The revelation also prompted the FA to announce that it would be examining the full text of the book in order to see whether there was a case to answer. Both Alf-inge Haaland and Manchester City also stated that they would be legally pursuing both Roy Keane and Manchester United for damages. Sir Alex Ferguson also weighed in with a defence of Keane, suggesting he had "no case to answer" regarding his admission of premeditated violence on Haaland. It was argued that Haaland's comments on a Web site had, jeopardised any case he had, having previously denied that Keane's tackle had any bearing on his long-standing knee injury.

As Manchester United prepared for their Champion's League qualifier in August of that year, the club's PR machinery attempted to deflect any suggestion that there were splits in the United camp following Keane's comments on an apparent lack of appetite for the game among some players. This is noted by several correspondents and reveals the cynicism of some journalists towards the new regime of football clubs and their "spin doctors."

In their desperation to play down any kind of resentment among the players with regard to Keane's remarks, United's press officers succeeded only in showing just how sensitive the entire club was over the accusations contained the book. When Keane claimed his teammates had lost their desire and accused them of being too obsessed with "Rolex watches, fast cars and mansions" rather than winning trophies, it was clear he was going to bruise a few high-profile egos (Mcdonnell, 2002).

When David Beckham denied any rift, it was actually clear Keane's comments had been poorly received by some of his teammates.

The to-and-fro of comments by the different parties reveal a classic scenario of utilising news source strategies to gain public support—as is often seen in political spin (Michie, 1998).

The United PR machine swung into action within minutes and it was pointed out that Beckham wanted to make it clear he was talking about the media and not, perish the thought, one of his teammates. You pays your money, in United's case, lots of it, and you takes your choice. Keane may not rule the roost when he wears the green of Ireland, but when he is in the red of United, it is a different story.

Both Ferguson and Keane have suggested that United's problems that season were partly due to players living in the comfort zone. Beckham, or rather United's PR department, were at pains to suggest that he was not referring to anyone from within the club when he defended the team (Curry, 2002).

Similarly, ghostwriter Eamon Dunphy came to Keane's aid by claiming he was responsible for the way the comments on Haaland were phrased. Dunphy was also interviewed by *The Observer* newspaper in an attempt to diffuse the focus on Keane.

> With Keane maintaining that his conscience was clear after playing a part in his team's 1–0 Premiership win over West Bromwich on Saturday, it was left to his ghostwriter Eamon Dunphy to begin a belated damage limitation process. Journalist and former Republic of Ireland midfielder Dunphy claimed yesterday that he had used "artistic licence" and had "paraphrased" many of Keane's opinions. Dunphy said: "There is the passage about Haaland and I am as much responsible for that, as a writer, rather than Roy. I should take the rap." However, Dunphy did admit that Keane read and approved the text (Ladyman, 2002).

On 30 August, Keane was sent off against Sunderland for elbowing his former Irish teammate Jason McAteer. The Premier League announced a three-match ban for the player and the FA charged Keane with two counts of bringing the game into disrepute. Both were linked to comments made in the book about the Haaland tackle. In the same week Manchester United announced that Keane would undergo a hip operation and would be out of action for at least 6 weeks.

In October of that year, the FA found Keane guilty of bringing the game into disrepute and profiting from this through the book. He was fined £150,000 (about 2 weeks' wages) and banned for five games.

CASE STUDY 3: FOOTBALL ON TRIAL: LEEDS UNITED AND REPUTATION MANAGEMENT

Reputation management in sport has been a growing field within public relations primarily due to the increased public interest in sporting celebrities who are exposed in media scandals. There have been numerous high-profile cases within sport where reputations have been irrevocably damaged and besmirched. Classically, where sports stars are involved in criminal court cases, their reputations as celebrities are brought into disrepute and are often radically transformed. Examples include former American football player OJ Simpson who faced murder charges in 1990, the former Heavyweight boxing champion Mike Tyson convicted of rape in 1992, and the late South African cricket captain Hanse Cronje who was found guilty of match-fixing in 2000.

In Britain, the two court cases against the Leeds United players Lee Bowyer and Jonathan Woodgate in 2001 for an attack on Asian student Safraz Najeib in January 2000 became the focus of intense media and public interest. While the circumstances of this particular case are specific to Leeds United, the case does offer a more generally applicable insight into the potential contradictions of public relations management and practice at times of crisis in the football industry.

The trial focused on a brutal attack on Najeib in Leeds City centre by a group of young men outside a popular nightclub allegedly involving Bowyer and Woodgate as key perpetrators. The case concluded in a conviction and 6-year prison sentence for Woodgate's friend Neil Caveney, while Woodgate was convicted of affray and sentenced to 100 hours' community service. Bowyer, who had changed his story from his original statement to police to his admissions in court, was found not guilty of affray but was labeled a "liar" by the judge, Mr Justice Henriques, who also left Bowyer to pay court fees of £1 million as a penalty for his dishonesty. The trial had gained exceptional notoriety, not only for the involvement of the players, but also due to the collapse of the first trial that began in January 2001.

The tabloid newspaper the *Sunday Mirror* had carried an interview with the victim's father containing allegations that the beating had been racially motivated. The claims ran contra to a pre-trial hearing, where the Crown Prosecution Service had ruled out racism as a motive for the attack. The judge, Mr Justice Poole, feared that the article would prejudice the case and collapsed the trial. The Mirror Group was charged with contempt of court under rules governing the reporting of criminal proceeding.

The whole event brought damnation on the players involved from the media and opposition supporters and severely damaged the reputation of the club that had begun to evolve as a preeminent force in the Premier League and European competition. In the light of the wider shifts in the football industry outlined above, the club had undergone significant change during the 1990s, restructuring its corporate management team and publicly floating as Leeds Sporting PLC (now Leeds United PLC). Therefore, financial- and football-related pressures to succeed were paramount and meant juggling the needs of investors, fans, and the media.

Both trials were subject to intense media scrutiny, and from the outset the club was eager to control how the players were managed and presented. However, although Bowyer was represented by Leeds United solicitors, Woodgate had distanced himself from the club's protection and employed his own defence team under instruction of his agent. The division in the defence of the players had a detrimental impact on the ability of the club to coordinate public statements, leaving them constantly open to media gossip and placing the club on the back foot. Even more problematic for the club was that one of the key witnesses, Leeds United defender Michael Dubery, who was cleared of any involvement in the attack during the first trial, revealed that he had been told to lie on the advice of Leeds United solicitors.

Leeds United's support of Bowyer, who was chaperoned by club officials from the court to Elland Road to play in vital Champions League matches, also brought criticism of the club management for supporting a player allegedly associated with such a violent incident. In a move to quell growing criticism of its overprotection of the players, the then club Chairman Peter Ridsdale (often portrayed as being among the most "media-savvy" of football club chairman) fined Woodgate and Bowyer 8 and 4 weeks' wages, respectively (the equivalent of £100,000 and £88,000). Bowyer, operating through his agent, steadfastly refused to pay the fine, claiming it went against his contract and PFA policy.

Bowyer's intransigence inflated the scandal further, ironically undermining any damage limitation instigated by the club. Ridsdale placed Bowyer on the transfer list, and a further round of media speculations ensued focusing on Bowyer's future and the crisis facing the club. *The Mirror* newspaper continued to attack Leeds United and Bowyer specifically, presenting itself as the moral arbiter of public opinion. On the news that Bowyer had been transfer listed, the tabloid newspaper ran a front-page tirade against the player with the following taunt:

> I'M THE VICTIM ... wails boozing, pot-smoking, violent, RACIST, cowardly, unapologetic, lying, odious, transfer-listed Lee Bowyer (NOW TRY TO SUE US YOU LITTLE SCUMBAG). (*Daily Mirror*, 19 December, 2001)

By this time, the club's attempts to dampen media focus on the club had spiralled out of control. Matters were worsened by the serialisation prior to publication of Leeds manager David O'Leary's autobiographical account of the troubled season in the *News of the World*. O'Leary's book, controversially titled *Leeds United on Trial*, was amazingly co-written by Leeds United's media director and club director, David Walker. Again, media criticism focused on the timing of the serialisation (less than 48 hours after the trial had finished) and, furthermore, the belief that O'Leary sought to gain financially out of the violent events. In the book, O'Leary openly criticised the players for damaging the reputation of the club.

O'Leary was coy over his payment for the serialisation and royalties for the book (reported figures ranged from £100,000 to £150,000). He remained adamant that he was not paid for the serial rights by the largest-selling Sunday newspaper, the *News of the World*, but the sports press were eager to point out that it was standard practice for such rights to be set against any royalty advance. O'Leary insisted his conscience was clear, even after his friend, BBC football pundit and *Mirror* columnist Mark Lawrenson, urged the Leeds manager to donate the money to charity in order to deflect personal criticism.

Although O'Leary defended the book, insisting that only two of the nine chapters dealt with the trial, as *The Times* football correspondent Kevin McCarra noted, "The existence of the book is a cause of greater concern than its contents" (*The Times*, 5 January, 2002). The inside revelatory stories from the Leeds manager criticised the players and included veiled criticism of the PLC, which he felt had placed added pressures on him to manage the club. Lack of success after a series of expensive signings (including Rio Ferdinand for £18 million) and O'Leary's decision to press ahead with the book ultimately led to his sacking in June 2002.

O'Leary had publicly washed the club's dirty linen in public at a time when the Chairman and the board had wanted to suppress media attention of the club's crisis. O'Leary's view that Bowyer should not have been excluded from England's 2002 World Cup campaign (a decision he believed was due to "political correctness" and a PR campaign instigated by the then Chief Executive of the Football Association, Adam Crozier) ran against Ridsdale's concurrence with the FA's policy.

The book was not well received by seasoned football journalists. The inability of O'Leary to understand that staying out of the media spotlight could at times improve public and media relations was apparent to all. As the following quotes from a selection of critiques of the Leeds manager illustrate, the whole saga represented a lesson in how not to manage and fight media scandals.

> That O'Leary involves sophistry against the charge that he has exploited one of the direst passages in the affairs of any leading football club highlights only one problem with the book, however. An equally serious one is that it puts him, and his football club, into the same dock he assigns to the Football Association for its refusal to allow the selection of either Bowyer or Woodgate for the national team while they still faced charges of such a serious nature. Hypocrisy, yells O'Leary, apparently without any notion of how the stance of his club sits, for starters, with the Asian population of Leeds. (Lawton, 2001)

O'Leary's was a story people were interested in but it was always going to be a risky venture. The golden rule seems to be for managers that they shouldn't be revealing secrets from within the changing room because they are in danger of losing the confidence of their players. (Quote from sports editor Ian Marshall cited in Rees 2002.)

One lingering perception of the club has been its disorganisation in coping with the crisis. The club appeared to stumble from one scandal to the next: from the trial itself to the publication of *Leeds United on Trial*; from accusations of institutionalised racism within the club to the embarrassment of hiring comedian Stan Bordman, who told a series of racist jokes during an after-dinner speech at the club's Christmas function. With lack of success on the field and financial crisis with escalating long-term debts in its failed attempt to qualify for the Champions League in 2002, the club's relations with the sports media reached a miserable low.

Summary on Football Scandals

As these examples of sports scandals demonstrate, public relations remains a crucial component in any attempt to manage reputation. Both cases suggest that attempts to manipulate public relations through direct intervention in the media, or through particular source strategies such as serialisation of memoirs, can quickly spiral out of control once information is in the public domain. In the case of Roy Keane, his forthright opinions of colleagues and opponents and the admission of violent intent against Haaland led to a weeklong media scandal.

As we have argued, Keane's reputation as an international sporting hero was undermined by the sporting press, who questioned the morality of the player and his motivation for publishing such damaging stories. Also of note were the attempts of the Manchester United PR office to iron out any rift between their star players and diffuse the threat of a lawsuit by employing Sir Alex Ferguson to downplay Keane's admission as nothing more than the words of an "honest professional."

In the case of the Leeds United trial, the inability to coherently control news sources by members of the club—players, agents, manager, and chairman—led to a series of contradictory statements and public fallouts. The divergence in the stories from the players (initially premised on a series of lies or "half-truths") was exacerbated by increasing divergence in the management of the situation by the club manager and the board of directors. The subsequent serialisation and publication of O'Leary's memoirs of the season served to inflate media interest in the scandal further, running against the club's attempts to diffuse the situation.

The Bowyer and Woodgate trial and subsequent poor publicity threw the club into a deep public relations crisis which continued to reverberate through the club's operation and management in the run up to the 2002/2003 season. As we discuss below, the crisis led the club to reassess not only its personnel—as well as sacking O'Leary, the club also released a number of staff from its Communications Department—but also to employ a new PR agent to handle the club's communication strategy. These events serve to illustrate the new set of commercial pressures and levels of media scrutiny clubs now face at the elite end of the sport.

CONCLUSION

As our case studies on football scandals have highlighted, the football industry is increasingly driven by stars and their newsworthiness. Football clubs focus much of their communications strategies and resources in this area in order to protect their substantial investment in star footballers and also to send positive signals out to their key publics: the fans, sponsors, and financial backers.

To this end, there has been a growing convergence of celebrity PR practice and the management of elite football stars. For example, in an attempt to counteract the negative consequences of the Bowyer/Woodgate trial, Leeds United appointed celebrity publicist Max Clifford to improve the club's image in the eyes of the City. With the resignation of Chairman Peter Risdale in 2003, Clifford also departed. Clifford, not renowned for his corporate PR work, is well equipped to deal with the celebrity culture that now surrounds the higher echelons of football and is an increasingly central part of the PR remit of any sports PR and marketing agencies operating in this sector.

A significant indicator of this shifting trend in football PR saw Jon Smith, the Chief Executive of First Artist Corp which manages more than 400 football players, becoming one of Clifford's clients. Smith was clear why, as a football agent, his clients needed Clifford's particular skills: "Footballers are the pop stars of the new age, so they have to be managed like pop stars and our industry doesn't have that sort of experience" (O'Connor, 2002, p. 2).

This particular area, which sees the convergence between celebrity-orientated management and the football industry, is one that looks set to grow over the coming years. It also offers the potential for conflict between the PR demands of the club and the individual's own PR agenda.

The wider structural changes that have occurred in the football industry over the last decade or so have also forced clubs to consider the role of PR in their wider communication strategies. However, this development has been at best uneven. While a number of elite clubs (such as Manchester United, Liverpool, and Celtic) with a global fan base have been developing a more proactive communication strategy, there still appears to be a degree of complacency among many clubs with regard to supporter loyalty and a lack of recognition of the value of PR to the club.

Clubs such as Manchester United have a range of financial and political stakeholders with whom they need to communicate, and PR activity is viewed as central in this process. They also recognise the importance of their fan base or, as they increasingly prefer to view these supporters, their domestic and international customers.

As branding in football continues to develop at the elite end of the sport, the associated role that PR plays in developing brands will increase. However, as journalist Michael Peters (2002) has argued:

> Taking a planned approach to developing, sustaining and nurturing sports brands won't end the growing conflict between the increasingly incompatible interests of the individual's brand and his/her team's brand.

Some football players such as Dennis Bergkamp, Ryan Giggs, and Henrik Larsson are using the Web to speak directly to supporters. Following its successful launch during Euro 2000, Icons.com signed up 90 players who provide weekly diary updates to supporters. Players use the site for promotional purposes and media outlets pay an annual fee to use the information (Gibson, 2002). However, issues around the importance of image rights for players and the relationship between commercial sponsors of individual players and those associated with their clubs are likely to continue to evolve with implications for the role of PR activity. Areas such as media relations are set to become more important to the PR activity associated with elite players.

Many clubs already have long-established football in the community programmes; often these attempt to build bridges with the ethnic communities who often appear excluded from the footballing mainstream. Other clubs, such as Celtic, have a specific social charter (a form of corporate responsibility charter) which places particular obligations on the club to interact with the communities which support the club (Boyle, 2004). As the television rights bubble bursts, many clubs are going to become once again much more dependent on supporters as a key source of revenue. As a result, it makes good business sense that clubs should be looking to enhance their community-based PR activity with a view to developing long-term relationships with their fan base.

Global clubs such as Manchester United view innovations such as their recently set up Fans Forum as important arenas allowing them to build long-term relationships and enabling fans to give feedback to the club. While the club's communications strategy is one which seeks to use a range of media platforms to convert fans into customers, other less high-profile clubs need to reconnect with their indigenous fan base, and a more proactive PR strategy should be one element in this process. Despite the increasingly globalised nature of the game, local support remains important for the long-term health of many clubs within the football economy.

As the boom time fuelled by television money comes to an end, the range of challenges that face the football economy over the next decade are significant. Whether you are an elite club operating on a global televisual stage or a small club seeking to survive in an increasingly difficult financial environment, communicating effectively with the stakeholders in the game is set to become more important. One challenge is to ensure that an effective, proactive, and committed PR strategy is integral to this process.

ACKNOWLEDGMENTS

We would like to thank those people who spoke to us during the research conducted for this chapter.

13

Public Relations in Sport, Health, and Tourism

Jacquie L'Etang
Stirling Media Research Institute

This chapter explores the interconnected domains of sport, health, and tourism as hitherto these have not been given a great deal of attention within public relations literature and certainly not in combination. As a first step this chapter aims to delineate areas of importance, not only for public relations theorists and practitioners but also for subject specialists, managers, practitioners, and social theorists. The approach taken has been to map the apparent role and scope of public relations' activities within the chosen fields as represented in the specialist literature and to consider the potential benefits that public relations perspectives could offer, not only to the respective fields under consideration but to our understanding of public relations' social role. Thus, at a deeper level the discussion indicates the potential that these areas have for illustrating and exploring the role of public relations in contemporary culture.

The selection of sport, health, and tourism as foci for discussion needs some explanation. First, these areas have been chosen because they are of fundamental importance in contemporary life and culture representing as they do well-being, entertainment, work, and the economy. Each area is a source of cultural cross-references and intertextuality. Second, the fact that these areas overlap (see Fig. 13.1) suggests the possibility for collaboration and conflict between and within organisations regarding policy priorities and future direction implying the need for communication, negotiation, and relationship management. Third, these intersecting worlds are to varying degrees beneficiaries and instruments of globalisation and a fundamental part of international communication and global society. At a base level, these subjects are deeply connected to the international economy, politics, policy, and the inevitable struggle over resource allocation. At the level of the individual, sport, health, and tourism are life choices and tools to construct individual identity. These interrelated areas offer a way of exploring organised communication and its relationship and impact upon culture, stakeholders, and individuals and their introspections (intra-communications and lifeworlds). Thus this chapter aims to create a

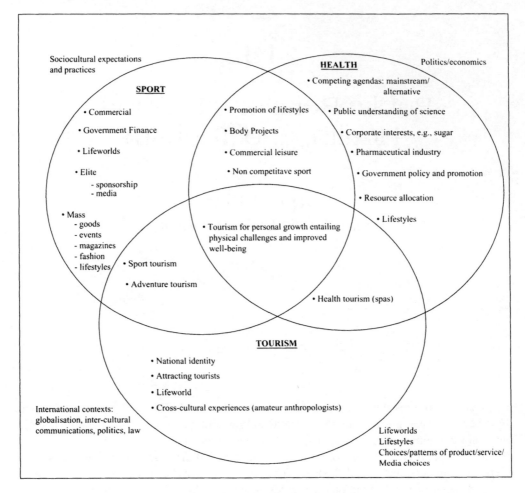

FIGURE 13.1. Domains for discussion.

new personal research agenda which includes a turn towards the cultural, functional and empirical. The scope of the project is ambitious and this chapter simply sketches out the territory. Figure 13.1 illustrates the overlapping areas and key issues.

Sport, health, and tourism have immense scope for controversy and drama and are major topics of news and entertainment in the media. As such, they contribute to media and public relations economies. Sponsorship, products, and services emanate from these apparently distinct sectors and each is an important driver of the economy. Yet, at the same time, these areas are interconnected and this chapter seeks to tease out some of the intersections and show how public relations perspectives can elucidate these relationships as well as indicating areas in which professional public relations can offer benefits in practice. Therefore, the chapter delineates areas for further empirical research.

Public relations provides rhetorical force in promotional culture in terms of persuasion and promotion and as such may be viewed largely as a subset of marketing. The chapter follows functional approaches to public relations where it suggests that the strategic role of public relations in terms of relationship and reputation management, environmental scanning, issues management, and evaluation has been given insufficient emphasis in the subject specialist literature to the detriment of the fields under consideration.

In terms of structure, the chapter proceeds through a discussion of public relations and sport, health, and tourism and the subfields that intersect these main areas: sport and health, sport and tourism, health and tourism, tourism and sport. In each area consideration is given to existing approaches as well as drawing out a research agenda for consideration. Part of this agenda is to suggest alternative approaches that may enlighten understanding of the fields under review. In particular it is suggested that a reorientation from news media to lifestyle and specialist media may be helpful in understanding publics (and *their* understanding of health and science, for example), their lifeworlds, and the contexts in which citizen debate does indeed take place.

PUBLIC RELATIONS AND SPORT

Public relations has the potential to contribute to three separate, though interconnected areas of sport: elite (professional) sport, mass participation (amateur leisure and recreation), and the promotion of sport as part of healthy living. Sport is a major structural feature of contemporary society, participated in by millions and watched by millions more. Governments allocate resources for citizen participation and for high-profile developments such as new stadia, sports complexes, and for mega-events such as the Commonwealth Games or Olympics. At the governmental levels, lobbying plays a crucial role both internationally between governments and national associations, and nationally in the competition for resources. International competition at this level means that sport is part of diplomacy and contributes to national identity. Sport is necessarily political as well as commercial, and sports organisations at all levels require communications expertise to achieve their political as well as economic goals. Non-governmental resources are lottery funding and sponsorship from the private sector, often as part of companies' corporate social responsibility or community relations budget. The vast sports market is comprised both of giants that encompass clothing, equipment, footwear, and to some degree fashion (Nike, Adidas) and niche specialists (De Rosa bikes, Slazenger Golf clubs, Aquaman wetsuits). All such commercial companies require public relations expertise beyond marketing not least to effect productive employee relations, partly through communicating an understanding of organisational culture and its relationship to organisational vision and mission and through seeking feedback.

Public relations can support elite sport via publicity, event management, and sponsorship and can contribute to mass participation in sport via sports participation programmes (that may or may not be linked to health communication) through publicity for products, services, and mass (mediated) events. In this chapter it is argued that public relations can offer more to both these areas in practice.

Turning to the sports literature, Gratton and Taylor's (2000) classic explanation of the industry clearly defines the structure of the sports industry in terms of goods and services, but its focus on business functionality means that it does not delineate the network of relationships that are implied and which may be influential in the development of enterprises. Gratton and Taylor defined commercial sport in terms of the production of sports goods and services including the manufacturing of sports equipment, clothing and footwear, distribution (retail and warehousing), spectator events, commercial leisure (private clubs), business services (including sports agents), sponsors, and the media (Gratton & Taylor, 2000, p. 143). The model in Figure 13.2 describes the sports industry context and relationships. It identifies key stakeholders, situated in political, sociocultural, economic and legal environments, and multitudinous relationships and networks that together contribute to the development of issues in contemporary sport, its images, identities and reputations, public opinion, and media representation. A broader relational approach points to a more strategic communications focus for the sector.

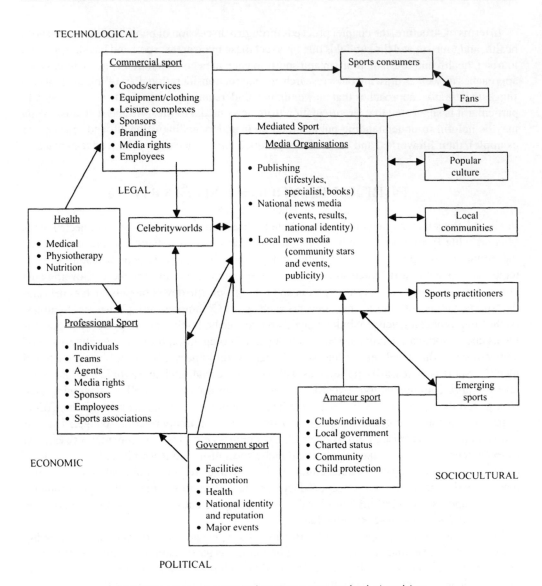

FIGURE 13.2. Sports industry context and relationships.

Figure 13.2 highlights the importance of values, connections to the world of celebrity (via the media) and popular culture, and to various key communities such as the local community, health community, medical and paramedical (especially physiotherapy), educational and so on. The model displays processes and relationships, some of which are mediated within the political, sociocultural, economic, legal, and technological environments.

Public relations as a discipline separate from marketing has not been given a great deal of attention in sports-related literature. Quite properly there is an emphasis on sporting experiences, the meaning of sport, national and international dimensions including identity construction and globalisation, gender and sexual orientation issues, class, ethnicity and disability, Olympism and 'post-Olympism', ideological and religious dimensions of sport, and there are specialist areas of sports marketing (including sponsorship and promotion) and events management (which also contributes to tourism). A number of texts also include media sociological considerations such as the media economy (ownership, politics and power), fans and fanzine literature, issues of content or representation, especially in news media, both quantitative and qualitative. Critical analyses uncover minority interests and practices, such as female body building, which are then methodically deconstructed to reveal a variety of insightful discourses and wider meanings. Inevitably much of the existing literature on sport and media and sport has been on economically dominant sports such as football and baseball and competitive sports.

Within media studies there have been comprehensive discussions of the business relationship between sport and the media and of sponsorship practices and relationships. Typically media studies sources analyse coverage (representation, genres, effects, hierarchies, dominance, hegemonies) but generally have not given so much attention to the application of concepts of source–media relations. The term "public relations" is sometimes not indexed or is assumed to be interchangeable with the term "media relations." While media relations and sponsorship are clearly an important part of PR work in this field, there are other areas worthy of attention.

In broad terms it seems that while marketing concepts have been integrated into media analyses alongside some basic promotional ideas, the more strategic approach of public relations has made little impact. By strategic is meant the development of communication vision, mission, aim, and measurable objectives to support organisational goals. Public relations conducted at this level conducts environmental analysis to identify, conceptualise, and then monitor issues and trends which arise and which may affect the organisation's relationships and reputation. The specialisms of issues and crisis management and that of community relations seem important for sports clients, particularly in relation to the management of mega events such as the Olympics and in the light of the increased chances of terrorism or ongoing issues such as drugs. Likewise, the substantial financial rewards and losses in the field suggest that the specialism of investor relations could be given further consideration. To date sports literature does not seem to appreciate that public relations defines and analyses key stakeholders and newly emerging publics and interest groups with a view to understanding not only their perceptions of, and relationships with, the organisation but also with each other. Since public relations practitioners seek to discover who influences whom and why, stakeholder and network analysis are important elements of the public relations research process. Analysing relationships requires research skills as well as the understanding of communication processes and public relations research has the capacity to identify gaps in knowledge or understanding between parties and then explore relationships which are troubled.

Public relations literature claims for its practitioners the complex task of monitoring not only external relationships but also internal ones as well, so the ability to understand and analyse organisational culture and climate and to conduct qualitative and quantitative research in the form of communication audits is crucial. As defined in the PR field, the strategic role of public relations practitioners requires them to feed back to top management assessments of internal as well as external relationships and to analyse issues which impact organisational reputation and affect the organisation's ability to achieve its mission. Public relations work encompasses discourse and plays a crucial part in co-creating organisational meaning.

Thus, a useful intervention could be made in terms of including concepts of organisational culture and climate and the practice of employee communications to analyses of sports organisations. Employee communications are vital for large sporting associations such as the Lawn Tennis Association or commercial operations such as Nike.

For public relations academics the field is defined as potentially much broader in operation and more significant than promotion or media relations. In the United States practitioners are defined as specialists in the field of "sports direction" and sports marketing, which encompass technical approaches, often linked to the marketing requirement for sales. The weakness of such approaches is that they leave undiscovered the complex dynamics of behind-the-scenes relationships in relation to evolving issues. It also suggests a rather restricted understanding of the processes that lie behind the public position of media sources and the way in which these are interpreted and represented.

Maguire, Jarvie, Mansfield, Bradley (2002) described "the media sport complex" that produces and consumes media as being comprised of "media organisations and personnel, sports organisations and personnel and marketing organisations and personnel" (p. 51), and they rightly go on to point out that:

> All of the groups represented in the media sport complex should be viewed as interdependent and located within a larger cultural, political and economic sphere. (p. 52)

"Interdependence" implies relationships and communication, aspects which could be given more emphasis. It could be useful to indicate the complex network of relationships that sports organisations need to manage, monitor, and evaluate on an ongoing basis with a view to teasing out the processes of identity construction, reputation management, source–media relations, and media effects on networks of key stakeholders, active publics, and opinion-formers. The model in Figure 13.3 presents a public relations perspective on the key processes in external relations (internal relations are not covered in this diagram). It attempts a more detailed schematic of relationships and processes between sports organisation, sports consumers and participants public relations, and the media (news, specialist and lifestyle) highlighting the importance of construction and interpretation of discourse and rhetoric as a key aspect of mediated sport. Thus, it builds into its framework the concept of source–media relations but also shows the other parts of public relations work that are necessary besides media relations. It indicates an active, discerning set of publics (who may be fans or active participants) who also filter and interpret information (some of which is mediated), thus pointing to the necessity of feedback and evaluation.

Identifying the responsibility for, and formulation of, communication objectives to support the overall aims of sports organisations implies an organisational focus which, as Henry and Theodoraki noted, has so far been something of a gap in the sports literature: "The application of organization theory in the sport domain has not in effect kept pace with that in the mainstream field of organizational analysis" (2002, p. 494).

Their quantitative study focusing on organizational types and structure concluded that sports organisations were largely simple, although some depicted bureaucratic features, often of a mechanistic rather than organic nature.

While there have been some specialist histories or case studies covering aspects of these concepts such as those conducted on Nike (Goldman & Papson, 1998; Strasser & Becklund, 1991), there is clearly further work to be done to understand better the role that sporting organisations play in culture. Furthermore, Henry and Theodoraki (2000) suggested that:

> Sporting organisations in "advanced" industrial societies... are operating in an increasingly volatile social, economic and political environment... The National Federation of Anglers for example, had had to allocate considerable amounts of money to research into water pollution, and the Royal Automobile Club and the British Gliding Association had had to lobby politicians in an attempt to create favourable opinions regarding the use of land for motor sport and of aviation air space respectively. (2002, p. 499)

This indicates the need for more sophisticated approaches to be taken by sporting organisations. There would be functional benefits for such organisations to engage in systemic analysis in order to facilitate a clearer understanding of external dynamic change and its potential for impact in terms of emerging issues and publics. This would also facilitate a greater

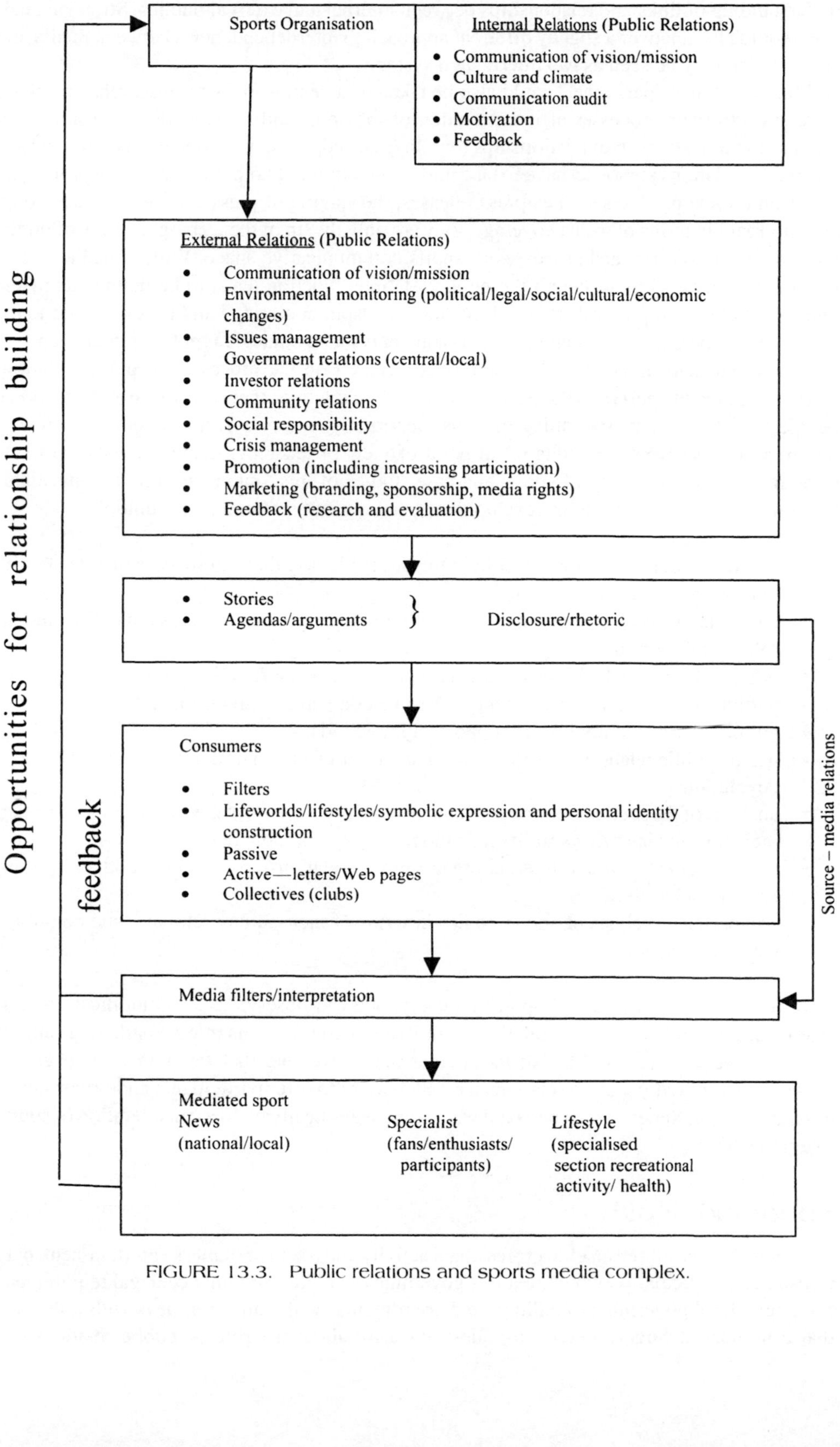

Opportunities for relationship building

Sports Organisation

Internal Relations (Public Relations)

- Communication of vision/mission
- Culture and climate
- Communication audit
- Motivation
- Feedback

External Relations (Public Relations)

- Communication of vision/mission
- Environmental monitoring (political/legal/social/cultural/economic changes)
- Issues management
- Government relations (central/local)
- Investor relations
- Community relations
- Social responsibility
- Crisis management
- Promotion (including increasing participation)
- Marketing (branding, sponsorship, media rights)
- Feedback (research and evaluation)

- Stories
- Agendas/arguments   } Disclosure/rhetoric

Consumers

- Filters
- Lifeworlds/lifestyles/symbolic expression and personal identity construction
- Passive
- Active—letters/Web pages
- Collectives (clubs)

feedback

Source – media relations

Media filters/interpretation

Mediated sport
News (national/local)

Specialist (fans/enthusiasts/ participants)

Lifestyle (specialised section recreational activity/ health)

FIGURE 13.3. Public relations and sports media complex.

understanding of links and relationships between internal and external publics. Strategic analyses would also uncover a slightly different approach to interdependencies between media and sport, which may be seen as two interrelated systems.

Maguire et al.'s "personnel" could also be taken as a central focus for research, especially in relation to their processes of interpretation of the sport and sport media environment in relation to the wider web of relationships (employees, suppliers, investors, local communities) that public relations personnel have to take into consideration. In other words, while promotion and promotional products such as press releases, the staging of press conferences, and so on are important in terms of media coverage, they are only the tip of the iceberg in terms of public relations responsibility and processes in sports communicative space. Within media studies generally, it does seem as though the public relations function tends to be defined as media relations and (in the political sphere) lobbying and "spin doctoring" and thus confined to the role of spokesperson rather than organisational analyst and strategic reputation manager.

At present there is no published empirical research on the processes of public relations work in the area of sport from the perspective of public relations theorists. From an educational perspective this may be something of a lost opportunity not only from the point of view of research but also from the pedagogical point of view of teaching: many students are likely to be interested in a variety of sports and case studies of this topic could provide invaluable teaching tools. To give just a few examples of teaching and research opportunities:

- the role of public relations in building national identity through success in elite sport or in hosting elite events;
- ethical analysis of sports companies in relation to corporate social responsibility and the role of public relations;
- public relations and lobbying strategies to influence resource allocation of elite and mass participation or between different sports in a competitive environment;
- public relations campaigns to support Olympic bids;
- use of public relations to support the recreation of national identities in the UK post-devolution;
- analysis of the public relations and reputational implications of media coverage of critical incidents and interviews (to include the role of sports "spin doctors");
- analysis of external and internal organisational relationships of sports bodies, sporting arenas, and media;
- comparative analysis of sports bodies in terms of their culture, climate, and communication orientations.

In understanding the role of sport in society, one can observe its commodification at all levels, a process to which public relations contributes, certainly in its role as marketing support. However, we can also see that in its broader discursive role that facilitates feedback and encourages reflexivity, public relations has much more to offer participants and organisations in sports worlds. Reflection on personal well-being leads neatly on to a consideration of sport's role in health.

Sport and Health

Sport may be considered an elite professional activity and a source of mass entertainment, but it is also mass participation which requires governmental policy and finance, legal requirements for safety, local government facilities, and coordination with education. It is within this area that a number of hugely interesting questions arise about the role of public relations. For example, while there have long been in the UK efforts to provide sports opportunities more widely in society and to encourage participation, the relationship between sport and health agendas has an intrinsic tension in relation to resource allocation and in terms of key policies and messages.

There has long been a political link between sport and health. In the mid-1930s there were extensive health campaigns to encourage the populace to drink more milk which ran concurrently with a get fit campaign. This followed Britain's lack of success at the Berlin Olympics and governmental awareness of Germany's extensive fitness movement and the Nazi government's promotion of ideals of Aryan physique (partly promoted through the film *The Olympiad* made by the infamous film director Leni Riefenstahl). The connection between national sporting prowess and national identity and reputation was thus clearly established even in an era where sport was largely amateur. As far as mass participation for health was concerned, Choi recorded that:

> At the beginning of the 1960s . . . The Council of Europe developed the "Sport for All" initiative and moderate physical exercise was promoted as a behaviour important for physical and psychological health. Thus, physical fitness became associated with health. (2000, p. 2)

In contemporary America and Britain, there is considerable debate and media coverage regarding increasingly overweight and sedentary populations. Politicians and health services are concerned about the costs of treating the inevitable degenerative diseases. Thus, through debates over health and future projections for resource allocation, sport has inevitably become entangled with health. From the health perspective, the imperative is to widen access and choice to maximise the possibility that higher numbers of the population will take up some form of regular exercise.

In fact, "sport" seems to be becoming increasingly equated with "exercise," a development that might concern some sports policy directors since it could dilute their mission. "Health" may be equated with slimness, an equation that may concern some health promoters. There are several examples of obesity becoming both entertainment (somewhat in the tradition of a "freak show") and competitive sport—in the BBC series *Fat Nation* (linked to a self-help book) and two ITV series, *Celebrity Fat Club* and *Fat Chance*. In *Fat Chance* two obese (in some cases morbidly obese) families comprising of four members compete over a period of 3 months to lose the most weight. Assisted by Jane the nutritionist and Peter the physical trainer, the two families are educated about lifestyle changes required to lose weight. Dramatic voiceover focusing first on one family and then the draws out comparisons in a pugilistic way, building tension to the monthly weigh-ins where typical comments include "putting that much on is a disaster" and "D has lost 6lbs, but Peter and Jane thought she'd lose a stone." The combative atmosphere is enhanced by disappointed participants threatening to withdraw ("That's it, show over, show over") and gladiatorial weigh-ins where suspense is created artificially by withholding announcements of weight loss until tension has built among participants and audience alike. The game is simple, about gain or loss (there is no reference to Body Mass Index, for example), and the prize is an all-expenses paid family holiday.

The health lobby encourages non-competitive sports such as aerobics (though in Continental Europe this is in fact a competitive sport covered on *Eurosport*), walking, "rambling" or now the trendily named 'power walking', recreational gym work and swimming. Recently, a new initiative introduced cheerleading for girls as a "trendier" way of increasing physical activity amongst a notoriously sedentary group. Such activities run somewhat counter to the Western ethos of sport as competitive, formalised, structured, and institutionalised. But as Coalter pointed out:

> The importance of the heterogeneous category of keep fit/yoga/aerobics/dance exercise for women cannot be over-emphasised and it accounts for a large proportion of the increase in female participation (from 12% of women in 1987 to 17% in 1996)... among all social classes. (1999, p. 31)

Nevertheless, while apparently non-competitive, it may be that competition is present in a different form. One does not have to attend too many of the larger aerobics/keep fit classes to understand the hierarchies. Typically, those who are regular attenders, experienced participants who are known to the instructor, will dominate the first row. Novices are more likely to inhabit the back row. Other new sports may be imported or created which combine aestheticism with a degree of competition such as Brazilian capoeira (knowledge about which, and enthusiasm for, has increased since its use in various TV ads) which combines dance, gymnastics and self-defence in non-body contact sparring and French *parkour*, an outdoor urban gymnastics using street furniture as hurdles and pommel horses. It may be that health professionals will turn to such rather outré sports to attract youngsters into activity rather than traditional forms. This would certainly be in tune with the cultural shift to 'Lifestyle' non-traditional sports such as snowboarding, skateboarding, rock-climbing.

Of common interest to those interested in sport and health is the production and marketing of specially designed sports drinks and bars, for example, High 5, Leppin, and Science in Sport (SIS). A wide range of these are available, usually specifically targeted at either endurance or strength athletes, both elite and amateur. While some nutritionists support and indeed contribute to the science behind such products, others are more cautious, particularly in relation to the supposed benefit to committed, but recreational participants (whose training levels are more likely to be up to 12–15 hours a week rather than 6 hours a day). For example, Nancy Clark, nutrition columnist for *New England Runner*, *Adventure Cycling*, and *Rugby* and regular contributor to *Shape* and *Runner's World*, advised:

> Expensive muscle-building supplements are not the answer [to bulking up]. The amount of protein in these formulas is often less than that which you might easily get through foods, but at two to four times the price. In addition, real foods provide a nice package of vitamins, minerals, and other nutrients that are often missing in engineered food. (2003, p. 177)

and she provides tabulated data to support this. The quote highlights the necessity for consumers to possess the ability to read science, as indicated by Campbell (chapter 11, this volume). For example, the Science in Sport (SIS) promotional leaflet and Web site (www.science in sport.com) contains considerable technical nutritional information to explain the articulation between their products structured within an energy "system" (carbo loading, energy and recovery drinks), a "protein kinetics system," and supplements (conjugated linoleic acid, creatine monohydrate, and glutanmine) and defining hypotonic, isotonic, and hypertonic solutions in terms of the implications for effective feeding of those involved in endurance sports. This market is becoming increasingly competitive with considerable efforts now going into branding and the building of reputation. This is especially interesting given the UK national context where there is a history of food scares, debate over the use of genetically modified (GM) foods and government (DTI) interest in 'health enhancing foods.' Trust has to be established and the SIS promotional brochure includes a section on "Our Credentials," where it is explained that:

> Science in Sport grew out of the desire to provide the best nutritional products and advice to athletes. The Company mixes qualified sport scientists, food technologists, and a physician with keen athletes and sports

people who have competed from local level to the world stage. As a result of all this experience they have an unprecedented knowledge of the nutritional needs of athletes. Science in Sport also collaborates with leading Universities on research projects, as well as getting involved at the sharp end of sports performance. Initially Science in Sport grew in cycling thanks to the use and endorsement of products by Chris Boardman who liked the Company ethos and helped to inspire the creation of REGO, total recovery sports fuel. It wasn't long before the word began to spread and Science in Sport's products became more popular at the top level of many other sports. To date Science in Sport have helped to win Olympic Golds, World Championships, Premiership Titles and set numerous World Records. Science in Sport designs, develops and manufactures its own products to ensure they are of the highest quality—they have to be, we don't know when an Olympic medal or World Cup may depend on it! (SIS information leaflet, 2004)

Unequivocal language is used such as "the best" or "unprecedented knowledge," "leading Universities," "total recovery," "more popular," "win," and "highest quality." One can note the emphasis on science (as opposed to nature) success, and association with a sporting star with whom most people will be familiar. Endorsement is achieved, not only by mention of the cyclist Chris Boardman, but also by the suggestion that the product is so effective that "word began to spread" and its increased popularity "at the top level." The level of technical sophistication of the leaflet is quite a contrast to some government-sponsored health campaigns and material. Interested, active, body-conscious publics are clearly more inclined to tackle complex messages, but one wonders whether some campaigns miss the mark because they are too simplistic and run the risk of patronising audiences. With this in mind it is worth considering the content, role, and effects of lifestyle magazines. Those such as *Health and Fitness* and *Zest* are entirely focused on well-being, mental and physical. These magazines take a holistic approach to wellness including mental and physical aspects and conventional and alternative therapies.

Specialised titles such as *Runner's World* or *Cycling Weekly* also make a link for their readers between their love of sport and health. Both of these magazines carry regular features on nutrition, for example, *Cycling Weekly's* Fitness Section has carried articles on "Eating for performance" and avoiding "the bonk" (glycogen depletion) and reviewing the use of the popular if controversial Atkins diet for endurance sport (Child, 2004, p. 35), often using mechanistic metaphors: "Always remember your body is a finely tuned engine that needs the right fuel to make it run as efficiently as possible" (*Cycling Weekly*, 22/1/05, p. 39). *Runner's World* carries many articles on diet and nutrition and on losing weight as well as regularly reviewing nutrition "systems" such as SIS and available sports nutrition and cereal bars for taste, edibility (and ease of eating on the move), digestibility, and effectiveness.

Sport and health overlap at state, institutional and individual levels and are becoming a site for contesting rhetorics. While there is some common ground between the sports and health lobbies, there is also a difference in emphasis. Both are concerned with mass participation, but whereas those within sport are ultimately concerned with facilitating merit and excellence, the other treats sport instrumentally as a way of helping citizens to enjoy "wellness." Drawing out these issues and the surrounding rhetoric and debates is beyond the scope of this chapter, except to argue that an exploration of these ideas within the contemporary public sphere is of importance to policymakers and to citizens since it has considerable implications for their long-term physical and economic well-being.

PUBLIC RELATIONS AND HEALTH

The role for public relations in health in the UK is immense, encompassing central and local government policy and provisions and political, economic, and ideological changes that have led to the privatisation and marketisation of some health services, as well as technological changes (especially the Internet, which is beginning to have a large impact on how citizens access information and relate to medical practitioners and health promotion). The focus here is on issues around health promotion, including some discussion of the challenges of scientific communication and the possibly unrecognised importance of lifestyle media.

Key issues in the area of health communication include those of the values of health educators and promoters and their relationships with stakeholders; risk and trust; the reliability of non-specialist public relations practitioners representing scientific, medical and health organisations or lobbies; source–media relations and the accuracy and interpretation of science by media and non-scientists; culture conflict between science and the media; media amplification and panics; the empowerment of publics; and the difficulties of evaluation in a multi-factorial field and consequent dangers of overpromising. The media are often seen as having a central and defining role, but that of public relations is probably less well researched and understood. D. Miller (1999, p. 206) has suggested that there is a flaw in the discussion of the communication of science in that it is often analysed from the perspective of only one group of actors. Therefore, he argued that:

> We find discussion of the coverage of particular issues, examinations of "lay perspectives" or public opinion, or attempts to evaluate the communication strategies of particular organisations. But we cannot properly understand the actual behaviour of "experts," the media or the public in isolation. Instead, they need to be examined in the context of their interactions with each other. (D. Miller, 1999, p. 206)

Miller thus proposed that the communication of science can be better understood by seeing it as the product of interaction between four sets of actors: (a) social and political institutions such as government, business and scientific research institutes, and think tanks; (b) the media including news and current affairs, popular science magazines, advice columns in popular magazines, and fiction; (c) the public; and (d) decision makers such as government, business, interest groups, universities, and scientific institutes which he sees as part of "the circuit of mass communication."

The "circuit of mass communication" helps us to appreciate the dynamism among the various actors and, according to Miller, enables us to explain "the rise and fall of scientific issues in the media and on the public and policy-making agenda" (D. Miller, 1999, p. 211). Miller highlighted the challenges facing the social and political institutions "translating" scientific advice into official reports and promotional material whilst maintaining accuracy and, in some cases, political advantage. Conflicting interests result in competitive media strategies often within or between governmental or scientific organisations. Nevertheless, Miller suggested, powerful institutions are advantaged by their ability to purchase public relations services.

The diversity of the media industry contains a range of perspectives funded from different sources. Scientific discrepancies are attractive to the media and may result in critical or aberrant readings, which may mitigate against rational discussion. For example, Miller cited the case of coverage on coronary heart disease where tabloids published headlines such as "Butter can slice heart attack" and "fatty food not a killer" (p. 216).

However, while the "circuit of mass communication" is useful in implying the dynamism of relationships and debate, there are some potential problems. First, decision makers and social and political institutions are described as overlapping but presented as separate. Second, it ignores private enterprise (food retailers, telephone companies) and the role of the market. Third, the public relations function is not represented and the process of communication seems overmediatised (the Internet is not presented). Fourth, interest groups are not present. Fifth, media selected seem to be those read by the highly literate, and sources of information in entertainment and lifestyle media are not taken into account. Sixth, the model might assume

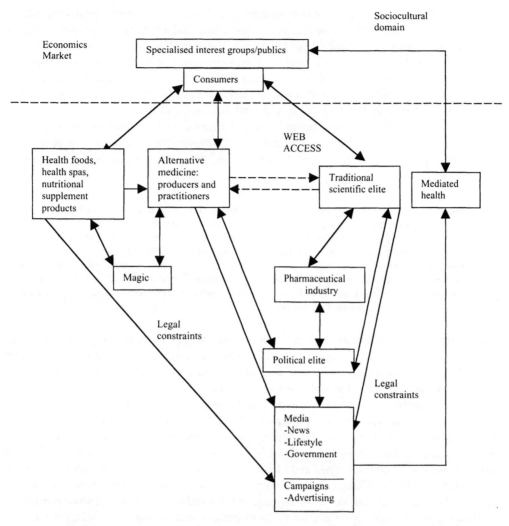

FIGURE 13.4.   Systems of mass communication in relation to health.

media effects. Finally, use of the term "public" seems to be overly homogenized. Taking these points into account a new model is presented in Figure 13.4.

This model tries to take into account not only the concerns of the scientific elite with regard to the rather pompously termed "public understanding of science," but also competing non-evidence-based perspectives such as alternative medicine, the health food movement, private health farms and spas, and the aforementioned nutritional supplements producers which are also part of the marketisation of health. The role of "magic" in contemporary modern culture is thus noted as relevant to some alternative perspectives and the importance of individual belief systems in this domain. It also indicates specialised publics, some of which are consumers, and the ability of these to source information directly via the Internet. Relationships and the promotional efforts of various parties are implied in this model by directional arrows.

Turning to the field of health promotion and education, it is only possible here to indicate the ideological shifts in the field. A major shift within the field has been that from seeing health promotion in terms of individual responsibility to change behaviours towards an approach which takes contextual and cultural factors into account in facilitating positive change that is determined by the individuals and publics in question. However, it is still the case that governments of all persuasions are more inclined to present health promotion as the responsibility of the individual. In the UK this ideology is linked to other issues such as revelations that government provision of pensions will be inadequate for those currently working so that individuals are now urged to save much harder for their old age.

The notion of "lifestyle" has entered political rhetoric and become linked to political ideology on health in the UK. For example, *The Independent on Sunday* reported under the headline "NHS offers free lifestyle 'MoT tests' for everyone" on its front page on 24 October, 2004:

> The National Health Service is to offer every patient in Britain a personal diet and fitness regime among its radical measures to force individuals to take greater responsibility for their own health ... Far-reaching proposals will include plans to screen children to identify those at risk of becoming obese ... The controversial measures amount to an unprecedented intervention into private individual's lifestyle choices and are sure to revive the charge of government "nannying." Ministers stress, however, that the individual health improvement programmes will be voluntary. Patients will be set specific goals monitored by their GP ... Progress will be monitored by e-mail ... Tony Blair has made public health the focus on NHS policy because of the spiralling cost to the taxpayer of so-called lifestyle diseases.

In broad terms public health specialists aim to encourage healthier living and to enhance the quality of health in communities, defined by WHO as "a state of complete physical, mental and social well-being and not merely the absence of disease." Public health objectives increasingly do not solely target individuals but take a holistic view and may aim to change societies in order to create improved understandings of behavioural outcomes. Increasingly campaigns have become orientated away from prevention of illness and scare tactics to emphasising life skills, positive health, and self-esteem linking physical and mental well-being. The field has been criticised in the past for displaying moral superiority, ideological health fascism, and indoctrination of healthy lifestyles and blamed for causing unhealthy obsessions (triggering anorexia, for example). These critiques demonstrate how language and the rhetoric employed are crucial to change at individual, community, and cultural levels. Public relations is essential to change processes and necessary for the management and evaluation of multiple relationships with stakeholders. Increasingly health promotion has become contextually focused on environments, institutions (for example, schools and workplaces), community, and families as crucial to gaining behavioural change rather than focusing on the individual as the unit of change. Health is central to our lives, a major topic of news, is politicised, underresourced, and a subject open to alternative perspectives so it is unsurprising that this sector of the public relations industry is expanding.

The content of health promotion material is familiar ground to public relations specialists since it uses common psychological frameworks such as elaboration likelihood and social learning and common campaign structures emphasising measurable objectives, feedback, and research and evaluation. Critical work in health campaigns has in the past, however, suggested that campaigners have been overdependent on the mass media, pointing to the dilution of messages that occurs when advertisements are displayed or broadcast around competitive anti-health messages (alcohol advertising, for example) or diluted by entertainment (soap operas or reality TV, which glamorise unhealthy behaviours; Wallack, 1989). There is a lesson here for public relations practice, which can still be overfocused on media content rather than researching effects and the overall impact of campaigns (including any non-media aspects).

Since the introduction of the modern health service after the Second World War, demand has always exceeded supply and health stories feature heavily in news and entertainment media. Health meets media news values requirements in that stories always involve human interest, often entail conflict, blame, and cover-ups and can be threatening, triggering fear. While scientific reporting of potential for longer-term future cures may be misrepresented as "new miracle cancer cure" (thus raising false hopes in sufferers) and inspirational stories of those who "beat cancer" recur, stories of doom and gloom remain attractive propositions.

The synchronicity of contemporary debates about health, fitness, and obesity also suggests the increasing importance of strategic public relations for retailers and fast-food chains, especially the increasingly troubled McDonald's, now planning something of a dietary about-face, scrapping super-size meals at the end of 2004 and advertising healthy breakfasts of porridge, bagels, and jam through TV ads and door-to-door mailings of a promotional leaflet that explains how:

> [We] would love to come round to your house to tell you how we're changing . . . we've made this book so that you can see all the fresh thinking going on in our restaurants—and we're inviting you to pop round . . . . and we're always cooking fresh meals . . . Mum and Dad, we've taken a look inside the brilliant Happy Meal box to see if we could pack some more good news in there. You care about your kids, we care about your kids . . . you can swap their fries for a fruit bag . . . but when you order fries . . . they'll get 23% less salt. And we know you know less salt is good . . . we've been back to our kitchens for some fresh thinking and prepared a range of new tastes and flavours that we call Salad Plus.

McDonald's reputation has been tarnished by public and media hostility. There awaits a fascinating case study of the decisions and communications strategy that lies behind this and the change of corporate identity reported in *The Herald* on 12 October, 2004:

> McDonald's is to axe its world-famous Golden Arches logo in a series of adverts aimed at shaking off the chain's unhealthy image. The company, pilloried by the movie documentary *Super Size Me*, is removing the symbol and replacing it with a golden question mark alongside pictures of healthier alternatives to burgers and fries. A global survey once found that the arches are a more internationally recognised symbol than the Christian cross. (p. 3)

In addition to news media and specialised programmes on current issues or health scares, many leisure and women's magazines also cover such topics. These can be categorised into specialist media, supermarket spin-offs, general magazines which have a significant and regular health section, and "body projects" media. Examples are displayed in Table 13.1.

The importance of lifestyle media to health issues may have been underplayed although they clearly offer some space to raise questions (both through letters pages and through specialised sections of magazines for readers' questions). However, as indicated by Campbell's useful analysis, the growth of this area of journalism has been seen as a negative development, distracting citizens from the important political concerns of the day to potentially sully pure journalism with content that is advertising centred. Campbell pointed out that:

> Lifestyle journalism . . . addresses audiences not in their role as public citizens concerned with the social and political issues of the day, but in their role as private individuals whose personal fears, aspirations, attitudes, and emotional experiences become the subject material. (2004, p. 221)

Yet it is surely precisely in this domain that one can learn more about health and fitness concerns, beliefs, and practices.

TABLE 13.1
Categories of Media

Mainstream Lifestyle Media
- *Health & Fitness*
- *Zest*
- *Ultrafit*
- *Women's Health*
- *Men's Health*
- *Healthy*
- *Here's Health*

Specialist Lifestyle Media (available through health food shops)
- *Positive Health*
- *Connections*
- *Kindred Spirit*
- *Healthy Way* (Holland & Barrett)

Supermarket spinoffs
- *Healthy Living* (Tesco)
- *Sainsbury's Magazine*

Mainstream magazines with a major health component
- *Good Housekeeping* ("How you feel")
- *Elle* ("Beauty & health")
- *Prima* ("Mind, body, soul")
- *Marie Claire* ("Health," "Lifestyle")
- *She* ("Health")
- *Woman* ("Health")
- *Woman's Own* ("Health")

Body projects media
- *Ultrafit*
- *Men's Fitness*
- *Men's Health*
- *Women's Health*
- *Slimming*
- *Weight Watchers*
- *Slimming World*
- *Rosemary Conley's Diet & Fitness*
- *Bodybuilding Monthly*
- *Flex*
- *Muscle & Fitness*
- *Natural Development*
- *Muscle Magazine International*

PUBLIC RELATIONS AND TOURISM

Tourism for leisure and business is the world's most important economic activity with massive sociocultural and environmental impacts which immediately imply a role for public relations in terms of corporate social responsibility, especially that of large companies that work in a globalised and transnational manner such as Holiday Inn.

Here the focus is on the notion of tourism in the modern world both as an example of globalisation and as an industry in which public relations plays a potentially crucial role. Tourism is an industry which has very specific requirements for strategic and tactical public relations. Indeed, there is much opportunity for research in the field. Tourism is an interdisciplinary area, with some academics focusing on it as an industry and others as a process (Page et al., 2001, p. 8). Tourism encompasses the temporary, or short-term movement of people, the industry that supports such activities, but also much bigger questions about why people travel, the impact of travel between guests and host nations, and the short- and long-term relationships that ensue from such travel. Thus, tourism is infinitely bound up with processes of intercultural communication and perceptions about the "global village."

Tourism encompasses a range of diverse activities and includes those who define themselves as "travellers" rather than tourists. It embraces an extraordinary range of activities from mass tourism to individually organised trips or even expeditions, which can last several months. Destinations are visited for purposes other than taking up permanent residence or employment remunerated from within the places visited (Chadwick, 1994, p. 65). The definition of "tourist" as opposed to "traveller" or "visitor" is problematic and has been much debated in the field. Even in Edwardian times, a certain snobbery existed about the hierarchical relationship between "traveller" and "tourist" which shows the symbolic importance of the concepts in terms of communicating status in society. Likewise, a glance at the serious British newspapers shows that the term "tourist" is not used as a way of capturing readers. Instead, sections are labelled "Travel" (for example, *The Daily Telegraph* and *The Guardian*) or, even more romantically, "Escape" (*The Observer*). The sheer diversity of holiday choices is spellbinding: biking in Finland, country house hotel in Wiltshire, Astanga yoga in the Peloponnese, Mysore or Ireland, train travel in the Andes, cultural visits, adventure travel, packaged sun sea and . . . the world is the Western tourist's oyster. To some degree, holiday for the tourist is an opportunity for lived fantasy and adult play. One can buy services which pamper such as health spas mentioned earlier or services that facilitate self-development and self-realisation.

Critical sociologists have suggested that mass tourism packages "pseudo-events" that present a caricature of the host culture, protecting the visitor from "the real world" (Urry, 2002, p. 7) even though the tourist seeks the authenticity of "otherness." Therefore, operators may act as:

> Surrogate parents . . . [and] relieve the tourist of responsibility and protect him/ her from harsh reality. Their solicitude restricts the tourist to the beach and certain approved objects of the tourist gaze. (Urry, 2002, p. 7)

This equally applies to "adventure" holidays off the beaten track where an illusion is created of exploration and a unique experience for the individual even though many have the opportunity to purchase the same holiday. There are extreme examples: for example, the now controversial guided trips up Everest or to remote places relatively undamaged by the human race such as Antarctica.

Photographer John Bentley reflected on what he saw as "the paradox" of "adventure travel":

> The parameters of travel that escalate it into an adventure are mostly connected to a possible uncertain outcome . . . Experiences outside the so-called "comfort-zone" are less easy to understand though the rewards are likely to be far greater . . . Travel is tough done in this way. To engage with the situation fully, to be absorbed by the variety in unfamiliar cultures . . . to be fearless, minimalist and sufficient according the resources around you . . . this is real travel . . . "I'm going on an adventure holiday" now means that you paid a company to pack you off with similarly unadventurous customers to a destination that is entirely predictable, where the itinerary has been agreed and booked in advance. Make no question about it: today's adventure travel is tourism in disguise. (TGO, February 2005, p. 41)

Even the most independent travellers, who wild-camp and organise their own leisure activities, cannot escape the definition of "visitor" because they are not part of the host culture. They are still participating in what John Urry has defined as "the tourist gaze" where:

Places are chosen to be gazed upon because there is anticipation, especially through daydreaming and fantasy of intense pleasures, either on a different scale or involving different senses from those customarily encountered. Such anticipation is constructed and sustained through a variety of non-tourist practices, such as film, TV, literature, magazines, records and videos which construct and reinforce that gaze. (2002, p. 3)

Examples of the latter might include the extensive travel pages in Sunday newspapers in the UK, travel programmes such as *Wish You Were Here*, or films that in themselves may promote a whole country as the *Lord of the Rings* films arguably did for South Island, New Zealand. The tourist industry therefore plays a big part in the construction of national identities as they are understood by external cultures. The creation of events (Olympics) or even the marketing of natural events (such as the near total eclipse in Cornwall in 2000) are examples that not only illustrate processes of symbolic construction and packaging for sale and the dependence of host countries on tourism for income but also the important role played by international media in global society in relaying those experiences for vicarious consumption. To some degree globalisation has stimulated tourism as well as being a consequence of it. For example, according to Pigram and Jenkins:

Economic globalisation and the consequent economic decline and restructuring of heavy industries in Western nations, led to a search for economic and employment alternatives by government at all levels, particularly in service industries. (1999, p. 136)

Likewise the increased movement of populations for reasons of migration can be partly seen as a consequence of globalisation, resulting from a greater awareness of alternative cultures and lifestyles. Migration in itself stimulates the globalisation process in that migrants take their culture with them and may "sell" part of their culture to the host country in ethnic restaurants or goods. Subsequent generations of immigrants may try to maintain or perhaps to reestablish links with their source culture and ethnically based tourism continues to expand. Thus, the modern world entails endless processes of cross-cultural travel and communication in which individuals may reflect upon their own individual identity and its relation not only to those of nation-states but also of diverse micro-cultures. Formal communications and media consumption are important aspects of this process. Travel has symbolic status in Western countries and tourists are carriers of Western brands that can acquire status in less-developed nations. The cultural impact of the dominance of Western goods and services impacts local expectations and raises issues of corporate social responsibility. According to Page:

Globalization has resulted in various forms of companies that operate in a globalized or transnational manner [which] comprise [of] . . . global corporations that operate throughout the world, such as the Holiday Inn; multinational corporations with operations in countries outside that of the main base or headquarters; smaller multinationals that operate in a limited number of countries. An organisation can adopt transnational strategies by franchising its operation to other businesses in different countries; licensing other companies to operate using its brand, logo or trademark; non-investment management agreements; acquisitions of overseas properties and interests; mergers to integrate business interests horizontally to operate in a number of countries. The homogenization of tourist services is most marked in the accommodation sector, where nearly 30% of the world's accommodation stock is owned by chains. (2003, pp. 165–166)

Public relations intersects with tourism in a number of ways. Public relations is an essential part of business practice and international tourism is a mammoth business. As Vellas and Becheral pointed out, tourism has become the world's most important economic activity, the principal source of job creation in many countries (employing more than 100 million people worldwide), and responsible for around 7% of global capital expenditure. In addition tourism affects social, environmental, and land development policies and has major consequences, not always positive, on levels of inflation, the environment, and traditions of local communities (Vellas & Bécherel, 1995, pp. xxii–xxiii). While rich foreigners may bring in much-needed hard currency to pay off debts, it is clear that tourism tends to perpetuate existing inequalities (Britton, 1982; cited in Page et. al., 2001, p. 390). Environmentalism has created reflexive tourists with concerns for sustainability (Franklin, 2003, p. 226), "green tourism," and a requirement for suppliers of tourist services to review their relationships with all stakeholders. The tourist business raises a number of ethical issues in relation to impact which implies an important role for public relations in terms of social responsibility and community relations. Sociocultural impacts of globalisation and tourism include language use (the ever-increasing dominance of English), health issues (the SARs crisis), religion, gastronomy, dress, leisure activities, drug use (Amsterdam), crime, sexual health (sex tourism), and so on. Public relations' relationship with tourism goes beyond business functionality since tourism encompasses nature and culture. In other words, public relations, through its focus on relationship building, has the capacity to go beyond marketing consumerism to contribute to deeper meanings and understandings of the tourism experience, contributing to reflexivity and improved inter-cultural understanding.

As far as the academic tourism literature is concerned, public relations is generally limited to the role of promotion (of businesses, tour operators, countries, airlines, tourist products and services, special events, tourist attractions, museums). The promotion of holidays, including the rhetoric employed in brochures and on Web sites, is clearly within the responsibility of "discourse workers" such as public relations practitioners, as is the management of relations with host communities, local guides, transport operators, insurance agents, investors, and employees, to name but a few. It is with public relations practitioners that the responsibility rests for ensuring that inspirational brochures are matched by behaviour, thus protecting organisational reputation.

However, there are far wider implications for the public relations role apart from promotion in terms of risk advice, destination reputation, and crisis communications. Swarbrooke, Beard, Leckie, and Pomfret (2003) cited Faulkner's (2001) judgement that while tourism is vulnerable to natural disasters and terrorism, few tourism organisations have developed disaster strategies. However, it is fair to say that much discussion of risk management in tourism literature does not address communication issues except in relation to crisis management. The impact of the catastrophic 2004 tsunami in Asia and the Indian Ocean goes way beyond mere tourism, but must surely impact present practice in terms of ethics and social responsibility in relation to contribution to affected local populations, ongoing community relations, destination recovery, consumer confidence and marketing (and retaining a cautious awareness of the dangers of rubbernecking), post-catastrophe communication with surviving tourists, and assessment and evaluation of existing systems of crisis communication.

A recently published volume on crisis management in the tourism industry (Glaesser, 2003) uses a wide variety of German and English literature from strategic management, risk communication, psychology and marketing, but does not seem to use any public relations sources, nor does it index the term. The only brief mention of the practice states that:

> Crisis communication includes elements of public relations as well as customer communication. On the other hand, it performs a public relations function, the aim of which is to create a positive and benevolent atmosphere for the organization, principally among the wider spheres of activity. On the other hand, crisis communication

also has concrete sales objectives that are normally reserved for advertising or sales promotion. The aim is to fulfil, in the most differentiated way possible, the tourists' increased need for information in the orientation, decision and holiday phases as well as in the wider spheres of activity. (Glaesser, 2003, p. 234)

Apart from this, however, Glaesser makes an extremely useful, strategic, and theoretically grounded contribution to the literature on crisis management covering analysis and prognosis, planning, and management instrumentation with a number of practical examples and real-life scenarios.

Public relations specialists who take a strategic approach will see the relevance of systems analysis and issues management to the industry. Part of this approach highlights the importance of a focus on corporate social responsibility because of the considerable environmental and social impact of the industry. In particular, the monitoring of relationships with local communities and involving them in the evaluation of process and change is of considerable importance from a public relations perspective. The international nature of tourism requires public relations practitioners to be conscious of the requirements for effective intercultural communication. For theorists and practitioners of tourism, it appears that a more cohesive approach to communication is required that brings together the key strategic elements of public relations with particular emphasis on long-term relationship management, ethical dimensions of communication, risk communication and reputation management.

There are also expanding markets in the specialist sectors of sports tourism and adventure tourism, both of which present physical risks to participants and highlight the importance of risk assessment and communication, for example, in promotional literature as well as in the aftermath of any accident. Bearing in mind the caveats expressed at the outset of this chapter regarding the real definition of "adventure," one can still recognise the expanding numbers of those who wish to spend holiday periods escaping the mundane or routine in search of the "peak experience" (Maslow, 1976; cited in Swarbrooke et al., 2003, p. 59) and "flow" which entirely eliminates thoughts of daily patterns of existence. "Flow" has been defined as:

the state in which people are so involved in an activity that nothing else seems to matter; the experience itself is so enjoyable that people will do it at great cost, for the sheer sake of doing it. (Csikszentmikalyi, 1992, p. 4; cited in Swarbrooke et al., 2003, p. 82)

Thus, there may be a more spiritual and transcendental motivation for hard physical challenge in escaping usual cultural norms and constraints. As Zuckerman suggested, maybe "those whose jobs fully satisfy their sensation-seeking needs [have] less need for extracurricular sensation seeking through risky sports" (Zuckerman, 1994, p. 165).

As far as physical activity in tourism is concerned, Franklin suggested that:

"Nature" and "body" are not only relatively new and important themes of the 1990s and 2000s but for the first time they are linked in many new and increasingly touristic ways . . . early tourism emphasised the disembodied subjectivity of the gazing tourist and the bodies of the Other as objects of their gaze, increasingly in recent years it is their *own* bodies that many tourists attend to . . . with embodied objectives such as fitness, thrill, spirituality, risk, sensual connection, sexuality, taste . . . and "flow." (2003, p. 213)

Turning to the tourism media, there are a number of specialist publications for consumers and travel enthusiasts, for example, *Wanderlust*, by-lined "passion for travel;" *Travelspirit*, by-lined "your holiday essential," published by ABTA; Conde Nast's *Traveller*, by-lined "Lifestyle magazine of the year;" and *Travel*, by-lined "Be informed. Be inspired. Be there," produced by *The Sunday Times*. These magazines carry extensive advertising and aim to titillate, inspire, and inform.

Increasingly in a globalised world issues around health and travel have come to the fore. Quite apart from natural disasters and the obvious safety factors entailed in more adventurous holidays, the spread of diseases, especially new diseases such as SARs, raises important challenges for public relations in terms of issues and crisis management. Doctors have long been interested in such affairs, as evidenced by the existence of the journal *International Travel Medicine* and the International Society of Travel Medicine and the challenges that many GPs face in dealing with patients who have exposed themselves to a variety of disease exotica.

While adventure and sports tourism may overlap in relation to physical risks and crisis communication, they are still separate domains. An expanding specialist market has developed in the area of sport and tourism distinct from adventure tourism's "adrenaline rush" artificialities such as bungee jumping (Swarbrooke et al., 2003 p. 39). Sports tourism includes fans and spectators travelling to mega-events such as the Olympics, just as did those who attended the truly spectacular Roman Games involving exotic beasts and other spectacles as well as more traditional gladiatorial battles. The fantastic cost of hosting such events has created the demand for event marketing and promotion specialists whose task, in addition to pure sales, requires liaison with design and the creation of "atmospherics."

There are, however, new forms of sport tourism arising, as "lifestyles" become more subtle and complex. For example, there are destinations marketed specifically for the "winter training" opportunities they offer professional and amateur alike, such as Club La Santa, Lanzarote (very popular with triathletes and host of one of the major Ironman competitions); Majorca (very popular with cyclists since it has good opportunities for hill-training); and Davos, Switzerland, which hosts an annual running festival culminating in a marathon event. This form of tourism links all the areas discussed in this chapter: sport, health, and tourism. Franklin suggested that:

> Muscular tourism became dominant as part of a generalised concern with exercise and fitness, particularly as a more significant component of health and well-being . . . the difference between the everyday and the holiday becomes blurred. (2000, p. 224)

Thus, according to this account, the holiday becomes part of an ongoing "body project" demonstrating cultural shifts in notions of "holiday" and "work" in which promotional communication and entertainment media, play a part.

CONCLUSIONS AND IMPLICATIONS: PUBLIC RELATIONS AND LIFESTYLE CHOICES IN HEALTH, SPORT, AND TOURISM

This chapter has outlined three interlinked domains which offer considerable potential for the analysis of public relations work. From a functional perspective, a review of existing specialist literature suggests that public relations theory has not yet had an impact on these areas and that public relations practice may have been subsumed into marketing, to the detriment of those clients. That has implications for public relations academics and in particular suggests the need for them to disseminate their knowledge in a variety of contexts and journals.

This chapter shows undeniably the relevance of public relations to the three domains and the intrinsic past that PR plays in these areas of cultural experience and practice through promotion, information management, and risk and crisis communication. The fact that domains overlap also implies the potential for differing agendas and the need for debate. In an era when many are alienated from politics, it may be that such areas have the potential to reveal alternative truths about the public sphere and the connection between organisational communication and publics.

The chapter reinforces the cultural linkages and opportunities for intertextuality that exist and also gives some insight into the role that organised communication (public relations) plays in the contemporary world and cultural experiences. As such, it is an early attempt to unpick complex social fabric to facilitate a deeper understanding of public relations and suggests that the PR role may be more diverse and less monolithic or uni-dimensional than is sometimes suggested. Furthermore, the conclusion can be drawn that only by exploring such intersections and attending to the detail and 'practice of everyday life' (Certeau, 1984) can we begin to understand the relationship between PR and culture.

ACKNOWLEDGMENT

Thanks are due to Karen Forrest, who patiently computer-processed the diagrams in this chapter.

IV

Professionalism
and Professionalisation

INTRODUCTION

The purpose of this section is to bring together an œuvre of our work focused on the public relations occupation in relation to its practice, knowledge systems, and aspirations to professional status. Our original interest in public relations education sprang from our experience of teaching public relations in the unsympathetic environment of a university marketing department within which status and power were bestowed on practitioners. As academics relatively new to the field of public relations, we were forced to engage in intellectual and political battles over our curriculum. Our efforts to understand these problems resulted in the chapter "Public Relations Education," which is presented in its reflexive and unabridged form in the final section of this book.

Subsequently, our work began to draw specifically on the sociology of the professions and, in the case of Pieczka, gravitate towards the sociology of work. The first chapter included in this section is a reprint from the seminal text *Handbook of Public Relations* (Heath, 2001b). This chapter clearly lays out a review of the literature on sociology of the professions and then proceeds to reflect on its application to the field of public relations. It points out that the public relations discipline was still using in a way the term profession in the 1990s which had been abandoned by sociologists of the professions in the late 1970s and that public relations academics became diverted into roles and gender research.

The next two chapters arise from Pieczka's recent project to explore public relations practice from an unusual perspective. Her research departs from the traditional sociological approach to the profession by excluding systematic investigation of academic institutions and practices relevant to the public relations occupation and makes no attempt to examine the body of abstract knowledge in public relations, academics as knowledge producers for the occupation, or to explore the relationship between academics and practitioners or education and practice.

Instead, she has set on one side expectations of PR's scientific or rational nature and focused on public relations knowledge as it derives from practice. Her first chapter focuses on public relations expertise and is based on participant observation of public relations trainers, a number of whom were former Presidents of the Institute of Public Relations; interviews with trainers; and analysis of a large number of Sword of Excellence entries. Pieczka offers a model of professional expertise as: picture of the world, conceptual frame, and working knowledge (comprising problems, tools, and truths).

In her second chapter, "Public Relations Jurisdiction," Pieczka takes the concept "jurisdiction" which has been elaborated in the first chapter in this section to address three key questions: How do public relations consultants get and deliver their work? What factors influence the process? How do the exigencies of routine work and conditions under which it is carried out influence the occupation in its self-identity and its behaviour? The chapter is based on interviews carried out during fieldwork in a consultancy and analysis of trade magazines. The analysis initially draws out the tension in public relations practitioners' discourse between rational professionalism and "chemistry" before proceeding to explore the Jekyll-and-Hyde nature of the occupation by reviewing the occupational practices which seek to shore up the weaknesses arising from split identity. Finally, the chapter reviews symbolic capital as communicated through the representation of practitioners who have a public persona in mass media. As part of this the chapter gives a detailed account of the revolving doors between public relations, politics, and the media which also demonstrates that while "the public image and status of the occupation are constantly under attack . . . at the same time there is a clear elite of practitioners who receive public signs of respect and recognition."

14

Public Relations and the Question of Professionalism

Magda Pieczka and Jacquie L'Etang
Stirling Media Research Institute

This chapter is about professionalism in public relations. Given the strong interest in professionalism on the part of educators, researchers, and practitioners, some critical reflection is needed to understand how this concept has been used. The chapter aims to bring a number of new concepts and empirical material into the field. A brief literature review of the sociology of the professions is presented, followed by a review of selected public relations literature in light of the sociological debates over the concepts of profession and professionalism. The resulting insights are contextualized by a brief review of the development of public relations in Britain so as to explore alternative interpretations of history and public relations.

UNDERSTANDING THE STUDY
OF PROFESSIONALISM

Professions as a subject of study can be traced back to the late 19th century and the work of sociologists such as Herbert Spencer, Emile Durkheim, and Max Weber but also of economists such as Cairnes (1887). A more systematic study developed during the 1920s and 1930s, the important early landmarks of this interest being Carr-Saunders and Wilson's (1933) study of 27 occupational groups and Parsons' (1939) article on professions and the social structure.

Like any field of inquiry, the sociology of the professions has been developing through a combination of empirical and theoretically driven research. Reviewing developments, one notices more or less consistent lines of research effort that sometimes run in parallel and sometimes in succession, one or two clear changes of direction, and a continuous chipping away at the problem from many bases while debating the merits of the various efforts. Underlying this diversity, however, the works of Durkheim (1933), Parsons (1939), and Weber construct the basic conceptual skeleton that has supported study of the professions from its early days. The profession is anchored in the social division of labour, instrumental rationality, and the institutional structures through which they are articulated. Thus, it is inextricably linked with the rise of the modern industrial society.

The history of this field normally is charted around the fissure of the paradigm shift that occurred sometime during the late 1960s. On the one side lies the *trait approach* allied with functionalist sociology; on the other lies the *power approach* and its extensions, indebted to the insights offered by interactionism but also to the revived interest in Marxism (for a detailed discussion, see Abbott, 1988; Burrage, 1990; Dingwall, 1983; Freidson, 1986, 1994; Macdonald, 1995). The following discussion is organized by the main concepts used by these different approaches before an analysis of the current situation is attempted.

The early writers and researchers agreed about—in fact, they took for granted—the important stabilizing role that professions play in the social structure (Durkheim, 1933, pp. 24–31; see also Macdonald, 1995, p. 2). This position was expressed in the following way by Carr-Saunders and Wilson (1933): "Professional organisations are stable elements in society . . . They engender modes of life, habits of thought, and standards of judgement which render them centres of resistance to crude forces which threaten steady and peaceful evolution" (p. 497). As a result, researchers' efforts up to the 1960s were focused on cataloging the traits that set professions apart from other groups in society and accounted for their prominent role. Thus, a profession was defined by its foundation on a body of "complex formal knowledge and skill along with an ethical approach to . . . work" (Freidson, 1986, p. 29). In fact, as Millerson's (1964) comparison of numerous definitions showed, a more detailed set of characteristics had been developed and well established in the field:

> The list covers familiar ground—a specialised skill and service, an intellectual and practical training, a high degree of professional autonomy, a fiduciary relationship with the client, a sense of collective responsibility for the profession as a whole, an embargo on some methods of attracting business, and an occupational organisation testing competence, regulating standards, and maintaining discipline. (Elliott, 1972, p. 5)

A corollary of the efforts to build an "ideal-type" definition of the phenomenon under study was the realization that a method also had to be found to account for the differences not only among the accepted professions but also between professions and occupations (for a discussion of definitions, see Freidson, 1986, pp. 21–33). Terms such as *semi-professions* (Etzioni, 1969), *paraprofessions* (Freidson, 1970b), and *status* and *occupational professions* (Elliott, 1972) were introduced to deal with the differences in autonomy or status that different occupational groups possessed.

There emerged a clear difference between the straightforward and descriptive nature of the trait approach (which viewed professions as a static phenomenon) and the process approach (which focused, as the name suggests, on the nature of the process by which occupations attain professional status; see, e.g., Vollmer & Mills, 1966). The process, called professionalization, was proposed as a historical model of the development of professionalism. This so-called natural history of professionalism, developed in the works of Caplow (1954) and Wilensky (1964), consisted of five stages: "(1) the emergence of the full-time occupation; (2) the establishment of a training school; (3) the founding of a professional association; (4) political agitation directed towards the protection of the association by law; [and] (5) the adoption of a formal code" (Johnson, 1972, p. 28).

Professionalization rendered itself to operationalization and, therefore, was used in empirical work dealing with structuration such as Hickson and Thomas' (1969) study in which they established a hierarchy of professions in Britain (for critical discussions of traits and professionalization, see Abbott, 1988; Johnson, 1972; Rueschemeyer, 1964; Spangler & Lehman, 1982).

But presenting the first few decades of the study of the professions as driven purely by the trait approach and by functionalism is too crude. An alternative approach developed within the Chicago School by Everett C. Hughes was present from the 1930s and became particularly prominent with the publication of his *Men and Their Work* (Hughes, 1958), and later his *The Sociological Eye* (Hughes, 1971) as well as the publication of his students' work—a classic ethnographic study, *Boys in White* (Becker, Greer, Hughes, & Strauss, 1961), and *Medical Dominance* and *Profession of Medicine* (Freidson, 1970a, 1970b).

In theoretical terms, the difference between these two approaches can be explained as the work of normative character linked to the concepts of the social structure and function and the work supported by the concepts of action and social interaction. The ethnographic approach used by the interactionist studies revealed aspects of professional practice and training that evaded other researchers, for example, the fact that young doctors developed cynicism rather than altruism in the course of their professional instruction. Thus, the term *profession* came to be seen as a symbolic label or ideology used by an occupational group:

> Ideal-typical constructions do not tell us what a profession is, only what it pretends to be . . . Everett C. Hughes and his followers are the principal critics of the "trait" approach and ask instead what professions actually do in everyday life to negotiate and maintain their special position. (Larson, 1977, pp. xii, xiv; quoted in Macdonald, 1995, pp. 7–8)

If one reads the early history of the sociology of the professions in the way presented heretofore and puts it in the context of theoretical and methodological changes within the social sciences beginning in the late 1960s (Denzin & Lincoln, 1994) and perhaps even broader social and political trends of that time, then one cannot avoid the impression of doors closing on certain ways of thinking and opening on others:

> The mood shifted from one of approval to one of disapproval, from one that emphasized virtue over failings to one that emphasized failings over virtues . . . This shift in evaluation and emphasis was reflected in a shift in conceptualization. The academic sociologists of the 1940s and 1950s were prone to emphasize as the central characteristics of the professions their especially complex formal knowledge and skill along with an ethical approach to their work . . . Writers from the late 1960s on, however, emphasized instead the unusually effective monopolistic institutions of professions and their high status as the critical factor. (Freidson, 1986, pp. 28–29)

This new way of looking at professions came to be termed the power approach, whereby power is understood, broadly speaking, as ways in which professions win social approval to define and control their work and their relationships with other actors such as clients (Macdonald, 1995, p. 5). There is an influential body of published work that either is directly focused on various manifestations of professional power or can be regarded as a development of such interests (Abbott, 1988; Freidson, 1970a, 1970b, 1986; Johnson, 1972; Larson, 1977). Although there sometimes are big differences among these authors, for the purposes of this review, it is more important to see them as advancing a broadly similar approach that has firmly shaped the conceptual map of the field.

The fundamental area of convergence among these authors has to be located in the theoretical sources from which they drew or, perhaps even more important, in their preoccupation with theorizing itself. The trait approach was *a*theoretical, and Parsons' conceptualization (which explains the place of professions in the social structure as defined by the special nature of the social functions they fulfill and by their "collectivity orientation") came under attack. The theoretical inspiration for this renewed interest in professions came in the form of a number of concepts borrowed from Hughes' interactionism, Weberian ideas, and Marxist modes of explanation.

Hughes contributed *licence* and *mandate*, that is, the idea that the profession depends on social approval to carry out certain activities in exchange for money and "to define, for themselves and others, proper conduct in relations to work" (Dingwall, 1983, p. 5). Weber's concept of "social closure" was introduced by Parkin (1974) and subsequently used by others. Another of Weber's ideas borrowed by the sociologists of the professions was the view that a profession represented an "interest group" whose actions are oriented toward common economic and social interests. Finally, Marxist influence raised questions about the profession's relations to the state and the position of professionals in the class system. It also produced a stream of work tracking the traces of proletarianisation of the professions (Braverman, 1974; Derber, 1982; Murphy, 1990), that is, their alleged loss of autonomy to bureaucratic systems that increasingly controlled the performance of professional work (Freidson, 1994, pp. 130–140).

The theorizing effort was further enriched by the study of professions outside the Anglo-American system, particularly studies of the French and German professions (Burrage, 1990, pp. 12–18). This Continental intervention highlighted the culture-specific nature of the concept by revealing a different model of the state's engagement with professions (Geison, 1984; Jarausch, 1990; Kocka, 1990). The differences begin with semantics (both French and German lack an exact equivalent of the term *profession* itself[1] but go deeper into the definition of the concept, showing its inextricable links to political culture:

> In the meritocratic ideology of "classless" America, the professions have come to be seen as the most obviously "legitimate" way to claim, attain, or retain elite status. In French (and German) political culture, the social standing of noncapitalist elites has had a less distinct connection with their occupational role, and the "liberal professions" in particular have generally been perceived as a much less important social and political force. (Geison, 1984, p. 5)

Thus, *profession* emerges recast from a new mould. First, it comes to be seen as a special case of a more general type of occupation. The old traits are reworked into a dynamic model that places a profession in relation to the state, political culture, and social groups, be they elites, other professions, or clients. Knowledge in this model can be reinterpreted as an instrument in the profession's competitive positioning. It also becomes clear that the study of professions, or of any profession for that matter, has to extend over three levels of analysis: "the level of general social change, the level of occupational organisation, and the level of individual life-cycle" (Elliott, 1972, p. 5).

Two such comprehensive models have been constructed and applied, known as the "professional project" (Larson, 1977) and the "system of professions" (Abbott, 1988; for a discussion of both, see Macdonald, 1995, pp. 8–35). Larson's (1977) work was inspired by the Hughesian approach, but at the same time it rests firmly on the idea of the market as the focus around which economy, society, and professions are organized:

> Professionalization is . . . an attempt to translate one order of scarce resources—specialist knowledge and skills—into another—social and economic rewards . . . The structure of the professionalization process binds together two elements . . . : a body of abstract knowledge, susceptible [to] practical application, and a market— the structure of which is determined by economic and social development and also by the dominant ideological climate. (pp. xvii, 40)

---

[1]The term *public relations* presents a similar problem. It either appears in English, as happens in Poland, or is covered by terms such as *relations publiques* in French and *Offentlichkeitsarbeit* in German. The problem with the terminology may be seen as merely an expression of deeper cultural differences.

Thus, the professional project unfolds along two dimensions: market control and social mobility. Its ultimate goal is complete social closure or elite status. Larson (1977) reused the old idea of professionalization, but in her account it is the combination of economics and the ideological mechanisms rather than social function that supplies the explanation. Professions no longer are neutral or detached from the class structure; rather, they very clearly are lodged in it by their "proximity to power" (p. xv).

There are two other features of Larson's (1977) model that are important to our analysis: her understanding of the operations that are performed on knowledge in the process of professionalization and her understanding of the role that professional training plays. The first is captured by the opposition of *codification* versus *indeterminacy* (p. 41). The first of the pair refers to the part of the cognitive base of the profession that can be standardized and mastered as rules; the second describes areas that escape codification and may be covered by explanations such as *talent*. Freidson (1970b), who had used the idea of indeterminacy before in the context of medicine, explained it as the "firsthand experience" of the clinician as opposed to "book knowledge" or science (p. 169). High indeterminacy helps in the exclusion of competitors from the field and, therefore, can be expected to play an important part in professionalization. The second important point is Larson's (1977) treatment of training, which she saw as "the cooperative activity of instructors and students—[which] appears indeed as the production of a marketable commodity, namely the special skill of the professional producer" (p. 211).

Abbott's (1988) work is founded on two points: (a) that "the evolution of professions... results from their interrelations" (p. 8) and (b) that professional work is constituted by tasks that the profession has successfully claimed for itself. The hold that a profession establishes over a set of tasks is known as *jurisdiction*. Jurisdictions are maintained, extended, and redefined on the basis of "a knowledge system governed by abstractions [because only abstraction] can redefine [the system's] problems and tasks, defend them from interlopers, and seize new problems" (p. 9). The new element is the concept of the system of professions as the level of generalization above that of a single profession. Thus, a change in one profession's jurisdiction affects jurisdictional changes in other professions. At the same time, Abbott's model includes the intraprofessional differentiation (by status, client, organization of work, and career pattern) and a sensitivity to broader environmental factors that he considered under the rubrics of social and cultural environments. To understand a profession, therefore, one needs to pay attention to its jurisdictional competitors. In the case of public relations, these might be journalists or marketing specialists. One also should see diversity beyond the homogeneity implied by the labels of *lawyer, doctor*, and *public relations specialist*.

It seems appropriate to finish this historical review of the sociology of the professions with Freidson, who occupies a special position in the field. Freidson has been publishing on the sociology of medicine since 1960, and since his *Profession of Medicine* (Freidson, 1970b) he has developed a strong theoretical position in the sociology of the professions that has influenced writers such as Larson and Abbott. What is particularly valuable in Freidson's approach is both the reworked definition of the profession "as an occupation which has assumed a dominant position in the division of labor so that it gains control over the determination and substance of its own work" (Freidson, 1970b, p xvii) and a more fundamental redefinition of the subject as the study of work based on application of knowledge to a variety of problems. The new element here is the retreat from the notion of objective knowledge to the notion of knowledge as a social construct (which for Freidson was not synonymous with extreme relativism):

   The profession claims to be the most reliable authority on the reality it deals with.... In developing its own "professional" approach, the profession changes the definition and shape of problems as experienced and interpreted by the layman. The layman's problem is re-created as it is managed—a new social reality is created by the profession. (p. xvii)

This leads logically to what Freidson (1970b) viewed as major questions that underpin the study of the profession: "First, one must understand how the profession's self-direction or autonomy is developed, organized, and maintained. Second, one must understand the relation of the profession's knowledge and procedures to professional organization as such and the lay world" (pp. xvii–xviii).

Freidson's (1970b) line of thought brought him to the following understanding of the current problems in the field. First, the trait approach—and he saw power as ultimately a version of the trait approach—cannot produce a theoretical basis for an explanation applicable to all manners of professions in all manners of countries (i.e., beyond its Anglo-American origins). Second, to build such a theoretical base, one must start with a comprehensive theory of occupations. Professions are to be treated only as special cases in which the claim made by the use of the title—Freidson called it "avowal" or "promise" (p. xvii)—has been successful. If the theory of occupations is to be general and abstract, then the theory of the professions should aim at explaining individual cases:

> The future of profession lies in embracing the concept as an intrinsically ambiguous, multifaceted folk concept of which no single definition and no attempt at isolating its essence will ever be generally persuasive ... Profession is treated as an empirical entity about which there is little ground for generalizing as a homogeneous class or a logically exclusive conceptual category. (Freidson, 1994, p. 25).

Thus, *profession* should be understood as a "socio-political artifact" and as a study of the "role of the title in the aspirations and fortunes of those occupations claiming it" (p. 26).

This brief summary of the development of profession shows how the concept has moved from the macro level of analysis to that of specific social and political location as well as how it has been problematized and changed from a sociological tool to a conscious occupational strategy. It is this changed understanding of the concept that frames our analysis and reflection in the sections that follow.

PROFESSIONALISM IN PUBLIC RELATIONS

Looking into public relations from the vantage point offered by the sociology of the professions, we are struck by two observations. First, the way in which profession is understood in our field reflects the view largely abandoned by the theorists of the professions since the late 1970s. Second, some of the interests observed in the field of the sociology of work and occupations also are present in public relations, notably gender and work itself. Finally, the comparison reveals a number of themes not present in public relations research.

The use of professionalism normally is linked in our field with the expression of a need to improve the occupational standing. The familiar troika—body of knowledge, ethics, and certification—is understood as the defining characteristics of a profession (Cutlip, Center, & Broom, 1994, pp. 129–163; J. Grunig & Hunt, 1984, pp. 66–69; Wylie, 1994), and there has been a consistent effort expounded by public relations professional associations and educators to develop these characteristics. American public relations, which seems to have the most developed institutional base for public relations with its big numbers of university courses, big numbers of practitioners associated with the Public Relations Society of America (PRSA), and its public relations journals, is the best example of this effort. In collaborative efforts,

American academics and practitioners since 1973 have striven to develop and implement common standards for public relations education through a number of Association of Education in Journalism and Mass Communication commissions (Ehling, 1992). Since 1987, there has been work conducted under the auspices of the PRSA to define and develop the necessary body of knowledge (PRSA, 1990). The International Association of Business Communicators committed itself to funding the *Excellence* project, which subsequently has produced at least two major publications (Dozier, L. Grunig, & J. Grunig, 1995; J. Grunig, 1992) and seemed to have worked as a focus for a lot of basic and applied research. Perhaps the most obvious symbol of these efforts is in the name of what was described as one of the "milestones on the road toward professionalism," that is, the Symposium on Demonstrating Professionalism (Ehling, 1992, pp. 442–443).

Thus, professionalism has become a loudly articulated group goal for public relations practitioners, guiding their efforts in developing public relations expertise but also inspiring a fair amount of introspective research (for a discussion, see J. Grunig & Hunt, 1984). Inspired by Wilensky (1964) and Vollmer and Mills (1966), J. Grunig's (1976) own research produced a scale operationalizing professionalism in public relations. Other researchers also have conducted studies based on measures of professionalism (McKee, Nayman, & Lattimore, 1975; Sallot, Cameron, & Lariscy, 1997; Wright, 1976).

Apart from research operationalizing professionalism, the occupational interests have been pursued in research dealing with gender (L. Grunig, 1995; Sereni, Toth, Wright, & Emig, 1997; Tam, Dozier, Lauzen, & Real, 1995), public relations roles, and other topics, extending in a more or less direct manner ideas best labeled as "public relations excellence" (Dozier, L. Grunig, & J. Grunig, 1995).

So far, the most extensive engagement within the field of public relations with practitioners' work has come from research built around the concept of role (Broom & Dozier, 1986; Broom & Smith, 1979; Creedon, 1991; Dozier, 1992; Dozier & Broom, 1995). Theoretically, this stream of research uses one of the fundamental sociological concepts. Empirically, it has been advanced through surveys of American practitioners and the use of factor analysis at the analytical stage.

Up to this point, public relations has engaged selectively with the range of issues found in the sociology of occupations. For example, gender is a prominent issue, as it is in the field of sociology of work and occupations, where we have located the study of the profession. Yet, the relations between groups of people identified by other criteria, such as the amount of power they wield in an organization, have not generated the same level of analysis. This lack of interest in how people at work really relate and communicate might perhaps be explained by the strong normative drive present in public relations theorizing that focuses on proving that dialogue is the best way in which to enact work relations or even all relations. This situation can be explained convincingly as resulting from professionalization efforts that necessarily rely on an idealistic understanding of the profession.

If research interest has been expounded on the study of public relations at the level of career and role (i.e., linking individual and institutional levels), then the larger scale interests (i.e., looking at public relations in terms of its engagement with the state and the big social structures of society) has remained a fairly marginal interest. Typically, this has meant that when we engage with knowledge and discourse (rhetoric) in public relations, we link them to improved effectiveness of public relations or, more critically, to the issue of image and presentation. We have not, however, been very bold in looking at the type of "social reality" that professional communication experts construct in their efforts to communicate more effectively.

PUBLIC RELATIONS IN BRITAIN
AND PROFESSIONALISM

In presenting a culturally specific take on the development of public relations, we are following Freidson's approach to professionalization, which recognizes the importance of unique sets of historical circumstances in particular cases. In adopting such an approach, we are clearly abandoning the American progressivist model of the development of public relations, which we see as reflecting the ideological and cultural context of the United States.

Existing narratives of the origins and development of the public relations occupation are dominated by the experience of the United States (see the British civil servant and cultural critic, Pimlott, 1951, as well as the more recent and better known Americans: Cutlip, 1994; Ewen, 1996; J. Grunig & Hunt, 1984; Olasky, 1987; Pearson, 1992; Tedlow, 1979). One interpretation has come to dominate mainstream public relations literature—the historical model developed by J. Grunig and Hunt (1984), which suggests that public relations historically has passed through four developmental stages: publicity, public information, two-way asymmetry, and symmetry. The model is also used to classify types of current practice and often is the basis for deductive applied research, which dominates the discipline. This interpretation has become the most widely known not only because it offers a clear framework for analysis but also because it has been used to underpin ideas about the role and ethics of public relations practice.

Much literature emanating from the United States promotes the idea that this evolutionary model is universally applicable both as a historical explanation and as a typology that satisfactorily explains professional practice. The difficulty with this sort of approach is that it can fail to take account of significant cultural and political factors in non-U.S. settings.

In this chapter, we present a brief summary of the evolution of public relations in Britain, which clearly shows a different pattern of development from that in the United States and, therefore, implies that the developmental model is not rigidly applicable. A fuller account of developments up to the formation of the Institute of Public Relations (IPR) in 1948 is detailed in L'Etang (1998c, 2004), but here we endeavor to illustrate the interplay between specific cultural, political, and economic experiences and development of the practice.

Origins of British Public Relations

The most significant feature of British developments was the large role played by local and central government and the relatively small contribution of the private sector (largely confined to advertising agencies and a few key organizations discussed in L'Etang [1998c] and not reviewed here). Although central government in Britain determines overall legislation, locally elected bodies implement policy within the constraints of their local budgets (partly raised directly from the local populace in the form of a property tax) from which a wide range of services are provided to the local communities. Nineteenth-century social reforms that attempted to deal with the social problems caused by the industrial revolution resulted in a greater role for local government. At this time, the relationship and communications between government officials and the local populace became an issue. As a result, officials began to consider their public relations role as well as their professional status. In 1922, local and central government officials combined to form the Institute of Public Administration and, in 1923, established a journal, *Public Administration*, that published many articles on public relations, showing that by the 1930s there was a fairly sophisticated definition of public relations and a clear understanding of the importance of good public relations to facilitate smooth administration in a democratic context. It was argued that "intelligence" (in current terminology, this translates as issues management) was an intrinsic role of public relations (Wood, 1936, p. 46) and that internal public relations should facilitate information flow within and between an organization and its environment (Kent Wright, 1936; Wood, 1936). Government officials' awareness and conception of public relations were demonstrated in articles declaring the following: "The first essential ... is to build up public understanding and appreciation of the services rendered to them [members of the public] and thus obtain their goodwill" (Whitehead, 1933, p. 272); "A public relations department exists ... not indeed for making policy palatable but for making it understood" (Wood, 1936, p. 45); and, "If the taxes branch is to be successful as it has been in the past, it must derive its strength from the goodwill and local cooperation of the general body of taxpayers" (Kliman, 1936, p. 290).

Another important influence was central government peacetime propaganda. Although there was extensive debate about the appropriateness of propaganda in a supposedly democratic country during peacetime, the view that propaganda had a role to play in assisting effective democracy through educating and informing citizens and facilitating feedback to civil servants was influential and spawned a number of public and health communication campaigns. Likewise, the collaboration between Stephen Tallents, secretary of the Empire Marketing Board that aimed to make the Empire "live as a society for mutual help" (Lee, 1972, p. 51), and John Grierson, the acknowledged leader of the British film documentary movement, was crucial. Grierson was a Scot who studied at the University of Glasgow and then the University of Chicago, where his views of democracy were influenced by Lippmann and after which he turned to film as the mass medium that could help to break down the barriers to informed citizenship. There is evidence that his views influenced public relations discourse in Britain (L'Etang, 1999), and an illustration is given in the following quotation from Alan Campbell-Johnson (1956), IPR president during 1956–1957:

[There is] a growing gulf between the active and passive elements in our community—the leaders and the led, the experts and the laymen, the players and the spectators. To cope with this cleavage, intensified as it is by the industrial and technical revolution around us, is, I believe, the central function of public relations. (p. 52)

Tallents' (1932/1955) vision was laid out in *The Projection of England* in which he envisaged a "school for national projection" (p. 40), and this document formed much of the basis for the British Council established in 1934— "to make the life and thought of the British peoples known more widely abroad and to promote a mutual interchange of knowledge and ideas with other peoples" (White, 1965, p. 7). The relationship between Britain's colonial past and public relations is explored in more detail in the next subsection.

During both world wars, the British government made substantial propaganda efforts both at home and overseas—in Allied, neutral, and enemy countries—using a range of media. Tactics included censorship and, particularly during World War II, the employment of "black propaganda" overseas involving the use of deception and subterfuge in disseminating misleading information. Some of those involved in such work (see L'Etang, 1998a, 1998c) became involved in public relations after the war, and the career paths of such individuals clearly suggests a difficulty in distinguishing between public relations and propaganda. It is evident that a background in propaganda was not seen as being problematic or in any way a barrier to public relations practice.

Politics, Economy, and the Post-War Development of Public Relations

In dramatic contrast to the United States, which after the war found itself the richest and most powerful nation, Britain ended the war the world's largest debtor nation, short of labour and food and with visible exports reduced to less than half of the pre-war level. Yet, Britain still attempted to maintain an imperial role and during the 1940s and 1950s was paying up to 8% of gross domestic product on defense as the Cold War escalated. The change to a Labour administration in 1945 brought about increased expenditure on social welfare, housing, and health. In this setting, there were several opportunities for public relations to become an established part of the socio-economic framework: there was a large amount of new social legislation that needed to be explained to the public; goods had to be promoted, initially to export markets and then, with the increase of consumer durables, to the home market; and the new administration's interventionist economic policies required some explanation and triggered opposition from business in rhetorical campaigns that often appealed directly to the public.

The wartime experience had forced local government into a much closer relationship with the communities for which it was responsible. After the war, the 1942 Beveridge Report, which laid out the vision of the welfare state, was implemented by the new Labour government. The mass of new legislation that resulted had to be explained to citizens, as did the reorganization and repairs to the infrastructure of the country, particularly in urban centers that had been badly damaged by bombing. Consequently, local government began to appoint officials into newly created public relations posts, and in 1947 these officials came together to define public relations as

> the deliberate, planned, and sustained effort to establish and maintain, by conveying information and by all other suitable means, mutual understanding and good relations between a firm, statutory authority, government, department, professional, or other body or group and the community at large. (Rogers, 1958, p. 12)

This definition reflected the debates in *Public Administration* during the 1920s and the stated aims of both the Empire Marketing Board and the British Council (L'Etang, 1998c). Local government officials also were instrumental in contacting others in public relations roles in private and public sectors and in formulating the mission of the IPR in 1948. They had the administrative skills needed to set up the Institute and contributed a strong sense of the importance of serving the public and the role of communication in facilitating democracy. Thus, local government played a substantial role in the formation of the public relations occupation in Britain and its early steps toward professionalization.

In terms of domestic politics, the major policy shift was that of nationalization whereby government took ownership of core industries away from the private sector to safeguard the interests of citizens by achieving economies of scale and reducing costs for consumers through a central planning model. There were strong ideological aspects of nationalization (public ownership based on principles of fairness and equity) versus anti-nationalization (free enterprise based on principles of efficiency through competition). Although Britain traditionally has had less state ownership than have other European countries, wars in 1914 and 1939 required major economic transformation and, therefore, acted as a stimulus to state ownership and management.

On its election, Labour swiftly nationalized the Bank of England, railways, road haulage, electricity, and civil aviation. Subsequent nationalizations were to include gas and, more contentiously, iron and steel. The threat of nationalization roused response from private enterprises in the form of special organizations that could lobby on their behalf. One such organization was

Aims of Industry, established in 1942 to protect free enterprise and oppose nationalization and "corporate socialism." According to Kisch (1964), Aims of Industry operated a covert strategy using Britain's old boy network" (p. 29) and making high-level contacts in building support. In contrast to the United States, Britain evidently had much stronger social networks, and these offered opportunities for public relations because networks could be used in a campaign (Sampson, 1969, p. 640). The policy of nationalization drove industry to seek public relations staff to promote their interests in the face of what were regarded by some as "political assaults" (Miller, 1960, p. 37).

The example of nationalization illustrates two important points. First, it indicates that public relations developed an interest in social elites apart from government and that public relations strategies entailed leveraging the power that social elites could offer. Second, it indicates the historical moment when public relations and business in Britain began to forge a closer alliance. Opposing views regarding the appropriate extent of government intervention and ownership as well as policies of nationalization and privatization (denationalization) from the postwar period to the present day have continued to have a substantial influence in creating opportunities for public relations practitioners to step in as advocates on behalf of business in response to government policy. Such policy is primarily explained on behalf of the politicians in power by technically neutral career civil servants in the Government Information Service, although since the 1980s government departments also have recruited public relations consultancies to help them explain their case (Miller & Dinan, 1998).

The postwar era threw up new challenges for the state, notably in its relationships with other countries, and the growth of public relations beyond Britain was, in some cases, stimulated by the process of decolonization. Again, such processes illustrate the difficulties in drawing clear boundaries between public relations, propaganda, intelligence, and psychological warfare operations, at least in the British context. For example, in Malaysia, there was a well-documented campaign to win over Malayan Chinese to the British government's side at the end of World War II. News management by the Malayan government sought to control information flow, to publicize the promise of independence in 1957, and to support counterinsurgency psychological warfare using a variety of tactics—leaflets, black propaganda newspapers, and "voice aircraft" (i.e., aircraft fitted with loudspeakers that either announce propaganda messages or play music or other distracting noises to intimidate local populations; Carruthers, 1995, p. 91). The Department of Publicity and Printing in Malaysia was established in 1945 and remained an important element once Malaysia had achieved independence in developing information campaigns to support government policy initiatives, particularly in the field of development (Van Leuven, 1996, p. 209; Van Leuven & Pratt, 1996, pp. 95–97).

Decolonization affected not only the British government but also organizations operating in the colonies. As one practitioner working for a major international organization recalled:

> The board realized that in postwar black Africa, there was going to be a big resurgence of political agitation working for independence from the British Commonwealth... [So, it was] proposed that we should practice public relations... solid, commonsensical, anticipating where African desires were going to lead and what sort of attitudes they were going to formulate with huge White imperialist companies that had been there for hundreds of years. We really learned by the seat of our pants. It was a question of impressing people with the idea that we were a good thing for them and their country... We ran... a strip cartoon [in a newspaper]..., and through it the Africans... would learn what capital was, what profit was, what employment was... all those basic things which would help them understand the company. (Interview, March 26, 1997)

Thus, the company tried to look after its own interest in the postcolonial world by persuading the African community of the benefits of capitalism through an educational campaign.

In this context, public relations seems to be a self-interested force for conservatism, developing personal relationships in the community in attempting to counteract the effects of any latent alienation or nationalism. Interestingly, the public relations effort is described both as "commonsensical" and as "seat of the pants;" on the one hand, it is obvious in that it is concerned with protecting the company's interests, yet on the other, the nature of the expertise cannot be described, perhaps because activities proceeded on a trial-and-error basis. In Britain, the inability to define specific expertise resulted in a jurisdictional struggle with journalists who thought that public relations practitioners were encroaching on their own domain (i.e., storytelling) as well as impeding the news-gathering process. The tensions that resulted forced practitioners to try to justify themselves and establish a clear identity, both of which played a significant role in the public relations professional project discussed in the next subsection.

Legitimation, Education, and Professional Discourse

Professional status was sought in an effort to establish social legitimacy. The expansion of public relations required the occupation to negotiate social approval or the concepts identified earlier in this chapter as mandate and licence. Social respectability was the aim of many within the IPR, and proving the occupation's value to society and democracy in general was a strategy easily drawn from the local government public service ethos. Practitioners declared that "the correct intelligent practice of public relations is something without which modern society would be immeasurably impoverished" (Hess, 1950, p. 5) and that "the philosophy of public relations is a policy of social responsibility" (Galitzine, 1960, p. 51). Thus, the route taken by public relations to legitimate itself was that of the public interest. However, there were competing legitimations within the practice, with some emphasizing truth telling and information (e.g., "The good public relations officer is one who is concerned with putting over facts which can be supported by the truth" [Paget-Cooke, quoted in "Eight Men," 1953, p. 20]) and others advocating persuasion and advocacy (e.g., "The public relations officer persuades... I suggest we become realists and not visionaries" [Garnett, 1951, p. 16]).

Education was, and is, an instrument for the public relations occupation to achieve status by contributing to the legitimizing process of social acceptance and by helping to define public relations expertise and the scope of its operation. However, as L'Etang (1998b) showed, attempts to impose a system of entry to the professional institute based solely on qualifications failed during the 1960s because "experience" remained a tradable commodity. Qualifications (the first of which was established in 1957) were seen as a way in which to improve the image of public relations, but compliance constantly was deferred and delegated to the next generation. Following Larson's (1977) insight cited earlier, it appears to be the case that in British public relations practice, there has been and remains a gap between ideals/aspirations and practice. Although there remains a reluctance to identify the necessary abstract knowledge required to practice, specific personal skills and qualities are articulated consistently, and following Abbott (1988), it seems useful to begin to explore these in understanding the occupation. The selection of quotes displayed in Table 14.1 gives the views of practitioners of all ages about the necessary qualities required to be a successful operator. Practitioners do not identify specific knowledge but rather focus on personal qualities such as creativity, lateral thinking, flexibility, articulateness, persuasiveness, common sense, and integrity. Beyond that also is the implication that a practitioner must know how to behave with senior people and to possess appropriate cultural capital. Such qualities reveal something of the self-perception of practitioners and

TABLE 14.1

Practitioners' Views About the Qualities Required of a Successful Operator

---

"A lot of those people in those early days... were people of integrity... who could mix in so many areas... acceptable to leaders and... to people ... They were able to handle people, and in some ways that's ideal for public relations." (Interview, 26/06/96)

"Great understanding, great forbearance, [and] a great spirit of attunement with one's fellow beings are essentials... He must possess an exceptional breadth of mind... A personal sensitivity... is infinitely more important than even the most methodical application of accepted techniques. There is no intellectual substitute for the human approach." (Hess, 1950, pp. 6–7)

"Personality [is important].... You are flitting daily from one thing [to] another, so you need your wits about you." (Interview, 28/06/98)

"One has to have lateral thinking like Edward de Bono." (Interview, 22/08/95)

"Common sense [is important]. You need to be reasonably practical. Organization is very important... You need to be able to communicate." (Interview, 25/06/91)

"Critical ability [is important, as are]... [being] persuasive in writing and verbally..., integrity..., personal courage..., [and] a sense of humor.... It doesn't matter if they can write a press release." (Interview, 25/06/91)

"[Practitioners. should be] ideas men who... wish to change things, and that's what I mean by being creative." (Interview, 25/07/96)

"People [who] speak up, who dress nicely, who've got something intelligent to say [can be successful].... The old slap-dash approach is just not good enough.... Personality and good interpersonal skills [are important]." (Interview, 13/03/97)

"Credibility [is important]... People who can operate at a senior level on very sensitive topics [can be successful]..., so the ability to have those relationships is more important, in a way, than technical training... There is a personality requirement... Salesmanship is a crucial skill for the top people in consultancy... In the noncommercial area, the key skill is persuasiveness." (Interview, 17/03/97)

"More character than anything else [is important]..., getting along with clients.... being relatively intelligent, a streetwise intelligence... [and] a sense of humor... [To be able to] come up with ideas and think at a bit of a tangent [is important]." (Interview, 28/01/97)

---

provide a link between legitimation processes and attempts to establish professional power. Although it is important to know how to deal with clients and to be credible in terms of convincing them that the public relations practitioner knows best, it is noticeable that there is no abstract knowledge claimed for the purposes of legitimation or definition of the expertise offered to employers and clients.

CONCLUSION

The main argument that we have pursued in this chapter is that professionalism has so far appeared in public relations discourse as merely an historical process but that it should in fact be regarded as a more or less consciously used mechanism that is to deliver specific occupational goals. First, we showed that the understanding of the term as it is used in public relations is strongly anchored in the more idealistic functionalist approach to professions. Then, taking our cue from more recent developments in the sociology of the professions, we presented public relations primarily as an occupational group pursuing its own interests in relation to the state and social elites as the source of cultural/ideological power. Therefore, our analysis should help practitioners to understand their own roles, not simply in terms of managerial/technical levels or organizational position but also in a much broader context in terms of the power of the occupational role in society. We suggest that further reflection on the nature of public relations expertise, particularly in view of its success in establishing itself as a distinct and commercially viable service, would be beneficial.

In advancing our argument, we chose to focus on a selected number of points relating to the prewar emergence and postwar development of public relations practice in Britain. Our starting point is the history of public relations, and the argument we put forward is that "history" is not just a dispassionate marshaling of facts but also a weapon in the struggle for improved status. A progressivist account of the development of the occupation tinged with claims of universal applicability could be seen as an ideological mechanism bestowing the status of universal truth on a particular account. In our view, a model drawn from one set of historical circumstances is likely to be of limited value in interpreting historical data elsewhere.

Our approach was to follow Freidson in seeing each case of public relations as explained by a unique configuration of "national" factors. In our case, this meant attending to the role played in the development of British public relations by a combination of institutional forces and the exigency of the state effort to manage national interests. Our analysis revealed a number of interwoven strands the British documentary film movement, local bureaucracy, central government wartime and peacetime propaganda, decolonization, and economic theories. Tracking the interplay among these multiple elements offers a fuller historical understanding than does dividing them into apparently distinct phases of development that might imply continual progress and improvement.

15

Public Relations
Expertise in Practice

Magda Pieczka
Stirling Media Research Institute

This chapter examines public relations expertise. It presents the results of an extensive empirical enquiry and is framed by the concept of *profession* and the sociological debates that surround it.[1] *Profession* here is understood as "an occupation which has assumed a dominant position in the division of labour, so that it gains control over the determination and substance of its own work" (Freidson, 1970b: xvii). Since my interest is not in ascertaining the status of public relations, *occupation* and *profession* may be used interchangeably. What is of central interest, however, is the role knowledge plays in the constitution of the profession and particularly the links between knowledge and professional practice. Abstract knowledge has been considered a defining feature of the professions by all schools of thought in the sociology of the professions. Here I follow Abbott's (1988) ideas, specifically his claim that professional work is constituted by tasks which the profession has successfully claimed for itself. "The tasks of professions are human problems amenable to expert service" (Abbott, 1988, p. 35). The hold a profession establishes over a set of tasks is known as *jurisdiction*.

The body of abstract professional knowledge, that is, its cognitive base, is codified in textbooks. However, the application of that knowledge in professional practice is a complex operation. The discrepancy between knowing and doing in the professional context has been described as the difference between "book knowledge" and "first-hand experience" (Freidson, 1970b, p. 169). In terms of internal structuring of the professions, there may be two distinct groups of professionals: those who produce the abstract knowledge and those who apply it in practice.

Given the fragmentary and poorly developed body of abstract knowledge in public relations and its weak institutional basis in academia, we need to understand more about the

---

[1] A review of the extensive literature, as well as my own view of its relevance to current debates about the public relations profession, have been presented elsewhere (Pieczka & L'Etang, 2001).

basis and nature of the expert services practitioners sell to their clients. If we cannot assume that public relations practice is based on the application of a body of abstract knowledge, what is it based on? What is public relations expertise? Here public relations expertise is defined as a body of practical knowledge which makes it possible for public relations practice to exist. *Practice* is to be understood both as what an individual public relations worker does and, perhaps more emphatically, as tasks and techniques shared by the occupational group.

I have excluded questions about public relations textbook knowledge, the formal education of practitioners, the status of the profession, and many others. Instead, I have followed, to use Bourdieu's phrase, the logic of its practice. If answering the earlier questions might tell us something about, for example, the bad press the profession consistently receives (at least in the UK), understanding the logic of its practice tells us how and why the occupational group is the way it is, how it manages to capture new markets, and why it survives.

In fact, the material presented in this chapter seems to lend itself to Bourdieu's ideas with some stimulating results. Public relations practice can be understood as emerging from a particular *habitus*, that is, "the system of structured, structuring dispositions" which is "constituted in practice and which constructs the objects of knowledge" (Bourdieu, 1992, p. 52):

> The practical world that is constituted in the relationship with the *habitus*, acting as a system of cognitive and motivational structures, is a world of already realized ends—procedures to follow, paths to take. (Bourdieu, 1992, p. 53)

But "[p]ractice has a logic which is not that of a logician," said Bourdieu (1992, p. 86), reiterating arguments made before by ethonomethodologists, and phenomenological thinkers before them (Pieczka, 1997). By focusing on training and the transmission of expertise, this research deals largely with accounts of practice, which are possible only if they embody a certain level of reflexivity (absent from the practice itself) and a theorising effort. The latter here means a discursive practice of translating one order of things (direct experience) into another (descriptions of the former, which may be offered in more or less theoretical, abstract terms). And this is precisely what public relations training seems to do:

> In your job [. . .] you build up a huge knowledge of examples and in the examples come all kind of rules and ways of doing things. The hard thing in doing a presentation like this—I guess it is the reason why it's quite good for people like me to do it—is that it forces you to get it out, sit down and work out why it is you say all these things. (Interview with trainer, 23/7/98a)

LOCATING EXPERTISE

Data used in this chapter were gathered during participant observation of a 3-week training course offered on a commercial basis in London in 1998 to an international group of practitioners. The trainers, with one notable exception (myself), were senior British public relations practitioners drawn from consultancies and in-house departments, or were full-time trainers exclusively. A number were past Presidents of the Institute of Public Relations (IPR) in the UK or otherwise well-known names in the occupation. I participated in the course as a trainer, observer, and full participant when invited to join in the practical activities by the students themselves. Data were gathered in the form of field notes, handouts distributed to the students, and interviews with 13 trainers.[2] Analysis was carried out in stages through a process of open coding. The interviews were analysed separately, with a different set of categories related to the interview guide.

Another data set consisted of 111 entries to the Sword of Excellence, an annual IPR competition for the best public relations campaign. As an illustration of the format of the competition, in 1998 there were 10 categories: City and Financial, Internal Communication, Public Affairs, Consumer Public Relations, Industry and Commerce, Issue and Crisis Management, Not-for-profit Organisation, Low Budget Programmes (under £10,000), Support of Sponsorship, and Use of New Technology. Each category may or may not have a winner in any given year, as well as a number of Certificates of Excellence awarded, effectively runners-up prizes. The best campaign in any given year is awarded The Sword of Excellence.

Entries must comply with the following rules:

Individuals or organisations are required to submit a *summary no longer than three A4 pages (maximum 1,500 words)* to describe a programme and cover points that include:

- The information stage—analysis, research, and definition of operational objectives.
- The planning stage—drawing up a strategy and costed plan of action.
- The action stage—communicating and carrying out the programme.
- The measurement stage—monitoring and evaluating process, results, and budgets; re-assessment and modification of programme as necessary. This should preferably include evaluative comment from the chief executive of the organisation for whom the programme was designed (Institute of Public Relations, 1998).

The cases were selected from the 1984–1988 and 1990–1998 published summaries of the campaigns chosen as winners in their categories by the IPR panel of judges.[3] The summaries have all been written by the entrants to the competition themselves, according to the competition guidelines, and reproduced without any substantive changes in a special "case history" publication published at the end of the annual round.

THREE COMPONENTS OF PUBLIC RELATIONS EXPERTISE

Professional expertise emerges from the analysis as a body of practical knowledge, diverse in its nature, and intricately structured. Its component parts are identified here as: picture of the world; conceptual frame; and working knowledge, which in turn is composed of problems, tools, and truths. Together they provide the occupation not only with the knowledge of what to do and how to do it, but they also enable the occupational group to read the world in which they practise in a way that makes it possible for them to lay a claim to their own jurisdiction. The following discussion will therefore proceed to describe each of the component parts and explain the function they play in the overall architecture of public relations expertise.

---

[2]Data drawn from trainers' presentations, as opposed to interviews, are referred to as training sessions. There were two sessions every day, each conducted by a different trainer. The references show dates followed by 'a' and 'b', for the morning or afternoon session.

[3]The 1989 set of summaries has not been recoverable and therefore has been excluded. The author believes that this gap is unlikely to be a serious limitation in view of the nature of analysis the rest of the material has been subjected to.

Picture of the World

"It's a changed world and it's a highly challenging world" (Training session, 23/7/98b). This statement is perhaps the best summary of both the picture of the world that emerges from the training observed and the reason for paying it the attention it receives here. As seen through the eyes of the trainers and as explained to the students, the world is being fundamentally reconfigured. The analysis shows this "Reconfiguration" of the known world in its social, economic, technological, and political dimensions before it proceeds ("Response") by focusing on a series of instrumental reinterpretations of problematic issues as well as a number of points which seem to contradict the grand narrative offered by "Reconfiguration." Finally, a fundamental unresolved tension at the centre of the occupational ideology is identified— *Reason and emotion.*

Reconfiguration

So we have a backdrop of fundamental social, political, economic and technological shifts as a result of the digital revolution, broader social and environmental concerns, a convergence of values and globalisation which will change the corporate approach to major decision-making . . . (Training session, 20/7/98a)

The advent of digital media and communications—and the Internet and the World Wide Web in particular—is changing the world in ways that were inconceivable just a few years ago. The shift from atoms to bites, from real to virtual, challenges all our notions of commercial relationships as well as the role of public institutions and the individual in society. (Training session, 31/7/98a)

PR practitioners evidently believe that power in society is moving away from its traditional centres in government and business and spreading over a wider social base; national boundaries are reconfigured as regional and global at the same time; legitimacy is defined away from the narrow understanding of what is legal and increasingly in terms of what is moral; citizenship is expressed through consumership, and all this is fuelled by the technological changes in communication and the resulting changes of the mass media. The interaction of these changes is well illustrated in the following statement:

As a result of digitalisation and the expansion of the Internet, individuals have become global citizens and consumers. [. . .] Companies now face a media environment shaping and determining the way they are perceived and evaluated on a global basis, twenty-four hours a day. [. . .] Active management of reputation, combined with relationship management of stakeholders . . . has become a strategic need, not just nationally, but regionally and on a global basis. (Training session, 20/7/98a)

The world is seen as becoming more homogeneous: it shares "increasingly similar political, civil and economic institutions" (Training session, 20/7/98a); aspirations—"international competitiveness and world class standards drive and shape the best national and international organisations" (Training session, 30/7/98a); and ideas of prosperity—"virtually every country wants to get the same industries (Training session, 21/7/98a).

In its extreme form, this world becomes the New Utopia where business works together with governments (whose role is declining) and with civil society to "create a dialogue with a whole range of new stakeholders to find common ground" (Training session, 20/7/98a); where compliance with legislation is replaced by the prerogative of earning social trust and approval; where crises are avoided by successful anticipation of issues due to "creative use of communications technology" (Training session, 20/7/98a); and where universities participate in the "building [of] the shared planetary mind" (Training session, 20/7/98a). The New Utopia does not appear as mere wishful thinking but a reasonable, if perhaps rather optimistic, projection of present trends into the future.

If the future appears as an extension of the present, the present takes shape in opposition to the past. The theme of the Old and the New identified in the analysis is a mixture of data from research companies such as MORI or Gallup and extrapolation of ideas from management gurus such as Charles Handy, Carl Naisbitt, Michael Porter, and Tom Peters; sources such as the *Economist, Financial Times, Fortune*, and *Reputation Management*; and business peers such as Michael Morley, Vice Chairman of Edelman; Jim MacNamara, CEO Asia/Pacific, Carma International; and Chris Green, Campaign Director, Greenpeace. The exact provenance of the ideas is almost impossible to establish as the presentation conventions of training do not seem to require that sources be acknowledged. What occurs, effectively, is the production and reproduction of popular knowledge.

The juxtaposition of the Old and the New shows that people are becoming more pessimistic about the general standards of knowledge, honesty, and health; more critical of big business in general with decreasing ratings for its ability to balance public interest with profit considerations; and more suspicious of the benefits of controversial industries such as the chemical industry. Perhaps the most comprehensive expression of the change over time was presented by an External Affairs specialist of a major oil company, under the heading of "Public Attitudes to Corporate Power," as summarised Figure 15.1.

This juxtaposition shows that the old structures of the social and economic world have been disappearing. Another element in the received wisdom shows the impact of new communication technology on the relationship of producers and consumers: from structured linear chain with producer and consumers at the two extreme ends linked by the product and preselected communication channels where producers control information; to unstructured, two-directional links over a central information sphere accessed and used by a number of stakeholders, undermining the primacy of producers in the production and information (Training session, 31/7/98a). Thus, the old certainties and controls have been eroded in the same way as the familiar structures.

Although statistics were quoted to substantiate this perception, there is also a certain element of nostalgia present in this evocation of the world where business was trusted and free to operate the most "logical" economies of scale. It has to be pointed out here that it was precisely the

Then	Now
trust granted	mistrust, scrutiny, questioning; perceived behaviour, less tolerant, less respectful
ownership	stewardship, stakeholder expansion
freedom within the law	license to operate, responsibility
economics of scale/ integrated operations	disaggregation and market test, e.g., diversification, joint ventures, alliances
big is best	big is too powerful, inefficient;
the big employers=people	no accountability=systems
confidentiality respected	transparency demanded
Government's problem	industry's problem

FIGURE 15.1. Summary of public attitudes to corporate power (Training session, 23/7/98b).

wide public distrust of big business in the United States in the late 19th century that gave the impetus for the development of corporate public relations, or perhaps even modern public relations as such (see Marchand, 1998). This mixture of the historical, the nostalgic, and the wished-for is well illustrated by another chart used in training: "External Affairs Role in Transition" (Training session, 23/7/98b), organised as *Past* (reactive, non-mainstream, separate from management), *Present* (moving to active role, taking place on management teams), and *Future* (integrated part of management team, creating competitive advantage, competitive tool, pool of expertise).

Response

Whether or not factually accurate, this perception of change has produced a clear response in terms of business philosophy, or business' understanding of its own place in the social world, and with it, to use a grand term, of public relations' philosophical grounding:

Business today has a new bottom line—public acceptance. (Training session, 23/7/98b)

... not just delivering economic but also environmental and social equity goals—the so called Triple Bottom Line. (Training session, 20/7/98a)

I thought license to operate only applied to nuclear energy business, but with expectations of corporate behaviour and greater media capacity to focus in on the issues, increasingly food, pharmaceutical, hotels and financial services companies are under scrutiny. (Training session, 20/7/98a)

The principle of public acceptance has given business the basis from which to reestablish its legitimacy. The process, in practice, is a continuous tense renegotiation of areas over which the principle extends, starting historically, according to one of the trainers, with the spectacularly controversial issue of nuclear power, but gradually including more and more areas. These areas of public life, called issues, are "environment, human and political rights, animal rights, aid and economic development, consumerism, food safety, health, religion" (Training session, 3/8/98a). Risk has hardly been mentioned by the trainers, yet it seems that the principle of public acceptance is linked, on the one hand, to the gradual widening of the scope of risk and risk management; and on the other hand to a retreat from the worldview of watertight divisions between economic, moral, and social spheres of public life.

Although the main line of response has been to accept the idea of "license to operate" (defined by one trainer as "social acceptability of corporate action;" Training session, 3/8/98a), attention to data in a more detailed way shows that there have been a number of smaller strategies in use which simultaneously limit and operationalise this principle in business practice. These strategies are a series of reinterpretations which can be labelled instrumentalism and evasion.

The most obvious example of the instrumental approach to problems thrown up by the fundamental reconfiguration of the world is the introduction of a toolkit of ideas and tactics, such as: stakeholder, issues management, crisis management, social corporate responsibility. All of these appeared in the training either as separate sessions or ideas used by trainers. Instrumentalism of these ideas and tactics is twofold: they are there to be used as instruments; and the way in which these instruments work defines the nature of engagement with the issues. Let us take as an example social corporate responsibility (referred to as "responsibility") and follow it through a number of statements made by the trainers. It is defined as "the responsibility of an organisation to its stakeholders beyond its duties to its members ... [it] involves choices based on ethical and moral principles, not processes of accountability" (Training session, 30/7/98a). Thus, social responsibility lies in "our contribution to social/societal goals" (Training session, 30/7/98a), which is beyond and above the basic duties of profitability and accountability. It is also very clearly allied with the principle of freedom, fundamental to Western culture, and with the Western myth of growth and development:

> [Is social responsibility] an issue for multi-nationals? Not if you want to be world class . . . Not if you want to compete in your own market . . . Not if you want national economic growth. [Yes] only if you enjoy decline or economic imperialism. (Training session, 30/7/98a)

The rhetorical "you" constructed here is being presented with an apparent choice: to embrace social responsibility in the way in which the exemplars of business success, that is, multinationals, do; or to turn your back on it, and thereby condemn yourself to inevitable decline and failure. Social responsibility is being bracketed with freedom and growth as attractive aspirations—in contrast to economic imperialism, commercial selfishness, and decline.

Another, parallel type of alignment is being articulated in the above statement: if moral principles are evoked, so are pragmatic, business ones—competitiveness and reputation. Indeed, this pragmatic alignment takes over when responsibility becomes part of communication expertise claimed by public relations/communication management: "Why be socially responsible? Survival, recruitment, acceptability, motivation through the organisation, investment, secure support for the future change" (Training session, 30/7/98a).

Social responsibility gets operationalised purely with reference to the organisation's identity and technical issues of credibility:

> Social responsibility should always relate to corporate goals, the business plan or operational objectives; [is] most effective at community level; involving employees and management secures commitment—an essential; need to be appropriate in scale to your organisation . . . ; initiatives must be monitored and evaluated. (Training session, 30/7/98a)

Thus, through a process of reinterpretation we have been moved from a position of clear separation of different kinds of considerations (ethical and economic) to a position where the two are supposed to blend into one, but instead the ethical considerations seem to be circumscribed:

> So, a Ford European environmental award needed to persuade the vehicle buying public that Ford Motor Company was more than a manufacturer of reliable cars and trucks, but also had a stake in the future of the environment and had the good of society at heart. To a certain extent it succeeded. *environment can equal responsibility in the public perception.* [emphasis added] (Training session, 31/7/98b)

The effect of this instrumental approach is double-edged: social responsibility is included in good business practice, but it is also made ambiguous by the mode of its inclusion. In fact, good business practice itself is a result of the same reinterpretation process whereby ethical considerations can be included into business thinking with no fundamental rethinking of business principles. To put it crudely, if you rename it, you do not have to rethink it:

> Is keeping employees informed a moral issue? The majority view seems to be that it is a business issue. It is part of standard good ways in which to run business. (Training session, 23/7/98a)

The answer is evasive, but at least the question is asked. Evasion, however, can be extended further to the point where the need for any reevaluation does not even arise. This seems to happen when problematic issues are evaded through the use of frameworks which are otherwise legitimate or comprehensive in their own right. For example, seeing the world in terms of purely business relations or in purely economic terms helps to evade more troublesome ethical questions which could not be dealt with as "good business practice:"

> In China, government support is particularly crucial to the success of a foreign venture, since the government develops the policies and laws that rule an organisation's operation, controls the multitude of approvals that allow your business to operate day-to-day and *is often your partner, customer and supplier.* [emphasis added] (Training session, 20/7/98b)

> As a reaction against increasing EU restrictions, tobacco companies are also going heavily into other markets— *the Middle East, Far East and Africa—where markets are growing, not declining.* [emphasis added] (Training session, 31/7/98a)

Finally, the clearest evasive technique of all is that of redistribution of responsibility:

> It is difficult to have a debate with stakeholders in tobacco industry or nuclear industry because it is such a polarised issue. [It is not the company's fault, it is the issue that society has to solve.] (Training session, 20/7/98a)

> It's not for a single company to solve big governance issues for the whole society. (Training session, 23/7/98b)

Which World?

So far, it seems that there is a fairly sharp picture of the world emerging together with a clear professional communication/management response to it. It would be wrong, however, to stop here: the picture may be sharp, but it is not without its own contradictions and tensions. This world seems to extend between the New Utopia and Dystopia.

In the utopian vision, business works together with government (whose role is declining) and with civil society to "create a dialogue with a whole range of new stakeholders to find common ground" (Training session, 20/7/98a). Business compliance with legislation is replaced by the prerogative of earning social trust and approval. Crises are avoided by successful anticipation of issues due to "creative use of communication technology" (Training session, 20/7/98a); and universities participate in the "building [of] the shared planetary mind" (Training session, 20/7/98a).

Yet, the "sameness" of the world may not be making it any more predictable or easier to deal with:

> Establishment and maintenance of trust and confidence is an increasing problem in a fast moving world where change is taking place all the time and people come and go and alter their loyalties as a matter of course. (Training session, 29/7/98a)

The unpredictability of the New World lies at the core of an alternative vision—the New Dystopia.

Reason and emotion

At the foundation of the New Dystopia lies the old division between logic/reason and emotion:

> Public opinion is increasingly a part of what we do, so are the emotional factors. (Training session, 20/7/98a)

> You can't rely on the rational arguments only. (Training session, 21/7/98b)

> [In] a battle between facts and emotions, emotions usually win the day. Don't just count on logic. (Training session, 28/7/98a)

The division can no longer be denied; in the New Utopia, however, the split can be repaired. In fact, the ambition to reunite reason with emotion is a driving force in the New Utopia:

> The old paradigm of defensive stance must be replaced by a high profile in public debate and facts and science working hand in glove with emotions and perceptions. (Training session, 20/7/98a)

Yet, as we have seen, people "come and go" and routinely refuse to be locked into relationships with organisations. They may like what you do and yet not like you, as it was demonstrated to the trainees with a MORI chart showing that satisfaction with a company's service is not linked to favourable attitudes towards it. It seems that this unmanageable fracture in the world is the location of the near-mythical status of pressure groups—Greenpeace either as itself or through references to the Brent Spar saga appeared in 7 out of 22 sessions (the next runner-up was British Airways with four appearances). The New Dystopia is, therefore, the vision of the permanently fractured world, unpredictable, driven by emotion, and spinning on forever-new issues.

Comparing the characterisation of pressure groups and companies produced by one of the trainers reveals the fault line, as seen in Figure 15.2.

The comparison, couched in loaded terms, sets emotion (pressure groups) against reason and science (companies); but it also reveals respect and recognition, if perhaps grudging, for qualities which would be praised in a public relations expert: well-informed, flexible, creative, professional, innovative, high PR skills. At least two other trainers who in the course of their sessions referred to pressure groups showed the same mixture of loathing and recognition. PR professionals recognise pressure groups as fundamentally like themselves in that they draw

Pressure groups	Companies
single issue driven but coalitions building	driven by traditional market values
intolerant, manipulative, unscrupulous, self-righteous	tendency to decide–announce–defend policies
driven more by values and emotions than facts	understand science, understand relative risk
distrust of business (look for, enjoy conflict)	becoming more aware of stakeholders
well-informed	
international networking	
flexible, innovative, creative, professional, self-perpetuating campaigners	still instinctively closed and suspicious
news-creating, publicity-hungry, high PR skills, search for simple solutions	tendency to overclaim problems with projecting trust and values

FIGURE 15.2. Characteristics of pressure groups and companies (Training session, 3/8/98a).

their power from the same source—their ability to impose discursive control over issues, the sites of complex power struggles in public life. At the same time, practitioners recognise the existence of a fundamental difference; in the words of one of the trainers, "I find that when I'm describing pressure groups, I could be describing one of the more extreme religions" (Training session, 3/8/98a).

Similar sentiments were expressed by another experienced professional in his "Comment" column contributed to *PR Week* (Hamilton, 1998, p. 11) almost at the same time as the training session were taking place:

> Pressure groups derive their strength by tapping into people's worries and fears and promoting grass roots issues that strike deep chords in many of us [. . .] They have learnt about creating and refining messages [. . .] They often have a good, instinctive feel for [the] moral high ground. We are all at it.

Again, beyond the point of fundamental similarities, the world splits: on the one side lies the madness of "screaming abuse, bullying and harassment;" on the other is a complex world whose ambiguity can only be negotiated by honesty and courage, helped by "steady nerves and a clear head:"

> Cast the shadow of bedlam aside for an honest, balanced argument. Do not give up, fight back and become a responsible pressure group yourself. (Hamilton, 1998, p. 11)

It seems that to PR professionals, pressure groups are in some ways twisted, frightening reflections of themselves. It is tempting to conclude that the difference hinges on the stance towards what constitutes true public interest. Yet, it might be too simplistic: such an explanation presupposes the existence of one, shared worldview within the occupation. As will be shown, examining the way in which the occupation defines its professional problems and its jurisdictional tactics necessitates a more complex explanation.

Conceptual Frame

If the picture of the world serves as the background, the conceptual frame pinpoints the space which the occupation calls its own and from which is gazes out into the world. The conceptual frame calls together ideas and concepts, thus providing the occupation with a locus; it also directs the occupation's attention towards others and other conceptual frames in a bid to improve status and secure both existing and new markets for public relations services.

One way to understand public relations expertise is by attending to its location in the world of action (see Fig. 15.3).

It is situated between client interests, whatever the expert's particular relation with the client might be (organisational sphere), and the sphere of public knowledge and opinion (public sphere). For the time being, we shall refer to this domain as "effective messages" in order to reflect practitioners' understanding of their work as helping "clients put their message across effectively" (Training session, 20/7/98b). "Effective messages" straddle the boundary between the client and the general public. On the public side, public relations intervenes in matters of public knowledge and opinion, as seen in practitioners' explanations of their work as:

> . . . The creation and distribution of public attention. (Training session, 20/7/98a)

> Public opinion is increasingly a part of what we do. (Training session, 20/7/98a)

> Changing attitudes . . . is one of the most difficult parts of public relations. (Training session, 21/7/98a)

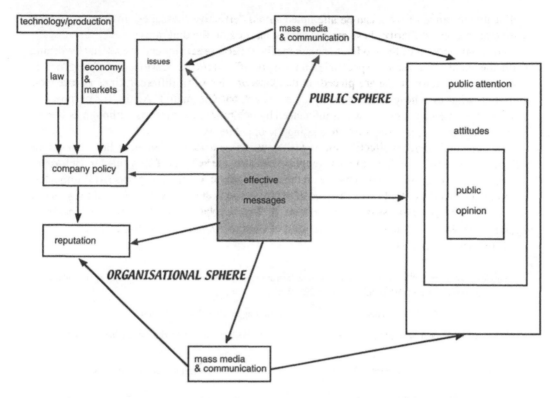

FIGURE 15.3. Public relations domain and lines of intervention.

"Issues" come into the model to represent the area of debate and struggle between different interests in society, and like the public relations domain itself, straddle the boundary between the public and the client side of the diagram.

On the company side of the model, issues are taken up by companies under social corporate responsibility, or broadly under company policy. The ultimate direction of efforts, however, goes to reputation—understood as a blend of business and non-business considerations (represented in the model by factors related to law, technology/production process, economy/markets, and issues). Practitioners, therefore, see their role in the following terms:

> Your responsibility is to advise your company . . . on the best policy. (Training session, 21/7/98b)

> Our work is to make sure that we know what needs to be communicated to protect the company's reputation. (Training session, 27/7/98a)

> Stakeholder philosophy [requires] the public relations function [to act] not just in its traditional box, but in tandem with other functions and close to the CEO, to co-ordinate knowledge management, correlating shareholder value and other business performance measures, such as productivity, innovation, quality, customer satisfaction with reputation, and developing methodologies for linking issues impacting on the company to company's involvement in broader activities than its traditional capitalist role. (Training session, 20/7/98a)

The lines of expert public relations intervention on the client side go to reputation, policy, and issues. Of course, all of these influence public relations while being influenced by it; they delineate the range of what can be attempted within "effective messages" in every particular case (for reasons of clarity, these arrows are not marked on the diagram).

The final element of the model, the mass media, reflects practitioners' views that "Working with the media is a major aspect of public relations" (Training session, 27/7/98a). Within the model, the mass media are placed on the boundary between different kinds of interests, although what or whose interests it represents is a debatable matter. Again, for purposes of clarity, mass media is only shown as influenced by public relations efforts, although as will be shown later, there is a strong influence going the opposite way.

As indicated above, "effective messages" is no more than a convenient label for public relations expertise, which is in fact a complex structure, the subject of this chapter. Before we move on to the examination of what lies at the core of public relations expertise, it is important to point out that the definition of the core of the expertise is driven by the needs of the practice and articulated as a process of differentiation. If "Public relations is about change" (Training session, 4/8/98b), it is about a particular kind of change, situated in the logic of management and organisational survival:

> Public relations must play more of an enabling role, instrumental in *strategic change and a source of sustainable success*. [emphasis added] (Training session, 20/7/98a)
>
> It is not about being "the organisation's conscience." (Training session, 30/7/98a), and
>
> What we do is deal with communication aspects ... [but] it's not my job to run the business. (Interview, 27/7/1998a)
>
> I employ [PR consultants] because they are communication specialists. (Training session, 6/8/98a)

Then again, if public relations is about communication, it has to be strategically understood communication:

> One reason why PR people have not managed to ascend to the company heights is because they have been so locked into the *communication process*. [emphasis added] (Training session, 21/7/98a)

At the core of public relations expertise lies an organisation understood as a sense of corporate self which is articulated and maintained in the face of a world full of challenges. This direction in the structuring of the expertise privileges the corporate entity but at the same time foregrounds the importance of the boundary between the corporate entity and its environment. The key concepts in this conceptual frame are: corporate identity, corporate culture, corporate reputation, and corporate image. Although extensive literature about them exists, of both a theoretical and applied nature, explanation or definitions did not seem of primary importance for trainers. Rather, systematic effort was made to link these concepts with others found in the managerial conceptual frame:

> Reputation management [is] the orchestration of discrete communications that are designed to protect your most valuable brand—your corporate reputation. (Training session, 20/7/98a)
>
> Management of reputation improves share value and acts as a crisis shield. (Training session, 20/7/98a)
>
> A strong sense of corporate identity is as important as slavish adherence to business unit financial results. (Training session, 21/7/98a)
>
> Nurturing corporate culture is useless unless the culture is aligned with a company's approach to competitiveness. (Training session, 21/7/98a)
>
> There is an almost straight line relationship between product recommendation and excellence of corporate image. (Training session, 21/7/98a)

The dynamic interlocking of knowledge (as a conceptual frame), its location in relation to other kinds of knowledge, and of action (as professional tools) is illustrated in Figure 15.4. The model is by no means a comprehensive map of public relations expertise, or even of its conceptual framework, but it captures the relationships between some of the key concepts, public relations tools, and their effects.

It is clear that the perspective adopted is that of looking from inside the company out towards others. Thus, the company's core are its employees, and around them the corporate culture and identity, which do not just exist but project towards "others," that is, stakeholders. They, on the other hand, have images of the company and form judgements about it, which are summarised as corporate reputation. In this symbolic realm, the organisational boundary is rather hazy, but it seems to lie in the area where identity and reputation overlap.

The other revealing fact in the above statements is the systematic juxtaposition of concepts from two different frames; the first dealing with the symbolic representation of the world, and the other; focused on the measurble, which has traditionally provided the managerial/business

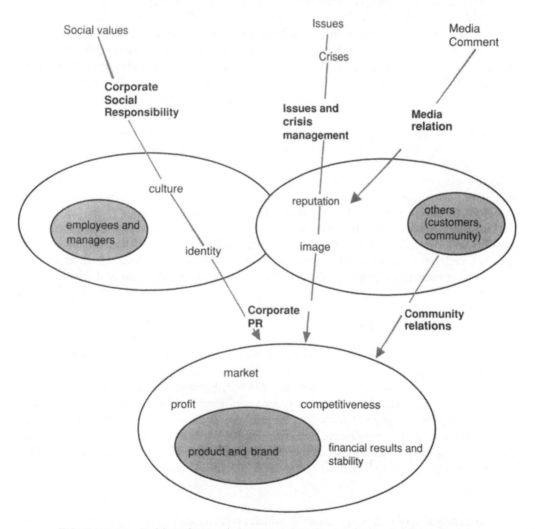

FIGURE 15.4. Public relations brings together the symbolic and the material.

raison d'être: reputation/share value; identity/financial result; culture/competitiveness; product/corporate image; and culture/brand. What this model also illustrates is the fact that this opposition is being abolished through expert action: the symbolic is stitched onto the material, with public relations tools being the metaphorical needle and thread in this process. We are, in effect, attempting to unravel the precise dynamics behind reputation strategy, explained by one of the trainers in the following way:

> The key notions are "thought leadership," "issue management," "share of mind" and "defining events" that are the building blocks of creating a reputation strategy. This thinking will be based on research among employees, customers, shareholders and "secondary" stakeholders. Phrases such as trust, responsibility, innovation, financial soundness, quality of products, vision of management and companies that other try to emulate. (Training session, 20/7/98a)

Reality and perception

An important element of public relations conceptual frame is the definition of reality. A clear ontological distinction is introduced: "not a fact, but . . . a perception" (Training session, 21/7/98b); "Perception, not reality" (Training session, 28/7/98b). Not only are perceptions and reality separate entities, but they are also different in nature: facts are hard and immutable; perceptions seem to have shape-shifting qualities—they can take on or be given different shapes. In the words of one of the practitioners, "It is possible to manipulate public perceptions, there is no doubt about it" (Training session, 28/7/98b). This quality of perception acquires a special significance for public relations practice when considered from a business point of view:

> Perceptions are a powerful fact in business, for example brand perceptions. There are few CEOs who realise that perceptions are outcomes of organised, planned action. (Training session, 20/7/98a)

A space is opened up, in terms of action and ideas, for public relations practice. If perceptions matter in business terms, then whatever their essence, they function like hard facts. It can, therefore, be said that "perception is reality" (Training session, 4/8/98a).

This simultaneous recognition and abolition of the difference between facts and perceptions not only underlies the conceptual effort of bringing together the symbolic and the material, but also of creating the space for occupational existence in the world of action, which as we have seen, lies between the fully open public sphere and the less accessible regions of organisational sphere.

Working Knowledge

Abstract knowledge has traditionally been regarded as one of the distinctive features of professions, but as it has been pointed out in the introduction, a profession normally has two different types of knowledge at its disposal: abstract, book knowledge produced by scholars; and practical, working knowledge used by practitioners. Here we are concerned specifically with the second type of knowledge, the everyday professional knowledge of practitioners. In public relations, this professional, working knowledge is made up of three elements: professional tools; problems to which these tools are applied; and, in the words of one of the trainers, "truths which we hold to be self-evident" (Training session, 27/7/98a).

Problems

An examination of real life problems to which professional knowledge is applied provides important information about the profession's jurisdiction as well as an insight into the process of professional diagnosis. The latter can be understood as a two-step operation of colligation and classification. Colligation, defined as "the assembly of a 'picture' of the client" (Abbott, 1988, p. 41), is a selective translation of real life into the profession's language—it therefore looks back to the conceptual frame; classification serves as a way of linking such pictures to professional solutions (treatments) by placing them in a category of recognised problems. As such, classification looks forward to what we call here professional tools. Although separated in this explanation, colligation and classification tend to be interdependent.

In order to reflect these different relationships between professional problems, knowledge, and reality, a two-step analysis has been performed on the Sword of Excellence case studies. First, objectives of work listed in each campaign were coded on the basis of the language used by practitioners (for details, see Pieczka, 2000). The aim of such an analysis was to reveal the presence of conceptual dimensions in the practice. In the second phase, problems have been defined on the basis of the information contained in the introductory parts of the cases which precede the statement of objectives chosen for a campaign. Such background information usually deals with the industry background, relevant history of the organisation or issue that lies at the heart of the campaign, specific market, or legislation. Analysing this information in connection with the objectives that follow has revealed the main thrust of the public relations effort in each case. Consequently, a professional problem is defined here as practitioners' identification of the object towards which their overall professional effort is directed in a given case.

In theoretical terms, one could argue that in public relations case histories, colligation is achieved through the information presented in the background and partly through objectives. The latter, by focussing on what needs to be achieved—for example, increasing knowledge or changing attitudes—hint at rather than name the professional problem and trigger the use of specific tools.

The analysis has revealed the existence of 10 types of objectives: Awareness, Image, Knowledge, Credibility, Involvement, Action, Sales/Financial, Framing Issues: Professional, and Instrumental. Except for the Instrumental and Professional categories, the typology was driven strongly by the language used and consequently focused around concepts such as awareness, image, sales, and profit. Professional objectives—which include statements about "launch[ing] the campaign to the general public," balancing "a national media strategy with a regional programme," or ensuring that communication is timely (employees get the news first) and within the regulatory limits set for mergers and takeovers—are concerned with the ways in which the solution is to be achieved, that is, with the characteristics of professional tools used. Examples of the instrumental objectives include statements about the need to: "promote the Commission's new policies," "present strong factual arguments in favor of a tax freeze," "demonstrate the advantages and application of the material," and so on. Such objectives define action in local rather than abstract terms (e.g., awareness, attitude). As such, they fail to classify the problem (Pieczka, 2000, p. 227). There are a number of possible explanation of this practice: poor diagnostic skills on the part of the practitioner, poorly developed professional classification system; alternatively, instrumental objectives could be seen as the extreme end of the diagnostic process, leaning firmly towards tools to be used.

In terms of their prevalence, the most frequently set objectives are Professional; followed by Instrumental, Action, Image, Sales/Financial, and Awareness. The popularity of these types of objectives is even clearer when we look at the proportion of campaigns in which they are used: approximately a third of all the campaigns studied used Professional and Action objectives (31% and 30%, respectively) and round a quarter of the campaigns included Awareness and Image objectives (28% and 25%, respectively). If campaign objectives refer to professional tasks, then the biggest task for public relations practitioners is to act professionally. Other sizeable tasks are the stimulation of desired behaviour, knowledge, or symbolic representation behaviour and public impression management (Action, Awareness, and Image; see Pieczka, 2000, pp. 226–227).

The analysis of campaign objectives has thus revealed both the conceptual skeleton of the practice and the collaborative effort of the practitioners and their occupational body to construct the meaning of professional practice. Extending the analysis in order to find the focus of work in each case has revealed six types of broad problem areas tackled in public relations practice: product promotion, profile work, corporate identity and culture, lobbying, public or health information campaigns, and presentation of special(ist) interests.

Product promotion taken literally is a somewhat misleading label; in fact, it covers efforts directed primarily at commercial promotion, that is, promotion with a financial gain in sight, of things conceived of as saleable commodity, for example: Magnesium-OK, a dietary supplement (The Public Relations Business, 1990); independent financial advice as sold by members of the Independent Financial Adviser Promotion scheme (Lansons Communications, 1994); less familiar species of fish, in order to manage the market for cod and haddock while the fishing quotas were restricted (Paragon Communications, 1992); Smirnoff as a brand (The Rowland Company, 1994b); Vodafone, as a new service provider, of a new service in an entirely new market—mobile cellular radio communications in 1986 (Racal, 1987). A clearly identifiable problem subset is represented by campaigns dealing with flotations (TSB Group plc, 1987), privatisation (Dewe Rogerson, 1985; 1997), and share issues (Valin Pollen International, 1990), that is, selling a very particular kind of commodity (shares) in a tightly regulated market.

Profile as a kind of professional problem refers to efforts directed at shaping the way— the actual terms—in which a client organisation is perceived publicly. One of the most direct examples of such an effort is the sponsorship of pub theatre awards by Guinness, in which a key objective reads: "to link Guinness with innovation and creativity, the key qualities of Guinness advertising" (Guinness plc, 1997, p. 43). Profile work, however, does not necessarily tie the client organisation in such a direct way to specified qualities. For example, in 1994 North West Water conducted a fund-raising campaign for WaterAid, the water industry charity engaged in supply of safe water and sanitation to communities in Africa and Asia. Although the only company-directed objective in the case was to do with encouraging teamwork, looking at the actual tools used (community outreach programme, appeal to customers, sponsored events) it becomes clear that, as it is stated in the final, evaluation section of the case, "North West Water has benefited too, from . . . the positive public relations generated from campaign activities" (North West Water, 1995, p. 28). If these examples show how profile work may address itself to qualities the client organisation wishes to associate with itself, the campaign conducted by Barnardo's in 1995 shows that profile work may also be used to inform the public about the organisation's core activities:

> Fourth of July 1995 marked the 150th birthday of Thomas Barnardo: a unique opportunity to raise profile as well as a PR challenge. At the beginning of the year, six out of ten people thought—wrongly—that Barnardo's ran homes for orphans. The strategy was to use the birthday to close the chapter on the children's home and focus attention on Barnardo's modern work. (Barnardo's, 1996, p. 30)

Finally, profile work is also used defensively and on behalf of not just individual organisations but wider, industry interests. A good example in hand is the 1986 campaign for the Chemical Industries Association (1987). Entitled "Chemicals are good for you," the case narrative begins in the following way:

> The chemical industry is one of Britain's most successful manufacturing sectors. [. . .] its products supply every other industry and are essential to modern society. Yet public evaluation of the chemical industry is poor

in terms of both familiarity and favourability. [...] Industry Year 1986 presented the ideal opportunity for chemical companies to win the goodwill of their local communities by a programme of events linked with the year's overall objectives. (Chemical Industries Association, 1987, p. 25)

The next problem area, *corporate identity and culture*, deals ultimately with employee motivation. The need for this kind of work may arise either out of structural changes which the organisation is undergoing, such as merges, takeovers, and new business development; or it may be linked to changes in work practices. An example of the first is the campaign prepared by public relations teams in Grand Metropolitan and Guinness when the two were merging to form Diageo (Diageo, 1998). The campaign spanned 6 months from the time immediately preceding the public announcement of the proposed merger till the time when the merger was formally completed. The campaign was clearly aimed at managing attitudes and behaviour of 85,000 employees all over the world by providing information about the proposed change, dealing with feelings of job insecurity, managing share price sensitive information, and keeping the normal operations going under these special circumstances. A more straightforward example of culture reengineering is illustrated by one of the winning campaigns of 1990, "Focus on the Customer" (ICI Paints, 1990). In the context of "dramatic restructuring" of the paints market:

The only way ICI Paints can respond is to be better than them [competitors] at meeting customer needs. The broad objectives are: to bring about a service orientated culture [...], to ensure that employees understand and subscribe to the concept of "internal customer" and to recognise that the quality of service that reaches the customer begins with the quality of service that people inside the company give each other. (ICI Paints, 1990, p. 11)

Lobbying refers here to efforts expanded in the public and political arena in order to change or prevent changes in the law, for example, regulating divorce (Fishburn Hedges, 1996) or taxation (Daniel J Edelman Ltd, 1987; Edelman PR Network, 1991); to influence government decisions about to be made, for example, on the disbandment of a military regiment (Quadrant Public Relations, 1992); or awarding of a big contract (The Rowland Company, 1994a). Although the cases mentioned so far focused on the national level of decision making, lobbying can also cut across the various levels of administration; for example, the operator of the port in Ramsgate embarked on a campaign in 1993 (Westminster Advisers, 1997) targeting local (Kent County Council), national (Westminster), and European (Brussels) levels of government—the first to seek a planning permission for building an access road, and the remaining two to attract funding for the project.

The remaining two problem areas are more difficult to define, perhaps because there was not enough information available to work from as they were the two smallest categories in this data set. Public information or health campaigns are represented by only six cases: two cases dealing with health issues, first aid (St John Ambulance, 1994) and breast cancer (Breast Cancer Care, 1998); the remaining four dealing with matters of public importance, or to put it differently, matters about which the public should be told. Out of the latter four, two are explained by the client organisation's statutory obligation to communicate—Cardiff Bay Barrage Act of 1993 in "Groundwater Protection Scheme" (Quadrant Public Relations, 1995); Wildlife and Countryside Act 1981 in "The Countryside Access Charter" (Charles Barker Lyons, 1986). The two remaining public information campaigns—informing the public about the introduction of a new coin (Shandwick Communications, 1993) and recruiting members of Children's Panel in Scotland, a body which deals, instead of the Juvenile Court, with certain types of young offenders (Strathclyde Regional Council, 1985)—seem to have a very strong public expectation attached to them as far as the appropriate dissemination of information is concerned. The health campaigns, conducted on behalf of charitable organisations, could be partially construed as profile work; on the other hand, their interest in matters of public health makes them similar to government-funded health campaigns (not represented in the data set). Thus, the common denominator in these campaigns appears to be public interest.

The final category of professional problems identified, presentation of specialist interests, is even more tentative than health and public information, but important nevertheless. As a category, it is very small (four cases) and a rag-bag of campaigns that could not be easily identified with any of the above problems: a campaign to promote a breed of dogs, to raise awareness of Feng Shui, to generate more interest for the government's Investors in People scheme, and finally to raise money for a local hospital. Of particular interest are the first two: they can be seen as promoting a cause, that is, make people take an interest in what is being promoted on the basis of its intrinsic values; they are broadly targeted; and there is no organisational muscle or financial resources behind the campaigns. Although in numerical terms, these specialist interest campaign barely register in the institutional account of PR excellence, they are important as an illustration of the uses to which public relations expertise can be put.

Two concluding points can be made here. First of all, in broad terms public relations deals with discourse about commodities, identities, and action, both on the level of the individual (customer, employee) and public institutions (policy). As the same areas are ploughed by other occupations, for example, marketers or advertisers, professional problems on their own cannot function as the sole base of professional differentiation for public relations. Second, the institutional account presented through the winning case studies shows product promotion and profile work (70% of all cases) as the prominent area of work. At the same time we have seen how the conceptual frame privileges an organisational perspective and concepts such as identity or reputation while attempting to imbue them with a commercial sense. It could be said that knowledge and work cannot be properly understood in separation from markets in which they are sold.

Tools

This element of public relations expertise can be understood as a repository of information about professional tools. It contains basic descriptions of all the tools as well as more detailed information about their structure, about how to apply them, and about the effects they may produce. PR tools appear to differ in their complexity and the types of outcomes they are meant to produce. Thus, we have a group of tools used to produce artefacts and events, for example: press release, pitch, press conference, photocall, corporate literature, speech writing. These may often be referred to as skills. Then there is a group of more complex tools, for example, issue management, investor relations, public affairs, media relations, internal communication, reputation management, and so one. These tools are otherwise seen as public relations specialisms, recognising the fact that they are larger structures, sold as programmes or campaigns in separate markets. Finally, there is a smaller group of tools used specifically for analytical purposes. These tend to have less standardised, more descriptive names, for example: "prioritising stakeholder demands," "reviewing internal tactics in issue management," "What information do employees want?," "assess your success," "media will ask three questions," "issue life cycle," "examine corporate behaviour."

Except for the analytical tools which serve as ways of organising information and illuminating problems, there is a strong common feature shared by public relations tools: they are understood and presented as a series of steps to be taken in providing a professional solution to a public relations problem. Their structure and application overlap with explanations given by the trainers, for example: "media interviews preparation: know your messages, research the journalist, anticipate difficult questions, think about responses in advance" (Training session, 28/7/98b). Occasionally, however, there may be additional information available specifically about application, that is, points to bear in mind while using a tool. For example, one of the trainers produced the following checklist for employee communication: "senior management commitment; clear objectives and purposeful; honest, truthful and non-patronising; communication medium in tune with the purpose and the message; regular; is it working?" Although there is a sense of structuring still present, the central point of this statement focuses on the qualities which should be built into an employee communication campaign.

Searching for the common denominator, we can say that tools are not only sequences of steps, but also largely the same sequence which can be summarised as situation analysis, objective setting, developing a strategy, and assessment of the work carried out (evaluation). This structure operates both for simple tools, like press releases, and for complex large programmes, like reputation management:

> Creating news releases: planning, content, style, checking. (Training session, 4/8/98b)

> Managing reputation consists of: understanding your environment, players, constraints/resources; setting goals (research); implementation, evaluation (research). (Training session, 20/7/98a)

Beyond structure and application, the tools repository also contains information about the effects produced by the tools. For example, the purposes to which corporate communication is put are listed as:

> [to] increase awareness; correct misimpressions, project truths, establish links, create climate of opinion; increase new product acceptability; develop influence; enhance morale. (Training session, 28/7/98b)

Finally, public relations tools rely on what is known in marketing as segmentation, and they aim at proactive management of the environment. Segmentation, more commonly known in public relations as "targeting," is a technique of breaking audiences into a number of more tightly defined groups relevant to the problem at hand in order to craft communication so that it takes account of the specific characteristics of these groups. Proactive approach to environment is aimed primarily at landscaping the organisation's environment in order to gain more control over public relations problems it might face.

To see how this repository works, let us take one tool, issues management, and follow the different types of information available about it. First of all, the tool is identified as such: "Issues management is something to have in your toolkit" (Training session, 3/8/98a), and then defined properly "Issue management is a disciplined business strategy to identify and understand external factors that influence organisation's relationship with stakeholders; identify sources and audience concerns of these factors; adjust communication and corporate behaviour to protect/enhance corporate reputation with these audiences" (Training session, 3/8/98a).

Although there is a sense of structure already present in this definition, a more explicit step-by-step explanation is also available:

> [Issue management] strategies: map the issues environment (understand the science); identify and prioritise publics; identify third parties, address internal processes and policies, prepare plan and timing, establish dialogue, communicate, monitor. (Training session, 3/8/98a)

Each of these steps is then broken down into another series of steps to be followed, producing, in effect, a very detailed manual. Additional information available to practitioners about issue management gives it an analytical framework for understanding the dynamics, or life cycle, of issues ("potential, emerging, current, crisis, dormant"). There are also points on application, not obvious from the basic structure of the tool, but crucial to the effects produced:

> Tactics: meet majority of criticism, satisfy moderate campaigners, isolate extremists. (Training session, 3/8/98a)

> Refocus the issue: challenge the emphasis, restate the problem, build new coalitions, help them to publicise their position, conduct research. (Training session, 3/8/98a)

Truths

In addition to professional knowledge encompassed in the problems and tools, public relations professionals are also guided in their practice by "truths which we hold to be self-evident." These truths are about public relations work and its effects, about others and the world. As a category, they are therefore clearly connected to the picture of the world and the conceptual frame; where they differ is in their form and complexity. Truths often sound like maxims, in that they are simple and so obvious as to be taken for granted. For example:

> Build goodwill before you need it. (Training session, 28/8/98b)

> Talk straight and simple. (Training session, 28/8/98b)

> Issues affect survival. (Training session, 3/8/98a)

> Green protesters can affect share prices of companies they target. (Training session, 3/8/98a)

Both the picture of the world and the conceptual frame incorporate elements of argument, reasoning, or abstract thinking; truths do not. They represent the level of knowledge which is least open to reasoning, discussion, or manipulation; maxims can be seen as unobtrusive instruments of teaching or inculcation (cf. Bourdieu, 1992, pp. 73–75 on the transmission of "practical mastery").

REPRODUCTION OF EXPERTISE

So far, this chapter has been devoted to describing public relations expertise. This final section takes a step back to investigate the process which has delivered the expertise to the trainees and to the researcher. The argument developed consistently through this chapter is that professional expertise is a complex structure integrating professional group interests arising out of a combination of socioeconomic factors, professional working knowledge, and action. So far this argument has been advanced by mapping out that particular structure in the way summarised briefly in the introduction to this chapter.

Here further evidence to support that argument is garnered from 13 interviews with the trainers. Our knowledge of public relations expertise will therefore be extended not only by reflecting practitioners' own understandings of what it is, but also by showing the role of reproduction in the actual production of the professional expertise. The specific areas of interest here are: understanding the meaning of the distinction between theory and practice clearly articulated by the trainers; understanding how trainers approach preparing for, in other words, constructing their sessions and therefore constructing specific bites of expertise for their audience's consumption.

Theory Versus Practice

In this section we return to the distinction made by theorists between professional knowledge and professional action, mentioned at the beginning of this chapter. If a profession is defined by its ability to apply abstract knowledge to real-life problems, then the nature of connections between knowledge and action, as well as connections between abstract knowledge and real-life situations, must be of crucial importance to the profession and its practitioners. Indeed, it comes out loud and clear from the way in which the interviewees consistently juxtapose textbook (theoretical) knowledge with operating in the "real world" and being "practical": we frequently deal with people who [. . .] can quote you theory after theory and all the book titles, but what they do not do is apply (Interview, 3/8/98b).

Thus, knowledge and action are not only different, but also may be entirely disconnected. Knowledge (theory) is "rigorous" and comprehensive, it speaks its own language, and it also seems to describe the world in such a way that information crucial to actually operating in the world is lost. Practice, or the real world, on the other hand, is shaped by time demands: "we are not going to have some fancy textbook or chart, in the real world we don't have the time" (Interview, 23/7/98a).

If there is no time to reflect, unambiguous direction for action is necessary, but

one of the difficulties [with] too many books is that you lose your sense of direction. (Interview, 28/7/98a

Real life is also about "commercial realities" and understanding "what business is all about." To sum up, being practical means possessing the ability to relate to the world through appropriate action. In a training situation, it is a source of trainer's credibility, as illustrated by the following mini-story about a trainer who was not being practical:

And [I] said to them when he'd finished, "What did you think of that?" [. . .] "It's not reality." "It's not based in fact." "It's not what it's like in the real world." [. . .] and he'd just died on his feet because they wouldn't believe him. His idea might be all right in the classroom, it might be all right on paper, it might be all right in a book—it just does not translate into reality. Can you take it back to the work place? (Interview, 3/8/98b)

Thus, if action and knowledge are to be linked at all it is through heuristic strategies delivered in training which select and translate abstract ideas into "handleable" tools. Training, however, is not conceived solely in these terms. In fact, trainers have given a whole range of objectives they planned to achieve.

Constructing Training

Figure 15.5 shows the range of factors trainers routinely take into account while preparing to deliver a training session; the model also shows how these factors are connected in the planning process. However, it is important to state that for the process the work not all the factors represented in the diagram have to be taken into consideration by an individual trainer.

Some of the logic behind the factors shown on the diagram from "Previous training or writing" through to "Interactive character of session," as well as their sequencing is clearly explained by the following statement:

I started with the framework content which is fairly standard. I did an article a couple of years ago on the same subject. The subject area is one with which I'm extremely familiar. [. . .] but it was also very clear that part of what I needed to do was to set it up in such a way as to encourage interaction. [. . .] I sat down with that

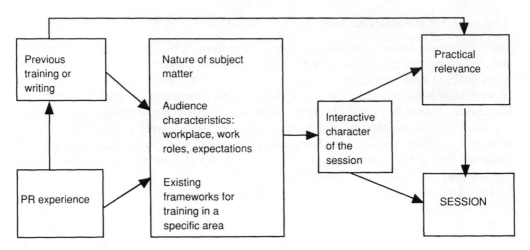

FIGURE 15.5.   Model of trainers' approach to delivering training sessions.

framework and argued with myself which were the best cases to use in order to get the maximum interaction.
[...] It was just about finding the right illustration to get people to participate. (Interview, 27/7/98a)

Let us now follow the final, and perhaps the most important, link in our model, that of the interactive character of training and its practical relevance to trainees. Relevance is understood here as the immediate applicability of what is learned to the trainees' "own experience or their own operation [organisation] or geographic context" (Interview, 30/7/97a). However, showing how general principles apply to particular situations is as much the trainer's as it is the trainee's job, with both sides actively participating in the process:

> You can put quite a lot of charts up until you go blue in the face with diagrams, principles, and so forth, but so
> much of it is actually thinking through problems. I must have mentioned common sense about sixteen times,
> it is actually about common sense being applied to problems. And therefore you have to encourage people to
> think that through for themselves (Interview, 23/7/98a)

Relevance and interactivity appear bound together in a kind of professional common sense which, in fact, is a joint effort on the part of the trainer and the trainee to redefine the world in terms of their specific professional expertise and therefore make it amenable to expert intervention. As such, training is nothing like the conveyer belt of knowledge suggested by "reproduction of expertise," but rather it appears as a joint, creative effort in which the expertise is as much produced as it is reproduced. Put simply by one of the trainers, "you often learn something yourself, which is quite fun" (Interview, 23/7/98a).

CONCLUSION

The main aim of this chapter has been to unpack PR expertise by setting aside expectations of its scientific or rational nature. The model of expertise constructed here is organised not through scientific classification of problems and theories, as textbooks might do, but by attending to practitioners' needs and uses to which concepts, ideas, and practical schemes are put. Public relations expertise is constituted and transmitted through practice. It is a complex interactive structure organised through past experience and current exigencies, which exists and modifies itself through action, that is, professional work and training. As such, it is strategic in its nature. Its conceptual frame includes concepts, not only because they might translate into useful tools, but also because they offer a professional/commercial *lingua franca*, a language understood by other important occupational groups, notably managers. It is supported by a broader and looser structure, the picture of the world, akin to a worldview. This is a more or less conscious reflection on the world as it presents itself to the practitioner. The picture of the world is thus a collage of ideas and facts already in public circulation, but equally importantly, accessible from the practitioner's location in the world of commercial interests. Truths, on the other hand, represent the taken-for-granted. They encapsulate values and norms as well as directions to appropriate professional behaviour. Truths construct what one might call the professional instinct.

Public relations expertise appears as practical knowledge, that is, knowledge which resonates with the practitioner's experience. This working knowledge must offer structured ways of acting which appear rational and effectual. Its persuasiveness is a crucial feature: working knowledge must present a convincing potential for successful enactment of the professional role to practitioners and, through them, to their clients. If professional training is unambiguously concerned with the practicality of the professional expertise, it is quite opaque in the way in which it deals with other kinds of claims relevant to professional knowledge, for example, its predictive nature. The role played by the esoteric, abstract knowledge is consequently not very prominent.

16

"Chemistry" and the Public Relations Industry: An Exploration of the Concept of Jurisdiction and Issues Arising

Magda Pieczka
Stirling Media Research Institute

"We feel we could work with these people"

The starting point for this chapter is the concept of *jurisdiction*, that is, tasks claimed by a profession and the way in which the claim is made. This concept was build into a theoretical framework explaining how professions exist and change by Abbott (1988). To simplify, one could say that a profession is defined by its jurisdiction: the work it does and whatever social or legal recognition it can win to claim that particular set of tasks. To be able to hold on to a jurisdiction, a profession requires a system of knowledge capable of supporting successful professional work, but it also requires public acceptance of this expertise and a certain public image helping to secure such approval. A profession in practice can be seen as constituted by constant competition: expertise, standard practices, and social standing are weapons used to secure the most advantageous outcome. A jurisdiction is also never completely safe as a challenge might come at any time driven by changes in neighbouring occupational jurisdictions, or by technological or legal change. From this point of view, we cannot talk about the public relations profession in a general sense, but need to take account of the competitive and time-dependent nature of this phenomenon.

This chapter examines public relations jurisdiction in Great Britain in the late 1990s. The main interest pursued here is to anchor public relations jurisdiction in the broader environment and to reconnect practitioners' routine practices with the forces and factors to which they as a profession need to respond. The approach taken in this chapter aims to answer three broad questions: How do public relations consultants get and deliver their work? What factors influence the process? Finally, how do the exigencies of routine work and conditions under which it is carried out influence the occupation in its self-identity and its behaviour?

A range of empirical material has been utilised to answer these two questions: interviews with practitioners conducted during fieldwork in a PR consultancy in January/February 1997;

observation of a professional training course in July/August 1998; and analysis of the relevant trade magazines—specifically *PR Week*—as a reflection of the topical issues, opinions, and attitudes.

The chapter consists of three sections. The first one focuses on routine elements of public relations practice, pitching and client management, as they are experienced by the individual practitioner. This section draws attention to the importance of what is often referred to as "intangibles," or "chemistry" between the practitioner and the client. It is claimed that PR practice is understood by practitioners in two, apparently contradictory, ways: one relies on the discourse of professionalism and instrumental rationality; the other evades such descriptions and emphasises the role of intuitive judgements and interpersonal relations. The second part of the chapter takes up the theme of the occupation's split personality and pursues it at the level of group action designed to counteract the occupation's weaknesses resulting from this unsettled identity. Two important debates are analysed here, about evaluation and regulation of the industry. If the first of these is an example of a tactic designed to improve the occupation's standing, particularly when competing against other occupations, the second one makes the point about the importance of wide public acceptance for public relations. The final section develops the point of the importance of the symbolic, reputation capital for the public relations occupation. The theme is pursued by analysing the representation and careers of practitioners who are thrust into the public eye (mass media) more than others due to the nature of their work or clients they serve.

GETTING AND DELIVERING THE WORK

Public relations practitioners work in two main work settings: in-house, in a range of commercial, public, and voluntary organisation; and in consultancy, either as employees of a consulting firm or as freelancers, working on their own. This section focuses primarily on consultancy for two reasons. First, studying public relations as a service sold in a competitive market to clients who need to be convinced about its effectiveness helps to focus on the presentation and value of public relations expertise. Second, little attention has been given to public relations consultancy in the existing literature. Writing about the emergence of the sector in the UK in 1948-1969, L'Etang commented on the "noticeable silence" (L'Etang, 2001, p. 101) in the literature about how the consultancy worked and, more generally, about its jurisdiction of work. At the same time, she pointed out the importance of the consultancy for the entire occupation:

> Within the context of professionalisation the establishment of consultancy services is of particular interest because specialists who serve clients represent an essential and concentrated form of the practice. They could be seen as standard-bearers for the occupation and owners of the knowledge systems that underpin practice. (L'Etang, 2001, p. 105)

Both observations still hold. Public relations seems to have been studied either generically as "practice" without clear distinctions being made between two sites of work, in-house and consultancy, or by focusing on the in-house practitioners. This chapter aims to help redress the balance.

THE PITCH

There appear to be two main ways in which consultants obtain clients and work: through a competitive pitch for an account or appointment with no pitch involved. The first is routinely used, especially for work considered by the client as substantial, both in terms of importance and expense. The latter usually depends on an existing level of knowledge and trust between the two parties from previous work, or a credible recommendation. The pitch is important in two ways: it is the first step in the client/consultant relationship; and it involves a necessary business risk: the cost involved in preparing a pitch more often than not has to be written off a loss, as there is approximately only a one in four or one in five chance of winning the account.

The pitch may be set for new work a client requires, or be part of a review process of either an existing account or an entire public relations area. PRCA guidelines for managing the pitch included in a *PR Week* feature on "a painless pitch process" offer a useful starting point:

PRCA Guidelines: dos and don'ts of agency reviews

- Don't ask more than five agencies to pitch.
- Establish what you want from your agencies before briefing them.
- Make sure that all agencies are given the same brief.
- Don't arrange for agencies to pitch if you are not serious about appointing one—don't just trawl the market for ideas.
- Don't expect detailed recommendations unless you are willing to pay for them.
- Don't ask an incumbent agency to repitch if you have already decided to ditch it.
- Don't drag out the pitch process. Make a decision as fast as you can.
- Have the courtesy to tell unsuccessful firms why they failed to get your business. (Gray, 1996b)

The process is managed on the client side either by a senior in-house PR specialist, or— particularly if there is no such post—by marketing, human resource managers, or even the CEO. In training, the process was described as starting with the identification of the specific needs for which a consultant should be appointed and then the putting together of a "long list" of possible agencies. This may either be done using existing listings (e.g., PRCA) or recommendations and previous experience. Assessing agency credentials is part of the process. Good practice here was summarised in training as:

What do we need to know about the consultancy before we appoint them: references, levels of experience, financial situation, size, basis for fee, evidence of previous work, ownership structure, CVs of key people, membership of professional bodies, awards won. (Training session 6/8/98a)

Very importantly, in the view of one of the experienced in-house practitioners, "you go to see them" for the presentation of credentials, and you refuse to give a brief at this stage: "otherwise they'll dig up everything they've ever done for your sector because they think they should prove to you their knowledge rather than present themselves, how they work" (Training session 6/8/98a).

The brief, offered to the shortlisted agencies, is the launchpad for the proposal presented to the client; in other words, it is the trigger for the expert analysis and solution. In reality, consultancies often complain about being given a poor brief, for example: "[. . .] one page briefs typed on Victorian typewriters [or] documents of 20 pages that look more like legal briefs" (R. Palmer, 1996). A more recent DTI-IPR study shows that the quality of the brief given by client organisations was rated by 75% of consultants as poor to mediocre (1–3 on a 6-point scale), as opposed to 25% as good to excellent (4–6 on a 6-point scale). Common problems included: lack of objectives; unrealistic expectations; failure to take account of the realities of programme planning; clients' lack of PR experience and business communications skills; standard procurement templates, notably in the public sector; and lack of a broad appreciation of PR issues. As a result, consultancies often have to educate clients in PR and the preparation of briefing documents (DTI and IPR, 2003, p. 34). Clients, for their part, judge pitches on a number of criteria—of which the actual response to the brief, that is, the display of expert knowledge, is only one: "Factors in judging competitive pitches: understanding of the brief, overall quality of response; budget/cost management; quality of the actual account team; account handling, chemistry" (Training session 6/8/98a).

So, at the very point of entry, the differing interests and resulting tensions between clients and consultants become apparent. At this stage, given the expense of mounting a pitch, the pitching consultancy will be focused on minimising the risk. The attention seems to have been focused, one might say paradoxically, not on the expert substance of what is proposed, but on presentation skills and beyond, on impression management. A set of telling connections is revealed in the following excerpt from a *PR Week* feature, which offers a brief historical background to this aspect of the practice. Businesses emerged from the recession of the early 1990s with a tighter grip on the cost base, including the purchase of PR services, which in turn led to more competitive pitching:

> Client companies are leaner and meaner and far more discerning. The retainers of the 1980s have been replaced by ad hoc projects and PR practitioners find themselves facing an increasing number of their peers in competitive pitches. As a result, more pressure is put on the pitch presentation. Time out of the office is expensive. Pitching for new business is time spent without earning fees. So what can be done to ensure a decent success rate from the client presentation to justify these costs and grow the business? (M. Smith, 1996)

As a result, the attention moved beyond the look of the presentation to its feel—the notorious, and somewhat magical, "chemistry."

> It is commonly accepted that even in the hi-tech 1990s no matter how flash the audio visuals and how well cut the suit at the final presentation, if the chemistry is missing from the first handshake, so is the business. (M. Smith, 1996).

It may sound somewhat vague, but there is no doubt about the crucial role of "chemistry" in selling PR services:

> There is this whole issue of intangibility of PR [...] chemistry is such an important factor. The clients who had appointed us were the ones who said they like us, they could work with us. [...] The decision-making process is "We feel we could work with these people." (Interview, 4/2/1997)

> Do [I] feel comfortable with these people? [Do] I feel comfortable that they should represent me [?] (Training session 6/8/98a)

> When I ask companies what made them choose one public relations consultancy over another, they usually tell me it was because they liked the people and felt they could work with them. The proposals might have been equally creative, the credentials evenly matched, but it was the personal chemistry that tipped the balance. (Stuart, 1996)

For consultants, "chemistry" may work partly as a substitute for detailed expert advice, which at this stage has not yet been paid for, while for clients it functions as a guarantee that an appropriate service will be obtained. There is a clear indication in the PRCA guidelines quoted above that asking agencies to pitch might be used as a cheap way of getting expert advice ("trawling for ideas"). According to a *PR Week* editorial, having your ideas "plagiarised" was a "long running complaint of agencies" ("Pitching for a fairer deal," 1996). The problem was succinctly laid out in a comment piece:

> Agencies pitching for new clients have always been on shaky ground. Do you lay all your cards on the table and risk your ideas being pinched and reproduced without you being hired, or do you hold back and risk not getting the account because you didn't demonstrate what you're capable of? It is a thin line and most agencies—particularly small ones—don't know which side of it they should be on. (Hamlett, 1998)

This state of affairs reveals a weakness on the part of the industry: while copyright protection could not be extended to pitches ("ideas" themselves are not protected), the evidence of the 1990s shows the industry's inability to introduce a standard solution obeyed by all agencies, which may require putting the industry's interests before commercial interests of an individual agency in any given pitch. When the Irish industry body (PRCA Ireland) introduced new rules imposing a charge for submission of creative proposals, a *PR Week* editorial claimed that such a solution could not be imposed in the UK:

> Attempts to introduce such diktats [payment for creative pitches] in the UK have floundered—mainly because there are more agencies outside the industry associations than within them, and, despite a return to growth, most are still feeling the pressure to undercut rivals where they can. ("Pitching for a fairer deal," 1996)

One reason for the agencies' vulnerability was the competitive nature of the market, undermining their ability to act as a group;[1] another was the nature of the services provided. Although in many respects the public relations consultancy industry is comparable to advertising (it employs the idea of creativity), it is not a creative industry in the sense of being based on the creation and exploitation of intellectual property, as the official definition used in the UK has it (Department of Culture, Media and Sport, 2001). In this respect, public relations consultancy is more akin to a traditional professional service—providing a diagnosis and treatment derived from a body of expert knowledge. A lawyer or doctor is paid for the ability to identify the client's problem as a specific medical or legal problem to which an appropriate solution can be applied. They may be paid for offering the same solution in innumerable cases. The expert solution is not protected by copyright; the fee is derived from the application of existing, publicly accessible knowledge.

Thus, the kind of knowledge that lies at the core of the occupation's expertise has profound implications for the way in which the occupation acts and presents itself. In recent years, as we shall see later in this chapter, the issue of measurability of results and of articulating a body of knowledge that can be employed with predictable results has come to occupy an important place on the industry's agenda. At the same time, however, references to "chemistry," "art," or "intangibles" persist, revealing other possibilities, other identities which public relations can or has assumed in the past.

---

[1]On 23 August 1996, *PR Week* printed a letter from Colin Thompson, a PRCA Financial Consultant, reminding readers of the PRCA guidelines on charging for creative pitches introduced in 1993. The only statement that can be read as a comment on the actual practice was "While the majority of consultancies are not members they are in essence averaging small incomes, with obvious expectations, even so the PRCA represents 80 per cent of the fee income for the industry. The cost of creative pitches can be very expensive and to expect consultancies invited to pitch as one of five, or even more, with odds of 5:1 or worse, can be a major strain on profitability which is one reason why so many consultancies who are here today will not be here tomorrow." The letter seems to hint that bigger, more powerful agencies do follow the guidelines. On balance, however, the extent of this practice remains unclear.

CLIENT RELATIONS

Client–consultant relationships (client relations, for short) are usually understood as those between an outside consultant and a client organisation. For the client organisation, the relationship is seen as a generic management of a supplier. It is framed by an articulation of "advantages: objectivity, anonymity, resources, skills, fixed fee, cross industry fertilisation, choice; and disadvantages: cost, learning curve" (Training session, 23/7/98b)—in other words, factors relating to the management of cost and access to standard professional skills as well as competitive knowledge. For consultants, the management of such relationships is treated as part of professional expertise and labelled *client management* or *client handling* (Field notes, 3/2/97). The key here is the need to inject more security and stability into a commercial relationship which by its nature is very tenuous:

> There is very little [...] that locks a purchaser in [...] there are an awful lot of companies out there and it's pretty easy to disentangle yourself as a purchaser if you want to. You don't think you are getting good value? You phone up and say "You're fired." (Interview, 4/2/1997)

Client–consultant relationships are supported by a legal infrastructure contained in the contract; their substantive definition, contained in the agreed programme of work; and a set of skills or tools employed by the consultant specifically to manage the relationship, rather than to discharge contractual duties. The contract usually deals with the consultant's fees, recovery of costs, mark-up on services bought in and managed by the consultant on behalf of the client, and finally with the extent and nature of any possible legal liabilities that might arise in the course of work. Who draws up the contract may be an area of power play in the relationship: consultancies usually have their own contracts, but from the point of view of service buyers, "You ... never ever sign their contract. Get your legal department to raise your own" (Training session, 27/7/98b).

There are two main types of financial arrangements between the consultancy and its clients: retainers and projects; while freelancers appear to be mostly paid on a daily rate basis (Fawkes, Fielden, & Tench, 2001). There is anecdotal evidence pointing to the shift away from retainers in the 1990s, which is explained either by a tighter cost control culture, mentioned in the previous section, or by the growth of in-house ("Don't ditch PR," 1997) presumably taking up a lot of the longer-term or cyclical work most suited to retainer agreements. Regular reporting of the hours worked on the account is part of good account management practice. It is underpinned by timesheet keeping. Both of these are sensitive issues as they raise questions about the accuracy of such reports, consultant skills, and ultimately honesty and power relations.

For example, a joke told by a trainer in the context of discussing account management, implies a practice of exaggerating the billable time.

> A PR consultant dies and goes to heaven. He is 25 years old. There is nothing wrong with him. At the gate, Saint Peter says, "Ah, Mr Smith." Smith says, "Excuse me, but I shouldn't be here. There is nothing wrong with me. I haven't been in a car accident or anything like that ...." Saint Peter says, "Oh, let me check." He taps into his computer. "Now, Mr Smith, according to your timesheets, you are one hundred years old!" (Training session, 22/7/98b)

However, there is another, more publicly recognised, issue related to time: overservicing, that is, not billing the client for all the time spent on their account. It appears to be a somewhat embarrassing fact of consultancy life; although an occasional public acknowledgement of its existence is made, there is a reticence to discuss it in too much detail.

"[I]sn't it time we all stopped repressing the most serious debate our industry faces—the fact that growth in turnover and profits is all too often at the expense of the employees who work such long hours overservicing clients, commonly with little reward or redress. [. . .] While giddy targets are set and reached, and fat bonuses pocketed, something unwholesome and downright immoral is going on underneath. Am I the only person to find the free-market motto of "no one gets sacked here, people sack themselves" a heartless denial of responsibility to staff? ("Stop feeding the egos," 1998)

For this angry correspondent, who signed himself "a boy in the boiler room," the issue is not so much that clients are overserviced, as the fact that this is made possible by the exploitation of staff, institutionalised in the free market value: the individual's effort and ability are an employee's personal asset for which the employer has no responsibility. But why does overservicing happen in the first place? Being able to identify and label the practice is evidence of managerial systems that are strong enough to prevent such practice. The reason lies elsewhere—in the power relations in the agency–client relationship. As we have seen, the relationship is enacted in the conditions of cutthroat competition between suppliers of PR services, virtually non-existent industry or professional regulation, and the considerable cost of obtaining new clients as well as the possibility of cutting the cost by obtaining more work from existing clients. It appears that these conditions give the upper hand in the relationship to the client.

[I]n client–consultancy relationship you never get to debate who's right, who's wrong. It's simple: consultancy is always wrong, because it's the client who's paying the cheques. And you've got to start from this point of view. (Interview, 4/2/97)

However, the straightforward financial aspect of the relationship may not be the entire explanation of the client's power: "Service we deliver cannot be extracted from the client. He is as much involved in delivering the service as we are" (Interview, 4/2/97).

If the service delivered is dependent on the client's involvement, managing the relationship becomes not just a question of earning a fee from the particular account, but of longer-term reputation building, which as we have seen is an important factor in gaining new work.

How is the relationship managed, then? Although it is focused on delivering the "tangibles" such as the product or service (i.e., the agreed programme), the process is dependent on building into the relationship a number of interlinked characteristics: reliability, responsiveness, managing the client's expectations, confidence and trust.

To my mind . . . reliability, performing dependently and accurately is more important than anything else. You can be the best PR adviser in the business, the most brilliant seller of stories to the media, but if the client doesn't know if you are gonna bother to turn up to a meeting, he is going to start doubting whether you are gonna bother giving him decent advice. (Interview, 4 /2/97)

The relationship is fashioned with the use of account management skills:

Use any excuse to keep in touch, have regular team meetings, diarise monthly client meetings, use contact reports, memos, keep track of hours spent. (Training session, 22/7/98b)

I always try to deliver in advance of when a client is expecting something. Part of the process of being able to deliver in advance [. . .] is being able to manage expectations of when a client needs it in order to set a deadline. Some clients want everything tomorrow so you have to prod them: prioritise . . . which of these can wait till next week . . . set out some sort of disciplined timetable for the client . . . as long as you deliver the day before [. . .], you build an atmosphere of willingness and that again helps build confidence and trust in the relationship. Doing these things makes delivering the actual work so much easier. (Interview, 4/2/97)

Although formal evaluation can track the delivery of the programme, it is the quality of the relationship that may be the key to getting repeat work and to the reputation that an agency acquires.

> It's about relationships, feeling the programme is working. This is not about hard evaluation. (Training session, 22/7/98b)

> Almost all my clients judge on feeling. I had a client for whom we'd done a great job [but] the client wanted to terminate the relationship because it "didn't feel right." These things are very instinctive. (Training session, 22/7/98b)

This trainer, a successful financial PR specialist, was very clear in distinguishing between the "tangible" and "intangible" elements in the public relations consultants' work. Paradoxically, "intangibles" are given a very tangible recognition in PR practice in the form of "restrictive covenants" in employment contracts in consultancy which prevent employees from poaching clients and setting up in business for themselves. A good example is offered by Shandwick Consultants and a breakaway firm, the Hogarth Partnership, set up in 1997 by "four board directors led by chief executive Chris Matthews" (Bevan, 1997c). The speculation at the time was about the number of key accounts which Shandwick might lose, a possible compromise arrangement of sharing accounts in view of the contractual constraints on ex-Shandwick, Hogarth founders, and the impact on the share price following a profits warning issued by Shandwick in August 1997, a few months after the split (Garside, 1997d).

Analyzing client relations has highlighted the importance of those characteristics of such relationships that tend to be difficult to unpack and measure meaningfully. The importance of "intangibles" in the practice appears also to differ depending on the level of analysis. For an individual practitioner, intangibles reflect a constant and important part of their professional lives which is not captured directly by standard business or professional measures. For PR businesses, intangibles are key assets protected by employment contracts. At the level of the industry or profession, they become an embarrassment, a rallying point for a campaign of self-improvement. The late 1990s saw an industry campaign to improve the standards and practice of evaluation.

JURISDICTIONAL SECURITY

So far in the chapter, we have focused on what happens close to the ground: how practitioners routinely go about and think about what they do, for example, pitching or dealing with clients. This section is concerned with the industry and the occupation, rather than individual practitioners. What was going on at this level? Why? How shall we understand such developments? Two key issues have been selected for analysis: evaluation and regulation.

EVALUATION

Evaluation was by no means a new issue in the 1990s. Industry and professional bodies as well as individual players had tackled the problem of what to measure, and how to do so, in order to evaluate PR effectiveness before. In one *PR Week* Platform column, a respected practitioner reminded readers that the debate

> has rumbled on among practitioner circles for more than 20 years [. . .] Going back further, to 1984, Burston-Marsteller dealt with the questions of evaluation in an excellent paper entitled "What's the Impact?." Walter

Lindenmann, vice-president of research with Ketchum PR in New York, has also discussed the topic exhaustively over the years. He is now working on yet another taskforce on evaluation with the Public Relations
Society of America. (J. White, 1999)

In fact, one gets a distinct impression that not much new could be added to the debate and
that there is possibly an element of ritual in the periodic resurfacing of such public discussions
and initiatives. An account of the 1996–2000 round of the debate is presented below, organised
around four questions: What was the debate about? Why was it necessary? Who were the most
active participants? What were the key moments?

In the late 1990s, the debate about evaluation focused on developing a standard system of
measuring public relations effectiveness that would be understood by clients and acceptable
from the PR expert point of view. Although *PR Week* ran a big feature on evaluation earlier
in 1996—hanging it on the hook of a survey showing that PR providers lagged behind
other marketing disciplines in that respect (Rogers, 1996b)—the debate was ignited by the
public launch of the "industry evaluation plan" in July 1996 at a conference organised by an
evaluation company, Cutting Edge Software. The proposal was to create a service calculating
the proportion of the "target population exposed to coverage" based on the existing audience
and readership data from bodies such as BARB, NRS, ABC, and RAJAR ("Crowe and Bell
Launch Industry Evaluation Plan," 1996). The service appears to have been a commercial
venture (viable for £250 a year at 400 subscribers minimum), but the reporting downplayed the
commercial aspect, framing this development as an industry response to a public/client need:

The plan was developed in response to client interest by a working group consisting of Crowe [marketing
manager, National Dairy Council] and Bell [former PRCA chairman], Norwich Union communications director
Raymond Wilson, and *PR Week* editor Stephen Farish. ("Crowe and Bell Launch Industry Evaluation Plan,"
1996)

Although the initial focus was on media analysis—thus simply equating evaluation with
media evaluation only—quite soon the discussion acquired a wider scope thanks to a reader's
letter:

Measures of content and potential audience reach won't satisfy more demanding users of public relations
[. . .] Equally, they won't be much use for programmes (of which there are many) which don't have media
relations as their prime focus. Something is needed to measure the results of PR in terms of attitudinal and even
behavioural change on the part of audiences. Surely with the industry's considerable combined purchasing
power, it shouldn't be impossible to devise a series of standard, low-cost research packages to track the
effectiveness of PR campaigns rather than simply analysing the techniques used. (Knight, 1996)

By late 1998, the topic had evolved to that of industry initiatives in developing not just
a standard measure but an accessible evaluation toolkit, eventually launched in April 1999
under the auspices of IPR, PRCA, and *PR Week*,[2] offering a practical illustration of a range of
methods to be understood as best practice in the area.

There is one main reason why this debate and these industry initiatives to improve evaluation
took place: the need to shore up public relations' position in relation to clients and competitors.

---

[2]Fairchild, Michael, *Research and Evaluation Toolkit*, IPR, PRCA, *PR Week*, London, 1999.

Following *PR Week's* coverage, we can identify various factors, the main one being the client demand for measurement:

> There does indeed seem to be an industry-wide acceptance that those who judge [PR] activity demand increasingly objective and professional measurement of achievement. (Rogers, 1996b)

Others invoke "respect," by which is meant "a fairer share of the budgets and the ear of decision-makers at board level" (Richardson, 1996); and a range of applications of research in planning work (Philips, 1998).

The leading participants in this evaluation round were the main industry and professional bodies in the UK (IPR and PRCA) as well as the International Committee of Public Relations Consultancies Associations (ICO), media evaluation companies, and *PR Week*, which participated in and reported on the developments at the same time. The magazine took a strong campaigning stance: for example, a minority of respondents to one particular survey who claimed that evaluation was "irrelevant" were blasted in an editorial as "living in cloud cuckoo land" ("Evaluating the strength," 1996). In the week when the proposal for the standard unit of measurement was launched, the editorial proclaimed that it was of vital importance:

> Evaluation is too important to the future of the PR business to let this opportunity go, which is why *PR Week* is putting itself firmly behind the campaign. [. . .] We want to hear from you. ("The final analysis," 1996)

Indeed, readers did write in and over the following 3 years the magazine published a number of their contributions.

If one is to write the story of the evaluation debate in the late 1990s, it is useful to start by recognising the commercial impetus behind it. Convincing and commercially viable evaluation methods were needed to attract custom; the participants in the debate all had a more or less directly commercial interest in evaluation being used and sold to customers. As we have seen above, the debate kicked off with a call for an industry-wide common evaluation standard and one industry body to deal with evaluation. Initially, the "industry" here meant the "media evaluation industry," effectively around 10 companies offering cuttings and media content analysis (see Rogers, 1996b). Despite the talk about the standard public relations measurement unit—referred to as Public Relations Point (Nicholas, 1996) or Media Relations Point (R. Wilson, 1997)—no common standard appears to have been adopted; while a single body for media evaluation companies, the Association of Media Evaluation Companies (AMEC) was formed quite quickly and appears to have embedded itself firmly amongst the important trade bodies in the area.

If we treat the Cutting Edge conference, mentioned above, as the first in a chain of initiatives, the next one was the meeting in November 1996 of the international media evaluators, including the recently formed AMEC, under the auspices of ICO. The meeting led to the production of a guide on the setting of measurable objectives and a consultation paper on the future of the evaluation industry to be presented to both ICO and IPRA boards during IPRA's conference in June 1997 (Nicholas, 1997b)—the connection between sound PR practice (objective setting) and its evaluation was thus reaffirmed.

That same year saw the publication of two practical guides, which could be seen as setting evaluation standards: AMEC's *The Power of the Media* (dealing with media evaluation techniques) and ICO's *How to Get Value From Public Relations* (dealing with measurable communication objectives and also suggesting that 12% of a PR budget should be spent on evaluation). The context to these initiatives was explained by the outgoing president of ICO in terms of jurisdictional competition: "If we don't move then other types of consultant will take work away from us" (Darby, 1997).

In 1998, *PR Week* turned up the pressure by conducting its own Proof Campaign, aiming "to encourage practitioners to allocate ten per cent of their PR budget to research and evaluation" (France, 1998, p. 11). The campaign was launched in February and developed through a combination of straw polls on relevant topics such as research and evaluation spend by different categories of clients; a discussion amongst a number of key practitioners on best evaluation practice (France, 1998); readers' letters; and later in that year, a joint initiative with other bodies to launch the industry guide to evaluation practice. The IPR launched its own Evaluation Taskforce in August 1998, and the discussion on the pages of *PR Week* quickly turned to the need for unity, both in terms of a common industry body and industry-wide consensus:

> The most important prerequisite is that the PR industry is seen to be totally united in its efforts to prove the worth of what is does [. . .] This means that any differences in approach or vested interests on the part of IPR, PRCA and other interested bodies need to be put to one side and a single, common standard agreed upon. (Fairchild, 1998)

In 1999, *PR Week* published the results of the Proof Survey (Cowlett & Nicholas, 1999), a commissioned piece of research attempting to quantify the extent of the evaluation practice and factors shaping it. The survey was conducted on a 200-strong sample of the magazine's readers and followed up with a number of qualitative interviews. Some of the key findings were: first, a sizeable minority of practitioners (around 20%) did not believe that their work could be evaluated; second, media content analysis and press cuttings were by far the most used measure (61% of respondents had actually used it; the next category, OTS,[3] was 27%, roughly half the size); third, the two main reasons for research and evaluation were to prove the value of PR (48%) and to show if the objectives had been met (38%); finally, the two main obstacles to planning and evaluation activity were difficulty in securing budgets (38%) and lack of definable measures (30%) (CARMA, 1999).[4]

These main findings are interesting if put in the context of the somewhat ambiguous identity of the public relations profession. They offer clear numerical evidence of the importance of the "intangibles" discussed in the previous section: one in every five practitioners thinks it is impossible to evaluate PR work. Consequently, we could say, they prove that the occupation's identity was not settled, and that it refused to be configured in purely rational, measurable terms, despite an outspoken industry-wide campaign.

The Proof Survey was swiftly followed by the publication in April 1999 of the *Research and Evaluation Toolkit*, representing the joint effort of the main industry players, reportedly "IPR, PRCA, AMEC, the Public Relations Standards Council, plus research company MORI, in-house practitioners and Michael Fairchild, author of ICO's publication *How to get real value from public relations*" (Leavy, 1998, p. 12). By 2001 the *Toolkit* was in its second edition and the industry had continued these joint efforts, having launched another initiative in October 2000:

> PRE-fix, the all industry initiative promoting the benefits of planning, research and evaluation as an integral part of PR programmes [. . .] is aimed at building on existing initiatives such as *PR Week's* Proof campaign and the Research and Evaluation Toolkit. [. . .] Initially this will be in the shape of a website [. . .] a complete listing

---

[3]OTS stands for Opportunities to See.

[4]The reported margin of error (7%) does not change the suggested reading of the key findings. More detailed breakdown figures had an even larger margin of error of 10–15%, making them effectively useless in terms of providing a clear picture of the practice.

of services of various R&E providers and a handful of case studies, [the] aim is to provide PR decision-makers with guidance on which methods suit which situations at which point in time. (Cowlett, 2001)

However, in 2003 PRE-fix was cancelled and it seems that the industry had come the full circle: the enthusiasm of the wide consensus dissipated under the onslaught of the economic downturn of the early years of the 21st century:

> No doubt, the PRCA and IPR will continue to undertake sterling work individually, but the failure of the industry to continue this campaign sends out an unfortunate message about its ability to co-operate on key issues.

> As in-house departments and agencies come under pressure to cut budgets to the bone, we are seeing a resurgence of the use of spurious methods such as AVEs.[5] It would seem that the need for initiatives such as PRE-fix has never been greater. ("The demise of Pre-fix," 2003)

To conclude, let us reflect briefly on the significance of this campaign. It is difficult to be precise about what was achieved by the campaign: although the *Toolkit* was noticed by the practitioners,[6] and remains an important statement by the profession about good practice, the extent of its impact in practice has not been assessed. The set of initiatives recounted above is significant as a way of making a public claim to the professional jurisdiction on the basis of values such as: rational action, professionalism, business acumen shown through responding to client needs, accountability to clients in measurable, ideally financial terms. At the same time, we see how the effort was counteracted by a number of factors, such as the fragmentation of the industry between work settings (in-house vs. consultancy; public sector vs. commercial sector) and disciplines (for example, financial PR specialists seem to hold the strongest allegiance to the belief in the "intangible," immeasurable nature of PR); commercial competition between PR companies; and weak governance due to a number of different industry bodies. In crude terms, the professionalisation of public relations is constrained by competition between practitioners, which in turn is influenced by macroeconomic conditions: as the market for PR services shrinks or grows, competition is more or less tough.

REGULATION

Evaluation was an important issue for the PR industry in the late 1990s, but there were others, notably the regulation of lobbying and financial public relations—the subject of this section. The debates and events relevant to these issues can be told as two separate stories connected by time, some of the major actors, and above all by the key dilemma of whether to support self-regulation of the industry or to push for statutory regulation by an outside body. Regulation, like evaluation, had been something of a perennial issue; the story told below covers 1996–2000 and is therefore just part of a longer saga.

The way in which PR practitioners debated the regulation of lobbying and the specific decisions they made about how to deal with the issue needs to be set against the backdrop of fairly recent events in the UK, specifically the Nolan Report; the continued work of the Committee on Standards in Public Life (for a discussion, see Schlesinger, Miller, & Dinan, 2001, pp. 189–194); the concurrent regulatory developments in the European Union; and devolution in Scotland, promoting a discussion about regulation in the devolved Parliament.

---

[5] AVE stands for Advertising Value Equivalent, a measure which relies on calculating the value of the coverage in terms of how much it would cost to pay for the same space if bought in as advertising. The measure, despite its strong condemnation by the industry, remains in use. See *PR Week* Platform column on 18 October 1996.

[6] The IPR Web site accessed in March 2004 showed that the *Toolkit* was in its third edition (http://www.ipr.org.uk).

In September 1996, Ian Greer and Neil Hamilton abandoned their libel case against *The Guardian* over allegations published by the newspaper on 20 October 1994 accusing Ian Greer Associates (IGA) of acting as conduit for cash payments from Mahomed Al Fayed to two MPs, Neil Hamilton and Tim Smith, for asking Parliamentary questions. The "cash for questions" affair, as it came to be known, had a number of important consequences.

The Committee on Standards in Public Life (CSPL) was set up in October 1994 by the Prime Minister John Major to deal with the affair. Initially, the remit of the committee did not extend to investigating individual allegations of misconduct (Nolan, 1995, p. 1). Instead, the focus was firmly on public life and public opinion. Crucially for this story, the Nolan Report made no recommendation on regulating lobbyists. The job of investigating allegations of individual misconduct was carried out in 1996–1997 by the newly appointed Parliamentary Commissioner for Standards, Sir Gordon Downey, and made public in July 1997 in what is commonly referred to as the Downey Report (Sheldon, 1997). The collapse of Greer and Hamilton's libel case was crucial as the evidence was now available to the Parliamentary inquiry enabling its completion. On publication of the report, *PR Week's* front page claimed "Report says Greer 'not guilty' of cash for questions" (Garside, 1997c). The article gave a rather misleading impression that Ian Greer was exonerated by the inquiry. First, the remit of the inquiry did not extend to non-MPs, such as Greer; second, although no evidence for cash payments was found, even *PR Week* was forced to admit that on other aspects of Greer's activity the report "was less conclusive" (Garside, 1997c). The affair cost Greer the collapse of his well-established company—the liquidators were finally called in January 1997.

In 1994, again in response to the cash for questions affair, a number of consultancies specialising in lobbying came together to form the Association of Professional Political Consultants (APPC; see Schlesinger et al., 2001, p. 205). The newly formed association immediately became an important player in issues relating to the regulation of lobbying. APPC gave evidence to the Nolan inquiry alongside other established bodies, PRCA and IPR. This, as well as the tone and the shifting substance of the views expressed by APPC, drew angry responses from some quarters, as evidenced by two letters published in *PR Week* on 25 October 1996. Responding to a statement made in a feature on lobbying (Beenstock, 1996), Shandwick's vice-chairman wrote angrily:

It is untrue that the [APPC] is "the regulatory body to which most lobbying companies belong." It is this kind of claptrap which has caused APPC to do so much damage in its very short life. Its pretentious evidence to the Nolan Committee sent that rather naïve body scurrying down the wrong track. We continue to read and watch APPC spokesmen making statements as if they were a long standing professional body rather than a recently plucked fig leaf.

It is perhaps noteworthy that it is two APPC members (IGA and GJW) who have attracted media attention over cash for questions and work for Libya respectively. Instead of self-appointed individuals claiming powers beyond their capacity, let us, for all our sakes use the present mood to insist that Parliament implements a fully transparent register of lobbyists. (McNally, 1996)

A director of Grandfield Public Affairs joined in, and it is worth quoting this letter extensively, too:

Lobbyists and public affairs specialists who are not members of the APPC will take grave exception to the claim from Michael Burrell of Westminster Strategy that "in pitching blue-chip clients are now careful to accept proposals only from APPC members."

This can only add to the growing suspicion that the APPC is an exclusive club with a veneer of self-regulation.

[. . .] As your editorial points out, APPC may well be "found wanting" partly because of the "cash for questions" shadow but also no doubt because of the exclusivity and lack of broader appeal to the industry as a whole. Reporting the APPC's "emergency meeting" *The Times* on 18 October said that the Association now "wants regulation by Parliament." At last. [...] But if it has abandoned the claim to be a self-regulator, what is the APPC for? (P. Kelly, 1996)

The letters highlight a number of important factors in the debate related to the depth of divisions in the industry and the potential commercial value of navigating the right course through these troubled waters. The industry was divided in its views toward regulation. If the need for regulation to signal transparency and respectability was understood, the extent and shape of the regulation were under discussion: some lobbyists thought statutory regulation the right solution; others were rather wary of solutions imposed by outsiders in the form of legislation, the prospect viewed by Bernard Ingham as "regrettable" (Beenstock, 1996). Another rift in the industry was caused by the question of representation: both IPR and PRCA claimed the right to represent the industry, and the swift rise to prominence of a new small body (APPC) was resented. Moreover, suspicion arose that the newcomer represented not the industry as such but rather a promotional strategy adopted by a small clique of companies.

Perhaps the speed of the events and the intensity of public attention on lobbying helped to build consensus. The Ian Greer affair was in the public eye from 1994 until July 1997. Its legacy to the industry was the establishment of two voluntary codes of conduct for lobbyists—one by IPR, the other by APPC—as well as a vigorous debate between supporters of self-regulation and those in favour of statutory regulation. In July 1998 another scandal brought lobbyists back to the front pages and under the renewed scrutiny of the Committee for Standards in Public Life—Cronygate or Drapergate, focused on Derek Draper, described by *The Observer* as "Labour insider-turned-lobbyist" (Palast, 1998). The essence of the *The Observer* investigative feature that sparked the renewed debate was the revelation that lobbying firms employing well-connected consultants boasted of having insider access to sensitive policy information. Derek Draper, ex-aide to the then all-powerful Peter Mandelson, at the time employed by GPC Market Access, was featured alongside the three founding partners of a lobbying consultancy, Lawson Lucas Mendelsohn, all of whom had previously worked for Tony Blair. For *The Observer*, the point seemed to have been as much about the ethics of lobbying as it was about the morality of New Labour:

Do any of these young men harbour misgivings about renting out their contacts? They see no reason for apology. It's their world after all. They are convinced they crafted New Labour and now they are merely charging admission to the show they produced. (Palast, 1998)

The furore led to the sixth CSPL inquiry chaired by Lord Neill, *Reinforcing Standards*, which reported in January 2000 (Cm 4557-I). As the inquiry was proceeding, IPR, PRCA, and APPC came to a shared view that statutory regulation of lobbying in the form of a public register policed by an independent body was desirable. IPR, PRCA, and APPC agreed a shared code of practice for lobbyists. Interestingly, in *PR Week's* portrayal of the interaction between the lobbying industry and the State, the lobbyists appear kept at "arm's length" by the Parliament unwilling to legislate despite calls from the industry for regulation ("Lobbying Laws," 1998). In the end, Lord Neill followed the line taken by the Nolan Report in deciding not to impose regulation on lobbyists.

Should we take *PR Week's* interpretation of these events at face value? How genuine was the appetite for regulation in the PR profession? Let us look at another regulation debate— regarding financial PR—which ran in parallel to that about lobbying. Like the question of regulating lobbying, the need to engage publicly with the issue of regulation over financial PR was also brought about by a scandal. In December 1995 the Takeover Panel rebuked Financial

Dynamics for disclosing to analysts sensitive information while acting for Amec, defending the company against a hostile takeover bid from Kvaerner (Bevan, 1996c). This prompted the IPR's City and Financial Group to start a consultation process with a view to presenting recommendations to the Securities and Investment Board, the regulator of financial markets. The position was to create a clear system of self-regulation in order to fend off the danger of statutory regulation: "Statutory regulation would be unwieldy, and possibly unenforceable. A form of self-regulation must be the way forward, although none of the existing industry bodies seem ideally positioned to make it work" ("Time for clarity," 1996).

As with lobbying, there were voices within the industry arguing that sufficiently clear rules of conduct already existed—laid down in the IPR Code of Conduct, or "Stock and Exchange's Listing Rules (Yellow Book), Takeover Code, (Blue Book), Criminal Justice Act 1993, Financial Services Act 1986 and Companies Act 1985" (Gray, 1997)—and what was required was simply policing the existing rules. But when in February 1997 another PR agency, Citigate, was reprimanded by the Takeover Panel for leaking sensitive information (Rogers, 1997), it was clear that action was needed. A sense of urgency was injected into this debate by the new Labour government's plans to reform the regulation of financial services (Gray, 1997). The reform took over 3 years to complete. It started with the announcement in May 1997 of plans to create a new regulator with combined responsibility for banking and investment sectors. In October 1997 the Securities and Investments Board became the Financial Services Authority (FSA) and by June 1998 banking was subsumed into its remit. The regulator was given statutory powers by the Financial Services and Markets Act 2000, implemented on 1 December 2001 (Financial Services Authority, 2004). In the summer of 1998 the FSA published its draft code of conduct for the London financial markets, proposing to regulate financial PR—with the powers of imposing fines for misconduct. The reported reaction of the IPR's City and Financial Group was that of endorsement and willing cooperation (Darby, 1998; "Writing the rules," 1998). However, 4 months later *PR Week* was obliged to report that the IPR's submission to the FSA did not request for "specific regulation of financial PR," but that there was an initiative underway to "examine the possibility of a voluntary, cross-industry financial PR code" (Greene & Garside, 1998). The chair of the IPR City and Financial Group was quoted as saying: "There is no guarantee that a voluntary code would prevent scandals, but we need to be prepared due to the increased interest the Government is showing" (Greene & Garside, 1998).

On the one hand, the statement could be read as a straightforward support for commercial freedom, and self-regulation as a defence mechanism against the threat of outside regulation. On the other hand, the statement is not straightforward at all. How serious was the threat if, as in this instance, the profession was effectively invited to write the rulebook? It also appears that there were no illusions about the effectiveness of self-regulation. It seems that the only way to interpret this statement is that it was asserting that the ultimate value is the freedom to act in the ways most advantageous at the time, while regulation, in any form, can only be disadvantageous.

These two regulation debates taken together lead to a similar conclusion—when all is said and done, above all else the industry values having the flexibility of a practice unconstrained by statutory regulation. But the price for this freedom is evidently paid in the reputation granted to the public relations industry. Bernard Ingham in one of his *PR Week* columns penned during Lord Neill's inquiry came down on the side of statutory regulation, arguing that it "would cement lobbyists into the fabric of public life" (Ingham, 1999). So far, however, the PR profession has opted out. Although at times it conducts itself as if seeking the status of a public institution, in reality it gets along well enough most of the time without having to assume the burden of being one.

PUBLIC IMAGE

Debates about evaluation and regulation in this period evidently revolved around the key issue of the occupation's public image. Individual practitioners and the various trade bodies were keenly aware of the need to appear respectable: being able to evaluate one's contribution (together with the knowledge and skills required to effect this) would build respectability in relations with clients; showing appreciation for the world of social values and public interest would provide respectability in the public sphere. But however hard the occupation tried to live up to this image, the old demons of lies and dubious morals could not be exorcised. In the UK in the late 1990s, the PR occupation's crusade to dissociate itself from Max Clifford was the most potent manifestation of this symbolic struggle.

MASTERS OF HYPE

The UK's most high-profile PR man dismissed suggestions that as a senior industry figure he had a responsibility to set an example to younger PROs on the importance of telling the truth. "Anyone who says that must know nothing about PR," he claimed. Launching an attack on industry figures whom he described as hypocrites, Clifford said: "Most in the PR industry lie through their teeth but don't admit it" ("Clifford and responsibility," 2000).

This excerpt contains all the staple ingredients of the story: Clifford's cheerful admission to lying; his insistence on lies being routine PR practice; his dismissive attitude towards the industry, which he sees as hypocritical and ineffectual; as well as his taste for controversy and the limelight. Clifford has been in business since the late 1960s doing publicity and media relations (Goddard, 1996). Many of his clients were famous or became well known as a result of Clifford's involvement, and scandal has been a staple ingredient of the cases he has handled. For example, in 1992 he represented an unknown actress who shot into the headlines when the story of her affair with a government minister, David Mellor, broke (see J. Davis, 1992); in 1996 he worked for OJ Simpson when the latter visited the UK on a 5-day tour.

Clifford expressed his view on PR and lies consistently and publicly throughout the 1990s, most importantly in two live appearances in the mass media (a BBC Radio Scotland programme "Who does he think he is" in January 1996 and a BBC TV chat show "Kilroy" in January 1997). In both programmes Clifford was confronted with a representative of the PR industry: Quentin Bell in his capacity as PRCA chairman; and Rosemary Brook, past IPR president, respectively. On both occasions, Clifford's views on PR and lies drew a furious response. The tactics adopted by Clifford's critics were twofold: distancing routine PR work from the type of publicity work carried out by Clifford, "[. . .] there is more to PR than the lurid '20 per cent' of Clifford's work that involves selling kiss-and-tell stories to the media" ("Bell tussles with Clifford," 1996), and a direct attack on his ethics, "Abortionists are doctors but similarities with GPs [General Practitioners] begin and end there" (Dowman, 1997). The industry's fury was sparked by Clifford's undermining of the basis of their claimed professional standing (ethical behaviour and public interest), but it was intensified by Clifford's being identified with the PR industry in the popular imagination: rightly or wrongly, in the public perception Max Clifford was what PR was all about. In fact, even the PR occupation was not as clear in its condemnation and exclusion of Clifford as one might by now expect. David Wynne Morgan, a veteran political activist turned PR consultant, wrote a *PR Week* Comment column lamenting the fact that PR practitioners increasingly put themselves in the limelight: "it is happening from the openly scurrilous Max Clifford, the self-professed master of hype, to the eminent Sir Tim Bell" (Wynne Morgan, 1997). A black sheep, no doubt, but a sheep none the less.

ONE OF THE BOYS: NETWORKS
OF RESPECTABILITY

For the PR occupation, Max Clifford became the embodiment of everything that was wrong with the profession and its image; at the same time, other practitioners came to symbolise the opposite: social and professional achievement, high status, and power.

PR Barons

On 14 August 1998 *PR Week's* Diary contained a short item entitled "Bell faces a Baron future in Belgravia," which began as follows:

> Sir Tim Bell was formally created a life baron last week. Following consultation on his *nomen dignitatus* with the Garter King of Arms and a rubber stamp from the Great Seal, he is from now on Baron Bell of Belgravia in the City of Westminster. Although Bell was made a peer some time after fellow Tory image consultants Peter Chadlington and Maurice Saatchi, he has the consolation of being baron of by far the most glamorous territory. ("Bell Faces a Baron Future," 1998)

Indeed, the magazine has always faithfully noted awards of high honours such as peerages, OBEs, or MBEs to PR professionals. It was front-page news when Peter Gummer, Shandwick's Chairman, and Maurice Saatchi, of Saatchi and Saatchi fame, were made life peers in 1996 (Dowman, 1996a), and front-page news again when Gummer adopted the title of Lord Chadlington of Dean ("Gummer adopts new title," 1996). On both occasions *PR Week* was expansive in discussing Gummer's business achievements, his insightful views on the PR profession, his role in public life, and his personal modesty and charm (Farish, 1996a, 1996b). The peerages were seen by the industry as excellent news, but drew public criticism from the Labour party, then in opposition, which dubbed the new peers "Lords of Lies" for their role in the Conservative negative advertising campaign in the run-up to the general election the following year.[7] In fact, looking at the various honours awarded to PR practitioners around that time (1996–1998), the furore appears to be political point scoring, as the practice of awarding such public recognition for service to a political party or cause seems to have been well established. For example, a number of PR practitioners featured in John Major's resignation honours list. There were MBEs for Jonathan Haslam, Sheila Gunn (Major's chief press secretary and press secretary), and George Bridges, Major's assistant political secretary; Charles Lewington, former communications director at the Conservative Party central office, was given an OBE. Others were rewarded on other occasions such as New Year's Honours Lists or Queen's Birthday Honours Lists, for example: a CBE for Jean Caines, former director of communications at the Department of Trade and Industry; an OBE for Sandi Rhys Jones of Rhys Jones Consultants for her work on the Construction Industry Board's Working Group on Equal Opportunities ("Caines and Rhys Jones," 1998); and an OBE to Angela Heylin, Charles Barker chairman, for her contribution to Citizen's Charter scheme (Murphy, 1997). At least

---

[7]The phrase came from Frank Dobson, Shadow Environment Secretary, and was widely reported on 21 August 1996; see, for example, R. Peston, "Maurice Saatchi among 14 new working peers." *Financial Times*, 21 August.

three Liberal-Democrats were made life peers while Conservatives or the Labour party were in government: Tom McNally (1995, Shandwick, previously Hill & Knowlton), Dick Newby (1997, Matrix Communications Consultancy), and Tim Clement-Jones (1998, Political Context).

In prestige terms, such awards clearly symbolise not only the social acceptability of the public relations occupation, but also its ability to connect with political elites. The symbolic role of the PR barons is well illustrated in this excerpt:

> Last month the Institute of Public Relations awarded Bell their President's medal for distinguished service to public relations. "Certainly, he's the closest thing we have to an industry champion and a very welcome antidote to Max Clifford," says Kate Nicholas, editor of *PR Week*. "He has shown that our industry is more than media relations." (Sanghera, 2001)

However, the extent to which such eminent practitioners influenced, rather than symbolised, the profession is less clear. Although Lord McNally did take a strong position in the lobbying debate speaking for statutory regulation both through *PR Week* and in the House of Lords, he seems to be an exception. There does not appear to exist a very strong allegiance to, or sense of, a common professional identity among high-status PR practitioners.

The Circuit of Power: Media, PR, and Politics

In the section above, a peerage was treated as a symbolic representation of the position PR holds in public and political life. In this section, an attempt is made to look behind such symbols and sketch out the underlying careers and professional networks. Three distinct groups constitute this circuit of power: journalists, elected politicians, and public relations experts.

PUBLIC RELATIONS PRACTITIONERS AND JOURNALISTS

The connections between journalism and public relations have a long lineage, going back to the early days of the PR occupation. A range of studies have shown that the two occupations have been connected by their tasks—provision (i.e., the supplying as well as the withholding) of information into the public domain, their fundamental activity—engagement with public opinion, as well as by the flow of practitioners from journalism into PR (see L'Etang, 2001, pp. 28–48; A. Davis, 2002, pp. 19–41). The tense relationship between the two has also been noted before (for example, L'Etang, 2001, pp. 117–122; DeLorme and Fedler, 2003) and it appears not to have changed much over the years, as shown by this contemporary picture of PR practitioners in a *Financial Times* feature on Tim Bell and the PR industry:

> Lord Bell [. . .] is the interviewee from hell. He's not difficult in the way that most PR people are difficult— he doesn't write rambling, illiterate press releases, for instance, or get my name wrong or make annoying, pointless calls—but he's difficult because he knows every trick in the media handbook. (Sanghera, 2001)

The reason for this tension, expressed here in the image of a PR practitioner as an incompetent and pushy peddler of his master's goods, stems partly from the fundamental difference in the professional identity of journalists and public relations practitioners. Journalism textbooks are unanimous in their explanation of the fundamentals (Randall, 2000, p. 3; Harcup, 2004, pp. 2–3; Sanders, 2003, p. 161), expressed most succinctly as:

[T]he purpose of journalism is to provide people with the information they need to be free and self-governing.[...]

1. Journalism's first obligation is to the truth.
2. Its first loyalty is to citizens.
3. Its essence is a discipline of verification.
4. Its practitioners must maintain an independence from those they cover.
5. It must serve as an independent monitor of power. (Kovach & Rosenstiel, 2001, p. 12)

These principles are also treated as universal, recognised by journalists all over the world (Burns, 2002, p. 10), and they serve to differentiate journalists from PR people:

Are public relations practitioners also journalists, because they are employees whose work is published in newspapers and magazines? The occupational group that is journalism, as represented by unions and associations, argues that these writers are not journalists, because their text is a form of advocacy, intended to persuade, rather than an articulation of the facts. (Burns, 2002, p. 17)

The professional identity of public relations practitioners is a more complex matter: it is a question of finding a compromise between serving the client and serving "the Truth." L'Etang (2001, pp. 63–68) showed the importance of the concept of the truth in the early years of the IPR when it was searching for the occupation's identity. Nowadays, while the practice is defined in various ways—for example, with reference to reputation, relationship, or communication management—values such as honesty, truth, and public interest tend to be articulated in codes of conduct and understood as a framework within which a set of technical, expert activities is conducted. Although PR is guided by the same values as journalism (see, for example, the IPR Code of Conduct), in practice these values may be refracted through the prism of client interests. These different frames of reference mean that on occasion journalists and PR practitioners clash over access to facts: where access is denied or manipulated through selection and presentation, journalistic hackles are raised.[8]

Here the relationship between the two occupations is tackled selectively by focussing on mentions of career moves between the two found in *PR Week*, in 1996–1998, and in some cases followed up in other print media. The trade magazine's news values skew such information towards high-level jobs, unexpected moves, or well-known personalities. As such, the source is not useful in showing the full extent to which practitioners move between the two professions, but it is helpful in drawing a picture of movements of people in prestigious jobs.

It is quite clear that people move between the two occupations predominantly in one way: from journalism, or more accurately, jobs in media organisations, to PR, both in-house and consultancy jobs. There is also a clear pattern of journalistic specialisms translating into PR specialisms: news, political reporting, and senior editorial roles in national newspapers or broadcast newsrooms are a path to PR jobs focused on media relations for political parties, government, or large organisations. For example, Conservative Party Central Office made a number of such appointments in 1995–1999, starting with two directors of communication: Charles Lewington (1996–1997; ex-*Sunday Express* political editor) and Amanda Platell (1999–2001; ex-*Sunday Express* executive editor). *PR Week's* article on changes at Conservative Central Office commented on Lewington's appointment as the Tory response to the role played by another ex-political journalist, Alastair Campbell, Tony Blair's press secretary at the Labour Party, before going on:

---

[8]An insider's view of the relationships within the circuit of power is offered by Jones (1997), who gave more detail on the work of some of the personalities mentioned here.

The new-look press office team—Sheila Gunn from the *Times* dealing with the lobby, Paul Hooper from the *Sun* handling the tabloids [. . .] has been less than entirely successful.[. . .] One thing Sheila Gunn will have learned is that the skills of a good journalist do not automatically translate into good PR handling. (Bevan, 1996b)

Other political parties continued to mine the same field for media relations expertise: for example, Jeff Postlewaite, local government correspondent for the *Evening Standard*, was reported as moving to a press secretary job for John Prescott, the Labour Party deputy leader (Rogers, 1996a); while, almost at the same time, Jane Bonham-Carter went from a career in current affairs (as producer and editor of well-known current affairs programmes for the BBC and later Channel 4) to head communications for the Liberal Democrats (Gray, 1996a). She became Baroness Bonham-Carter of Yarnbury in 2004. Such career changes were by no means a new development, as David Walker reminded *Guardian* readers by pointing out that ex-journalists had served as press secretaries to a number of previous Prime Ministers (Francis Williams, Joe Haines, and Bernard Ingham working for Clement Attlee, Harold Wilson, and Margaret Thatcher, respectively; D. Walker, 1998).

Expertise gained from covering the city or business beats appears to have been a well-established route to financial PR. A number of such career changes were reported, for example: in 1996 Mike Tate, ex-city editor at *The Times*, which he had left in 1992, joined Ludgate consultancy from the *Observer* ("Tate takes on account director role," 1996); Marc Popiolek, former editor of the *Daily Telegraph* Questor column, moved to Gavin Anderson after more than 2 years with Financial Dynamics (Dowman & Bevan, 1996); John Eisenhammer, financial editor at the *Independent*, was recruited by Lowe Bell Consultants; in 1997 Allan Piper joined Citigate Communications from his job as the news editor of the *Financial Mail on Sunday* (Garside, 1997b); Peter Rogers, *Independent* financial editor, was appointed chief press spokesman at the Bank of England (Kavanagh, 1997); and in 1998, Michael Walters joined Square Mile Communications from the city editor job at the *Daily Mail*. Again, career changes from business journalism to financial PR were nothing new in the 1990s: in the first generation of financial PR specialists, those who went into practice around the late 1960s, many were ex-journalists, such as Roddy Dewe, one of the founders of Dewe Rogerson; and John Coyle, billed by *The Observer* as "one of the founding fathers of financial PR" (Coyle, 2004).

However common such career changes might have been, there is evidence to show that they could be difficult for the people involved. For many ex-journalists, it did not take long to beat a retreat from PR back into journalism. To mention just one example, Jeff Randall, who moved to Financial Dynamics in 1995 from the post of city editor at the *Sunday Times*, and after only 6 months back to the same paper as assistant editor, reportedly taking a pay cut (Bevan, 1996a). As careers of others show, the door between PR and journalism could also swing both ways: Andy Cornelius left the *Daily Telegraph* (city news editor) for Dewe Rogerson in 1996, then he went to the *Independent* as business and city news editor to leave after 8 months in 1999 for a directorship at Citigate Dewe Rogerson ("Cornelius Quits *Independent*," 1999). Another financial journalist who moved between the two occupations, Peter Krijgsman, offered this explanation of his brief tenure, of a few days only, at Gavin Anderson in 1988:

Gavin Anderson was a pretty small agency at that time and was struggling to make itself felt, recalls Krijgsman. "Essentially I was joining a marginal agency from a marginal trade magazine [*Corporate Money*] and it wasn't serving either of us well. If I had been a heavy hitter from the *Sunday Times* I might have been able to build up business." (Joyce, 1997)

This is a clear indication that the value of journalists to a PR company resides in their business contacts as well as in their knowledge of the media.

PUBLIC RELATIONS PRACTITIONERS
AND POLITICIANS

If movements between journalism and public relations were, and judging by more up-to-date reports, still remain, based on media expertise, jobs in public relations and politics were swapped on the basis of expertise in policy making and (political) campaigning. Following career developments mentioned in *PR Week* in 1996–1998 which spanned the worlds of PR practice and national politics, reveals a number of jobs which seem to draw on the same expertise: politicians, that is, elected Members of Parliament (MPs); PR consultants, described either as lobbyists or public affairs specialists; PR specialists working for the government (permanent civil servants); special advisers;[9] researchers, working for MPs or for political parties; and PR practitioners, usually described with labels using the term "communications," at political parties, trade unions, or other organisations. In comparison with media relations and journalism, there is less of a sense of one route in the world of careers in politics and PR. It is possible to build up the required expertise in any one of these jobs and exploit it in almost any other. Let us follow a few such career routes.

A career in the world of politics and communication could be based on expertise developed in-house working for a trade union, and then gather momentum moving through public affairs consultancy and/or other high-powered in-house jobs. Chris Savage's professional history since the late 1990s is a good example: in 1997 he left the Trades Union Congress (TUC) where he was a senior policy adviser (head of the industry policy unit) to join a lobbying consultancy called the Public Policy Unit (Macrae, 1997). After roughly a year, he joined Shandwick ("Savage moves from PPU," 1998) where he stayed until his next move to Central Railway, a railway company, in 2001, before he went back into consultancy, at Foresight Communications, in 2004 (Chandiramani, 2004).[10] His work in all of these jobs revolved around transport, regulation and competition, utilities, and defence—all in his beat while at the TUC.

The CV of another successful PR practitioner, Colin Byrne, shows that well-rounded experience of politics and campaigning is also a solid basis for a career in public affairs, and that strengthening such credentials with personal ties to powerful individuals can only help. Byrne's career started in 1981 at the Automobile Association and subsequently encompassed PR jobs for the National Union of Students, the Prince of Wales' business leaders' forum, and the National Union of Farmers, before a 5-year period in the Labour Party's press office, from where he moved into consultancy life, becoming a director of Shandwick in 1996, managing director of Shandwick Public Affairs in 1997, joint CEO of Weber Shandwick in 2001, and in 2003, CEO of Weber Shandwick UK and Ireland (Freedman, 2003). On at least two occasions in 2003 *PR Week* reminded its readers that Byrne had excellent New Labour contacts, notably

[9]The role of special advisers became particularly controversial during the first years of the Labour government and was eventually dealt with by CSPL in its Ninth Report, *Defining the Boundaries within the Executive: Ministers, Special Advisers and the permanent Civil Service* (Cm 5775). Special advisers were defined as government servants, i.e., paid out of the public purse, but temporary—their appointment is tied to the tenure in office of the appointing minister. Although their actions are governed by some of the same principles as those applying to Civil Servants, their role is a political one.

[10]There is a discrepancy in the two *PR Week* reports of Savage's career referred to here in that the later one, dated 1 July 2004, has him joining Shandwick straight from the TUC.

Peter Mandelson, who had been best man at Byrne's wedding, and to whom Byrne referred as "friend and mentor" (Freedman, 2003; "Paul Dacre... you took hell of a beating," 2003).

Labour credentials were more than just a matter of the social circles in which one moved; they were an asset that rapidly appreciated in value in the run-up to and immediately following the general election of 1997. After three terms in government, the Conservative Party looked vulnerable and lobbyists and their clients were taking notice. Amongst references to new appointments and job changes, *PR Week* talked about "an expected flood of former Labour researchers" moving into lobbying (Bevan, 1997a) and Labour "front bench advisers and party workers looking to move into the commercial world following the election" (Nicholas, 1997a). Indeed, a number did move, some in advance of the election, others in the immediate aftermath. For example, Anne Rossiter (researcher to Labour MP Glenda Jackson) joined Fishburn Hedges in 1996 ("News," 1996). In 1997, Pete Metcalfe (researcher to Labour shadow energy minister, John Battle) became a public affairs manager for British Nuclear Fuels (Bevan, 1997a). Another post-election appointment was that of Steve Barwick (adviser to Margaret Beckett while shadow Health Secretary and then shadow Trade and Industry Secretary) to a job at GPC Connect, a public affairs consultancy. New Labour credentials and contacts were important not only for individual careers, but also for consultancies: Tim Bell's corporate and public affairs consultancies suffered "a drop in business" around the time of the election (Garside, 1998), the implication being that their past close association with the Conservartive Party was to blame.

The changing political landscape in Britain in the late 1990s makes it a particularly interesting period for analysing public affairs networks. The strain put on the system through years of political sleaze and the public investigation of lobbying in the media and through CSPL inquiries and reports made lobbyists and politicians conscious of the need to tread carefully. Before the 1997 general election, there was an anticipation of imminent changes in the political culture, personalities, and policies, accompanied by some anxiety as to what the exact shape of these changes would be:

> It is widely believed that a whole new climate of open government is about to sweep over Westminster and Whitehall and lobbyists who want to survive will have to adapt. Not only have some well-established figures— cabinet ministers among them—disappeared, but the composition of Parliament is younger and there are more female MPs. New relationships will have to be forged. (Lee, 1997)

The movement of people within the circuit, shown above, was one way in which the public affairs world was adjusting to the new political landscape. Another response to change, hinted at in an account offered by a practitioner, was to rethink, or at least re-present, the expertise sold to clients:

> These were heady days for lobbyists. The business community and other key sectors knew that change was about to happen but were uncertain about its nature. They needed advice on the likely policy agenda and help dealing with the key decision makers. The old days of launch at the Carlton Club were to become as irrelevant to lobbying as socialism was to become to New Labour. (Bingle, 1997)

Lobbyists began to talk about "ethical lobbying," "strategic lobbying," "new lobbying," or (new) public affairs: the industry was at pains to get away from the image of fixers selling access and contacts, and to be seen as policy experts and strategists selling advice:

> The industry as a whole needs to stress that while face-to-face access to ministers and their advisers can be important [...] it is not central to public affairs. What really matters is knowledge of political processes and expertise in drawing up and implementing strategy. (Gray, 1998)

As in other matters, such as regulation, the reputation-building effort was publicly under-mined by other, perhaps more pragmatic, views, such as: "[t]he process hasn't changed. What has changed is access. Those lobbyists who can't get access talk about strategy" (Garside, 1997a).

Interestingly, this opinion was offered by the same practitioner, Peter Bingle, who 2 weeks after this quote appeared in print was explaining on the pages of *PR Week*: "Why it's goodbye lobbying, hello new public affairs" (Bingle, 1997).

Elected politicians, whether at the national level, serving as Members of Parliament, or at the local level, serving as Councillors, are key elements of what is here referred to as the circuit of power, that is, a network of prestigious jobs in the media, public relations, and politics. Politicians as decisions makers are the lobbyists' targets, but some of them are also lobbyists themselves. A year ahead of the election, *PR Week* commented on "the lure of Parliament," estimating that the Conservative Party alone had more than 20 prospective parliamentary candidates for the next election who "currently work in public affairs or communications" (Gray, 1996c). Immediately after the election, a headline in the magazine claimed that "PR proves fast track to Parliament" reporting that "at least 16 new MPs come from PR and lobbying backgrounds," nine of them sitting on the Labour benches (Bevan, 1997b). A lobbying consultancy, Rowland Sallingbury Casey, had employed three of the new MPs. This was not a coincidence; equally there could not have been many organisations that could boast to have had one, let alone three MPs, among its employees.

The relationship between lobbyists and politicians could be seen as that between suppliers and purveyors of political influence. Viewed in the context of individual careers, it is more a matter of acquisition and exploitation of the key resource—political influence—consisting of knowledge of the political processes and personalities as well as an ability to read the prevailing political climate, policy initiatives, and the ebb and flow of power through political networks. One way in which this expertise could be acquired and used across various jobs is demonstrated in the CV of John Bercow, MP for Buckingham (Conservative) in the House of Commons since 1 May 1997. His official political biography (www.dodonline.co.uk) suggests that he went from student politics in 1984–1987 into local politics (Lambeth Borough Council, 1986–1990), and then consultancy—6 years with Rowland Sallingbury Casey—before becoming a special adviser to Virginia Bottomley, Heritage Secretary, in 1995. He left in 1996 to work part-time as a consultant for Westminster Strategy and to campaign in his prospective constituency (Dowman, 1996b). Bercow had contested two general elections (1987, 1992) before being elected to the House of Commons, where he joined the front benches in 2001 as Shadow Chief Secretary to the Treasury and then Shadow Secretary for International Development (2003–2004). Should his party win an election, a CV like Bercow's makes him a potential candidate for a government post. Here we have an example of the same expertise being used, without any apparent difficulty or conflict, in different jobs—public office and commercial consultancy. Bercow's career choice seems to have been politics, while consultancy was a useful sideline.

Jack McConnell, MSP, Scottish First Minister, is another politician who used a job in lobbying as "a staging post," to borrow a phrase from *PR Week*, in his case to the Scottish Executive. After years of leading the Scottish Labour Party (1992–1998), McConnell became the Chief Executive of Public Affairs Europe (1998–1999), a lobbying consultancy, a joint venture between a successful Scottish PR consultancy (Beattie Media) and lawyers Maclay Murray and Spens ("McConnell quits Scottish Labour," 1998). In this case, the lobbying job proved more problematic when in 1999 a sting operation by *The Observer* led to an exposé, similar to that of Drapergate, of lobbying in Scotland. Lobbygate, as it came to be known, focused on a Beattie Media employee, Kevin Reid, son of the then Secretary of State for Scotland, John Reid, apparently trading on this connection. This raised concerns about close links between lobbyists and politicians in Scotland, and McConnell's name inevitably came centre stage (for a detailed account, see Schlesinger et al., 2001, pp. 226–244).

Connections between journalists, lobbyists, and politicians have been treated as a threat to standards in public life both in institutional and critical terms. It has been argued in media comment, in official inquiries, and in critical analysis (B. Franklin, 1994, 1997, 2003) that standards are being eroded. In the 1990s, the attention focused on spin, particularly on the way in which the Labour government managed media coverage of its policies and personalities; on the politicisation of the Government Information and Communication Service; and the weakened boundaries between public and private interests, which lay at the heart of the lobbying scandals. At the same time, however, the movement of people through the circuit continued, and if anything, the tracks were getting deeper. This raises a question about the actual, practical value of public image to an occupation. Whatever might have been said about PR, there is no evidence that fewer people work in it, fewer organisations use it, or that there is a long-term trend of diminishing expenditure on such services. Judging by the place communications specialists routinely occupy at the high table—whether in politics, business campaigns, or public feasts of honour, as we have seen looking at PR barons—the precise damage, if any, to the occupation resulting from its poor public image is difficult to locate.

CONCLUSION

In the introduction to this chapter, a question was asked about the main factors which influenced UK public relations practice in the late 1990s. As has subsequently been shown, there have been a number of interlinked influences, which could be summarised as clients, competition, and public image.

The relationship practitioners build with their clients appears to be critical in establishing a consultant's security that goes beyond contractual commitments. This may in turn bring more work without the need for expensive pitching. Another outcome of good client relations is felt in the reputation the consultancy acquires, which circulates through recommendations. Client relations are managed by recognised account management skills (for example, accounting for decisions made, work undertaken, time spent on tasks, results achieved). At the same time as shaping routine, daily work, client relations are partly responsible for overservicing, which in turn is a hidden cost, possibly borne mostly by the junior consultancy juniors. In this way, client relations may influence economic basis of the business and its labour market.

Key to understanding client relations is the notion of "chemistry," by which practitioners mean intuitive judgements—made by both partners—and the ensuing level of trust and comfort in the relationship. Studies of management consultants in recent years have problematised both the concept of knowledge and of the profession. For example, Reed (1996) showed that that there are different ways in which the knowledge base, occupational power strategies, and organisational forms are inter-related. He differentiated between three types of expert groups: independent/liberal professions (doctors, architects, lawyers), organisational professions (managers, administrators), and knowledge workers (financial and business consultants, computer and IT analysts). Fores, Glover, and Lawrence (1991) pointed out that traditional approaches to the study of professionalism foreground one side of the professional practice—that based on abstract knowledge—at the expense of another—"the more important qualities of skill, creativity, judgement, and *savoir faire*, and the constructive response to the uncertain and unprogrammable" (Fores et al., 1991, p. 97; cited in Alvesson, 1993, p. 999). A similar distinction between tacit and explicit knowledge has also been made in studies of organisational knowledge (see Tell, 2004, pp. 443–445). Alvesson in his study of knowledge workers redefined the role of knowledge in professional work in the following way:

> [w]ithout denying that knowledge may be a functional resource that is directly applied in work [. . .] other functions of knowledge and knowledge-talk become central. Knowledge plays other roles such as (a) a means for creating community and social identity through offering organizational members a shared language and promoting their self esteem; (b) a resource for persuasion in, for example, PR work and interactions with customers; (c) providing the company with a profile (an intended image targeted at the market); (d) creating legitimacy and good faith regarding actions and outcomes, and (e) obscuring uncertainty. (Alvesson, 1993, p. 1005)

In public relations consultancy both types of knowledge (formal or professional; personal or intuitive) play their part. While chemistry is emphasised in dealing with clients, evaluation, and the technical knowledge of quantification associated with it, becomes important in competitive situations where other occupations such as marketing or advertising might be involved. Evaluation is also an important image building tactic directed primarily at potential clients. As we have seen, in the debate discussed in this chapter, evaluation was clearly perceived as a tool of persuasion, and, perhaps less explicitly, as a way of obscuring the uncertainty involved in the highly complex contexts for PR work.

Competition between providers of PR—which hardly gets a mention in standard PR textbooks or academic research—is nevertheless fundamental to any explanation of the state of the occupation. Competition appears to be the constant factor undermining all attempts at professionalisation. We have seen the role it played in the institutional efforts at standardising evaluation practice; we have all seen competition at work in the efforts aimed at improving the public image of public relations. The occupation's stance on regulation articulated how the occupation perceived its public image and the ambitions it harboured in this respect—becoming a public institution. The ambition was frustrated by disagreements rooted in the positions occupied in the competitive market by practitioners.

The importance of the symbolic representation of public relations, underscoring its public image, was made clear in the publicly articulated endorsement or rejection of values represented by well-known individual practitioners. Names by which the practice should be known were another site of this symbolic effort. A range of terms are used routinely in PR practice, for example, a lobbyist may go as a public affairs specialist, but would bridle at "public relations." Wood and Higgins' (1999) survey of Scottish organisations showed a range of departmental titles given to the function, for example, communications (& media/public affairs), public relations, corporate communication, corporate affairs, internal communication, press office, and publicity. The occupation's well-demonstrated awareness of how such denominations function could be observed early in 1996, when Burson-Marsteller renamed itself as a "perception management consultancy," rather than a public relations one (Bevan, 1996d)—*PR Week's* editorial was critical of the move ("PR shouldn't be a shameful term," 1996).

The public image and status of the occupation are constantly under attack, but at the same time there is a clear elite of practitioners who receive public signs of respect and recognition. It seems this paradox can be explained with a reference to a classic profession, medicine, that is invoked by all aspirants to the title. Instances of poor practice by individual doctors are often reported and there are abundant media stories about them. At the same time, nobody would seriously suggest that the institution of medical practice is of dubious value to society. It seems that the opposite happens in public relations: the practice—there is no "institution"—is seen as highly suspicious, but individual practitioners may command recognition and trust.

V

Critical Perspectives Revisited

INTRODUCTION

This section includes a number of chapters from the book *Critical Perspectives*, published by ITBP in 1996. Pieczka's chapters on "Paradigms, systems theory, and public relations" and "Public opinion" appear as they did in that text. Since the chapter on systems in particular aroused the ire of those within the dominant paradigm (Grunig in Heath, 2001), it seemed sensible to reprint the original article so that future scholars can more easily track paradigm debates. Likewise, the chapter on "Public relations education" has been included because it records educational issues and institutional relationships and problems at the outset of public relations education in the UK and so it has been left untouched, defensiveness and all. The remaining chapters have all been revised to varying degrees.

The chapter "Paradigms, systems theory, and public relations" begins with a review of three clearly defined manifestations of systems thinking in sociology and organizational studies. The chapter traces the development of systems ideas, showing how these came to be adopted in public relations theory. In the second part of the chapter, Pieczka, takes a critical look at discourse in public relations within academia and argues that systems thinking has become dominant paradigm.

"Public relations and rhetoric" explores classical and more contemporary ideas in rhetoric for insights into the role and ethics of public relations. It argues that questions of ethics cannot be addressed without consideration of recent and contemporary intellectual debates in rhetoric, epistemology, and postmodernism. The chapter has been re-edited for greater clarity of argument.

"Public relations as diplomacy" draws comparison between the emergence of public relations and diplomacy as areas of academic study and practice. The chapter also now includes some historical examples of public relations practitioners interpreting their work as a form of diplomacy. The critical arguments in relation to the concept of symmetry and its implication for hegemony and organisational boundaries have been retained.

The theme of symbolic communication is picked up in "Corporate identity and corporate image," where Meech presents a review of the terminological debates around image and identity and the notion of corporate personality before turning to corporate identity as a practice. More recent examples have been incorporated into the chapter together with updated literature.

The chapter on "Corporate social responsibility" remains critical of functional approaches to the practice, though this is leavened by the inclusion of a much wider range of contemporary business views and thus is less black and white than the original. Much more historical material is included on the Quakers and sources from strategic management and marketing have also been introduced. The chapter explores the relationship between public relations and notions of corporate social responsibility by means of discussions of crisis management and community programmes. Utilitarian and Kantian moral theory are used as analytical tools to expose contradictions in these two practices. The analysis draws out the motivation behind corporate social responsibility, crisis management, and issues management to expose the essential tension that lies between the fight for organisational survival and concern for the public interest. There is also some analysis of the claim that public relations itself is intrinsically ethical and socially responsible and the discussion is linked to broader questions about relationships between government, society, and business.

"Public opinion and public relations" reviews debates and key concepts in relation to public relations practice and research. The chapter highlights the empiricist stranglehold on the concept of public opinion and explores the connections between public opinion and mass communication. The essay concludes with a discussion of the conceptual and methodological links between public opinion and public relations research to demonstrate the assumptions implicit in public relations theory. As part of the discussion, the chapter reveals the source of public relations' claims to be a neutral and enabling function in society as well as proposing that the close link between public relations and political science should be articulated more openly.

L'Etang and Pieczka's chapter on "Public relations education" provides an historic link with the earlier section on "Professionalism, professionalisation, and education." Indeed, it is a matter for debate as to whether it might have been usefully included in that section. However, the decision was made to keep material from the original volume together. After a cursory summary of some early developments in public relations in the UK (which date back to the early 1950s), the chapter reviews educational developments as they obtained in the UK in the late 1980s and early 1990s and discusses the nature of the public relations discipline, the appropriate location of courses, and proposes a radicalisation of the curriculum. The chapter suggests that the functionalist nature of courses in the United States and the UK can be linked to pressures from the industry, and argues that this emphasis could potentially threaten the academic freedom and credibility of the subject. It is suggested that public relations education needs instead to be rooted more firmly in its conceptual origins and to resist being equated with basic training. It is argued that public relations academics should be producing a wide variety of theoretical and applied research and that students should be educated to think independently and critically, not simply taught to conform to existing industry norms and values. The chapter thus reflects the historical concerns of some educators in the late 1980s and early 1990s.

Much has changed in the last decade in the UK, especially in the relationship between the Institute of Public Relations (IPR)[1] and higher education. Where once the IPR's position was driven by an Education Committee led by distrustful practitioners, the Institute has been professionalised and appointed personnel who have experience and knowledge of further and higher education and whose desire is to collaborate rather than control. The IPR's growing

---

[1] In February 2005 the IPR was granted Chartered Status and changed its name to Chartered Institute of Public Relations (CIPR).

commitment to education, continuous professional development, and particularly to research and evaluation in practice has undoubtedly defused many tensions that existed. There are other areas that remain to be explored, for example, the gender and class origins of public relations students and the reported (L'Etang, 2002) high incidence of stress and eating disorders among public relations students in what is clearly a very image-conscious occupation.

17

Paradigms, Systems Theory, and Public Relations

Magda Pieczka
Stirling Media Research Institute

One of the presuppositions underpinning current public relations theorizing is the concept of a system; or, to be more precise, the belief that organizations behave in ways that can be conceptualized as closed or open systems (Grunig & Hunt, 1984; Botan & Hazleton, 1989a; Cutlip et al., 1985; J. E. Grunig, 1992). This presupposition has far-reaching consequences in terms of attempts at building public relations theories per se, but also for the nature of emerging academic public relations discourse. This chapter attempts to address broader methodological questions by focusing on the way in which systems theory underpins current public relations theory. The aim is to fill a gap in public relations literature by showing the origins of fundamental presuppositions currently made by most academic writers in the field. The chapter thus presents both a critique and a source of references for those who wish to acquaint themselves with debates more fully.

Those who wish to tackle only the argumentative parts of the chapter as opposed to the careful mapping of the field may wish to proceed directly to the section "Public relations discourse," as it is from this point onwards that critical points about public relations theory are developed. The sections entitled "Systems theory and public relations theory" and "Implications" focus strongly on public relations theory and literature and critically analyse a number of key public relations texts for their treatment and use of systems theory.

In order to make its point, this chapter has to proceed in a particular manner: by introducing analytical tools and terminology, discussing relevant debates, and, finally, presenting a set of concepts taken from public relations literature and analysing them within the framework provided by the first two sections. There is a fair amount of detail and referencing, which readers might find laborious but which is necessary for understanding the analytical approach and the structure of the argument. Briefly, the structure of this chapter can be compared to three different maps of the same intellectual area drawn from three different perspectives. The maps are imposed one upon another to achieve a more complete, 3-dimensional picture. References and terminology provide the constants, the points with the help of which the maps can be fitted together.

The first map, "Models of systems: an historical perspective," discusses the concept of "system" and its different incarnations in natural as well as social sciences over the last 300 years or so. The purpose is to make it clear that "system" was not discovered by the general system theory in the 1950s. In fact there had been a long tradition of explaining all kinds of phenomena as systems, however these might have been conceptualized. To appreciate the influence of this tradition on general systems theory, a review of terminology connected with the concept is provided. As a result, "system" emerges as an ambiguous concept that can be linked, for example in organization studies, to different theoretical positions.

The discussion then moves on to "The battle of paradigms," the second map, to show the relationship between organization theory, metatheoretical positions (paradigms), and systems theory. The vantage point chosen is that of Burrell and Morgan's (1979) work, which reviewed the field of organization theory using a four-paradigm framework constructed by the authors. The book made a strong impression, particularly with its argument about the functionalist dominance in the field. As the book was published in 1979, a further discussion was needed to show what happened to the debate about paradigms with the onslaught of postmodernism. The purpose of this section within the whole argument, then, is to introduce the metatheoretical dimension, necessary for any discussion of discourse(s).

Finally, our third map, "Public relations discourse," shows how systems thinking shapes the terrain of public relations theory. This aim can be achieved only by marshalling detailed evidence and analysing it using the framework constructed by earlier sections of the chapter. To manage the potentially massive amount of detail, the discussion presents clusters of related concepts as "units of analysis." The analysis itself moves from terminology to discussion of the worldviews behind it in order to reflect on the public relations discourse revealed through such a discussion.

A similar interest was expressed by Pearson (1990), who also used Burrell and Morgan as his starting point. The main thrust of his discussion was a distinction between functionalism and a holistic approach emphasizing interdependence—each using a systems approach in rather different ways—to explore their implications for public relations. Pearson seems to have been influenced by Habermas in his approach to the role of communication activity in social life, and he developed this interest as a result of an exploration of ethics in public relations. To summarize crudely, Pearson believed that there was a choice for public relations between a narrow functionalist approach, that is, an organization as a system driven by the need to attain its goals, and an ethical holistic approach as the basis for the practice. We shall refer to Pearson's argument in more detail later in the chapter, but, unlike Pearson, the author here is more interested in critiquing frameworks than in building them.

MODELS OF SYSTEMS:
AN HISTORICAL PERSPECTIVE

The three models by which systems approach can be applied to understand human organizations (whether large organizations such as societies or smaller units such as commercial companies) are referred to in the literature as either mechanistic, organismic, or social system models (Buckley, 1967; Burrell & Morgan, 1979; Morgan, 1986; Gharajedaghi & Ackoff, 1994). Buckley (1967) discussed the concept of the social system in the sociological tradition, and in so doing presented the following three models: equilibrium, homeostatic, and the process or adaptive system. These correspond to the mechanistic, organismic, and "social system" models of Gharajedaghi and Ackoff (1994). It should be pointed out that the terminology used by Gharajedaghi and Ackoff can be confusing, as they see the "social system" as a particular model of social systems within a more general understanding of the term. These terms are often used interchangeably in the literature and will be used so in this chapter, but we shall start with Buckley's terminology for the purposes of introduction and definitions. The equilibrium model describes systems "which, in moving to an equilibrium point, typically lose organization, and then tend to hold that minimum level within relatively narrow conditions of disturbance" (Buckley, 1967, p. 40). Homeostatic models "apply to systems tending to maintain a given, relatively high, level of organization against ever-present tendencies to reduce it" (ibid.). And finally, there is the process or complex adaptive system model, which describes a system capable of elaboration or evolution of its organization and which "depend[s] on 'disturbances' and 'variety' in the environment" (ibid.).

THE EQUILIBRIUM MODEL

The roots of this model lie in the advances in physics, particularly mechanics (dealing with the motion of bodies: for example, Kepler's laws of planetary motion or Newton's laws of motion), and in mathematics in the 17th and 18th centuries. These developments were so impressive in offering a rational deductive approach (in which true laws are developed from true assumptions through logical reasoning) that they came to be accepted as a paradigm for thinking about man and society.

Within this perspective, a universe is viewed as a clockwork mechanism, and a human being as a sophisticated machine whose actions can nevertheless be explained according to the same mechanistic principles that apply, for example, to planets.

> In "social mechanics," society was seen as an "astronomical system" whose elements were human beings bound together by mutual attraction or differentiated by repulsion; groups of societies or states were systems of balanced oppositions. Man, his groups, and their interrelations . . . constituted an unbroken continuity with the rest [of] the universe. (Buckley, 1967, p. 8)

Terminology and concepts borrowed from mechanics, such as attraction, inertia, equilibrium (a state of perfect balance) or entropy (a measure of disorder), were thus applied to society by a number of sociologists, particularly from the end of the 19th century, producing concepts such as social entropy, fields of force, social equilibrium, and social coordinates. What this clearly demonstrates is that the influence of mechanics produced a mechanical model of society.

Vilfredo Pareto (1848–1923), an Italian economist and sociologist, is credited with developing this early, mechanistic view of society as a system consisting of "interrelated parts with a boundary, and usually tending to maintain equilibrium" (Buckley, 1967, p. 9). The implication of such a definition is that society is determined by forces acting upon it. The dynamics of such forces revolve around the pivotal point of equilibrium, so that any force directed away from equilibrium is counterbalanced by changes directed at restoring the balance. Pareto saw the concept of equilibrium as a useful analytical tool which could be applied in the social sciences, although for his followers there seemed to have been some ambiguity whether this was to be understood purely as an abstract, analytical concept or rather as a description of social reality (Burrell & Morgan, 1979, p. 47).

Pareto's main work, *Trattato di sociologia generale*, originally published in 1916, strongly influenced the Harvard School of Sociology in the 1930s, as can be seen in the work of a number of sociologists such as Mayo (1933), Homans (1950), and, perhaps most significantly, Parsons (1951).

THE HOMEOSTATIC MODEL

If the above mechanistic model offers one paradigm, the advances in biology epitomized by the Darwinian revolution—the theory of the evolution of the species—established a different approach, often referred to as the organic or organismic approach. The analogy between a living organism and society has an ancient lineage, yet it reappeared in a new shape in the early 19th century in the work of Auguste Comte, recognized as the founder of both positivism and sociology; and in the late 19th century in the work of Herbert Spencer, representing social Darwinism.

It was Comte's view that the science of society should adopt the model of the natural sciences with their positive methods whereby the observation of empirical facts and reasoning leads to the discovery of universal laws governing the phenomena under study. In his own writing society is, for purposes of analysis, compared to an organism. Spencer took from Comte both the methodological interest in applying natural sciences methods to sociology and also the organismic analogy. The enormous impact of the theory of evolution—which by that time was well established, even if seen as strongly controversial—made the analogy a persuasive one.

In very broad terms, in Spencer and his followers we find a school of thought which sees society as consisting of a number of parts performing specific functions and in this way contributing to the existence of the whole organism/society. This perspective assumes a fundamental "unity, interdependence, and ordered nature of constituent relationships" (Burrell & Morgan, 1979, p. 43); the focus on evolutionary change is linked to the interest in functional differentiation and specialization. However, as Buckley pointed out (Buckley, 1967, pp. 12–13; Burrell & Morgan, 1979, p. 43), the unitary perspective resulting from the application of evolutionary principles at the microscopic level of organism is in contradiction to the Darwinian principles of the struggle for survival and the process of natural selection.

If we follow the history of the organismic analogy beyond Spencer, we find a line of thinkers who are grouped together as the functionalist school in sociology. Durkheim, although critical of Comte and more sympathetic to Spencer, did accept both the principle of a social reality which can be investigated scientifically and the "integrationist" framework (Burrell & Morgan, 1979, p. 13) which resulted from a belief in the holistic nature of society, in which the concept of functional differentiation is linked to that of the interdependence of parts; in other words, society is held together by "organic solidarity" (ibid., pp. 41–46).

Structural functionalism, although originally articulated theoretically by two anthropologists, Malinowski and Radcliffe-Brown, became the predominant mode of sociological analysis until the rise, in the 1970s, of Marxism, ethnomethodology, poststructuralism, and symbolic and cultural analysis (Reed, 1993, p. 163). Both Malinowski and Radcliffe-Brown in their studies of "primitive" societies employed the concept of function as the basis for explanation: anthropological facts could be understood in terms of the functions they performed in the system of culture under study. Radcliffe-Brown, in his theoretical work, consciously referred to the organismic analogy, placing a strong emphasis on the distinction between structure and process, which in his work appears as a distinction between social morphology and social physiology (Radcliffe-Brown, 1952; Burrell & Morgan, 1979, pp. 51–54). Talcott Parsons, one of the most influential functionalist sociologists, preoccupied himself with the study of the latter, that is, the explanation of how social structures function. Such an explanation needs to address four "functional imperatives" (Parsons, 1959; Rocher, 1974; Burrell & Morgan, 1979): adaptation, goal attainment, integration, and latency or pattern maintenance, across all of which a system's equilibrium is to be maintained.

This brings us to an interesting point, namely the continued reference to the concept of equilibrium—derived originally from the mechanistic analogy, but now found in a framework clearly built on the organismic model. Burrell and Morgan (1979, pp. 57–63) pointed out that this theoretical inconsistency was made apparent by von Bertalanffy's work on general systems theory and open systems theory (von Bertalanffy, 1950, 1956), in which equilibrium is, according to the second law of thermodynamics, a state inevitably attained in a closed system isolated from its environment, that is, the type of system that is described by conventional physics. Open systems, on the other hand, are engaged in a constant exchange with environment (input, output) and may, though this is not a necessary condition, achieve a state of holistic balance within this flux (homeostasis). Von Bertalanffy's work can therefore be seen as establishing the widely accepted distinction between mechanistic, closed systems and homeostatic, organismic, open systems.

Pursuing the connection between sociology and organization theory, we have already mentioned Pareto, Romans, and Mayo as followers of the first model; we have also mentioned Parsons' work as combining elements of both. Classical management is linked with the closed systems model (Morgan, 1986, p. 45); whereas the open systems perspective can be found in the work of Katz and Kahn (1966), the Tavistock group—in the concept of a socio-technical system (Emery & Trist, 1946)—and as the basis for contingency theory (Lawrence & Lorsch, 1967). This organismic, open systems approach typically operates a number of concepts, such as boundary, process, input, output, feedback, homeostasis, systems behaviour, subsystems, and boundary transactions (Burrell & Morgan, 1979, p. 63; Morgan, 1986, pp. 46–47).

Gharajedaghi and Ackoff (1994), in their review of the three models, established clear links between the models as theoretical tools and the empirical reality of organizations that fit these categories. The mechanistic organization is reductionist, inflexible, preoccupied with control and coordination, and, consequently, centrally controlled and hierarchically structured. Organismic organizations are preoccupied with survival and its necessary condition, growth; individual parts possess a certain degree of self-control; the structure is less formal and supported by direct communication between parts; there is also more two-way communication. Finally, introducing the social systems model, the focus of their discussion, holism and synergy seem to be the main features. These three models are also linked to types of system behaviour as identified by Ackoff and Emery (1972, pp. 30–31): "most systems display some combination of these types of behaviour. Nevertheless, it should be noted that mechanistically conceptualized systems are modelled as predominantly reactive; organismically conceptualized systems as predominantly responsive [goal-seeking]; and socially conceptualized systems as predominantly active [purposeful]" (Gharajedaghi & Ackoff, 1994, p. 34).

THE PROCESS OR ADAPTIVE SYSTEM MODEL

This model was proposed by Buckley (1967) as a critique of the traditional mechanistic and organismic models. His interest lay in explaining the process of structure elaboration (morphogenesis) and in doing so he addressed issues such as conflict, deviance and social control, which traditional models are unable to deal with. Theoretically, he attempted to "synthesize the whole range of functionalist paradigm—from interactionist [Mead, Simmel and Blumer] to the social systems theory [Homans and Parsons]—and makes passing references to ... Marx" (Burrell & Morgan, 1979, p. 99).

The process model uses cybernetics as its analogy to avoid any teleological bias in explanations of goal-seeking behaviour, often inseparable from organismic analogies. This model also helps to focus on the role of information in the system's dynamics. The sociocultural system thus "emerges from a network of interaction among individuals in which information is selectively perceived and interpreted in accordance with the meaning it holds for the actors involved" (Burrell & Morgan, 1979, p. 100).

Gharajedaghi and Ackoff (1994) concluded their review of these three system models and their practical implications by equating mechanistic management with its prime interest in efficiency; organismic management with a focus on growth and survival; and social-system management with the overriding interest in development, defined as "the process in which individuals increase their abilities and desires to satisfy their own needs and legitimate desires, and those of others" (Gharajedaghi & Ackoff, 1994, p. 36). Organizations operating on these principles are said to serve

> the purposes of the system, its parts, and its containing systems. There may be conflict between these levels or within them. Therefore, resolution, or dissolution of conflict is one of management's principal responsibilities. A social system should be viewed as an instrument of those it affects. Its principal function is to encourage and facilitate their development. For management of social systems, planning should consist of designing a desirable future and inventing or finding ways of approximating it ... Such management should attempt to maximize the freedom of choice of those it affects. Only from experience of choice can one learn, hence develop. (Gharajedaghi & Ackoff, 1994, p. 39)

Ironically, this interpretation of Buckley, originally published in 1984, seems to bring us back to our starting point, and we could draw out a number of familiar characteristics from this extract. It is functionalist in its acceptance that not only an organization but also, it seems, the whole social world is a system of interdependent, cooperating parts. Although the existence of conflict is acknowledged, the whole emphasis of the social system is on maintaining unity. This, interestingly, is achieved through the intervention of management, which apparently possesses both the knowledge and the ability to devise and implement rationally ways in which conflict can, and should, be worked out of the system. We find, then, a clear normative approach demonstrated, and linked to a rational view of human nature, which under favourable conditions (freedom) tends towards "socially responsible" action. So, social systems are designed to provide freedom, which allows individuals to satisfy their needs and which also produces social harmony.

AUTOPOIESIS AND SOCIAL SYSTEMS

When general systems theory emerged in the 1950s, it was greeted with a considerable degree of excitement:

> Under the banner of systems research ... we have witnessed a convergence of many specialized contemporary scientific developments ... These research pursuits and many others are being interwoven into a co-operative research effort ... We are participating in ... the most comprehensive effort to attain a synthesis of scientific knowledge yet made. (Ackoff, 1959, p. 145)

The ambitious final statement here may have echoed von Bertalanffy's aim of achieving "a unity of science," made possible since general systems theory started uncovering the "isomorphy of laws in different fields" (von Bertalanffy, 1956, p. 8; quoted in Burrell & Morgan, 1979, p. 58). Rapoport referred to general systems theory as "a direction in the contemporary philosophy of science" (Rapoport, 1968, p. 452); and Buckley seemed to have views similar to those already quoted above, defining general systems theory as:

A common vocabulary unifying the several "behavioural" disciplines;
A technique for treating large, complex organizations;

An operationally definable, objective, non-anthropomorphic study of purposiveness, goal-seeking systems behaviour, symbolic cognitive process, consciousness and self-awareness, and sociocultural emergence and dynamics in general. (Buckley, 1967, p. 39)

By the end of the 1960s, functionalism and systems theory were going out of fashion. "The problematic of order" by the late 1970s had been displaced by "the problematic of domination"; and the 1980s, in turn, saw the emergence of "the problematic in which the construction of organizational reality, through the skilled utilization of largely arbitrary linguistic and cultural representation or 'language games' has become the central concern" (Reed, 1992, pp. 10–11; see also Ackroyd, 1992). Put differently, systems-based contingency approaches focusing on "the adaptability of organizational designs to environmental imperatives" came to be criticized for relying on "devalued theoretical capital" (Reed, 1992, pp. 2–3). This explains a shift in the 1970s away from the static view of organizations—units constrained by the environment—to an interest in organizational reproduction and transformation through a cultural and political process, which could not be explained by the systems approach with its "logic of effectiveness." Hence alternative approaches to the study of organizations started emerging, such as action frame of reference (Silverman, 1970), negotiated order (Strauss, 1978), ethnomethodology (Cicourel, 1968), and political theories of organizational decision making (Pettigrew, 1973; Pfeffer, 1981; see Reed, 1992, pp. 2–3). Finally, from the late 1970s and throughout the 1980s the range of interests and approaches was widened still further:

First, then, there was an increasingly potent emphasis on the cultural and symbolic processes through which organizations were socially constructed and organizational analysis academically structured (Turner, 1990). Second, the macro-level power relations and ideological systems through which organizational forms were shaped became a central theme for analysis (McNeil, 1978). Third, the retreat from natural science conceptions of organizational analysis seems to make an intellectual and institutional space available for approaches focused on the complete interaction between theoretical innovation and social context (Morgan, 1990). (Reed, 1992, p. 4)

The above discussion is, as is every generalization, a broad and probably simplified account of changes in organization studies. There is, however, one specific strand of theorizing that emerged in the social sciences in the mid-1980s which requires more attention from our point of view—the concept of autopoiesis and its applications. Originally, autopoiesis, or the autopoietic model of systems, was proposed in 1974 by two Chilean biologists, Varela and Maturana, in cooperation with the systems theorist Uribe. It was taken up in social science following Luhmann's pioneering work (1984, 1986; see Kickert, 1993, p. 263).

The originality of autopoiesis lies in its presenting a fundamentally different model of the relationship between the system and its environment. Instead of the traditional view that systems adapt to the environment, the new model sees systems as self-referential and closed. The system is driven by its need to survive, but survival is understood as the maintenance of self-identity. Environment exists for the system only as a projection of its self-identity—or, to simplify, it is constructed by the system.

The original, biological, model focused on redefining the nature of "living" and in the process redefined the concept of the system. But for Varela. and Maturana, a living system is primarily a "network of interactions of components" and

instead of looking at what makes a living system reproduce the parts of the system . . . [Varela and Maturana] looked at the organization of the living system that is reproduced . . . not reproduction as such, but rather the reproduction of the organization of the living system . . . which makes it "living." (Kickert, 1993, p. 263)

The autonomy of such a system lies in its unity, which "consists of a network of component-producing processes such that the interactive components recursively generate the same network of processes" (Kickert, 1993, p. 264).

This proved an intriguing new idea which received a lot of attention from systems theorists. As Burrell and Morgan observed, following von Bertalanffy's conceptualization of the closed system as being isolated from the environment, social scientists had decided that it was an inadequate model to apply to social phenomena. It became fashionable to criticize Weber and classical management theory as examples of outmoded, closed-system thinking. In fact, the very notion of the closed system tended to be avoided like a "dreaded disease" by the social sciences (Burrell & Morgan, 1979, p. 60). Varela and Maturana's ideas about autonomy and closure as the way in which systems survive seemed to turn this traditional concept of the closed system on its head, and promised a new lease of life for systems theory.

Although Varela and Maturana themselves argued very strongly against autopoiesis being applied outside biology, Kickert (1993, pp. 265–266) listed a number of elaborations and applications of the model "outside the realm of living": notably Jantsch (1981), who related it to notions of chaos and order; and Ben-Eli (1981), who linked autopoiesis and self-referentiality with evolution. Following its career among systems theorists, autopoiesis eventually found its way to the social sciences when Luhmann applied it to the social system, and also introduced the idea of "a paradigmatic shift in systems theory from the holistic notion of parts and whole, via the distinction of system and environment, towards a theory of self referential systems" (Kickert, 1993, p. 267).

In the light of our discussion so far, Luhmann's paradigmatic shift could be seen as focusing on the differences between the mechanistic, organismic, and process models of systems discussed earlier in this chapter, although such a comparison has to be conducted rather cautiously.

So by 1984 (that is, in about a decade) autopoiesis had not only become well established in the social sciences, but also undergone some important changes in the process. First, the requirement of closure was considerably relaxed, or even dropped; second, from the original concept of self-reproduction, we seem, via self-organization, to have arrived at a much broader concept of self-referentiality, as employed by Luhmann (Kickert, 1993, p. 267).

Autopoiesis comes into our orbit of interest in Morgan's metaphor of flux and transformation (Morgan, 1986, pp. 235–240), where he explained an autopoietic system as producing "images of reality as expressions or descriptions of its own organization" (ibid., p. 238) and interacting with these images, the way, for example, a human brain does. Interestingly, Morgan linked Weick's concept of enactment with autopoiesis:

> The ideas on autopoiesis add to our understanding of . . . enactment, in that they encourage us to view organizational enactments as part of the self-referential process through which an organization attempts to tie down and reproduce its identity. For in enacting the environment an organization is attempting to achieve the kind of closure that is necessary for it to reproduce itself in its own image. (Morgan, 1986, p. 241)

Pearson, in his discussion of systems theory in public relations, argued that the prevalent approach is that "which emphasized processes and uses terms like *input, throughput,* and *output*" and is attentive to the concept of interdependency, taking a holistic view of a system; while simultaneously referring to management by objectives, viewing a system as goal-seeking (Pearson, 1990, p. 222). In terms of the models identified above, this is perhaps closest to the homeostatic, or organic, model. This approach, Pearson claimed, lies clearly within the functionalist tradition; and his interest, therefore, focused on examining the implications of this "metatheoretical perspective, or paradigm" (ibid., p. 220) for the discipline of public relations.

Although Pearson referred to Burrell and Morgan, his assumption about systems theory constituting a paradigm seems to be incompatible with their definition of a paradigm. This explains perhaps why Pearson could see as meaningful the question of when systems theory is not functionalist. He argued that taking the idea of holism to its logical conclusion, one arrives inevitably at a completely different framework—an ethical rather than a goal-directed view of behaviour. Similarly, if one considers the differences between the three system models presented so far, the adaptive system—close in many respects to the self-referentiality of autopoiesis—poses a serious question about the metatheoretical assumptions behind it: is it or is it not functionalism? In order to explore this problem, however, it is necessary to understand what a paradigm is and how theories are related to paradigms.

THE BATTLE OF PARADIGMS: ORGANIZATION STUDIES AND PUBLIC RELATIONS

The word "paradigm" is just about the most over-used in the philosophical lexicon. In fact, professional philosophers tend to avoid it like the plague, and today it is much more commonly used by sociologists, scientists, and journalists . . . Part of the problem is that the word "paradigm" is as slippery as the word "God." Everyone who uses it means something slightly different. Too frequently the term is used as a propaganda tool, bolstering the pretensions of some supposed major breakthrough: paradigm founder today, Nobel prize winner tomorrow, burial in Westminster Abbey the day after that. (Ruse, 1993, p. 118)

This discussion of the debate about paradigms in organizational studies is introduced, quite consciously, by questioning the meaning and usage of the term itself. It seems that the following discussion can be enlightening in many respects and useful to public relations, and my intention is to reflect on how public relations as a discipline "thinks," or at least on some aspects of this question. As a new discipline, public relations seems to be rather sensitive about its academic status; but this position is neither unique nor can it be solved by bolstering false pretensions. The term "paradigm" has therefore been avoided as far as possible so far, but will be used, without any apologies, in the context where it seems legitimate, that is, the debate about philosophical positions underlying theories in sociology and organization studies, which I shall attempt to extend to public relations.

The debate about paradigms has already begun in public relations (Botan, 1993; Everett, 1993; Hallahan, 1993). It is seen as a sign of the discipline maturing and developing a range of different approaches; at the same time the process is not seen as advanced enough for a full-blown paradigm struggle, or debate, to be able to take place (Botan, 1993, p. 108). Although the term paradigm is used, and although it is a notoriously ambiguous term, the meaning with which it has appeared so far in public relations is rather narrow—a model with a group of followers seems to be sufficient to merit the term. The difficulty with this interpretation is that it leads to unnecessary fragmentation and confusion, precisely the problem which Burrell and Morgan tried to get away from by suggesting their four-paradigm scheme for discussing organizational theory (Burrell & Morgan, 1979, pp. x–xiv).

There are two slightly different accounts of how and when the debate started in organization studies. Reed (1993) traced the beginning back to Silverman (1970); Ackroyd (1992) looked to Burrell and Morgan (1979), who, in turn, seem to be in agreement with Reed about the pivotal role played by Silverman in opening the floodgates for alternative approaches to organization and challenging the systems orthodoxy. It seems that the point of disagreement between Ackroyd and Reed is over whether Silverman organized his work on the principle of Kuhnian paradigmatic shift—Ackroyd's point (1992, p. 171)—or according to a "serial" approach, in which theories follow one another and constitute series, admittedly sometimes very short ones (Reed, 1993, p. 110). Avoiding taking sides on this point, I shall take Burrell and Morgan as central to this debate in view of their later contributions.

Before we step into the thick of the debate itself, a number of other introductory comments must be made. First, Burrell and Morgan's work should be seen against the background of, on the one hand, dissatisfaction with functionalism and the contingency approach dominating at the threat of stopping other developments and, on the other hand, the lack of debate, if not hostility, between theorists representing various approaches. Burrell and Morgan's response was to create an "effective synthesis of diverse approaches to theory" by mapping these approaches within a single "general frame [which] denied exclusive authority to one approach to organization" (Ackroyd, 1992, p. 111). They consequently dealt with the apparent differences as being attributable to simpler expositions. However, there was a danger inherent in the design of their "general framework": in suggesting the desirability of paradigm closure, and therefore the necessity to choose between them, Burrell and Morgan reinforced inadvertently the imminent "fragmentation of organizational studies into querulous and squabbling factions" (Reed, 1993, p. 172).

Second, as hinted before, there are other ways of categorizing or grouping theories of organizations. Aldrich provided an interesting discussion of ecological, institutional, and interpretative approaches differentiated on the basis of "their products rather than the process of their construction" (Aldrich, 1992, p. 18). Gergen (1992) proposed an approach that follows the process of theory construction, that is, he uncovered the influence of romanticism, modernism, and postmodernism. Thus, romantic dimensions can be found in the work of the Tavistock Institute, theories drawing on psychoanalysis (Zeleznick), theories drawing on Jungian archetypes (Denhardt, Mitroff), research presuming fundamental human needs (Mayo, Maslow, McGregor), approaches to leadership based on personal resources (Fiedler, Hollander), and Japanese management theory (Ouchi). Modernist conceptions include time and motion studies, general systems and their extensions (Lawrence and Lorsch), exchange theories (Homans), cybernetic theories, trait methodology presuming the stability of individual patterns of behaviour (Fiedler), cognitive theories, and theories of industrial societies based on the rational laws of economic organizations. Finally, there are postmodern approaches inspired by the work of Wittgenstein, Quine, Kuhn, Garfinkel, Goodman, Foucault, and feminist critiques; Morgan's metaphorical approach to organizations is one of only a few examples identified in organizational studies.

Burrell and Morgan started by considering a variety of assumptions about the nature of science (nominalism–realism in ontology; anti-positivism–positivism in epistemology; voluntarism–determinism in debates about human nature; ideographic–nomothetic theory in methodology); and assumptions about the nature of society (the order–conflict debate). This discussion allows them to produce four paradigms placed along the horizontal axis of "subjective–objective"; and the vertical axis of "regulation–radical change." The four paradigms are: the functionalist paradigm (containing objectivism, social system theory, pluralism, theories of bureaucratic dysfunction, action frame of reference); the interpretative paradigm (containing hermeneutics, phenomenological sociology, phenomenology, and solipsism); the radical humanist paradigm (containing solipsism, French existentialism, anarchic individualism, and critical theory); and, finally, the radical structuralist paradigm (containing contemporary radical Marxism, conflict theory, and Russian social theory).

Each paradigm is then discussed in terms of its main assumptions and thinkers, and then again in connection with theories of organization, providing a way of both grouping various theories and tracing their origins in terms of metatheory. Functionalism, for example, is primarily objectivist and concerned with the sociology of regulation:

> It is characterised by a concern for providing explanations of the *status quo, social order, consensus, social integration, solidarity, need satisfaction* and *actuality*. It approaches these general sociological concerns from a standpoint which tends to be *realist, positivist, determinist* and *nomothetic*. (Burrell & Morgan, 1979, p. 26)

The roots of this paradigm are traced to Comte, Spencer, Durkheim, and Pareto; but also to Weber, Simmel and Mead, whose work, seen as incorporating elements of German idealism, found its place in the least objective region of functionalism. Burrell and Morgan's extensive discussion of the functionalist paradigm has already been referred to, but in order to summarize and to facilitate making links with the discussion of public relations, I shall identify those writers and works in organizational studies which are seen as operating within this paradigm.

As we have seen, there are clear groups of approaches within this paradigm: social systems theory and objectivism, under which we find classical management theorists and industrial psychologists (Taylor, Fayol, Mooney, Urwick; Mayo, Roethlisberger, and Dickson); and, separately, post-Hawthorn objectivist studies of job satisfaction and human relations (Liken, Maslow, Herzberg). Burrell and Morgan continued their discussion with socio-technical systems (Trist), grouped together with the work of Argyris; equilibrium theories of Bernard and Simon; the structural functionalism of Selznick, and the open systems perspective (again invoking the Tavistock researchers Trist and Emery, but also Katz and Kahn); finally we find empirical studies of the Aston group and similar work in the United States carried out by Hall, Hage, Aitken, and Blau. The latest of the discussed approaches which was inspired by the open systems theory is Lawrence and Lorsch's contingency theory.

The action frame of reference is represented by Silverman—a position with which Reed (1993, p. 172) took issue, seeing it as an illustration of the futility of the whole paradigm debate; other important writers mentioned are Goffman and Turner. Theories of bureaucratic dysfunction, influenced by Mertonian theory of cultural and social structure, are represented by Selznick, Gouldner, and Blau. The last approach within the paradigm is pluralist theory. The tack Burrell and Morgan adopted in this section was to refer to the pluralist strand within the work of writers already classified elsewhere (Selznick, Gouldner, Goffman, Silverman, Blau). In doing so the authors emphasized the point made earlier about various traditions feeding into individual theories and approaches, often across the paradigmatic divisions.

None of the three remaining paradigms produced discussions as extensive as functionalism, or, for that matter, as many examples of their application in organizational studies. This quantitative imbalance was not a matter of design and led to the conclusion that the bulk of theory and research is located within a narrow range of theoretical possibilities.

> This concentration of effort in a relatively narrow area defines what is usually regarded as the dominant orthodoxy within the subject. Because this orthodoxy is so dominant and strong, its adherents take it for granted as right and self-evident. (Burrell & Morgan, 1979, p. xi)

Let us briefly summarize Burrell and Morgan's views on the three alternative paradigms. The interpretative paradigm is traced back mostly to the work of early German idealists (and beyond that to Kant), with the more recent influence of Dilthey (hermeneutics), Husserl (phenomenology), and Weber. Within organizational studies in this paradigm the authors distinguished ethnomethodological approaches to the study of organizational activities to be found in Bittner, and to a certain extent in Zimmerman and Silverman; and phenomenology in the work of symbolic interactionists (Sundow, Emerson).

Radical humanism derives its main origins from the work of Hegel and "Young Hegelians" like Feuerbach and the young Marx. The separate strands of thought within the paradigm are critical theory (the Frankfurt School), anarchistic individualism (Max Stirner), and French existentialism (Jean-Paul Sartre). This framework, applied to organizational studies, produced anti-organization theory (Clegg, 1975; Silverman & Jones, 1976; Beynon, 1973). The problem with which these theories are preoccupied is alienation, and the seemingly objective forces impinging on human consciousness. Burrell and Morgan (1979, p. 323) broke these problems down into a list of more specific factors in which anti-organization studies are interested: the concept of purposive rationality; rule and controls within which the purposive rationality is exercised; roles as limiting human activity; language and the Habermasian concept of communicative distortion; ideological mechanisms within the workplace which support roles; the worship of technology as a liberating force; and reification as applied to concepts of work, leisure, profitability, and scarcity.

Radical structuralism originated from Marx's later work and in some respects from Weber's concern with the "iron cage," that is, bureaucracy as social domination: Burrell and Morgan described it as "a fusion of plurality of philosophical, political and social traditions" (Burrell & Morgan, 1979, p. 333). There are three broad approaches distinguished within the paradigm: Russian social theory (Plekhanov, Bukharin) and, connected with it, anarchistic communism (Kropotkin); contemporary Mediterranean Marxism (Althusser, Colletti); and conflict theory (Rex, Dahrendorf). In organizational studies these approaches can be seen as either a radical Weberian position or a Marxian structuralist approach. The former is interested in problems such as the role of the State and the general process of bureaucratization, corporatism, and power relationships; writers discussed in this context are Miliband (1973), Eldridge and Crombie (1974), and McCulloch and Shannon (1977). The latter is to be found in Baran and Sweezy (1968), Braverman (1974), and Allen (1975).

The above summary is too brief to do justice to Burrell and Morgan's discussion; it should be taken more as a rough map of the vast intellectual territory traversed, or as an early skirmish in the paradigm battle before it became further complicated by the arrival of postmodernism on the field of organizational studies. There have been many voices in this most recent phase of the debate: there are writers whose work has explored organizations in a postmodern world; there have also been those writing "on a more self-consciously theoretical level" (for discussion of postmodemity as an epoch and postmodernity as a philosophical position, see M. Parker, 1992). It seems easier for the purposes of this review to focus on the latter and in doing so give examples of the first group of writers.

In 1988 *Organization Studies* started publishing a series of papers discussing the relevance of "postmodernist concerns for the study of organizations" (M. Parker, 1992, p. 4). Cooper and Burrell's (1988) was the introductory article, which approached the debate via "a return to Weber's concerns about the 'iron cage' of rational bureaucracy" (M. Parker, 1992, p. 4). Taking this as their focal point, Cooper and Burrell examined the concept of rationality as underlying the modernist discourse, and contrasted this with the postmodernist discourse seen as a critique of rationality.

Modernism is supported by the well-established rationalist tradition in philosophy, starting from Kant (critical modernism), and in sociology, right at its source in the work of Saint-Simon and Comte (systemic modernism). The common area for both forms of modernism is their belief in Reason as the foundation for the world, which is, therefore, intrinsically logical and meaningful.

> This takes two forms: (1) that discourse mirrors the reason and order already "out there" in the world, and (2) that there is a thinking agent, a subject, which can make itself conscious of this external order. (Cooper & Burrell, 1988, p. 97)

In the case of systemic modernism, system is the agent. Since it works according to "cybernetic discourse," its logic is accessible through the application of scientific methods of enquiry; and the logic resides within the system, rather than its parts. For critical modernism, the thinking subject is the network of interacting individuals who "through the commonsense of ordinary discourse, can reach a 'universal consensus' of human experience" (Cooper & Burrell, 1988, p. 97).

Searching for the expression of modernist discourse in organization studies, it appears that systemic modernism expressed as instrumental rationality is the dominant type. The authors cited as an example D. Bell's (1974) interpretation of the post-industrial society as organized through theoretical knowledge for control and innovation, thus offering a way of managing the complex, large-scale systems characteristic of the modern world. Apart from the large-scale unitary system, Bell also pointed out another characteristic feature—the economizing mode, operationalized as productivity and performance. Similar ideas are developed further by Luhmann, where society becomes a gigantic organization, like a corporation, governed by performativity, or "the optimization of the global relationship between input and output" (J-F. Lyotard, 1984, p. 11; quoted in Cooper & Burrell, 1988, p. 96).

Critical modernism occupies a somewhat ambiguous position in this debate: although criticized implicitly for being modernist in the first place, it seems to have some redeeming features—its interest in language and, more generally, its opposition to the "cybernetic-like monolith of systemic modernism" (Cooper & Burrell, 1988, p. 97). Critical modernism is discussed briefly by exposition of Habermas' interest in language as the medium of reason, and in the process of "the colonization of the life-world by systemic reason" (ibid.), that is, rationalization rather than rationality.

It is impossible to present any comprehensive discussion of postmodernism in two paragraphs, and it is virtually impossible to summarize Cooper and Burrell's discussion of it in such a brief way either. I shall, therefore, resort to focusing on those elements of their paper that are of interest in this context, while trying not to lose their original sense.

For Cooper and Burrell, "difference" is perhaps the key concept around which they build their discussion of postmodernism. It allows them to draw together the work of Derrida (1973), Foucault (1977a, 1977b, 1980), and Lyotard (1984), and to contrast it with the modernist position (Habermas, 1984). Difference is defined as:

> a form of self-reference in which terms contain their own opposites and thus refuse any singular grasp of their meanings. Difference is . . . a unity . . . divided from itself, and . . . it is that which actually constitutes human discourse . . . the human agent is faced with a condition of irreducible indeterminacy. (Cooper & Burrell, 1988, p. 98)

These ideas produce two irreconcilable positions. The modernist discourse is referential; it legitimizes itself by reference to "some grand narrative such as the dialectics of Spirit, the hermeneutics of meaning, the emancipation of the rational or working subject, or the creations of wealth" (Lyotard, 1984, p. xxiii; quoted in Cooper & Burrell, 1988, p. 94). Postmodern discourse, however, sees systems as self-referential; thus, any attempt to analyse them in terms of purpose and meaning is purely an interpretative position. What postmodernist discourse attempts to do is "to show that the world of commonsense structures is the active product of a process that continually privileges unity, identity and immediacy over the differential properties of absence and separation" (Cooper & Burrell, 1988, p. 100).

Postmodernist effort, then, can be seen as focused on deconstructing concepts of unity and identity.

Cooper and Burrell's article provoked other writers to respond and take positions on different sides of the question about whether or not the modern and postmodern paradigms can be reconciled. Cooper, Burrell, and Gergen believed they cannot and suggested that a way forward for organizational studies is to pursue the postmodern critique (Cooper & Burrell, 1988; Gergen, 1992). M. Parker (1992), while believing that the paradigms are ultimately irreconcilable, advocated a need for "cross fertilization" between these two positions. Tsoukas talked about "soft" postmodernism, which is ontologically close to reflexive rationalism (critical modernism), while challenging "the cognitive monopoly of an allegedly omniscient subject-centred rationality" and thus investigating the postmodern concepts of instability and discontinuity (Tsoukas, 1992, p. 648). Reed (1992) rejected the paradigm mentality altogether as unhelpful, fostering a "camp" mentality, and Ackroyd seemed to share his view when he wrote about the "silliness" that such forms of thinking may produce (Ackroyd, 1992, p. 172).

An obvious question to ask at this point is whether any postmodern work has actually been produced by organizational researchers, or whether the debate is a purely "academic" event, in the worst sense. Hassard (1993, pp. 16–17), in his discussion of postmodernism and organizational analysis, pointed to Clegg (1990) and his identification of de-differentiated postmodern organizational structures consistent with theories of flexible specialization and post-Fordism (see Piore & Sabel, 1984; Pollert, 1988; C. Smith, 1989; Hirst & Zeitlin, 1991). Postmodernism—not as an epoch (postmodernism) but an epistemological position—is more problematic for organizational analysis. First of all, there is the problem with theory construction as being essentially dependent on the belief in "the factual nature of a knowable universe" (Hassard, 1993, p. 18), which cannot be easily reconciled with the postmodern belief in the unconquerable ambiguity of the universe, which is both constructed and at the same time obscured by language. However, if one persists, examples can be found: Gergen's relational theory of power (Gergen, 1992), which operates somewhere in the "middle ground between the 'strong' epoch and epistemology traditions" (Hassard, 1993, p. 20); or ethnographic research, known as the organizational culture and symbolism movement (for further discussion, see Hassard & Parker, 1993).

P. Thompson (1993), in his outspoken criticism of postmodernism in organizational studies, pointed out that the characteristics of a postmodern organization as defined by Clegg (1990) appear at the centre of contemporary pop-management. The broad themes running through the work of writers such as Handy (1987, 1989), Naisbett (1982), T. Peters (1987), Peters and Waterman (1982), and Deal and Kennedy (1982) are broadly those of flexibility and disorganization. More specifically, postmodern interests are conceptualized by Clegg (1990, p. 203) as diffusion, democracy, trust, and empowerment; and he juxtaposes them with the modernist focus on specialization, bureaucracy, mistrust, and disempowerment.

What conclusions can be drawn from this debate about paradigms, and how can it be relevant to public relations? The debate represents a period in the development of organization studies characterized by intensive methodological introspection. As late as 1979, Burrell and Morgan wrote about the functionalist dominance in the field (although many would dispute their definition of the functionalist paradigm), and in their review they chose to highlight not particular theoretical solutions to particular practical problems, but the big ontological and epistemological questions underlying such solutions. The subsequent explorations of postmodern concepts and their application to the study of organizations intensified the introspective process. Having grappled with the idea of paradigm closure and the effects of the postmodernist onslaught, organization studies began to re-form in "the renewed quest for a sustained dialogue which has direction and gives the field an identifiable coherence" (Reed, 1993, p. 174). Although the tendency of this introspective debate to encourage polarized positions cannot be dismissed, the methodological awareness it brings with it can be used constructively, in the

> making and re-making of intelligible narratives concerning organization theory's historical development and its significance for present-day concerns.... [This] will extricate organizational studies from the intellectual paralysis and "collective amnesia" which came to pervade as a result of the "triumphalism" of systems orthodoxy or the "forgetfulness" of postmodernist thinking. (Reed, 1993, pp. 174–175)

What seems to be emerging out of this period of strife is a more mature discipline, at ease with the idea of its own identity as being continually remade, a discipline that is open to issues beyond its own limits at any particular time and capable of accommodating theoretical and methodological variety without disintegrating. Armed with this knowledge, let us take a critical look at the emerging discourse of public relations within academia.

PUBLIC RELATIONS DISCOURSE

The first part of this chapter has presented a review of the systems approach in sociology and organizational studies. Three models, or strands, of thinking about social systems have been identified, in order to supply the analytical framework for discussing the application of systems theory in public relations. These three models, as we shall see, have indeed been recognized and used in public relations. My aim is to sketch a critique of that awareness and its broader implications.

The data for analysis consist of a selection of examples of particular uses or applications of systems theory in a number of public relations academic texts. The books chosen for consideration are:

Grunig, J., & Hunt, T. (1984). *Managing Public Relations.*
Cutlip, S. M., Center, A. H., & Broom, G. (1985, 1994). *Effective Public Relations,* 6th and 7th ed.
Botan, C., & Hazleton, V. (Eds.). (1989). *Public Relations Theory.*
Grunig, J. (Ed.). (1992). *Excellence in Public Relations and Communications Management.*

There are a number of reasons for this particular selection. First, there seems to be a general consensus, arising from the documentation of historical developments and the educational tradition in the field of public relations, that American scholars lead in the field. Second, American academic textbooks in the field of public relations seem to dominate the market, at least in the UK, which offers further support for the claim of the strong position of American scholars. Third, within the field the more practice-oriented textbooks make only a cursory reference to systems theory, if any, and have therefore been disregarded. Finally, the choice of textbooks rather than other texts has been decided on the assumption that within the category of "published work" in the academic context, a textbook is firmly associated with the establishment, in the sense of representing the views central to the field and containing an up-to-date body of knowledge. In other words, a textbook serves as a medium through which the direction of the development in a field is reaffirmed, and also functions as a mechanism for self perpetuation. The following analysis assumes that the application of systems theory to public relations as observed in the texts considered is representative of this academic field in English-speaking countries.

Another point that should be clarified here is the fact that despite citing a number of textbooks as the data, I focus mainly on the work of James Grunig and a group of researchers contributing to the "Excellence" study in public relations. There are four reasons for this focus: first, James Grunig's position as a researcher who has been active for about 20 years; second, the enormous influence of his views and his achievements in providing a theoretical basis for public relations, claiming for it the status of an academic discipline (see Botan, 1993); and third, his leading position as the director of the research team for the "Excellence" study, which itself is a unique project within public relations. The "Excellence" study is a project funded by the International Association of Business Communicators (IABC) and initiated in 1985. *Excellence in Public Relations and Communication Management* was published after 7 years and represents the first stage of the project, theory building, which is to be followed by empirical research. A project of this length and size would constitute a serious research effort in any discipline and, to date, is outstanding in public relations. Fourth, and finally, the core of the theoretical effort represented in *Excellence,* such as the definition of public relations and its presuppositions of a public relations theory, can be traced to Grunig's earlier work (see Grunig & Hunt, 1984; Botan & Hazleton, 1989).

Systems Theory and Public Relations Theory

Systems theory appears in public relations directly as systems theory in chapters bearing the appropriate headings—"A 'system' focus" (in Grunig & Hunt, 1984), "The systems approach" (in Cutlip et al., 1985); or applied as a framework to particular problems: "The systems concept of management" (in Grunig & Hunt, 1984), "The systems perspective of effectiveness" (in Grunig, 1992).

There is also a more indirect route whereby systems theory is applied to a problem, but the acknowledgement or clarification is not found directly in the title of the appropriate section or chapter, though it can be traced through the book's index: "What are the community publics," indexed under "systems theory in community relations," and "The concept of linkages," indexed under "systems theory, interpenetrating systems related to linkages" (both in Grunig & Hunt, 1984).

Finally, there is the indirect route, whereby concepts derived from systems theory enter public relations via a different source, often under a different term. These are more difficult to identify, but are also more pervasive in Grunig (1992) than in any other of the texts, given the nature of this particular book: a combination of extensive literature review and theorizing, more useful for the purposes of academic research than as support for straightforward instruction. Perhaps the most useful way of identifying such influences is by clusters of concepts. I examine these concepts in the four, numbered sections that follow, showing in each of them the sources referenced by the authors in their discussion. This signposting technique should help relate the two parts of the discussion presented in this chapter. In other words, I shall attempt to superimpose our rough map sketched out in "The battle of paradigms" on to the mainstream public relations writing and see what happens. As noted previously, the following discussion can only provide a rough sketch, in view of the amount of material available even within the limits of my selection.

(1) I shall begin with concepts of autonomy, interdependence, and relationships in a chapter dealing with organizational effectiveness, "What is an effective organization?" (Grunig, 1992, chap. 3). The way in which this chapter speaks systems language is by focusing on concepts such as goal-attainment as a measure of organizational effectiveness (Pfeffer & Salancik, 1978). The concept of autonomy, defined as independence from environmental intrusion, is juxtaposed with that of interdependence, traced back in a more or less direct way to the work of a number of writers (Katz & Kahn, 1966; Parsons, 1960; Gouldner, 1959; Perrow, 1961;

Blau & Scott, 1962; Etzioni, 1964; J. L. Price, 1968). The need for an organization to be open to its environment is also linked to the concepts of cooperation (Hage, 1980; Quinn & Hall, 1983) and interaction (Buccholz, 1989).

Interdependence is based in relationships which the organization has with groups, internal and external, that compete for power. Following Mintzberg (1983), the authors of this chapter—Grunig, Grunig, and Ehling—accepted that competition for power can lead to a high degree of "politicization." This, however, is ultimately a positive factor, as it "kills organizations that are not well-suited to their environments" (Grunig, 1992, p. 69), a view reminiscent of Darwinian survival of the fittest and the ecological perspective in organizational studies. Other important sources in the discussion of relationships seem to be Aldrich (1975) and Zeitz (1975).

Finally, requisite variety and enactment (Weick, 1979) are invoked: the argument seems to be that the more variety, the more effective the process of enactment. The conclusion to the chapter is a proposition linking the various elements discussed with the practice of public relations: its contribution to organizational effectiveness lies in building relationships with strategic constituencies (which are quantifiable in monetary terms). The work of a public relations practitioner can be effective only if public relations is part of the dominant coalition, that is, if it participates in strategic decisions of goal-setting and identifying strategic constituencies (Grunig, 1992, p. 86).

(2) In his discussion of management decision-making, in "Public relations and management decision making" (Grunig, 1992, chap. 4), the key concept is that of boundary-spanning, which is necessary for organizations which are open to environment. Environment, as such, is defined as a "construction built from the flow of information into the organization" (Grunig, 1992, p. 92). The construction itself is a process of selecting some of that information for further analysis; in other words, the process of enactment.

This constitutes an introduction, which is followed by a review of literature on decision making with references to, for example, Mintzberg et al. (1976) and Pfeffer (1981). Boundary-spanning is also strongly linked with the concept of meaning as a "cultural artifact" (Grunig, 1992, p. 99). Strangely, the authors, White and Dozier, do not offer any references here to literature on culture or symbolism. In fact, rather uncharacteristically they do not offer any references in this particular section.

The concept of requisite variety reappears as "requisite scenarios" (Grunig, 1992, p. 100). Decision making is thus seen as an iterative process fully dependent on managers' ability to produce scenarios ("simplified models of possible future")—that is, their imagination—"and the perceptions/meaning they bring to the decision-making process."

The discussion is summarized in a number of propositions, which warrant a longer comment:

Proposition 1: The more environmental scanning that practitioners conduct, the greater their participation in management decision making.

Proposition 2: The more turbulent and uncertain the organisational environment, the more environmental scanning practitioners will be expected to conduct.

Proposition 3: The more turbulent and uncertain the organizational environment, the greater the participation of practitioners in management decision-making.

Proposition 4: The greater the conflict between practitioner provided input and existing language/codes/frameworks, the greater the mistrust of practitioner loyalty to the organization.

Proposition 5: The greater the conflict between practitioner-provided input and existing language/codes/frameworks, the better the quality of the decision provided.
(Grunig, 1992, p. 106)

These propositions seem to be based on a number of unrevealed metatheoretical assumptions. Environment is external to the organization and constructed from information brought into the organization. The more information is available, the clearer the picture, and thus we are faced with the positivist belief in the objectively existing world, which organizations reconstruct from information. On the other hand, this objectivist belief is moderated by the realization that it is the human being that acts as the information-processing unit, and therefore the whole process has to take account of human sense-making strategies. Thus, on the one hand we are presented with the picture of the organization as separate, but dependent on the environment, and on the other hand we seem to be moving towards a more interpretative framework with the human being, rather than a system, in the centre.

Finally, conflict seems to play an important role within this scheme. There is an implicit acknowledgement that conflict between the organization and its environment, if not inevitable, is likely to arise. Indeed, the more extreme it appears, as revealed through the work of the public relations practitioner, the better for the decision making within the organization. It seems fair to interpret this proposition as saying that the more divorced the organization is from its environment, the more imperative the process of adaptation or alignment. Public relations appears as an element in the negative feedback loop. The worldview in which such an explanation makes sense is that of systemic modernism, ruled by performativity.

(3) "What is excellence in management?" (Grunig, 1992, chap. 9) is of interest to this discussion for two reasons. First, it takes the excellence framework as proposed by Peters and Waterman (1982), but also by other writers interested in distinguishing between good and poor organizations on other than purely financial factors (Grunig, 1992, pp. 222–223). Second, there is a clear attempt to link the distinction between mechanistic and organic structures with a discussion of how organizational structure influences organizational effectiveness.

The chapter attempts to bring together two different models of systems, factors linked to ideas of excellence, and Grunig's models of public relations. In a section devoted to organic structure (Grunig, 1992, pp. 225–229), Grunig makes an explicit distinction between "centralized, formalized, stratified and less complex" organizations, referred to as mechanical; and organic ones characterized by a lesser degree of centralization, formalization and stratification, and a larger degree of complexity. The key to this distinction is autonomy (understood as the extent of discretion employees have in their jobs). This provides a good vantage point for reviewing various ideas on what constitutes excellence and linking these ideas to a systemic approach. The chapter goes on to discuss intrapreneurship, that is, "an innovative, entrepreneurial spirit," and claims a clear link between human resources, organic structure and intrapreneurship, which are likely to occur together and, from the public relations perspective, to be facilitated by excellent public relations (Grunig, 1992, p. 248).

Other elements of excellence are identified as strong cultures, symmetrical communication systems, empowering leadership, decentralization of strategic planning, and social responsibility. The implication drawn out for the public relations function is that "excellent public relations probably cannot exist within mechanical structures" (Grunig, 1992, p. 229).

If we follow the theme of synthesizing various models of systems, models of public relations and a deterministic view of relationships between organizational structure and environment, we find it explored further in Dozier and Grunig's chapter "Organization of public relations function," which draws on Hage and Hull's typology linking "overall organizational structure to the environmental niche in which the organization fits" (Grunig, 1992, p. 403). The press agentry/publicity and the public information models are seen as reflecting the closed-system orientation; two-way asymmetric and symmetric models are based on an open systems view of organizations. In terms of Hage and Hall's typology organized around concepts of scale and complexity, press agentry is associated with craft organizations; mechanical organizations are linked with the public information model; the organic organization tends to practise two-way symmetric public relations and the mixed organization practises both two-way models (Grunig, 1992, pp. 403–404).

(4) "Public relations management and operational research" (Grunig, 1992, chap. 10) starts by locating the source of operational research firmly within the development of cybernetics. The function of operational research is to help managers make decisions; it is "the approach to problem-sorting that examines the system (a set of interacting entities) in which the decision problem is contained" (Richmond, 1968; quoted in Grunig, 1992, p. 258). In conclusions to this chapter, Ehling and Dozier wrote:

> The point of this chapter is not to suggest that every strategic communication of public relations decision must be made fully operationalized as a mathematically designed decision-making model; it is the kind of thinking that is more rigorous, more demanding, and more benefit oriented than the questionable "by-guess-and by-gosh" methods so frequently employed by those who manage "by the seat of their pants." (Grunig, 1992, p. 281)

"In contrast, operations research thinking calls for careful planning and designing of public relations and communication programs of action and constant evaluation of program performance" (Grunig, 1992, p. 281). Operations research thinking requires that a manager be mindful that the goals and end-states of public relations and communications activities must be:

- socially warranted
- ethically acceptable
- conceptually well-specified
- organizationally relevant
- structurally distinguishable
- administratively feasible
- operationally attainable
- empirically measurable
- economically optimal. (Grunig, 1992, p. 281)

There are, again, a number of interesting points that invite more comment. Although there is a clear insistence that not every decision has to be worked out in a mathematical model, the requirement that it has to be empirically measurable does imply that public relations should aspire to using quantitative methods of research as the final proof of its effectiveness.

Organizational goal-states are clearly linked to economic factors, but also to moral considerations, apparently on the assumption that what is socially warranted is also ethically acceptable. Perhaps more interestingly, the manager appears to be in a position to decide what is in the public interest and what is ethically acceptable. This claim can only be sustained if one accepts an unambiguous and generally accepted normative system.

So how is systems theory used in public relations as it emerges from *Excellence*? In broad terms it seems to be consistent with the Parsonian four imperatives (adaptation, goal attainment, integration, and latency). More specifically, in terms of system models, there is a very consciously argued preference for organic (open) systems. Yet, if we look back to Buckley's adaptive model, or even more interestingly to Gharajedaghi and Ackoff, we cannot fail to notice that the inclusion of the ethical dimension of social responsibility implies a shift closer to the adaptive (purposeful) system. It seems that there is some degree of ambiguity about which model is being applied, or why more than one. If we look back to the discussion of the connection between models and paradigms (see also Pearson, 1990), it becomes clear that the difference is not merely between different analogies used, but possibly also between different metatheoretical presuppositions. Yet again, the focus of the project on the question of effectiveness pulls us back into the organic model with its logic of goal-attainment and environmental fit. This is not necessarily an inconsistency, if we accept the argument that most systems exhibit a combination of various types of behaviour.

This particular point, however, draws our attention to another characteristic: the ease of moving across different approaches. For example, the sources revealed in the chapter on effectiveness—Hall, Hage, Perrow, Lawrence and Lorsch, Pfeffer, Blau and Scott, Etzioni, Gouldner—represent a whole spectrum of functionalist approaches as defined by Burrell and Morgan (1979), which seems to be consistent with the hybrid nature of many of these approaches but at the same time does not seem to pay any attention to debates and difference within the paradigm. The choice of the paradigm, or worldview, itself is not surprising, given the focus of the study; but it is more problematic when one looks at the sources in the discussion of a concept such as power (Grunig, 1992, pp. 483–501). True, it has been explored within the functionalist paradigm; nevertheless, the apparent lack of other points of view (critical theory, Marxism, postmodernism) has to be noticed. This is not to say that there is any obligation to explore all possible perspectives, but not doing so becomes then a choice with reasons behind it. In this case, the choice might be explained by, on the one hand, the problem-solving approach and, on the other, the theory-building agenda and therefore the need for internal consistency.

In fact, the drive for internal consistency, the need to translate into systems language, may produce some curious effects, such as using the argument of requisite variety to support the entrance to the profession for minorities; no doubt well intentioned, and by no means the full extent of the argument, it creates an apparently irreconcilable tension. Is there not some degree of confusion between an organization's instrumental reason for a particular action and a moral principle of a different order?

One could also speculate whether it is the need for internal consistency which is responsible for "Excellence" not exploring the concept of self-referentiality and organizational identity. Morgan (1986) made the connection from autopoiesis to enactment; and there is also, as we have seen, a connection from autopoiesis to concepts of evolution and chaos. The perspective adopted for the study of effectiveness has the organizational fit as the focus; self-referentiality does not, which perhaps explains why this particular line is of no interest to the study.

Models of Public Relations

This brings our discussion directly to questions about paradigms, or worldviews, a term preferred by Grunig in "symmetrical presuppositions as a framework for public relations theory" (Botan & Hazleton, 1989) and in "The effect of worldviews on public relations theory" (Grunig, 1992), a chapter co-written with White. There is a considerable degree of overlap between these two chapters, although the later version seems to present a more extended discussion not just of Grunig's own approach, but also of alternative approaches as far as the social role of public relations is concerned.

The asymmetrical model is supported by seven presuppositions (J. E. Grunig, 1989, pp. 32–33; Grunig, 1992, p. 43): internal orientation (inability to see the organizations as outsiders do), a closed system (information flows out but not in), efficiency (control of cost more important than innovation), elitism (leader of the organization knows best), conservatism (resistance to change) tradition (as culture-generating, thus providing the organizational glue), and central authority (autocratic organizations, no autonomy for employees).

On closer examination these characteristics seem to collapse one into another. For example, a closed (mechanistic) system is defined by its inward orientation. The idea that information flows out of but not into the organization is difficult to reconcile with any model of systems thinking, though again the mechanistic one in perhaps the most feasible (see earlier discussion of von Bertalanffy's work). Efficiency, conservatism and tradition, as defined by Grunig, may refer to the same trait—inability to sustain organizational change. Central authority and elitism seem to describe the concentration of authority and organizational wisdom at the top of the hierarchical structure. Thus, it appears that the asymmetrical model is a closed system model and therefore corresponds to mechanistic organization.

The symmetrical view of organization, on the other hand, presupposes (Grunig, 1989, p. 38; Grunig, 1992, pp. 43–44) holism, interdependence (with other systems in the environment), an open system (free exchange of information across the boundary) and moving equilibrium (this is not within the organization but with other organizations). In addition to presuppositions specifically derived from open systems approach, there are eight more presuppositions. The first of these, in fact the first on the list, is "communication leads to understanding," derived from symmetrical models of communication (Newcomb, 1953; Chaffee & McLeod, 1968). An effort is made to distinguish symmetrical communication from persuasion, as the latter is regarded as less desirable.

The remaining presuppositions are equity (equal opportunities and respect for members of the organization) autonomy (seen as the degree of individuals' discretion over their tasks and linked to job satisfaction), innovation (new ideas privileged over tradition and efficiency), decentralization of management (decentralized and collective; increasing autonomy, employee satisfaction, and innovation), responsibility (i.e., social responsibility), conflict resolution (through negotiation, communication, and compromise), and interest-group liberalism.

The concept of open system, interdependence, and moving equilibrium can in fact be summarized as some of the basic features of an organismic model. Autonomy, innovation, and decentralization are elements of the open system, but also almost exact opposites of elitism, efficiency and central authority; this points to a conscious juxtaposition of mechanistic and organismic models of social systems. Reinterpreted in this way, concepts of systemic closure and openness seem to be used almost symbolically, in a way which seems to be very conscious of "the dreaded disease" symptom pointed out by Burrell and Morgan (1979). "Closed" (and for Grunig press agency/public information and two-way asymmetrical models) connotes "bad" and "old-fashioned"; "open" (two-way symmetrical model) connotes "good," in fact more than that, "excellent."

The last three characteristics of the excellent model of public relations are responsibility, conflict resolution, and interest-group liberalism. These are not derived from systems theory and originate from a consciously taken theoretical and ethical position. An excellent public relations theory, argued Grunig and White (Grunig, 1992, p. 338), must fulfil internal criteria (logical, coherent, unified, and orderly); external criteria ("effective in solving organizational problems as judged by relatively neutral research or history"); and ethical (concerned with building "caring—even loving—relationships"). These criteria in turn lead to the view that excellent public relations is "symmetrical, idealistic or critical, and managerial."

The first characteristic, symmetry, is derived from a number of sources: theories of symmetrical communication; game theory and negotiation; and Gouldner's (1960) norm of reciprocity, which solves the problem of unequal power in social relationships and thus serves "to inhibit the emergence of exploitative relations which would undermine the social system and the very power arrangements which had made exploitation possible" (Gouldner, 1960, p. 174;

quoted in Grunig, 1992, p. 47). The idealistic stance seems to refer both to the social role of public relations and the normative character of the proposed theory. It means that "public relations serves the public interest, develops mutual understanding between organizations and their publics, contributes to informed debate about issues in society, and facilitates a dialogue between organizations and their publics" (Grunig, 1992, p. 53). Idealistic also means "exemplary" and thus supports public relations ethics. If public relations takes a critical position, it contributes by revealing the areas of practice or theorizing that are at odds with the normative view. A further possible source for the idealistic position can be interest-group liberalism, which champions the interests of citizens against the government; or which is, to quote another of Grunig's sources, the kind of liberalism which

> possesses a strong faith that what is good government is good for society . . . sees as both necessary and good a policy agenda that is accessible to all organized interests and makes no independent judgement of their claims . . . it defines the public interest as . . . the amalgamation of various claims. (Grunig, 1989, p. 39)

The managerial characteristics of public relations come from research into roles (Grunig, 1992, chap. 12), which makes a basic distinction between public relations technician and manager. For public relations to be effective, the practitioner must participate in strategic decision making. In other words, if public relations is to serve as an effective adaptive subsystem, it must have a say in the highest level of decision making, concerned with relating the system to its environment.

On the face of it, the theory is seamless—it is carefully constructed, and offers coherent explanations of a range of problems and a promise of empirical evidence. There is a clear awareness of the metatheoretical basis for the position taken, and there is also a discussion of alternatives, with reasons why they have been rejected. In addition to these, the sheer size of the project and the range of literature searched suggest a definitive theory. Not only does Grunig not make any such claims, but he also even states that the theory may well be reworked following the empirical stage of the project (Grunig, 1992, p. 2); yet, the above characteristics of the work have already made it immensely influential. If this is the case, it is even more important to scrutinize both the basis of this theory and its implications.

IMPLICATIONS

As we have seen, the research on which the theory seems to be based is predominantly functionalist, in the broad sense given to the term by Burrell and Morgan. At the same time, however, there are other sources cited, notably Weick and Peters and Waterman, which could just as easily be seen as coming from beyond the modernist framework. This kind of discussion or comment does not seem to be necessary and one could ask how methodologically conscious, therefore, the theory-construction process really has been. One could, however, also ask what it matters which paradigm the ideas come from, especially since the whole debate about paradigms has been abandoned in organization studies as unhelpful.

In presenting the debate about paradigms, I have tried to show the importance of methodological introspection and the knowledge it brings with it: paradigms rest on different ontological and epistemological bases which cannot simply be ignored. True, intense paradigm battles might be seen as disruptive, but that does not mean that metatheoretical presuppositions can be freely mixed. It is also worth remembering that our knowledge of paradigm struggle here is derived from organizational studies; yet in terms of history and volume of academic research, organizational studies and public relations are in rather different positions and, if anything, more theoretical variety might be healthy for public relations development.

Let us start with the nature of the excellence study: it is a project funded by a professional body and with research questions very specifically defined from the outset:

1. When and why are the efforts of communication practitioners effective?
2. How do organizations benefit from effective public relations?
3. Why do organizations practice public relations in different ways?
   (Grunig, 1992, p. 1)

One could argue that such an approach puts answers before questions, in the sense of limiting the possibilities of what the answers might be. This process of limitation stems from the original assumptions present in the questions (the bottom-line imperative which implies systems theory rather than other approaches), which in turn influence, in this case, the selection of literature relevant to the problem. Methodologically, the project seems to be designed as a deductive process, so the original selection of literature comes in turn to be translated into hypotheses to be tested empirically at a later stage. If the sources are too restricted, or used without due consideration being given to their broader context, all the subsequent research steps might be affected.

To complicate matters further, we are dealing with an attempt not only to answer the research questions but also to propose a normative theory of excellent public relations. What such a position means is that vast areas of activity (three of the four of Grunig's models) can be seen as public relations that is not quite right, dysfunctional. Although there may be objective causes, such as the structure of the organization, which do not allow the excellent model to be practised, there nevertheless is an implication of failure.

But what exactly is wrong with believing in improvement, in the call for progress implicit in such a theory? What is wrong with a normative theory? Well, what is wrong with the Ten Commandments? Only that they make perfect and profound sense to the converted, but appear problematic to those who operate outside them. To carry on with this religious metaphor, one finds a somewhat proselytizing approach emanating from the theory of excellent public relations: if public relations practitioners resist or do not understand the excellence ideas, it is because they do not know any better, even if through no fault of their own.

> Practitioners often do not understand or accept theories like ours because they work from a pragmatic or conservative worldview. We argue that practitioners with a pragmatic worldview have a set of asymmetrical presuppositions even though they do not realize it. They take an asymmetrical view, usually a conservative one, because their clients hold that view. (Grunig, 1992, p. 10)

This is rather reminiscent of Victorian missionaries explaining savages' habits of walking about naked or praying to rain by their lack of civilization. It is not a bad explanation; but it is a good one only from a particular point of view.

The all-inclusive approach to the sources at an early stage can also lead to internal tensions within the resultant theory. For example, how can it be possible to talk about decentralizatian, empowerment and trust, and at the same time claim that to be effective public relations needs to be in the dominant coalition. In other words, no matter how strongly one believes that organizations should be diffused and autonomous in relation to their employees, there is still a centre of power and to make a difference one has to be in this centre.

Let us look at the ethical dimension of the theory. On the one hand, we see that ethics in this context is defined as "a process of public relations rather than an outcome" (Grunig, 1992,

p. 308). So the outcome, which could be a compromise not consistent with the views of any of the parties involved, is ethical if arrived at through two-way symmetrical communication. On the other hand, at the core of public relations ethics is the concept of public interest. Ultimately, it seems, we can arrive at a paradoxical situation whereby what is good for the whole society/system is not good for any of the groups it consists of. How is it possible to arrive at such a position?

Lippmann (1954a), in "The Image of Democracy," presented an interesting argument about the historical circumstances surrounding the crystallization of Jefferson's ideas about democracy and their subsequent career which could be helpful in addressing the problem at hand. Jefferson, he claimed, conceived his ideas in a specific historical context, when communities were small and fairly isolated. In such conditions, a community has a very real and clear set of rules derived from the same education received, the same religious beliefs shared, and a real participation of citizens in the matters of government which were to do with their families, properties, security, and the provision of communal services for themselves and others in the community. If differences of opinion arose, these were likely to stem from a misunderstanding of some of the shared norms or their application. A free debate could, therefore, reveal the misinterpretation and resolve the conflict. Although the specific conditions have disappeared, people seem to operate explanations about the mechanisms of social life as if modern society were still such a rural township. Ironically, systems theory can be seen as providing a modern way of recreating the rural township.

It is ineffective, even practically impossible, as a public relations practitioner to be concerned with everyone, since not everyone has an impact on the organization or vice versa. A way of selecting who the organization should be concerned with is by segmenting the environment into publics. In public relations literature this constitutes a preliminary step to building relationships. The outcome of such a process is an approximation of the rural township. Logically, then, communication should lead to conflict resolution, if conflicts arise. Unfortunately, what holds this recreated township together is likely to be issues, not shared norms.

If one cannot be sure that a failure in reasoning is the only cause of misunderstanding, the focus shifts from the substance of the debate on to the process of debate itself, and we seem to be left with the form only—dialogue. The moral imperative for public relations seems to be about rule clarification (Grunig, 1992, p. 60); in other words, creating conditions for dialogue. But who does the organization's talking? Who writes newsletters, scripts, speeches, briefing documents, letters to customers? Who advises on community relations? The process of talking involves saying; that is, taking positions, making judgements, stating opinions—even facts are not unequivocal, objective entities. Can the distinction between form and substance be made so easily? The tension within the theory that can be gleaned from this example is that it seems to advocate the inseparability of moral involvement from the practice of public relations, yet avoids dealing with the implications of this position by claiming that moral values for public relations practitioners reside in the formal rather than the substantive element of their activities. In other words, if the game is played by the rules, the outcome must be satisfactory.

This chapter has attempted to provide support for the argument that the theory of public relations presented in "Excellence" is in fact more than just a theory; it has grown into a discourse—not just a tentative proposition about relationships between phenomena, but a way of thinking. If, however, we stop and think about how the theory so far has been constructed, we realize that it is, and should be treated as, a particular point of view; a view that is firmly based in the belief that society exists around the equilibrium of consensus. It is not a dramatic saga of a heroic stance in a society pulled apart by antagonistic forces, but a story of a well-ordered household proving to itself how civilized it is.

There is nothing wrong with choosing one of these views over another, as long as it is clear that as a result of the choice certain questions do not get asked. These might be questions about power and knowledge or power and language; or they might be questions about the position of the public relations practitioners, and researchers, within the scheme of things: is knowledge independent of the one who knows? Could one not see society as organized not around consensus, but struggle?

The lesson that can be drawn from the debate about paradigms is that ignoring such broad philosophical considerations leads to privileging one point of view over another. Public relations research revealing potential for other approaches has already been published (see Botan & Hazleton, 1989a; Toth & Heath, 1992), and hopefully we shall see the range of research interests and perspectives extended even further.

To summarize, this chapter has endeavoured to show the origins, development, scope, and limitations of systems theory and the way in which it has been adapted in public relations. It is argued that the process of adoption has so far not been clearly charted and that this creates the possibility of contradictory assumptions being built into the model created. The lack of critical work in public relations compounds the problem, as the lack of challenge leads to the development of a somewhat confused or hybrid form of systems theory achieving the status of ideology within the public relations canon.

18

Public Relations and Rhetoric

Jacquie L'Etang
Stirling Media Research Institute

This chapter explores the connections between rhetoric and public relations. Key terms such as "persuasion", "rhetoric", and "public relations" are compared and contrasted. Ideas about public relations, persuasion, ethics, and public opinion are explored partially through the description and analysis of key classical texts from which contemporary ethical and political implications are drawn out and discussed in the context of public relations theory. The debates which emerge from this analysis are related to the idea that the role of public relations practitioner is that of organizational rhetor.

The term "rhetoric" is taken to mean persuasive strategies and argumentative discourse. However, the term has a long history and connotes a variety of meanings. The origins and development of rhetoric are discussed in relation to a variety of intellectual positions. It is argued that the study of rhetoric is of relevance to public relations in terms of its definition, its ethics, and its epistemology. The chapter takes a broadly historical approach in that it tackles the classical concept of rhetoric prior to the review of contemporary developments in the field and a discussion of the relevance for public relations. The connections between classical and more contemporary debates are explored by relating Greek ideas to modern concepts and considering the implications for contemporary practice. This facilitates an understanding of the enduring nature of some of the fundamental debates concerning communications practices in society.

THE ORIGINS OF RHETORIC

The first formal usage of the term rhetoric (from the Greek *rhetorike*, public speaking) is thought to have been in one of Plato's dialogues, *Gorgias*, around 386 B.C. (Gagarin, 1994, pp. 46–48). The *Gorgias* is alleged to have been largely responsible both for the popularization

359

of the term and for the development of ideas which condemned the practice. Plato's unflattering representation of the practice continues to the present day, with the pejorative use summed up in the phrase "empty rhetoric". For the Greeks, rhetoric was closely associated with logic and the development of persuasive speech. Rhetoric became a formal branch of learning in medieval Europe and was one of the seven liberal arts or sciences (the others being grammar, logic, arithmetic, geometry, astronomy, and music) but did not survive as a subject after the Reformation (Hartley, 1994, p. 264). The study of rhetoric gradually became absorbed into the study of literature and the philosophy of language.

There are different elements to the meaning and use of the term rhetoric, which is now recognized as a distinct yet interdisciplinary academic field. Especially important for an analysis which focuses on rhetorical aspects of public relations is the persuasive element; for Aristotle in particular, rhetoric was a technical skill which could be acquired to achieve persuasive effects. Persuasion is effected through the use of rhetoric, which is the application of techniques combining patterns of language and specific structures of argumentation, together with emotional appeals which can be expressed orally (oratory) or in written form. Aristotle's version of rhetoric can be interpreted as "social scientific" in its approach since it combines what we would define as the use of behaviouristic psychology and logic in order to persuade. The final and most controversial element is the ethical dimension: since Plato, writers have debated the ethics of persuasion. From the Classical period onwards, the concept of rhetoric encompassed not only analytical elements focused on the structure of language and the practical application of rhetoric in terms of persuasive effects, but also debate regarding its social consequences. It is this broader approach which potentially links the debate about persuasion to concepts of public relations and propaganda. Classical texts define these various aspects of rhetoric and clearly illustrate the conceptual difficulties involved. These difficulties are also reflected in the writing of recent and contemporary analysts.

The roots of classical rhetoric began with a class of professional reciters who presented oral versions of Homeric texts known as *rhapsodes*, a word derived from the Greek *rhaptein*, which means "to weave together" (Thomas & Webb, 1994, p. 10). The skills thus developed were then applied by the Sophists and others for purely temporal ends (financial and social rewards). However, even where the ethics and application of such a skill are doubted, as they were most clearly by Plato, the importance of good argument is recognized as a contribution to social dialogue. Thus, Socrates stated in *Phaedrus* that speeches must be carefully constructed:

> Any speech ought to have its own organic shape, like a living being; it must not be without either head or feet; it must have a middle and extremities so composed as to fit one another and the work as a whole. (Plato, 1986, p. 79)

The technical aspects of rhetorical skill, however, developed in a specific historical social context which both facilitated and encouraged men to acquire such skills, as will now be explored.

THE CONTEXT OF CLASSICAL RHETORIC

The historical, cultural, and political context of the texts of classical rhetoric demonstrate the original conceptions about the purpose of rhetoric and the role it played in society. Included in this review, which is largely based on Thomas and Webb (1994), is some discussion of various interpretations that can be made of the classical texts and their presentation of the term "rhetoric". From the outset rhetoric has been associated with the development of varying forms of democracy. The standard interpretation is that rhetoric's origins were in Syracuse in the second quarter of the 5th century B.C. after the tyrant Phrasybulus had been deposed and a form of democracy established. Newly enfranchised citizens flooded the lawcourts with litigation to recover property that had been confiscated during the reign of the despot (Corbett, 1965, p. 536). A Sicilian, Corax, assisted such citizens in pleading their claims in court and subsequently, with his compatriot Isias, allegedly produced the first handbooks on effective speaking, which included "examples of effective verbal argument" (Thomas & Webb, 1994, p. 13). These handbooks were the first steps towards an analytical and critical approach to oral language forms. This approach influenced those who became known as "Sophists", the name derived from the Greek word for wisdom (*sophistes*, a wise man). The term "Sophist" may be used in a variety of ways. It is sometimes used to describe travelling professional speakers who gave lectures on a range of philosophical topics, especially ethics, politics, epistemology, and philosophy of language and of the mind (Lacey, 1990, p. 227). Sometimes the term is used to specify pre-Socratic philosophers, and on other occasions it is used in a pejorative sense to define later philosophers who made their living out of teaching argument that was effective but misleading. Later in this chapter specific examples of this last type will be explored since they show how ethical issues became so bound up with questions of rhetoric.

In 427 B.C., Gorgias, a Sicilian diplomat, brought the practice with him when he was posted to Athens, "where democratic processes caused it to flourish" (Thomas & Webb, 1994, p. 5). The Sophists advised others on the structure and style of speeches and on their dramatic presentation. They operated as "consultants", charging fees for their advice, which was based on their research into the effectiveness of various speech styles and structures of argument (Lawson-Tancred in Aristotle, 1991, p. 4). As writing technology developed, so did the opportunities for creating permanent records and new applications and products for the Sophists to sell "to ambitious young men from the Athenian upper classes for whom rhetorical training performed the same function as a modern university degree" (ibid.). In the context of Athenian democracy, the ability to present ideas and arguments in such a way as to sway an audience was a very important skill for citizens. Debates within the small citizen body determined policy and political appointments as well as legal cases, and, in the absence of professional barristers, a man's individual presentation skills and impression management might be required to help him defend his property, his position, or even his life (Hamilton in Plato, 1988, p. 7).

On one interpretation, the popularity of the Sophists owed as much to fears about democracy as to a rejoicing in it. It has been suggested that the institution of rhetorical training developed into a "craze" and that "The idea spread rapidly through the political elite that the worst consequences of opening up the constitution to mass accountability, in both the assembly and the law courts, could be mitigated by the mastery of new arts from abroad" (Lawson-Tancred in Aristotle, 1991, p. 4). Consequently, the ability to persuade and influence public opinion was no longer assumed to be a gift but a transferable skill that could be taught by specialists who did not necessarily have any familiarity or expertise with the context or even the content of a given speech. There are clear similarities to be drawn here between the role of rhetoric and the modern practices of lobbying, mass media, and advertising (Irwin in Plato, 1989, pp. 117, 131). In both public relations and rhetoric, practical emphasis on persuasive technique can distract from the political and philosophical implications of such a role, such as the importance of social, economic, and political power in influencing the public agenda and dominating the public sphere. The potential of organizational rhetors to dominate discourse is clearly greater than that of most individuals (royalty, celebrities, and leading politicians are potential exceptions), and a society structured around large organizations is likely to give more space for organizational rather than individual discourse.

However effective the Sophists may have been in their oral presentations and application of good argument, ultimately their reputation management was poor and their image in the literature arising from their contemporaries is not good and, "they were accused, especially by Plato, of logic-chopping and subversiveness, but also of pandering to popular tastes" (Lacey, 1990, p. 227).

The Sophists were criticized in a number of texts, notably in Aristophanes' plays *The Wasps* and *The Clouds*. In *The Clouds* Strepsiades is

> driven by mounting debt to study with Socrates, who is pictured as a representative Sophist, so that he can learn how to escape from his creditors, whose cases against him are otherwise valid. Strepsiades' only reason for wanting to learn the tricks of the sophist is to cheat others. (Gagarin, 1994, p. 47)

In *The Wasps* Aristophanes describes the typical Athenian juror as "blinded by prejudice and utterly unconcerned with the truth of a litigant's case" (Gagarin, 1994, p. 47).

The concerns regarding rhetoric in classical literature were largely focused on the lack of protection for society from evil men using rhetoric for their own ends. The "essence" of rhetoric in terms of its definition, its moral content, and its role in society was the subject of much debate by philosophers. In particular, the role of rhetoric in producing knowledge or truth was a major concern, as can be seen in the next section which summarizes criticisms made at the time.

GORGIAS AND THE CRITICISMS OF RHETORIC

One of the sharpest critiques of rhetoricians is that presented in *Gorgias* by Plato, through the character of Socrates, Plato's mentor and teacher. The main approach which Plato takes in his critique in *Gorgias* is to raise questions about the ethics of the Sophists. Quite apart from his personal feelings and extreme bitterness about the fate of Socrates (who was coerced into taking poison by the Athenian people in 399 B.C. because he refused to recognize their gods and was thought to be corrupting the younger generation), Plato was concerned with the implications for society of the role which the Sophists had begun to play and the influence which they appeared to be able to wield. The Sophists claimed that their practice was a distinctive skill or art which could be learned and applied to any body of knowledge to secure influence for those who could afford either to pay for such representation or to learn these skills themselves. Plato argued that the practice could lead to injustice being perpetrated in society even though the Sophists were presenting their craft as a neutral skill. Plato regarded the practice as potentially evil and also as an intellectual threat to his philosophical position, which sought to identify universal answers to the question "How should a man live?" The Sophists' position, by contrast, appeared to be a relativist one. Some of the questions which Plato raised are useful in thinking about the role of public relations today and are reviewed in the following discussion of the dialogue *Gorgias*.

Gorgias expresses Plato's overall concern about the power and effects of oratory in society and his particular concern that a good orator may have the power to mislead his listeners. Through the dialogic medium the author explores the merits and demerits of the role of the persuasive communicator. Those taking part include a famous orator, Gorgias; a young man named Polus, who has written a thesis on oratory; a young and ambitious Athenian, Callicles; the host Chaerophon; and, of course, the philosopher Socrates.

The debate begins with Socrates questioning Gorgias about the nature and definition of oratory. Gorgias has some difficulty with this and Socrates teases him by suggesting that the power of oratory is almost supernatural. (It is of interest to note that public relations, especially of the "spin doctoring" nature, is often referred to as "the black art".) Eventually, Gorgias arrives at the following definition:

> GORGIAS: I mean the ability to convince by means of speech a jury in a court of justice, members of the Council in their Chamber, votes as a meeting of the Assembly, and other gathering of citizens whatever it may be. By the exercise of this ability you will have the doctor and the trainer as your slaves, and your man of business will turn out to be making money not for himself but for another; for you, in fact, who have the ability to speak and convince the masses.

> SOCRATES: Now, Gorgias, I think that you have defined with great precision what you take the art of oratory to be, and, if I understand you aright, you are saying that oratory is productive of conviction, and that this is the be-all and end-all of its whole activity. (Plato, 1988, p. 28)

Gorgias clarifies his position, that "Oratory serves ... to produce the kind of conviction needed in courts of law and other large assemblies, and the subject of this conviction is right and wrong" (Plato, 1988, p. 31). In response to this Socrates distinguishes between two kinds of conviction, that resulting in knowledge and that resulting in belief. The discussion ranges over the nature of conviction and the effect of orators on public opinion as Plato tries to show how rhetoric raises some problematic ethical issues. Socrates suggests that it is always important to consult subject specialists rather than orators, so that if one was building a wall one would consult an architect, not an orator. Gorgias responds to this by citing an occasion where the siting of Athens' dockyards and harbour walls was decided not only by professional builders but also as a result of the debate between Themistocles and Pericles: "And you can see that when there is a choice to be made of the kind that you spoke of just now it is the orators who dictate policy and get their proposals adopted" (ibid., p. 32).

Gorgias suggests in debate that powerful orator does not need to be an expert in the subject he is speaking about. The example given is that on matters of health an orator could be more convincing than a doctor:

> SOCRATES: The orator need have no knowledge about things: it is enough for him to have discovered the knack of convincing the ignorant that he knows more than the experts.

> GORGIAS: And isn't it a great comfort, Socrates, to be able to meet specialists in all the other arts on equal terms without going to the trouble of acquiring more than this single one? (Plato, 1988, p. 38)

Similarly, one might raise questions about the credibility and ethics of public relations officers in the fields of science, technology, or medicine where individuals do not possess specialist qualifications in the relevant scientific field. On what basis might one believe such a person if he or she makes claims about the safety of their product, installation or industry? In this case it appears that it is only their power to convince, not their knowledge, which has influence.

When pressed, Socrates himself defines oratory as a knack, a "spurious counterfeit of a branch of the art of government" (Plato, 1988, p. 44) and his criticisms focus on what he calls "pandering", which he defines as the practice of giving the audience what they want (often in terms of entertainment) without regard to truth, justice, or the general welfare. Socrates defines rhetoric as a skill which enables the orator to persuade others about matters of truth and justice while conveying neither knowledge nor understanding in listeners, only conviction. From this he argues that rhetoric is concerned only with appearances and is as far from justice as cooking is from medicine (Plato, 1988, p. 8; Gagarin, 1994, pp. 47–48).

ARISTOTLE AND THE ART OF RHETORIC

Aristotle's *The Art of Rhetoric* is often presented as being the first formal attempt to define a science of persuasion. At that time persuasion was usually seen as an intrinsic gift. While the early Sophists attempted to define practical advice based on the analysis of texts, they were not able to evolve clear principles from their research and so their contribution was limited, in the same way that some public relations teaching can be limited by practitioner "case studies" which describe processes and actions without reference to underlying principles. Aristotle, however, sought to develop a methodical and rigorous approach to, and analysis of, the subject and it is really at this point that rhetoric shifts focus from a philosophical tradition based on essentialism and universal values to an approach akin to that of contemporary applied social science. Plato's criticism of the Sophists, while apparently focused on moral debate, is a strong critique of relativist ethics and an argument about epistemology.

The Art of Rhetoric is basically a manual of persuasion which explores the principles underlying various types of proof. It clearly anticipates contemporary communications, psychological and sociological research into persuasive communication, as well as the numerous practical guides on selling, advertising, and public relations published in recent years. For example, its focus on the structure of argument is reflected in the contemporary application of social psychology, and there are elements which imply and anticipate the use of psychological understanding about personality types, persuasibility, and the effects of engendering different emotions to enhance persuasive effects. Aristotle's work specifies a much broader role for the rhetorician than that of mere orator, a role which encompasses that of an adviser or counsellor role in the devising and production of convincing arguments and proofs.

> It is this that justifies the definition of rhetoric not, as in earlier studies, as the artificer of persuasion, but as the technique of discovering the persuasive aspects of any given subject matter, and it is this too that justifies the close parallel frequently drawn with dialectic. (Lawson-Tancred in Aristotle, 1991, p. 65)

Aristotle, therefore, clearly separated the act of communication (oratory) from preparatory research and the planning of logical argument structures.

Other writers discussing classical rhetoric have made some shrewd points about the importance of trustworthiness and reputation in terms of contributing to the process of conviction. There is a familiar feel to the ideas expressed in terms of public relations practice; for example: "Openness, manifested explicitly in a readiness to reveal things which one might be expected to conceal, or a promise to tell the whole story from the beginning helps to establish trust" (Carey, 1994, p. 37). There is a clear similarity here with the guidance offered in crisis management texts in terms of media relations and in the management of corporate reputation.

RHETORIC AND PERSUASION

The relationship between rhetoric and persuasion is one of fundamental importance because a number of ethical and epistemological issues are contingent upon it. In rhetoric and persuasion there are examples of definitions which are more instrumental and others which highlight ethical considerations and fears of manipulation and coercion. The concept of free will is important in separating persuasion from negative connotations of manipulation, coercion, "brainwashing", and propaganda. These terms raise a fundamental point about who is to define a piece of communication as persuasive, manipulative, or coercive. Some sociologists (Barker, 1984; M. Smith, 1982) have argued that such definitions should be subjectively arrived at by the receiver of the communication. Perloff suggested that persuasion and coercion are not "polar opposites" but part of a continuum:

> The differences are subtle; often they are not discernible to outside observers who use the term coercion to describe a social influence attempt that they disapprove of and employ terms like persuasion or information campaign to describe influence attempts that are consistent with their values. (Perloff, 1993, p. 13)

Research into persuasion has focused strongly on the identification and measurement of the attitudes of those who have been the target of a particular persuasive communication in order to determine the effectiveness of different persuasion strategies. Such a scientific approach takes an "objective" stance to the concept of persuasion, arguing that it is a neutral skill which can be applied for both good and evil ends and can be seen as descending from the Sophists. The argument about neutrality may be linked to that which proposes that public relations contributes to pluralist or liberal democracy because it helps the process of ensuring that all views get aired. There is an important tension here between the view that public relations is a neutral and technically driven operation which may be employed to promote the view of either party in a dispute and that which states that public relations is concerned with "the truth".

The concept of rhetoric has implications for criteria of knowledge and truth. If we accept the position that universal truths are achievable, then in a situation in which two parties take different positions we will believe that only one of them can be right. Alternatively, if we do not believe that there is only one right answer, we are accepting the (relativist) point that there may be different perspectives which can be derived only from analysing rhetor, rhetoric (the rhetor's product) and the audience of the rhetoric.

Public relations construed as rhetoric argues for a particular perspective or version, that is, "the truth" is relative. On this account, then, the question of whether ethics is also relative must be considered. How is one to arrive at an acceptable ethic for public relations from a rhetorical perspective? This is a question to be returned to later, but it should be noted that it is very difficult to make a case for ethics within the postmodern perspective (a concern in the contemporary field of rhetoric) which is implied by the rhetorical stance outlined above. For this reason, public relations scholars seeking ethical justification for the practice have based their arguments on modernist, rationalist constructs.

CONTEMPORARY DEVELOPMENTS IN RHETORIC

Rhetoric has had something of an intellectual renaissance due to the influence of structuralism, poststructuralism, semiotics and postmodernist thinking, streams of thought which move away from essentialist conceptions of society and knowledge towards relativist and phenomenological approaches: society and knowledge are explained as being the result of certain intellectual structures which arise partly from cultural experience and language. Debates which spring from structuralism and poststructuralism focus on the relationship between thought and language, and between the thinking, articulate subject and the object. Structuralism and semiotics explore the sources and signs of culture, and the ways in which our experiences and knowledge are influenced and structured by these. Structuralism abandoned the idea that there was an intrinsic "essence" or meaning in a text or that the author's intention was either obvious or of paramount importance (Hartley, 1994, p. 302). Work in the structuralist tradition tries to identify systems of structural patterns within a text which enable the reader to generate meaning. This philosophical position led to the form of analysis known as deconstruction, in which the critic or reader tries to extract that which is missing or suppressed, or regarded as deviant in the discourse(s) or power relations present in the text under review (ibid., p. 304). A "text" in this context has a very broad meaning and can refer to not only literary works but also dramatic performances, films, television, and public or cultural events. Poststructuralism emphasized the reader rather than the text as a site of enquiry and therefore focused more on psychoanalytical influences on the interpretation of meaning and on external structures, such as ethnicity and gender, that facilitate meaning processes (ibid., p. 304). Postmodernism presents an epistemology based on "multiple and fragmentary worlds . . . that overlap, compete and transform themselves continuously" (Halloran, 1993, p. 114).

These intellectual currents imply that the relationship between thought, language, signification, dialectics and knowledge is contested, dynamic, and intrinsically rhetorical. Rhetoric focuses on the sign system, the devices, and strategies that operate within texts and the sense-making function of specific discourses (Hartley, 1994, p. 266). As Bizzell and Herzberg noted, "Twentieth-century theories of rhetoric, in formulating the relationships between language and knowledge and in re-examining the powers of discourse, have extended the concerns of rhetoric to include nothing less than every instance of language use" (Bizzell & Herzberg, (1990, p. 921) cited in Enos & Brown, 1993, p. viii). Hartley also suggested that the forms of the cultural produce with which we are surrounded are "highly rhetorical" and that "publicity, advertising, newspapers, television, academic books, government statements and so on, all exploit rhetorical figures to tempt us to see things their way" (Hartley, 1994, p. 266).

Rhetorical thinking is thus connected to debate, argument (intentional communication), and persuasion (instrumental communication). The views of Sophists and ancient Sceptics anticipate relativism and postmodernism in their rejection of a universal standard in favour of a range of different perspectives. This is of importance to public relations for two reasons: first, because it suggests that there is no one overall standard with regard to those interests on behalf of which public relations operates, and, second, because it also suggests that there is no one overall standard for public relations practice itself. Much of the debate about the ethics of public relations has focused on its social role and conflict between client and public interest, such as the promotion of causes thought to be unjustifiable. Some have tried to get around this problem by arguing that public relations is intrinsically ethical because it promotes democracy and good citizenship. This move necessitates consideration of questions of power and access since these elements will influence ability to communicate as well as how a piece of communication is regarded. A discussion about the social role and ethics of public relations should at least acknowledge important linked debates about knowledge acquisition and communication ethics. The field of rhetoric is an important part of such a discussion, not only because of its historical link to public relations but also because currently it directly confronts questions of dialogue, debate and persuasion within a framework which takes account of ethics and postmodernist thought.

Contemporary developments in rhetoric have returned to explore the tension between philosophy (based on foundational and universalist principles) and rhetoric (seen as relativist) and thus to the problematic of the ethics of rhetoric. The renewed interest in the ancient concept of rhetoric began in the 1950s and the expansion and development of the field has been dubbed "The New Rhetorics" (Enos & Brown, 1993, pp. vii–xiii). Work in this area connects with a wide range of analytical work in discourse analysis and postmodernism, as well as with more practical application of languages and argument in Departments of English or Schools of Communication and Writing. Thus, it can be seen that the twin streams of analysis and practice, present in the classical tradition, have also been more recent concerns.

Cohen (1994, pp. 69–82) identified a number of separate perspectives in the New Rhetorics. These include an extension of the traditional understanding of rhetoric as a methodology for the study of argument; an attempt to overcome the traditional hostility between philosophy and rhetoric by using rhetoric itself as a way of explaining dialectical principles; the use of rhetoric as an analytical tool for fictional narrative; and the attraction of rhetoric for postmodernists because of its rejection of philosophical conceptions of universals such as truth and knowledge. The New Rhetorics was said to be marked by diversity, transformation, and dialogue in order to achieve a broad understanding of what "our contending viewpoints reveal about skilled human discourse" (Bazerman, cited in Enos & Brown, 1993, p. x). These different approaches are reflected in a variety of contemporary definitions of "rhetoric" reflecting different aspects of the historical, political, and cultural baggage that the term encompasses. Bazerman suggested that the field can be approached in a variety of ways that reflect and "characterize our approach to dividing up and studying the symbolic domain" (Bazerman, 1993, p. 4). So, for example, one approach might look specifically at symbolic activity which seemed primarily motivated by persuasion, whereas an alternative approach might analyse the nature and focus of organizational rhetors and rhetoric. Bazerman argued from an instrumental perspective that most rhetorical study is concerned with its practical application and that our thinking about this matters because:

> Symbolic action is a major dynamic of society to be wielded for public and private ends. Prescriptions for traditional rhetorics, proscriptions for traditional rhetorics, proscriptions against stigmatized rhetorics, projections of new rhetorics—all advance social visions, perceived by their advocates to improve the human condition. (Bazerman, 1993, p. 4)

The relevance of rhetoric to public relations lies not only in its communicative function but also in its symbolic and structural role managing meaning within and between organizations and publics and in the claim to be contributing to a better society by assisting the flow of information. Rhetoric, however it is defined, is important to public relations at both the technical and theoretical levels and impacts upon both the practice and the interpretation of public relations.

PERSUASION AND PUBLIC RELATIONS

At this point it will be useful to review the role of persuasion in public relations and the way in which persuasion has been historically presented in the public relations literature. Practical "how-to-do-it"-type manuals have equated public relations goals with persuasive goals: "If you're a PR consultant you're in the persuasion business. By definition that means that your primary goal in life is to change the attitudes and subsequent behaviour of others to those viewpoints of your own (or your clients')" (Q. Bell, 1991, p. 24).

This approach is common in practice but has been defined and critiqued as the asymmetrical model of public relations (Grunig & Hunt, 1984; Grunig, 1992). Grunig argued that the asymmetrical approach, defined as "a way of getting what an organization wants without changing its behaviour or without compromising" (Grunig, 1992, p. 39), leads to actions which are unethical, socially irresponsible, and ineffective. Grunig also argued that "Organisations get more of what they want when they give up some of what they want" (Grunig, 1992, p. 39). While it is possible to imagine a continuum, at one end of which is coercion and manipulation and at the other end of which lies negotiation and cooperation, with persuasion somewhere in the middle, it is also possible to argue that if the organizational goal remains getting "more of what they [organizations] want", "symmetry" collapses into "asymmetry".

A rather different view was put forward by Miller (1989), who defined public relations as a process which attempts to manage symbolic control over the environment. He argued that effective persuasion and effective public relations are "virtually synonymous because both are primarily concerned with exerting symbolic control over relevant aspects of the environment" (G. Miller, 1989, p. 45). Miller proposed a model of persuasion which entails active participation by the persuadee, who in effect self-persuades. This is achieved through a process in which the persuadee is given the opportunity to become involved in the creation of the persuasive message through a dialogical process.

A consideration of the role of ethics in persuasion raises questions over the nature of evaluation methodology. Persuasion could be evaluated empirically in terms of effectiveness (an instrumental approach). In this case, questions arise as to what counts as effectiveness and the basis on which this should be decided. For example, in cases regarding public health it might be argued that decisions should be based on scientific and medical knowledge, which might be presented as a conception of "the truth", and some concept of a majoritarian "public interest", which may permit the infringement of the rights of a minority (to smoke, for example). Persuasion might be justified in such cases but there are clearly cases where "hard" evidence is not forthcoming and so persuasion is based on a myriad of conceptions and opinions, shaped partly by argument but also by experience and knowledge. This is why arguments about concepts of "truth" and the way in which knowledge is acquired and shaped are of such importance in public relations. Alternatively, persuasive acts might be judged in terms of the relationship between the parties concerned and their views of each other (a co-orientation approach). This would raise issues of the nature of the communication between parties, such as the degree of "openness", a concept which has received much attention in public relations theory.

The argument that can be presented on behalf of rhetoric is that it has the capability to publicise or make known "truth" or "facts", and for Aristotle this function served a justifiable and scientifically neutral purpose in society. On this account, rhetoric is simply a neutral conveyor of the truth which is apparently only available to the few. For Scott, this

> suggests the dynamic of an elite, those who are ... situationally fortunate, leading those who are not. One may call the process "rhetoric" by which the elite govern, but, if so, one should realize the set of assumptions about people and knowledge in the world that accompanies the label. (Scott, 1993, p. 122)

Public relations literature has presented the function as a set of skills which can be used to promote a client's case. As suggested earlier, however, the role may effectively be promoting what Scott called "second-rate truth[s]" (Scott, 1993, p. 124), or ideas which are not amenable to the scientific method of research. But he pointed out that even "scientific" evidence is structured within certain discourses which are subject themselves to rhetoric, so that scientific knowledge is to some degree socially constructed. If only certain qualified people have access to those truths there are social implications in terms of the evolution of various "knowledge elites" which exchange privileged material between themselves and structure discourse for others. Examples of these might include scientific journalists, politicians, members of "think tanks", and public relations practitioners.

Scott went on to argue that if there are no prior truths (because he suggested that these in themselves are subject to rhetorical creation and promotion), then rhetoric has a role in creating a concept of truth which is dynamic and evolutionary, ever subject to testing through dialectics. Porter argued that postmodernism shows that "methods themselves are rhetorically invented entities. Dialectic is not prior to or free of rhetoric; it is itself subject to rhetoric" (Porter, 1993, p. 212).

The public relations academic Pearson argued that:

> The strongest claim about the epistemic role of rhetoric is that all epistemological endeavour is rhetorical... According to Leff (1978) this view collapses the empirical into the symbolic: We live in a symbolic world, and all knowledge is a function of how communities of knowers construe and manipulate symbols. (Pearson, 1989b, p. 116)

It is this sort of approach which has led to a greater ethical focus on the process of communication rather than the specific content and is of value in discussing public relations.

THE RHETORICAL SCHOOL OF PUBLIC RELATIONS

The initial claim for a rhetorical approach to contemporary public relations studies was that of Elizabeth Toth and Robert Heath, whose work views "the organisation as speaker" (Toth, 1992, p. 3) and gave emphasis to the impact of public relations in society. However, such an approach may still be instrumental in intention in evaluating "the effectiveness of organizational messages in successfully advocating organizational stances" (ibid., p. 6) even though it may take account of and evaluate rhetorical messages in terms of their "ethical value to the public interest" (ibid., p. 6).

Toth and Heath promoted the concept of the organizational advocates who, through "a dialectic process...use symbolic exchange to come to agreements about cultural structures, events and actions" (Toth, 1992, p. 6). On this account, rhetoric is fundamental to the functioning of society and to communicative action. It acknowledges self-interest and argues that rhetoric facilitates the negotiation of relationships. This particular approach to rhetorical studies in public relations focused on identifying symbols and expressing and arguing opinions "dialogically to search for truth" (Heath, 1992, pp. 19–20). Heath suggested that although rhetoric can imply manipulative one-way communication, it can also be used to create a contested debate about issues and positions. Heath argued that while "truth" is required as the basis for rhetoric if rhetoric is not to mislead, relativism is a necessary feature because of the necessity to interpret and debate issues: "Indeed, 'facts' demand interpretation as to their accuracy, relevance, and meaning. Not only do people argue about facts, but also they contest the accuracy of conclusions drawn from them" (ibid.).

The issue of relativism and its relevance for ethics and for public relations is addressed directly by Pearson (1989a). Pearson suggested that public relations was "situated at precisely that point where competing interests collide" (Pearson, 1989a, p. 67) and that public relations problems could be defined in terms of "the collision, or potential collision, of these interests" (ibid.).

Following his identification of this crux, Pearson's argument had two threads: the first is that he suggested that empirically, public relations consultants are relativists who see themselves as serving different interests (clients). Pearson proposed that in order to escape the difficulty of there being different views about the ethics of policies being advocated, efforts to reconcile difference should be refocused on to the "type of communication system [that] can most likely mediate among these interests" (Pearson, 1989, p. 70). Pearson stated that the important structural elements in ethical communication are Grunig and Hunt's (1954) communication, negotiation, and compromise. Pearson suggested that support for these ideas is to be found in Ehling's (1984, 1985) message exchange or communication-as-conversation, Ackerman's

(1980) concept of neutral dialogue, and Habermas' (1984) communication symmetry. Pearson used Ackerman and Habermas to bolster Grunig's concept of "symmetrical communication", and thus was the first to provide a substantial (grounded in ethically based theory) claim that symmetrical communication was more ethical.

Habermas' theory of communicative action (1984) proposed that all linguistic communication takes place on the assumption that certain communicative norms exist; these norms not only encompass the technical aspects of language (grammar) but also recognize that different types of intention lie behind different types of statement and that to common understanding reality comprises external objects, cultural norms, and internal (private) intentions. Habermas' concept of conversation entailed a constant probing and testing of claims made, and in an ideal speech communication either party should feel free to make such challenges, to introduce new concepts, and to move from one level of abstraction to another. Habermas argued that the potential of communication to provide rational emancipation for all individuals was hindered by power relations. Habermas suggested that humans operate on the assumption and expectation of rationality in order to reach consensus and that this is necessarily reflected in the way in which communication takes place; any distortion in the process, such as an unequal distribution of power, is therefore irrational and inhibits the potential for "the general symmetry requirement" or "ideal speech communication" (Ray, 1993, p. 26).

Pearson argued that Habermas' theory of the ideal speech communication act, which proposes a number of key rules which would promote the ideal speech communication situation, is "couched in the language of symmetrical communication" (Pearson, 1989a, p. 72).

The difficulty in applying these ideal concepts to public relations is that participants are clearly not equal. The power and resources of government will be greater than those of many organizations, and the power and resources of many organizations and knowledge elites possessing cultural capital will be greater than those of many publics. Furthermore, symmetrical communication and its associated concepts of negotiation and mutuality seem not to take account of the role of the media in mediating, reinterpreting, or amplifying the "conversation" between participants. The application of Habermas' framework and the concept of symmetry (which Pearson offered as a potentially practical and measurable framework when combined with a co-orientation communication model) somewhat oversimplifies the context within which public relations operates. Within the new rhetorical school in public relations, there is the possibility of bringing organizational communication down to the individual level of spokespersons for the organization. This could obscure consideration of the collective responsibility for organizational rhetoric, policy making and action, and inhibit comprehension and acknowledgement of the power which lies behind the organizational rhetor. The framework's focus on spokespersons (orators) not only conceals the organizational dialectical dynamics which lead to the position adopted (a substantial rhetorical and political dimension) but also presumes an openness or transparency about all organizational communication which may not be justified, for example, in the areas of public affairs and lobbying.

It also remains unclear whether a distinction between the concepts of symmetry and dialogue is to be made clear or is of importance in public relations. Both are presented as end-states which are desirable in themselves and partially achieved through debate and agreement (i.e., dialogue and symmetry) over communication rules which would facilitate those end-states. The argument thus appears to be circular: dialogue and symmetry can only be achieved through dialogue and symmetry. Pearson presented a choice between "symmetry" (dialogue) and "asymmetry" (monologue/persuasion) but does not explore the social or political contexts which allow certain interests an enhanced position in which they have more choice in the nature and type of communicative acts they carry out.

The development of rhetorical ideas in public relations is clearly a route through which the subject can be connected to important arguments in ethics and epistemology and seems likely to be a rich area for future debate. It should, however, be noted that to date self-proclaimed rhetorical scholars within public relations have not really presented an alternative paradigm, in that they still have sought to work within the systems framework. Heath, for example, argued that although the rhetorical paradigm acknowledges self-interest it "is not antithetic to the symmetry paradigm ... the assertion of self-interest can only go as far as others are willing to allow it to do so" (Heath, 1992, p. 318).

CONCLUSION

Pearson's approach appears to site ethical value in the power of dialectic. There is disagreement by rhetorical scholars on the relationship between rhetoric and dialectic. For some (Rowland & Womack, 1985, pp. 13–31), dialectic is characterized by its truth-seeking function whereas rhetoric is simply a persuasive communicative technique. For such thinkers rhetoric in itself cannot be described as moral or immoral; it is as ethical as the ends to which it is put.

The challenge in addressing the ethical issue is not so much in justifying the activity as a legitimate enterprise, but in untangling the nature of public relations and the assumptions which lie behind the concept. Such discussion requires careful definition and exploration of concepts, epistemology, methodology, and ethics.

It is sometimes said that public relations is a recent phenomenon, but it is clear that its purpose and role in society and the type of communication entailed raise questions that have been asked of rhetoric "for nearly two and a half millennia" (Scott, 1993, p. 122). Since much of the relatively recent academic arm of public relations is located within instrumental or applied traditions, students and practitioners are often ill-equipped to respond to (often superficial) criticism of their discipline. Consequently, they may be tempted into making sweeping (and sometimes contradictory) statements which try to emphasize the positive aspects of the role of public relations. A theoretical approach to public relations and rhetoric may reveal the negative aspects of public relations as traditionally and originally publicized by Plato, but may also reveal understanding about and justifications for the discipline.

This chapter has tried to show that a discussion about public relations and its relationship with rhetoric has implications for ethical and normative theory in public relations. It is clear that developing ideas about public relations are related to fundamental issues in communication, ethics, politics, and sociology. Consequently, it is proposed that basic theory-building in public relations should be informed by an understanding of debates in epistemology, linguistics, structuralism, poststructuralism, modernism, and postmodernism. Approaches which take account of arguments from these traditions seem to have the potential to develop subtle and important theories about public relations which can improve our understanding of this major force in contemporary society. Finally, it is suggested that the importance of media studies in understanding public relations and rhetorical processes is of fundamental significance and has been insufficiently explored in discussions to date.

ACKNOWLEDGEMENT

The author wishes to acknowledge that the original inspiration for this chapter came from the teaching of Professor Sandra Marshall, formerly Head of the Department of Philosophy, University of Stirling.

19

Public Relations as Diplomacy

Jacquie L'Etang
Stirling Media Research Institute

This chapter contrasts the practice and academic disciplines of public relations and international relations and illustrates the point that such a comparative approach can yield many ideas of use in understanding the immature discipline of public relations. Three main themes are pursued: practical or craft concerns, the evolution of the academic disciplines, and, finally, the conceptual convergence of the two areas. The last-named theme is given most emphasis and detailed explanation.

The discussion of the practical similarities in the role of public relations and diplomacy is explored largely through academic literature and contextualised with practitioner perspectives which illustrate that aspiration to diplomatic status could offer public relations the kudos it currently lacks. The discussion of the emergence of the distinctive academic disciplines of public relations and international relations (diplomacy) illustrates common sources and similar problematics such as tension between academics and practitioners and methodological debates. The review of conceptual convergence describes the overlap between the framework in international relations and the dominant framework in public relations, and attempts to draw out possible implications for public relations theory from the more developed international relations model. In drawing out the implications from this analysis, the author critiques the concept of symmetry as it is presented in the public relations model and suggests that assumptions about its positive benefits may not be justified.

It will be shown that, rather than being underpinned by separate and distinct theoretical and philosophical frameworks, existing traditions in international relations, which have tackled diplomacy from a theoretical rather than a purely practical perspective, can be applied to public relations. It will be seen, therefore, that public relations theories are linked to well-established philosophical positions not currently referred to in the standard literature in the field and, consequently, that public relations can be seen neither as unique nor as neutral, as is implied in a number of texts. Rather, its degree of disinterestedness is contingent upon any one of a range of specific philosophical positions that may be applied to it.

It should be noted that diplomacy is sometimes identified as an aspect of "international theory," which is usually seen as falling within the field of international relations, also known as international affairs. Here, the term "diplomacy" is used to describe the practice and its role in international society. However, in referring to broader theoretical issues I allude to international theory, and when referring to the various schools of thought I make reference to international affairs or international relations following the sources used. The emergence of public relations and diplomacy as fields of academic study is also briefly discussed, highlighting the conflicts which have arisen during that evolutionary process.

DIPLOMACY AND PUBLIC RELATIONS: ROLE AND SCOPE COMPARED

Diplomacy may be described as the managing of a country's relationships with other countries so as best to further the principal country's aims, whether they be benevolent or otherwise. Formal diplomacy concerns the managing of political relationships and political intercourse with other countries and is conducted by means of permanent representative of other nations on international bodies such as NATO or the UN.

Cultural diplomacy, on the other hand, is directed at the populations of other countries rather than solely their political elites with the aim of raising positive attitudes towards the principal country. It is termed "cultural diplomacy" since it uses cultural aims and means to achieve medium term foreign policy ends. The aims and means of cultural diplomacy are manifold but they all revolve around the central idea of using a principal nation's cultural capital by offering wider access to it to target countries with the aim of rendering opinion formers in those countries better disposed towards the principal country. The aim is to win supporters and cultivate the rising generations and, through cultural access (via language, education, science, technology, and the arts), to inculcate sympathy towards the principal country's values and ideology. In brief, such efforts are argued to increase the circle of "shared meaning" between the principal and the recipient. In some ways, cultural diplomacy is the corporate social responsibility of national politicians. While cultural institutions argue that such activities support political and diplomatic efforts and lead to commercial benefits, methodological problems in quantifying such benefits have dogged cultural practice as in public relations.

It is possible to trace a number of related functions in public relations and diplomacy in the existing public relations literature: rhetoric, oratory, advocacy, negotiation, peacemaking, counselling, intelligence gathering. There appear to be three orders of function here: representational (rhetoric, oratory, advocacy), dialogic (negotiation, peacemaking), and advisory (counselling). The function of intelligence gathering describes research and environmental scanning and underpins the issues management function. This is a very interesting function because it carries with it connotations of a military function carried out at least partly secretly. The representational functions acknowledge self-interest and suggest strategies of promotion and persuasion. They also imply processes of planning and impression management, and possibly a degree of rigidity in terms of maintaining one's own position.

The dialogic metaphors—those of negotiation, peacemaking, and, to an extent, counselling—imply some degree of neutrality or objectivity. This seems to be linked to public relations' aspiration to professional status and its desire to sanitize its generally sleazy image: there is a substantial qualitative difference in terms of status and respectability between a "spin doctor" and a "corporate diplomat."

Public relations as counsellor explains the advisory role to management. In diplomatic circles the post of counsellor is a senior embassy post, junior to minister or ambassador but senior to the first secretary. Another potential metaphor that can be derived from this terminology is a legal one, since "counsel" is a British term for a barrister or advocate, as in "Queen's Counsel," and "counsellor" is the American term for a lawyer, particularly one who conducts cases in court. Both imply the "asymmetrical" advocacy role. Examples of how this may be represented in the literature emphasize the advisory role; for example, "Advice on the presentation of the public image of an organisation" (Black & Sharpe, 1983, p. 19), "Advise management on policy" (Wilcox et al., 1986, p. 7), and the very term originally promoted by Bernays (1955), "PR Counsel."

Clearly these various functional approaches to public relations practice may not necessarily be applied in isolation from one another and several might be used in the course of a relationship, but the strategy adopted at any one moment builds in different assumptions about the nature of the relationship between sender and receiver and this, in turn, will affect the quality and process of subsequent communication acts. Sensitivity to such issues is clearly important in relationship management but difficult to express in a single definition or mission statement.

Many definitions of public relations are all-encompassing, including both advocacy and mutual understanding within the same framework. A seminal article on the many definitions by Rex Harlow (1976, pp. 34–42) set an unfortunate precedent for those that followed, in that the article at no stage makes clear whether definitions are descriptive or normative—he does not distinguish these as different orders of definition, nor does he attempt to classify these in any way. The effect of all this is that public relations definitions are apparently constructed in an attempt to be all things to all people simultaneously.

CORPORATIONS: THEIR POLITICS, DIPLOMACY, AND DIPLOMATS

At a personal and functional level, there are clear similarities in the work of diplomats and public relations practitioners. Theoretical support for this comes from various studies in communication which highlight the stressful "boundary-spanning" role of both parties, which sees them crossing cultures (whether organizational or national) and bridging cultural gaps. Both parties have interpretative and presentational roles and both attempt to manage communication about issues. Both diplomats and public relations practitioners conduct much of their business via the media and are media-trained to provide appropriate "sound-bites" on the issues of the day. In communications literature, the political role of organizational diplomats is recognized:

> There is now a substantial level of international business diplomacy. (Fisher, 1989, p. 407)

> Numerous large organisations today explicitly act in a political manner and see themselves as doing so. (Cheney & Vibbert, 1987, p. 188)

The political role for diplomats and public relations practitioners has come to depend increasingly upon the management of public opinion. Conventional diplomats have long recognized the power of public opinion, and the diplomat Sir Harold Nicolson credited Richelieu as being the first to do so, realizing that "no policy could succeed unless it had national opinion behind it" (Nicolson, 1954, p. 51). According to Nicolson's interpretation, Richelieu also recognized the concept of "opinion leaders" or "opinion formers" since he sought to "inform, and above all to instruct, those who influenced the thoughts and feelings of the people as a whole. He was the first to introduce a system of domestic propaganda" (ibid., pp. 51–52). Richelieu wrote and circulated pamphlets which were intended to educate and "create a body of informed opinion favourable to his policies" (ibid., p. 52).

Techniques of political communication are therefore fundamental to the diplomatic role. While the term "diplomacy" normally implies a political role and context, its application to the organizational context reveals a number of insights. First, it implies a specific interest in power-broking at an elite level; and second it implies the need for representative agents (Mitnick, 1993, passim).

Organizations are active in seeking to influence national and international political decisions in their favour and also to manage the way in which issues are perceived and media agendas set. Cheney and Vibbert suggested that organizations are faced with a dilemma, in that while they act politically and consciously develop their own political goals they also have to direct political influence without being identified as political groups. They must proclaim political messages without at the same time being represented as political bodies in the discourse of other corporate and political rhetors (Cheney & Vibbert, 1987, p. 188).

It is also in organizations' interests to identify their opponents as political actors in order to position them both as ideologically motivated and as solely self-interested (ibid.), which is surely what lies behind pejorative terms such as "activist groups," "single-issue publics," or "social activists." Such groups are often presented as being the reason why organizations need public relations.

Organizational politics targeted externally is conducted through the public relations specialities of public affairs, issues management, and lobbying. The ambitions of practitioners to lay claim to strategic high ground in terms of their own political positions within organizations can match the needs of organizations for reliable agents or diplomats to act on their behalf. Mitnick argued that corporate political activity is thus a game of agents in a democracy which can be seen as a system of competition as to which agents will govern and which goals of which principals those agents will seek to advance (Mitnick, 1993, p. 1). It is clear, however, that some principals have more resources than others and can therefore buy more or better agents than others, so that a free-market system will invariably favour some actors over others. It may also be argued that the creation of a corporate political elite which is effectively shadowing legitimate accountable political elites, both national and international, is a move which leads not only to an institutional domination of the public sphere but also to the creation of a particular elite culture sharing privileged information and thus power. Since elite persons and groups are always "newsworthy," the chance of these groups being able to shape communication and politico agendas is considerable. Organizational agents negotiate space for the organizational mission partly through the symbolic management of meaning. This influence may not always be obvious: the agents may effectively be secret, as is argued in Gandy's (1982) analysis of source–media relations and "information subsidies."

While one is likening the collectivity of an organization to a country in adopting the diplomatic metaphor, it is a truism that many multinational organizations are economically as big as or bigger than small or developing countries. However, they are not as accountable politically. Although they are ostensibly limited by national and international law, the relationship between themselves and governments is one of collusion; governments are highly dependent upon industries and industry agents can use government agents as their own to secure their ends. In other words, the relationship between government and business elites may lead to the formation of a wider diplomatic culture within which an extended chain of agency relationships exists; these agency relationships may not be formalized or even recognized.

One of the great historical figures of British public relations, Alan Campbell-Johnson, pointed out in an interview that:

[The growth of] public relations involved an extension of the diplomatic capability into business into the commercial field and I still think that there is an element of diplomacy involved in PR. (Interview, March 1994)

Likewise, the rather younger Traverse-Healy commented on comparative styles of public relations between the United States of America and UK:

I thought that in the UK we were an extension of the industrial diplomacy process . . . industrial statesmanship, whereas in the US it seemed to me that they were an extension of the communication industry and they were far more concerned about the size of the budget than they were with the virtues of the case they were promulgating. (Interview 25/6/91)

Sam Black, one of the most active IPR members also agreed that:

diplomacy and education [are] very important parts of publics relations. (Interview 25/6/91)

The trade journal *PR Week* described the then Director-General of the British Nuclear Industry Forum as "every bit the corporate diplomat" *(PR Week*, 1993, p. 16). The Director-General, Roger Hayes, a close contact of Traverse-Healy, described his own role as follows:

I think the real role of a public affairs PR person like myself is to act as a catalyst, helping corporations play a much bigger role in setting the agenda of our society. That's what I call corporate diplomacy. That's my mission (ibid., p. 16).

Turning to the diplomatic field, it is clear that Nicolson saw the evolution of shared values between diplomats as significant in the political process. He pointed out that officials in capitals around the world had similar levels and standards of education and similar peripatetic lifestyles, and that they shared objectives. Often, members of this international diplomatic corps had served in the same foreign capitals together. In short, they shared a professional culture and camaraderie which, according to Nicolson, meant that:

They desired the same type of world . . . they tended to develop a corporate identity independent of their national identity . . . they all believed, whatever their governments might believe, that the purpose of diplomacy was the preservation of peace. This professional freemasonry proved of great value in negotiation. (Nicolson, 1954, p. 75)

If we apply this notion to public relations, a number of interesting issues arise. First, as public relations professionalizes we might assume that the occupational identity strengthens. In a globalised world public relations agents who share craft knowledge, expertise, and, increasingly, educational concepts are likely to develop an increasingly coherent occupational culture that transcends national boundaries. Understanding the values and mores of the occupational culture should therefore be a research priority.

The scope and boundaries of public relations occupational culture, however, is complicated by the close relations some practitioners have with journalists and politicians: "revolving doors" suggest rather opaque boundaries. A key question here would be, "What kind of 'professional freemasonry' is developing and what social and political costs and benefits develop?"

PUBLIC RELATIONS AND DIPLOMACY

Considering the degree of at least superficial similarity between the roles of diplomacy and public relations, there has been relatively little discussion comparing the two functions. Much has focused on the role that public relations, specifically in its media relations role, can play in facilitating diplomacy and international relations rather than focusing on the role itself (Traverse-Healy, 1988b; Grunig, 1993a; Signitzer & Coombs, 1992). Here I give most attention to Signitzer and Coombs (1992), who analysed the conceptual relationship between public relations and diplomacy. The authors noted the lack of attention given to diplomacy by public relations academics and observed that the main focus of public relations texts which tackled "international public relations" was purely practical, focused on the problems which arise for multinational organizations in communicating with multinational publics. They identified a gap in public relations literature and argued that:

> How nation-states, countries or societies manage their communicative relationships with their foreign publics remains largely in the domain of political science and international relations. Public relations theory development covering this theme has yet to progress beyond the recognition that nations can engage in international public relations. (Signitzer & Coombs, 1992, p. 138)

Another way of approaching this is offered by writers in international relations, two of whom have pointed out that the revolution in communications and technology means that nation-states can also be seen as activist groups:

> A senior British practitioner, the diplomat Brian Crowe... argued in an academic journal recently that "in our new global village and with the spread of *intermestic* issues... domestic opinion on domestic matters in individual countries is becoming more and more a matter for concern to others."[1] (Hill & Beshoff, 1994b, p. 223; italics mine)

In the era of globalisation the scope of diplomacy and public relations becomes broader as technology facilitates communication across national frontiers and creates more publics. This approach is well anticipated in Traverse-Healy's paper (1988b), which provides a practitioner's perspective and documents a number of international examples of politicians and governments achieving credibility and influence with foreign publics through careful impression and media management.

Signitzer and Coombs focused on the concept of "public diplomacy" or the way in which activist groups (which they defined as including governments as well as pressure groups) influence public opinion to shape a government's foreign policy decisions, rather than on "traditional diplomacy," which, they suggested, "conjures up images of nation-states sending formal documents to other nation-states" (Signitzer & Coombs, 1992, p. 138). Public diplomacy may be used to exert an influence on foreign audiences "using persuasion and propaganda" (ibid. p. 138) through the dissemination of political information via the news media, which is designated the "tough-minded" approach. The alternative, referred to as cultural diplomacy, is designated the "tender-minded" approach, which, through the use of cultural, educational and artistic exchanges can transmit "messages about lifestyles, political and economic systems and artistic achievements." The authors argued that in the "tough-minded" approach:

> Objectivity and truth are considered important tools of persuasion but not extolled as virtues in themselves... the supreme criterion for public diplomacy is the raison d'état defined in terms of fairly short-term policy ends. (ibid. p. 140)

---

[1] The term "intermestic" is used to described international communication targeted at the domestic publics of other nations.

The article goes on to contrast the "tough-minded" approach with information and cultural programmes, the aim of which "is not necessarily to look for unilateral advantage"; rather they "must bypass foreign policy goals to concentrate on the 'highest' long-range national objectives. The goal is to create a climate of mutual understanding... truth and veracity are considered essential, much more than a mere persuasive tactic" (ibid., p. 140). Signitzer and Coombs proceeded to compare the motivation of these two "schools" of thought with the four models of Grunig and Hunt (1984) and to argue that basic concepts and motivations are shared.

While both Signitzer and Coombs and Traverse-Healy acknowledged overlap between the fields of public relations and diplomacy, their respective analyses fail to uncover deeper similarities between the two occupations in terms of international and national political structures and competition. Traverse-Healy came closest to this where he acknowledged that "international competition between states is comparable to commercial competition between business organisations in one national setting" (Traverse-Healy, 1988b, p. 3). This interpretation, however, underplays the political role of business organizations and does not seem to acknowledge the degree to which economics and politics are intertwined.

I would argue that Signitzer and Coombs' review of public diplomacy, especially cultural diplomacy, implies a deformalization of diplomacy and the involvement of non-governmental organizations and their personnel in the diplomatic process. They argued that the purpose of such exchange is "mutual understanding." This phrase used to be part of the British Council's mission statement and their argument depends on a key source, Mitchell, a professional cultural diplomat whose distinguished career saw him reach Assistant Director-General level of the British Council. Signitzer and Coombs suggested that cultural relations has a "nobler goal, that of information exchange" (Signitzer & Coombs, 1992, p. 142), broadly equated with that of Grunig and Hunt's (1984) symmetrical communication, but they did not explore the implications of this position in the context of international relations or the degree to which national goals may really by adjusted. The relationship between traditional diplomacy and cultural diplomacy remains underexplored—for example, the funding arrangements between central government and cultural agencies may be crucial in determining the "real" goals of the latter, which could be considerably more tough-minded than the publicly expressed statements of such organizations. Signitzer and Coombs' presentation of cultural organizations emphasizes artistic and academic exchanges rather than the scientific, medical, technical, and language work that many such organizations carry out. Increasingly, too, such agencies are having to prove their worth, and this might increasingly be linked to trade agreements.

Another difficulty in Signitzer and Coombs' analysis is an underlying but unacknowledged instrumentalism which is at odds with their stated aim to explore conceptual links between public relations concepts and ideas drawn from public or cultural diplomacy. Concern is expressed for "what works" and consideration as to whether the tough- or tender-minded school "function[s] best" (Signitzer & Coombs, 199, p. 141). Definitions of, and assumptions about, what is best or ideal are not stated. The underlying deductive approach becomes clear towards the end of the article, where it is stated that:

> the exact ideas/concepts which can be transferred from one area to the other have yet to be fully delineated and tested... researchers should test which concepts best transfer... Only a series of theory-based empirical studies will facilitate this convergence of research traditions. (ibid. pp. 145–146)

Certainly quantitative research into values and concepts would be useful, but so also would be more anthropologically based work and triangulated case work.

Grunig's article addressing diplomacy and international affairs sets out to "analyse the effects and ethics of... international campaigns and derive recommendations for how public relations can contribute to global diplomacy without obfuscating or corrupting the process" (Grunig, 1993a, p. 139). It is argued that asymmetrical and unethical public relations has been "prevalent in international public relations throughout history" (ibid., p. 147) with a view to influencing political events and public opinion. Asymmetrical public relations is associated with, if not actually defined as, propaganda: "The terms 'promoters, propagandists, and lobby-ists' seem to describe the press agentry, two-way asymmetrical and personal influence models of public relations, respectively" (ibid., p. 149). This view presents a role for public relations of facilitating international relationships which are "ethical." Grunig did not define what is meant by "ethical," but it looks as though it is the dialogic aspect of symmetry which makes commu-nication moral rather than immoral,[2] and it is argued that:

> When practised symmetrically, public relations is a valuable component of the public communication systems of a country and of the world . . . If public relations is practised according to the principles of strategic man-agement, public responsibility and the two-way symmetrical model, it is an important element of the global communication system. (Grunig, 1993a, p. 149)

This quote clearly indicates the importance given to the role of public relations in influ-encing the political architecture. The role for public relations can be seen as influential and interventionist in national policies. Such intervention might not "obfuscate" or "corrupt" (ibid., p. 130) international communication, but it clearly is intended to effect change and influence public relations practice in one way rather than another.

If international relations is the discipline which tries to explain political activities across state boundaries (Taylor, 1978), it is difficult to see how the communications aspect of this—public relations—can be entirely separated from political action. Public relations is profoundly concerned with the establishment and maintenance of the reputation and credibility of client organizations, and this is done explicitly to maintain the client's ability to influence key publics and to be identified by the media as a contributor to debate on particular issues. Furthermore, as has been noted, governments themselves employ such techniques—though in this case these are sometimes referred to as information or propaganda.

DEVELOPMENT OF THE DISCIPLINE OF DIPLOMACY

Literature on diplomacy falls within the field of international relations, which is a relatively new area of study in itself. There is some potential confusion in the terminology since the terms "international theory" and "diplomacy" are sometimes used interchangeably, as are the terms "international affairs" and "international relations." The term "international theory" is used to define the theoretical as opposed to historical or applied aspects of the field of international relations, and the term "international relations" may be used metonymically to stand as representative of any of these more specialized aspects. The inconsistent use of terminology appears to arise from continued debate over the definitions and boundaries of the field, a feature held in common with public relations. I shall continue to refer to the specific role of diplomacy but in the remainder of the chapter will reflect the literature and refer to theories of diplomacy and international theory interchangeably, following the sources used in the discussion. When discussing the emergence of diplomacy as an area of study, I shall do so

---

[2]It seems as though in the recent past writers within the Grunig school (such as Pearson, 1992) have suggested that Grunig's position is supported by Jürgen Habermas' Theory of Communicative Action (see chapter 18).

largely under the umbrella term of international relations because this describes the academic area and degrees awarded by universities.

Within the field of international relations, there has been surprisingly little theoretical work specifically on diplomacy. Diplomacy, it seems is only interesting insofar as it contributes to specific political decisions or crises and is treated descriptively rather than analytically. It is not, therefore, seen as a field of study in itself, but as a technique used to achieve certain ends, similar in some respects to a marketing view of public relations. Such work as there is on diplomacy is very much of the "how to do it" variety. *Satow's Guide to Diplomatic Practice* (Gore-Booth, 1978), first published in 1917, is still used by the British Foreign and Commonwealth Office and describes in great detail diplomatic customs and precedent but does not include any conceptual discussion. The other key British source is Nicolson, who again adopted an uncritical approach, asserting that the "essence" of diplomacy is common sense (Nicolson, 1954, pp. 50, 132, 144), a view apparently shared by a number of public relations practitioners. A theoretical study of public relations or diplomacy must go beyond practical guidance and consider the motivations, values, beliefs and conventions of the practice, its organizational and social effects, as well as the underlying assumptions and political configurations that go along with these practices.

Important common ground is shared by international relations and public relations partly because they are relatively new fields of study and relate to clearly defined areas of practical application. There have been a number of common concerns: the relationship between academics and policy-makers or practitioners, debate over the purpose and appropriate orientation of the discipline, debate over epistemology and methodology, and questions of ethics. Some of these similarities confront any new discipline; questions of boundaries, legitimacy, credibility, and methodology. Other similarities arise from a response to similar intellectual currents; for example, systems theory was important to international theory in the 1970s. By the 1980s systems theory was not a significant force, and academics in the field responded to work developing in anthropology and psychology and became focused on debates emerging around structuralism, critical theory, and postmodernism. Public relations became somewhat fossilized at the systems theory stage, and it has proved difficult for academics to escape the totalizing net of systems theory. For example, some have used ideas taken from different intellectual traditions, such as critical theory, but used these to support a systems perspective (see chapters on systems theory and rhetoric for detailed discussion). Interestingly, the aspect of Habermas' work which has received most attention from public relations academics, that of the Theory of Communicative Action, has also been the focus of interest in international theory, the two possibly unconsciously sharing a motive to

reinscribe the emancipatory potential within IR [PR]—both as a discipline and a social practice. Much of this work is informed by Habermas's arguments regarding communicative rationality as the basis for discourse ethics which allows the uncovering and construction of "truths." (Hoffman, 1994, p. 38)

The relationship between academics and practitioners is debated in both international relations and public relations. Because both areas are practice-based, it can be difficult for academics to obtain access to certain types of information or activity regarded as politically or commercially sensitive. The relationship between academics and practitioners may be difficult because of their differing perspectives on the purpose of the discipline. One very eminent academic in the field of international relations, Christopher Hill, Montague Burton Professor of International Relations at the London School of Economics, identified the following key questions arising from the relationship between academics and practitioners in international relations:

- How far do academics and policy-makers define problems in the same way? Can the theoretical debate about competing "paradigms" illuminate policy choices?
- Do decision-makers increasingly rely on outside sources of expertise, whether technical, historical or regional?
- Is theory, as Friedrich van Hayek once suggested, the ultimate source of power because new ideas promote change?
- Do International Relations academics take too many cues from politicians? What are the proprieties which should govern the agenda and conduct of research?
- How can academic findings be conveyed to the world of action? Is the indirect route (i.e. via scholarly publication) enough, or should knowledge be mobilised through the use of media, conferences and political contacts? (Hill & Beshoff, 1994a, p. 4)

These questions have considerable resonance in public relations as with other applied fields.

Hill presented a dichotomous choice for academics between the role of popular commentator and that of traditional academic. He argued that the existence of this choice means that the academic world of international relations is divided between the "ivory-tower" academics and those actively involved in contemporary affairs. This picture is reflected in the nature and scope of professional and academic journals, which can largely be divided between those that are policy-driven and those that are academic.

Hill and Beshoff rightly pointed out the dangers posed to academics by pursuing the latest *Zeitgeist* or by overdependence on research funded by policy-makers:

> The point is not that scholarship should not respond to major changes in the world; it is rather that the opportunity costs of so doing are not always appreciated in terms of the atrophying of important but suddenly unfashionable areas where the lack of expertise may indeed be keenly felt once the wheel eventually turns again in their favour . . . academics [may] become, almost without noticing it, reactive to the initiatives of others, rather than pursuing their own professional concerns, which would otherwise intersect with policy issues only occasionally . . . Creativity is thus attenuated . . . It is difficult indeed to free oneself from the pressures and conventional wisdoms of one's own time. But that is exactly what is supposed to characterise a good academic; the ability to pursue an independent line of thought. (Hill & Beshoff, 1994a, p. 8)

The debate over the purpose of a discipline involves broader epistemological, metatheoretical, and methodological issues which are now emerging in public relations.

Another area of convergence for public relations and international relations lies in a number of ethical and political issues which arise from a number of their practitioners servicing large and powerful collectivities. The questions about the relative rights and responsibilities of these collectivities and their relationships to their citizens and publics takes international relations and public relations into the realms of political philosophy; and thus requires those writing in these fields to deal with questions of ideology, something that some practitioners might prefer to remain between the covers of books.

The development of both subjects within academia shows interesting similarities. Both subjects can trace their "roots" back to classical literature—in the case of diplomacy to Thucydides' *History of the Peloponnesian War* and Machiavelli's *The Prince* and *The Art of War*; in the case of public relations, useful reference can be made to Aristotle's *The Art of Rhetoric* and Plato's *Gorgias* and *Phaedrus*. The first Chair in International Relations in the UK was created at the University of Aberystwyth in the 1920s. The first full-time academic to be appointed at the professorial level in public relations in the UK was Anne Gregory, Leeds Metropolitan University. The early years of both subjects were marked by uncertainty and hostile debate over the extent and role of the areas under review. Critics claimed that international relations was not a subject in its own right because it lacked unity of knowledge and depended on many other disciplines. Not only were the boundaries of the international relations discipline in dispute, but it was also claimed that there were "no obviously valid theories nor self-evident methods of obtaining them" (Taylor, 1978, p. 8). Many public relations academics have found themselves in unfriendly, even hostile homes such as marketing departments. In the bureaucratic university environment such academics may find that work published in public relations journals is unrecognised or held in low esteem. Alternatively, they may be required to change intellectual direction in order to publish in marketing journals, and so on.

Within international relations there was bitter methodological debate between the traditionalists, who argued that accurate prediction was impossible in international relations and who produced explanations centred on concepts of power and national interest, and the behaviouralists, who advocated that all assumptions should be clearly spelt out and only empirically verifiable hypotheses should be produced. The field expanded dramatically post-World War II, fuelled by the Cold War and work in strategic studies focused on case studies, computer modelling of game theory, theories of deterrence, theories of crisis management, and an increasing amount of action research by peace researchers. There are some similarities to be noted here with regard to public relations, for example, the use of case studies both as a teaching tool and as a research method and a clear overlap in subject matter in the area of crisis management. Both public relations and diplomacy deal in trust and use strategies of negotiation and impression management while guarding the reputation of their clients. Thus, it can be seen that diplomacy and public relations are comparable occupations and have certain similarities in their development as disciplines. The degree to which they share common problems in terms of theorization and justification will be explored in the remainder of this chapter.

THEORIES OF DIPLOMACY—WIGHT'S FRAMEWORK

One of the few examples of a substantial attempt to theorize about diplomacy was made by Wight in the 1950s. His series of lectures at the London School of Economics (LSE) have remained a landmark although there have been few attempts since to develop such work further. Wight's approach was that of political philosophy and he pursued it in defiance of the behaviouralists, who "sought a kind of theory that approximated to science" (Wight, 1994, p. x). The behaviouralists sought to exclude moral issues from the subject matter of international relations on the grounds that they lay beyond the scope of scientific behaviour, whereas Wight placed these questions at the centre of his enquiry (ibid., p. x).

Wight conceptualized diplomacy as consisting of three main approaches in terms of diplomatic style and underlying assumptions about political intercourse and international society. Wight identified these three positions as Machiavellian (characterized as pragmatic but one-sided), Grotian (after Hugo Grotius, the Dutch diplomat, whose *De Jure Belli et Pacis* was published in 1625 and whose style of diplomacy was moderate negotiation), and Kantian (diplomacy based an the sentiments expressed in Kant's *Perpetual Peace*, published in 1795 and which basically argued that the human condition could only be overcame by belief that it had the potential for transformation). Somewhat confusingly he also referred to these three types of diplomacy as realist, rationalist, and revolutionist. These positions did not have rigid boundaries and occasionally collapsed into one another. Wight's method was to analyse historical ideas and events in relation to political philosophy in order to reveal the fundamental sources of the positions adopted.

The Machiavellian or realist position was based on the assumption that international politics was equal to international anarchy and that each state should therefore pursue its own interest in a free-market Hobbesian world where the only relationships that count are those based on contract. The authority, dignity, and coherence of individual states was emphasized at the expense of any concept of international society or the suggestion that the state is a member of a wider society of states (Wight, 1991, p. 33). In other words, the realist sees international relations as an arena for competition and conflict rather than a society. The realist assumes that interests will conflict and that the intelligent position to adopt is therefore that of the application of pressure and the offering of inducements in pursuit of one's own interests. The approach is supported by assumptions that the world is constantly in flux and transformation, that people and states are driven by fear and greed, and that the sensible way to respond is to use all the techniques of bargaining to negotiate from a position of strength. The characteristic realist response to political change can be summed up as "adapt, fore-stall, facilitate and control," and the basic quality for a diplomat is argued to be that of adaptability to change (ibid., p. 189). The following quotation could easily be from a public relations book on issues management: "the capacity to adapt oneself to change is the minimum diplomatic requirement. A higher achievement is to anticipate change, to see the dirty weather ahead and avoid it or outflank it" (ibid., p. 190).

The Machiavellian or realist position is clearly represented in the public relations literature. This position is clearly self-interested and seeks to persuade publics to fall into line and governments to accommodate organizational interests. In this there are similarities with much of the writing on issues management, where military terminology is readily used. It assumes a hostile, difficult, changeable, and competitive world in which strategic alliances and sympathetic agents are sought out to enhance the organizational position. The specific public relations role is to secure "the willing acceptance of attitudes and ideas" (Black, 1989, p. 7); the public relations person must be a "professional persuader" (Hayward, 1990, p. 3). The approach might be characterized by the title of Edward Bernays' book *The Engineering of Consent* (1955). Hiebert acknowledged directly that "too much public relations is Machiavellian" (Hiebert, 1966, p. 317). The approach is also rhetorical in its focus on the persuasive function and the intention to seek and develop arguments that will persuade publics to change their views in line with organizational wishes.

The rationalist or Grotian tradition focuses on continuous international and institutional intercourse based on concepts of mutuality. The Grotian style was based on building relationships through truthfulness and promise-keeping, which helped to build a good reputation for reliability and trustworthiness. Diplomacy is seen as something akin to commerce and international society is defined as the sum of customary (and often commercial) exchanges. It acknowledges, therefore, that there is something called international society but that its form is distinct from that of a state. The principle of reciprocity is important and was used to justify colonialism, which was argued not to be pure philanthropy but of reciprocal benefit (Wight, 1991, p. 79). The paternalistic concept of trusteeship was also important. Both these arguments are of a similar nature to those often employed in the justification of corporate social responsibility. The position of enlightened self-interest raises problems, in that it pre-supposes that you can estimate the interests of other parties. This problem is clearly shared by public relations practitioners claiming to be working in the public interest. The Grotian or rationalist tradition emphasizes enlightened self-interest and reciprocity and can be likened to claims in the public relations literature which emphasize mutual understanding as an organizational goal. Much literature emphasizes that the role of public relations is to achieve mutually beneficial acts for both organization and public. Leading writers (Grunig & Grunig, 1990) have latterly been recommending "Negotiation, collaborative mediation" as the prime role in two-way public relations. Grunig went so far as to claim that the two-way symmetrical model bases public relations on negotiation and compromise (Grunig, 1993a, p. 146), and it is clearly an important element of his approach. It is an appealing ideal, emphasizing dialogue, truth and "win/win" end-states, but possibly underplays negative outcomes such as lying and manipulation, defence-attack spirals, and so on. It also ignores the possibility of organizational hegemony and the domination of the public sphere.

The third tradition, that of the Kantian or revolutionist, is based on the assumption that the multiplicity of sovereign states form a moral and cultural whole. This whole is imbued with an authority which transcends that of individual states but which, in a somewhat Rousseauian way, represents the will of the people. It conceives of an international society comprised of a world-state empowered by individuals in a world where nation-states have diminished influence. Concepts of ideological homogeneity and doctrinal imperialism (whether Stalinism or capitalism) are of importance in the creation of an international citizenship. International tension is seen as an irrational obstacle to the fulfilment of human potential and the assumption is clearly made that existing national governments manipulate public opinion to their own ends.

The revolutionist or Kantian approach emphasizes a peacemaking approach in which the public interest is served by a world order which limits the influence of nation-states. In public relations this is represented by the strong emphasis on public relations' potential to achieve transcendental mutual satisfaction and understanding between peoples. For example, J. Carroll Bateman, President of IPRA in 1980, "referred frequently to public relations professionals as 'peacemakers' of world society. He appropriately did so in recognition of public relations' value and importance to world peace in facilitating communications and understanding between the governments and the publics that constitute nations" (Black & Sharpe, 1983, p. vii). The late DeWitt C. Reddick, Dean Emeritus of Journalism and Communications at the University of Texas at Austin, called public relations "the lubricant which makes the segments of an order work together with the minimum friction and misunderstanding" (ibid., p. vii).

This type of aim and argument seems clearly linked to the revolutionist tradition and it raises similar questions over what counts as peace, consensus, or mutual understanding and who defines this. The approach may lead to the complacent imposition of traditional orders with little space for those who wish to deviate from the accepted norm. The following quotations give examples of perceptions of the peacemaker function in public relations:

> In the two-way symmetric model, finally, practitioners serve as mediators between organisations and their publics. Their goal is mutual understanding between practitioners and their publics. (Grunig & Hunt, 1984, p. 22)

> I believe the more we understand one another, the more we will reduce the changes of war, or terrorism, and of man's violence against man. Fortunately, public relations can aid us in that understanding. (Hiebert, 1988, p. 1)

> Public relations must be a two-way activity and is all about creating both goodwill and understanding. (Hayward, 1990, pp. 4–5)

> Public relations serves society by mediating conflict . . . PR plays a major role in resolving cases of competing interests in society . . . Blessed are the peacemakers. (Black & Sharpe, 1983, p. vii)

> Public relations . . . should be ethical in that it helps build caring—even loving—*relationships* with other individuals and groups they affect in a society or the world. (Grunig, 1992, p. 38)

These idealistic goals are utilitarian, in that they maximize happiness, but in instances of irreconcilable difference between organization and public it is likely that organizational interests will prevail. This is not to say that majority interest is not taken into account, but it may only be considered to the degree that is prudent for the organization. In such circumstances the notion that the aim of organizational public relations is to create goodwill, understanding, and peace suggests that the concept of what constitutes goodwill, understanding, and peace may be determined principally by the organization. There is also something slightly unreal and a little sinister in the idea that agreement can always be reached and that this is a desirable state of affairs. Given that public relations largely represents organizations, it seems that the potential for individual or minority interests may be compromised. In short, I am suggesting that the very notion of symmetry or understanding can be doctrinally imperialist.

Another characteristic which can be found in justifications offered for public relations and which can be interpreted as revolutionist thought in action is that of the public relations obsession with democracy. Arguments in public relations literature highlight the contribution that public relations makes to "democracy," in terms of enhancing the free flow of information in society. It is significant that the nature of this "democracy" is never clearly articulated and defined since public relations very clearly enhances the flow of subsidized institutional information. It may claim to "serve the public interest by providing a voice in the public forum for every point of view, many of which would not otherwise be given a hearing because of limited media attention" (Hayward, 1990, pp. 4–5).

The implications of this view are that public relations facilitates the articulation of various and possibly conflicting points of view and also manages to increase the media's attention span. However, in reality the public relations industry clearly does not take upon itself responsibility for ensuring that all views are heard—it simply represents those who pay for its services.

IMPLICATIONS

At a societal level there are clear overlaps between public relations and diplomacy since they both have to do with concepts such as power, negotiation, coercion, manipulation, propaganda, principal, agent, publics and public opinion, with issues management and lobbying functions bearing perhaps the closest relationship to diplomacy. Cultural or "soft" diplomacy could be likened to corporate social responsibility.

Thus, the three positions identified by Wight can be identified in the public relations literature. The Machiavellian or realist position overlaps with both the "press agentry" and "asymmetrical" models. The Grotian or rationalist position overlaps with the "public information" and "asymmetrical" models. The Kantian or revolutionist position seems to have strong similarities with the "symmetrical" model. These overlaps suggest that the problems of public relations are not unique but relate to particular views about the way the world operates and how collectivities, whether organizations or countries, ought to behave. The overlap also suggests that the public relations models should not be presented as some discrete form of historical development; on the contrary, they relate to existing but heretofore unacknowledged, unresearched roots. They arise from a particular interpretation of events leading to the evolution of the public relations industry in one country (the United States), but it is not self-evident that they have the normative power often ascribed to them. The presentation of historical development as necessarily logical and progressive has long been controversial and a matter for intense debate.

The "symmetrical" or revolutionist position is the one of most interest here because the meaning and implications of this position have not been exhaustively debated. Symmetry is presented as being a noble (and more effective) organizational goal which can result in peaceful coexistence. The question that is neither raised nor answered is "What kind of peace do you want?"[3] Symmetry implies an open form of negotiation, something that Nicolson criticized in his historical sweep of diplomatic practice, where he argued against Wilsonian democracy and its imposition on international practice because transparency inhibited genuine negotiation as it led to posturing and propaganda speeches for media consumption. Furthermore, Nicolson suggested, Wilson's view of the conduct of international relations was both naive in its understanding of human nature and imperialistic in its imposition of American doctrine.

The claims made for the potential of symmetrical public relations are quite substantial: "Symmetrical public relations would eliminate most ethical problems of international public relations. More importantly, it would make public relations more effective in producing international understanding and collaboration" (Grunig, 1993a, p. 162). The argument seems to imply an extremely powerful role for public relations advisers in the international scene while underplaying the strong desire for gain of those involved in international relations.

Revolutionist doctrine in international relations posits an international state or community which can override nation-states. Symmetrical doctrine in public relations does not currently propose an equivalent body which can override organization-states. The implications of the convergence of public relations theory and international theory may be that we have to rethink our concept of organizations, organizational goals, and organizational boundaries. Public relations and diplomacy both deal with an ensemble of inter-penetrating relationships and overlapping publics, principals, agents, and cultures in a social world which is the product of creative human activity undergoing continuous transformation. For these reasons it is important to see diplomacy and public relations in structural contexts which have the potential for change. Of crucial importance is the relationship between international society and the State, the status of corporate actors in these contexts, and the perception of these by public relations practitioners. It seems that the diplomatic function of public relations is to perform a political role on behalf of organizations in national and international society.

In theoretical terms I am arguing that the concept and implications of "symmetry" in public relations theory could be more fully delineated and justified. The definitions and practice of symmetry are presented as unproblematic, and the social and political impact of the approach is not explored. Drawing the contrast between the frameworks of Wight and Grunig demonstrates some theoretical convergence but also shows that the critical implications of symmetrical thought are more developed in international theory than in public relations theory.

It is also clear that in international theory the revolutionist (symmetrical) position implies fundamental change in political architecture, but the potential for transformation is not explored in public relations theory. This raises a problem for the public relations theory where there seems to be a tension between achieving the goal of symmetry and retaining existing structural and organizational frameworks. The concept of "symmetry" has implications for the potential disintegration of organizations as we know them and their possible transformation as they reintegrate in some different form.

Public relations and diplomacy negotiate with publics on behalf of principals. The ways in which each is conducted and the aims they profess to have are based on particular positions about how organizations should be organized and how they should relate to one another, and the extent to which they should order our political and social affairs, both nationally and internationally. Through "boundary-spanning," the functions of public relations and diplomacy also have a role in maintaining boundaries and thus in protecting the status quo. This was represented symbolically in diplomacy between the 15th and 19th centuries, when on occasion European princes met each other at the centre of a bridge and spoke to each other through a stout oaken lattice (Nicolson, 1954, p. 38). The attempt to participate in or define symmetrical public

---

[3]I owe this question to Jim Wyllie, Senior Lecturer in Strategic Studies, University of Aberdeen.

relations threatens those boundaries and raises the prospect of an as yet undefined but rather different organizational and political life. What could be described as the "pax symmetrica" is itself based on the imposition and acceptance of a particular worldview of common sense, and is thus intrinsically hegemonic in that one overall framework may be applied and the potential for disagreement may be restricted. For example, Heath (1992, p. 318) saw the value of public relations as "its ability to contribute to the collective shared reality that brings harmony, a shared perspective that leads people to similar compatible conclusions." Because there is so little content to the concept of "symmetry," the term appears to have become a euphemism for "good." "Symmetry" appears to offer liberation and free expression simultaneously, but it is also a potentially totalitarian ideology.

This chapter argues that public relations can usefully be considered in tandem with international relations, not simply because it performs a (publicity) function in the process of diplomacy and international relations, but because it is linked to fundamental positions about the way individuals organize themselves into collectivities (whether publics or nations), form identities, and relate to other collectivities. Assumptions about what is considered appropriate in organizational and international intercourse and about the rights of organizations and nations to define and fulfil their destinies are as important as the communicative acts that are undertaken in the name of those represented.

Finally, this chapter reveals shared normative conceptions with ideas in international theory. These frameworks and the intellectual currents they sprang from are a rich potential source for public relations academics which will enable them to connect public relations with political, economic, and social architecture and elites.

20

Corporate Identity and Corporate Image

Peter Meech
University of Stirling

Identity and image have commanded the attention of thinkers and scholars across a range of disciplines from at least the time of the ancient Greeks. Corporate identity, by contrast, has a relatively brief history. As a term it has established itself in common use, but despite this there is a lack of consensus over what it actually means. It can be regarded, on the one hand, as a modern label for an age-old phenomenon, and, on the other, as an activity of comparatively recent standing. This chapter begins with a discussion of the use of the key terms in the field and of the factors which have determined the growth of corporate identity consultancy. The claimed strategic benefits of a corporate identity exercise are considered, as is the controversy that the practice continues to attract. There follows an account of the process involved in a corporate identity exercise. Finally, a case study is presented to illustrate some of the points previously considered. While the focus in this chapter is mostly on the visual, it needs stressing from the outset that this is only one, albeit particularly salient, aspect of a complex organizational phenomenon.

ISSUES OF TERMINOLOGY

Corporate identity is of professional interest not simply to specialist practitioners such as graphic designers, corporate communication advisers, and public relations consultants but also to academics and students in corresponding disciplines. It is, or should be, of concern too to CEOs and other senior managers, for reasons which will become clear later. Given the range of practical aspects and theoretical perspectives involved, it is scarcely surprising that a degree of confusion exists regarding the relevant concepts. What follows is a consideration of the terms most frequently used by writers on the subject.

CORPORATE IMAGE

To begin not with the organization but with those with whom it has significant dealings may appear to be putting the cart before the horse. It certainly reverses the order in which it is traditional to approach the topic. But in doing this we are acknowledging the key role that publics, stakeholders, or target audiences play in the process. The term most widely used by practitioners to signify the impression these groups have of an organization is "image," often qualified by evaluative adjectives such as good, poor, positive, or negative. David Bernstein had no qualms in using "image" in the title of his book on the subject, even referring to it as "a 'true reality'" (Bernstein, 1984, p. 233). But a number of academic writers are more circumspect, not to say highly sceptical, because of the term's multifarious uses (Cutlip, Center, & Broom, 1985; Grunig, 1992). In particular, the contrast with "reality" suggests something illusory and hence dubious. This negative image of "image" itself is due in large part to Daniel Boorstin's influential discussion of the creation by the U.S. media and public relations of "pseudo-events" (Boorstin, 1961) and from the similarly caustic attitude taken by left-wing cultural theorists in the UK. Raymond Williams, for instance, commented:

> [Image] is in effect a jargon term of commercial advertising and public relations. Its relevance has been increased by the growing importance of visual media such as television ... This technical sense in practice supports the commercial and manipulative processes of image as "perceived" reputation or character. (Williams, 1976, pp. 130–131)

But perceptions, whether manipulated or not, are a form of reality. For some people, including many postmodernists, they are indeed the only reality.

For the purposes of the present discussion, "image" will be used to signify the sum impression gained of an organization by an individual. This derives partly from the explicit, controlled ways in which an organization communicates with its various publics, through the graphic design and verbal tone of its advertising and other visual material, and, not least, through its choice of corporate logo. But communication in this sense is too narrowly conceived and takes no account of the messages conveyed, for example, by face-to-face dealings between employees and customers. Nor does this addition exhaust the factors affecting an organization's image. Other information which can play a role includes media coverage of any one aspect of an organization's activities, including the pay and working conditions of its staff or those of its suppliers (Klein, 2000). Interpersonal communication, hearsay, and gossip—activities beyond the immediate control of an organization—also have a potential impact to make. But corporate image is affected too by an individual's personal experiences of an organization's products or services, including its after sales performance, and the resulting sense of satisfaction and pleasure (or their lack) and value for money (or its opposite). In short, the interaction between organizations and their publics is often multi-faceted and works on different levels. A simile by James Grunig is particularly apt here: "symbolic and behavioral relationships are intertwined like strands of a rope" (Grunig, 1993, p. 123).

It is a commonplace in the literature that different publics have different perceptions of an organization, each responding to it, as it were, en bloc. But while allowing for a degree of differentiation, this approach does not go far enough. Composed of a multiplicity of elements, as noted above, an organization's image is better conceptualized as likely to vary from one individual to another. In one and the same person it may also be many-sided or even contradictory in character, since he or she may be simultaneously both an employee and a customer or both a supplier and a shareholder. Hence, factual knowledge may be at variance with emotional attitude. Nor is an image compelled to remain static, but may undergo change over time. Furthermore, it is not necessarily something an individual is fully conscious of or can adequately put into words when asked to. The point to note here is that the individually specific circumstances of message reception interact with the changing behaviour and communication activities of an organization to produce a plurality of corporate images. So to assert, as Clive Chajet did, that identity management can secure a good image is thus to oversimplify (Chajet, 1989, p. 18). In a case study of an Illinois insurance company's image, Mary Anne Moffitt provided empirical confirmation of some of the contingencies involved (Moffitt, 1994). Using a theoretical articulation model deriving from work in British cultural studies on media audiences, she examined the personal, social, environmental, and organizational factors that compete to determine corporate image and the circumstances under which shared meanings are possible.

A single, unitary image and its management are both idealized accounts of a complex and, in the final analysis, unpredictable process. But if "corporate image" is best conceptualized as the impressions—both cognitive and affective—produced within individuals in specific social settings, what of the other terms that are regularly encountered in the literature? How, in particular, are we to distinguish between "corporate identity," "visual identity" and "corporate personality"? There is a measure of agreement here among writers on the subject, but also sufficient differences to warrant investigation. The main problem concerns the first term, for which there would appear to be four principal uses.

CORPORATE IDENTITY

In ordinary speech and in much media coverage, corporate identity is typically equated with a company logo and little if anything else. This understanding of the term is buttressed by those graphic design businesses, many of them online, offering "CI packages" which, for just a few hundred dollars or pounds, comprise a selection of logo designs. A second sense of the term involves a broadening of its scope, but still within the limits of planned communications. Thus, for Bernstein, "Corporate identity . . . is the sum of the visual cues by which the public recognises the company and differentiates it from others" (Bernstein, 1984, p. 156). Similarly, Chajet remarked: "Corporate identity is the most visible element of a corporate strategy" (Chajet, 1989, p. 18). This use of the term is by far the most common in the specialist literature.

Before considering the third use, we should note that the term "visual identity" has been coined in an attempt at conceptual clarification. Thus, when used of an organization, it signifies "not just its logo, but the various other aspects of its physical presentation, such as its standard layouts, typography, colour schemes and interior design" (Keen & Warner, 1989, p. 13). A major focus here is on publications such as annual reports, brochures, instruction manuals, letterheads, business cards, press releases, invoices, flyers, CD-ROMs, and Web sites. But equally important are the signs on buildings (Kinneir, 1980), the buildings themselves, vehicles, uniforms, and, where relevant, the product and its packaging. Visual identity equates most closely with corporate identity in the second sense, although it has still to establish itself as widely as a distinct concept. Understanding corporate identity in this way by concentrating on the visual aspects of communication is the approach traditionally taken by designers. The addition of a musical phrase or jingle, for example in the area of broadcasting, suggests the need for the related concept of "aural identity" (Brownrigg & Meech, 2002).

For most of the writers considered here, corporate identity certainly embraces the visual elements of self-presentation but takes in also the numerous additional ways in which an organization communicates with people, both internally and externally. At one level this means considering, for instance, not just the uniform (style, colours, material, and fit) of, say, airline flight attendants, but also their body language, manner of speech, and, above all, their actual treatment of passengers. At another level it comprises the speed and efficiency with which an organization copes with a crisis as well as the degree of openness to the media, in good times and in bad. An organization's corporate identity, like its image, will inevitably vary according to circumstances. In the case of a company, the persona it desires to present to its shareholders reflects its profitability and future strategy at one end of the spectrum and, at the other, its efficiency in running an annual general meeting and its informative, well-designed annual report. Increasingly, a company's social responsibility programme is coming to play a part, too. However, this external face may be at odds with the one it presents to its own workforce, for whom low rates of pay, unsatisfactory working conditions, and a company newsletter which is merely a management mouthpiece are the daily reality of the company. There again, the two versions may coincide. Clearly congruence is preferable for an organization, since the exposure of a glaring discrepancy could indicate a lack of cohesiveness or, worse still, corporate hypocrisy.

Given the vital role played by the various elements that make up a corporate identity, it is not surprising that there is widespread agreement that it should be the subject of close and continuous attention by senior management, preferably by chief executives themselves. In the third sense, then, corporate identity includes everything from products or services (what you make, sell, or offer), environments (the place where you make, sell, or offer it), information (how you describe and communicate what you do) to behaviour (how people within the organization behave to each other and to outsiders; Olins, 1989, p. 29). In this all-encompassing sense corporate identity is the aggregate of an organization's activities and artefacts, everything it does and says, both deliberately and unintentionally, built up over a period of time.

Finally, there is a fourth sense in which "corporate identity" occurs. Nicholas Ind, for example, referred to it as "the term most commonly used to define the programme of communication and change that a company undertakes in conjunction with an external consultancy" (Ind, 1990, p. 19). This sense differs from those previously discussed in treating corporate identity as a specific project, usually undertaken with external professional help. The typical stages involved in such a corporate identity exercise are discussed later.

CORPORATE PERSONALITY

For analytical purposes, there is a case for recognising "corporate personality" as a distinct concept. Whereas corporate identity can be equated with everything an organization does or says, its personality might be thought of as its own sense of self. Both corporate culture and corporate vision and strategy are integral parts of this multi-faceted entity. Mission statements are potentially of importance here as codified expressions of corporate aims, though they are sometimes too idealistic to indicate the actual character of the organization and too platitudinous to assist in identifying features which make it distinctively different from others.

But can there be such a thing as a stable, unitary corporate personality? Just as the concept of corporate image has been characterized as protean, so too corporate personality is perhaps better regarded as highly differentiated and dynamic, yet capable of manifesting continuity (Gorb, 1992). Members of an organization, differentially situated in terms of power, status, earnings, interests and geography, will inevitably have different perspectives from which they form their perceptions. This is not to condemn a corporate personality audit as the pursuit of a will-o'-the-wisp. Both the findings of such an exercise, and indeed the process itself, may very well have practical benefits—the latter insofar as a heightened self-awareness may lead to other kinds of beneficial change. But any attempt to determine corporate personality must take account of the plurality of views in an organization in as nuanced and objective a manner as possible, and to recognize even then the partial and ephemeral nature of the picture gained.

This discussion of one set of concepts concludes with Bernstein's summary account of three of the terms treated: "[p]ersonality made manifest by identity is perceived as image" (Bernstein, 1984, p. 60). For operational purposes this may be a useful aid to research, but as a description of the complex field of relationships involved it needs qualification. First, the changeable and ultimately indeterminate nature of corporate personality must be noted. Second, the visual, as already noted, is only one dimension of corporate identity. And third, "perceived as image" implies the communication process between sender and receiver is straightforward and automatic, thereby downplaying the negotiation of meaning on the part of the latter.

At a more basic level there is a further set of terms which calls for elucidation. The term "logo" (from the Greek *logos* = speech, word, reason) is generally used to refer to the ways in which organizations represent themselves in graphic terms, whether or not verbal language as such is involved. The more specific "logotype" applies to the use of the full name of an organization and "monogram" to its initials, when these are designed for identification purposes. There are many examples of organizations which have simply employed a logotype or a monogram version of their name (e.g., Sony and CNN, respectively). Others have incorporated a pictorial element into their logo. Some symbols may have an iconic resemblance to physical objects which are specially appropriate, for example, the World Wildlife Fund's panda (www.wwf.org). Alternatively, they may be seemingly arbitrary in their relationship with the organization, for example, construction company Bovis Homes' hummingbird (www.bovishomes.co.uk), MSN's butterfly (www.msn.com), or the wholly abstract Nike swoosh (www.nike.com). Whatever their degree of motivation, these examples illustrate Yusaku Kamekura's remark (concerning trademarks): "Ideally they do not illustrate, they indicate. They are not representational, but suggestive" (Kamekura, 1966, p. 6).

Whether the links are direct or indirect, symbols are chosen both to prompt recognition (their denotative function) and to evoke positive associations (their connotative function). As Keen and Warner demonstrated, the British university sector provides examples of each of these categories (Keen et al., 1989, p. 14). Oxford Polytechnic (as it then was) used to employ a logotype version of its name, whereas the University of East Anglia preferred the monogram "UEA." By means of its shield symbol, the Open University (formally established in 1969) aligned itself with long-standing institutions of higher education, which had always identified themselves through this heraldic device, if not a complete coat of arms. However, a more innovative institution was suggested by a superimposed circle ("O") on a plain shield ("U"), by a sans serif monogram, and by bold blue and white or yellow colour schemes (www.open.ac.uk). With the abolition of the distinction between universities and polytechnics in the early 1990s, the latter undertook major visual identity programmes to reposition themselves. A common element in these was the design of new visual symbols that boldly deviated from the heraldic norm. The University of Greenwich's ship's compass is a case in point, alluding as it does to the area's own maritime heritage rather than to any generic similarity with other ancient institutions of learning (www.gre.ac.uk). By the start of the 21st century, the movement away from conventionally drawn shields initiated by the Open University and taken further by the former polytechnics had been joined by most of the pre-1992 HE institutions. It is exemplified by a long-established university such as Newcastle, which revamped its corporate design by modernizing a classic symbol of tradition, the heraldic lion passant (www.ncl.ac.uk).

Organizations come in all shapes and sizes; many are commercial, others non-profit making; most are geographically circumscribed, but some are global in their reach. The corporate identity issues that confront a large transnational conglomerate differ radically from those of a small-scale charity or a school, both in degree and scope. To assist an understanding of these differences and similarities, two classificatory schemes devised by Olins may be found helpful. The first, touched on already, identifies the dominant mode of communication an organization has with what may be regarded as its main audience. Thus, the priority of a manufacturing company is the quality, reliability, design, price, and availability of a product, whereas for an upmarket department store an atmosphere of exclusivity produced by decor is likely to be paramount. In contrast, for an institution such as the police the emphasis will be on behaviour towards the public (Olins, 1989, p. 29).

The second relates an organization's visual identity to its corporate structure (Olins, 1989, pp. 78–129). Three broad categories are suggested, applicable to a wide range of concerns: the monolithic, the endorsed, and the branded. Such a classification scheme runs the risk of oversimplifying a complex reality, of appearing too neat and tidy, as Olins himself readily admitted. Nevertheless, it has been accepted by other writers as a useful working model. Ind, for one, adopted the same three basic types of structure, but employed different terms in two cases ("unitary" for "monolithic," and "diversified" for "endorsed" (Ind, 1990, p. 121). Rowden (2000) preferred the simpler "mono-identity" and "multi-identity."

The monolithic concern organizes itself, as the term implies, in a highly centralized way, with each section intended to perceive itself an integrated part of the larger whole. In the case of a manufacturer, the company's subsidiaries and their products all bear the same corporate name and corporate design, as with Mitsubishi. At the other end of the spectrum, the branded approach is associated with greater decentralization and diversification and the use of a variety of product names, for example, Unilever's traditional approach to its range of foodstuffs, washing powder, and soap (www.unilever.com). In between, the endorsed identity applies to those organizations where the two coexist: individual parts enjoy a degree of autonomy and public presence but within an overarching identity framework. Thus, the multinational Nestlé added its own name to that of Kit-Kat on the wrappers of the chocolate biscuits when it acquired the brand. A service sector example is provided by the regional operations of the BBC, where sensitive local affiliations are given a degree of recognition, for example, BBC Wales (www.bbc.co.uk/wales).

CORPORATE IDENTITY AS A PRACTICE

The term "corporate identity" was coined in the United States in the Post-World War II era by Walter Margulies, who together with Gordon Lippincott had founded the New York design consultancy Lippincott & Margulies in 1945 (it became Lippincott Mercer in 2003). His intention was to differentiate and "add value" to the work he was carrying out for major U.S. companies in contrast to the simpler styles being produced by his competitors. In the UK corporate identity work was already being undertaken by design consultants by the early 1960s, but Wolff Olins, established in 1965, claims to be the first company in the country to call itself a corporate identity consultancy (www.wolff-olins.com). As a professional practice, corporate identity gained wider acceptance in the course of the following decade, a period characterized, in the UK at least, by a dramatic increase in acquisitions, mergers, and management buyouts. The commercial climate of the time made it necessary to heighten awareness on the part of the financial community of the merits of individual companies, both predators and those vulnerable to takeover bids. In addition, the problems of integration following the merging of previously distinct companies—each with its own culture, behaviour, and symbols—brought into sharp focus the need for corporate identity programmes, as did the increasingly global character of many concerns.

During the course of the 1980s successive UK governments under Margaret Thatcher implemented a policy of privatizing the public utilities (e.g., gas, water, and electricity), together with such publicly owned companies as British Aerospace and British Steel. The process initially involved raising the profile of each of these concerns (in the case of the utilities from a very low level). There followed a significant growth in corporate advertising, especially in the press and on television, which rapidly became a lucrative source of revenue for media owners. The strategy was to generate an awareness of and a positive attitude towards these new commercial institutions and, additionally, to attract potential investors, both institutional and private. For much of this period the rise of advertising agencies and public relations consultancies, some of whom had also successfully promoted the Conservative Party, appeared inexorable (Miller & Dinan, 2000). In the process a widespread view developed that the "image business" had almost magical powers to influence perceptions of organizations and the behaviour of customers. In the words of Klaus Schmidt, writing before the dot-com era, the 1980s were "the decade of the identity bubble" (Schmidt, 1995, p. 8). During this period graphic design experienced a boom, becoming the most profitable part of the design industry, as companies queued up for corporate makeovers. In similar fashion, the dot-com phenomenon of the late 1990s provided employment for many in design, PR, and advertising agencies as well as dramatically boosting advertising revenue for media companies (though both were to prove short-lived).

While design has recently played a key role in the development of corporate identity in an increasingly visually aware culture such as that of the UK, other ways of defining the essential values of an organization clearly predated it. Philanthropic activity, for one, has long identified certain commercial organizations. Historically, this work was often associated, as might be expected, with Quaker companies like Cadbury's or Rowntree's. Such activities, often local in scope, have recently been augmented by a more overt concern on the part of many organizations about their role in society. "Corporate social responsibility" has come to define attitudes and practices which distinguish those companies which take heed of the wider consequences of their activities rather than being motivated by considerations of profit alone. The consumer awareness movement from the 1960s on played an important part in effecting this ethical change, but it is perhaps environmentalism which in recent years has intensified the pace and broadened the scope. The energy consumed and the environmental impact caused by a product's manufacture, distribution, use, and disposal are factors that only a few years ago no one but specialists was likely to have bothered about. Nowadays more and more people are believed to be taking such matters into account when making purchasing decisions, if only on the basis of secondhand, incomplete information. Hence, the efforts made by companies to be identified by their various publics as "green" and "caring," not least as regards their explicit corporate identity programmes. Companies active in sensitive areas or with a controversial track record, such as those in the oil and petroleum sector, are particularly exercised in trying to shape public opinion in this way (Prakash, 2000). The Exxon Mobil Corporation, for example, in its 2002 *Citizenship Report* (www.exxonmobil.com), highlighted the various health, educational, and similar programmes with which it was involved, commenting, "To us that is what being a good corporate citizen is all about." However, the sum involved, while substantial, still represented less than 0.6% of the company's total revenues.

While external factors such as green issues have transformed the external environment in which organizations operate and helped modify their identities, many organizations have instituted major internal changes, too. The adoption of less hierarchical structures is one such example. Employees working in a more collaborative organization are often expected to have a more positive perception of that organization by virtue of a greater sense of involvement and "ownership" than those whose work is mechanistically organized. Likewise, there is increasing recognition of the contribution made by organizational culture (Hatch & Schultz, 2000).

Though management has a part to play in helping to produce patterns of shared meanings, this culture is to a large extent organic and self-generating, that is, not imposed from above. One potentially significant way in which it is expressed is through institutional storytelling or the construction of narratives, an activity which has recently begun to receive academic recognition (van Riel, 2000), though dismissed by some as a mere management fad (Kellaway, 2004).

In order to survive and prosper, an organization needs to know what its *raison d'être* is and to ensure as far as possible that all groups with which it is strategically involved do, too. Communicating this idea clearly and effectively, both internally and externally, is thus an activity of considerable importance. The means adopted will vary, but a common objective is to solicit goodwill, leading to such desired actions as purchasing, investing, donating, voting, or joining. The identity of an organization, as of a person, a brand or a country, is formed from many components (Kapferer, 1992; Schlesinger, 1991). Not all of these manifest themselves at any one time. But it is an assumption which managers and consultants alike proceed from that every organization has its own identity, however difficult this may be to define or to measure. Furthermore, a recognizable corporate identity is considered a potential asset in an increasingly competitive environment, since it functions simultaneously to distinguish the organization in question from others and to provide its own members with a collective sense. However, an early example of a very different approach was that taken by the General Electric corporation from the 1890s. As Nye (1985, p. 29) noted: "It refused to maintain a single identity—that implied in the legal fiction of the corporation as a private person—and instead multiplied versions of itself." Thus, while GE presented itself to its different publics in different guises, "[t]he company's huge photographic file [of over one million images] was the only site where the multiple General Electrics existed side by side" (ibid.).

The origins of corporate identity as a practice, as already noted, are usually traced back to the U.S. design sector in the 1940s. In the course of the next half-century practitioners and theorists came to adopt a more holistic approach, arguing that the colours, shapes, and typefaces which signify an organization have to be integrated with wider aspects of communication and behaviour if they are to have more than purely decorative value. Meanwhile, many marketing theorists and practitioners have extended their focus on brands from the product or service level to that of the corporation. Corporate branding has become an important strategic tool, as the organizations behind products and services position themselves for competitive advantage (Ind, 1997; Olins, 2003). Redefining the notion of branding to include everything an organization produces, does, and says makes it virtually synonymous with corporate identity in the broadest sense of the term. Thus another area opens up for jurisdictional disputes between marketing and public relations specialists.

More than anything else names are the key symbolic means of identification, an aspect not limited to individuals or countries. Preserving the same name over many years is a priority for most organizations concerned with consistency, reliability, and tradition (for example, BMW). Others, however, deliberately alter theirs to signal a planned change in corporate structure or strategy (Wathen, 1987). Many succeed (e.g., PricewaterhouseCoopers), but there have been several examples in the UK in recent years of ill-conceived attempts at (re)naming. In 2002 the sportswear firm Umbro was obliged to rebrand a range of trainers, after belatedly realising that the name Zyklon had been that of the gas used the Nazis at Auschwitz. A particularly high-profile example was that of the Post Office, which decided in 2001 that after 350 years its name no longer reflected the current range of its activities or international ambitions. It consequently adopted the freshly minted "Consignia" to suggest, it was said, activities beyond that of delivering mail. The decision caused widespread bewilderment and scorn, which, coupled with an increased level of complaints about declining standards of service, forced Consignia's management after a mere 18 months to abandon the controversial name change.

For a small organization a simple design based on its name may be sufficient to help establish an initial presence and as a means to motivate staff. But as an organization matures and expands, it is almost inevitable that the earlier, intuitive character will change and become more diffuse, if left to itself. To guard against this a common management practice is to undertake periodic reviews and thereby to seek to protect an asset. In the case of a multinational conglomerate, for example, a full-scale corporate identity programme can last for many months, entail painstaking research, generate a significant change in internal and external perceptions and behaviour, produce a modified visual identity, and cost a great deal of money. Yet it may still provoke hostile media comment.

It is not simply journalists who in recent years have expressed outrage at corporate identity exercises; ordinary members of the public have joined in, too, as the practice has spread well beyond large corporations. The usual target is the logo (and sometimes the name, too, as in the case of Consignia) and the characteristic response one of incomprehension at the incommensurability of the changes and costs involved. A typical example was the reaction to the commissioning by British Petroleum of a redesign in the late 1980s. "A million pounds for that?" began one otherwise informative business-section article, mimicking the standard complaint. "The new BP logo, unveiled last week, had children playing spot-the difference and adults marvelling at how so little could cost so much" (*Sunday Times*, 1989).

Supposedly naive and profligate managers, like the clothes-conscious Emperor and his courtiers in the Hans Christian Andersen story, find themselves publicly pilloried for having been duped by clever, but cynical advisers. Pitcher (2000), for example, lambasted both groups:

> The obsessives are those who spend millions of their shareholders' value on one of the most spurious of management mountebanks of the late 20th century: The corporate identity consultant.... They have qualitative research that leads to perceptions analysis through focus groups, followed by brain-storming and customer audits, before developing a mission statement that reflects the core brand values that cascade through the management structure and, finally, can be launched as a new global identity. They then lean the company's initials slightly to the left, alongside a simpler logo in a different shade of the same old corporate colour. Oh, and they change the letterhead.

Changes to the BP or ICI logos in the 1980s are cases in point, where the very subtlety of the alterations fuelled the moral indignation of many commentators in the press. In response, corporate identity practitioners will point out that little or no attention is usually paid to the invisible benefits of such programmes. These can include bringing the symbolic into alignment with the strategic, as in the case of BP's shift to "Beyond Petroleum" (www.bp.com), or the boost to staff morale after a painful process of restructuring.

Despite such negative reporting by the media, visual identity programmes have proliferated in recent years. The spread of market forces into areas which were previously exempt has played a crucial role in this as in other areas of social life. Nowadays it is not just companies which routinely invest large sums of money in this way, but government departments, political parties, media organizations, trade unions, hospital trusts, educational institutions, local councils and charities, to name but a few. Indeed, so widespread is the practice that it might be argued that not to undertake such a change periodically can today be interpreted as a sign that the organization concerned lacks the capacity to respond imaginatively to a changing environment. Consultants, not surprisingly, continue to be mostly involved with large-scale commercial operations, and the literature on the subject tends to reflect this (e.g., Olins, 1989; Schmidt, 1995; Rowden, 2000).

THE CORPORATE IDENTITY EXERCISE

There are many reasons why an organization believes it is in its strategic interest to undertake a corporate identity exercise. It may have been suffering from unwelcome public attention which has damaged its credibility and/or reduced the value of its shares. In such a case a simple change of name is likely to have little impact and may be indeed only make matters worse by being perceived as a rather cynical cosmetic exercise. For instance, part of Windscale, the UK nuclear power plant, became Sellafield in 1981 with little or no obvious benefit to its reputation. Alternatively, a company might be expanding into commercial activities with which it has not been previously associated, either by organic growth or acquisition. Or it might be separating off an aspect of its business, as in the case of the management consulting division of the former accountancy firm Arthur Andersen, which became Accenture. Here major structural changes brought about a new business entity requiring its own identification, for both external and internal purposes. A third category (which, incidentally, by no means exhausts the range of possibilities) comprises organizations which are neither reacting to bad publicity nor being transformed in some way. Instead, they wish to achieve the best fit between the messages they send out and the way these are received, an activity that ideally should take place at regular intervals. Coca-Cola, for instance, while retaining its distinctive logotype and colours, has nonetheless tweaked them at various times over the past century (www.coca-cola.com).

A prerequisite for undertaking a review of an existing corporate identity is to recognize the organization's dominant mode of communication and its basic structure. Any subsequent recommendations should attempt to take these factors into account and be congruent with them. Let us assume an organization has resolved on a corporate identity exercise, has set a budget, and has appointed an appropriate consultancy to undertake the work. The sketch which follows of the ensuing process is a necessarily simplified account, condensing it into four main stages: research, development, introduction, and implementation. It is augmented by discussion of certain problematic aspects.

The first stage concentrates on determining as accurately as possible the status quo regarding the organization's visual identity, its personality, and perceptions of it among the different groups with which it has dealings. Special attention focuses on any discrepancy between how an organization thinks it is perceived and how it actually is or would like to be perceived. All writers on the subject emphasize that it is a stage that requires to be undertaken as thoroughly and dispassionately as possible. Because of the multiple aspects involved, present discussion of this stage is disproportionately long.

Empirical research conducted by consultants into the intangible areas of corporate personality and image is typically reliant on a mix of interviews, questionnaires, and focus group discussions to elicit a cross-section of opinion (van Riel, 1995, pp. 47–72; Fox, Balmer, & Wilson, 2001). Inevitably, the more extensive and detailed the process of information and opinion gathering, the more labour-intensive and expensive the exercise becomes. The temptation for a client is to cut costs by settling for a consultation with a handful of senior executives and journalists, for example, or to forgo one altogether. At its best, an audit can provide valuable insights. However, many aspects of an organization's complex personality may still elude the standard techniques. By contrast, participant observation, a research instrument of anthropologists and sociologists, involves extensive immersion in a culture or institution. Theoretically informed fieldwork of this kind has a greater capacity to capture the unspoken values, the tacit assumptions—in short, the many taken-for-granted features of an organization's culture. Such ethnographic work is time-consuming, its objectives not usually instrumental, and the findings rarely framed for executive-style reading. It is, nonetheless, a valuable alternative research technique, providing rich insights that are unlikely to be registered otherwise.

However, constraints of time and finance render it less attractive for routine commercial purposes.

The study of the visual statements made by an organization involves producing an inventory of every kind of printed material from advertising to business cards, from vehicle livery to uniforms, from exhibition stands to Web presence. This allows a check to be made of the degree of consistency with which the existing house-style is being applied across the board. Such an audit is in principle a relatively straightforward process, though in practice it can be lengthy, particularly in the case of a large, complex, and geographically dispersed organization. With manufacturing companies the exercise will also extend to consideration of the packaging of the goods they produce. Existing typefaces, colours, layouts, logos, and slogans may best be evaluated by comparing them with those of competitors, a process which can benefit from a semiotic analysis of each element and of the visual identity as a whole. Although often ignored in the literature on the subject, semiotics provides a potentially valuable way of understanding how meanings are produced. Individual elements, or signs, are distinctively different from other, similar signs in the same category (be they words, sounds, colours, etc.) and combine to form larger wholes (sentences, music, paintings, etc). At both levels these are organized in informal codes which vary from both culture to culture and through time. It is clear, therefore, that a knowledge of these socially determined codes is vital for a full understanding of individual signs and their interaction with others in complete messages. Roland Barthes, in his essay "Rhetoric of the Image," provided a classic semiotic analysis of how an advertisement by the food manufacturer Panzani is "constructed" to evoke associations with Italianness, freshness, domesticity, and even fine art (Barthes, 1977, pp. 32–51). In the case of Barthes the results can be perceptive and illuminating, but inevitably much depends on the analytical skills of the individual undertaking the study and the cogency of the resulting interpretation. Even so, there can be no guarantee that the meanings discerned will be wholly shared by others. Also, such a qualitative analysis is likely to be criticized by the positivistically inclined for its lack of methodological rigour.

But since visual identity is only a part of corporate identity, other factors ideally require auditing as well to determine what they reveal about the organization. Chief among these are the physical environment, the external appearance of buildings and surrounding grounds (if any), and the interior look of offices, reception areas, laboratories, or wards. Here attention will be focussed on the choice of colour schemes, lighting, and furnishings, as well as their care and maintenance. An examination of these physical aspects can provide revealing insights into an organization's corporate identity. Ideally, they need to be supplemented by audits of how the organization communicates with its external and internal audiences and how it behaves towards both. These would typically include, on the one hand, an appraisal of everything from its advertising to its staff notice-boards and, on the other, from its career development schemes to the efficiency of its online services and the civility of its counter staff.

After the data have been collected and analysed, the findings produced, and recommendations made, a brief is agreed. On this basis the consultancy team starts its work of devising a new name and/or designing visual schemes for the new identity programme. This, the second stage of the exercise, inevitably involves a series of consultations with the client. Practical considerations, such as the range of surfaces involved, the possible display in pixels or the suitability of full-colour images for black-and-white photocopying, must be taken into account. Then there are questions of meaning. Will it actually be recognized as a logo and, if so, is it sufficiently distinctive? What are the connotations of the overall design—sober tradition, maybe, or edgy creativity? Do the colours or the shape of the symbol have unfortunate associations or are they likely to evoke only positive responses? Such questions, while not always articulated, nonetheless require to be answered before the definitive design scheme is finally agreed. For organizations operating in foreign markets, in different languages and cultures, the potential problems of interpretation and acceptability are only multiplied. With the advent of the World Wide Web in 1990, a new means of communication and trading became available to organizations of all varieties and sizes with the means to make use of it. Since then the rapid growth of the Web industry has given rise to the equally rapid growth of professional Web site designers, many of whom advertise their services on the Web.[1] In addition to the normal design considerations, those employed in this sector need to bear in mind the impact of their work on Web page accessibility and usability or risk frustration on the part of computer and mobile phone users (Schofield, 2003).

The third stage, the introduction, may be phased in gradually, and unheralded, over a period of time for economic reasons. In this way the cost of repainting vehicles or reprinting stationery can often be met out of normal maintenance or consumables budgets. Alternatively, a full-scale public relations operation may be undertaken. Most common in the case of larger organizations, this aims to solicit media attention and coverage, as happened with the Prudential in 1986, when it launched its new visual identity (Traverso & White, 1990). Whichever approach is taken, the need to first introduce the new visual identity to staff is a sine qua non for most writers on the subject. It is employees above all, they are surely right in arguing, who need convincing of the merits of such symbolic changes if the side benefits of improved morale and a renewed sense of collective endeavour are to be realized (Williams & Beaver, 1990). Also, the workforce must be convinced of the value of the exercise or their scepticism may undermine their capacity to act as corporate advocates in the community.

The implementation stage offers the opportunity to make explicit not only a new corporate strategy but a (possibly new) cohesiveness within the various parts of an organization. In order for this to be expressed most effectively, a high degree of discipline is required in the ways in which the design scheme is put into practice. A standard procedure is for a manual of implementation rules to be part of the package produced by the consultancy. These typically lay down precisely what is and what is not permissible in the use of the new design, usually in the form of templates. However, there is a danger that such rules can also engender resentment on the part of those disposed to see in the exercise an expression of an authoritarian management style. For this reason, some consultants prefer to speak of guidelines, which may or may not permit greater flexibility. What matters most is that anyone obliged to use the new corporate design, having been fully consulted and made aware of its intended benefits, agrees to relinquish some autonomy in the interests of overall consistency.

Finally, although not always treated as a stage as such, but crucial nonetheless, is the subsequent monitoring and evaluation of the visual identity exercise as part of a wider corporate identity change. This completes the communication loop, providing feedback which may eventually lead to the process starting all over again.

A SCOTTISH CASE STUDY

While many writers on the subject include an account of the process of researching, devising and implementing a corporate identity programme, this is usually normative, detailing how the process should take place, often in checklist form, for example, "Ten Key Points to Remember" (Ind, 1990, p. 198). And when actual case studies are included, they are typically exemplars of good practice (e.g., Williams & Beaver, 1990; Schmidt, 1995). The use of such case studies can clearly be justified from a pedagogical point of view, but the absence of discussion of

---

[1]In July 2004 "web design" generated 14,900,000 Google links compared with 6,190,000 for "Christianity."

failures or near-misses gives a somewhat unrealistic quality to these accounts. Practitioners such as Ind, Olins, or Schmidt are understandably reluctant to publicize any projects that do not redound to their own credit and to that of their clients. The following discussion is a modest attempt to right the balance by looking at a less than successful corporate (= visual) identity exercise.

Among suppliers of goods and services television companies arguably impinge more than most on the consciousness of the general public through the frequency with which they identify themselves on-air in the junctions between programmes (Meech, 1996c). For half a century Scottish Television has held the ITV franchise for the Central Scotland region without interruption. During much of the period from 1957, it was content simply to fulfil its requirements to provide local programming to viewers and to sell airtime to advertisers wishing to communicate with its potential audience, the majority of the Scottish population. The absence of an alternative vehicle for television commercials and the relative lack of competition for viewers for a generation, until the start of Channel 4 in 1982, were responsible for weaknesses in respect of corporate personality, visual identity, and public image. The company was highly successful commercially, but the programmes it produced, with some notable exceptions, betokened a complacent attitude. One of the smaller players in the ITV network of UK commercial television, the company had long since settled for a quiet life, interrupted from time to time by complaints from Scottish intellectual and artistic circles about the poor quality of its output. Shareholders stayed loyal as the company maintained the highly profitable tradition already established by 1959, the year it was referred to by its then Chairman, Roy (later Lord) Thomson, as "a licence to print money."

The 1980s were a period in which Scotland underwent a profound renewal, at least in the cultural field. By mid-decade the company—driven by its advertising sales department—decided to highlight its Scottish national identity so as to enhance its positioning within the domestic and overseas television markets. The name by which the company was known, STV, and its monogram logo were judged by management to lack distinctiveness and emotional appeal and to need replacing by something more arresting and obviously meaningful. The process by which a replacement came about is instructive. It is no secret that the atmosphere within the company at this time was anything but cooperative, with much of the tension due to poor industrial relations between management and the unions. In this climate the company management commissioned the designer of Channel 4's innovative logos, Martin Lambie-Nairn, to produce a design that could be used both on-screen, in computer animated form, and off-air. At the same time the company name was introduced in its full form, with all the hoped-for benefits that would accrue from associations with the word "Scottish."[2]

But four factors conspired to make the project less of a success than it might have been. First, no research was undertaken into the existing visual identity and corporate image. Second, the commission went ahead only as a design project and quasi-renaming exercise (STV to Scottish Television). Third, Robinson Lambie-Nairn as a company were relatively new to the field, were self-confessedly ignorant of the strategic implications, and were "only a few pages further forward" than STV's own in-house designer (Interview with Martin Lambie-Nairn, 1994). Their lack of confidence in dealing with only their second client led, for example, to a reluctance to insist on a postponement, when, just 2 weeks in advance of the launch, the broadcaster changed its mind about the design.[3] Lastly, the in-house design staff had not been

[2]The various versions of the on-air ident can be seen at 625: Andrew Wiseman's TV Room (http://625.uk.com/tv_logos/index.htm).

[3]It is noteworthy that Martin Lambie-Nairn, in his account of his company's extensive and exemplary work, made no reference to the Scottish project (Lambie-Nairn, 1997; www.lambie-nairn.com).

adequately consulted, felt alienated from the new motif, and allegedly sabotaged its effective screening. The outcome was that the company started to use its full name, but found itself stuck with an expensive logo featuring a stylized thistle (the national symbol), which was flawed in design terms on the grounds of inflexibility. One senior executive of the company later referred to it an "insult," adding "It actually won a prize as the worst piece of graphic design" (Interview, 1994). Nor did the change achieve much in boosting morale within the company. Externally, though, the change of name and the introduction of the thistle motif did at least help to emphasize the Scottishness of the broadcaster more than the previous visual identity and this became indelibly associated with the company (Meech, 1996b).

In contrast, Scottish Television adopted a more textbook approach in 1991–1992 to coincide with major structural changes both within the company and in the industry as a whole. This time a specialist consultancy was brought in to research audience perceptions of the company's programming and its visual identity. On the basis of these findings, a strategy was produced for retaining the Central Scotland franchise. The findings also assisted in-house designers with the task of updating the corporate logo. Versions were tested on groups of viewers on this occasion, although little or no effort was made to sound out the opinions of employees, who were presented with a fait accompli (www.scottishtv.co.uk).

Further change came about in 1997 when Grampian Television, the other main ITV licensee north of the border, joined Scottish Television as part of Scottish Media Group plc. The move was unpopular in the Grampian transmission area (Highlands and North East Scotland), where it was feared that regional interests would be neglected in pursuit of cost-cutting and the centralizing of production. As a way of expressing the new relationship between the two broadcasters—part of the process of creating a new corporate identity—their individual logos were replaced by a single near-identical logo. This took the form of a square in the national colour (blue), incorporating a smaller, lighter blue square and the words "Scottish TV" (www.scottishtv.co.uk) or "Grampian TV" (www.grampian.co.uk). Along with other design manifestations of the previously unrelated companies, this example of an endorsed visual identity represents a politically astute compromise between homogenization and regional autonomy. The fact that the process happened in the year of the referendum on a Scottish parliament indicates the importance of external factors in corporate identity change (Interviews with current and former Scottish TV staff, August 2002).

CONCLUSION

At the start of *Corporate Identity*, still the most influential UK work on the subject, Olins reminds us that there is a long history to the symbolic display by institutions of their actual or would-be nature (Olins, 1989). Visual symbols, in particular, have traditionally been used by dominant groups to communicate institutional distinctiveness, common goals and values, and a sense of belonging, both to subordinates and to outside groups. His 19th-century examples—the U.S. Confederacy, the British Raj, and successive French Republics—associate the phenomenon exclusively with Western political-military formations involved in the hegemonic struggle of nation building. There is an apparent assumption here that corporate identity is socially progressive. Absent from the discussion, for instance, is the example of Nazi Germany (or that of other 20th-century totalitarian regimes), as a more recent corporate identity programme of note.[4] In the case of the Third Reich striking symbols, such as the swastika, and a highly distinctive overall visual style helped to brand a whole nation. In this they played a significant

---

[4]Olins, to be fair, dealt briefly with the Third Reich's corporate identity in his earlier book (Olins, 1978, pp. 22–25).

part in the process of *Gleichschaltung*, the enforced coordination of beliefs, values, goals, and practical activities for maximum internal and external effect. Citing the example of Hitler's Reich in this context is not to argue that a corporate identity programme which encourages a collective sense of purpose and belonging is inevitably repressive in intent or consequences. There are, after all, many benign examples to refute such a view. It serves merely as a reminder of Morgan's point that "Most discussions of organization attempt to be ideologically neutral" (Morgan, 1986, p. 316). This is of relevance here since much of the literature on corporate identity has been written by practitioners in the field, employing a managerial, rather than a social scientific perspective.

Though it has yet to achieve the same status as finance or human resource functions within organizations, corporate identity has clearly established itself as a professional practice. It is unthinkable, for instance, that a new company, healthcare organization, or quango would risk stinting on an identity programme. Similarly, existing organizations are more than ever likely to seek help in periodically updating the visual symbols through which they communicate to their various audiences. And as many organizations become global concerns and introduce outsourcing or teleworking, an increased use of corporate symbols can be anticipated to help obviate the loss of shared physical space and reduced human contact.

The process itself remains an expensive one, with a fee the standard means of remuneration for each discrete project. However, in the future, if some practitioners are to be believed, a greater degree of continuity may be assured by the hiring of consultants on a retainer basis. These would act as permanent advisers on corporate identity matters, monitoring existing arrangements and perceptions, and making recommendations for change when appropriate. In short, there would be a shift towards a public relations orientation compared with that conventionally adopted by design agencies. But for this to happen, however, two things would be necessary. First, a change of attitude would need to be inculcated in the relevant sections of the design community, typically used to responding to problems with one-off solutions. Second, organizations would require to be convinced of the value of undertaking foundational research and of investing long-term in an activity the cost-effectiveness of which is notoriously difficult to demonstrate. Whether or not such a development takes place remains to be seen. Meanwhile, issues of corporate identity will continue to be important for organizations both large and small, global and local, commercial and non-profit, since each inescapably has its own personality and reputation, whether or not it attempts to manage them. A visual identity has an obvious role to play in the process, but, no matter how eye-catching or stylish, it remains a supporting one.

21

Corporate Responsibility and Public Relations Ethics

Jacquie L'Etang
Stirling Media Research Institute

This chapter explores the relationship between public relations and corporate responsibility. The chapter begins by reviewing the origins and development of the concept and practice of corporate responsibility and the relationship between business and society. The motivation behind, and the relationship between, corporate social responsibility, crisis management and issues management is debated to expose the essential tension that lies between the fight for organizational survival and concern for the public interest. The role of public relations both in managing community programmes and as a socially responsible occupation is debated and a number of problematic issues raised. There is also a review of the debate concerning issues of corporate responsibility and liability.

The chapter is written from a normative moral philosophical perspective and applies the classical philosophical moral frameworks of utilitarian and Kantian thought but does not relate these to the relativist and postmodern perspectives raised in some other chapters.

MORAL FRAMEWORKS

Moral[1] theories do two things: they give an account of what is "good" and they judge "right" actions. These frameworks of principles can be applied in a consistent fashion and used to evaluate situations or human behaviour. The frameworks used here define goodness differently and give different weightings to the importance of the motivation and the effects of actions in judging rightness of behaviour.

The utilitarian framework is probably the most familiar to non-philosophers and can be most simply described as "the greatest happiness of the greatest number." For a utilitarian, "good" is

---

[1] It should be noted that the terms "moral" and "ethical" may be used interchangeably.

defined as happiness and a "right" action is that which increases happiness by at least as much as any other option open to the agent at the time. Utilitarianism is a type of consequentialism because it makes the rightness of actions solely dependent upon their consequences.

An alternative moral framework is a deontological (from the Greek *deon*, duty) approach, in which goodness is seen as being intrinsic to an act within the context of a relationship. This sort of approach is derived from Immanuel Kant, whose formulations about morality encompassed a number of key points of relevance to corporate social responsibility. Kant argued that a right act was one which was done out of duty and conformity to universal law and not out of inclination. He thus thought less highly of generous actions done through an impulse of sympathy or generosity and more highly of those motivated strictly out of duty. He attributed the action done out of duty with moral worth because the action arose from a rational process and included an understanding of obligation and duty. Kant argued that the moral worth of an act should be judged by asking whether one was willing for the act to become a universal law. An important aspect of this framework is that where self-interest plays a part in the motivation of the action, then that action is regarded as prudential[2] and cannot be regarded as a morally right action.

DEFINITION OF THE TERM "RESPONSIBILITY"

The term "responsibility" may be used in a number of different ways in the context of the moral responsibility of business, and perhaps it is this which leads to some confusion over the morality of both the practice of corporate social responsibility and the role of public relations in the field. When the adjective "responsible" is used predicatively, as in "Company X was responsible for the pollution" or "Company X was responsible for the creation of new jobs," a statement is made about a causal link between the acts or omissions of the company and a subsequent state of affairs, which may be seen as either good or bad. There is no single negative equivalent of the adjective "responsible" as used in this way: a company cannot be "irresponsible" for pollution or job creation. When the adjective is used attributively, as in "Company X is a responsible company," a simple statement is made about the company's being answerable for its acts or omissions; however, a more important statement is also made in an evaluative and approving manner regarding the overall behaviour of the company. The negative equivalent can be used to show a lack of responsibility in this sense: "through its irresponsible conduct, Company X caused the pollution." Thus, while the term "corporate responsibility" can have many meanings, it is most widely used in an evaluative and laudatory manner, describing the conduct of business as a whole or of a corporation above and beyond its purely economic function. It is not that approval in itself is a bad thing but that approval needs to be based on a clear framework or rationale.

By exploring the philosophical principles behind corporate responsibility, together with a discussion of moral frameworks, we can begin to distinguish between corporate responsibility based on sound moral principles and that which is not. It is important to analyse the justifications offered in favour of corporate social responsibility and the arguments which are presented against its practice so this chapter focuses on the idea of the corporate social responsibility as a theory of obligation to society. It will be argued that the very term "corporate responsibility" implies a contractual, rights-based approach because of the use of the term "responsibility" and that therefore the most natural and coherent justification will be in terms of rights and duties.

---

[2]An action characterized by care and caution with regard to one's own interests.

CORPORATE RESPONSIBILITY: ORIGINS AND DEVELOPMENT

The concept of corporate responsibility is a broad one and includes a variety of ideas and practices. In terms of this discussion it will be useful to define the two main applications of corporate responsibility, the first of which is those apparently voluntary and benevolent (though not necessarily beneficial) actions taken by corporations in society outside their primary economic function, and the second those actions taken by corporations in response to corporate disasters. In public relations these two areas present themselves directly in the fields of crisis management and community programmes.

Although corporate responsibility in the UK is presented as a modern concept and business practice it has its theoretical roots in philosophical debates and its practical roots in the activities of 19th-century philanthropists. Of particular note were the Quaker dynasties Cadbury, Rowntree, and Bournville. The link with Quakerism was not coincidental since this strand of the Christian faith emphasises social justice and both corporate and collective responsibility, for example:

> We are for justice and mercy and peace and true freedom, that these may be exalted in our nation, and that goodness, righteousness, meekness, temperance, peace and unity with God and with one another, that these things may abound. (Edward Burrough, 1659, from *Quaker Faith and Practice*, 1999, 23.11)

and

> Seeking at all times in a divine order of life, Quakers have always considered social service part of Christianity. (William Charles Braithwaite, 1919, from *Quaker Faith and Practice*, 1999, 23.13)

These philanthropists might appear to have been to an extent both paternalistic and self-interested, but some were inspired by radicalism, for example, Joseph Rowntree (1836–1925), a chocolate manufacturer, was clearly well aware of the dangers inherent in sentimentally motivated charity. His trusts were intended to carry forward his Quaker principles and to fund research and political action to make possible the necessary changes in society:

> Charity, as ordinarily practised, the charity of endowment, the charity of emotion, the charity which takes the place of justice, creates much of the misery which it relieves, but does not relieve all the misery it creates ... Much of the current philanthropical effort is directed to remedying the more superficial manifestations of weakness and evil, while little thought or effort is directed to search out their underlying causes. The soup kitchen in York never has difficulty in obtaining financial aid, but an enquiry into the extent and causes of poverty would enlist little support. (Joseph Rowntree, 1865, from *Quaker Faith and Practice*, 1999, 23. 17–18)

With such principles as inspiration, George Cadbury, a third-generation Quaker, created Bournville and a miniature welfare state for his employees which included space for leisure and relaxation in specially designed gardens to offer alternatives to alcohol. Bournville included a cross-section of incomes and occupations but was also pragmatic since it assumed a healthy and contented workforce would be more productive. The company subsidised a pension scheme, non-contributory sickness scheme, sick benefits (not then available to UK citizens from the state), evening classes, and physical training.

Quaker values and practice are emphasised here partly because it is quite clear that this was the origin of *British* practice and therefore it is not the case that the concept was invented by the United States in the 1960s in response to public criticism of big companies and then exported to the UK. There does seen to be a trend in which each management and public relations generation "discovers" corporate responsibility and thinks it is something new. Recently some media sociologists have also discovered the topic and set up a web-based organisation 'SpinWatch' which,

> exists to provide public interest research and reporting on corporate and government public relations and propaganda...spin techniques are much more extensive than is generally realised, encompassing media management, lobbying, corporate social responsibility, investor relations and corporate dirty tricks and spying...We aim to campaign against the manipulations of the PR industry in the public interest (http://spinwatchserve101.com/index.php).

This remit encompasses a number of different activities but can be broadly defined as anti-corporate activism. It does not, however, add to our understanding of the CSR concept. Nor does it appear to take account of the seriousness with which some corporates take of the critiques which emerged from the field of business ethics from the 1960s onwards. It is also a good example of academic critique developing into activism.

Some business leaders also seem to be unaware of the historical ethical principles. For example, Lord Sheppard of Didgemere, Chairman of Grand Metropolitan PLC suggested:

> It *is* true that companies such as Cadbury and Rowntree were giving help to their local communities in Victorian times, but this help was the result of *individual* generosity. The activity was paternal and altruistic. *Today's* good corporate citizen believes that involvement in the community is not something separate from business but an integral part of it. The motive for it is not altruism, but vision and common sense...companies are discovering that their reputation as citizens influences both their ability to sell and their ability to attract investment. (*First Forum*, 1995, p. 47)

Some corporate authors use the terms "philanthropy" and "social responsibility" interchangeably, perhaps without realising that the language connotes different values. Philanthropy is generous charity whereas social responsibility implies an obligation and duty. Thus, the motivation for engaging in corporate social responsibility is important and determining intentions may assist in judging the morality of a particular corporate social responsibility programme. Drumwright and Murphy raised important issues when they wrote:

> That is, do the company's intentions for engaging in marketing with a social dimension matter? If the outcomes for society are positive, then does it matter that the company's objectives are predominantly or even completely economic? From a managerial perspective, several findings have a bearing on this question...when initiatives have both non-economic and economic objectives, there is a tendency over time to gravitate toward greater emphasis on the non-economic objectives. Second, individuals who initially oppose the social initiative but become engaged in it for economic reasons tend to convert. That is, the socially responsible behavior "takes," and commitment to the cause increases. Third, corporate societal marketing, whatever the motivation, can have positive social benefits...one might [therefore] argue that intentions might be irrelevant. (Drumwright & Murphy, 2001, pp. 175–176)

From an academic perspective, philanthropy implies charitable and benevolent actions done beyond legal requirements or the call of duty. Philanthropic or charitable acts are voluntary, done out of beneficence, and the recipient of such acts has no right to expect or demand that such acts will take place. This is in contrast to the underlying implications of the term "social responsibility" that there is a specific obligation and a relationship in which there are reciprocal rights and duties.

Despite its strong British historical legacy, it is fair to acknowledge that a major 20th-century influence on corporate responsibility as a business practice was stimulated by developments in the United States and subsequently reinvented in Britain and Europe. Advocates preached the idea that affluent companies could well afford charitable donations to those less well off in society. The sense of obligation was nourished by social activists in the 1960s and 1970s, many of whom criticized the role of large corporations and power elites in society and argued that political and economic justice could only be achieved through a redistribution of goods and power. These sorts of arguments tend to promote an idea that increased power should bring with it increased responsibility and an obligation not to exploit or take advantage of individuals and small communities. In some literature the idea of obligation is encapsulated in the notion of contract, which will be discussed later.

Business writers and practitioners have not always been comfortable using ethical terminology implicit to the debate and some use a euphemism such as "integrity" in preference to a standard moral philosophical term such as "ethics" (see Nash, 1990). For example, White and Mazur cited Werner Baier, Henkel's Director of Corporate Communication, as saying, "I think it is completely necessary to have values but I prefer not to talk about ethics but about our responsibilities. If you talk about ethics some people mentally shy away" (White & Mazur, 1995, p. 8). In the 1980s executives were less inclined to try and define what they meant by corporate responsibility than is now the case: the growth of organizations such as Business in the Community and conferences and publications in the area of business ethics have made an impact. Now corporate social responsibility is seen as "an essential element of modern business practice" (Novar Annual report and accounts, 2003, p. 23), and a business competitive element can be apparent. For example, Pearson's Director wrote in their 2003 Annual Review that:

> For the first time this year we've included a special section on corporate social responsibility in our annual report. This is not because we have just discovered it. Weetman Pearson, who led the company more than a century ago, had a reputation as one of the most enlightened employers of his time. (Pearson Annual Review 2003, p. 22)

This quote demonstrates the need to establish long-term commitment and respectability. The reference to historical practice is clearly intended to defuse criticism that Pearson might be jumping on the bandwagon.

The concept of corporate responsibility has become ever more closely associated with public relations as the function has extended its strategic scope. For example, John Koten, then President of the Wordsworth Group, argued in 1997 that:

> One of the tools available to the public relations executive to help fashion a favourable public identity is the company's contributions program. Ideally, this function falls within the corporate communications department . . . Developing an effective contributions strategy can assist the corporation in establishing a positive identity with each of its key stakeholder groups. (Koten in Clarke, 1997, p. 149)

The emergence of issues management in America in the 1970s coincided with that of corporate responsibility. Issues management is linked to corporate social responsibility at a strategic level because emerging issues are often of a social nature, to which organisations may need to respond either through issues advocacy advertising, public relations campaigns, or programmes of corporate social responsibility. For example, Glaxo Smith Kline's annual report clearly states the link between corporate social responsibility, issue management, and reputation:

> Glaxo Smith Kline has a Corporate Responsibility Committee of non-Executive Directors, which has oversight of corporate responsibility matters. It advises the Board on social, ethical and environmental issues that have the potential to impact seriously Glaxo Smith Kline's business reputation. (Annual Report 2003, p. 27)

Likewise, Pearson's Annual Review stated in its corporate social responsibility section that:

> Managing our risks, especially reputational risks, is very important to us ... we regularly review our social, environmental and ethical risks as part of our normal risk management processes ... We consider the most important to be compliance with the UN Global Compact ... the environmental impact of our products and our ethical standards ... (Pearson Annual Review 2003, p. 29)

The danger is that corporations develop an incoherent, reactive approach to their social responsibility programmes, responding to external issues or trends rather than defining their moral responsibilities in a rational manner. Public relations is necessarily implicated because of its representational role and responsibility for managing relationships and reputation.

Grunig argued that corporate responsibility and excellent public relations "balance ... the private interests of the organization with the interests of publics and of society" (Grunig, 1992, p. 240), citing Steiner's opinion that:

> This is not solely a matter of defending the corporation but involves a deep interest in resolving major social problems, injecting more economic rationality into the political processes, helping to assure that our sociopolitical system works in the interests of everyone, and preserving political and economic freedom. (Steiner, 1983, p. 29)

This value-driven quote clearly suggests that organizational response to social issues may facilitate strategic interventions in public policy. Thus, it marks a more self-interested approach to CSR than the Quaker conception.

A more recent example of instrumentalism comes from David Finn, former CEO of Ruder and Finn, when he lamented that:

> Companies and their leaders don't get enough credit for what they do for society and, out of fear of criticism, they don't make the effort to tell what they and their companies are doing for their communities and nation. The public may approve or condemn a specific corporate action, but if it knows what kind of person is responsible for the company's policies and what values he or she believes in, it is possible to be responsive to that leadership. Instead of being anonymous instruments of impersonal corporate interests, top executives can be understood as conscientious individuals doing their best to fulfil their responsibilities to society which they believe to be of great importance. (Koten in Caywood, 1997, p. 150)

Koten suggested that "today's CEO takes this a step further and seeks to find out how the company contributions program also can be used to meet the company's self interest as well" (ibid.).

Whetton et al. provided an excellent analytical review of the strands in business ethics and corporate social responsibility which includes historical twists and turns in the field. It is, however, notable that their chapter does not address the communicative aspects of the practice, or mention public relations. This gap is also apparent in the rest of the excellent volume in which it is included: *Handbook of Strategy and Management* (Pettigrew, Thoms, & Whittington), published in 2002. That such a major work, which (as with all Sage handbooks) summarises and defines a field, its paradigms, knowledge base and key developments, does not even index either public relations or communications, speaks volumes for public relations' status and its failure to make any impact or jurisdictional claim over this area of knowledge.

Interestingly, turning to the account of "Public relations and social responsbility" in Sage's equivalent volume for public relations (Daugherty in R. Heath (Ed.), *Handbook of Public Relations*, Sage 2001), corporate social responsibility is included as part of "Defining the practice" which suggests its centrality to academic notions of public relations practice. Initial emphasis is given to global activism (the use of the term "activists" suggests opposition, even hostility to corporate mission) and public relations practitioners in this field defined as, "community builders responsible for helping to link socially, politically, geographically, culturally diverse and often competing interests" (p. 389).

Daugherty drew on a range of business and public relations literature to conclude that public relations role is to close the "legitimacy gap" and to act as the "corporate conscience" (p. 390) and to suggest that "public relations is the practice of social responsibility" (p. 392). Her analysis, however, did not include any discussion of ethical principles and a relativist view was clearly put forward when she argued:

> Corporate responsibility is constantly redefined when stakeholders and activists demand new standards, industry groups want higher operating performance of their members or another industry, or government regulators enforce codes of operation. In other words the ideology of society reshapes the standards of behavior. (p. 394)

Where there is some congruence between Daugherty and Whetton et al. is in the stress given to the importance of the stakeholder concept and issues management. However, it is clear that while Daugherty has drawn on some of the similar sources to Whetton, the reverse does not apply, and as she lamented, "unfortunately, public relations practitioners are not playing key roles in ethics and policymaking for their organisations" (p. 400), and she speculated as to whether

> public relations functions are increasingly being placed in the hands of other individuals because many public relations practitioners are unprepared to handle the responsibilities of continuously monitoring attitudes and expectations of stakeholders, preparing executives to develop strong relationships with stakeholders and truly understanding the relationship between an organization and its many constituents. (p. 401)

This suggests the need for practitioners to have greater facility with research and evaluation skills, as has long been argued, and for public relations academics to publish even more widely than is now the case in the key management and marketing journals.

BUSINESS AND SOCIETY

Having established the strategic importance of corporate responsibility to business as part of issues management, it will be useful to discuss arguments for and against the practice. If one were forced to identify an historical and historiographical "turning point" in the debate about the role of business in society, the article written by the Nobel Prize winner Milton Friedman (1970) would provide the locus, and it has remained a critical piece cited in virtually all discussions of the subject. Friedman's ideas are pursued in some detail here partly because of their historical importance but also because they present the sharpest critique of corporate social responsibility. Friedman's view was that business is socially responsible by virtue of its profit-making function and he saw altruistic acts carried out on behalf of business as a violation of business' function and obligations (which are purely economic). This is part of a wider set of arguments about the role of morality in business which suggest that business does not have to be concerned with issues of morality. Friedman's ideal society maximized individual freedom (which he saw as the greatest good) and limits regulation (by government) and the responsibilities of corporations. It was a strongly libertarian view and consequently portrays an individualistic and atomistic society, stressing individual not collective responsibilities.

Friedman did not promote an amoral view as such; for him business was intrinsically ethical because it promoted free enterprise and freedom.

Yet economic activity is not separate from moral activity and, as has been pointed out elsewhere, the free market institution itself is a product of convictions about the nature of a good society and what constitutes a *fair* distribution of goods and services; economic goals *are* social and political goals (Hoffman & Moore, 1990, p. 2).

Friedman was profoundly opposed to the concept of corporate responsibility, which he defined as corporations donating resources to charities or local communities. He thought that the practice is inimical to democracy and freedom because it turns corporations into instruments of public policy though they are neither elected representatives of the people nor subject to them (as civil servants are). In fact, he argued, such an expansion is akin to the growth of government via the back door of corporate social responsibility: if corporations are not maximizing profit but embarking on other socially desirable ends, they are in effect imposing taxes on those to whom they are directly and primarily responsible—their shareholders. For Friedman, neither government nor business should contribute to the welfare of the needy in society; this activity should be left entirely to the actions of individual philanthropists.

The only way in which corporate social responsibility could be acceptable for Friedman was if it was motivated entirely out of self-interest and justified on the grounds that such actions were being carried out to promote the company's interests. But he also argued that if it was in the long-term interest of companies to cover up their real intentions (of self-interest) by pretending to be motivated by some sense of duty or social obligation, then that was also acceptable. For Friedman, therefore, the only acceptable justification for corporate social responsibility was self-interest, and he was happy for the corporate representatives to deceive publics (consumers, media, shareholders) as to their real motivation.

If we reject the Friedman argument, we must find some sound moral grounds for the justification of corporate social responsibility. Friedman's analysis was based in the right to freedom, and one route to justifying the practice is to argue that the right to freedom attracts complementary duties as part of a contract between business and society quite apart from the reciprocal rights and duties that arise from the relationship between business (as part of society) and government. Friedman himself did not believe that the concept of "society" was viable, claiming that it did not exist, but contemporary business views are rather different, with chief executives working in ways to ensure that their companies can be described as "good corporate citizens."

A contractarian account of corporate social responsibility attempts to balance the conflicting rights and duties of citizens and business. In reality the debate which arises from this conflict focuses on large and influential businesses and their response to pluralist interest groups in society such as environmental groups and consumer lobbies. The nature of corporate obligation and the idea of corporate duties raise the question of the extent to which government has the right to regulate business. In the area of the environment, for example, legislation may be drafted to protect consumers, employees, and the environment from risk. To avoid government restrictions, business may choose to acknowledge responsibilities to society and, as part of its contract with government, self-regulate in return for being allowed to maintain a larger degree of freedom.

The concept of contract has been identified by several writers (Baier, 1984; Harrington, 1978; Lodge, 1986) as a significant component of capitalist ideology in relation to the exchange of money, goods and property, and as a method of avoiding conflict in society. Such writers find their sources of inspiration in Hobbes, Locke, and Darwin. Contracts are seen by philosophical contractarians as a way of improving the lot of citizens, specifically by reducing conflict. For Hobbes, civil society is only arrived at through the implementation of contract, which creates the status of citizen. In politics the term "social contract" is also seen as a way of ameliorating conditions or relationships between government and governed, such as the Labour government of 1974. Social contract is a way of mediating the claims of autonomous and free citizens and a centralized, powerful state to the mutual benefit of both (Turner, 1986, p. 106).

While contract theory is a strong theme in business ethics literature, the concepts of contract theory in the corporate social responsibility sphere are by no means clear-cut. A properly defined contract between business and society should make it clear what business can and ought to be responsible for. For corporate social responsibility, contract theory must be an ideal and not an historical contract. It is an implicit contract, but not one to which all businesses subscribed over time as a practice which is of intrinsic benefit to society; rather, "justice established itself by a kind of convention or agreement; that is, by a sense of interest, suppos"d to be common to all, and where every single act is performed in expectation that others are to perform the like" (Hume, 1980, p. 498). This interpretation suggests that contract is a technique to achieve and formalize a particular type of relationship. The concept of fair dealing is implicit to contract, together with an understanding that the arrangement is a cooperative venture of benefit to both parties and that neither party should be coerced to contract. The practice of corporate social responsibility is potentially a way of redressing the balance and redistributing benefits and burdens in society on the grounds that business benefits from publicly funded infrastructures and considerable economic, social, and political power and that this accumulation of power should lead to increased responsibility.

An analogy could be made between the concept of a government–society contract and a business–society contract; however, this cannot be sustained in its entirety because society is not given the option to vote for or against business leaders and policy-makers. The individuals who are promoted to run the companies and direct policy are subjected only to organizational hustings, often of a clandestine nature.

The idea that corporations have a requirement to redistribute further profit into the community is contentious and dependent on a society's arrangements for distributive justice and the extent to which arguments about sharing benefits and burdens predominate. It is important to maintain a clear distinction between corporate social responsibility activities which relate directly to a corporation's economic function linked to particular relationships (stakeholders) and those which do not; the latter should properly be described as philanthropy since they are supererogatory (above and beyond the call of duty). Clearly all corporate social responsibility activities are dependent upon the economic health of organizations, and recession inevitably threatens such activities. What becomes important, however, is that companies can justify particular donations in terms of the interests of their stakeholders, including the local community, and not simply in terms of corporate branding and as part of their promotional budget when times are good. A contractual relationship does not alter according to the economic climate.

PROGRAMMES OF CORPORATE SOCIAL RESPONSIBILITY: COMMUNITY PROGRAMMES

Corporate social responsibility programmes include a wide range of activities, often far removed from the corporation's economic function. Examples of such activities include sponsorship of sport or the arts, donations to charity and contributions in either cash or kind such as office facilities, equipment, professional advice, training, and technology. Such gifts are normally given towards public- or voluntary-sector activities in the community in which the organization operates. The dominant view of corporate social responsibility is that it is a practice which benefits both society and business. It could be argued that public relations practitioners can potentially serve the public interest through programmes of social responsibility.

Corporate social responsibility is often managed by public relations practitioners for public relations ends, and therefore corporate social responsibility is seen as part of the public relations portfolio and as a technique to establish relations with particular groups (for example, in the local community) and to enhance reputation with key stakeholders.

Consequently, public relations practitioners may be responsible for proposing corporate social responsibility activities and identifying relevant publics, objectives, and messages. In this way public relations practitioners are directly involved in policy formulation. It is not, therefore, a question of senior management working out their organizational responsibilities and then the public relations practitioner communicating the policy or actions, but of public relations actively driving the programme and setting corporate objectives.

Corporate social responsibility has become important to public relations because such programmes offer the opportunity to build goodwill by promoting the benefits of the company to its stakeholders; corporate social responsibility delivers target audiences to those managing the corporate image. Corporate social responsibility falls within the public relations portfolio because it affects a company's image and reputation. It may well be seen as an investment against the day when a crisis occurs and the company needs all the goodwill it can muster. In addition to its strategic role in formulating policy and making recommendations as to the donation which will yield the most publicity, public relations also provides the necessary techniques to promote these activities among target publics, which may include not only the media but also other individuals seen to be of influence and important to the corporation. The rationale given in corporate publicity varies from the explicitly self-interested to that which implies that corporations must recognize specific obligations to the community, that a community has rights and the corporation has duties.

The justification that corporate social responsibility is enlightened self-interest of mutual benefit to both donor and beneficiary is questionable on a number of grounds. But there is clearly something wrong about claiming moral capital while at the same time being driven largely by self-interest. The term "enlightened self-interest" seems to imply that the recipient's benefit is seen of being of equal value to the benefit which accrues to the company either through ensuring a healthier economic climate in which the company operates or in terms of improved image and competitive edge for the company. This is an unsatisfactory justification because the company stands to gain so much more in terms of long-term benefits and because the phrase seems to imply a far more equal relationship based on equal exchange than is usually the case in corporate social responsibility. For example, donors choose beneficiaries, activities and the amount of money, resources and the length of commitment so that the recipient has little, if any, autonomy in the decision-making process. In short, it appears that what may be important for the corporation is what the recipient can do for the corporation in terms of enhancing their reputation and not what the company can do for the recipient.

Thus, some companies become involved in corporate social responsibility because of its perceived benefits. The motivation behind corporate responsibility may become explicitly self-interested. For example, "Whatever its more altruistic role, proactive corporate social responsibility, and more particularly, the successful generation of public awareness and appreciation of it, is good for business" (Mannheim & Pratt, 1989, p. 9).

The appeal to mutual benefit arising for donor and beneficiary appears to be based loosely on utilitarianism. A utilitarian approach does not take account of concepts of rights and responsibilities or ideas about just relationships, which seem to be embedded in much of the language used in defining and discussing corporate social responsibility. If companies which adopt a utilitarian line of justification do not attempt to evaluate the effects of their corporate social responsibility programmes, not only in their own terms of media coverage but also by seeking the evaluation of beneficiaries, then they will not be in a position to claim that they have contributed to happiness. In short, corporate social responsibility justified on utilitarian grounds needs to demonstrate cost–benefit analysis from the perspectives of donor, recipient, and society in general. If public relations is involved in identifying or choosing beneficiaries, then it would seem to be appropriate for the public relations practitioner to conduct a social audit based on sound research methodology in order to understand the different arguments and alternative perspectives of beneficiaries, stakeholders, and "public opinion."

Drumwright and Murphy seemed to suggest that evaluation focused on relationships and communication, using more qualitative methodologies, may be appropriate:

> However, intentions and objectives matter greatly in terms of how success is measured. For example, initiatives with heavily weighted economic objectives often are evaluated using conventional methods such as copy testing, number of media impressions, tracking studies, and sales. The more conventional the measures, the higher the hurdles for corporate societal marketing and the more likely the initiatives are to be "scapegoats" when the company's economic performance is disappointing. As the emphasis on non-economic objectives increases, evaluation methods tend to become both more qualitative and more informal as companies assess the initiative's impact on employees and key constituents. Because corporate societal marketing tends to be more robust in meeting objectives related to communicating with and motivating key constituents, it is more likely to be perceived as successful when measured in these terms. (Drumwright & Murphy, 2001, pp. 175–176)

A Kantian approach to corporate social responsibility focuses on the motivation behind the programme and the nature of the relationship between donor and recipient. For Kant, a corporate social responsibility programme needs to demonstrate that it is motivated by duty, not self-interest. Self-interested or prudential motivation renders corporate social responsibility programmes immoral, not only because they are wrongly motivated but also because they treat beneficiaries as a means to an end. Kant argued that one was obliged to have regard for people's autonomy and to treat people with respect. On a Kantian account, corporate social responsibility is not a moral practice because it may be wrongly motivated and because beneficiaries may be used as a means to the end of improving the company's image. If corporations took on board Kantian principles, then their programmes and accompanying publicity might look very different and closer to Quaker ideals. A Kantian approach might exclude evaluation which focused on the benefits to the corporation and instead focus on the careful identification of corporate duties and responsibilities and on allowing the beneficiaries full scope in defining the relationship between the corporation and themselves.

And lest it should be thought that cynicism is the preserve of the academic, it should be borne in mind that journalists, consumers, and other stakeholders may also be cautious of CSR benefits claimed in Annual Reports. Indeed, "evidence does exist that a company's intentions or motives regarding its corporate social marketing matter to consumers" (Drumwright & Murphy, 2001, pp. 175–176).

Thus, the terminology used in the area of corporate social responsibility has considerable implications in terms of moral discourse which may not be fully taken into account. In some cases corporate literature is confusing because it appears to appeal to both utilitarian and Kantian principles yet apparently delivers on neither. This poses a difficult challenge for the public relations practitioner, who may be seen as contributing to the instrumental and self-interested approach while simultaneously claiming moral credit. The area of corporate social responsibility thus highlights a dilemma which arises generally in the role of public relations: the tension between organizational goals and declared responsibility for "the public interest." Whetton et al. drew attention to:

> an emerging effort to finesse the use of instrumental arguments to justify moral behavior . . . several scholars and practitioners have argued that internal and external stakeholders are so essential to the effectiveness of a company that partnering and collaborating with stakeholders are essential strategic activities . . . [and they posit] that the ability to do so effectively is a strategic asset—a source of competitive advantage. This perspective asserts that collaborating with, rather than the management of, stakeholders requires a positive, rather than a defensive or manipulative orientation towards stakeholders. Empirical evidence is used by supporters of this position to suggest that the quality of stakeholder relations may be synonymous with the quality of management. (Whetton et al., 2002, p. 395)

Such an approach presumes a focus on relationships that could potentially position public relations at the centre of public relations activities. It could also imply the importance of the qualitative paradigm in seeking deeper insights into the nature of those relationships.

One way of conceptualizing the field in which organizational and other discourse takes place is that of the public sphere. Habermas' ideas are important to public relations because of the presentation of the theoretical space for rational debate which is presented as the source for "public opinion" to emerge from. Habermas' ideal conception of the public sphere of an arena for rational debate separate from economic and political considerations is threatened where certain interests have greater access and substantial resources with which to dominate. This was also important to economist John Kenneth Galbraith when he argued that companies should not be allowed to make contributions to the community because it gave them the opportunity to use undue influence in social and economic affairs (Koten in Caywood, 1997, p. 150).

Public relations increases the visibility and impact of large organizations, thus potentially reducing available space for citizens. Far from liberating or facilitating public debate and dialogue or the expression of "public opinion," public relations is profoundly instrumental, both intellectually and in terms of praxis. The use of largely positivist methodologies to "measure" public opinion empowers clients, not publics. The use of the concepts of "opinion leaders" or "opinion formers" and "networking" suggests that concepts of public opinion and democracy are as limited as they were in Habermas' coffee houses and as subject to elitism and class interests. Public relations may facilitate the relationship between business and the media at the expense of others and thus contribute to the erosion of the public sphere. Public relations in itself is not accountable but may be largely hidden in its contribution to predominating and deterministic "market forces."

PUBLIC RELATIONS AS THE "CONSCIENCE" OR "ETHICAL GUARDIAN" OF THE ORGANIZATION

In the showcase volume of public relations research, *Handbook of Public Relations* (Sage 2001), there is a discussion of public relations ethics (Day et al., 2001, pp. 403–409) and an accompanying chapter, "Ethics in public relations: theory and practice" (Curtin & Boynton, 2001, pp. 411–421). Taken together these contributions note concerns with unethical practice, the consequent effect on the occupation's reputation, and the necessity to address these issues in order to achieve the necessary legitimacy for social acceptance, "licence to operate," and professional status.

The eminent public relations academic, Robert Heath, has argued:

> Corporate actions are evaluated by key publics. For this reason, corporate responsibility is value-informed choice-making. Ascertaining appropriate ethical responses is a rhetorical problem vital to strategic planning used by excellent organizations that aspire to build and maintain mutually beneficial relationships. Public relations persons enjoy an ideal position to counsel executives on which values fit best with the interests of their markets, audiences and publics. (Heath, 2001a, p. 46)

Thus are corporate social responsibility and public relations' status entwined.

These claims for the public relations role suggest that within the organization public relations is acting as the "conscience" of the organization. For this reason it is sometimes suggested that public relations should be involved in setting up organizational codes of ethics and maintain a watching brief on organizational ethics. The scope of this brief could include monitoring the environment for publics' views on values; making company officials aware of prevailing ethical standards; helping companies refine their concepts of social responsibility; helping develop codes of ethics that are properly incorporated into planning, operating, and appraisal procedures; developing strategies for explaining to publics how values shape company actions and decisions; and helping senior managers to avoid crises that can damage reputation (Heath & Ryan, 1989, pp. 23–24).

The idea of public relations as the "conscience" of the organization sounds moral and alluring perhaps because of its appeal to the idealistic concept of public relations acting as a peacemaker breaking down barriers between the organization and its publics. In practical terms, however, the "conscience" concept seems to have specific implications which are rather less idealistic. It is quite clear that ultimately all the listening and soul-searching is directed towards organizational survival and that public relations is naturally only responsible to senior managers, not to employees or publics. In any case, a major implication is that the practitioner would need some knowledge of moral philosophy and applied ethics in order to manage discussion sensibly. Without this expertise, it is hard to see how morality could avoid being subjected to organizational goals given the situation and role of the practitioner as outlined above.

The choice of the term "guardian" implies responsibility for others, in this context, the public interest, and is also suggestive of high status (L'Etang, 2003, p. 55). The term resonates with the ideal of public service, so important to the evolution of public relations in the UK. It so clearly opposes notions of manipulation and "spin" that it can seem an innocuously benevolent term. However, accountability and transparency remain major issues for the occupation. These become more acute at times of public wrongdoing, corporate accidents, and crises.

CORPORATE ACCIDENTS AND BLAME

Discussion of corporate responsibility often relates to specific disasters. Such discussion often concerns the possibility of attaching blame to someone or something—either the corporation itself, one of its principals, or an agent acting on its behalf. Here I shall review debates in the field and draw out implications for the role of public relations.

The approach taken here follows Wells (1993) in discussing how a corporation may be regarded as criminally liable. The discussion relates to corporations because the concept of "corporation" "enables legal liability, whether criminal or civil, to attach to the enterprise itself rather than, or as well as, to any one person within it" (Wells, 1993, p. 1). Most countries currently do not recognize criminal liability for corporations. The English common law system recognizes corporate liability to criminal prosecution, but only where a senior official who personifies the corporation can also be prosecuted (Vidal & Cordahi, 1995, p. 5). In Australia and Canada companies can be prosecuted even if no single person or collection of individuals can be identified for prosecution (ibid.). The rest of continental Europe uses civil law (which generally does not recognize corporate liability to criminal prosecution), and some countries such as Holland have specifically related environmental criminal law to corporate responsibility (ibid.).

The key issue is whether a corporation in itself could be held criminally liable or whether blame should be devolved to particular individuals held responsible for their actions. The argument rests on a particular conception of the nature of a corporation and its relationship to its constituent parts: its managers, shareholders, and employees. Much of the legal discourse which has taken place on this issue is concerned with philosophical interpretations of legal concepts of organizations arrived at through a number of cases in legal history.

De George (1983) suggested that individuals and corporations may both be held culpable even though he accepted that the corporation in itself is not a moral agent, because the people within it are and actions done by them on behalf of corporations should be morally evaluated. He argued that:

> People cannot be rid of their moral or legal responsibility simply by disclaiming it, or by seeking anonymity in corporate decisions, or by pretending decisions are impersonal or made by a corporation or organization that is not a moral being and so not morally accountable. (De George, 1983, p. 164)

In practice, the legal conception of a corporation is an anthropomorphic legal fiction. On this account a corporation is an abstraction which possesses neither human mind nor human body and therefore is not capable of expressing intention. Intention is critical in criminal law as it applies to individuals, where judge and jury must determine whether a person was guilty because he or she had a "guilty mind" (*mens rea*). Therefore, the corporation's

> active and directing will must consequently be sought in the person of who for some purposes may be called an agent, but who is really the directing mind and will of the corporation, the very ego and centre of the personality of the corporation. (Viscount Haldane, cited by Lord Morris of Borth-y-Gest in *Lennard's Carrying Co. Ltd. v Asiatic Petroleum Co. Ltd.* [1915] AC 713)

This makes it very difficult to hold corporations criminally responsible since the emphasis is on finding persons who can be identified as responsible and then deciding whether they work in the "brain area" of the organization or whether they are simply the "hands" or "a cog in the machine." If a corporation delegates full powers of responsibility to an individual, then he or she can be held responsible as part of the "directing mind and will" or "alter ego" of the corporation and the corporation may be held liable. If, however, an individual is deemed to have been "directed" to perform certain functions and has failed to do so, then the individual is counted as "another person" (not part of the corporate persona) and, provided the corporation can prove that it established adequate systems of line management and supervision, the corporation cannot be held responsible.

Some (Friedman, 1970; Velasquez, 1983) have argued that a corporation cannot be held responsible for actions because a corporation is not a human agent. Others (L. May, 1986) argue that a corporation only acts in a vicarious way through the acts of those who are members of the corporation. Friedman (1970) argued that organizations cannot be moral agents with moral responsibilities because they are only "artificial persons." In his view, managers and employees are agents of the shareholders, directly responsible to them "to conduct the business in accordance with their desires, which will generally be to make as much money as possible while conforming to the basic rules in society, both those embodied in law and those embodied in ethical custom" (Friedman, 1970, p. 249).

For Friedman, employers are principal moral agents only when acting on their own behalf in their private lives. Friedman did not comment on the responsibilities of corporations in the event of corporate disasters, nor did he discuss the responsibilities of shareholders with regard to the corporations in which they invest. Velasquez (1983) focused on the relationship between physical action and intention in order to argue that moral and criminal responsibility can only be attributed to an agent for actions which originated in the agent. Blaming the corporation is like blaming agents who were not involved in the action in question, which appears to infringe moral principle by effectively blaming the innocent. Velasquez argued that it is not correct to infer that the action of corporate members is the same as corporate action because the individual corporate members are autonomous and possessed of free will.

In contrast to Velasquez, French (1979) argued that corporate intentions may be inferred not only from individual actions but also from a corporation's official policies, decision-making procedures, and lines of authority, which French referred to as "CID" (Corporate Internal Decision structure). French's CID can be seen as a kind of group mind and is objected to because it encourages us to see and accept the corporation as a large-scale personality. Velasquez suggested that the danger here is that if the corporation is seen as an organic whole, then the interests and well-being of individuals both within and without the organization may be sacrificed to the organization's interests. As Wells pointed out:

> There is a public welfare in prevention of harm done to individuals by individuals as well as that done to individuals by collectivities and that done to the "community" by collectivities. The state has a legitimate interest in all these. (Wells, 1993, p. 7)

The suggestion that corporations should be more carefully restricted by legislation raises political issues and is likely to be strongly resisted by those who support free enterprise. In addition to these arguments, one could also point out that companies do in fact deliberately promote themselves as personalities, developing expensive logos as symbols of their corporate identity in an attempt to cultivate a strong sense of corporate culture among their personnel. Public relations can be seen to be engaged in a process of symbolic management which helps both to define and then to capture, enhance, and promote an identity or persona that stands for the organization, "survival is understood as the maintenance of self-identity." The scope of public relations in facilitating and promoting organizational totalitarianism in this context is considerable but currently quite outside both practitioner and academic public relations discourse.

As can be seen, there are a number of different positions on what constitutes corporate responsibility in the context of corporate accidents. While there are arguments for and against aggregating all individual actions, attributing responsibility to those in control or to those who were present when an accident occurred, there is considerable difficulty in identifying what might count as organizational as opposed to individual intent or recklessness. The central problem in dealing with a collectivity is that power and responsibility are almost always unevenly distributed within it. This problem becomes more apparent when one starts to consider what sort of punishment might be appropriate for an organization. While it seems just that in a hierarchical structure more blame should be attached to those responsible for conceiving and implementing policies, that is, the "mind" of the organization, the legal system is limited by the convention of criminal liability to attribute fault to individuals, not collectivities. The problem of attributing intention, mentioned at the outset, becomes an issue because "individual liability is ... grounded in a theory of culpability based in mental states ... not everyone is convinced that corporations can be said to possess a mental state" (Wells, 1993, p. 95). The practical dilemma which arises from this is that "the more diffuse the company structure, the more it devolves power to semi-autonomous managers, the easier it will be to avoid liability" (Feld & Jorg, 1991, p. 150).

The process of individuation makes it difficult to prosecute corporations as entities and it also seems to inhibit discussion of another option: that of aggregating individual culpability and calculating the corporate responsibility from a quantitative as well as a qualitative evaluation. It certainly seems unjust that a corporation can escape criminal prosecution for manslaughter in cases where individual members have been allowed to carry out their duties in an irresponsible way. Wells suggested that if the "concept of individual culpability is unsuitable for corporate conglomerates" (Wells, 1989, p. 150), then an alternative standard and procedure may need to be developed. On the other side, Rafalko argued that "the lesson of the Nuremberg trials is that guilt is individual; the notion of collective guilt has no place in American law" (Rafalko, 1989, p. 923).

Rafalko went on to argue that even the notion of individual guilt has its problems in a corporate setting because individuals may make a distinction between their private and work roles. He cited the Union Carbide/Bhopal case as an example where events highlighted this dilemma. Union Carbide's Chairman, Warren Anderson, initially pronounced personal moral responsibility and claimed that he would devote the rest of his life to helping people who had suffered during the tragedy, but a year later he said he had "overreacted" when making this statement (Rafalko, 1989, p. 923). The *New Yorker* magazine suggested that "what Mr Anderson meant ... perhaps, is that at first he reacted as a private man but in the intervening months he has remembered—or been reminded—that he is the head of a corporation" (quoted in Rafalko, 1989, p. 923).

Even if one rejects the idea of a corporation possessing legal personhood, it has to be accepted that the corporation provides the context for moral action. Since a corporation has a certain amount of power and influence that derives from its position in society—for example, power gained through the ability to attract media interest or conduct campaigns of public affairs and lobbying—it seems right that this should be balanced by a legal recognition of the corporation's moral responsibility. The appropriate punishment for organizations is also an area for debate. While at present erring companies may be fined, certain radical and imaginative writers have suggested that such companies should be "beheaded" by wholesale sacking of top management or executed through compulsory nationalization (Rafalko, 1989, p. 923).

What are the implications of the legal debate for the role of public relations? The role of public relations is likely to be extremely constrained by legal considerations and restricted to that of orator, dependent upon the advice of legal advisers: apologies and regrets must be carefully phrased. So public relations is here performing a subordinate role, not an advisory role. In such a situation there is only room for advocacy of the managerial position, not of that of employees within the organization. External reputation may depend partly on success in attaching blame to one or two employees; public relations seems to be operating in an expedient way rather than on any considerations of ethics or justice. Finally, public relations acts on behalf of organizations to create corporate personae for marketing benefits. In this process it reinforces the sentimental and anthropomorphic conceptions of organizations which prevent us from seeing them for what they often are: autocratic and totalitarian.

CONCLUSION

Corporate social responsibility as it is practised does not appear to conform to any theory of obligation (supported by contractual and deontological frameworks) as may be implied by the language and concepts utilized by practitioners and corporate publicity. Corporate social responsibility seems largely dependent on some utilitarian concept of supererogatory action which benefits donor and recipient. However, the conceptualization of corporation appears to be somewhat different in the two distinct areas of corporate social responsibility that can be identified: those of crisis management and community programmes. In the field of crisis management, the process of conceptualization has been subject to much dispute and debate as corporate minds have been wonderfully concentrated by the potential threat of legal action; in this area it is in their interests to devolve responsibilities. However, in the field of community programmes, the corporation is very much presented as a moral person who can do good in society to the benefit of all. The notion of agency here is scarcely addressed, except insofar as it relates to the role of employees in such programmes. The contractual notions present in debates about crises are underdeveloped in terms of community relations since there is no sense in which the contract is negotiated or arbitrated: the corporation determines the playing field and referees the game. This is less true of community programmes, which are focused on stakeholders or responsibilities arising from the economic role of the corporation, but there is no satisfactory justification for a deontological approach to non-stakeholders. The ability of corporations to determine the nature and scope of moral "contracts" means that the only real bargaining occurs between state and business. This is where the conceptualization of the public sphere helps us to see the degree of domination present in our apparently democratic and open society. The role of public relations appears to be working to support that domination and thus working against, not for, democratic principles.

Corporate social responsibility is presented in public relations largely as a technique or tool for enhancing reputation. This chapter has shown that the field of corporate responsibility is a highly complex one involving ethical and political issues. Only if practitioners engage with such issues can they avoid the charges of superficiality and cynical exploitation of target audiences. The role of public relations is necessarily partisan on behalf of client or employer which makes it difficult to claim that the function necessarily operates in the public interest.

One of the main conclusions which arises from this analysis is that public relations is implicated in a range of ethical and political issues of fundamental importance. Public relations can be seen to be intrinsically linked to power-broking initiatives in society and therefore a profoundly conservative force in society; the popular concept of public relations as "neutral" may privilege the existing order over justice.

ACKNOWLEDGMENTS

The author would like to acknowledge the contribution made to the development of ideas in this work by the late Dr Murray MacBeath, who supervised her dissertation for the M.Phil. in Social Justice at the University of Stirling in 1991.

22

Public Opinion and Public Relations

Magda Pieczka
Stirling Media Research Institute

This chapter aims to review the concept of public opinion and the research traditions in the field in order to discuss their relevance to public relations. The first part of the chapter concentrates on definition and the development of public opinion research. The main focus of the second part is the concept of "public" itself and the implications for public relations practice of the various definitions employed.

The literature on all aspects of public opinion with which this chapter is concerned is quite extensive; much of it is well known and often cited. The difficulty, therefore, is in balancing the requirements of a useful review accessing this literature for a public relations student against the danger of being merely repetitive. Oddly, while public relations literature demonstrates awareness of both the concept and the reality of public opinion, it has not been very attentive to the debate in the field of public opinion research. This chapter attempts to fill this gap for students and to reflect on exactly why the concept of public opinion is relevant to public relations.

As in chapter 19, I have cited a substantial range of useful references to show the origins and development of the concept. The citation of sources is also intended to help the student see which concepts public relations writers have borrowed and which have become absorbed into public relations literature, sometimes without question. It should also be noted that the section on public opinion research assumes some familiarity with methodological terminology.

WHAT IS PUBLIC OPINION?

Traditionally, definitions of public opinion have been seen as falling into two categories: those which view public opinion as akin to Rousseau's "general will"; and the majoritarian definitions in which public opinion is the opinion that matters, that is, the majority opinion in a democracy (V. Price, 1992, p. 13; Herbst, 1993, p. 49).[1] The first type of definition derives from the work of the Enlightenment thinkers, such as Rousseau, who were preoccupied with the problem of how a state should be governed in the age when the institution of monarchy based on the monarch's divine right was gradually getting out of step with a society transformed by a range of economic, cultural, and religious factors. This process of transformation, with its attendant rise of public opinion, is discussed in detail by Habermas, who conceptualized it as the rise of the "public sphere" (Habermas, 1989; Speier, 1980).[2] Chapter 3 defines the concept of public sphere and discusses its relevance in considering the role of public relations in democracy.

From its beginning the concept of public opinion has been rooted in political science, and it has remained so despite the extensive interest it has aroused throughout the 20th century among sociologists, psychologists, and communication experts. If one reviews the history of the concept, it appears to have been created in its early form by the English (Locke, Hume), then taken over by the French (Rousseau) and Americans (Madison), and again by the English (Mill, Bentham). The cross-Channel, indeed, cross-Atlantic, nature of the endeavour can be easily explained by the timing of the political and social changes taking place in England, its American colonies, and France from the 1640s to the mid-19th century.

It is generally accepted that Locke's law of opinion or reputation is the first explicit recognition of the mechanism of public opinion. The philosopher worked on this, and other ideas contained in his *Essays Concerning Human Understanding*, in the 1670s, although it appeared in print for the first time in 1690. The work was inspired, perhaps very appropriately for the subject of public opinion, by a discussion with friends on human knowledge and principles of politics, which must have been influenced by the political struggle taking place in England. The next generation of thinkers developed Locke's ideas further: Hume, in his *Treatise of Human Nature* (1740), formulated his basic principle that "It is . . . on opinion only that government is founded" (quoted in Noelle-Neumann, 1979, p. 146); the principle was subsequently endorsed in 1788 by Madison in the Federalist paper No. 49 (ibid., p.146) as the basis for the emerging American democracy.

English politics was watched keenly from across the Channel in France, which around the 1750s started moving quite clearly towards "a politics of contestation" (K. Baker, 1990, p. 168). Montesquieu, in *De L'Esprit des lois* (1748), admired the type of "modern state, free and individualistic" (ibid., p. 177) that England had become; and that was his inspiration for proposing the "theory of separation and balance of powers" (ibid., p. 173) which lies at the foundations of the modern democratic state. It is Rousseau, however, who is credited with using the term public opinion (*opinion publique*) for the first time, in his *First Discourse*(1750) (ibid., p. 186).[3] For him, public opinion was a social rather than political phenomenon which could be defined as "the collective expression of the moral and social values of a people, the shared sentiments and convictions embodied in a nation's customs and manners and applied in its judgements of individual action" (ibid., p. 186).

This was very much how the phenomenon was conceptualized and used until the 1780s in France, when the definition changed and public opinion was no longer seen as the "generalized social practice", but as "the enlightened expression of active and open discussion of all political matters, the free exercise of the public voice regarding the daily conduct of affairs, the institutional remedy for the administrative secrecy and arbitrariness that was threatening France with despotism" (ibid., p. 188).

---

[1] See also Katz et al., 1954, p. 50.
[2] For a discussion of Habermas, see also Calhoun, 1993.
[3] See also Noelle-Neumann (1979, p. 147), who gives the date as 1744 rather than 1750.

It is impossible to overestimate the influence not only on the development of modern democracy, but also on the debate about public opinion, of the political storms of the late 18th century—American Independence and the French Revolution—with the role that constitutional debates played in them, and with the resulting declarations of basic philosophical principles, in the form of the Bill of Rights (1791) and the Declaration of the Rights of Man and Citizens (1789). Both declarations were based on the firm belief in the rational nature of men, the equality of all men and therefore their ability, and right, to govern themselves and their equals through a process of communal decision making, whatever the particular structure of that process might be.

In the debates of the French National Assembly on the exact shape of the constitution to be adopted, evidence can be found of strong interest in the current American and English solutions, but equally in Rousseau's social contract and the concept of the general will. In fact, the solution finally adopted in 1791 was a compromise between different opinions and factions. The "Rousseauian principle of the inalienable sovereignty of the general will" (Baker, 1990, p. 303) was upheld: the constitution was not a pact between the king and the people, but an expression of the laws of the nation binding the king as much as any other citizen. On the other hand, the general will as a discursive process taking place in the Assembly was abandoned in favour of the practice of representation, in which individual wills had to be balanced, a solution that created a danger of subverting the general will by partisan interests. In the course of the deliberations many points were raised, such as whether the general will (i.e., the public opinion) can err and the clear possibility of the majority oppressing minorities in a representative form of government based on opinion—doubts echoed by later commentators and public opinion researchers.

A few decades later, within the context of rapid economic and social changes, utilitarian philosophers, most famously Mill and Bentham, provided ethical justification for the rule of majority. Their basic premise was that society consists of self-interested individuals, and a way of managing the unavoidable conflict was, in accordance with the general happiness principle, to govern by listening to the majority opinion.[4] It appears, then, that within roughly 100 years public opinion evolved from being first conceptualized as the general will through a complex process of political, economic, and social change in America, England, and France into the widely accepted 19th-century definition of public opinion as the opinion of the majority of citizens,

It could be argued that the writers whose ideas have been discussed so far concerned themselves with establishing the concept of public opinion and deliberating on how it was present in the principles and effort of government. However, as the practice of popular government was becoming well established, the critical interest turned perhaps more towards observing complexities and paradoxes of government and public life in democracies. This is not to say that the concept itself had become finally clarified and defined—in fact, this aim has yet to be achieved—but conceptual ambiguities were considered alongside the practicalities, or for that matter impracticalities, of the relationship between public opinion and democratic institutions.

One of the best-known and most quoted works of that nature is Bryce's *The American Commonwealth*, published in 1888. The author's insight is impressive and, despite all the technological and social changes of the last 100 years and the staggering amount of public opinion research published in the last 60 years, many of Bryce's points are easily compatible with the contemporary scientific knowledge in the field. For example, Bryce postulated a five-stage process of opinion formation which included elements such as—to use 20th-century terminology—the agenda-setting role of the mass media, group influence, simplification of

---

[4]See Price, 1992, pp. 12–14.

the opinion in the process of a "yes" or "no" electoral choice, and the apparent "uniformity", meaning possibly generalizability, of public opinion, equated again with a vote outcome.

Equally interesting are Bryce's comments on definitions of public opinion:

> The difficulties ... arise from confounding opinion itself with the organs whence people try to gather it, and from using the term to denote, sometimes everybody's views,—that is, the aggregate of all that is thought and said on the subject,—sometimes merely the views of the majority. (Quoted in Berelson & Janoyitz, 1966)

This points to yet another type of definition in addition to the original historical distinction suggested at the beginning of this chapter. A useful discussion of the dilemma and a typology was presented by Herbst (1993), who proposed four definitional categories: aggregation, majoritarian, discursive/consensual, and reification. The most common understanding of the term "public opinion", that of aggregation, underlies polling, surveys, elections, and referenda. It assumes "that public is an atomized mass of individuals, each with a set of opinions" (Herbst, 1993, p. 439) and consequently sees public opinion as the sum of opinions people hold. The majoritarian view also depends on counting individual opinions, but it assumes that opinions are not equal in weight. Earlier in this discussion we saw how it was decided in modern democracy that it was the opinions of the majority that counted. An important condition was added to this definition by Lowell, who believed that numerical supremacy was not sufficient in itself and that there had to be willingness on the part of the minority to accept the majority opinion as a binding solution (ibid., p. 439). The discursive/consensual approach concentrates on the role of communication in the process of opinion formation. Similarly to Rousseau's, such definitions assume that public opinion emerges in the process of rational public discourse (Habermas). Paradoxically this approach can also focus on the censorial nature of such public discourse (Locke, Noelle-Neumann). Finally, the last type of definition is based on the assumption "that public opinion does not exist at all—it is a reification or fictional entity" (Herbst, 1993, p. 440). Lippmann expressed such a view in *The Phantom Public* (1925); as did Bourdieu (1979), who came at the problem from a Marxist perspective.

This typology represents the knowledge of some 200 years of reflection before the empirical tools of public opinion were developed in the 20th century, as well as the cumulative knowledge that 60 years of such empirical research has produced. The following section will provide an overview of public opinion research as a social-scientific activity and facilitate a sideways move to the consideration of some relevant aspects of public relations at a time when clear aspirations to a social-scientific status have been expressed in the field (Grunig, 1992; Pavlik, 1987; Broom & Dozier, 1990).

PUBLIC OPINION RESEARCH

Writing in 1957, Lazarsfeld (1981) commented on the fierce antagonism in public opinion research since the late 1940s between the supporters of what he called the classical tradition and the modern empiricists.[5] Following Berelson, he defined the classical stage in the development of public opinion research as "a general feeling that something called public opinion was important. As a result, prominent writers developed broad speculations about it" (Lazarsfeld, 1981). Modern empiricists, in contrast, had been able to learn from earlier attempts at gathering empirical data, from debates about a suitable methodology, and from "intellectual neighbours" such as psychology and anthropology. This made possible a phase "in which

---

[5] See also Berelson, 1956.

systematic propositions on public opinion [were] being developed: public opinion [had] become an empirical social science" (ibid.).

The turning point between these two traditions, or perhaps more appropriately stages in the development reminiscent of the different stages in the scientific of "hypothetico-deductive" method, came in the 1930s. By that time attempts at opinion polls had become quite popular in America, but it was the success of the 1936 poll conducted by Gallup, Roper, and Crossley which predicted "the Roosevelt landslide" in the presidential elections that gave such a strong impetus to the survey approach (Converse, 1987, S12).

The year 1937 saw the publication of the first issue of *Public Opinion Quarterly*, which was founded by prominent academics who "hoped to promote the scientific study of interrelationships among three potent new social forces: *mass opinion . . . mass communication . . .* and *public opinion measurement and reporting . . .* based on scientific sampling" (Beniger, 1987, S46). The editors decided to dedicate the journal to these new social forces, which they summarized as public opinion, and to study them from "the perspective of "scholarship, government, business, advertising, public relations, press, radio, motion pictures" (ibid., S46).

However, the journal did not develop quite in this way and a short digression here might provide a useful illustration of the development of the public opinion research in general. Davison, writing in the 50th anniversary special issue, commented on the long-term trends from such content analyses of the journal as were available. It appears that since the late 1940s the proportion of articles devoted to propaganda and public relations has steadily declined, while the number of articles either based on quantitative methods or devoted to their discussion has risen (Davison, 1987, S6). There is, it seems, an interesting set of questions here for public relations researchers: Was the journal's mission statement based on an overoptimistic assessment of public relations' potential for academic development, or was the early promise unfulfilled? Is there, perhaps, a completely different explanation capable of dealing sensibly with this apparent non-engagement of public relations with public opinion research?

What the above digression confirms is the empiricists' hold over the field of public opinion. This was by no means a unanimously applauded development. At the 1947 annual meeting of the American Sociological Society, Herbert Blumer presented a paper which articulated the nature of the disagreement between the two factions. The empiricists were criticized for a mistaken approach to the problem: they started from the premise that public opinion was what the polls measured rather than from a generic definition from which systematic propositions could be derived—in short, they reversed the accepted order of scientific enquiry, or at least seemed to have omitted an important initial stage. Their narrow instrumentalism could "leave or raise the question of what the results meant. Not having a conceptual point of reference the results [were] merely disparate findings" (Blumer, 1954, p. 71). It is fair to say that the other major criticism Blumer made referred to the practice of weighting all opinions in a survey equally, whereas in reality some opinions, he believed, were more important, or effective, than others. His own definition attempted to capture both the social dynamics of the process and its effectiveness: the character of public opinion in terms of meaningful operation must be sought in the array of views and positions which enter into the consideration of those who have to take action on public opinion" (ibid., p. 73). Public opinion as defined by opinion poll outcomes appears out of its natural social context: because it captures only the views of disparate individuals, it appears static. Blumer's direct attack provoked equally direct responses, the main arguments of which as well as the flavour of the debate might be gathered from Newcomb's and Woodward's comments (D. Katz et al., 1954, pp. 78–84).[6]

---

[6]See also Converse, 1987.

A way to reconciliation was opened in 1957 by Lazarsfeld (1981), who suggested that the empiricists had learnt from the classics and returned the favour, as it were, by shining conceptual tools that might allow further development of the classical ideas. Converse (1987) offered support to Lazarsfeld's views on the matter; and Noelle-Neumann's "Public opinion and the classical tradition: A re-evaluation" (1979) provided an example of how modern research could both be inspired by classical writers and provide a scientifically backed reworking of their ideas.

So far this chapter has looked at the origins of the classical tradition and at the debate between the supporters of this tradition and the modern empiricists. It should be clear how the battle started and what it was all about, but what has not been explained is where the empiricists came from in the first place. Lazarsfeld gave the following account of the beginnings:

> The empirical tradition in opinion and attitude research began...in Germany with...laboratory experiments on problem solving...[then came] the work of the Chicago school of sociologists, which brought the study of attitudes and values into play...thereafter, the psychometricians...introduced the...problem of measurement. (Lazarsfeld, 1981)

Another important early influence was the theme of mass society, apparent in the first issue of *Public Opinion Quarterly*. Beniger (1987, S46–S48) offered a succinct discussion of how the interest in mass society developed among American scholars. He pointed to the European influence, which reached America in the 1930s through translations of works such as Ortega y Gasset's *The Revolt of the Masses* (1930), Durkheim's *Division of Labor in Society* (1933), and Parson's synthesis of the work of European mass theorists in *The Structure of Social Action* (1937), assimilating the work of Toennies and Weber into the English-speaking sociology even though the actual translations appeared in the United States in the 1940s. Last but not least, the Frankfurt School moved to New York in 1933. Beniger, however, also pointed to the already existent American interest in mass society: Lippmann's *Public Opinion* (1922/1954) and *The Phantom Public* (1925); Bernays, *Crystallizing Public Opinion* (1923), Dewey's *The Public and Its Problems* (1927), and Lasswell's *Propaganda Techniques in the World War* (1927).

The concept of mass society, in very general terms, grew out of the intense process of industrialization and bureaucratization, which were accompanied by increasing scepticism about traditional liberal values. The mixture of angst and exhilaration at the possibilities offered by this urban industrial civilization were vividly captured by Modernist art: alienated individuals in the midst of a mass of their likes, like the voice of T. S. Eliot's poetry; the Futurists' fascination with the city and the machine; the anarchy of Dada; and the bizarre alliance of ideology and the subconscious in Surrealism, to mention just a few examples.

> Born in this intellectual context, on the advent of world war involving several totalitarian states, the mass society model of public opinion formation and change continued to dominate the field for almost three decades [i.e., until the 1960s]. (Beniger, 1987, p. 345)

Central to this model was the belief that the mass media influence individuals, rather than people as members of social groups, and that such influence is direct. Similar assumptions, of course, underpinned the "large-scale probability sampling model used in public opinion surveys" (Beniger, 1987, S49), which could therefore be criticized for reducing social science to "aggregate psychology", an argument offered by Coleman in 1964 (ibid., S49). Klapper's intervention in 1960, "codifying" (E. Katz, 1987, SS6) the model of limited effects, turned the tide against the notion of the passive, atomized audience and the powerful media. The new trend coincided with communication studies being abandoned by sociologists and political scientists when it could no longer offer a theory clearly linking public opinion and mass communication (Beniger, 1987, S50).

Despite mounting criticism, the direct effects model was not entirely discredited or abandoned. McQuail pointed to the arrival of television as a new popular medium in the 1950s and "the revival of (new) left thinking in the 1960s" (McQuail, 1987, pp. 254–255) as being responsible for the return of the concept of the all-powerful media and consequently the view of "public opinion as an effect of mass communication" (Beniger, 1987, S51). The old model, however, was not just revived but also reworked. For example, Converse's work (1964) on the role of ideology in public opinion brought back the old doubts about the idealized picture of democracy and democratic citizens (Lippmann, 1954, pp. 38–39) at the same time as it led to a view of society as composed of overlapping issue publics. The agenda-setting approach, while accepting the limited effects of mass media, proposed that the media's power to delineate issues and their public presence or absence goes deeper than direct effects. The "spiral of silence" went even further, to claim that in addition to setting agendas the media perform a kind of social-control function by constraining individual courage, as it were, to express unpopular views. Finally there is cultivation analysis, which defines mass media as the source of the ubiquitous, manufactured discourse (see Beniger, 1987).

In the 1980s a paradigmatic shift in mass communication, which had started in the mid-1970s, became apparent. It can be summarized as "a change in dependent variables from attitudes to cognitions, as a shift in independent variables from persuasive communication to less directed media processes ranging from 'framing' through 'discourse' to the social construction of reality" (Beniger, 1987, S52–S53). Like many previous research agendas and approaches, this new paradigm utilized concepts which had been noted by classical writers or by its intellectual neighbours—for example, Tolman's "cognitive maps" or Lippmann's "enlisted interest" (ibid., S55). The logical, or rather methodological, consequence of the emergence of the new paradigm, referred to as the cognitive perspective, has been the widening of the range of data collection techniques to include content analysis, focus groups, and quasi-experiments in addition to the traditional attitudinal survey. The change produced seven different strands of research: uses and gratifications, knowledge gap, co-orientation models, work on political cognition, various approaches to audience decoding, studies of media events, and hegemonic models (ibid., S57).

PUBLIC OPINION RESEARCH AND PUBLIC RELATIONS

"Only fools, pure theorists, or apprentices fail to take public opinion into account," wrote Necker, who served as the crown minister of finance to Louis XVI and who is described as one "among the first to propose systematic governmental public relations" (Price, 1992, p. 12). Many contemporary public relations practitioners can be described, like Necker, as placed within the classical approach as Lazarsfeld explained it: they realize that public opinion is an important factor and take it into account, but not on the basis of a scientific theory. In Necker's case, of course, no such scientific basis was available; for many contemporary practitioners it is a question of working on the basis of lay theories, not entirely without any link with or resemblance to the up-to-date body of knowledge, but at the same time more implicit and not entirely rigorous frameworks.

Herbst's (1993) research on lay theories of public opinion and their relation to political activity and ideology is worth further comment here. Although the design of the study did not permit generalizations, Herbst found some evidence indicating resistance to scientific definitions, and a conviction that public opinion is a fiction and that the Habermasian public sphere simply does not exist. Even more unexpected was the lack of any relationship between such beliefs and respondents, ideological positions uncovered by this exploratory study. It would be interesting to see what a similar research project might reveal about theories of public opinion on the basis of which public relations practitioners work. In the absence of such data, an indirect answer might be given on the basis of what public relations theory has to say about public opinion.

Cutlip et al. (1985, 1994) represent perhaps the most comprehensive source of information on public opinion for a public relations student. The authors' approach is fairly standard, acknowledging the problems in defining the term and providing a discussion of its constituent elements, "public" and "opinion".[7] Public opinion is defined as "[representing] a *consensus, which emerges over time, from all the expressed views that cluster around an issue in debate, and that this consensus exercises power*" (Cutlip et al., 1985, p. 157) and as "the aggregate result of individual opinion on public matters" (ibid., p. 162).

In terms of Herbst's typology, the definitions fall clearly in the class of "aggregation", which, as we have seen, underlies the empirical tradition of public opinion research. However, the definition changes in the latest edition to: "[public opinion] reflects a dynamic process in which ideas are "expressed, adjusted, and compromised en route to collective determination of a course of action" (Cutlip et al., 1994, p. 243). The latest definition, with its focus on the public opinion formations process, is more comfortably placed in the discursive/consensual category.

It seems reasonable to explain the change as linked to the developments in public relations theory that emerged in the years between the two editions, namely the situational theory proposed by Grunig and Hunt in 1984 for identifying publics, and the augmentation of the position of the co-orientation model at the basis of the theory of excellence in public relations (Grunig, 1992). Cutlip et al. devoted a section to a discussion of situational theory (Cutlip et al., 1994, pp. 245–247), which is followed by a discussion of the co-orientation model (ibid., pp. 247–254). As far as the definition itself is concerned, it seems to reflect the line of argument linking Grunig's original interest in co-orientation with his awareness of Habermas' concepts of communicative action and public sphere, as mediated by Pearson (1989a, 1989b; see also chapters 19 and 21); this provides not only a discursive definition of public opinion but also a justification for the (excellent) practice of public relations:

> Communication system [as created by public relations] is based on two-way exchange of messages . . . It takes the form of . . . a dialogue and argument about politics and issues that goes beyond the revealing of private opinion to the forming of public opinion—the same sense in which Habermas referred to public opinion. (Ehling et al., 1992, p. 388)

Public relations, in this definition, seems to act as the enabling mechanism for public debate, and therefore for public opinion and the public sphere. If this is how the practice appears, where then should the study of public relations as a discipline be located in the social sciences? In other words, which disciplines are the nearest intellectual neighbours? In chapter 1 the editors point out a range of answers to the question of the problem of academic location; on the basis of the present discussion it appears that the answer hinges on co-orientation, and therefore mass communication and the process approach to communication. Grunig and Hunt (1984, p. 143) made this connection even more explicit in the situational theory which in conceptual terms is derived from Blumer—and originally from Dewey's *The Public and Its Problems*

---

[7]See Allport, 1954; Young, 1954; Blumer, 1954; Price, 1992.

(1927)—and which, in methodological terms, represents the instrumental approach dominating public opinion research.

Dewey's work has to be noted here for its contribution to interest group theory; it should also be remembered that group liberalism is cited as one of the presuppositions of symmetric models of public relations (see chapter 19). Somewhat indirectly, public relations seems to be positioning itself in relation to its unmentioned intellectual neighbour—political science. The view of society that seems to be assumed is that in which various interest groups (and publics) are unavoidably pitched one against another but where conflict can always be resolved by the process of negotiation, which breeds at least as much mutual understanding as is necessary for compromise. Government, not as a public or a client but as a social and political mechanism, seems to be conceptualized in traditional democratic terms as "based on opinion" and, at least in principle, acting to safeguard public interest. Inherent in this vision, of course, is rationalism as the steering mechanism of social life. Reason, within this scheme of things, is not merely the instrumental intelligence needed to figure out the course of action leading to the fulfilment of self-interest, but rather the reason that guides the general will.

Public relations practice anchored in those wider social concerns as they appear in the above discussion is in a position to claim an ethical stance and at the same time to give an impression of neutrality, of being merely an enabling mechanism. Whether or not any ethical responsibility is claimed, public relations still works from a particular set of assumptions. The principles of the discursive/consensual model of the relationship between private actions and social outcomes are so deeply ingrained in our political culture that we accept them almost as common sense, but they still articulate a set of beliefs, a point of view: and what are these in the political sphere if not ideology?

23

Public Relations Education

Jacquie L'Etang and Magda Pieczka
Stirling Media Research Institute

The practice of public relations has aspirations to professionalize itself, and public relations education is a tool which can help achieve that status. However, the nature of curricula and the purpose of courses is a matter for discussion, and sometimes difference, between academics and practitioners. The context of the debate in the United Kingdom is one in which Government explicitly encourages vocational education. Education is thus increasingly required to serve business and industrial interests.

This chapter explores the relationship between public relations practice, education, and research in the late 1980s and early 1990s. The discussion includes an overview of educational developments in the United Kingdom in this early phase, which are contrasted with developments in the United States and continental Europe. The chapter presents an argument for academic freedom in the design and delivery of courses.

REVIEW OF EDUCATIONAL DEVELOPMENT IN THE CONTEXT OF PROFESSIONALIZATION

Professional status is important to public relations because such recognition could achieve social respectability and satisfy social aspirations as well as facilitate a clear separation from propaganda. The drive for professionalism in the UK has been articulated to a certain degree through debates over the structure and content of academic syllabuses and their location, aspects of which we will be discussing later in this chapter.

Within public relations literature concerned with the concept of professionalism, there is a strong tendency to treat it as something which is applied to the individual rather than the occupation as a whole. Grunig and Hunt claimed that "we could say that an occupation becomes

433

a profession when a majority of its practitioners qualify as professionals" (Grunig & Hunt, 1984, p. 66).

This leaves wide open the question of what exactly is the size of majority required and also seems a convenient way of moving debate away from important questions about the role of public relations in society. The process of individuation carried out here by Grunig and Hunt is similar to that in the area of public relations ethics, which is often narrowed down to questions of individual behaviour. It is not that such an approach in itself is not of interest; the problem lies in the lack of alternatives, which creates a substantial gap in the literature on the sociology of public relations. Doubtless this gap will in due course be filled, by those academics in public relations whose backgrounds or interests in sociology, politics, and media studies equip them better to address such questions.

Many of those writing about professionalism claim that public relations can already be described as a profession on the grounds that:

> Public relations [in the US] has a body of knowledge, a professional society, a code of ethics, a system for accreditation of practitioners by examination, a process for reporting violations including reviewing and censuring, a foundation for furthering public relations research and education, specified curricula at university level. (Wright, 1979, p. 20)

Others simply describe public relations as though it had already achieved professional status, sometimes ignoring key criteria that emerge from sociological literature, for example:

> Although public relations is often dismissed as a young profession and therefore not to be taken too seriously as an academic discipline, the professional practice of public relations can be dated logically from 1923 when Ed Bernays published the first textbook on public relations and taught the first university course. (Public Relations Education Trust, 1991, p. 9)

The published record of educational developments in the field of public relations has been dominated by the American experience. In part, this reflects the fact that the two academic journals in public relations to date, *Public Relations Review* and *Journal of Public Relations Research,* are based in America and largely devoted to American research and academic orientations. The representation of the European scene has been very general and not always as accurate as it might be; publication in refereed journals about the British scene is limited to one article (Hatfield, 1994, pp. 189–201) published 8 years after its submission and consequently so outdated as to be very inaccurate. Another article (Hazleton & Cutbirth, 1993, pp. 187–197) generalized about the "European system of education" on the basis of research in Austria, Hungary, and Germany. Both of these articles are written by Americans, not Europeans.

Educational developments in the United Kingdom seem to have been stimulated in the first instance largely by professional bodies. The Institute of Public Relations (IPR) set up its own courses and examinations in the 1950s. Teachers were recruited from the band of existing practitioners who delivered teaching at the Department of Management Studies, Regent Polytechnic, London, and the first Intermediate Examination was taken in July 1957. In the late 1950s the Education Committee of the IPR reported the early awakenings of interest in the university sector at the University of Sheffield, where there was talk of a Chair in Public Relations; at the London School of Economics, where there was to be a Lecturer in Advertising; and at Keele College (later University), where it was proposed that a Chair in Communications be appointed (IPR Education Committee Minutes IPR 3/7/2 History of Advertising Trust). At this stage there was an emphasis on technical skills such as film-making, photography, typography and advertising, and the most theoretically driven topic appeared to be opinion research. Examiners' reports and minutes of the Education Committee indicate concern over the scope of teaching of "public relations principles" and the absence of appropriate texts. Assessment was by two-stage examination (Intermediate and Final), including a viva voce examination designed to "enable the Board of Examiners to assess a candidate's personality and his ability to think and express himself clearly and concisely on a specific public relations problem" (Education Committee Minutes, 24/4/59, IPR 3/7/2).

In the late 1970s and early 1980s, IPR Education Committee members explored the possibilities for degree-level education with a number of educational institutions, largely in the then polytechnic sector. The International Public Relations Association (IPRA) produced two policy documents on education (Gold Papers 4 and 7) which reviewed the role and scope of public relations education in relation to the professionalization of the practice and made a number of specific recommendations in relation to the content and level of degree courses and the appropriate qualifications for those teaching the subject.

We shall concentrate our attention here on the second, more recent, of these papers. The main themes emerging can be summarized as concern over the academic and professional standards of those who teach public relations, the establishment and maintenance of independence from other disciplines, the role for practitioners in making contributions to education, the balance between academic and practical work, and the importance of education in contributing to the professionalization of the field. The paper presents a model which places public relations theory and practice as an academic subject at the centre of two concentric circles (the Wheel of Education) containing topics such as editing, research and advertising, which can be seen as developing relevant skills; and in the outer circle, a number of subjects, such as business administration, humanities, natural sciences and statistics, which could be drawn on to develop theoretical underpinnings for public relations and furnish future practitioners with knowledge rather than just skills. The model offers an enlightened view of what is required of a good public relations practitioner and a good educational programme; at the same time, it is revealing about the authors' perspective. We shall reflect on a few points which can be inferred from the model or which are directly stated in the paper itself, in order to provide an educational and academic response.

The main focus of the paper is on what is needed in terms of developing academic courses and research for public relations to be able to achieve the status of "more traditional professions" (IPRA, 1990, p. 5). There is no definition of what such a profession is, but the examples provided are law, medicine, and theology (lawyers, medics, and clergy). This is an interesting selection, revealing perhaps more about the aspirations of public relations than about the concept of profession or professionalism. The three professions chosen have traditionally been highly respectable middle-class occupations; entry to each of them has required formal academic qualification, and additional vocational training for lawyers and medics, in effect a period of often hard and exploitative apprenticeship. The nature of these professions is also of some interest here: in general terms, they seem to be concerned with correction and prevention of physiological, spiritual, or social malfunctions. The nature of the service these professions provide, and therefore the professionals' relationship with clients, puts the professionals in a position of power based either on the specialised knowledge possessed or the special social status accorded to the system of beliefs they represent (clergy). In brief, one does not normally tell the doctor or the lawyer how they should go about providing the service that is being paid for. Perhaps it is the aspiration to this kind of social position and relationship with the client that underlies some of the current ideas in public relations, such as the need, expressed in many definitions, to be counted as a management function (Grunig, 1992; White & Mazur, 1994; Cutlip et al., 1994); as a member of the dominant coalition (Grunig, 1992); or the organizational conscience.

More importantly perhaps from our own point of view, the paper is also very revealing about what the authors understand to be a sound methodology, how public relations theory is supposed to be built and, finally, how academics work. In terms of methodology the paper noted that:

> Insofar as public relations is concerned, "basic research" is of the type conducted by sociologists, psychologists and other social scientists ... research in the social sciences seldom produces the same kinds of definite statements of principle that are evolved in the "hard" sciences. (IPRA, 1990, p. 19)

The paper also recommended "that public relations be taught as an applied social science with academic and professional emphasis" (ibid., p. 13) and that there is a need in public relations for a balance between theory and the requirement of acting on "solid, empirically tested foundations and concepts" (ibid., p. 7). There are two obvious questions that must be asked at this point. If producing "definite statements" is not really possible for the social sciences, where are the "solid, empirically tested foundations" supposed to come from? If basic research for public relations is to be done by other disciplines, if public relations is to be "an applied social science", where is public relations theory supposed to come from? It appears that public relations aspires to the status of a social science, but at the same time is not ready to conduct basic research or accept that positivism is not the only worldview. This position, in our view, is symptomatic of a young discipline eager to graduate to long trousers and grow a moustache.

The IPRA paper speaks of "theory of public relations", thus assuming its existence. To date, it would seem more appropriate to speak of a theory—represented by the research effort of Professor Grunig and the "Excellence" team—and a growing body of empirical and critical research, as conducted by Broom, Dozier, Pearson, and White, to mention just a few prominent names. However, the use of theory to indicate a well-developed discipline combining a diversity of theories and approaches, such as communication studies, seems to be an aspiration rather than a factual statement.

The above inconsistencies or overgeneralizations could be attributed to the rather simplistic understanding of the academic environment. True, the authors admitted that education and consultancy require different skills, and that suitable teachers coming directly from the practice "will be exceptions", but in the same breath they talked about substituting "lengthy and appropriate years of experience for academic credentials" (ibid., p. 11). The move from consultancy to teaching and research is seen as unproblematic, based purely on consulting experience, and presumably intellectual ability combined with the acceptance of a likely salary cut. In fact, it represents a major career change: to become a professional academic one probably needs several years to become a fully trained and competent lecturer, catch up on reading in a number of disciplines in the case of public relations, and start producing and supervising research—all this on top of a normal routine of teaching, student counselling, and academic administration. To achieve this transition successfully requires at least high motivation on the part of the new recruit and a sympathetic academic environment.

The respect for public relations in academia which the paper calls for can only come from a sufficient body of academics performing the duties described above to standard academic performance indicators and, much more importantly, from a large volume of respectable published research. This, in turn, is facilitated by a culture which encourages research; in practical terms this means manageable teaching loads, senior colleagues sympathetic to the discipline, financial support to attend conferences, opportunity to tackle doctoral and postdoctoral research, a structure of appropriate academic appointments, and, of course, the infrastructure mentioned in the Gold Paper. How many of those teaching and researching public relations can claim to have such support? In reality it seems that many colleagues in the area are employed to teach lucrative undergraduate programmes with little thought being given to their academic development or the future of the discipline.

Differences between academics and practitioners with regard to the development of theory and research in public relations have already been debated in published research. Typical empirical studies of this nature include Terry's (1989) study of educator and practitioner differences on the role of theory in public relations and research into the gap between professional and research agendas in public relations journals (Broom et al., 1989). These studies clearly illustrate a major difference in interest, and in understanding of and use of research. In the early 1990s a study (White & Blamphin, 1994) was conducted in the United Kingdom to explore practitioner and academic perceptions in relation to the research agenda.

The Delphi study, carried out in May, June and July 1994, replicated a similar American study carried out in 1992 by Professor McElreath of Towson State University with the help of John Blamphin, who collaborated with Jon White on the British study. The report produced contains the following general summary:

> Among the Delphi group, most felt that the important research topics were those dealing with the scope of practice, the contribution public relations makes to strategic management, and measurement and evaluation of the practice. A number of people felt that the list was focused too much on the professional concerns of public relations practitioners, and further study was needed of management and client expectations. One academic commented on the list [of research topics generated] as one of subject headings rather than a true guide to research. The overriding conclusion at the Symposium [held in November 1994] was that there is a need for a translation service, or research digest, which would interpret findings from the social sciences so as to make them relevant for practitioners. (White & Blamphin, 1994, p. 4)

There was a fair degree of disagreement and a wide range of opinions were expressed by the participants both in the research paper and at a meeting held in November 1994 which one of the authors (Pieczka) attended. If one can at all generalize from the results presented, it would appear that people in public relations are searching for a confirmation of their professional identity (scope of practice, management and client expectations); of their status and perceptions of the practice (contribution to organizational strategy, evaluation, and client expectations); and of their own professionalism in terms of working on the basis of scientific findings.

Published literature has highlighted the different perspectives of educators and practitioners with regard to the role, scope, and content of public relations education. There appears to be some lack of clarity among some practitioners and some teachers regarding the distinction between education and training. Practitioners are naturally keen that relevant practical skills should be taught but often express doubts about the value of underpinning theory, as noted in the preceding section. Some practitioners (and even some academics) are uncomfortable with the notion that academics may adopt critical perspectives. The lack of critical work in public relations has already been noted:

> Considerably more work is needed to enhance our understanding of the "sociology" of public relations . . . the role of public relations in this process and the "manufacturing" of PR communications is an important area of future research . . . critical research has been virtually non-existent. (Pavlik, 1987, p. 123)

> Most critical researchers tend to be Marxist Europeans, with few Americans embracing the challenge to engage in a process that is by definition disruptive. Perhaps American public relations scholars, working to promote a positive image of public relations, find that challenge problematic. (Cottone, 1993, p. 169)

Practitioners are keen that those teaching public relations should not only already possess practical experience but also "continue to develop their professional experience while they hold teaching appointments" (IPRA, 1990, p. 11). Such comments reveal a lack of understanding not only of the educational role but also of the educational culture and the professional requirements and priorities for academics. Academic performance indicators in the United Kingdom consist of research, teaching and administration, and every academic is evaluated yearly against preset objectives; failure to achieve in any of these fields can result in the termination of an individual's contract. It perhaps has not been fully realized that educators and practitioners inhabit different cultures and attempts to maintain or impose public relations' occupational roles and norms within the academy are likely to be frustrated. Attempts by industry to dictate or control the research agenda may well be resisted once academics realize the potential threat to academic freedom and the subsequent loss of academic credibility within education. Too cosy a relationship between education and practice threatens the development of the academic discipline: "public relations is compromised when educators allow practitioners to view universities as production houses for business interests, rather than as entities that should engage in critical research" (Cottone, 1993, p. 173).

D. Morris (1994) found that there was a difference of opinion as to the role of the Institute of Public Relations and the extent to which it should lead educational developments. Whereas some expressed the view that education should reflect practice, a number of interviewees in her study thought it was important for a clear distinction to be made between academia and practice and that part of the educational role was to challenge and critique the practice. One academic was quoted as saying:

> It's up to academics to challenge the definitions set by the people who are practising public relations... we shouldn't have limitations in education... We're not here to produce clones, we're here to educate people... One of the things that industry has got wrong is thinking that we're a training school, because we're not, so there's bound to be a discrepancy, because if there weren't we'd be doing something wrong—we're not teaching to serve practice, we're educating and it's quite a different thing. (D. Morris, 1994)

Perhaps the appropriate metaphor for understanding the relationship between educator and practitioner is that of artist (practitioner) and critic (educator); both are expert but have to be judged on different criteria. Education goes beyond training, and to fulfil their role in academic life educators must move beyond the purely pragmatic.

Educators in the United Kingdom have been slow to cooperate with one another and to develop an agenda of their own. While a number of educators in the UK are tackling PhDs in public relations, many educators do not publish regularly in refereed articles in their chosen field. Public relations courses recruit well and academic institutions fully exploit their economic potential. Public relations courses often have high number of students and public relations lecturers often easy teaching loads that prohibit research activity. Morris found that most academics in the field had practical experience in public relations and commented that

> it is problematic that so few have postgraduate qualifications... without input from credible academics, public relations will not be accepted as an academic discipline, certainly not at postgraduate level. If public relations degrees are being taught by those who only have practical experience—no matter how extensive that experience may be—not only may public relations be ridiculed for the lack of faculty's "necessary academic requirements" (IPRA, 1990, p. 11) but research will suffer. A lack of public relations educators with PhDs means there is an absence of faculty qualified to supervise public relations students undertaking postgraduate study and PhDs. Thus, a lack of research will not facilitate growth of the body of knowledge. (D. Morris, 1994)

One aspect which does not appear to have received much attention in the literature is the appropriate role of practitioners in education. It is clearly very important for students to receive teaching from practitioners. Such sessions can be quite inspirational for students, as well as conveying invaluable practical information attractively packaged in anecdotal form. However, the nature of such presentations tends to be very different from academic lectures, and students need to be prepared for this so that they can get the most out of the experience; for them the practitioners themselves are as much an object of study as the content of the presentation. To give one example of the differences between academic and practitioner approaches, the IPRA Gold Paper (No. 7) specifically recommended "the use of guest lecturers . . . to keep professors updated on developments in areas such as case studies" (IPRA, 1990, p. 12).

Guest lecturers offer an invaluable link to the practice though their understanding and presentation of, for example, "case studies" is very different from that of an academic. For a practitioner, "case study" tends to mean "story" told as a narrative and usually ending with a moral. An academic understanding of "case study" is considerably more demanding methodologically, requiring demonstration of triangulation and explanation of the multiple methodologies applied.

The drive to professionalization evident in IPRA Gold Paper no. 7, and which has been referred to in this chapter, has led to educational developments but there is a long way to go before academic credibility and autonomy are achieved.

ACADEMIC DEBATES: DEVELOPMENT AND POSITIONING OF THE DISCIPLINE

Public relations in the United Kingdom has developed largely in the former polytechnic sector, which has traditionally specialized in more vocational and innovative courses. A Diploma in International Public Relations was set up in 1987 at Watford College, followed by a Master's degree in 1988 at a traditional university, Stirling, in Scotland (in 1991 the Stirling degree was made available via distance learning to meet the needs of practitioners). Undergraduate degrees followed in England at Bournemouth, the College of St Mark and St John (University of Exeter), and Leeds Business School. The College of St Mark and St John (University of Exeter) also participated in an innovative master's degree jointly with a number of European institutions. On this degree students from participating institutions study in a variety of languages and universities. By 1994 these courses had been added to by two more postgraduate qualifications, a degree in public relations at the new university Manchester Metropolitan and a diploma in journalism at the University of Wales.

As indicated earlier, little attention has been given to the educational scene in the United Kingdom in the existing literature. Hatfield's (1994) article was published several years after it was written and gives a journalistic overview mostly of practitioner views about what public relations education should consist of and achieve for its graduates. The article is interesting from a couple of points of view in the light of subsequent developments. It is quite noticeable that the American author has sought practitioner rather than academic perspectives. Ten practitioners were interviewed but the views of only one academic (Dr Jon White, then of Cranfield Institute of Technology, later Visiting Professor at City University) are represented. It is quite clear that the assumptions of the author and those she interviewed are that the role of education is to produce qualified people for industry: "The British public relations profession has recognized that through the development and support of a sound educational programme it can direct and shape its own future" (Hatfield, 1994, p. 198).

There is considerable emphasis on skills and the legitimation of public relations as a profession. In contrast to literature recording the American scene, there is no discussion or debate about the academic content or the location of courses as the appropriate home is presented as being business and management.

American academics Hazleton and Cutbirth (1993) also surveyed the European scene with a view to exploring educational paradigms. Much of what they said, however, relates to continental Europe only and not to the European Community in general. For example, British academics, like their American counterparts, are under extreme pressure to publish in refereed journals, especially since the introduction of governmental research exercises which review all departments and allocate funding according to research productivity. Another point of difference is that academics in Britain are not referred to as "Professor Doctor", nor are they accorded the respect accorded to continental Europeans. In terms of public relations education, the British model has tended to follow the American rather than the continental European model of education. This has led to an emphasis on skills and business education rather than the rigorously academic teaching which is available in countries such as Germany, Denmark, and the Netherlands. In continental Europe, as opposed to Britain, public relations is generally studied in departments of mass communication. In contrast to the situation in America, where public relations courses tend to be housed in Schools of Journalism, the majority of public relations courses in Britain are housed in business schools and departments of marketing or advertising. D. Morris (1994) argued that the placement of public relations courses in marketing and business departments was likely to inhibit, not facilitate, the professionalization process. Therefore, there seems to be a strong argument for placing public relations education in departments which facilitate an interdisciplinary style of teaching encompassing communications, media studies and cultural studies, management and organizational behaviour, and public relations theory and practice.

TOWARDS A RADICALIZATION
OF THE CURRICULUM

Public relations offers an opportunity for developing stimulating and broad curricula producing graduates with good skills and an understanding of a range of subjects from psychology, politics, sociology, and organizational behaviour to media and cultural studies. Public relations practitioners must be generalists and a wide-ranging curriculum helps to ensure that they are; it also has another educational aim in developing a habit of flexibility and a sensitivity to different ways of seeing the world, as different subjects bring their own conceptual frameworks and cultures. There are, however, also clear dangers: inviting a range of subject specialists to contribute to teaching may produce a fragmented and confusing course. It is therefore necessary for public relations educators to develop a required level of expertise in a number of subjects to ensure that the delivery of the curriculum does take public relations as the focal point.

Public relations courses are expected to produce graduates who can "hit the ground running", in other words, fit in smoothly into any public relations operation without Account Directors and Managers having to spend too much time on training or supervising junior staff. They are also expected to produce graduates with good analytical skills and capable of developing into seasoned "counsellors"; and, finally, public relations courses are where research is supposed to come from. All this should happen, well, preferably now. It seems that public relations has waited to become a "traditional profession" for so long that it is running out of patience. While this is understandable, the attitude also produces undesirable effects by pushing towards research agendas geared to instantaneous solutions and is responsible for some confusion as to what exactly a curriculum should do. While the opinions of practitioners are a valuable guide to many decisions that educators need to take in designing their courses, it is ultimately the professional educator who should be trusted with the task.

We suggest that a sensible course of action for academic institutions which offer public relations courses to take under these demanding circumstances is to start with educational aims rather than a checklist of techniques and applications suggested by the Gold Paper no. 7. The difference of approach can be best illustrated by an example. Let us imagine a situation where a pupil needs to be taught perfect table manners to last a lifetime in a rather short space of time. There are two approaches that could be taken. A simple way would be to compile a list, as comprehensive as one can make it or as comprehensive as one knows the pupil will need to be familiar with, of things to do and not to do. The time of instruction would be spent on making sure the pupil has memorized the rules, applies them appropriately, is familiar with all the types of implements and has rehearsed all the useful conversation topics to be tried on, for example, a young female stranger who is the hostess' cousin, or an old family friend who might be a lawyer or doctor. While pupils with a natural gift and better memory could do quite well, one can easily imagine the less confident ones getting the rules embarrassingly mixed up. An alternative is to leave all the three- and four-pronged forks till later and spend some time first of all talking about the history of table manners, the dynamics of a social interaction at a dinner party, food, maybe amuse the student with some well-chosen reading; and, having in this way mastered the "why", progress to the "how". No doubt the pupil would make mistakes, but at the same time would be much better prepared to deal with a wider range of problems and be confident in confronting completely unknown situations which might arise—for example, in different cultures.

A similar approach has influenced change in medical education in the United Kingdom. Although medical syllabuses have, of course, always differed between the various medical schools, traditionally students have been required to undergo an intensive course of factual learning. Now some medical schools are adopting an approach in which student work in small groups with a facilitator to focus on particular problems and analytical concepts. The idea underlying this approach is twofold: first, students will be required to carry out research in their chosen field from an early point in their career; and second, they will understand that their career will consist of continual research, updating, and problem-solving. Students may possess less factual knowledge when they qualify, but they will have been given the ability to think for themselves, conceptualize problems, and find things out for themselves. This represents a fundamental shift in educational practice from a system of intensive cramming of facts, many of which may be forgotten once finals are over, and where academic or conceptual learning is thought to be something which occurs between the ages of 18 and 25 or 26, to a system where it is clearly understood that the graduate may not know all procedures but has a greater capacity for identifying problems.

Curricula in medical schools in the UK are determined by individual universities; there is no attempt by the General Medical Council (GMC) to prescribe a list of skills that students must acquire beyond two or three core skills such as cardiopulmonary resuscitation and the ability to set up an intravenous line. Instead, the GMC make very broad recommendations which the universities consider and take into account as they revise and update educational aims, objectives, and curricula. GMC recommendations in the 1990, proposed moves away from departmentally focused teaching to integrative system-based teaching to facilitate the intellectual development of research, conceptual, and communication skills as discussed above.

Whatever approach one chooses in education, it can only succeed if the pupil is willing to trust the teacher's judgement and, as it were, willingly suspend disbelief. It is also to some extent a question of a pupil's personality. Some will be happy to engage with your way of teaching, even if the engagement is rebellious and demands proof every stage of the way;

some will take the attitude that they know what is needed and refuse to engage with what they perceive as academic rubbish. It is a perfectly reasonable reaction—the trouble is it is only reasonable on the basis of what the student knows at the time; consequently, the student, impatient to learn "useful stuff", limits his or her own potential for future development.

If public relations practice chooses to look up to medicine or law, it should also be prepared at least to tolerate the study of some seemingly non-practical subjects such as Roman law or Latin. This is not to say that choices made by educators about curriculum details should go unquestioned; but a more liberal attitude and an understanding that every graduate will still need on-the-job training would be a constructive and beneficial approach.

It is our view that public relations education should be integrated and interdisciplinary, taught by academics who can move comfortably between the traditional disciplines as they help students learn to see different perspectives and the varied implications of any particular situation. If this approach is taken, students can be encouraged to be curious, to play "devil's advocate", question received truths, and develop moral courage—all qualities they will need as public relations counsellors.

Public relations taught in an interdisciplinary way demands intellectual flexibility from academics and students. As such, it is a field in which there is the potential to deliver an excellent education regardless of whether its young graduates decide to pursue careers in public relations or not. It is a subject with opportunities to connect students with the challenging and important ideas which will confront them not only as public relations practitioners but also as citizens.

It is our view that the responsibility of academics in the field of public relations is to define and unpack concepts in use in practice and to identify the sources of ideas in order to reflect upon their significance to the world we inhabit. While it is the case that public relations has only recently become an area of study in Europe, it is not the case that the ideas underpinning it are unique and that the subject has to be invented from scratch. The educator's role is surely to bring to bear upon public relations ideas from moral philosophy, epistemology, philosophy of language, sociology, communications, and media studies, as well as from some of the more technical subjects such as psychology, management, and marketing. This we see as education's contribution to the process of the professionalization of public relations.

References

A Guide to the Practice of Public Relations. (1958). Institute of Public Relations. London: Newman Neame.

Abbott, A. (1988). *The system of the professions: An essay on the division of expert labor.* Chicago, London: University of Chicago Press.

Abbott, J. (1998). Tough times caring for the nurses. *Independent on Sunday*, 13 December, p. 15.

Abercrombie, N. H. S., & Turner, B. S. (1894). *Dictionary of sociology.* London: Penguin Books.

Abraham, L. (1999, August). Visual literacy in a multicultural environment: Integrating aesthetic with critical visual awareness. Paper presented to Association for Education in Journalism and Mass Communication conference, New Orleans.

Achrol, R. (1991). Evolution of the marketing organization: New forms for turbulent environments. *Journal of Marketing, 55*(4), 77–93.

Ackerman, B. (1980). *Social justice in the liberal state.* New Haven, CT: Yale University Press.

Ackoff, R. L. (1959). Games, decisions, and organizations. *General Systems 4*, 145–150.

Ackoff, R. L., & Emery, F. E. (1972). *On purposeful systems.* London: Tavistock Publications.

Ackroyd, S. (1992). Paradigms lost: paradise regained? In M. Reed & M. Hughes (Eds.), *Rethinking organization* (pp. 102–119). London: Sage.

Adams, T. (1999). *Addicted.* London: HarperCollinsWillow.

Adams, L., Amos, M., & Munro, J. (Eds.). (2002). *Promoting health: Politics & practice.* London, Sage.

adidas-Salomon. (2003). *Behind our brand: Social and environmental report 2002.* Retrieved 29 June, 2004, from http://www.adidas-salomon.com/en/sustainability/reports/default.asp.

adidas-Salomon. (2004). *Staying focused: Social and environmental report* 2003. Retrieved 29 June, 2004, from http://www.adidas-salomon.com/en/sustainability/reports/default.asp.

Ahlers, C. (1979). Öffentlichkeitsarbeit des Staates—Propaganda, Mitteilung, Dialog? In C. Ahlers, G. Baum, et al. (Eds.), *Der öffentliche Dienst und die Medien* (pp. 183–198). Bonn: Godesberger Tachenbuch-Verlag.

Aldrich, H. E. (1975). An organization-environment perspective on cooperation and conflict between organizations in the Manpower training system. In A. R. Negandhi (Ed.), *Interorganizational theory.* Kent, OH: Kent State University Press.

Aldrich, H. E. (1992). Incommensurable paradigms? Vital signs in three perspectives. In M. Reed & M. Hughes (Eds.), *Rethinking organization* (pp. 17–45). London: Sage.

Aldrich, H. E. (1999). *Organizations evolving.* Thousand Oaks, CA: Sage.

Allan, S., Adam, B., & Carter, C. (Eds.). (2000). *Environmental risks and the media.* London and New York: Routledge.

Allen, V. (1975). *Sociological analysis: A Marxist critique and alternative.* London: Longman.

Allern, S. (1997). *Når kildene byr opp til dans* /When news sources ask for a dance. Oslo: Pax Forlag.

Allport, F. (1954). Toward a science of public opinion. In D. Kate, D. Cartwright, S. Eldersveld, & A. McClung Lee (Eds.), *Public opinion and propaganda.* New York: Holt, Rinehart & Winston (originally published 1937, *Public Opinion Quarterly, 1*, 7–23).

Alvesson, M. (1993). Organizations as rhetoric: Knowledge intensive firms and the struggle with ambiguity. *Journal of Management Studies, 30*(6), 997–1015.

Anderson, A. (1991). Source strategies and the communication of environmental affairs. *Media, Culture & Society, 13*(4), 459–476.

Anderson, A. (1997). *Media, culture and the environment.* London: UCL Press.

Andrewes, A. (1986). *Greek society.* London: Penguin.

Andriof, J., Waddock, S., Husted, B., & Sutherland Rahman, S. (Eds.). (2002). *Unfolding stakeholder thinking, theory, responsibility and engagement.* Sheffield: Green Leaf Publishing Limited.

Anonymous. (1989). Making a mark is big business. *The Sunday Times*, 5 February.

Anthony, A. (2001, October 7). A hard act to follow. *Observer Sports Magazine*, p. 12.

Apostopoulos, Y., Leviadi, S., & Yiannakis, A. (1996). *The sociology of tourism: Theoretical and empirical investigations.* London: Routledge.

Arendt, H. (1968). The crisis in culture: Its social and political significance. In *Between past and future: Eight exercises in political thought* (pp. 197–226). New York: The Viking Press.

Argyris, C. (1964). *Integrating the individual and the organization.* New York: Wiley.

Aristophanes. (1972). *The Wasps.* London/Harmondsworth: Penguin.

Aristotle. (1991). *The art of rhetoric.* London/Harmondsworth: Penguin.

Arlt, H-J. (1998). *Kommunikation, Öffentlichkeit, Öffentlichkeitsarbeit. PR von gestern, PR für morgen—das Beispiel Gewerkschaft.* Opladen: Westdeutscher Verlag.

Asante, M. K., & Gudykunst, W. B. (Eds.). (1989). *Handbook of international and intercultural communication.* London: Sage.

Attwater, D. (Ed.). (1961). *A Catholic dictionary.* New York: Macmillan.

Atuahene-Gima, K., & Li, H. (2002). When does trust matter? Antecedents and contingent effects of supervisee trust on performance in selling new products in China and the United States. *Journal of Marketing, 66* (July), 61–81.

Baggott, R. (1995). *Pressure groups today.* Manchester, UK: Manchester University Press.

Baier, K. (1984). Duties to one's employer. In T. Regan (Ed.), *Just business: New introductory essays in business ethics* (pp. 60–99). New York: Random House.

Baker, K. (1990). *Inventing the French Revolution.* Cambridge, UK: Cambridge University Press.

Baker, S. (2000, March). The theoretical ground for public relations practice and ethics: A Koehnian analysis. Paper presented to Public Relations Society of America Educator's Academy Communication Sciences Division conference, Miami.

Bakhtin, M. M. (1981). *The dialogic imagination*, ed. M. Holquist (trans. C. Emerson & M. Holquist). Austin: University of Texas Press.

Bakhtin, M. M. (1984). Toward a reworking of the Dostoevsky book. (1961). In *Problems of Dostoevsky's poetics* (Ed. and trans. C. Emerson), *Theory and history of literature*, Vol. 8 (pp. 283–302). Minneapolis: University of Minnesota Press.

Bale, J., & Christensen, M. (2004). *Post-Olympism? Questioning sport in the twenty-first century.* Oxford: Berg.

Ball, P. (2001). *Morbo: The story of Spanish football.* London: WSC.

Banks, S. (2002). *Going down: Football in crisis*. Edinburgh and London: Mainstream.

Baran, P., & Sweezy, P. (1968). *Monopoly capita.* Harmondsworth, UK: Penguin.

Barbe, B. (1998). *Santiago Apostol: Semblanza biografica y Novena en su honor.* Barcelona: Grafiques, S.A.

Barker, E. (1984). *The making of a Moonie: Choice or brainwashing?* Oxford, UK: Blackwell.

Barker, Sir Ernest. (Ed.). (1966). *Social contract.* London: Oxford University Press.

Barnardo's (1996). 150th birthday of Thomas Barnardo. *The IPR Sword of Excellence Awards 1996*, Institute of Public Relations: London, pp. 29–32.

Barney, R. D., & Black, J. (1994). Ethics and professional persuasive communications. *Public Relations Review, 20*(3), 233–248.

Barnouw, E. (1974). *Documentary: A history of the non-fiction film.* New York: Oxford University Press.

Barsamian, D., & Chomsky, N. (2001). *Propaganda and the public mind.* London: Pluto Press.

Barthenheier, G. (1988). Public relations—Öffentlichkeitsarbeit heute —Funktionene, Tätigkeiten und berufliche Anforderungen. In G. Schulze-Fürstenow (Ed.), *PR-Perspektiven.* Neuwied: Luchterhand.

Barthes, R. (1977). *Image-music-text.* London: Fontana.

Bate, R. (Ed.). (1999). *What risk?* London: Butterworth-Heinemann.

Baudrillard, J. (1983). *In the shadow of the silent majorities.* New York: Semiotext.

Bauman, Z. (1997). *Postmodernity and its discontents.* Cambridge, UK: Polity Press.

Bazerman, C. (1993). A contention over the term "rhetoric". In T. Enos & S. C. Brown (Eds.), *Defining the new rhetorics* (pp. 3–7). London: Sage.

BBC News. (2003). Nike settles 'free speech' court case. BBC News UK Edition Web site, 13 September, 2003. Retrieved 29 June, 2004, from http://news.bbc.co.uk/go/pr/fr/-/1/hi/world/americas/3106930.stm.

Beauchamp, T. L., & Bowie, N. E. (Eds.). (1988). *Ethical theory and business.* Englewood Cliffs, NJ: Prentice-Hall.

Beck, U. (1992). *Risk society towards a new modernity.* London: Sage.

Beck, U. (1994). The reinvention of politics: Towards a theory of reflexive modernization. In U. Beck, A. Giddens, & S. Lash. *Reflexive modernization: Politics, tradition and aesthetics in modern social order* (pp. 1–55). Stanford, CA: Stanford University Press.

Beck, U. (1997). *The reinvention of politics—rethinking modernity in the global social order.* Cambridge, UK: Polity Press.

Beck, U., Giddens, A., & Lash, S. (1994). *Reflexive modernization: Politics, tradition and aesthetics in the modern social order.* Stanford, CA: Stanford University Press.

Becker, H. S., Greer, B., Hughes, E. C. and Strauss A. L. (1961). *Boys in white.* Chicago: University of Chicago Press.

Beckwith, B. (1999, December). Visiting the land where Jesus was born. *St. Anthony Messenger, 107*, 18–23.

Beder, S. (1997). *Global spin: The corporate assault on environmentalism.* Melbourne: Scribe Publications.

Beenstock, S. (1996, October 18). Under fire from all sides. *PR Week*, 16.

Beetham, D. (1994). Key principles and indices for a democratic audit. In D. Beetham (Ed.), *Defining and measuring democracy.* London: Sage.

Bell, D. (1974). *The coming of post-industrial society.* London: Heinemann.

Bell, E. (1986). The origins of British television documentary: The BBC 1946–1955. In J. Corner (Ed.), *Documentary and the mass media.* London: Edward Arnold.

Bell faces a baron future in Belgravia. (1998, August 14). *PR Week*, p. 32.

Bell tussles with Clifford in radio debate. (1996, January 12). *PR Week*.

Bell, Q. (1991). *The PR business.* London: Kogan Page.

Ben-Eli, M. U. (1981). Self-organization, autopoiesis and evolution. In M. Zeleny (Ed.), *Autopoiesis: A theory of living organization.* New York: North-Holland.

Beniger, J. (1987). Toward an old new paradigm: Half century flirtation with mass-communication. *Public Opinion Quarterly, 51*, S46–S66.

Bennett, L., & Manheim, R. (2001). The big spin, communication and the transformation of pluralist democracy. In L. Bennett & Entman (Eds.), *Mediated politics. Communication in the future of democracy.* Cambridge, UK: Cambridge University Press.

Bennett, P., & Calman, K. (Eds.). (1999). *Risk communication and public health.* Oxford, UK: Oxford University Press.

Bennie, L. G. (1998). Brent Spar, Atlantic oil and Greenpeace. *Parliamentary Affairs, 51*(3), 397–410.

Bentele, G. (1998). *Berufsfeld PR.* Berlin: PR Kolleg.

Bentele, G., & Wehmeier, S. (2003). From literary bureaus to a modern profession: The development and current structure of public relations in Germany. In D. Verčič & Sriramesh (Eds.), *The global public relations handbook. Theory, research and practice* (pp. 199–221). Mahwah, NJ: Lawrence Erlbaum Associates.

Bentley, J. *The Great Outdoors,* February 2005, p. 41.

Berelson, B. (1956). In L. White (Ed.) *The study of the social sciences.* Chicago: Chicago University Press.

Berelson, B., & Janowitz, M. (Eds.). (1966). *Reader in public opinion and communication* (2nd ed.). New York: Free Press; London: Collier Macmillan.

Bergmann, V. (1993). *Power and protest movements for change in Australian society.* St. Leonards: Allen and Unwin.

Bernays, E. (1923). *Crystallizing public opinion.* New York: Boni & Liveright.

Bernays, E. (1955). *The engineering of consent.* Norman: University of Oklahoma Press.

Bernays, E. L. (1965). *The biography of an idea: Memoirs of public relations counsel Edward L. Bernays.* New York: Simon & Schuster.

Bernstein, D. (1984). *Company image and reality.* Eastbourne: Holt, Rinehart & Winston/Advertising Association.

Bethell, A. (1998). Pleasure plus principle. *The Guardian* (part 2), 2 February, pp. 4–5.

Bettinghaus, E. P., & Cody, M. J. (1994). *Persuasive communication.* Orlando, FL: Harcourt Brace.

Bevan, S. (1996a, March 1). FD loses Randall back to Sunday Times. *PR Week,* 1.

Bevan, S. (1996b, January 12). Filling the PR vacuum at Tory central office. *PR Week,* 1.

Bevan, S. (1996c, February 16). IPR fires debate on position of financial PR. *PR Week,* 1.

Bevan, S. (1997a, May 9). Labour researcher takes BNFL public affairs role. *PR Week,* 2.

Bevan, S. (1997b, May 9). PR proves fast track to parliament. *PR Week,* 3.

Bevan, S. (1997c, February 21). Shandwick plays down Hogarth breakaway. *PR Week,* 1.

Beynon, H. (1973). *Working for Ford.* Harmondsworth, UK: Penguin/Allen Lane.

Binder, E. (1983). *Die Entstehung unternehmerischer Public Relations in der Bundesrepublik Deutschland.* Münster: University Dissertation.

Bingle, P. (1997, October 24). Comment: Why it's goodbye to lobbying, hello to public affairs. *PR Week,* 9.

Birch, D., & Glazebrook, M. (2000). Doing business—doing culture: Corporate citizenship and community. In S. Rees & S. Wright (Eds.), *Human rights, corporate responsibility: A dialogue* (pp. 41–52). Annandale, NSW: Pluto Press.

Birrell, S., & Cole, C. (Eds.). (1994). *Women, sport, and culture.* Leeds, UK: Human Kinetics.

Bivins, T. (1995). *Handbook for public relations writing.* Lincolnwood, IL: NTC Publishing Group.

Bizzell, P., & Herzberg, B. (1990). *The rhetorical tradition: Readings from classical times to the present.* Boston: Bedford.

Black, S. (1962, 1976). *Practical public relations.* London: Pitman.

Black, S. (1989). *Introduction to public relations.* London: Modino Press.

Black, S., & Sharpe, M. (1983). *Practical public relations: Common-sense guidelines for business and professional people.* Englewood Cliffs, NJ: Prentice-Hall.

Blau, P., & Scott, W. R. (1962). *Formal organizations.* San Francisco: Chandler.

Bliss, T. (2002). Citizen advocacy groups: corporate friend or foe?. In J. Andriof, S. Waddock, B. Husted & S. Sutherland Rahman (Eds.), Unfolding stakeholder thinking, theory, responsibility and engagement (pp. 251–265). Sheffield: Green Leaf Publishing Limited.

Blumer, H. (1948). Public opinion and public opinion polls. *American Sociological Review, 13,* 542–554.

Blumer, H. (1954). Public opinion and public opinion polls. In D. Katz, D. Cartwright, S. Eldersveld, & A. McClung Lee (Eds.), *Public opinion and propaganda.* New York: Holt, Rinehart & Winston. (Originally published 1948, *American Sociological Review*, *13*, 542–554).

Blumer, H. (1966). The mass, the public and public opinion. In B. Berelson (Ed). *Reader in public opinion and communication* (pp. 45–50). New York: Free Press.

Blumler, J., & Gurevitch, M. (1981). Politicians and the press. An essay on role relationships. In Nimmo, D. & Sanders, D. (Eds.), *Handbook of political communication.* London: Sage.

Blumler, J., & Gurevitch, M. (1995). *The crisis of public communication.* London: Sage.

Boadt, L. (2002, May 30). In the Old Testament. *The Florida Catholic*, p. A18.

Boggs, C. (1978). *Gramsci's Marxism.* London: Pluto Press.

Boorstin, D. (1961). *The image.* London: Weidenfeld & Nicolson.

Boorstin, D. (1962). *The image.* London: Weidenfeld & Nicolson.

Bostrom, A. (1997). Vaccine risk communication: Lessons from risk perception, decision making and environmental risk communication research. *Risk: Health, Safety & Environment* Vol. 8, available at http://www.fplc.edu/risk/vol8/spring/bostrom.htm.

Botan, C. (1992). International public relations: Critique and reformulation. *Public Relations Review*, *18*(2), 149–159.

Botan, C. H. (1989). Theory development in public relations. In C. H. Botan & V. Hazleton (Eds.), *Public relations theory* (pp. 99–110). Hillsdale, NJ: Lawrence Erlbaum Associates.

Botan, C. H. (1993). Introduction to the paradigm struggle in public relations. *Public Relations Review*, *19*(2), 107–110.

Botan, C. H., & Hazleton, V. (Eds.). (1989a). *Public relations theory.* Hillsdale, NJ: Lawrence Erlbaum Associates.

Botan, C. H., & Hazleton, V. (1989b). The role of theory in public relations. In C. H. Botan & V. Hazleton (Eds.), *Public relations theory* (pp. 3–16). Hillsdale, NJ: Lawrence Erlbaum Associates.

Bourdieu, P. (1979). Public opinion does not exist. In A. Mattelart & S. Siegelaub (Eds.), *Communication and class struggle.* New York: International General.

Bourdieu, P. (1989). *Distinction: A social critique of the judgement of taste.* London: Routledge.

Bourdieu, P. (1992). *The logic of practice* (trans. R. Nice). Cambridge, UK: Polity Press.

Bowden, G., McDonnell, I., Allen, J., & O'Toole, W. (2001). *Events management.* Butterworth-Heinemann.

Bower, T. (2003). *Broken dreams: Vanity, greed and souring of British football.* London: Simon and Schuster.

Bowman, P. (1988). Professional attitudes. In W. Howard (Ed.), *The practice of public relations* (3rd ed., pp. 238–248). Oxford, UK: Heinemann Professional Publishing.

Bowman, P., & Ellis, N. (1969). *The manual of public relations.* London: Heinemann.

Boyle, R. (2000). *Sports clubs or media corporations?* Paper presented at Clubs or public corporations: Management and social representations of sport in modern society. Institut d'Estudis Catalans, Barcelona, 13 April.

Boyle, R. (2004). Football and social responsibility in the New Scotland: The Case of Celtic. In Wagg, S. (Ed.). *Football and social exclusion* (pp. 186–204), London: Routledge.

Boyle, R., Dinan, W., & Morrow, S. (2002). Doing the business? The newspaper reporting of the business of football. *Journalism, 3*(2), 149–169.

Boyle, R., & Haynes, R. (2000). *Power play: Sport, the media and popular culture.* Harlow: Longman.

Boyle, R., & Haynes, R. (2002). *Football, new media and community in the digital age.* Paper presented at the International Association of Mass Communication Research (IAMCR), Media and Sport Working Group, Barcelona, 24 July.

Boyle, R., & Haynes, R. (2003). New media sport. In N. Blain & A. Bernstein (Eds.), *Sport in the media age.* London: Frank Cass.

Boyle, R., & Haynes, R. (2004). *Football in the new media age.* London: Routledge.

Braverman, H. (1974). *Labor and monopoly capital.* New York: Monthly Preview Press.

Breast Cancer Care (1998). Focusing on breast health. *The IPR Sword of Excellence Awards 1998,* Institute of Public Relations: London, pp. 33–36.

Brebner, J. H. (1949). *Public relations and publicity*. London: Institute of Public Administration.

Brendon, P. (1991). *Thomas Cook: 150 years of popular tourism*. London: Secker & Warburg.

Britton, S. (1982). The political economy of tourism in the third world. *Annals of Tourism Research, 9*, 33–58.

Brooker, W., & Jermyn, D. (2003). "It's out there ... somewhere": Locating the audience for the *Audience studies reader*. In W. Brooker & D. Jermyn (Eds.), *The audience studies reader* (pp. 1–11). London: Routledge.

Broom, G., Cox, M. S., Krueger, E. A., & Liebler, C. M. (1989). The gap between professional and research agendas in public relations journals. In J. E. Grunig & L. A. Grunig (Eds.), *Public Relations Research Annual*, vol. 1, (pp. 141–154). Hillsdale, NJ: Lawrence Erlbaum Associates.

Broom, G. M., Casey, S., & Ritchey, J. (2000). Concept and theory of organization-public relationships. In J. A. Ledingham & S. D. Bruning (Eds.), *Public relations as relationship management* (pp. 3–22). Mahwah, NJ: Lawrence Erlbaum Associates.

Broom, G. M., & Dozier, D. M. (1990). *Using research in public relations*. Englewood Cliffs, NJ: Prentice-Hall.

Brown, R. (2003). St Paul as a public relations practitioner: A metatheoretical speculation on messianic communication and symmetry. *Public Relations Review, 29*, 229–240.

Brownrigg, M., & Meech, P. (2002). From fanfair to funfair: The changing soundworld of UK television idents. *Popular Music, 21*(3), 345–355.

Bruning, S. (2000, March). Phases in organization-public relationships: Managing organization-public relationships in development and deterioration. Paper presented to Public Relations Society of America Educator's Academy Communication Sciences Division conference, Miami.

Bruning, S. (2002). Relationship building as a retention strategy: Linking relationship attitudes and satisfaction evaluations to behavioral outcomes. *Public Relations Review, 28*, 39–48.

Bruning, S., & Ledingham, J. (1998). Organizational-public relationships and consumer satisfaction: The role of relationships in the satisfaction mix. *Communication Research Reports, 15*, 199–209.

Bruning, S., & Ledingham, J. (1999). Relationships between organizations and publics: Development of a multi-dimensional organizational-public relationship scale. *Public Relations Review, 25*(2), 157–170.

Bruning, S., & Ledingham, J. (2000a). Organization and key public relationships: Testing the influence of the relationship dimensions in a business to business context. In J. Ledingham & S. Bruning (Eds.), *PR as relationship management: A relational approach to the study and practice of public relations* (pp. 159–173). Mahwah, NJ: Lawrence Erlbaum Associates.

Bruning, S., & Ledingham, J. (2000b). Perceptions of relationships and evaluations of satisfaction: An exploration of interaction. *Public Relations Review, 26*(1), 85–95.

Bruning, S. D., Langenhop, A., & Green, K. A. (2004). Examining city-resident relationships: Linking community relations, relationship building activities, and satisfaction evaluations. *Public Relations Review, 30*(3), 335–345.

Bruzzi, S. (2000). *New documentary: A critical introduction*. London and New York: Routledge.

Buccholz, R. A. (1989). *Business environment and public policy* (3rd ed.). Englewood Cliffs, NJ: Prentice-Hall.

Buckley, W. (1967). *Sociology and modern systems theory*. Englewood Cliffs, NJ: Prentice-Hall.

Buchmaster, M. (1953). *Specially Employed*. London: Batchworth Press.

Bull, H., & Watson, A. (1984). *The expansion of international society*. Oxford, UK: Oxford University Press.

Burgmann, V. (1993). *Power and protest movements for change in Australian society*. St. Leonards: Allen and Unwin.

Burkart, R. (1993a). *PR als Konfliktmanagement*. Wien: Braumüller.

Burkart, R. (1993b). Verständigungsorientierte Öffentlichkeitsarbeit. Ein Transformationsversuch der Theorie des kommunikativen Handelns. In G. Bentele & M. Rühl (Eds.), *Theorien öffentlicher Kommunikation* (pp. 218–227). München: Ölschläger.

Burkart, R. (1996). Verständigungsorientierte Öffentlichkeitsarbeit. Der Dialog als PR Konzeption. In G. Bentele, H. Steinmann, & A. Zerfaß (Eds.), *Dialogorientierte Öffentlichkeitsarbeit. Grundlagen, Praxiserfahrungen, Perspektiven* (pp. 245–271). Berlin: Vistas.

Burkart, R., & Probst, S. (1991). Verständigungsorientierte Öffentlichkeitsarbeit. Ein Transformationsversuch der Theorie des kommunikativen Handelns. *Publizistik, 30*(4), pp. 56–76.

Burke, K. (1957). *The philosophy of literary form.* New York: Vintage.

Burns, L. S. (2002). *Understanding journalism.* London: Sage.

Burrage, M. (1990). Introduction: the professions in sociology and history. In M. Burrage & R. Torstendahl (Eds.), *Professions in theory and history: Rethinking the study of the professions* (pp. 1–23). London: Sage.

Burrell, G., & Morgan, G. (1979). *Sociological paradigms and organisational analysis.* London: Heinemann.

Buß, E. (1992). Propaganda. *PR-Kolloquium,* Heft 4.

Buttle, F. (1996). Relationship marketing. In F. Buttle (Ed.), *Relationship marketing: Theory and practice* (pp. 1–16). London: Paul Chapman Publishing.

Cain, A. (1956). Editorial. *Public Relations, 8*(2), 1.

Caines and Rhys Jones in Queen's Birthday Honours. (1998, June 19). *PR Week.*

Cairnes, J. E. (1887). *Some leading principles of political economy newly expounded.* London: Macmillan.

Calhoun, C. (1992). Introduction: Habermas and the public sphere. In C. Calhoun (Ed.), *Habermas and the public sphere* (pp. 1–50). Cambridge, MA: MIT Press.

Calhoun, C. (Ed.). (1993). *Habermas and the public sphere.* Boston: MIT Press.

Campbell, D. (2002a). Spent forces. *The Observer Sports Monthly,* May, No. 25.

Campbell, D. (2002b). In a league of his own. *Football Business International,* June.

Campbell, V. (2000). You either believe it or you don't. . . : Television documentary and pseudo-science. In J. Izod & R. Kilborn (Eds.), *From Grierson to the docu-soap* (pp. 145–157). Luton: University of Luton Press.

Campbell, V. (2004). *Information age journalism: Journalism in an international context.* London: Arnold.

Campbell-Johnson, A. (1956). A consultant's point of view. *Public Relations, 8*(2), 53.

Canary, D. J., & Cupach, W. R. (1988). Relational and episodic characteristics associated with conflict tactics. *Journal of Social and Personal Relationships, 5,* 305–325.

Canary, D. J., & Stafford, L. (1992). Relational maintenance strategies and equity in marriage. *Communication Monographs, 59*(3), 243–267.

Caplow, T. (1954). *Sociology of work.* Minneapolis: University of Minnesota Press.

Cardwell, J. (1997). Career paths in public relations. In C. L. Caywood (Ed.), *The handbook of strategic public relations and integrated communications* (pp. 3–14). New York: McGraw-Hill.

Carey, C. (1994). Rhetorical means of persuasion. In I. Worthington (Ed.), *Persuasion: Greek rhetoric in action* (pp. 26–45). London: Routledge.

Carey, A. (1997). *Taking the risk out of democracy: Corporate propaganda versus freedom and liberty.* University of Illinois Press.

Carlson, R. (Ed.). (1975). *Communications and public opinion.* New York: Praeger.

CARMA. (1999). PR Week readers' attitudes to measuring and evaluating PR activity. Godalming, England: CARMA.

Carmichael, S., & Drummond, J. (1989). *Good business: A guide to corporate responsibility and business ethics.* London: Business Books, Century Hutchinson.

Carr-Saunders, A. M., & Wilson, P. A. (1933). *The professions.* Oxford: The Clarendon Press.

Carruthers, S. (1995). *Winning hearts and minds: British governments, the media, and colonial counterinsurgency, 1944–60.* Leicester, UK: Leicester University Press.

Cashmore, E. (1990). *Making sense of sports.* London: Routledge.

Castells, M. (1996). *The information age: Economy, society and culture: The rise of the network society.* Oxford: Blackwell.

Castells, M. (1997). *The information age: Economy, society and culture: The power of identity.* Oxford: Blackwell.

Castells, M. (1998). *The information age: Economy, society and culture: The end of the millennium.* Oxford: Blackwell.

Castells, M. (2001). *The Internet galaxy: Reflections on the Internet, business and society.* Oxford: Oxford University Press.

Catholic Online. (1999). Saint James the Greater. [Online: http://saints.catholic.org]. (Accessed November 17, 1999).

Cayward, C. L. (Ed.). (1997). *The Handbook of Strategic Public Relations and Integrated Communications.* New York McGraw. NY.

Center, A. H., & Jackson, (2003). *Public relations practices: Managerial case studies and problems.* Oxford, NJ: Prentice-Hall.

Cerny, P. (1990). *The changing architecture of politics: Structure, agency, and the future of the state.* London: Sage.

Certeau, M. (1984). The practice of everyday life. Berkeley: University of California Press.

Chadwick, R. (1994). Concepts, definitions and measures used in travel and tourism research. In J. R. Brent Ritchie & C. Goeldner (Eds.), *Travel, tourism and hospitality research: A handbook for managers and researchers* (2nd ed.). New York: Wiley.

Chaffee, S., & McLeod, J. (1968). Sensitization in panel design: A coorientation experiment. *Journalism Quarterly, 45,* 661–669.

Chajet, C. (1989). The making of a new corporate image. *Journal of Business Strategy,* (May/June), 18–20.

Chandiramani, R. (2004, July 1). Foresight hires Savage to boost new business. *PR Week UK.*

Charles Barker Lyons (1986). The Countryside Access Charter. *The IPR Sword of Excellence Awards 1986,* Institute of Public Relations: London, pp. xii–xiii.

Chemical Industries Association. (1987). Chemicals are good for you. *Public Relations: The Quarterly Journal of the Institute of Public Relations, 6*(1), 25–26.

Cheney, G., & Dioniopsoulos, G. N. (1989). Public relations? No, relations with publics: A rhetorical-organizational approach to contemporary corporate communications. In C. H. Botan & V. Hazleton (Eds.), *Public relations theory* (pp. 135–158). Hillsdale, NJ: Lawrence Erlbaum Associates.

Cheney, G., & Vibbert, S. L. (1987). Corporate discourse: Public relations and issues management. In F. Jablin et al. (Eds.), *Handbook of organizational communication* (pp. 165–196). London: Sage.

Childs, H. (1965). *Public opinion: Nature, formation, and role.* Princeton, J.N.: D. Van Nostrand Comp.

Child, R. D. (2004, April 24). 'The Atkins Diet: fact or fad' *Cycling Weekly,* p. 35.

Child, R. D. (2005, January 22). Cycling Weekly 'Eating for Performance', p. 39.

Chisman, F. (1976). *Attitude psychology and the study of public opinion.* University Park: Pennsylvania State University Press.

Choi, P. (2000). *Femininity and the physically active woman.* London: Routledge.

Christensen, L. T. (2002). Corporate communication: The challenge of transparency. *Corporate Communications: An International Journal, 7*(3), 162–168.

Cicourel, A. (1968). *The social organization of juvenile justice.* New York: Free Press.

Clark, C. E. (2000). Differences between public relations and corporate social responsibility: An analysis. *Public Relations Review, 26*(3), 363–380.

Clark, N. (2003). *Nancy Clark's sports nutrition guidebook* (3rd ed.). Champaign. IL: Human Kinetics.

Clarke, R. (2002). *The future of sports broadcasting rights: A SportsBusiness Report, Executive Summary.* London: SportsBusiness.

Clegg, S. (1975). *Power, rule and domination.* London: Routledge & Kegan Paul.

Clegg, S. (1990). *Modern organizations: Organization studies in the postmodern world.* London: Sage.

Clifford and responsibility. (2000, November 24). *PR Week UK.*

Coakley, J., & Donnelly, P. (Eds.). (1999). *Inside sports.* London: Routledge.

Coakley, J., & Dunning, E. (2002). *Handbook of sports studies.* London: Sage.

Coalter, F. (1999). Sport and recreation in the United Kingdom: Flow with the flow or buck the trends? *Managing Leisure, 4,* 24–39.

Cobb, R., & Elder, C. (1972). *Participation in American politics: The dynamics of agenda-building.* Baltimore: Johns Hopkins University Press.

Cockerell, M. (1988). *Live from number 10.* London: Faber.

Cockerell, M., Hennessey, P., & Walker, D. (1984). *Sources close to the Prime Minister.* London: Macmillan.

Cohen, B. (1963). *The press and foreign policy.* Princeton, NJ: Princeton University Press.

Cohen, D. (1994). Classical rhetoric and modern theories of discourse. In I. Worthington (Ed.), *Persuasion: Greek rhetoric in action* (pp. 69–84). London: Routledge.

Cohen, J., & Stewart, I. (2002). *Evolving the alien: The science of extraterrestrial life.* London: Ebury Press.

Cole, W. R. (1996). The decline of dissent? *DOX: Documentary Film Quarterly, 10* (Winter), 16–18.

Collison, D. (n.d). Corporate propaganda: Its implications for accounting and accountability. Unpublished paper, Department of Accountancy and Business Finance, University of Dundee, Scotland.

Death of Eric Stenton (1979, March). *Communicator,* p. 8.

Concello de Santiago Departamento de Turismo. (1994). *Santiago de Compostela.* Santiago de Compostela: Concello de Santiago Departamento de Turismo.

Conn, D. (1998). *The football business: Fair game in the 90s.* Edinburgh and London: Mainstream.

Connor, T. (2002). *We are not machines,* Oxfam Community Aid Abroad. Retrieved 29 June, 2004, from http://www.caa.org.au/campaigns/nike/reports/machines/

Converse, P. (1964). The nature of belief systems in mass publics. In D. Apter (Ed.), *Ideology and discontent.* New York: Free Press.

Converse, P. (1987). Changing conceptions of public opinion in the political process. *Public Opinion Quarterly, 51,* S12–S24.

Cook, T. (1989). *Making laws and making news. Media strategies in the US House of Representatives.* Washington, DC: The Brookings Institution.

Coombes, P., & Watson, M. (2001). Corporate reform in the developing world. *McKinsey Quarterly Special Edition, 4,* 89–92.

Coombs, W. T. (2001). Interpersonal communication and public relations. In R. Heath (Ed.), *Handbook of public relations* (pp. 105–114). London: Sage.

Cooper, R., & Burrell, G. (1988). Modernism, postmodernism and organizational analysis: an introduction. *Organization Studies, 9*(1), 91–112.

Corbett. E. P. J. (1965). *Classical rhetoric for the modern student.* New York: Oxford University Press.

Cornelius quits *Independent* to return to Citigate. (1999, April 2). *PR Week,* p. 1.

Corner, J. (1996). *The art of record: A critical introduction to documentary,* Manchester: Manchester University Press.

Corner, J. (2000). What can we say about "documentary"? *Media, Culture & Society, 22,* 681–688.

Cottone, L. P. (1993). The perturbing worldview of chaos: Implications for public relations. *Public Relations Review, 19*(2), 167–177.

Coup de Frejac, J. (1999, October). Action, trends and transitions in international public relations. Speech presented to the Public Relations Society of America, Anaheim.

Cowlett, M. (2001, January 26). Total R & E. *PR Week UK.*

Cowlett, M., & Nicholas, K. (1999, March 12). The Proof Survey. *PR Week.*

Coyle, J. (2004, April 18). Flattery will get you everywhere. *The Observer.*

Cracknell, J. (1993). Issue arenas, pressure groups and environmental agendas. In A. Hansen (Ed.), *The mass media and environmental affairs* (pp. 3–21). Leicester: Leicester University Press.

Craib, I. (1992). *Modern social theory from Parsons to Habermas.* Hemel Hempstead: Harvester Wheatsheaf.

Creswell, J. W. (2003). Research design: Qualitative, quantitative, and mixed methods approaches. Thousand Oaks, CA: Sage.

Crick, M. (2002). *The boss: The many sides of Alex Ferguson.* London: Simon & Shuster.

Cropp, F., & Pincus, J. D. (2001). The mystery of public relations: Unraveling its past, unmasking its future. In R. L. Heath (Ed.), *Handbook of public relations* (pp. 189–204). London: Sage.

Crowe and Bell launch industry evaluation plan. (1996, July 12). *PR Week,* p. 7.

Cruz, J. (1984). *Relics.* Huntington, IN: Our Sunday Visitor.

Csikszentmihalyi, M. (1992). *The psychology of happiness.* Rider.

Culbertson, H., & Chen, N. (1997). Communitarianism: A foundation for communication symmetry. *Public Relations Quarterly, 42*(2), 36–41.

Culbertson, H. M., & Jeffers, D. W. (1992). Social, political, and economic contexts: Keys in educating the true public relations professionals. *Public Relations Review, 18*(1), 53–67.

Curran, J. (1991). Mass media and democracy: A reappraisal. In J. Curran & M. Gurevitch (Eds.), *Mass media and society* (pp. 82–117). London: Edward Arnold.

Currie, M. (1998). *Postmodern narrative theory*. Basingstoke: Palgrave.

Curry, S. (2002, August 14). Becks bites back. *Daily Mail*, p. 78.

Curtin, P., & Boynton, L. (2001). Ethics in public relations: Theory and practice. In R. Heath (Ed.), *Handbook of public relations* (pp. 411–421). Thousand Oaks; London: Sage.

Cusick, J. (1994, February 13). Golfers suffer trauma of TV. *Independent on Sunday*, p. 7.

Cutlip, S. M. (1994). *The unseen power: Public relations. A history*. Hillsdale, NJ: Lawrence Erlbaum Associates.

Cutlip, S. M. (1995). *Public relations history: From the 17th to the 20th century*. Hillsdale, NJ: Lawrence Erlbaum Associates.

Cutlip, S., Center, A., & Broom, G. (1985). *Effective public relations* (6th ed.). Englewood Cliffs, NJ: Prentice-Hall.

Cutlip, S. M., Center, A. H., & Broom, G. M. (1994). *Effective public relations* (7th ed.). London: Prentice-Hall.

Cutlip, S., Center, A., & Broom, G. (2000). *Effective public relations* (8th ed.). Upper Saddle River, NJ: Prentice-Hall.

Dahl, R. (1998). *On democracy*. New Haven, CT: Yale University Press.

Dalrymple, W. (1992, August). Pilgrimage to Galicia. *Conde Nast*, 104–122.

Dalton, R. (1988). *Citizen politics in Western democracies*. Chatham, NJ: Chatham House Publishers.

Daniel J Edelman Ltd. (1987). Face the facts; freeze the tax. *Public Relations: The Quarterly Journal of the Institute of Public Relations, 6*(1), 17–19.

Darby, I. (1997, October 31). Public relations people stand up to be counted. *PR Week*, 1.

Darby, I. (1998, June 19). PR agencies face fines under FSA draft code. *PR Week*, 1.

Darwin, C., & Burrows, J. W. (Eds.). (1982). *The origin of species: Or the preservation of favoured races in the struggle for life*. London: Penguin Books.

Davis, A. (2002). *Public relations democracy: Public relations, politics and the mass media in Britain*. Manchester, UK: Manchester University Press.

Davis, J. (1992, August 6). Notoriety, money and the Max factor. *Daily Mail*.

Davison, W. P. (1987). A story of the POQ's fifty-year odyssey. *Public Opinion Quarterly, 51*, S4–S11.

Dawkins, R. (1989). *The selfish gene*. New York: Oxford University Press.

Dawkins, R. (1998). *Unweaving the rainbow*. London: Penguin.

Day, K., Dong, Q., & Robins, C. (2001). Public relations ethics: An overview and discussion of issues for the 21st century. In R. Heath (Ed.), *Handbook of public relations* (pp. 403–409). Thousand Oaks, CA: Sage.

Daymon, C. (2000). On considering the meaning of managed communication: Or why employees resist "excellent" communication. *Journal of Communication Management, 4*(3), 240–252.

De Cremer, D., & Dewitte, S. (2002). Effects of trust and accountability in mixed-motive situations. *Journal of Social Psychology, 2003, 142*(4), 541–543.

De George, R. T. (Ed.). (1978). *Ethics, free enterprise and public policy: Original essays on moral issues in business*. New York: Oxford University Press.

De George, R. T. (1983). The social business of business. In W. L. Robison, M. S. Pritchard, & J. Ellin (Eds.), *Profits and professions*. Clifton, NJ: Humana Press.

De Winter, R. (2001). The anti-sweatshop movement: Constructing corporate moral agency in the global apparel industry. *Ethics and International Affairs, 15*(2), 99–115.

Deal, T., & Kennedy, A. (1982). *Corporate cultures*. Reading, MA: Addison- Wesley.

Deetz, S. (1992). *Democracy in an age of corporate colonization*. New York: State University of New York Press.

Deetz, S. (1995). *Transforming communication, transforming business*. Cresskill, NJ: Hampton Press.

DeLorme, D., & Fedler, F. (2003). Journalists' hostility toward public relations: An historical analysis. *Public Relations Review, 29*, 99–124.

Denzin, N. K., & Lincoln, Y. S. (Eds.). (1994). *Handbook of qualitative reserch*. Thousand Oaks, CA: Sage.

Department of Culture, Media and Sport. (2001). *Creative industries mapping document.*

Department of Trade and Industry and Institute of Public Relations. (2003). *Unlocking the potential of public relations: Developing good practice.* London: DTI, IPR.

Der Derian, J. (1987). *On diplomacy: A genealogy of western estrangement.* Oxford, UK: Blackwell.

Derber, C. (Ed.). (1982). *Professionals as workers: Mental labor in advanced capitalism.* Boston: G.K. Hall.

Derrida, J. (1973). *Speech and phenomena.* Evanston, IL: Northwestern University Press.

Derriman, J. (1964). *Public relations in business management.* London: University of London Press.

Deutsch, K. (1963). Nation-building and national development: Some issues for political research. In K. Deutsch & W. Foltz (Eds.), *Nation-building* (pp. 1–16). New York: Atherton.

Deutsch, K. (1966). *Nationalism and social communication.* Cambridge, MA: MIT Press.

Dewe Rogerson (1985). British Telecom flotation. *The IPR Sword of Excellence Awards 1985,* Institute of Public Relations: London, pp. 13–14.

Dewe Rogerson (1997). The Deutsche Telekom IPO. *The IPR Sword of Excellence Awards 1997,* Institute of Public Relations: London, pp. 10–13.

Dewey, J. (1927). *The public and its problems.* Denver: Swallow.

Diageo (1998). Merger communication at Grand Metropolitan and Guinness. *The IPR Sword of Excellence Awards 1998,* Institute of Public Relations: London, pp. 5–8.

Dickie, R., & Rouner, L. (1986). *Corporations and the common good.* Notre Dame, IN: University of Notre Dame Press.

Dingwall, R. (1983). Introduction. In R. Dingwall & P. Lewis (Eds.), *The sociology of the professions* (pp. 1–13). New York: Macmillan.

Donelan, M. (1992). *Elements of international political theory.* Oxford, UK: Oxford University Press Clarendon Paperbacks.

Don't ditch PR in the hour of need. (1997, June 13). *PR Week.* p. 9.

Doob, L. (1966). *Public opinion and propaganda.* Hamden, CT: Archon.

Doob, L. W. (1997 [1950]). Goebbels' principles of propaganda. In R. Jackall (Ed.), *Propaganda* (pp. 190–216). New York: New York University Press.

Dorer, J. (1997). Die Bedeutung der PR Kampagnen für den öffentlichen Diskurs. Ein theoretischer Ansatz. In U. Röttger (Ed.), *PR-Kampagnen. Über die Inszenierung von Öffentlichkeit* (pp. 55–72). Opladen: Westdeutscher Verlag.

Dornan, C. (1990). Some problems in conceptualising the issue of "science and the media". *Critical Studies in Mass communication,* 7(1), 48–71.

Dowman, R. (1996a, August 23). PR praise and Labour brickbats for Lord Gummer. *PR Week,* 1.

Dowman, R. (1996b, April 12). Westminster strategy gains Bercow expertise. *PR Week,* 4.

Dowman, R. (1997, January 17). Clifford claim triumph despite industry critics. *PR Week.*

Dowman, R., & Bevan, S. (1996, April 19). Popiolek departs from FD as Lloyd joins. *PR Week,* 1.

Dozier, D. M. (1995). *Manager's guide to excellence in public relations and communication management.* Hillsdale, NJ: Lawrence Erlbaum Associates.

Dozier, D. M., & Lauzen, M. M. (2000). Liberating the intellectual domain from the practice: Public relations, activism and the role of the scholar. *Journal of Public Relations Research,* 12(1), 3–22.

DPRG e.V. (1958). Satzung. Köln.

Drake, S. (1957). *Discoveries and opinions of Galileo.* New York: Anchor Books.

Drijvers, J. (1992). Community broadcasting: A manifesto for the media policy of small European countries. *Media, Culture and Society,* 14, 193–202.

Drucker, P. (1989). *The new realities.* Oxford: Heinemann Professional Publishing.

Drumright, M. E., & Murphy, P. (2001). Corporate social marketing. In P. N. Bloom & G. T. Gundlach (Eds.), *Handbook of marketing and society* (pp. 162–183). Thousand Oaks; London: Sage.

Duck, S. (1984). Social and personal relationships. In M. L. Knapp & G. R. Miller (Eds.), *Handbook of interpersonal communication* (pp. 655–686). Beverly Hills, CA: Sage.

Duffield, C. (2000). Multinational corporations and workers' rights. In S. Rees & S. Wright (Eds.), *Human rights, corporate responsibility: A dialogue* (pp. 191–209). Annandale, NSW: Pluto Press.

Dunn, M., & Davidson, L. (1994). *The pilgrimage to Santiago de Compostela: A comprehensive, annotated bibliography*. New York: Garland.

Dunn, M., & Davidson, L. (Eds.). (1996). *The pilgrimage to Compostela in the Middle Ages*. New York: Garland.

Durkheim, E. (1933). *The division of labor in society* (G. Simpson, Trans.). New York: Free Press.

Edelman PR Network. (1991). Tobacco tax and tobacco retailer. *Public Relations: Journal of the Institute of Public Relations, 10*(2), 15–17.

Ehling, W. (1992). Public relations education and professionalism. In J. Grunig (Ed.), *Excellence in public relations and communications management* (pp. 439–466). Hillsdale, NJ: Lawrence Erlbaum Associates.

Ehling, W., Grunig, J., & White, J. (1992). Public relations and marketing practices. In J. Grunig (Ed.), *Excellence in public relations and communications management* (pp. 357–394). Hillsdale, NJ: Lawrence Erlbaum Associates.

Ehling, W. P. (1984). Application of decision theory in the construction of a theory of public relations 1. *Public Relations Research and Education, 1*(2), 25–39.

Ehling, W. P. (1985). Application of decision theory in the construction of a theory of public relations II. *Public Relations Research and Education, 2*(1), 4–22.

Ehling, W. P. (1992). Estimating the value of public relations and communication to an organization. In J. E. Grunig, D. M. Dozier, W. P. Ehling, L. A. Grunig, F. C. Repper, & J. White (Eds.), *Excellence in public relations and communication management* (p. 622). Hillsdale, NJ: Lawrence Erlbaum Associates.

Ehling, W. P. (1992). Public relations education and professionalism. In J. E. Gruning (Ed.), *Excellence in public relations and communication management* (pp. 439–363). Hillsdale, NJ: Lawrence Erlbaum Associates.

Eight men in serach of answer. (1953). *Public Relations, 6*(1), 11–20.

Eldridge, J., & Crombie, A. (1974). *A sociology of organisations*. London: George Allen & Unwin.

Eldridge, J., Kitzinger, J., & Williams, K. (1997). *The mass media and power in modern Britain*. Oxford, UK: Oxford University Press.

Elliott, P. (1972). *The sociology of the professions*. New York: Herder and Herder.

Ellis, J. (2000). *John Grierson: Life, contributions, influence*. Carbondale and Edwardsville: Southern Illinois University Press.

Ellis, N., & Bowman, P. (1963). *The handbook of public relations*. London: George Harrap & Co.

Ellul, J. 1962(1966). *Propaganda*. New York: Knopf.

Emery, F., & Trist, E. (1946). Socio-technical systems. In C. Churchman & Verhulst (Eds.), *Management science, models and techniques, vol. 2*. London: Pergamon.

Enos, T., & Brown, S. (Eds.). (1993). *Defining the new rhetorics*. London: Sage.

Entman, R. (1993). Framing: Toward clarification of a fractured paradigm. *Journal of Communication, 43*(4), 51–58.

Ericson, R. et al. (1989). *Negotiating control. A study of news sources*. Milton Keynes/London: Open University Press.

Etzioni, A. (1964). *Modern organizations*. Englewood Cliffs, NJ: Prentice-Hall.

Etzioni, A. (1969). *The semi-professions and their organization: Teachers, nurses and social workers*. New York: Free Press.

Etzioni, A. (1998). Introduction. In A. Etzioni (Ed.), *The essential communitari an reader*. Lanham, MD: Rowman & Littlefield.

Eusebius. (1981). *The history of the Church* (trans. G. Williamson). New York: Penguin. (Original work published c. 324).

Evaluating the strength of PR. (1996, July 5). *PR Week*, p. 9.

Evans, N., Campbell, D., & Stonehouse, G. (2003). *Strategic management for travel and tourism*. London: Butterworth-Heinemann.

Everett, I. The ecological paradigm in public relations theory and practice. *Public Relations Review, 19*(2), 177–185.

Ewen, S. (1976). *Captains of consciousness. Advertising and the social role of the consumer culture*. New York: McGraw-Hill.

Ewen, S. (1996). *PR! A social history of spin*. New York: Basic Books.

Ewing, R. P. (1990). Moving from micro to macro issues management. *Public Relations Review* (Spring), 19–24.

ExxonMobil. (2004). *2003 corporate citizenship report: Summary*. Retrieved 29 June, 2004, from http://www.exxonmobil.com/corporate/Citizenship/Corp_citizenship_report_archive.asp.

Fairchild, M. (1998, September 4). Letter: Seize the momentum to evaluate PR. *PR Week*, 9.

Fairclough, N. (1989). *Language and power.* London and New York: Longman.

Fairclough, N. (1992). *Discourse and social change.* Oxford, UK: Polity Press.

Fairclough, N. (1995). *Critical discourse analysis: The critical study of language.* London and New York: Longman.

Fairclough, N. (2001). The dialectics of discourse. *Textus, 14*(2), 231–242.

Falb, R. (1992). The place of public relations education in higher education: Another opinion. *Public Relations Review, 18*(1), 91–97.

Farish, S. (1996a, August 23). Editorial: Gummer earns himself the recognition of his peers. *PR Week*, 3.

Farish, S. (1996b, October 18). Gummer: PR of the realm. *PR Week*, 10–11.

Faulkner, B. (2001). Towards a framework for tourism disaster management. *Tourism Management, 22*(2), 135–147.

Faulstich, W. (1992). *Grundwissen Öffentlichkeitsarbeit: kritische Einführung in Problemfelder der Public Relations.* Bardowick: Wissenschaftlicher Verlag.

Fawkes, J. (2001). Public relations and communications. In A. Theaker (Ed.), *The public relations handbook* (pp. 13–23). London: Routledge.

Fawkes, J., Fielden, S., & Tench, R. (2001). *Freelancing in the communications and events industries.* Leeds Metropolitan University, UMIST.

Fedler., F., & Smith, R. (1992). Faculty members in ad/PR perceive discrimination in academia. *Public Relations Review, 18*(1), 79–91.

Feifer, M. (1985). *Going places.* London: Macmillan.

Feld, S., & Jorg, N. (1991). Corporate liability and manslaughter: Should we be going Dutch? *Criminal Law Review* (March), 50.

Ferguson, M. (1984, August). *Building theory in public relations: Interorganizational relationships.* Paper presented at the annual convention of the Association for Education in Journalism and Mass Communication, Gainesville, Florida.

Ferris, T. (1999). Interstellar spaceflight: Can we travel to other stars? *Scientific American Presents, 10*(1), 88–91.

Financial Services Authority. (2004). FSA Web site. http://www.fsa.gov.uk/history/ [Accessed 24 May 2004].

First Forum 8(4). (1995). Special issue on corporate social responsibility.

Fishburn Hedges (1996). Divorce: A fair deal for families. *The IPR Sword of Excellence Awards 1996,* Institute of Public Relations: London, pp. 5–8.

Fisher, G. (1989). Diplomacy. In M. Asante & W. Gudykunst (Eds.), *Handbook of international and intercultural communication* (pp. 407–422). London: Sage.

Fisher, R., & Brown, S. (1988). *Getting together: Building a relationship that gets to yes.* Boston: Houghton Mifflin.

Fisher, R., & Ury, W. (1991). *Getting to yes.* New York: Random House Business Books.

Fishman, M. (1980). *Manufacturing the news.* Austin: University of Texas Press.

Fiske, J. (1993). *Introduction to communication studies.* London: Routledge.

Fitzpatrick, L. (2004). The small pool: How can we identify the next generation of internal communication specialists? *Profile, 46,* November/December, 19.

Florini, A. (1998). The end of secrecy. *Foreign Policy,* Summer, 50–63.

Football Business International. (2002). Harverson unites PR role. June.

Foley, K. (2004). *History of women's PR group,* M.Sc. dissertation, University of Stirling.

Fores, M., Glover, I., & Lawrence, P. (1991). Professionalism and rationality: A study in misapprehension. *Sociology, 25,* 79–100.

Foucault, M. (1972). *The archaeology of knowledge.* London: Routledge.

Foucault, M. (1977a). *Language, counter-memory, practice*. Ithaca, NY: Cornell University Press.

Foucault, M. (1977b). *Discipline and punish: The birth of the prison*. London: Allen Lane.

Foucault, M. (1978). *The history of sexuality*, vol. 1: An Introduction, (trans., Robert Hurley). Harmondsworth: Penguin.

Foucault, M. (1980). *Power/knowledge*. Brighton: Harvester Press.

Foucault, M. (2000). The ethics of the concern for the self as a practice of freedom. In P. Rabinow (Ed.), *Ethics: Subjectivity and truth* (trans. R. Hurley et al.), *Essential works of Foucault 1954–1984*, vol. 1 (pp. 281–301). London: Penguin.

Foucault, N. (1980). *Power/knowledge: Selected interviews and other writings 1972–1977*. New York: Pantheon.

Fowles, J. (1996). *Advertising and popular culture*. London: Sage.

Fox, T., Balmer, J., & Wilson, A. (2001) *Corporate identity management: Applying the ACID Test*. www.crmuk.co.uk/downloads/ACID01.pdf.

Fox, J. A., and Zawitz, M. W. (1999) Homicide trends in the united States, Bureau of Justice Statistics, accessed 1/10/2002, at [http://www.ojp.usdoj.gov/bjs/homicide/homtrnd.htm]

France, S. (1998, April 24). Driving hard for one formula. *PR Week*, 12–13.

Franklin, A. (2003). *Tourism: An introduction*. London: Sage.

Franklin, B. (1994). *Packaging politics. Political communications in Britain's media democracy*. London: Edward Arnold.

Franklin, B. (1997). *Newzak and news media*. London: Arnold.

Franklin, B. (2003). "A good day to bury bad news?": Journalists, sources and the packaging of politics. In S. Cottle (Ed), *News, public relations and power* (pp. 45–61). London: Sage.

Franklin, J. (Ed.). (1998). *The politics of risk society*. Cambridge, UK: Polity Press.

Fraser, N. (1989). *Unruly practices: Power, discourse and gender in contemporary social theory*. Minneapolis: University of Minneapolis Press.

Freedman, G. (2003, September 25). Profile: Colin Byrne, Weber Shandwick—Though but loyal Byrne takes control at WS. *PR Week UK*.

Freidson, E. (1970a). *Medical dominance: The social structure of medical care*. Chicago: Aldine-Atherton.

Freidson, E. (1970b). *Profession of medicine*. New York: Harper & Row.

French, P. A. (1979). The corporation as a moral person. *American Philosophical Quarterly, 16*(3).

Freidson, E. (1986). *Professional powers: A study of the instutionalization of formal knowledge*. Chicago, London: University of Chicago Press.

Freidson, E. (1994). *Professionalism reborn: Theory, prophecy and policy*. Cambridge: Polity Press.

Frey, N. (1998). *Pilgrim stories: On and off the road to Santiago*. Berkeley: University of California Press.

Friedman, M. (1970, September 13). The social responsibility of business is to increase its profits. *New York Times Magazine*.

Friedman, M. (1993). The social responsibility of business is to increase its profits. In G. D. Chryssides & J. H. Kaler (Eds.), *An introduction to business ethics* (pp. 249–253). London/Glasgow: Chapman & Hall.

Friedman, S. M. (1994). The media, risk assessment and numbers: They don't add up. *Risk: Health, Safety & Environment*, Vol. 5, at http://www.fplc.edu/risk/vol5/summer/friedman.htm.

Fynn, A., & Guest, L. (1999). *For love or money: Manchester United and England—the business of winning*. London: Andre Deutsch.

Gagarin, M. (1994). Probability and persuasion: Plato and early Greek rhetoric. In I. Worthington (Ed.), *Persuasion: Greek rhetoric in action* (pp. 46–68). London: Routledge.

Galitzine, Y. (1960). The philosophy of public relation. *Public Relations, 12*(4), 49–55.

Gandy, O. (1982). *Beyond agenda-setting. Information subsidies and public policies*. Norwood, NJ: Ablex.

Gans, H. J. (1979). *Deciding what's news*. New York: Pantheon.

Garnett, A. A. (1951). That definition [Letter to the editor]. *Public Relations, 3*(3), 16.

Garnham, N. (1986). The media and the public sphere. In P. Golding, G. Murdock, & P. Schlesinger (Eds.), *Communicating politics: Mass communications and the political process* (pp. 37–54). Leicester: Leicester University Press.

Garside, J. (1997a, October 10). Labouring under the illusion of strategy. *PR Week*, 7.

Garside, J. (1997b, August 22). Piper quits the Mail on Sunday to take director role at Citigate. *PR Week*, 1.

Garside, J. (1997c, Juky 11). Report says Greer "not guilty" of cash for questions. *PR Week*, 1.

Garside, J. (1997d, August 8). Shandwick banks on international results. *PR Week*, 7.

Garside, J. (1998, April 3). General election hits Bell Pottinger profit margins. *PR Week*, 3.

Gauntlet, D. (1995). *Moving experiences: Understanding television's influences and effects.* London: John Libbey.

Gergen, K. J. (1992). Organisation theory in the postmodern era. In M. Reed & M. Hughes (Eds.), *Rethinking organization* (pp. 207–226). London: Sage.

Gharajedaghi, J., & Ackoff, R. (1994). Mechanisms, organisms and social systems. In H. Tsoukas (Ed.), *New thinking in organizational behaviour* (pp. 25–39). Oxford, UK: Butterworth-Heinemann.

Gibson, O. (2002). Shooting from the lip. New Media, *The Guardian*, 2 September.

Giddens, A. (1991). *Modernity and self-identity: Self and society in the late modern age.* Cambridge, UK: Polity Press.

Gillard, D. (1996, January 13–19). Making a song and dance. *Radio Times*, 18–20.

Gillman, F. C. (1978). Public relations in the United Kingdom prior to 1948. *International Public Relations Review* (April), 43–50.

Gilovich, T. (1991). *How we know what isn't so: The fallibility of human reason in everyday life.* New York: Free Press.

Gitlin, T. (1980). *The whole world is watching.* Berkeley: University of Californa Press.

Glaesser, D. (2003). *Crisis management in the tourism industry.* London: Butterworth-Heinemann.

Glasser, B. (1999). *The culture of fear: Why Americans are afraid of the wrong things.* New York: Basic Books.

Glaxo Smith Kline Annual Report. (2003).

Glover, J. (1970). *Responsibility.* London: Routledge & Kegan Paul.

Goddard, L. (1996, May 24). Biggest splash in the PR pond. *PR Week.*

Golding, P., & Murdock, G. (1991). Culture, communications, and political economy. In J. Curran & M. Gurevitch (Eds), *Mass media and society*, (pp. 15–32). London: Edward Arnold.

Golding, P., Murdock, G., & Schlesinger, P. (Eds.). (1986). *Communicating politics: Mass communications and the political process.* Leicester: Leicester University Press.

Goldman, R. (1992). *Reading ads socially.* London and New York: Routledge.

Goldman, R., & Papson, S. (1998). *Nike culture.* London: Sage.

Goldstein, T. C. (2003). *Nike v Kasky* and the definition of "commercial speech". *Cato Supreme Court Review*, 63–79. Retrieved 29 June, 2004, from http://www.cato.org/pubs/scr2003/commercialspeech.pdf.

Gonstedt, A. (1997). The role of research in public relations strategy and planning. In C. L. Caywood (Ed.), *The handbook of strategic public relations and integrated communications* (pp. 34–59). New York: McGraw-Hill.

Gorb, P. (1992). The psychology of corporate identity. *European Management Journal, 10*(3), 310–314.

Gore-Booth, L. (1978). *Satow's guide to diplomatic practice* (5th ed.). London: Longman.

Gormly, E. (1999). The study of religion and the education of journalists. *Journalism & Mass Communication Educator, 54*(2), 24–39.

Gouldner, A. (1959). Organizational analysis. In R. K. Merton, L. Broom, & L. S. Cottrell (Eds.), *Sociology today.* New York: Basic Books.

Gouldner, A. (1960). The norm of reciprocity: A preliminary statement. *American Sociological Review, 25*, 161–178.

Graef, R. (1993). Inside story of a fight for survival. *The Times*, 17 February, 30.

Graham, B. (2000a, April). *Letter.* Minneapolis: Billy Graham Evangelistic Association.

Graham, B. (2000b, July). *Letter.* Minneapolis: Billy Graham Evangelistic Association.

Grahame, E. (2002, August 1). *Ewing Grahame reflects on an undignified saga.* The Herald [Glasgow], p. 33.

Gramsci, A. (1971). *Selections from the prison notebooks of Antonio Gramsci* (trans. Q. Hoare & G. Nowell Smith). New York: International Publishers.

Grant, C. (1991). Friedman fallacies. *Journal of Business Ethics, 10*, 907–917.

Grant, M. (1994). *Propaganda and the role of the state in inter-war Britain.* Oxford Claverdon Press.

Grant, W. (1995). *Pressure groups, politics and democracy in Britain* (2nd ed.). London: Phillip Allan.

Gratton, C., & Taylor, P. (2000). *Economics of sport and recreation.* London: Spon Press.

Gray, R. (1996a, June 28). Bonham-Carter wins the Liberal Democrat PR vote. *PR Week*, 1.

Gray, R. (1996b, March 22). Planning to deliver a painless pitch process. *PR Week*, 7.

Gray, R. (1996c, April 4). PR people fall prey to the lure of Parliament. *PR Week, 7.*

Gray, R. (1997, August 22). New RO prompt for PR to sort out regulation. *PR Week*, 7.

Gray, R. (1998, October 30). Fighting to rebuild a tattered image. *PR Week*, 13– 16.

Greene, K., & Garside, J. (1998, November 13). IPR rejects calls for tighter City PR regulation. *PR Week*, 1.

Greenwood, M. R. (2001). *Community as a stakeholder in corporate social and environmental reporting.* Monash University, Caulfield, Australia.

Grierson, J. (1941). Education and the New Order. Winnipeg. John Grierson Archive, University of Stirling G4:19:1, p. 1.

Grierson, J. (1943). The necessity and nature of public information. (Delivered at the annual meeting of the American Informational Association in Montreal 3 June, 1943). John Grierson Archive, University of Stirling, G4:20:13.

Grierson, J. (undated) Art in action. John Grierson Archive, University of Stirling, G4:21:4.

Grierson, J. (1944). The film in international relations. 21 November, 1944. John Grierson Archive, University of Stirling, G4:20:22.

Grierson, J. (1943). Propaganda and education. 15 November, 1943. John Grierson Archive, University of Stirling, G4:19:5.

Grierson, J. (1945). The changing face of propaganda. January 1945. John Grierson Archive, University of Stirling, G4A:3:2.

Grierson, J. (1946/1966). *Grierson on documentary*, London: Faber.

Grierson, J. The film industry's public relations in war and peace. *Variety* 38th Anniversary number, Wednesday January 5, 1944. John Grierson Archive, University of Stirling G4:34:26.

Grierson, J. Propaganda: A problem for educational theory and for cinema. *Sight and Sound*, Winter 1933–34, p. 119. John Grierson Archive, University of Stirling G3A:5:1.

Grönroos, C. (1994). From marketing mix to relationship marketing. *Management Decision, 32*(1), 4–20.

Grönroos, C. (2000). Relationship marketing: The Nordic perspective. In J. N. Sheth & A. Parvatiyar (Eds.), *Handbook of relationship marketing* (pp. 95–118). Thousand Oaks, CA: Sage.

Groom, A., & Light, M. (Eds.). (1994). *Contemporary international relations: A guide to theory.* London: Pinter.

Gross, H. (1951). *Moderne Meinungspflege.* Düsseldorf: Droste-Verlag.

Groth, O. (1948). *Die Geschichte der Deutschen Zeitungswissenschaft.* München: Weinmayer.

Grunig, J. (1989). Symmetrical presuppositions as a framework for public relations theory. In C. Botan & V. Hazleton (Eds.), *Public relations theory* (pp. 17–44). Hillsdale, NJ: Lawrence Erlbaum Associates.

Grunig, J. (1993a). Public relations and international affairs: Effects, ethics and responsibility. *Journal of International Affairs, 47*(1), 137–162.

Grunig, J. (1993b). Image and substance: From symbolic to behavioral relationships. *Public Relations Review, 19*(2), 121–139.

Grunig, J. (1997). A situational theory of publics: Conceptual history, recent challenges and new research. In D. Moss et al. (Eds.), *Public relations research: An international perspective* (pp. 3–48). London: Thompson.

Grunig, J. (2001). Two-way symmetrical public relations: Past, present and future. In R. L. Heath (Ed.), *Handbook of public relations* (pp. 11–30). London: Sage.

Grunig, J., & Grunig, L. (Eds.). (1989). *Public Relations Research Annual*, vol. 1. Hillsdale, NJ: Lawrence Erlbaum Associates.

Grunig. J., & Grunig, L. (1990). Models of public relations: A review and reconceptualization. Association of Education in Journalism and Mass Communication (AEJMC).

Grunig, J., & Hunt, T. (1984). *Managing public relations.* New York: Holt, Rinehart & Winston.

Grunig, J. E. (1989). Symmetrical presuppositions as a framework for public relations theory. In C. Botan & V. Hazelton (Eds.), *Public relations theory* (pp. 17–44). Hillsdale, NJ: Lawrence Erlbaum Associates.

Grunig, J. E. (1990). Theory and practice of interactive media relations. *Public Relations Quarterly, 35*(3), 18–23.

Grunig, J. E. (1992). Communication, public relations and effective organizations: An overview of the book. In J. E. Grunig et al. (Eds.), *Excellence in public relations and communications management* (pp. 1–28). Hillsdale, NJ: Lawrence Erlbaum Associates.

Grunig, J. E. (2000). Collectivism, collaboration, and societal corporatism as core professional values in public relations. *Journal of Public Relations Research, 12*(1), 23–48.

Grunig, J. E., (Ed.). (1992). *Excellence in public relations and communication management.* Hillsdale, NJ: Lawrence Erlbaum Associates.

Grunig, J. E., & Grunig, L. A. (1992). Models of public relations and communication. In J. E. Grunig (Ed.), *Excellence in public relations and communications management* (pp. 285–325). Hillsdale, NJ: Lawrence Erlbaum Associates.

Grunig, J. E., & Grunig, L. A. (1998). Does evaluation of PR measure the real value of PR? Jim & Laui Grunig's Research. Insert of *PR Reporter, 41*(35), 4.

Grunig, J. E., Grunig, L. A., & Verčič, D. (1998). Are the IABC's excellence principles generic? Comparing Slovenia and the United States, the United Kingdom and Canada. *Journal of Communication Management, 2*, 335–356.

Grunig, J. E., & Huang, Y. (2000). From organization effectiveness to relationship indicators: Antecedents of relationships, public relations strategies, and relationship outcomes. In J. A. Ledingham & S. D. Bruning (Eds.), *Public relations as relationship management: A relational approach to the study and practice of public relations* (pp. 23–53). Hillsdale, NJ: Lawrence Erlbaum Associates.

Grunig, J. E., & White, J. (1992). The effect of worldviews in public relations theory and practice. In J. E. Grunig (Ed.), *Excellence in public relations and communication management* (pp. 31–64). Hillsdale and Hove: Lawrence Erlbaum Associates.

Grunig, L. A. (2000). Public relations research: A tripartite model. *Corporate Communications, 5*(2), 75–80.

Grunig, L. A., Grunig, J. E., & Ehling, W. P. (1992). What is an effective organization? In J. E. Grunig et al. (Eds.), *Excellence in public relations and communications management* (pp. 65–90). Hillsdale, NJ: Lawrence Erlbaum Associates.

Grunig, L., Grunig, J., & Dozier, D. (2002). Activism and the environment. In L. Grunig, J. Grunig & D. Dozier, *Excellent public relations and effective organizations: A study of communication management in three countries* (pp. 442–479). Mahwah, NJ: Lawrence Erlbaum Associates.

Gudykunst, W. B. (1995). Anxiety/uncertainty management (AUM) theory. In R. L. Wiseman (Ed.), *Intercultural communication theory* (pp. 8–58). Thousand Oaks, CA: Sage.

Guinness plc (1997). Guinness Awards for Pub Theatre. *The IPR Sword of Excellence Awards 1997*, Institute of Public Relations: London, pp. 43–46.

Gummer adopts new title for "very active" role in the House of Lords. (1996, October 18). *PR Week*, p. 1.

Gunter, B., Kinderlerer, J., & Beyleveld, D. (1999). The media and public understanding of biotechnology. *Science Communication, 20*(4), 373–394.

Gwyn, R. (2002). *Communicating health and illness.* London: Sage.

Habermas, J. (1976). *Legitimation crisis* (trans. T. McCarthy). London: Heinemann.

Habermas, J. (1979). The public sphere (FRG, 1964). In A. Mattelart and S. Siegelaub (Eds.), *Communication and class struggle* (Vol. 1, pp. 198–201). New York: International General.

Habermas, J. (1984). *The theory of communicative action 1: Reason and the rationalization of society.* Boston: Beacon Press.

Habermas, J. (1987). *The theory of communicative action* (trans. T. McCarthy) (Vol. 2). Cambridge, UK: Polity Press.

Habermas, J. (1988a). *Theorie des kommunikativen Handelns.* Band 1. Frankfurt a.M.: Suhrkamp.

Habermas, J. (1988b). *Theorie des kommunikativen Handelns.* Band 2. Frankfurt a.M.: Suhrkamp.

Habermas, J. (1989a). *The structural transformation of the public sphere: An inquiry into a category of bourgeois society* (trans. T. Burger with the assistance of F. Lawrence). Cambridge, UK: Polity Press.

Habermas, J. (1989b). *The structural transformation of the public sphere: An inquiry into a category of bourgeois society*. Cambridge, MA: MIT Press.

Habermas, J. (1996). *Between facts and norms: Contributions to a discourse theory of law and democracy* (trans. W. Rehg). Cambridge, MA: MIT Press.

Habermas, J., & Luhmann, N. (1971). *Theorie der Gesellschaft oder Sozialtechnologie*. Frankfurt a.M.: Suhrkamp.

Hage, J. (1980). *Theories of organizations: Form, process, and transformation*. New York: Wiley.

Hager, N., & Burton, B. (1999). *Secrets and lies: The anatomy of an anti-environmental PR campaign*. Nelson, NZ: Craig Potton.

Hainsworth, B. E. (1990). The distribution of advantages and disadvantages. *Public Relations Review* (Spring), 33–39.

Hall, S. et al. (1978/1993). Policing the crisis. Mugging, the state, and law and order. London: Macmillan.

Hall, S. (1988). *The hard road to renewal. Thatcherism and the crisis of the Left*. London: Verso.

Hall, S., Critcher, C., Jefferson, T., Clarke, J., & Robert, B. (1978/1993). *Policing the crisis. Mugging, the state, and law and order*. London: Macmillan.

Hallahan, K. (1993). The paradigm struggle and public relations practice. *Public Relations Review, 19*(2), 197–205.

Hallahan, K. (2000). Inactive publics: The forgotten publics in public relations. *Public Relations Review, 26*(4), 499–515.

Hallin, D. (1986). *The uncensored war*. Oxford UK: Oxford University Press.

Halloran, S. M. (1993). Further thoughts on the end of rhetoric. In T. Enos & S. C. Brown (Eds.), *Defining the new rhetorics* (pp. 109–119). London: Sage.

Hamel, J., Dufour, S., & Fortin, D. (1993). *Case study methods*. Newbury Park, CA: Sage.

Hamil, S., Michie, J., & Oughton, C. (Eds.). (1999). *The business of football: A game of two halves?* Edinburgh and London: Mainstream.

Hamil, S., Michie, J., Oughton, C., & Warby, S. (Eds.). (2000). *Football in the digital age: Whose game is it anyway?* Edinburgh and London: Mainstream.

Hamilton, K., & Langhorne, R. (1995). *The practice of diplomacy: Its evolution, theory and administration*. London: Routledge.

Hamilton, P. (1998). Learning to apply the appropriate PR pressure. *PR Week*, 3 July, 11.

Hamlett, A. (1998, March 6). Don't leave your pitch ideas open to thieves. *PR Week*, 9.

Hammarberg, T. (2001). Searching the truth: The need to monitor human rights with relevant and reliable means. *Statistical Journal of the UN Economic Commission for Europe, 18*(2/3), 131–141.

Handy, C. (1987). *The future of work*. Oxford, UK: Blackwell.

Handy, C. (1989). *The age of unreason*. London: Business Books.

Hansen, A. (1994). Journalistic practices and science reporting in the British press. *Public Understanding of Science, 3*(2), 111–134.

Harcup, T. (2004). *Journalism: Principles and practice*. London: Sage.

Hardy, F. (Ed.). (1966). *Grierson on documentary*. London and Boston: Faber & Faber.

Hargreaves, J. (2000). *Heroines of sport: The politics of difference and identity*. London: Routledge.

Harkner, R., Makar, C., & Wilkes, C. (1990). *An introduction to the work of Pierre Bourdieu: The practice of theory*. London: Macmillan.

Harlow, R. (1976). Building a public relations definition. *Public Relations Review 2*(4), 34–42.

Harrington, M. (1978). Corporate collectivism: A system of social justice. In R. T. De George & J. A. Pilcher (Eds.), *Ethics, free enterprise and public policy: Original essays and moral issues in business*. New York: Oxford University Press.

Harris, R. (1991). *Good and faithful servant*. London: Faber.

Hart, N. A. (Ed.). (1995). *Strategic public relations*. London: Macmillan Business.

Hart, R. (1987). *The sound of leadership: Presidential communication in the modern age*. Chicago: University of Chicago Press.

"Harrerson units PR role". (2002, June). *Football Business International*, p. 38.

Hassard, J. (1993). Postmodernism and organizational analysis. In J. Hassard & M. Parker (Eds.), *Postmodernism and organizations*. Newbury Park, CA: Sage.

Hassard, J., & Parker, M. (Eds.). (1993). *Postmodernism and organizations*. London/ Newbury Park/New Delhi: Sage.

Hatch, M. J., & Schultz, M. (2000). Scaling the Tower of Babel: Relational differences between identity, image and culture in organizations. In M. Schultz, M. J. Hatch, & M. Holten Larsen (Eds.), *The expressive organisation* (pp. 11–35). Oxford, UK: Oxford University Press.

Hatfield, C. R. (1994). Public relations education in the United Kingdom. *Public Relations Review, 20*(2), 189–199.

Haynes, R. (1996). *The football amagination: The rise of football fanzine culture*. Aldershot: Arena.

Hayward, R. (1990). *All about public relations* (2nd ed.). London: McGraw-Hill.

Hazleton, V., & Cutbirth, C. (1993). Public relations in Europe: An alternative educational program. *Public Relations Review, 19*(2), 187–197.

Heath, R. (1992). The wrangle in the marketplace: A rhetorical perspective of public relations. In E. Toth & R. Heath (Eds.), *Rhetorical and critical approaches to public relations* (pp. 17–36). Hillsdale, NJ: Lawrence Erlbaum Associates.

Heath, R. (1993). A rhetorical approach to zones of meaning and organizational prerogatives. *Public Relations Review, 19*(3), 141–157.

Heath, R. (1997). *Strategic issues management*. Thousand Oaks, CA: Sage.

Heath, R. (2001a). A rhetorical enactment rationale for public relations. In R. Heath (Ed.), *Handbook of public relations* (pp. 31–50). Thousand Oaks: Sage.

Heath, R. (2001b). Shifting foundations: Public relations as relationship building. In R. Heath (Ed.). *Handbook of public relations* (pp. 1–9). Thousand Oaks, CA: Sage.

Heath, R. (2001c). The dynamics of change in public relations practice. In R. Heath (Ed.). *Handbook of public relations* (pp. 183–188). Thousand Oaks, CA: Sage.

Heath, R. (Ed.). (2001b). *Handbook of public relations*. Thousand Oaks: Sage.

Heath, R., & Cousino, K. (1990). Issues management: End of first decade progress report. *Public Relations Review* (Spring), 6–18.

Heath, R., & Nelson, R. (1986). *Issues management: Corporate public policymaking in an information society*. London: Sage.

Heath, R., & Ryan, M. (1989). Public relations' role in defining corporate social responsibility. *Journal of Mass Media Ethics, 4*(1), 21–38.

Heath, R. L. (1997). *Strategic issues management organizations and public policy challenges*. London: Sage.

Heath, R. L. (2000). A rhetorical perspective on the values of public relations: Crossroads and pathways towards concurrence. *Journal of Public Relations Research, 12*(1), 69–91.

Heath, R. L., & Bryant, J. (1992). *Human communication theory and research: Concepts, contexts and challenges*. Hillsdale, NJ: Lawrence Erlbaum Associates.

Heltzer, M. (1999). *The dream job: Sports publicity, promotion and marketing*. Athens, OH: University Sports Press.

Hendrix, J. A. (2001). *Public relations cases*. Belmont, CA: Wadsworth Thomson Learning.

Henry, I., & Theodoraki, E. (2000). 'Management, Organization and Theory in the Governance of Sport. In Coakley. J. S. Dunning E. (Eds.). *Handbook of sports studies*, (pp. 490–503). London: Sage.

Herbst, S. (1993). The meaning of public opinion: Citizens' constructions of political reality. *Media, Culture and Society, 15*, 437–454.

Herbst, S. (1998). *Reading public opinion. How political actors view the democratic process*. Chicago: University of Chicago Press.

Hermansson, J. et al. (1999). *Avkorporativisering och lobbyism*/De-corporatism and lobbyism. Stockholm: Liber (SOU 1999: 121).

Hess, A. (1950). Conference speeches. *Public Relations, 3*(2), 5.

Heywood, A. (1992). *Political ideologies: An introduction*. New York: St. Martin's Press.

Hibberd, M., R. Kilborn, B. McNair, S. Marriott, & P. Schlesinger (2000). *Consenting Adults?*, London: Broadcasting Standards Commission.

Hickson, D. J. & Thomas, M. W. (1969). Professionalisation in Britain: A preliminary measurement. *Sociology 3*, 37–53.

Hiebert, R. E. (1966). *Courtier to the crowd: The story of Ivy Lee and the development of public relations*. Ames: Iowa State University Press.

Hiebert, R. E. (Ed.). (1988). *Precision public relations*. London: Longman.

Hiebert, R. E. (2003). Public relations and propaganda in framing the Iraq war: A preliminary review. *Public Relations Review, 29*, 243–255.

Higham, C. (1920). *Looking forward*. London: Nisbet.

Hill, C., & Beshoff, P. (Eds.). (1994a). *Two worlds of international relations*. London: Routledge.

Hill, C., & Beshoff, P. (1994b). The two worlds: Natural partnership or necessary distance? In C. Hill & P. Beshoff (Eds.), *Two worlds of international relations* (pp. 211–225). London: Routledge.

Hirst, P., & Zeitlin, J. (1991). Flexible specialisation versus post-Fordism. *Economy and Society, 20*(1), 1–56.

Ho, S. S. M., & Wong, K. S. (2001). A study of corporate disclosure practice and effectiveness in Hong Kong. *Journal of International Financial Management and Accounting, 12*(1), 75–103.

Hobbes, T. (1974). *Leviathan*. Glasgow: Collins/Fontana.

Hoffman, M. (1985). Normative approaches. In M. Light & A. Groom (Eds.), *International relations: A handbook of current theory* (pp. 27–44). London: Pinter.

Hoffman, M. (1994). Normative international theory: Approaches and issues. In A. J. R. Groom & M. Light (Eds.), *Contemporary international relations: A guide to theory*. London: Pinter.

Hoffman, W., & Moore, J. (1990). *Business ethics: Readings and cases in corporate morality*. New York: McGraw-Hill.

Hofstede, G. (2001). *Culture's consequences: Comparing values, behaviours, institutions and organizations across nations*. Thousand Oaks, CA: Sage.

Hollinger, R. (1994). *Postmodernism and the social sciences*. London: Sage.

Hollingsworth M., (1991). *MPs for hire*. London: Bloomsbury.

Holmberg, S., & Weibull, L. (1998). Opinionssamhället. In *Opinions–Samhället*/The Opinion Society. Göteborgs universitet: The SOM Institute.

Holtzhausen, D. R. (2000). Postmodern values in public relations. *Journal of Public Relations Research, 12*(1), 93–114.

Holtzhausen, D., & Voto, R. (2002). Resistance from the margins: The postmodern public relations practitioner as organizational activist. *Journal of Public Relations Research, 14*(1), 57–82.

Holz, S. (1998). *Public relations on the Net*. New York: AMACON.

Homans, G. C. (1950). *The human group*. New York: Harcourt, Brace & World.

Hon, L., & Grunig, J. (1999). *Guidelines for measuring relationships in public relations*. [Online] Available: http://www.instituteforpr.com/pdf/1999_guide_measure_relationships.pdf [Accessed 29 August 2005]

Hon, L. C., & Grunig, J. E. (1999). *Guidelines for measuring relationships in public relations*. Paper presented to the Institute for Public Relations, Gainesville, FL [online]. Available at URL: http//: www.instituteforpr.com [accessed October 2001]. http://ReclaimDemocracy.org/nike/ nyt_nikesettles. html http://www.caa.org.au/campaigns/nike/reports/machines/ http://www.nike.com/nikebiz/news/ pressrelease.jhtml?year=2003&month=09&letter=f http://www.thebodyshop.com/web/tbsgl/images/ tbs_employee_stakeholder_survey_2000.pdf.

Honeth, A., & Hans, J. (Eds.). (1991). *Essays on Jurgen Habermas' The theory of communicative action* (trans. J. Gaines & D. Jones). London: Policy Press.

Horne, J., Tomlinson, A., & Whannel, G. (1999). *Understanding sport: An introduction to the sociological and cultural analysis of sport*. London: Spon Press.

Horner, S. (2004). *International cases in tourism management*. London: Elsevier, Butterworth Heinemann.

Horrie, C. (2002). *Premiership: Lifting the lid on a national obsession*. London: Pocket Books.

Horsman, M. (1997). *Sky high: The rise and rise of BSkyB*. London: Orion Business Books.

Hornby, L. (1958). 'It's purpose and function'. In institute of public relations. *A guide to the practice of public relations*. London: Newman Neame.

Houlihan, B., & White, A. (2002). *The politics of sports development: Development of sport or development through sport?*, London: Routledge.

Howard, W. (Ed.). (1988). *The practice of public relations*. London: Heinemann.

Howe, E. (1967, 1972). *Astrology and psychological warfare during World War II*. London: Rider & Co.

Huang, Y. (2001a). Values of public relations: Effects on organization-public relationships mediating conflict resolution. *Journal of Public Relations Research, 13*(4), 265–301.

Huang, Y. (2001b). OPRA: A cross-cultural, multiple-item scale for measuring organization-public relationships. *Journal of Public Relations Research, 13*(1), 61–90.

Hughes, E. C. (1958). *Men and their work*. New York: Free Press.

Hughes, E. C. (1971). *The sociological eye: Selected papers*. Chicago: Aldine.

Hume, D. (1980). *A treatise of human nature*. Oxford, UK: Oxford University Press.

Hundhausen, C. (1937). Public relations. *Die Deutsche Werbung*, Heft 19.

Hundhausen, C. (1951). *Werbung um öffentliches Vertrauen: Public Relations*. Essen: Girardet.

Hundhausen, C. (1959). Zur Gründung der Deutschen Public Relations Gesellschaft. *Wirtschaft und Werbung*, 1.

Hundhausen, C. (1969). *Public Relations. Theorie und Systematik*, Berlin: de Gruyter.

Hung, F. (2000, March). Relationship maintenance strategies and outcomes. Paper presented to Public Relations Society of America Educator's Academy Communication Sciences Division conference, Miami.

Hutson, S., & Liddiard, M. (2000). Exclusionary environments: The media career of youth homelessness. In S. Allan, B. Adam, & C. Carter (Eds.), *Environmental risks and the media* (pp. 160–170). London & New York: Routledge.

Hutton, J. (1999). The definition, dimensions, and domain of public relations. *Public Relations Review, 25*(2), 199–214.

Hutton, J. G. (2001). Defining the relationship between public relations and marketing. In R. L. Heath (Ed.), *Handbook of public relations* (pp. 205–214). London: Sage.

Iannone, A. (Ed.). (1989). *Contemporary moral controversies in business*. New York: Oxford University Press.

ICI Paints. (1990). Focus on the customer. *Public Relations: Journal of the Institute of Public Relations, 9*(2), 11–12.

I'm the victim, (2001, December 19). *Daily Mirror*, p. 1.

Ind, N. (1990). *The corporate image: Strategies for effective identity programmes*. London: Kogan Page.

Ind, N. (1997). *The corporate brand*. Basingstoke: Palgrave Macmillan.

Information and Tourism Ministry. (1972). *Santiago en Toda Espana*. Madrid: Publicaciones Espanolas.

Ingham, B. (1991). *Kill the messenger*. London: Fontana.

Ingham, B. (1999, April 2). Statutory regulation is needed to keep lobbying respectable. *PR Week*, 3.

International Monetary Fund (cited as IMF). (1999). *Code of good practices on transparency in monetary and financial policies: Declaration of principles*. URL: http://www.imf.org/external/np/mae/mft/code/index.htm.

Institute of Public Relations. (1998). *Sword of Excellence Awards*, London: Institute of Public Relations.

International Public Relations Association. (1990). Public relations. The Institute of Public Relation (1958) *it quids to use practise of public relations*. London. New man Neame. Education—recommendations and standards. Gold Paper no. 7.

Institute of Public Relations Archive, History of Advertising Trust, Beccles, England.

Irwin, R., Sutton, W., & McCarthy, L. (2002). *Sport promotion and sales management*. Champaign IL; Leeds: Human Kinetics.

Istel, W. (1974). *Städtische Öffentlichkeitsarbeit*. Hereford: Maximilian Verlag.

Izod, J., Kilborn, R., & Hibberd, M. (Eds.). (2000). *From Grierson to the docu-soap: Breaking the boundaries*. Luton: University of Luton Press.

Jablin, F., Putnam, L., Roberts, K., & Porter, L. (Eds.). (1987). *Handbook of organizational communication*. London: Sage.

Jackall, R. (1995). The magic lantern: The world of public relations. In R. Jackall (Ed.), *Propaganda* (pp. 351–399). New York: New York University Press.

Jacobs, L. (1979). *The documentary tradition*. New York: Norton.

Jahansoozi, J. (2002). *Public relations and the relational perspective: An exploration of relationship characteristics*. Paper presented at the 9th Bled Public Relations Symposium, Slovenia.

Jahansoozi, J., & Koper, E. (2004). *The public relations catalyst model: Towards a new approach to explore public relations and knowledge management concepts*. Paper presented at The Fourth International Conference on Knowledge, Culture and Change in Organizations. Greenwich, August.

Jahn, H. E. (1953). *Vetrauen, Verantwortung, Mitarbeit. Eine Studie über Public Relations Arbeit in Deutschland*. Oberlahnstein: Fritz Nohr.

Jakobson, R. (1960). Concluding statement on linguistics and poetics. In T. Sebeok (Ed.), *Style in language*. Cambridge, MA: MIT Press.

Jamieson, K. H. (2003). *The press effect. Politicians, journalists, and the stories that shape the political world*. Oxford University Press.

Jantsch, E. (1981). Autopoiesis: A central aspect of dissipative self-organization. In M. Zeleny (Ed.), *Autopoiesis: A theory of living organization*. New York: North-Holland.

Jefkins, F. (1977, 1986). *Planned press and public relations*. Glasgow, London: Blackie.

Jensen, I. (1997). Legitimacy and strategy of different companies: A perspective of external and internal public relations. In D. Moss, T. MacManus, & D. Verčič (Eds.), *Public relations research: An international perspective* (pp. 225–246). London: International Thomson Business Press.

John Grierson Archive, University of Stirling G5:16:1, p. 1.

John Grierson Archive, University of Stirling G4:19:21, p. 3.

John Grierson PRO BT 64/86 6880, p. 2, cited in I. Aitkin (1990), *Film and reform: John Grierson and the documentary film movement*. London: Routledge, p. 98.

Johnson, S. (2001). *Emergence*. London: Penguin.

Johnson, T. (1972). *Professions and power*. London: Macmillan.

Johnson, B. B. (1993). Advancing understanding of knowledge's role in lay risk perception. Risk: Health, Safety & Environment, 4: 189–213, available at http://www.fplc.edu/RISK/vol4/ summer/johnson.htm.

Jolley, R. (2001). Sport needs to raise its game. *Revolution*, 25 July.

Jones, L., & Sidell, M. (2002).*The challenge of promoting health: Exploration and action* (2nd ed.). Basingstoke: Open University in association with Palgrave.

Jones, N. (1997). *Campaign 1997: How the general election was won and lost*. London: Indigo.

Jowett, G., & O'Donnell, V. (1992). *Propaganda and persuasion*. Newbury Park, CA: Sage.

Jowett, G., S., & O'Donnell, V. (1986). *Propaganda and persuasion*. London: Sage.

Joyce, J.-P. (1997, January 17). An editorial withdrawal. *PR Week*, 28.

Juan Carlos y Santiago Apostol. (1999, July 25). *El Nuevo Herald*, 2.

Kamekura, Y. (1966). *Trademarks and symbols of the world*. London: Studio Vista.

Kant, I. (1983). *Perpetual peace and other essays* (trans. T. Humphrey). Indianapolis: Hackett.

Kapferer, J. (1992). *Strategic brand management*. London: Kogan Page.

Katz, D., Cartwright, D., Eldersveld, S., & McClung Lee, A. (Eds.). (1954). *Public opinion and propaganda*. New York: Holt, Rinehart & Winston.

Katz, D., & Kahn, R. L. (1966). *The social psychology of organizations*. New York: Wiley.

Katz, D., & Kahn, R. L. (1978). *The social psychology of organization*. New York: Wiley.

Katz, E. (1987). Communication research since Lazarsfeld. *Public Opinion Quarterly, 51*, S25–S45.

Katz, J., & Perberdy, J. (2000). *Promoting health: Knowledge and practice*. Open University.

Kavanagh, M. (1997, January 24). An Independent appointment for Bank of England. *PR Week*, 2.

Keane, R. (2002). *Keane: The autobiography*. London: Michael Joseph/Penguin.

Kearney, R. (1998). *Poetics of imagination: Modern to postmodern*. Edinburgh: Edinburgh University Press.

Keen, C., & Warner, D. (Eds.). (1989). *Visual and corporate identity*. Banbury: HEIST.

Kellaway, L. (2004). Once upon a time, we had managers, not storytellers. *Financial Times*, May 10.

Kelley, S. (1956). *Professional public relations and political power*. Baltimore: John Hopkins University Press.

Kelly, J. (1986). *The Oxford dictionary of popes*. Oxford, UK: Oxford University Press.

Kelly, P. (1996, October 25). Letter. *PR Week*, 9.

Kendall, R. (1996). *Public relations campaign strategies*. New York: HarperCollins.

Kent, M. L., & Taylor, M. (2002). Toward a dialogic theory of public relations. *Public Relations Review*, *28*, 21–37.

Kent Wright, C. (1936). Intelligence and public relations: Local authorities. *Public Administration, 14*, 49–58.

Kepplinger, H. M., & Fritsch, J. (1981). Unter Ausschluss der Öffentlichkeit. Abgeordneter des 8. Deutschen Bundestag. *Publizistik, 26*, 33–55.

Kickert, W. J. (1993). Autopoiesis and the science of (public) administration: Essence, sense and nonsense. *Organization Studies, 14*(2), 261–278.

Kilborn, R. (1996). New contexts for documentary production in Britain. *Media, Culture & Society, 18*(1), 141–150.

Kilborn, R., & Izod, K. J. (1997). *An introduction to television documentary: Confronting reality.* Manchester: Manchester University Press.

Kinast, R. (1999, May 6). When the calendar flipped from 999 to 1000. *The Florida Catholic*, A23.

Kinder, D., & Sears, D. (1985). Public opinion and political action. In G. Lindzey & E. Aronson (Eds.), *The handbook of social psychology*, (3rd ed.), vol. 2.

Kingston University. (2002). *The Body Shop employee stakeholder survey 2000: Summary report.* Centre for Stakeholding and Sustainable Enterprise, Kingston University: Kingston Surrey. Retrieved 29 June, 2004, from http://www.thebodyshopinternational.com/web/tbsgl/images/tbs_employee_ stakeholder_survey_2000.pdf.

Kinneir, J. (1980). *Words and buildings: The art and practice of public lettering.* London: Architectural Press.

Kisch, R. (1964). *The private life of public relations.* London: MacGibbon & Kee.

Kitto, H. (1986). *The Greeks.* London: Pelican.

Kitzinger, J. (1990). Audience understanding of AIDS media messages: A discussion of methods. *Sociology of Health & Illness, 12*(3), 319–335.

Kitzinger, J. (1993). Understanding AIDS: Researching audience perceptions of Acquired Immune Deficiency Syndrome. In J. Eldridge *Getting the message: News, truth and power* (pp. 217–304). London: Routledge.

Klein, N. (2000). *No logo: Taking aim at the brand bullies.* London: Flamingo.

Kliman, M. (1936). Correspondence with the public. *Public Administration, 14*, 276–290.

Knight, G. (1996, July 26). How can we ensure that PR measures up. *PR Week*, 11.

Knorr, R. H. (1984). *Public Relations als System-Umwelt-Interaktion.* Wiesbaden: Verlag für Dt. Wittschaftsbiographien.

Koehn, D. (1994). *The ground of professional ethics.* New York: Routledge.

Koranteng, J. (2001). *European football channels.* London: A SportBusiness Report.

Kordes, W., & Pollmann, H. (1989). *Das Presse und Informationsamt der Bundesregierung.* Düsseldorf: Droste.

Koten, J. A. (1997). The strategic uses of corporate philanthropy. In C. L. Caywood (Ed.), *The handbook of strategic public relations and integrated communication* (pp. 149–172). New York; London: McGraw-Hill.

Kovach, B., & Rosenstiel, T. (2001). *The elements of journalism.* London: Guardian Atlantic.

Kovacs, R. (2001). Relationship building as integral to British activism: Its impact on accountability in broadcasting. *Public Relations Review, 27*, 421–436.

Kruckeberg, D., & Starck, K. (1988). *Public relations and community. A reconstructed theory.* London: Praeger.

Kunczik, M. (1993). *Public Relations: Konzepte und Theorien.* Koln: Böhlau.

Kunczik, M. (1994). Public Relations: Angewandte Kommunikationswissenschaft oder Ideologie? Ein Beitrag zur Ethik der Öffentlichkeitsarbeit. In W. Armbrecht & U. Zabel (Eds.), *Normative Aspekt der Public Relations* (pp. 265–280). Opladen: Westdeutscher Verlag.

Kunczik, M. (1997). *Geschichte der Öffentlichkeitsarbeit.* Köln: Böhlau.

L'Etang, J. (1996a). Corporate responsibility and public relations ethics. In J. L'Etang & M. Pieczka (Eds.), *Critical perspectives in public relations* (pp. 82–105). London: International Thomson Business Press.

L'Etang, J. (1996b). Public relations and rhetoric. In J. L'Etang and M. Pieczka (Eds.), *Critical perspectives in public relations* (pp. 106–123). London: International Thomson Business Press.

L'Etang, J. (1996c). Public relations as diplomacy. In J. L'Etang & M. Pieczka (Eds.), *Critical perspectives in public relations* (pp. 14–34). London: International Thomson Business Press (ITBP).

L'Etang, J. (1997). Public relations and the rhetorical dilemma: Legitimate "perspectives", persuasion, or pandering? *Australian Journal of Communication, 24*(2), 33–53.

L'Etang, J. (1998). State propaganda and bureaucratic intelligence: The creation of public relations in 20th century Britain. *Public Relations Review, 24*(4), 413–441.

L'Etang, J. (1998a, July). *The development of British public relations in the twentieth century.* Paper presented at the meeting of the International Association of Mass Media Communication Research, History division, Glasgow, Scotland.

L'Etang, J. (1998b, September). *Public relations education in Britain, 1948–73.* Paper presented at the Public Relations Educators' Forum, Leeds, UK.

L'Etang, J. (1999, January). *Grierson's influence on the formation and values of the public relations industry in Britain.* Paper presented at "Breaking the Boundaries: The Stirling Documentary Conference," Stirling, Scotland.

L'Etang, J. (2000). Grierson and the public relations industry in Britain. In J. Izod, R. Kilborn, & M. Hibberd (Eds.), *From Grierson to the docu-soap: Breaking the boundaries* (pp. 83–96). Luton: University of Luton Press.

L'Etang, J. (2002). Public relations education in Britain: A review at the outset of the millennium and thoughts for a different research agenda. *Journal of Communication Management, 7*(1), 43–53.

L'Etang, J. (2003). The myth of the "ethical guardian": An examination of its origins, potency and illusions. *Journal of Communication Management, 8*(1), 53–67.

L'Etang, J. (2001). *The professionalisation of British public relations in the twentieth century: A history* PhD thesis. Department of Film and Media Studies, University of Stirling.

L'Etang, J. (2004). *Public relations in Britain: A history of professional practice in the 20th century.* Mahwah, NJ: Lawrence Erlbaum Associates.

L'Etang, J., & Pieczka, M. (1996). *Critical perspectives in public relations.* London: International Thomson Business Press.

Lacey, A. (1990). *A dictionary of philosophy.* London: Routledge.

Laclau, E., & Mouffe, C. (1985). *Hegemony and socialist strategy: Towards a radical democratic politics* (trans. by W. Moore & P. Cammack). London: Verso.

Ladyman, I. (2002, August 19). Alfie can't win, *Daily Mail*, pp. 71–72.

Lambie-Nairn, M. (1997). *Brand identity for television, with knobs on.* London: Phaidon.

Lansons Communications (1994). TaxAction: The war on wasted tax. *The IPR Sword of Excellence Awards 1994*, Institute of Public Relations: London, pp. 10–12.

Larsson, L. (1998). *Nyheter i samspel/*News in interplay. Göteborg/Gothenburg: Göteborg University.

Larsson, L. (2002). Journalists and politicians: A relationship requiring manoeuvring space. *Journalism Studies, 3*(1), 21–34.

Larsson, L. (2005). Opinions makarna/The opinion makers. Lund: Studentlitteratur.

Lashley, C., & Lee-Ross, D. (2003). *Organization behaviour for leisure services.* London: Butterworth-Heinemann.

Lasswell, H. D. (1927). *Propaganda techniques in the World War.* New York: Smith.

Lasswell, H. D. (1934, 1995). Propaganda. In R. Jackall (Ed.), *Propaganda* (pp. 13–35). New York: New York University Press.

Lauer, J. (1993). Rhetoric and composition studies: A multimodal discipline. In T. Enos & S. C. Brown (Eds.), *Defining the new rhetorics* (pp. 44–54). London: Sage.

Lawton, J. (2001, December 18). O'Leary's shameful rag-bag of poses, *The Independent*, p. 20.

Lawton, J. (2002, August 12). Adam Crozier, Chief Executive, Football Association: On the attack. *The Independent*, p. 11.

Lawrence, P., & Lorsch, J. (1967). *Organizations and environment.* Cambridge, MA: Harvard Graduate School of Business Administration.

Lazarsfeld, P. (1981). Public opinion and the classical tradition. In M. Janowitz & P. Hirsch (Eds.), *Reader in public opinion and mass communication* (3rd ed.). New York: Free Press.

Leavy, S. (1998, November 13). A united front. *PR Week*, 11–14.

Lechte, J. (1994). *Fifty contemporary thinkers*. London: Routledge.

Ledingham, J. A. (2000). Guidelines to building and maintaining strong organization-public relationships. *Public Relations Quarterly*, *45*(3), 44–47.

Ledingham, J. A. (2001). Government-community relationships: Extending the relational theory of public relations. *Public Relations Review*, *27*, 285–295.

Ledingham, J. A., & Bruning, S. D. (Eds.). (2000). *Public relations as relationship management: A relational approach to the study and practice of public relations.* Mahwah, NJ: Lawrence Erlbaum Associates.

Ledingham, J. A., Bruning, S. D., & Wilson, L. J. (1999). Time as an indicator of the perceptions and behavior of members of a key public: Monitoring and predicting organization-public relationships. *Journal of Public Relations Research*, *11*(2), 167–183.

Lee, F. (1997, May 9). New Labour, new ways of lobbying. *PR Week*, 7.

Lee, J. M. (1972). The dissolution of the EMB. *Journal of Imperial and Commonwealth History*, 1.51.

Leeper, R. (2001). In search of a metatheory for public relations: An argument for communitarianism. In R. Heath (Ed.), *Handbook of public relations* (pp. 93–104). Thousand Oaks, CA: Sage

Leeper, R., & Leeper, K. (2001). Public relations as "practice": Applying the theory of Alasdair MacIntyre. *Public Relations Review 27*, 461–473.

Leff, M. (1978). In search of Ariadne's thread: A review of the recent literature on rhetorical theory. *Central States Speech Journal*, *29*, 73–91.

Leipziger, D. (2003). *The corporate responsibility code book*. Sheffield: Green Leaf.

Leitch, S., & Neilson, D. (1997). Reframing public relations: New directions for theory and practice. *Australian Journal of Communication*, *24*(2), 17–32.

Leitch, S., & Neilson, D. (2001). Bringing publics into public relations: New theoretical frameworks for the practice. In R. Heath (Ed.), *Handbook of public relations* (pp. 127–138). London: Sage.

Lessnoff, M. (1986). *Social contract*. Basingstoke: Macmillan Education.

Lewis, J. (1998). *Constructing public opinion*. New York: Columbia University Press.

Liebert, T. (1995). *Zur Geschichte kommunaler Öffentlichkeitsarbeit in Deutschland*. Leipzig.

Lievrouw, L. A. (1990). Communication and the social representation of scientific knowledge. *Critical Studies in Mass Communication*, *7*(1), 1–10.

Lippman, W. (1922, 1997). *Public opinion*. New York: Free Press.

Lippman, W. (1925, 1995). The phantom public. In R. Jackall (Ed.), *Propaganda* (pp. 351–399). New York: New York University Press.

Lippmann, W. (1925). *The phantom public*. New York: Harcourt Brace.

Lippmann, W. (1954). The image of democracy. In D. Katz et al. (Eds.), originally published 1922, *Public opinion*. New York: Macmillan Co.

Lipscombe, E. (1953). Let's get lost. *Public Relations*, *5*(4), pp. 69–72.

Liptak, A. (2003). Free speech: Nike move ends case over firms' free speech. Reclaim democracy.org, first published *New York Times*, 13 September. Retrieved 29 June, 2004, from http://reclaimdemocracy.org/nike/myt_nikescttes.htm.

Livesey, S. M. (2001). Eco-identity as discursive struggle: Royal Dutch/Shell, Brent Spar, and Nigeria. *Journal of Business Communication*, *38*(1), 58–91.

Lloyd, H., & Lloyd, P. (1963, 1989). *Teach yourself public relations*. Sevenoaks, UK: Hodder & Stoughton.

Lobbying laws can no longer be put off [Editorial]. (1998, July 10). *PR Week*.

Lodge, G. C. (1986). The large corporation and the new American ideology. In R. B. Dickie & L. S. Rouner (Eds.), *Corporations and the common good*. Notre Dame, Indiana: University of Notre Dame Press.

Luhmann, N. (1984). *Soziale systeme*. Frankfurt: Suhrkamp.

Luhmann, N. (1986). The autopoiesis of social systems. In F. Geyer & J. van der Zouwen (Eds.), *Sociocybernetic paradoxes*. London: Sage.

Lund, M. (1985). The development of investment and commitment scales for predicting continuity of personal relationships. *Journal of Social and Personal Relationships, 2*, 3–23.

Lupton, D. (1994). *Medicine as culture: Illness, disease and the body in Western societies.* London: Sage.

Lupton, D. (1999). *Risk.* London: Routledge.

Luttberg, N. (1974). *Public opinion and public policy: Models of political linkage.* Homewood, IL: Dorsey.

Lyotard, J. (1977). The unconscious as mise-en-scène. In M. Benamou & C. Caramello (Eds.), *Performance in postmodern culture.* WI: Center for Twentieth Century Studies and Coda Press.

Lyotard, J-F. (1984). *The postmodern condition: A report on knowledge.* Manchester: Manchester University Press.

Lyotard, J-F. (1988). *The differend: Phrases in dispute* (trans. George Van Den Abeele). Minneapolis: University of Minnesota Press.

Lyotard, J-F. (1989). Lessons in paganism. In A. Benjamin (Ed.), *The Lyotard reader* (pp. 122–153). Oxford, UK: Basil Blackwell.

Macarthur, J. (1992). *Second front: Censorship and propaganda in the Gulf War.* New York: Hill & Wang.

Macdonald, K. M. (1995). *The sociology of the professions.* London: Sage.

Machiavelli, N. (1981). *The prince.* Harmondsworth: Penguin Classics.

Machiavelli, N. (1983). *The discourses.* Harmondsworth: Penguin Classics.

Macpherson, C. (1976). *The life and times of liberal democracy.* Oxford, UK: Oxford University Press.

Macrae, J. (1997, September 12). Public Policy Unit puts its faith in Rock and Savage. *PR Week.*

Maeckling, C. (1983). The future of diplomats. In W. Olson (Ed.), *The theory and practice of international relations.* Englewood Cliffs, NJ: Prentice-Hall.

Maguire, J., Jarvie, G., Mansfield, L., & Bradley, J. (2002). *Sport worlds: A sociological perspective.* Champaign, IL; Leeds: Human Kinetics.

Maletzke, G. (1972). Propaganda. Eine begriffskritische Analyse. *Publizistik, 17*, 153–164.

Malkiel, B. G. (1999). *A random walk down Wall Street.* New York: Norton.

Mancini, P., & Swanson, D. (1996). Politics, media and modern democracy: Introduction. In D. Swanson & P. Mancini (Eds.), *Politics, media, and modern democracy.* London: Praeger.

Mann, Christopher, Publicity and Press Agent to Grierson regarding possible appointment of agency for media relations on behalf of the Empire Marketing Board. Refers to importance of journalists' requirements. John Grierson Archive, University of Stirling, G4:22:9.

Mannheim, J. B., & Pratt, C. B. (1989). Communicating corporate social responsibility. *Public Relations Review, 15*(2), 9.

Marchand, R. (1998). *Creating the corporate soul: The rise of public relations and corporate imagery in American big business.* Berkeley: University of California Press.

Marlin, R. (2002). *Propaganda and the ethics of persuasion.* Ontario: Broadview.

Marsh, K., & Fraser, C. (Eds.). (1989). *Public opinion and nuclear weapons.* London: Macmillan.

Martin, B. (1998 September/October). 'Coincidences: Remarkable or random?', *Skeptical Inquirer, 6*(4): 23–28, at [http://www.csicop.org]

Matrat, L. (1990). Good citizenship and public relations. *International Public Relations Review, 13*(2), 8–12.

Maturana, H., & Varela, F. (1980). *Autopoiesis and cognition: The realization of the living.* London: Reidl.

May, C. (2002). *The information society: A sceptical view.* Cambridge, UK: Polity.

May, L. (1986). Corporate property rights. *Journal of Business Ethics, 5.*

Mayhew, L. (1997). *The new public. Professional communication and the means of social influence.* Cambridge, UK: Cambridge University Press.

Mayo, E. (1933). *The human problems of industrial civilisation.* New York: Macmillan.

McBirnie, W. (1977). *The search for the Twelve Apostles.* Wheaton, IL: Tyndale House.

McBride, G. (1989). Ethical thought in public relations history: Seeking a relevant perspective. *Journal of Mass Media Ethics, 4*(1), 5–20.

McCarra, K. (2002, January 5) Jury still out on O'Leary's talent as manager, *The Times*, Sport section.

McConnell quits Scottish Labour for agency post. (1998, April 10). *PR Week.*

McCulloch, A., & Shannon, M. (1977). Organization and protection. In S. Clegg & D. Dunkerley (Eds.), *Critical issues in organizations.* London: Routledge & Kegan Paul.

McDonald's. (2002). *McDonald's social responsibility report.* Retrieved 29 June, 2004, from http://www.mcdonalds.com/corp.html.

Mcdonnell, D. (2002, August 14). Only Fergie has got the right to criticise us (in other words: Shut it, Roy!). *The Mirror*, p. 46.

McDowell, B. (1991). *Inside the Vatican.* Washington, DC: National Geographic Society.

McHoul, A., & Grace, W. (1993). *A Foucault primer: Discourse, power and the subject.* Carlton: Melbourne University Press.

McLean, F. (1997). *Marketing the museum.* London: Routledge.

McLeod, J. M., & Chafee, S. H. (1973). Interpersonal approaches to communication research. In Steven H. Chaffee and Jack M. McLeod (Eds.). *Interpersonal perception and communication. American Behavioral Scientist [Special issue], Vol. 16*(4), 483–488.

McLellan, D. (Ed.). (1984). *Karl Marx: Selected writings.* Oxford: Oxford University Press.

McNair, B. (1988). *Images of the enemy.* London: Routledge.

McNair, B. (1989). Television news and the 1983 election. In C. Marsh & C. Fraser (Eds.), *Public opinion and nuclear weapons.* London: Macmillan.

McNair, B. (1991). *Glasnost, perestroika and the Soviet media.* London: Routledge.

McNair, B. (1995). *An introduction to political communication.* London: Routledge.

McNair, B. (1996). Performance in politics and politics of performance: Public relations, the public sphere and democracy. In J. L'Etang & M. Pieczka (Eds.), *Critical perspectives in public relations* (pp. 35–53). London: International Thomson Business Press.

McNair, B. (2000). *Journalism and democracy.* London: Routledge.

McNally, T. (1996, October 25). Letter. *PR Week*, 9.

McNeil, K. (1978). Understanding organizational power: Building on the Weberian legacy. *Administrative Science Quarterly, 23*(1), 65–90.

McQuail, D. (1987). *Mass communication theory: An introduction* (2nd ed.). London: Sage.

McQuillan, M. (2000). Introduction—aporias of writing: narrative and subjectivity. In M. McQuillan (Ed.), *The narrative reader* (pp. 1–33). London: Routledge.

Meech, P. (1996a). Corporate identity and corporate image. In J. L'Etang & M. Pieczka (Eds.), *Critical perspectives in public relations* (pp. 65–81). London: International Thomson Business Press.

Meech, P. (1996b). The lion, the thistle and the saltire: National symbols and corporate identity in Scottish broadcasting. *Screen, 37*(1), 68–81.

Meech, P. (1996c). Watch this space: The on-air marketing communications of UK television. *International Journal of Advertising, 18* (3), 291–304.

Meijer, I. C. (1998). Advertising citizenship: An essay on the performative power of consumer culture. *Media, Culture & Society, 20,* 235–249.

Melczer, W. (1993). *The pilgrim's guide to Santiago de Compostela.* New York: Italica Press.

Mercer, D., Mungham, G., & Williams, K. (1987). *The fog of war.* London: Heinemann.

Michie, D. (1998). *Invisible persuaders: How Britain's spin doctors manipulate the media.* London: Bantam Press.

Milchen, J., & Kaplan, J. (2003). Saving corporations from themselves? Reclaim democracy.org. Retrieved 29 June, 2004, from http://ReclaimDemocracy.org/nike/nike_court_case_oped_6272003.html.

Miles, M., & Huberman, A. M. (1994). *Qualitative data analysis: An expanded source book.* London: Sage.

Miliband, R. (1969). *The state in capitalist society.* London: Quartet.

Mill, J. S. (1975). *Three essays.* London: Oxford University Press.

Mill, J. S., & Bentham, J. (1987). *Utilitarianism and other essays.* Harmondsworth: Penguin.

Miller, C. (1991). *Lobbying: Understanding and influencing the corridors of power.* Oxford: Blackwell.

Miller, D. (1994). *Don't mention the war.* London: Pluto.

Miller, D. (1998a). Mediating science: Promotional strategies, media coverage, public belief and decision making. In E. Scanlan & S. Yates (Eds.), *Communicating science: Contexts and channels* (pp. 206–226). London: Routledge.

Miller, D. (1998b). Public relations and journalism. In A. Briggs & P. Cobley (Eds.), *The British media: An introduction* (pp. 65–80). Harlow: Longman.

Miller, D. (1999). Risk, science and policy: Definitional struggles, information management, the media and BSE. *Social Science & Medicine, 49*, 1239–1255.

Miller, D. (Ed.). (2003). *Tell me lies: Propaganda and media distortion in the attack on Iraq.* London: Pluto Press.

Miller, D. & Dinan, W. (1998, July). *Public relations and promotional culture.* Paper presented at the meeting of the International Association of Mass Media Communication Research, Political Communication division, Glasgow, Scotland.

Miller, D., & Dinan, W. (2000a). The rise of the PR industry in Britain, 1979–1998. *European Journal of Communication, 15*(1), 5–35.

Miller, G. (1989). Persuasion and public relations: Two "Ps" in a pod. In C. Botan & V. Hazleton (Eds.), *Public relations theory* (pp. 45–66). Hillsdale, NJ: Lawrence Erlbaum Associates .

Miller, G. R. (2002). On being persuaded. In J. P. Dillard & M. Pfau (Eds.). *The persuasion handbook: Developments in theory and practice* (pp. 3–16). Thousand Oaks, CA: Sage.

Miller, H. (1960). A private view of public relations. *Public Relations, 13*(1), 37.

Miller, J. (1981). *The world of states.* London: Croom Helm.

Millerson, G. (1964). *The qualifying associations: A study in professionalisation.* London: Routledge & Kegan Paul.

Mills, C. (1975). *The power elite.* New York: Oxford University Press.

Mills, S. (1997). *Discourse.* London: Routledge.

Ministerio de Comercio y Turismo. (1995). *Santiago de Compostela.* Madrid: Ministerio de Comercio y Turismo.

Ministerio de Economía y Hacienda. (1995). *Santiago de Compostela A Coruña.* Madrid: Ministerio de Economía y Hacienda.

Mintzberg, H. (1983). *Power in and around organizations.* Englewood Cliffs, NJ: Prentice-Hall.

Mintzberg, H., Reisinghani, D., & Theoret, A. (1976). The structure of unstructured decision processes. *Administrative Science Quarterly, 21*, 246–275.

Mitnick, B. (1993). *Corporate political agency: The construction of competition in public affairs.* London: Sage.

Moffitt, M. (1994). A cultural studies perspective toward understanding corporate image: A case study of State Farm Insurance. *Journal of Public Relations Research, 6*(1), 41–66.

Moloney, K. (2000). *Rethinking public relations: The spin and the substance.* London and New York: Routledge.

Mooij, M. K. de. (1998). *Global marketing and advertising—understanding cultural paradoxes.* London: Sage.

Moore, G. (2002). Crash that threatens even the giants. *The Independent,* European Football supplement, 15 August.

Morgan, G. (1986). *Images of organization.* Newbury Park/London: Sage.

Morgan, G. (1989). *Creative organization theory.* London: Sage.

Morgan, G. (1990). *Organisations in society.* London: Macmillan.

Morgan, G. (1992). *Imaganization.* London: Sage.

Morgan, G. (1997). *Images of organization.* Beverley Hills, CA: Sage.

Morgan, R. M., & Hunt, S. D. (1994). The commitment-trust theory of relationship marketing. *Journal of Marketing, 58* (July), 20–38.

Morneau, R. (2000, August). Spirituality for the new millenium. *St. Anthony Messenger, 107*, 12–16.

Morris, D. (1994). Public relations in the UK: An overview of the marketing/public relations debate. Unpublished master's dissertation, University of Stirling.

Morris, N. (1995). *Puerto Rico: Culture, politics, and identity.* Westport, CT: Praeger.

Morris, S. (1995, November 5). The force is always with us. *The Sunday Times* (The Culture), 10.

Morriss, S. (2000, November 6). The end is nigh, perhaps. *The Guardian,* at: http://www.guardian.co.uk.

Morrison, D. (1989). *Understanding Black Africa: Data and analysis of social change and nation-building.* New York: Irvington.

Morrow, S. (1999). The new business of football: Accountability and finance in football. Basingstoke: Macmillan.

Motion, J., & Leitch, S. (1996). A discursive perspective from New Zealand: Another world view. *Public Relations Review, 22*(3), 297–309.

Motion, J., & Weaver, C. K. (2005). A discourse model for critical public relations research: The Life Sciences Network and the battle for truth. *Journal of Public Relations Research*, 17, 1. 49–68.

Mowlana, H. (1997). International interactions: Travel and tourism. In *Global Information and world communication: New frontiers in international relations* (pp. 131–145). London: Sage.

Mullins, E. (1974). *The pilgrimage to Santiago*. London: Martin Sacker and Warburg Ltd.

Murcott, A. (Ed.). (1998). *The nation's diet: The social science of food choice*. London: Longman.

Murphy, C. (1997, June 20). Heylin wins OBE for Citizen's Charter. *PR Week*, 3.

Murphy, J. A. (1996). Retail banking. In F. Buttle (Ed.), *Relationship marketing*. London: Paul Chapman.

Murphy, R. (1990). Proletarianization or bureaucratization: The fall of the professional? In R. Torstendahl & M. Burrage (Eds.), *The formation of the professions: Knowledge, state, and the strategy* (pp. 71–96). London: Sage.

Murray, D., Schwartz, J., & Lichter, S. R. (2001). *It ain't necessarily so: How media make and unmake the scientific picture of reality*. Oxford, UK: Rowman & Littlefield.

Murray, R. (1955). *Red scare: A study of national hysteria, 1919–1920*. Westport, CT: Greenwood.

Murray Milne, F. (1950). What they said. *Public Relations, 2*(4), 8.

Myerson, G. (1994). *Rhetoric, reason and society: Rationality as dialogue*. London: Sage.

Naisbett, J. (1982). *Megatrends*. New York: Warren Books.

Nardin, T., & Mapel, D. (Eds.). (1992). *Traditions of international ethics*. Cambridge, UK: Cambridge University Press.

Nash, L. (1990). Ethics without the sermon. In W. M. Hoffman & J. M. Moore (Eds.), *Business ethics: Reading and cases in corporate morality* (2nd ed.). New York: McGraw-Hill.

National Science Foundation. (1998). *Science & Engineering Indicators 1998*, USA: NSF, at: http://www.nsf.gov/sbe/svs/seind98/start.htm.

Naude, P., & Holland, C. (1996). Business-to-business relationships. In F. Buttle (Ed.), *Relationship marketing*. London: Paul Chapman.

Neill, (2000). *Sixth report of the Committee on Standards in Public Life: Reinforcing standards*. (Cm 4557-I).

Nelson, J. (1989). *Sultans of sleaze*. Monroe: Common Courage Press.

Nelson, R. (1990). Bias versus fairness: The social utility of issues management. *Public Relations Review, 16*(2), 98–104.

Nelson, R. (1994). Issues communication and advocacy: Contemporary ethical challenges. *Public Relations Review, 20*(3), 225–233.

Nessmann, K., (2000). The origins and development of public relations in Germany and Austria. In Moss et al (Eds.). Perspectives on Public relations Research, London, Routledge.

Nessmann, K., (2000). Public relations in Europe: a comparison with the United States, *Public Relation Review. 21*, 2, 151–160.

Nessmann, K. (2004), Austria. In B. R. Van Ruler and Verčič, D. (Eds.). *Public Relations and Communications Management of Europe: A nation-by-nation introduction to public relations theory and practice*, Berlin, Monton de Grayter.

New American Bible. (1970). Washington, DC: Confraternity of Christian Doctrine.

New Zealand Public Relations Council Letter to John Grierson 2 June, 1939. John Grierson Archive, University of Stirling, G3:15:17.

Newcomb, T. (1953). An approach to the study of communicative arts. *Psychological Review, 60*, 393–404.

Newman, W. (1993). New words for what we do. *Institute of Public Relations Journal* (October), 12–15.

Newsom, D., Turk, J., & Kruckeberg, D. (2000). *This is PR: The realities of public relations*. Belmont, CA: Wadsworth/Thomson Learning.

News: Stop Press. (1996, May 31). *PR Week*, p. 2.

Nichols, B. (1991). *Representing reality: Issues and concepts in documentary*. Bloomington: Indiana University Press.

Nicholas, K. (1996, October 4). A step closer to standard unit for PR measurement. *PR Week*, 1.

Nicholas, K. (1997a, May 23). GPC Connect has the right mix for Beckett adviser. *PR Week*.

Nicholas, K. (1997b, November 20). One giant step for evaluation. *PR Week*, 3.

Nicolson, H. (1954). *The evolution of the diplomatic method*. London: Constable & Co.

Nike Inc. (2001). *Corporate responsibility report 2001*. Retrieved 29 June, 2004, from http://www.nike.com/nikebiz/nikebiz.jhtml?page=29.

Nike Inc. (2003, September 12). Nike, Inc. and Kasky announce settlement of Kasky v. Nike First Amendment case. Media release. Retrieved 29 June, 2004, from http://www.nike.com/nikebiz/news/pressrelease.jhtml?year=2003&month=09&letter=f.

Noelle-Neumann, E. (1979). Public opinion and the classical tradition: A re-evaluation. *Public Opinion Quarterly, 43*, 143–156.

Noelle-Neumann, E. (1984). *The Spiral of Silence: Public opinion-our social skin*. Chicago: University of Chicago Press.

Noelle-Neumann, E., & Schulz, W. (Eds.). (1971). *Publizistik*. Frankfurt a.M.: Fischer.

Nolan, M. P. (1995). *First report of the Committee on Standards in Public Life*. London: HMSO.

Norris, P. (2000). *A virtuous circle. Political communications in post-industrial societies*. Cambridge, UK: Cambridge University Press.

Novar Annual Report (2003).

North West Water (1995). Thirsty world. *The IPR Sword of Excellence Awards 1995*, Institute of Public Relations: London, pp. 26–28.

Nozick, R. (1990). *Anarchy, state and Utopia*. Oxford, UK: Blackwell.

Nye, D. (1985). *Image worlds: Corporate identities at General Electric*. Cambridge, MA: MIT Press.

O'Connor, A. (2002). The most cynical game in football. *The Game, The Times,* 23 September.

O'Donnell, C. (1999). *The veneration of relics*. Gervais, OR: Carmelite House of Studies.

O'Keefe, D. (1990). *Persuasion: Theory and research*. London: Sage.

O'Keefe, D. (2002). *Persuasion: Theory and research*. Thousand Oaks, CA: Sage.

O'Leary, D. (2002). *Leeds United on trial*. London: Time Warner Paperbacks.

O'Sullivan, T., Hartley, J., Saunders, D., Montgomery, M., & Fiske, J. (Eds.). (1994). *Key concepts in communication and cultural studies*. London: Routledge.

Oeckl, A. (1964). *Handbuch der Public Relations. Theorie und Praxis der Öffentlichkeitsarbeit in Deutschland und der Welt*. München: Süddeutscher Verlag.

Oeckl, A. (1976). *PR-Praxis: Der Schlüssel zur Öffentlichkeitsarbeit*. Düsseldorf: Econ-Verlag.

Oeckl, A. (1988). Ausbildung unt Fortbildung in einen zukunftsberuf. PR-magazine. 10 pp. 36–38.

Oeckl, A. (1994). Die historische Entwicklung der Public Relations. In W. Reineke & H. Eisele (Eds.), *Taschenbuch der Öffentlichkeitsarbeit*. Heidelberg: Sauer.

Olins, W. (1978). *The corporate personality*. London: Design Council.

Olins, W. (1989). *Corporate identity*. London: Thames & Hudson.

Olins, W. (2003). *On brand*. London: Thames & Hudson.

Oliver, C. (1990). Determinants of interorganizational relationships: Integration and future directions. *Academy of Management Review, 15*, 241–265.

O'Sullivan, T. Hartley, J. Saunders, D., M. Montgomery, & J. Fiske (Eds.). (1994). *Key concepts in communication and cultural studies* (2nd ed.). New York: Routledge.

Otazo, J. (1972). Monopoly on the road to Santiago. Unpublished Master's thesis, University of Florida, Gainesville.

Otero, X. (1974). *Museo de Arte Sacro: Monasterio de San Pelayo de Antealtares*. Santiago de Compostela: El Eco Franciscano.

Otero, X. (1998). *Santiago de Compostela*. La Coruna: Editorial Everest, S.A.

Oxfam Community Aid Abroad. (2002). The price of milk in Sri Lanka. *Horizons, 2*(2), June, 14–15.

Page, S. J. (2003). *Tourism management: Managing for change*. London: Butterworth-Heinemann.

Page, S. J., Brunt, P., Busby, G., & Connell, J. (2001). *Tourism: A modern synthesis*. London: Thomson.

Palast, G. (1998, July 5). Secrets for cash. *The Observer*.

Palenchar, M. J., & Heath, R. (2002). Another part of the risk communication model: Analysis of communication processes and message content. *Journal of Public Relations Research, 14*(2), 127–158.

Palmer, J. (2000). *Spinning into control: News values and source strategies*. London: Leicester University Press.

Palmer, R. (1996, December 6). Tell me what you want, what you really, really want. *PR Week*, 9.

Paragon Communications. (1992). New fish on the block. *Public Relations: Journal of the Institute of Public Relations, 11*(2), 9–11.

Paragon Communications. (1994). Smirnoff International Fashion Awards 1993. *The IPR Sword of Excellence Awards 1994*, Institute of Public Relations: London, pp. 29–31.

Parker, I. (1992). *Discourse dynamics: Critical analysis for social and individual psychology*. London: Routledge.

Parker, M. (1992). Post-modern organizations or postmodern organization theory. *Organization Studies 13*(1), 1–17.

Parkin, M., & King, D. (1995). *Economics* .Wokingham, UK: Addison-Wesley.

Parsons, T. (1939). The professions and the social structure. *Social Forces, 17*, 457–467.

Parsons, T. (1951). *The social system*. London: Free Press.

Parsons, T. (1959). *Economy and society*. London: Routledge & Kegan Paul.

Parsons, T. (1960). *Structure and process in modern societies*. New York: Free Press.

Paton, H. J. (1948). *The moral law: Kant's groundwork of the metaphysic of morals*. London: Hutchinson.

Paul Dacre, Gavyn Davies, Prince Charles . . . you took hell of a beating. [Diary]. (2003, December 11). *PR Week UK*.

Pavlik, J. V. (1987). *Public relations: What research tells us*. Newbury Park, CA: Sage.

Pearson Annual Review. (2003).

Pearson, R. (1989a). Beyond ethical relativism in public relations: Co-orientation, rules and the idea of communication symmetry. In J. E. Grunig & L. A. Grunig (Eds.), *Public Relations Research Annual*, (vol. 1, pp. 67–86). Hillsdale, NJ: Lawrence Erlbaum Associates.

Pearson, R. (1989b). Business ethics as communication ethics: Public relations practice and the idea of dialogue. In C. H. Botan & V. Hazleton (Eds.), *Public relations theory* (p. 111–135). Hillsdale, NJ: Lawrence Erlbaum Associates.

Pearson, R. (1990). Ethical values or strategic values? Two faces of systems theory in Public relations. In L. Grunig & J. Grunig (Eds.), *Public Relations Research Annual*, (vol. 2, pp. 219–235). Hillsdale, NJ: Lawrence Erlbaum Associates.

Pearson, R. (1992). Perspective on public relations history. In E. L. Toth & R. L. Heath (Eds.), *Rhetorical and critical approaches to public relations*. Hillsdale, NJ: Laurence Erlbaum Associates.

Perkins, J. M., & Blyler, N. (1999). *Narrative and professional communication*. Stamford, CT: Ablex.

Perloff, R. M. (1993). *The dynamics of persuasion*. Hillsdale, NJ: Lawrence Erlbaum Associates.

Perrow, C. (1961). The analysis of goals in complex organizations. *American Sociological Review, 32*, 194–209.

Peston, R. (1996, August 21). Maurice Saatchi among 14 new working peers. *Financial Times*.

Peters, H. P. (1995). The interaction of journalists and scientific experts: Co-operation and conflict between two professional cultures. *Media, Culture & Society, 17*(1), 31–48.

Peters, M. (2002, August 21). Brand-new spin to taking your chances in sport. *The Guardian*.

Peters, T. (1987). *Thriving on chaos*. London: Macmillan.

Peters, T., & Waterman, R. (1982). *In search of excellence*. New York: Harper & Row.

Pettigrew, A. (1973). *The politics of organizational decision-making*. London: Tavistock.

Pettigrew, A., Thoms, H., & Whittington, R. (2002). *Handbook of strategy and management*. London: Sage.

Pfeiffer, J. (1978). *Organizational design*. Arlington Heights, IL: AHM.

Pfeffer, J. (1981). *Power in organizations*. Boston: Pitman Press.

Pfeffer, J., & Salancik, G. (1978). *The external control of organizations: A resource dependence perspective*. New York: Harper & Row.

Philips, D. (1998, May 15). Evaluators need to prove their worth. *PR Week*, 9.

Philo, G., & Miller, D. (2001). Cultural compliance. In G. Philo & D. Miller (Eds.), *Market killing: What the free market does and what social scientists can do about it* (pp. 3–95). Harlow: Pearson Education.

Pieczka, M. (1996). Paradigms, systems theory and public relations. In J. L'Etang & M. Pieczka (Eds.), *Critical perspectives in public relations* (pp. 124–156). London: International Thomson Business Press.

Pieczka, M. (1997). Understanding in public relations. *Australian Journal of Communication, 24*(2), 65–79.

Pieczka, M. (2000). Objectives and evaluation in public relations: What do they tell us about expertise and professionalism? *Journal of Public Relations Research, 12*(3), 211–233.

Pieczka, M., & L'Etang, J. (2001). Public relations and the questions of professionalism. In R. Heath (Ed.) *Handbook of public relations* (pp. 223–235). Thousand Oaks, CA: Sage.

Pimlott, J. A. R. (1951). *Public relations and American democracy.* Princeton, NJ: Princeton University Press.

Pigram, J., & Jenkins J. (1999, reported 2002 & 2003). *Outdoor Recreation Management.* London: Routledge.

Piore, M., & Sabel, C. (1984). *The second industrial divide.* New York: Basic Books.

Pitcher, G. (2000). Better off branded. *Business Life.* February, 69.

Pitching for a fairer deal. (1996, July 26). *PR Week.* p. 11.

Plato. (1986). *Phaedrus.* Harmondsworth: Penguin.

Plato. (1988). *Gorgias* (trans. and with an introduction by W. Hamilton). Harmondsworth: Penguin.

Plato. (1989). *Gorgias* (trans. with notes by T. Irwin). Oxford: Clarendon.

Plowman, K. D., Briggs, W. G., & Huang, Y. H. (2001). Public relations and conflict resolution. In R. Heath (Ed.), *Handbook of public relations* (pp. 301–310). London: Sage.

Pollert, A. (1988). Dismantling flexibility. *Capital and Class, 34*, 42–47.

Porter, J. (1993). Developing a postmodern ethics of rhetoric and composition. In T. Enos & S. C. Brown (Eds.), *Defining the new rhetorics* (pp. 207–226). London: Sage.

Porter, J. E. (1998). *Rhetorical ethics and internetworked writing.* Greenwich, CT: Ablex.

Pousa, X. (2001, November). Paper presented to the 1st International Seminar on Communication and Tourism, Viña del Mar.

PR shouldn't be a shameful term. [Editorial]. (1996, February 23). *PR Week.*

PR Week 1993, September 23, p. 16.

Public Relations Society of America. (1990). *Public relations body of knowledge.* New York: Author.

Prakash, A. (2000). *Greening the firm: The politics of corporate environmentalism.* Cambridge, UK: Cambridge University Press.

Price, J. L. (1968). *Organizational effectiveness: An inventory of propositions.* Homewood, IL: Irwin.

Price, V. (1992). *Public opinion.* Newbury Park, CA: Sage.

Pritchard, F. (1950). "Persuasion". Conference presentation. *Public Relations, 2*(4), 20.

Profile 46, November/December 2004.

Public Relation Education Trest, (1991).

Public relations in industry [Editorial]. *Public Relations 1*(1), 1948, p.1.

Public Relations Society of America. (1990). *Public relations body of knowledge.* New York: Author.

Pusey, M. (1987). *Jurgen Habermas.* London: Ellis Harwood.

Quadrant Public Relations. (1992). Save the Royal Welsh Fusiliers. *Public Relations: Journal of the Institute of Public Relations, 11*(2), 19–21.

Quadrant Public Relations (1995). Groundwater protection scheme. *The IPR Sword of Excellence Awards 1995,* Institute of Public Relations: London, pp. 32–35.

Quaker Faith and Practice. (1999). The yearly meeting of on Religious Society of Friends in Britain.

Quinn, R. E., & Hall, R. H. (1983). Environments, organizations and policymakers: Towards an integrative framework. In R. H. Hall & R. E. Quinn (Eds.), *Organizational theory and public policy.* Beverly Hills, CA: Sage.

Racal. (1987). Introducing Voda. *Public Relations: The Quarterly Journal of the Institute of Public Relations, 6*(1), 20–23.

Radcliffe-Brown, A. (1952). *Structure and function in primitive society.* London: Cohen & West.

Rafalko, R. J. (1989). Corporate punishment: A proposal. *Journal of Business Ethics, 8*, 923.

Rakow, L. (1989). Information and power: Toward a critical theory of information campaigns. In C. Salmon (Ed.), *Information campaigns: Balancing social values and social change.* Newbury Park, CA: Sage.

Randall, D. (2000). *The universal journalist*. London: Pluto.

Rapoport, A. (1968). General systems theory. In Sills (Ed.), *International encyclopedia of social sciences*. New York: Macmillan/Free Press.

Rasmussen. D. M. (1990). *Reading Habermas*. Oxford, UK: Blackwell.

Rawls, J. (1988). *A theory of justice*. Oxford, CA: Oxford University Press.

Ray, L. (1993). *Rethinking critical theory*. London: Sage.

Reardon, K. K. (1991). *Persuasion in practice*. London: Sage.

Reconciliation, the only road to peace. (2002, June). *FMA Focus*, 13.

Reddi, C. (1978). *Public relations in municipal government*. Hyderabad: Sharada.

Reed, M. (1992). Introduction. In M. Reed & M. Hughes (Eds.), *Rethinking organization* (pp. 1–16). London: Sage.

Reed, M. (1993). Organizations and modernity: Continuity and discontinuity in organization theory. In J. Hassard & M. Parker (Eds.), *Postmodernism and organizations*. London/Newbury Park/New Delhi: Sage.

Reed, M. (1996). Expert power and control in late modernity: An empirical review and theoretical synthesis. *Organization Studies, 17*(4), 573–597.

Rees, J. (2002, July 3). When a book deal turns into a sending-off. *Evening Standard*, p. 55.

Regan, T. (Ed.). (1984). *Just business: New introductory essays in business ethics*. New York: Random House.

Reineke, W., & Eisele, H. (1994). *Taschenbuch der Öffentlichkeitsarbeit*. Heidelberg: Sauer.

Reinarman, C & Duskin, C. (1992). Dominant Ideology and Drugs in the Media, *International Journal on Drug Policy, 3*(1), 6–15.

Reynolds., P. (1980). *An introduction to international relations* (2nd ed.). London: Longman.

Rheingold, H. (1995). *The virtual community: Homesteading on the electronic frontier*. Reading, MA: Addison-Wesley.

Rice, R., & Atkin, C. (Eds.). (1989). *Public communication campaigns* (2nd ed.). Newbury Park, CA: Sage.

Rice, R., & Atkin, C. (Eds.). (2001). *Public communication campaigns*. London: Sage.

Richardson, D. (1996, October 11). This evaluation method is better by design. *PR Week*, 11.

Richmond, S. B. (1968). *Operations research for management decisions*. New York: Ronald Press.

Rines, S. (2000). *Driving business through sport*. London: International Marketing Reports.

Riordan, J., & Kruger, A. (1999).*The international politics of sport in the 20th century*. London: Spon Press.

Robins, K., Webster, F., & Pickering, M. (1987). Propaganda, information and social control. In J. Hawthorn (Ed.), *Propaganda, persuasion and polemic* (pp. 1–17). London: Edward Arnold.

Robison, W., Pritchard, M., & Ellin, J. (Eds.). (1983). *Profits and professions: Essays in business and professional ethics*. Clifton, NJ: Humana Press.

Rocher, G. (1974). *Talcott Parsons and American sociology* (trans. B. Mennell & S. Mennell). London: Nelson.

Rogers, D. (1996a, June 21). Have the campaigners spun out of control? *PR Week*, 7.

Rogers, D. (1996b, March 29). Measure of results valued like gold. *PR Week*, 11–14.

Rogers, D. (1997, February 14). Regulations returns to haunt City PR agencies. *PR Week*, 7.

Rogers, N. (1958). The birth of the institute, *Public Relations, 10*(2), 9–12.

Roman Missal. (1999). Washington, DC: National Conference of Catholic Bishops.

Ronneberger, F. (1977). *Legitimation durch Information*. Düsseldorf: Econ-Verlag.

Ronneberger, F., & Rühl, M. (1992). *Theorie der Public Relations*. Opladen: Westdeutscher Verlag.

Roper, E. (1954). Who tells the storytellers? *The Saturday Review, 37*(31), 25–32.

Roper, J. (2005). Symmetrical communication: Excellent public relations or a strategy for hegemony? *Journal of Public Relations Research, 17*, 1, 69–87.

Rosenthal, A. (Ed.). (1988). *New challenges for documentary*. Berkeley, Los Angeles, London: University of California Press.

Rosiko, J. (2000). *The Madonnas of Europe*. Warsaw: Rosiko Press.

Rotha, P. (1952). *Documentary film*. London: Faber and Faber.

Röttger, U. (2000). *Public Relations—Organisation und Profession.* Westdeutscher Verlag: Wiesbaden.

Rousseau. J.-J. (1968). *The social contract.* Harmondsworth: Penguin.

Rowden, M. (2000). *The art of identity. Creating and managing a successful corporate identity.* Aldershot: Gower.

Rowe, D. (1997). The anatomy of the sports scandal. In J. Lull & S. Hinerman (Eds.), *Media scandals.* Cambridge, UK: Polity Press.

Rowland, R. C., & Womack, D. F. (1985). Aristotle's view of ethical rhetoric. *Rhetoric Society Quarterly, 15,* 13–31.

Rueschemeyer, D. (1964). Doctors and lawyers: A comment on the theory of professions. *Canadian Journal of Sociology and Anthropology, 1,* 17.

Ruffin, C. (1997). *The Twelve: The lives of the apostles after Calvary.* Huntington, IN: Our Sunday Visitor.

Ruse, M. (1993). *The Darwinian paradigm: Essays on its history, philosophy and religious implications.* London: Routledge.

Ryan, C. (1991). *Prime time activism/media strategies for grassroots organizing.* Boston: South End Press.

Sabato, L. (1981). *The rise of political consultants. New ways of winning elections.* New York: Basic Books.

Salinas, C. (2000). *Toward a critical rhetoric of images: Design/writing within a corporate web site.* Doctoral dissertation, Purdue University, West Lafayette, Indianapolis. Retrieved 29 June, 2004, from http://communication.utsa.edu/salinas/research/research.html.

Salmon, C. T. (Ed.). (1989). *Information campaign: Balancing social values and social change.* Newbury Park, CA: Sage.

Sampson, A. (1969). *The anatomy of Britain.* London: Book Club.

Sanders, K. (2003). *Ethics and journalism.* London, Sage.

Sandman, P. (1994). 'Mass media and environmental risk: Seven Principles', *Risk: Health, Safety & Environment,* 5: 251–260, available at [http://www.fplc.edu/risk/vol5/summer/sandman.htm]

Sanghera, S. (2001, May 8). The case for defence. *Financial Times.*

Saunders, B., & Rae, A. (1991). *Bluff your way in PR.* London: Ravette Books.

Savage moves from PPU to Shandwick. (1998, March 6). *PR Week,* p. 2.

Saxer, U. (1991). Public Relations als Innovation. *Media Perspektiven,* Heft 5, 273–290.

Saxer, U. (1992). Public Relations als Innovation. In H. Avenarius & W. Armbrecht (Eds.), *Ist Public Relations eine Wissenschaft? Eine Einführung* (pp. 47–76). Opladen: Westdeutscher Verlag.

Schamber, L. (1991). Core course in visual literacy for ideas, not techniques. *Journalism Educator, 46*(1), 16–21.

Scheidges, R. (1991). Kommunikationsverschmutzung: zur "übergreifenden Theorie" der PR. In J. Dorer & K. Lojka (Eds.), *Öffentlichkeitsarbeit* (pp. 20–27). Wien: Braumüller.

Schlesinger, P. (1991). *Media, state and nation. Political violence and collective identities.* London: Sage.

Schlesinger, P., Miller, D., & Dinan, W. (2001). *Open Scotland? Journalists, spin doctors and lobbyists.* Edinburgh: Polygon.

Schlesinger, P., & Tumber, H. (1993). Fighting the war against crime. *British Journal of Criminology, 33*(1) (Winter), 19–32.

Schlesinger, P., & Tumber, H. (1999). Reporting crime: The media politics of criminal justice. In H. Tumber (Ed.), *News: A reader* (pp. 257–266). Oxford, UK: Oxford University Press.

Schmidt, K. (Ed.). (1995). *The quest for identity. Corporate identity strategies, methods and examples.* London: Cassell.

Schofield, J. (2003, July 31). Are most commercial websites designed by children? *Guardian.*

Schöneberger, M. (1981). *Diplomatie im Dialog: Ein Jahrhundert Informationspolitik des Auswärtigen Amtes.* München: Olzog.

Schudson, M. (1986). *Advertising. The uneasy persuasion. Its dubious impact on American society.* New York: Basic Books.

Schürmann, F. (1992). *Öffentlichkeitsarbeit der Bundesregierung: Strukturen, Medien, Auftrag und Grenzen eines informalen Instruments der Staatsleitung.* Berlin: Duncker und Humbolt.

Schweda, C., & Opherden, R. (1995). *Journalismus und Public Relations: Grenzziehungen im System lokaler politischer Kommunikation.* Wiesbaden: Dt. Universitätsverlag.

Scott, R. (1993). Rhetoric is epistemic: What difference does that make? In T. Enos & S. C. Brown (Eds.), *Defining the new rhetorics* (pp. 120–136). London: Sage.

Seale, C. (2002). *Media and health.* London: Sage.

Seidman, S. (1994). *Contested knowledge social theory in the postmodern era.* Oxford, UK: Blackwell.

Seth, J. N., & Parvatiyar, A. (2000). *Handbook of relationship marketing.* Thousand Oaks, CA: Sage.

Sethi, S. P. (1977). *Advocacy advertising and large corporations: Social conflict, big business image, the news media, and public policy.* Lexington, MA: D.C. Heath.

Shandwick Communications. (1993). The introduction of the New 10 pence coin. *The IPR Sword of Excellence Awards 1993* (pp. 24–25). London: Institute of Public Relations.

Shank, M. D. (2002). *Sports marketing: A strategic perspective* (2nd ed.). Upper Saddle River, NJ: Prentice-Hall.

Sharpe, M. (1990). Harmonizing ethical values in the global village: The public relations professional challenge! *International Public Relations Review, 13*(3), 21–25.

Sharpe, M. L. (2000). Developing a behavioral paradigm for the performance of public relations. *Public Relations Review, 26*(3), 345–361.

Shaw, E. (1993). *The Labour party since 1979.* London: Routledge.

Sheldon, R. (1997). *First report, session 1997–1998: Complaints from Mr Mohamed Al Fayed, the Guardian and others against 25 Members and former Members.* London, HMSO.

Shugart, H. A. (2003). An appropriating aesthetic: Reproducing power in the discourse of critical scholarship. *Communication Theory, 13*(3), 275–303.

Sidell, M., Jones, L., Katz, J., Peberdy, A., & Douglas, J. (Eds.). (2003). *Debates and dilemmas in promoting health* (2nd ed.). Basingstoke: Palgrave Macmillan/Open University.

Sigal, L. (1973). *Reporters and officials. The organization and politics of newsmaking.* Lexington, MA: D.C. Heath and Company.

Signitzer, B., & Coombs, T. (1992). Public relations and public diplomacy: Conceptual convergences. *Public Relations Review, 18(2),* 137–147.

Silcock, B. (1994, August). Television news coverage of the Maastricht Summit testing theories of the global newsroom. Paper presented to the Association for Education in Journalism and Mass Communication conference, Atlanta.

Silverman, D. (1970). *The theory of organizations.* London: Heinemann.

Silverman, D., & Jones, J. (1976). Getting in: the managed accomplishments of "correct" selection outcomes. In J. Child (Ed.), *Man and organisation.* London: George Allen & Unwin.

Silverstone, R. (1986). The agnostic narratives of television science. In J. Corner (Ed.), *Documentary and the mass media* (pp. 81–106). London: Edward Arnold.

Simmons, M. (1991). Santiago: Reality and myth. In J. Myers (Ed.), *Santiago: Saint of two worlds* (pp. 1–32). Albuquerque: University of New Mexico Press.

Smith, A. (1987). *The wealth of nations, books I–III.* Harmondsworth: Penguin.

Smith, B. (1984). *Spain: A history in art.* Garden City, NY: Doubleday.

Smith, C. (1989). Flexible specialization, automation and mass production. *Work, Employment and Society, 3*(2), 203–220.

Smith, C. (1996). The geography and history of Iberia in the *Liber Sancti Jacobi.* In M. Dunn & L. Davidson (Eds.), *The pilgrimage to Compostela in the Middle Ages* (pp. 23–41). New York: Garland.

Smith, M. (2000). *American business and political power. Public opinion, elections, and democracy.* Chicago: University of Chicago Press.

Smith, M. J. (1982). *Persuasion and human action: A review and critique of social influence theories.* Belmont, CA: Wadsworth.

Smith, M. J. (1993). *Pressure, power and policy: State autonomy and policy networks in Britain and the United States,* Pittsburg: University of Pittsburgh Press.

Smith, W. (1996, November 29). The art of achieving perfect pitch. *PR Week,* 13–15.

Sorell, T. (1990). Ethics and public relations. *Business ethics?* University of Stirling.

Sotelino, B. (1999, June 18). Rock. *La Voz de Galicia,* 16.

Spangler, E., & Lehman, P. M. (1982). Lawyering as work. In C. Derber (Ed.), *Professionals as workers: Mental labor in advanced capitalism* (pp. 63–99). Boston: G.K. Hall.

Speier, H. (1980). The rise of public opinion. In H. Lasswell, D. Lerner, & H. Speier (Eds.), *Propaganda and communications in world history*, vol. 2. Honolulu: University Press of Hawaii.

Spicer, C. H. (2000). Public relations in a democratic society: Value and Values. *Journal of Public Relations Research, 12*(1), 115–130.

Splichal, S. (2001). Public opinion and democracy today. In S. Splichal (Ed.), *Public opinion and democracy, vox populi-vox dei?* Cresskill, NJ: Hampton Press.

Springston, J. K., & Keyton, J. (2001). Public relations field dynamics. In R. Heath (Ed.), *Handbook of public relations* (pp. 115–126). London: Sage.

St. James the Apostle. (1996). Madrid: Aldeasa.

St John Ambulance (1994). Breath of life campaign. *The IPR Sword of Excellence Awards 1994*, Institute of Public Relations: London, pp. 21–23.

Stafford, L., & Canary, D. J. (1991). Maintenance strategies and romantic relationship type, gender and relational characteristics. *Journal of Social and Personal Relationships, 8*, 217–242.

Stam, J. (2002). *Head to head.* London: HarperCollinsWillow.

Starkie, W. (1957). *The road to Santiago.* New York: Dutton.

Stauber, J., & Rampton, S. (1995). *Toxic sludge is good for you! Lies, damn lies and the public relations industry.* Monroe, ME: Common Courage Press.

Steiner, G. A. (1983). *The new CEO.* New York: Macmillan.

Stewart, D. (1967). *Early Islam.* New York: Time-Life Books.

Stone, J. (1927). *The cult of Santiago: Traditions, myths and pilgrimages, a sympathetic study.* London: Longmans, Green.

Stop feeding the egos of the fat cats of PR. [Letter]. (1998, September 18). *PR Week*, p. 9.

Stout, D. A. (1990). Internal process of corporate advocacy. *Public Relations Review* (Spring), 52–62.

Strasser, J. B., & Becklund, L. (1993).*Swoosh: The unauthorised story of Nike and the men who played there.* New York: HarperBusiness.

Strauss, A. (1978). *Negotiations.* New York: Wiley.

Strathclyde Regional Council. (1985). Help put back the pieces. *The IPR Sword of Excellence Awards 1985* (p. 14), London: Institute of Public Relations.

Street, J. (2001). *Mass media, politics and democracy.* London: Palgrave.

Strinati, D. (2000). *An introduction to studying popular culture.* London and New York: Routledge.

Stuart, C. (1996, March 22). Technology never won a business pitch. *PR Week*, 9.

Sugden, J., & Tomlinson, A. (1998). *Fifa and the contest for world football.* Cambridge, UK: Polity Press.

Swann, P. (1989). *The British documentary movement, 1926–1946.* Cambridge, UK: Cambridge University Press.

Swanson, D., & Mancini, P. (1996). Patterns of modern electoral campaigning and their consequences. In D. Swanson & P. Mancini (Eds.), *Politics, media, and modern democracy.* London: Praeger.

Swarbrooke, J., Beard, C., Leckie, S., & Pomfret, G. (2003). *Adventure tourism: The new frontier.* London: Butterworth-Heinemann.

Szymanski, S. (2002). Collective selling of broadcast rights. *Soccer Analyst, 3* (1).

Tallents, S. (1932, 1955). *The projection of England.* London: Olen Press.

Tate takes on account director role at Ludgate. (1996, November 5). *PR Week*, p. 3.

Taylor, M. (2000). Toward a public relations approach to nation building. *Journal of Public Relations Research, 12*(2), 178–210.

Taylor, M. (2001). International public relations: Opportunities and challenges for the 21st century. In R. L. Heath (Ed.), *Handbook of public relations* (pp. 629–637). London: Sage.

Taylor, M., & Botan, C. (1997). Strategic communication campaigns for national development in the Pacific Rim: The case of public education in Malaysia. *Australian Journal of Communication, 24*(2), 115–130.

Taylor, M., & Kent, M. (1999). Challenging assumption of public relations: When government is the most important public. *Public Relations Review, 25*, 131–144.

Taylor, T. (Ed.). (1978). *Approaches to theory in international affairs*. Longman: New York.

Tedlow, R. S. (1979). *Keeping the corporate image: Public relations and business 1900–1950*. Greenwich, CT: JAI Press.

Tell, F. (2004). What do organizations know? Dynamics of justification context in R & D activities. *Organization, 11*(4), 443–471.

Terry, K. E. (1989). Educator and practitioner differences on the role of theory in public relations. In C. H. Botan & V. Hazleton (Eds.), *Public relations theory* (pp. 281–298). Hillsdale, NJ: Lawrence Erlbaum Associates.

The demise of Pre-fix is a mistake. (2003, January 17). *PR Week UK*.

The final analysis on PR evaluation. (1996, July 12). *PR Week*, p. 9.

The Guardian. (2004). It's a hell of a town. 19/5/04, 14.

The need for mutual understanding [Editorial]. *Public Relations 7*(3), 1955, p. 16.

The place of public relations in management education. (1991). Public Relations Education Trust.

The Public Relations Business. (1990). Wassen international magnesium OK. *Public Relations: Journal of the Institute of Public Relations, 9*(2), 11–12.

The Sunday Times. (1989, 5 February). Making a mark is big business.

The Rowland Company (1994a). Trident—battle of the dockyards. *The IPR Sword of Excellence Awards 1994*, Institute of Public Relations: London, pp.16–18.

The Rowland Company (1994b). Smirnoff International Fashion Awards 1993. *The IPR Sword of Excellence Awards 1994*, Institute of Public Relations: London, pp. 29–31.

Theis, A. M. (1992). Inter-Organisationsbeziehungen im Mediensystem: PR aus organisationssoziologischer Perspektive. *Publizistik, 37*(1), 25–35.

Thomas, C., & Webb, E. (1994). From orality to rhetoric: An intellectual transformation. In I. Worthington (Ed.), *Persuasion: Greek rhetoric in action*. London: Routledge.

Thomas, T., & Eyers, B. (1998). Why an ethical business is not an altruistic business. In *Visions of ethical business* (Financial Times Professional Limited), Journal.

Thompson, D. (Ed.). (1995). *The concise Oxford dictionary of current English*. New York: Oxford University Press.

Thompson, J. (1995). *The media and modernity*. Cambridge, UK: Polity.

Thompson, J. B. (1988). Mass communication and modern culture: Contribution to a critical theory of ideology. *Sociology, 22*(3), 359–383.

Thompson, K. (1983). The moral dilemma of diplomacy. In W. Olson (Ed.), *The theory and practice of international relations*. Englewood Cliffs, NJ: Prentice-Hall.

Thompson, P. (1993). Postmodernism: Fatal attraction. In J. Hassard & M. Parker (Eds.), *Postmodernism and organizations*. London/Newbury Park/ New Delhi: Sage.

Thompson, T., Dorsey, A., Miller, K., & Parrott, R. (Eds.). (2003). *Handbook of health communication*. Mahwah, NJ: Lawrence Erlbaum Associates.

Thomson, O. (1977). *Mass persuasion in history: A historical analysis of the development of propaganda techniques*. Edinburgh: Paul Harris Publishing.

Thorne, K. S. (1994). *Black holes and time warps: Einstein's outrageous legacy*. London: Papermac.

Thucydides. (1987). *History of the Peloponnesian War*. Harmondsworth: Penguin Classics.

Thurston, S., & Attwater, D. (Eds.). (1996). *Butler's lives of the saints*. New York: HarperCollins.

Tilson, D. (1999). Against the common good: The commodification of Latin America. *Media Development, 46*(3), 69–74.

Tilson, D. (2000). Devotional-promotional communication and Santiago: A thousand-year public relations campaign for Saint James and Spain. Paper presented to the 2000 Invited Seminar, University of Stirling, Stirling Media Research Institute, Stirling, Scotland.

Tilson, D., & Chao, Y. (2002). Saintly campaigning: Devotional-promotional communication and the U.S. Tour of St. Thérèse's relics. *Journal of Media and Religion, 1*(2), 81–104.

Time for clarity in financial PR. [Editorial]. (1996, January 26). *PR Week*, p. 9.

Tomlinson, J. (1997). "And besides the wench is dead": Media scandals and the globalization of communication. In J. Lull & S. Hinerman (Eds.), *Media scandals* (pp. 65–84). Cambridge, UK: Polity Press.

Toth, E., (1992). The case for pluralistic studies of public relations: Rhetorical, critical and systems perspectives. In E. Toth & R. Heath (Eds.), *Rhetorical and critical approaches to public relations* (pp. 3–16). Hillsdale, NJ: Lawrence Erlbaum Associates.

Toth, E., & Heath, R. (Eds.). (1992). *Rhetorical and critical approaches to public relations.* Hillsdale, NJ: Lawrence Erlbaum Associates.

Touraine, A. (1981). *The voice and the eye. An analysis of social movements.* Cambridge, UK: Cambridge University Press.

Touraine, A. (1988). *Return of the actor.* Minneapolis: University of Minnesota Press.

Traverse-Healy, T. (1988a). Public relations and propaganda: Values compared. International Public Relations Association Gold Paper No. 6.

Traverse-Healy, T. (1988b). The credibility factor and diplomacy: A public relations perspective on public affairs. Koeppler Memorial Lecture, Baylor University, Waco, TX, 15 November, unpublished lecture.

Traverso, M., & White, J. (1990). The launch of the Prudential's corporate identity. In D. Moss (Ed.), *Public relations in practice* (pp. 25–37). London: Routledge.

Trujillo, N., & Toth, E. L. (1987). Organizational perspectives for public relations research and practice. *Management Communication Quarterly, 1*(2), 199–281.

TSB Group plc. (1987). How five million people said "yes". *Public Relations: The Quarterly Journal of the Institute of Public Relations, 6*(1), 10–12.

Tsoukas, H. (1992). A reply to Martin Parker. *Organization Studies, 13*(4), 643–650.

Tsoukas, H. (Ed.). (1994). *New thinking in organizational behaviour.* Oxford, UK: Butterworth-Heinemann.

Tunstall, J. (1970). *The Westminster lobby correspondents—a sociological study of national political journalism.* London: Routledge & Keegan.

Tunstall, J. (1993). *Television producers.* London and New York: Routledge.

Turner, B. (1986). *Citizenship and capitalism: The debate over reformism.* London: Allen & Unwin.

Turner, B. (1990). The rise of organizational symbolism. In J. Hassard & D. Pym (Eds.), *The theory and philosophy of organizations* (pp. 83–96). London: Routledge.

Turney, J. (1998). *Frankenstein's footsteps: Science, genetics and popular culture.* London: Yale University Press.

Turow, J. (1997). *Breaking up America.* Chicago: University of Chicago Press.

Tye, L. (1998). *The father of spin: Edward L. Bernays and the birth of public relations.* New York: Crown.

United States Catholic Conference. (1994). *Catechism of the Catholic Church.* Washington, DC: U.S. Catholic Conference.

Urry, J. (2002). *The tourist gaze* (2nd ed.). London: Sage.

Valin Pollen International. (1990). Euro Disneyland pan-European investor marketing and launch. *Public Relations: Journal of the Institute of Public Relations, 9*(2), 27–28.

van Herwaarden, J. (1980). The origins of the cult of St. James of Compostela. *Journal of Medieval History, 6,* 1–35.

Van Leuven, J. (1996). Public relations in South East Asia from nation building campaigns to regional interdependence. In H. M. Culbertson & N. Chen (Eds.), *International public relations: A comparative analysis* (pp. 207–222). Mahwah, NJ: Lawrence Erlbaum Associates.

Van Leuven, J., & Pratt, C. (1996). Public relations' role: Realities in Asia and Africa south of the Sahara. In H. Culbertson & N. Chen (Eds.), *International public relations: A comparative analysis* (pp. 93–105). Mahwah, NJ: Lawrence Erlbaum Associates.

van Riel, C. (1995). *Principles of corporate communication.* London: Prentice-Hall.

van Riel, C. (2000). Corporate communication orchestrated by a sustainable corporate story. In M. Schultz, M. J. Hatch, & M. Holten Larsen (Eds.), *The expressive organisation* (pp. 157–181). Oxford, UK: Oxford University Press.

Van Ruler, B. (1997). Communication: Magical mystery or scientific concept? Professional views of public relations practitioners in the Netherlands. In D. Moss, T. MacManus, & D. Verčič, (Eds.), *Public relations research: An international perspective* (pp. 247–263). London: International Thomson Business Press.

Van Ruler, B., & Verčič, D. (2004). *Public relations and communication management in Europe: A nation-by-nation introduction to public relations theory and practice.* Berlin: Mouton de Grouter.

Vande Berge, L. (1998). The sports hero meets mediated celebrityhood. In L. A.Wenner (Ed.), *MediaSport.* London: Routledge.

Vasko, P. (1999, September). A Pilgrimage. Speech given to the Southeastern Lieutenancy of the Equestrian Order of the Holy Sepulchre of Jerusalem, Naples, Florida.

Vasquez, G. M. (1993). A homonarrens paradigm for public relations: Combining Bormann's symbolic convergence theory and Grunig's situational theory of publics. *Journal of Public Relations Research, 5*(3), 201–216.

Vasquez, G. M., & Taylor, M. (2001). Research perspectives on "the public". In R. L. Heath (Ed.), *Handbook of public relations* (pp. 139–154). London: Sage.

Velasquez, M. G. (1983). Why corporations are not morally responsible for anything they do. *Business and Professional Ethics Journal, 11.*

Vellas, F., & Bécherel, L. (1995). *International tourism: An economic perspective.* Basingstoke: Macmillan.

Verčič, D., Grunig, L., & Grunig, J. (1996). Global and specific principles of public relations: Evidence from Slovenia. In H. Culbertson & N. Chen (Eds.), *International public relations: A comparative analysis* (pp. 31–65). Mahwah, NJ: Lawrence Erlbaum Associates.

Verčič, D., & Tkalac, A. (2004). *A local point of view: Application of the coorientation theory on communication problems in international relations: The case of Slovenia and Croatia.* Paper presented at the 11th Bled Public Relations Symposium, Slovenia.

Verčič, D., Van Ruler, B., Butschi, G., & Flodin, B. (2001). On the definition of public relations: A European view. *Public Relations Review, 27*(4), 373–387.

Victoria Women's Sexual Assault Center (VWSAC). (1994). *Crisis counselor training manual.* Victoria, Canada: VWSAC.

Vidal, J., & Cordahi, C. (1995). A question of guilt. *The Guardian* (23 August), 5.

Vigor del Camino. (1999). Santiago de Compostela: San Martin.

Vincent, M., & Stradling, R. (1994). *Cultural atlas of Spain and Portugal.* Abington: Andromeda Oxford Limited.

Vollmer, H. M., & Mills, D. L. (Eds.). (1966). *Professionalization.* Englewood Cliffs: Prentice-Hall.

Von Bertalanffy, L. (1950). The theory of open systems in physics and biology. *Science,* 3.

Von Bertalanffy, L. (1956). General systems theory. *General Systems, 1,* 1–10.

Von Bertalanffy, L. (1972). General systems theory—a critical review. In J. Beishon & G. Peters (Eds.), *Systems behaviour.* London: Harper Ross for the Open University Press.

Von Furstenberg, G. M. (2001). Hopes and delusions of transparency. *North American Journal of Economics and Finance, 12*(1), 105–121.

Waddington, I. (2000). Sport and health: A sociological perspective. In J. Coakley & E. Dunning (Eds.), *Handbook of sports studies* (pp. 408–421). London: Sage.

Wakefield, G., & Cottone, L. (1992). Public relations executives' perceptions of disciplinary emphases important to public relations practice for the 1990s. *Public Relations Review, 18*(1), 67–79.

Waldman, M. (1997). Inside track. *The Guardian* (part 2), 5 January, 16–17.

Walker, D. (1998, August 6). Government PR: Getting the choir singing from the same sheet. *Guardian.*

Walker, M. Urban. (1998). *Moral understandings: A feminist study in ethics.* New York: Routledge.

Wallack, L. (1989). Mass communication and health promotion: A critical perspective. In R. Rice & C. Atkin (Eds.), *Public communication campaigns* (2nd ed. pp. 353–368). Newbury Park, CA: Sage.

Walsh, A., & Brown, A. (1999). *Not for sale!* Edinburgh and London: Mainstream.

Walsh, M. (Ed.). (1991). *Butler's lives of the saints.* New York: HarperCollins.

Ward, K. (1989). *Mass communication and the modern world.* Basingstohe: Macmillan.

Wartick, S. L., & Rude, R. E. (1986). Issues management: Corporate fad or corporate function? *California Management Review* (Fall), 124–140.

Wathen, M. (1987). Names people play. *Public Relations Journal,* May, 14–16.

Weaver, C. K. (2001). Dressing for battle in the new global economy: Putting power, identity, and discourse into public relations theory. *Management Communication Quarterly, 15*(2), 279–288.

Weaver, C. K., & Motion, J. (2002). Sabotage and subterfuge: Public relations, democracy and genetic engineering in New Zealand. *Media Culture & Society, 24*(3), 325–343.

Weaver, D., & Elliott, S. N. (1985). Who sets the agenda for the media? A study of local agenda-building. *Journalism Quarterly, 62*, 87–94.

Webster, R. (2000). Highs and lows of letting ITV's cameras loose at 30,000 feet. *The Observer*, 27 August, 5.

Weed, M., & Bull, C. (2004). *Sports tourism: Participants, policy and providers*. London: Elsevier, Butterworth-Heinemann.

Weick, K. (1969). *The social psychology of organising*. Reading, MA: Addison-Wesley.

Weick, K. (1979). Cognitive processes in organizations. *Research in Organizational Behaviour, 1*, 41–74.

Wells, C. (1989). The decline and rise of English murder: Corporate crime and individual responsibility. *Criminal Law Review* (March).

Wells, C. (1993). *Corporations and criminal responsibility*. Oxford Monographs on Criminal Law and Justice. Oxford, UK: Clarendon Press.

Wernick, A. (1991). *Promotional culture. Advertising, ideology and symbolic expression*. London: Sage.

Westminister Advisers (1997). Port Ramsgate relief road. *The IPR Sword of Excellence Awards 1997*, Institute of Public Relations: London, pp. 21–23.

Wetherbee Phelps, L. (1993). Writing the new rhetoric of scholarship. In T. Enos & S. C. Brown (Eds.), *Defining the new rhetorics*. London: Sage.

Whannel, G. (1992). *Fields in vision*. London: Routledge.

Whannel, G. (2002a). Sport and the media. In J. Coakley & E. Dunning, (Eds.), *Handbook of sports studies*. London: Sage.

Whannel, G. (2002b). *Media sports stars: Masculinities and moralities*. London: Routledge.

Whetton, D. A., Raids, G., & Godfrey, P. (2002). What are the responsibilities of business to society? In A. Pettigrew, H. Thomas, & R. Whittington (Eds.), *Handbook of strategy and management* (pp. 373–408). London: Sage.

White, A. J. S. (1965). *The British Council: The first 25 years, 1934–59*. London: British Council.

White, J. (1991). *How to understand and manage public relations*. London: Business Books.

White, J. (1999, March 26). Evaluation must now show it can have an impact. *PR Week*, 13.

White, J. (2001). Lecture notes, University of Stirling.

White, J., & Blamphin, J. (1994). Priorities for research into public relations practice in the United Kingdom. Unpublished report from a Delphi study carried out among UK practitioners and public relations academics in 1994.

White, J., & Mazur, L. (1994). *Strategic communications management: Making public relations work*. Wokingham: Addison Wesley.

White, S. (1990). *The recent work of Jürgen Habermas*. Cambridge, UK: Cambridge University Press.

Whitehead, H. (1933). Salesmanship in the public service: Scope and technique. *Public Administration, 11*, 267–276.

Who Was JONAH? (2002, May). *Decision*, 37.

Wight, M. (1994). *International theory: The three traditions*. Leicester: Leicester University Press for the Royal Institute for International Affairs.

Wilcox, D., Ault, P., & Agee, W. (1986). *Public relations: Strategies and tactics*. New York: Harper & Row.

Wilcox, D., Ault, P., & Agee, W. (1992). *Public relations: Strategies and tactics*. New York: HarperCollins.

Wilcox, D., Ault, P., Agee, W., & Cameron, G. (2000). *Public relations: Strategies and tactics*. New York: Longman.

Wilensky, H. L. (1964). The professionalization of everyone? *American Journal of Sociology, 70*, 137–158.

Williams, J., & Beaver, W. (1990). Barnados: Relaunching Britain's biggest children's charity. In D. Moss (Ed.), *Public relations in practice*. London: Routledge.

Williams, K. (1998). *Get me a murder a day! A history of mass communications in Britain*. London: Arnold.

Williams, R. (1976). *Keywords*. Glasgow: Fontana/Croom Helm.

Williams-Thompson, R. (1951). *Was I really necessary?* London: World's Press News.

Wilson, D. (1980). The British documentary movement. In R. Roud (Ed.), *Cinema: A critical dictionary* (pp. 154–4). New York: Viking.

Wilson, L. J. (1940). Corporate issues management: An international view. *Public Relations Review* (Spring), 40–51.

Wilson, P. A. (1937). *Some modern business problems.* London: Longman.

Wilson, R. (1997, June 24). The ultimate measure of effectiveness. *PR Week*, 9.

Winchester, S. (1994, February). The long, sweet road to Santiago de Compostela. *Smithsonian*, 65–76.

Winston, B. (1995). *Claiming the real.* London: BFI.

Wise, G. (1980). *American historical explanations: A strategy for grounded inquiry.* Minneapolis: University of Minnesota Press.

Wolbring, B. (2000). *Krupp und dieÖffentlichkeit im 19.Jahrhundert.* München: C. H. Beck.

Wolfers, A. (1966). *Discord and collaboration: Essays in international politics.* Baltimore: John Hopkins University Press.

Wood, E., & Higgins, M. (1999). *Scottish corporate communications survey 1999: Internal communications trends.* Edinburgh: Carter Rae Communications.

Wood, S. H. (1936). Intelligence and public relations. *Public Administration, 14,* 41–48.

Worthington, I. (Ed.). (1994). *Persuasion: Greek rhetoric in action.* London: Routledge.

Wright, D. K. (1979). Professionalism and social responsibility. *Public Relations Review,* 20–33.

Writing the rules of financial PR. [Editorial]. (1998, June 19). *PR Week*, p. 9.

Wylie, F. W. (1994). Commentary: Public relations is not yet a profession. *Public Relations Review, 20,* 1–3.

Wynne Morgan, D. (1997, August 15). PR must shake itself out of this star-struck state. *PR Week.*

Xunta de Galicia. (1997). *Galicia 1997.* Vigo: Xunta de Galicia.

Yeoman, I., Robertson, M., Al-Knight, J., Drummond, S., & McMahaon-Beattie, U. (2004). *Festival and events management: An international arts and culture perspective.* Amsterdam; Oxford: Elsevier Butterworth-Heinemann.

Yin, R. K. (2003a). *Case study research: Design and methods.* Thousand Oaks, CA: Sage.

Yin, R. K. (2003b). *Applications of case study research.* Thousand Oaks, CA: Sage.

Young, K. (1954). Comments on the nature of "public" and "public opinion". In D. Katz, D. Cartwright, S. Eldersveld, & A. McClung Lee (Eds.), *Public opinion and propaganda.* New York: Holt, Rinehart & Winston (originally published 1948, *International Journal of Opinion and Attitude Research, 2,* 385–392).

Zedtwitz-Arnim, G-V. (1961). *Tu Gutes und Rede Darüber.* Berlin: Ullstein.

Zeitz, G. (1975). Interorganizational relationships and social structure: A critique of some aspects of literature. In A. R. Negandhi (Ed.), *Interorganizational theory.* Kent, OH: Kent State University Press.

Zeller, J. (1992). *The nature and origins of mass opinion.* Cambridge, UK: Cambridge University Press.

Zeno, K. (2000, January 2). Remembering the "holy house" of Mary. *Our Sunday Visitor,* 17.

Zhang, Y., & Cameron, G. T. (2004). *Journal of Communication Management,* 8(3), 307–321.

Zipfel, A. (1997). *Public Relations in der Elektroindustrie. Die Firmen Siemens und AEG 1847–1939.* Köln, Weimar, Wien: Böhlau.

Zucherman, M. (1994). Behavioural Experience and Biosocial Basis of sensation seeking Cambridge, Cambridge University Press.

Zwirek, D. (2002). *The Football Association and public relations.* Unpublished MSc. Public Relations dissertation. Stirling: University of Stirling.

Author Index

Subject Index

Lightning Source UK Ltd.
Milton Keynes UK

173071UK00005B/7/P